THE DEFINITIVE NOTTS COUNTY F.C.

Keith Warsop & Tony Brown

A *SoccerData* Publication

Published in Great Britain by Tony Brown,
4 Adrian Close, Beeston, Nottingham NG9 6FL.
Telephone 0115 973 6086. E-mail soccer@innotts.co.uk
First published 2007

© Keith Warsop and Tony Brown, 2007

All rights reserved. No part of this publication may be reproduced, stored in a retrieval system, or transmitted in any form, or by any means, electronic, mechanical, photocopying, recording or otherwise without the prior permission in writing of the Copyright holders, nor be otherwise circulated in any form or binding or cover other than in which it is published and without a similar condition including this condition being imposed on the subsequent publisher.

Cover design is by Bob Budd.

DEDICATION

This book is dedicated to the memory of Paul Wain,
our colleague as Magpie historian.

There are now twenty-three clubs in the 'Definitive' series. Other SoccerData publications include yearbooks and books of statistical and historical interest. Please contact the publisher for a catalogue.

Printed and bound by the Cromwell Press, Trowbridge, Wiltshire

ISBN 978-1-899468-99-7

CONTENTS

Notts County's history at a glance............................4
Magpies A-Z... 8
Introduction to the statistics pages........................62
Results grids 1864 to 2007..................................63
League tables..197
Results against other clubs................................202
Player lists...204
Results of friendly games..................................220

1931/32: Ferguson, Mills, HR Smith, Dowsey, Coglin, Bisby, Jakeman, Andrews, Lawrence, Maw, Taylor, Keetley, Haden

NOTTS COUNTY: THE CLUB'S HISTORY AT A GLANCE

1862/63
The original Notts County footballers played practice matches in The Park near Barrack Lane.

1864/65
Club placed on a formal basis (December 7th 1864). Colours of amber and black hoops adopted. First match v outside opponents on Meadows Cricket Ground, which was used until 1877. Nickname of "Lambs".

1865/66
First match v Nottingham Forest, who had been recently formed in December 1865.

1877/78
Moved to Beeston Cricket Ground. First match in F.A.Cup, v Sheffield FC (h, November 3rd 1877, drew 1-1).

1878/79
First F.A.Cup match v Forest (h, November 16th 1878, lost 3-1). Notts County played Derbyshire FC at Trent Bridge under floodlights.

1880/81
Moved to Castle Cricket Club ground in the Meadows. Colours changed to chocolate and blue halves.

1882/83
Reached F.A.Cup semi-finals, losing to Old Etonians.

1883/84
Moved to Trent Bridge Cricket Ground. In the F.A.Cup semi-finals again, losing to Blackburn Rovers.

1885
Turned professional soon after F.A. legalised payment to players (July 20th).

1885/86
Beat Rotherham Town 15-0 in F.A.Cup 1st round, County's record victory.

1888
Founder members of Football League (April 17th). Notts were represented by secretary Edwin Browne.

1888/89
First match in Football League, v Everton (a, September 15th 1888, lost 2-1). Finished next to bottom but successfully applied for re-election to League.

1889/90
Third from bottom but again applied successfully for re-election.

1890
Became limited company as Notts Incorporated FC. Colours changed to black and white stripes, bringing nickname of "Magpies".

1890/91
Losing F.A.Cup finalists to Blackburn Rovers at Kennington Oval in first final to use goal nets. Finished third in the Football League.

1892/93
Relegated from Division 1 via test matches.

1893/94
F.A.Cup winners 4-1 v Bolton Wanderers at Goodison Park, first Division 2 club to win Cup. Reached League test matches but lost and so failed to win promotion.

1894/95
Beat Burslem Port Vale 10-0, club's first double-figure League victory. Played in League test matches for second successive season but again lost, so stayed in Division 2.

1896/97
Champions of Division 2 and promoted to Division 1 via test matches. England beat Ireland 6-0 at Trent Bridge, the only full international ever staged at a Notts County ground.

1900/01
Third in Division 1, still their equal best League position along with 1890/91.

1904/05
Bottom of Division 1 but saved from relegation when League was enlarged.

1909/10
Last match at Trent Bridge, v Aston Villa (April 16th 1910, 2-3).

The last game at Trent Bridge, v Aston Villa

1910/11
First match at Meadow Lane, v Forest (September 3rd 1910, 1-1).

The Lord Mayor's party at the opening of the County Ground

1912/13
Relegated from Division 1.

1913/14
Albert Fisher appointed as club's first manager. Champions of Division 2 and promoted.

1915-19
Wartime regional competitions.

1919/20
Relegated from Division 1.

1921/22
Reached F.A.Cup semi-finals, losing to Huddersfield Town.

1922/23
Champions of Division 2 and promoted.

1925
New stand opened, on what is now the County Road side, with the familiar formation date gable.

1925/26
Change in offside law. Relegated from Division 1. Goalkeeper Albert Iremonger played his final match to reach a club record 564 League appearances.

1929/30
Relegated from Division 2.

1930/31
Champions of Division 3S and promoted. Centre-forward Tom Keetley set up club's seasonal scoring record with 39 goals in 34 matches.

1934/35
Colours changed back to chocolate and blue. Relegated from Division 2.

1935/36
Changed colours back to black and white stripes.

1939-46
Wartime regional competitions.

1941
Bomb damage to Meadow Lane pitch.

Not fit for football!

1946/47
Colours changed to white shirts with black facings.

1947/48
Signed England centre-forward Tommy Lawton from Chelsea for the then British record transfer fee of £20,000 (November 13th 1947).

1948/49
Club's record League win, 11-1 v Newport County. Topped 100 League goals in a season for first time with 102 in 42 matches.

1949/50
Record Meadow Lane League attendance of 46,000 for match v Forest (April 22nd 1950). Champions of Division 3S and promoted.

1950/51
Jackie Sewell became first Notts County player to top 100 League and Cup goals (97 League, 7 F.A.Cup). Later this season he was transferred to Sheffield Wednesday for new British record transfer fee of £34,500.

Leuty and Lawton congratulate Jackie Sewell on his record transfer

1951/52
Tommy Lawton completed his century of League and Cup goals for the Magpies (90 League, 13 F.A.Cup). Later this season he was transferred to Brentford.

1952/53
Colours changed back to black and white stripes. First set of Meadow Lane floodlights installed and opened with friendly v Derby County on March 23rd 1953.

1954/55
Reached F.A.Cup 6th round, losing to York City 1-0 when all-time Meadow Lane attendance record of 47,310 set up (March 12th 1955). Best-ever season by Reserves who won Midland League championship.

1955/56
Tragic early death of club skipper Leon Leuty from leukaemia.

1957/58
Relegated from Division 2.

1958/59
Divisions 3 and 4 formed from Divisions 3S and 3N. Relegated from Division 3.

1959/60
Promoted from Division 4, topping goals century for second time with 107 in 46 matches.

1960/61
First match in new F.L.Cup, v Brighton and Hove Albion (h, October 20th 1960, lost 3-1).

1961/62
Club celebrated centenary with match v England XI (May 2nd 1962, lost 3-1).

1962/63
Colours changed to white shirts with black facings. New set of floodlights opened v Port Vale (Division 3, October 11th 1962).

1963/64
Eddie Lowe appointed club's first player-manager and colours switched back to black and white stripes. Reached 5th round of F.A.Cup. Relegated from Division 3.

1965/66
Club saved from possible extinction by £10,000 cash injection from local businessman Bill Hopcroft.

1966/67
Saved on goal average from having to apply for re-election to Football League.

1969/70
Jimmy Sirrel appointed manager (November 19th 1969).

1970/71
Champions of Division 4 and promoted.

1971/72
Tony Hateley became first Notts County player to top 100 League goals, ending up with 109.

1972/73
Promoted from Division 3. Also outstanding F.L.Cup run to 5th round, knocking out Division 1 clubs Southampton and Stoke City.

1974/75
Ian Scanlon scored a hat-trick in less than three minutes against Huddersfield Town.

1975/76
Another fine F.L.Cup run to 5th round, beating Sunderland, Leeds United and Everton before narrow 1-0 defeat to Newcastle United. Jimmy Sirrel resigned as manager for Sheffield United job (October 16th 1975).

1977/78
Further new floodlights installed for start of season. Jimmy Sirrel returned as manager (October 6th 1977). Les Bradd reached club career record aggregate of 125 League goals.

1978
Demolition of Meadow Lane stand, which had been brought from Trent Bridge to new ground in 1910.

The original Meadow Lane stand

1980/81
Promoted from Division 2.

1981/82
Three points for a win introduced by League, replacing previous two points which had lasted since 1888/89.

Iain McCulloch scores Notts' first goal back in Division 1, at Villa Park, August 1981

1982/83
County supporters dipped into their pockets in an unsuccessful attempt to keep on-loan Glenn Roeder at the club.

1983/84
Reached 6th round of F.A.Cup, going out 2-1 to Everton. Relegated from Division 1.

1984/85
Relegated from Division 2. Jimmy Sirrel back for third spell as manager (April 20th 1985).

1987
Derek Pavis took control of Notts County from chairman Jack Dunnett.

1987/88
Notts reached Division 3 play-off semi-finals under new manager John Barnwell but lost to Walsall.

1988/89
Neil Warnock appointed manager (January 5th 1989).

1989/90
Promoted from Division 3 via play-offs with club's first-ever match at Wembley Stadium.

Play-off winners 1990

1990/91
Reached 6th round of F.A.Cup where they lost 2-1 to Tottenham Hotspur. Promoted from Division 2 via Wembley play-offs again.

1991/92
Relegated from Division 1 and so failed to become founder members of new F.A. Premier League.

1992
First stage of rebuilt Meadow Lane stadium with further new floodlights, leaving just Main Stand to be replaced.

1994
Main Stand also rebuilt to complete all-seater stadium.

1994/95
Anglo-Italian Cup winners at Wembley Stadium. Relegated from (renumbered) League Division 1.

1995/96
Lost (renumbered) Division 2 play-off final at Wembley Stadium.

The teams line up for the presentation before County's last game at the old Wembley, against Bradford City

1996/97
Relegated from Division 2.

1997/98
Champions of (renumbered) League Division 3 under manager Sam Allardyce, setting up various club records along the way. Promotion clinched in March with six games left to play.

2000/01
Albert Scardino signed deal with Derek Pavis to take over club (November 15th 2000).

2001/02
More than 15,000 in the County Ground for a last day 'great escape' from relegation after a 2-1 victory over Huddersfield Town.

2002
Club put into administration with debts stated to be around £5 million.

2002/03
Supporters Trust set up (March 12th 2003) to help to raise funds and rescue the club from threatened Football League expulsion.

2003/04
Notts County out of administration when Football League accepted Blenheim 1862 Limited as new owners (December 3rd 2003). Relegated from Division 2 into renamed League 2 (formerly Division 3).

2005/06
Notts were in danger of falling out of the League on the last day of the season. A 2-2 draw with Bury saved the day.

Supporters celebrate after the Bury game

2006/07
Excellent F.L. Cup results with wins against Premiership Middlesbrough and two Championship clubs, Crystal Palace and Southampton. Supporters Trust acquired majority shareholding for control of Notts County FC.

MAGPIES A TO Z

A NOTE ON THE TEXT
There have been four tiers or levels of the Football League that have been subjected to renumbering or rebranding. These are as follows: The original Football League became Division 1 in 1891 when Division 2 was created, then in 1992 the entire Division 1 clubs resigned to become founder members of the F.A. Premier League. Consequently, the Football League Divisions 2, 3 (formed 1920) and 4 (formed 1958) were renumbered 1, 2 and 3. A Football League rebranding exercise took place in 2004 with the three divisions renamed the Championship; League 1 and League 2. In order to signify these changes, the 1992 and 2004 titles have an asterisk attached (e.g. Division 1*, League 2*). After the formation of Division 3 in 1920, the League introduced southern and northern sections the following year which lasted until 1958; the Magpies spent a number of seasons in the southern section. This is given here as Division 3S.

The Football Association Challenge Cup is shown as the F.A.Cup and the Football League Cup as the F.L.Cup, otherwise abbreviations have been avoided apart from (h) and (a) for home and away.

Games played to determine certain promotion and relegation issues, the test matches (1892-97) and play-offs (1988-96), have been counted in Notts County's League records but mention is usually made of this in the affected entries. Appearances as a substitute are usually shown as part of a player's overall record.

Sponsored competitions are to be found under the generic name where there is one (e.g. F.L.Cup and not Carling Cup) though all sponsorship titles are entered and cross-referred to the appropriate section. The Notts F.A. County Cup is not included in the overall first-class competitive records but it does have its own entry.

ABANDONED MATCHES
Notts County have been involved in the following instances of Football League matches having to be abandoned through weather conditions:

- November 23rd 1889, Football League, v Stoke (a), fog, 90 mins. Score: 2-2. Notts scorers: Harry Daft and Harry Walkerdine.
- December 13th 1890, Football League, v Sunderland (h), fog, 62 mins. Score: 1-1. Notts scorer: an own goal.
- January 19th 1895, Division 2, v Grimsby Town (a), rain, 44 mins. Score 2-3. Notts scorers: John Allan and Jimmy Logan.
- January 12th 1901, Division 1, v Bolton Wanderers (a), fog, 25 mins. Score: 0-0.
- March 30th 1903, Division 1, v Aston Villa (a), rain, half-time. Score: 0-1.
- January 6th 1906, Division 1, v Bolton Wanderers (a), rain, half-time. Score: 0-2.
- October 12th 1912, Division 1, v Tottenham Hotspur (a), fog, 82 mins. Score: 3-1. Notts scorers: Jimmy Cantrell 2 and Albert Waterall.
- March 10th 1934, Division 2, v Bradford Park Avenue (h), rain, 16 mins. Score: 0-0.
- December 25th 1937, Division 3S, v Gillingham (a), fog, 37 mins. Score: 0-1.
- December 3rd 1960, Division 3, v Halifax Town (h), rain, half-time. Score: 0-2.
- March 25th 1965, Division 4, v Millwall (h), rain, half-time. Score: 1-2. Notts scorer: Derek Pace.
- December 28th 1965, Division 4, v Tranmere Rovers (h), fog, 14 mins. Score: 0-0.
- December 11th 1976, Division 2, v Burnley (h), frost, half-time. Score: 0-0.
- November 3rd 2002, Division 2*, v Bristol City (a), rain, 49 mins. Score: 1-0. Notts scorer: Paul Heffernan.

Though 90 minutes were played in the Stoke match of 1889 the result was declared void because of the fog. The rearranged match was also drawn, 1-1. The Division 1 match v Birmingham (a) on September 19th 1925 was halted for 50 minutes because of torrential rain but play was resumed and the match completed. Notts won 1-0.

A wartime Midland Section league match v Huddersfield Town (a) on February 9th 1918 was abandoned at half-time with the score 0-0. Huddersfield won the rearranged fixture 2-1. Two other wartime league games were abandoned but the results were allowed to stand. These were a Midland Section match v Bradford City (a) on January 26th 1918 (0-0 after 60 minutes) and a F.L.Cup North game v Mansfield Town (a) on January 15th 1944 (0-1 after just 15 minutes).

In recent seasons stricter rules for referees mean that games are often called off well before kick-off if conditions are bad. On January 10th 1987 the players did not agree with the referee when he postponed the scheduled game with Newport County so they held a practice match on the Meadow Lane pitch!

ABSENTEES
Only once has the club taken the field a man short for a major competitive fixture. The occasion was v Preston North End (a), Division 1, March 31st 1893. The absentee was goalkeeper George Toone who missed the train. For economy reasons the directors had not sent a reserve player for the match so full-back Jack Hendry went into goal and the Magpies, playing with ten men, lost 4-0.

In pre-Football League days there were a number of times when the side took the field with only ten and a few times with nine players but the record for absentees must be v Lincoln (a), February 8th 1872 when no fewer than **SEVEN** selected players failed to turn up. The side was made up to eleven from spectators at the Lincoln ground but despite this Notts lost by only 1-0!

See also **Goalkeepers** under **Stand-in goalkeepers**.

ADMINISTRATION: see under Crises and Limited Company

AGE
Oldest
The oldest player to appear in a Football League match for Notts County is goalkeeper Albert Iremonger who was 41 years 320 days old when he played against Huddersfield Town (h), Division 1, on May 1st 1926. Next comes half-back Bill Corkhill whose final appearance was v Barnsley (a), Division 2, on September 12th 1951 when he was 41 years 142 days. These are the only players on record to appear for the Magpies when aged over 40.

Oldest (debut)
Player-manager Eddie Lowe was 38 years five months when he made his debut for the Magpies v Oldham Athletic (a), Division 3, on December 26th 1963.

Youngest
When making his debut v Brentford (a), Division 3, on April 3rd 1961 full-back Tony Bircumshaw was 16 years 54 days, the youngest player to represent the Magpies in a Football League match. However midfielder Jermaine Pennant was only 15 years 341 days old when he came on as substitute v Hull City (h) in the Associate Members Cup 1st round match on December 22nd 1998.

AMATEURS
Until the legalisation of professionalism by the F.A. on July 20th 1885, all players were nominally amateurs. In 1974 the F.A. abolished the distinction between professionals and amateurs.

Amateur internationals
The following Notts County players gained Amateur International honours: Len Barry (1) England v Ireland 1923/24; Bryn Jones (1) Wales v Scotland 1934/35 (one of three players named Jones signed from Swansea Town in 1934, he never appeared in the Magpies first team); Terry McCavana (1) Ireland v Scotland 1948/49.

University Blues
Players in the Oxford v Cambridge University Match who also represented Notts County: Leonard Gillet (Oxford) 1882; Alfred Harrisson (Cambridge) 1894; Arthur Henfrey (Cambridge) 1890 and 1891; Tinsley Lindley (Cambridge) 1885, 1886, 1887 and 1888; John Morgan (Cambridge) 1877; John Walker (Oxford) 1892, 1893 and 1894.

ANGLO-ITALIAN CUP

Phil Turner clutches the trophy, with Steve Cherry following, after County's 2-1 win against Ascoli in 1995

This was introduced in 1992/93 and was competed for by clubs from Division 1* of the Football League and Division 2 of the Italian League.

The competition excited little interest except for Magpies fans who were rewarded by two Wembley finals producing a defeat in 1993/94 and success in 1994/95. County's best win was 4-2 over Ascoli (h) in an intermediate round match on October 12th 1993 and their worst defeat was by the same score v Derby County (a) in the preliminary round on September 2nd 1992. Total Notts record: P.18 W.7 D.7 L.4 F.25 A.23.

A previous version of the Anglo-Italian Cup had been played in the early 1970s. See also under **Wembley Stadium** for details of the two finals involving Notts.

ANGLO-SCOTTISH CUP
Formerly the Texaco Cup and originally including Irish clubs as well as English and Scottish, it developed into a pre-season qualifying tournament with knock-out stages being played during the season proper. The Magpies first took part in 1976/77 and their first match was on August 7th 1976 v Nottingham Forest (h) when they drew 0-0. From their three matches Notts secured only one point and failed to qualify for the quarter-finals.

In 1977/78 they finished level with Sheffield United and won the play-off for a place in the quarter-finals. There they beat Motherwell 2-1 on aggregate but lost 2-1 to St. Mirren on aggregate in the semi-finals. In 1980/81 Notts went one better by reaching the final after dispatching Kilmarnock 7-3 on aggregate in the semi-finals. However they lost the final v Chesterfield 2-1 on aggregate after extra time in the second leg at Meadow Lane.

After Scottish clubs withdrew in 1981 the competition was continued as the Football League Group Cup in 1981/82, the last time the Magpies entered. Its final season was 1982/83 as the Football League Trophy. Complete Notts record: P.29 W.12 D.8 L.9 F.37 A.36. Biggest victory 5-2 v Kilmarnock (h), semi-final 2nd leg, November 18th 1980; biggest defeat 3-0 v Norwich City (a), group stage, August 22nd 1981.

APPEARANCES

Albert Iremonger

Consecutive (League)

The record number of consecutive Football League appearances for Notts County is held by goalkeeper Albert Iremonger with 211 in Division 1 from February 9th 1907 to October 19th 1912. As he also played in 11 F.A.Cup ties during this period, his overall sequence was 222 games. Runner-up is another goalkeeper, Steve Cherry, who clocked up 149 matches between April 18th 1989 and August 25th 1992, a total which includes six play-offs. During the same period Cherry also played in all of the Magpies' various cup-ties taking his overall sequence to 177.

Others to top the century mark are centre-half Alex Gibson with 141 outings between October 24th 1964 and November 18th 1967; centre-half Arthur Clamp, October 19th 1907 to January 28th 1911 with 128; right winger George Taylor, March 7th 1931 to December 2nd 1933 with 112; left-back Alf West, September 2nd 1911 to March 28th 1914 with 110; right-back Aubrey Southwell, October 19th 1946 to March 26th 1949 with 108; central defender David Needham, March 23rd 1974 to November 27th 1976 with 107; goalkeeper George Toone, December 1st 1894 to January 3rd 1898 with 102 (including five test matches); goalkeeper George Smith, August 22nd 1959 to September 23rd 1961 with 102; outside-right Jon Nixon, August 22nd 1970 to September 30th 1972 with 102 (including three as substitute); left-back Jack Hendry, September 9th 1890 to February 3rd 1894 with 101 (including one test match).

Most appearances

Record number of Football League appearances for the Magpies: Albert Iremonger with 564 followed by David Needham with 429 (one as substitute). Record number of F.A.Cup games: Harry Cursham with 43. The F.L.Cup record is 39 by Pedro Richards. Iremonger lost four years to the First World War when at the peak of his career otherwise his total would probably have been around 700. He did play 93 games in the wartime leagues and these, along with his 37 F.A.Cup games, took his overall Notts County appearances to 694.

The following is a list of players who have made 350 or more appearances for Notts County in all first-class competitive games:

	Career	Total	League	F.A.Cup	F.L.Cup	Others
Albert Iremonger	1904/05 to 1925/26	601	564	37	–	–
Brian Stubbs	1968/69 to 1979/80	486	426	21	24	15
Pedro Richards	1974/75 to 1985/86	485	399	19	39	28
David Needham	1965/66 to 1976/77	471	429	17	21	4
Don Masson	1968/69 to 1981/82	455	402	17	23	13
Les Bradd	1967/68 to 1977/78	442	395	22	17	8
Percy Mills	1927/28 to 1938/39	434	407	20	–	7
Billy Flint	1908/09 to 1925/26	408	376	32	–	–
David Hunt	1977/78 to 1986/87	408	336	22	29	21
Dean Yates	1984/85 to 1994/95	394	320	20	24	30
Ray O'Brien	1973/74 to 1982/83	386	323	11	25	27
Tristan Benjamin	1974/75 to 1986/87	386	311	17	30	28
Teddy Emberton	1904/05 to 1914/15	382	365	17	–	–
Alex Gibson	1959/60 to 1968/69	373	347	10	16	–
Aubrey Southwell	1945/46 to 1956/57	358	328	30	–	–
George Smith	1955/56 to 1966/67	352	323	15	14	–

(appearances in play-offs included in Dean Yates' League total; substitute appearances also included where applicable)

Other players who have totalled over 300 senior outings are: Jack Montgomery (1898/99 to 1910/11) 339 (316 in League); Steve Cherry (1988/89 to 1994/95) 328 (272); Davey Calderhead (1889/90 to 1899/1900) 321 (285); Gary Lund (1987/88 to 1994/95) 316 (253); Haydn Kemp (1920/21 to 1930/31) 312 (286); John Sheridan (1957/58 to 1965/66) 308 (287); George Toone (1889/90 to 1901/02) 308 (272); Walter Bull (1894/95 to 1903/04) 306 (285); Phil Turner (1988/89 to 1995/96) 306 (243); Darren Ward (1995/96 to 2000/01) 302 (254); and Sam Haden (1927/28 to 1936/37) 301 (289).

Divisional records

Most appearances in each division of the Football League are as follows:

Player	Divisional career	Total	
Albert Iremonger	1904/05 to 1925/26	440	Division 1
Ray O'Brien	1973/74 to 1980/81	279	Division 2
Dean Yates	1985/86 to 1989/90	218	Division 3

(he also made five Division 3 play-off appearances)

| Percy Mills | 1930/31 to 1938/39 | 204 | Division 3S |

(he also made two Division 3S appearances in the cancelled 1939/40 League season)

| Alex Gibson | 1959/60 to 1968/69 | 215 | Division 4 |

(modern renumbered League divisions have been considered under their previous titles; e.g. League 2 = Division 4).

Ever-presents

The most seasons in which one player has appeared in every Football League match is seven. The record is held by Albert Iremonger who was an ever-present in 1907/08 to 1911/12 inclusive, 1913/14 and 1914/15. Next comes Walter Bull with four seasons, 1895/96, 1896/97, 1899/1900 and 1901/02.

The most ever-presents in a single League season is five on two occasions. In 1890/91 Jack Hendry, Andrew McGregor, Tommy McInnes, Jimmy Oswald and Archie Osborne played in all 22 matches while in 1908/09 Jimmy Cantrell, Arthur Clamp, Teddy Emberton, Albert Iremonger and Bill Matthews appeared in the 38 games. In more modern times the record is four in 1978/79 when Iain McCulloch, Eric McManus, Ray O'Brien and Brian Stubbs were the ever-presents in the 42 matches, and also in 1987/88 when Gary Mills, Geoff Pike, Paul Smalley and Dean Yates were the 46-game ever-presents.

Meadow Lane

David Needham has made the most Football League appearances at Meadow Lane with 221 though Brian Stubbs edges ahead of him in all competitive games with 244. Nine players top the 200 mark as follows: Stubbs 244 (217 League), Needham 241 (221), Pedro Richards 238 (198), Don Masson 225 (199), Les Bradd 224 (202), Percy Mills 217 (208), Albert Iremonger 205 (193), David Hunt 202 (165) and Billy Flint 201 (185). But for missing two entire seasons through injury, Dean Yates would surely have joined this "200 Club" as he totalled 194 (159).

Trent Bridge

The most Football League appearances at Trent Bridge were made by Walter Bull with 128 (including one test match) and he also holds the record in all competitions with 139. Close on his heels comes Jack Montgomery with 138 (127 League) and Davey Calderhead, also 138 (126 League including one test match). A few games behind these three is George Toone on 132 (120 League including one test match).

ASSOCIATE MEMBERS CUP

This knock-out tournament began in 1983/84 and has been known under seven different sponsorship titles. Associate Members were those League clubs in the lower divisions who did not have full voting rights. Although all League clubs now have the vote, this competition for the two lowest divisions continues as the Football League Trophy under various sponsors' names. For consistency, entries in this A-Z use the original title of Associate Members Cup.

The Magpies competed from 1985/86 to 1989/90 and again from 1995/96 to date. Their best seasons were 1987/88 and 1989/90 when they lost on aggregate both times in the southern final. In the former season they went out to Wolverhampton Wanderers 4-1 on aggregate and in the latter to Bristol Rovers 1-0 on aggregate. Their biggest victory was 5-1 over Brighton and Hove Albion (a) in the southern semi-final on March 9th 1988. Worst defeat 5-0 against Gillingham (h) in the preliminary round on November 24th 1986. Complete record: P.40 W.13 D.8 L.19 F.41 A.55.

The competition had the following names in the seasons involving Notts: 1985/86 and 1986/87 Freight Rover Trophy; 1987/88 and 1988/89 Sherpa Van Trophy; 1989/90 Leyland-DAF Cup; 1995/96 to 1999/2000 Auto Windscreens Shield; 2000/01 to 2005/06 LDV Vans Trophy; 2006/07 Johnstone's Paint Trophy.

ATTENDANCES

It was only with the introduction of turnstiles that it became possible to provide accurate attendance figures. Previously these had been estimated from the amount of money taken at the gate – hence the occasional modern use of "gate" to mean attendance.

High attendances

Record attendance at Meadow Lane: 47,310 v York City, F.A.Cup 6th round, March 12th 1955.
Record League attendance at Meadow Lane: 46,000 v Nottingham Forest, Division 3S, April 22nd 1950.
Record since stadium rebuilding: 17,911 v Nottingham Forest, Division 1*, February 12th 1994.
Other 40,000-plus Meadow Lane attendances:
- 46,500 v Portsmouth, F.A.Cup 4th round, February 2nd 1952.
- 45,116 v Swansea Town, Division 3S, December 26th 1947.
- 45,014 v Aston Villa, F.A.Cup 2nd round, January 29th 1921.
- 44,195 v Preston North End, Division 2, September 23rd 1950.
- 44,087 v Nottingham Forest, Division 2, September 15th 1951.
- 44,000 v Burnley, F.A.Cup 3rd round, January 7th 1950.
- 43,906 v Torquay United, Division 3S, April 8th 1950.
- 42,676 v Walsall, Division 3S, October 29th 1949.
- 42,489 v Leicester City, Division 2, February 2nd 1957.
- 41,457 v Chelsea, F.A.Cup 5th round, February 19th 1955.
- 41,023 v Coventry City, Division 2, August 19th 1950.
- 40,192 v Ipswich Town, Division 3S, December 26th 1949.

Record attendance for any match involving Notts: 61,003 v Liverpool (Anfield), F.A.Cup 4th round, January 29th 1949.
Other 48,000-plus attendances:
- 59,940 v Brighton & Hove Albion (Wembley), Division 2 play-off final, June 2nd 1991.
- 53,138 v Sheffield Wednesday (Hillsborough), F.A.Cup 4th round, January 29th 1955.
- 53,000 v Birmingham City (St.Andrew's), F.A.Cup 3rd round, January 10th 1948.
- 49,737 v Everton (Goodison Park), F.A.Cup 3rd round, January 9th 1954.
- 49,604 v Everton (Goodison Park), Division 2, October 20th 1951.
- 49,491 v Aston Villa (Villa Park), F.A.Cup 2nd round replay, February 2nd 1921.

Record attendance at Trent Bridge: 25,000 v Tottenham Hotspur, F.A.Cup 3rd round, February 23rd 1907; and v Everton, Division 1, December 28th 1908.
First 30,000-plus attendance for any match involving Notts County: 37,000 v Bolton Wanderers (Goodison Park), F.A.Cup final, March 31st 1894.

Low attendances
Lowest home attendance in League matches: Estimated 200 v Crewe Alexandra (Trent Bridge), Division 2, February 17th 1894 (the only Trent Bridge League attendance below 1,000).
Lowest at Meadow Lane: 1,779 v Tranmere Rovers, F.L.Cup 2nd round 1st leg, September 16th 1997.
Lowest in League at Meadow Lane: 1,927 v Chesterfield, Division 4, April 2nd 1966.

There were lower Meadow Lane attendances in the Division 3S Cup and the Associate Members Cup; in the former 1,000 v Watford, 2nd round, on November 10th 1937; and in the latter 1,020 v Wigan Athletic, 1st round, on October 22nd 2002.

The 1965/66 record Meadow Lane low v Chesterfield listed above is the only League attendance at the ground to fall below 2,000. However, there have been a number of occasions in away games when this figure has not been reached. Those below 1,800 are as follows:
   1,279 v Brighton and Hove Albion, Division 3*, December 3rd 1997.
   1,339 v Newport County, Division 4, February 28th 1970.
   1,702 v Accrington Stanley, League 2*, January 13th 2007.
   1,749 v Newport County, Division 4, March 29th 1969.
   1,749 v Workington, Division 4, April 8th 1969.
   1,768 v Darlington, Division 4, November 22nd 1969.
   1,781 v Halifax Town, Division 3, May 7th 1963.
   1,797 v Hartlepool United, Division 4, March 2nd 1970.
In the early days of the Football League, the following away estimated attendances were below 1,000:
   100 v Crewe Alexandra, Division 2, January 16th 1895.
   300 v Preston North End, Football League, December 12th 1891.
   500 v Crewe Alexandra, Division 2, October 5th 1895.
   500 v Rotherham Town, Division 2, November 16th 1895.
   900 v Wolverhampton Wanderers, Football League, October 17th 1891.
   912 v Bury, Division 1, January 6th 1900.

Average attendances
The best season for attendances at County's games, home and away, was 1949/50 when an average of 28,064 saw the 42 League matches. The worst season was 1895/96 when the average was 3,328. In recent times the worst season was 1985/86 with 4,405 for 46 games.

For home matches only, the highest average attendance was 35,176 in 1949/50 and in fact the five seasons of the Lawton era, 1947/48 to 1951/52, are the only occasions in which the Meadow Lane average has topped 20,000. The lowest of the five was 1947/48 with 25,380 while both 1948/49 and 1950/51 averaged above 30,000. Apart from the Lawton years the highest average was 19,391 in 1952/53 and the highest since 1959 was 13,941 in 1971/72. To date 6,154 in 2002/03 is the highest in the 21st century while the record during the Trent Bridge years was 10,676 in 1898/99.

The 4,239 average in 1996/97 was the lowest ever at Meadow Lane with 4,354 in 1966/67 running it close. So far in the 21st century the lowest is 4,974 in 2006/07. All Trent Bridge attendances since 1897 averaged over 8,000 and for the lowest we have to go back to 1893/94 with 3,121 while 3,133 in 1895/96 fills second place.

Notts' seasonal home and away attendance details in League matches are listed in a later section.

AUTO WINDSCREENS SHIELD: see Associate Members Cup

AWAY RECORDS (Football League matches only)
Best away seasons:
Two points for a win

	P	W	D	L	F	A	Pts	Div.
1971/72	23	9	9	5	32	25	27	Div.3
1970/71	23	11	5	7	30	24	27	Div.4
1980/81	21	8	9	4	23	23	25	Div.2
1965/66	23	10	4	9	29	28	24	Div.4
In Division 1								
1923/24	21	5	7	9	23	34	17	
1924/25	21	5	7	9	13	19	17	
In Division 3S								
1930/31	21	8	7	6	39	33	23	
1936/37	21	8	7	6	30	29	23	
Three points for a win								
1997/98	23	15	5	3	41	23	50	Div.3*
1987/88	23	9	8	6	29	25	35	Div.3
1990/91	23	9	7	7	31	27	34	Div.2
2000/01	23	9	6	8	25	33	33	Div.2*
1989/90	23	8	8	7	33	35	32	Div.3
2006/07	23	8	8	7	26	28	32	Lge 2*
In Division 1								
1981/82	21	5	3	13	29	36	18	

Worst away seasons:
Two points for a win

1888/89	11	1	0	10	16	41	2	League
1963/64	23	2	1	20	16	66	5	Div.3
1892/93	15	2	1	12	19	46	5	Div.1
1891/92	13	2	1	10	14	39	5	League
1934/35	21	1	4	16	17	64	6	Div.2

In Division 3S

1948/49	21	4	2	15	34	49	10

In Division 4

1966/67	23	3	4	16	22	47	10

In Division 1 (programme of 21 matches)

1925/26	21	2	3	16	17	48	7

Three points for a win

1994/95	23	2	5	16	19	38	11	Div.1*
1982/83	21	3	3	15	18	46	12	Div.1

In Division 2*

1996/97	23	3	5	15	13	34	14
2003/04	23	4	3	16	18	51	15

In League 2*

2005/06	23	5	5	13	18	37	20

Most wins in a season: 15 in 1997/98 (Division 3*, 23 matches).
Fewest defeats in a season: 3 in 1997/98 (Division 3*, 23 matches).
Fewest wins in a season: 1 in 1929/30; 1934/35; and 1977/78 (all Division 2, 21 matches). 1 in 1912/13; and 1914/15 (both Division 1, 19 matches). 1 in 1888/89 (Football League, 11 matches). In a 23-match programme: 2 in 1963/64 (Division 3); 1968/69 (Division 4); 1992/93; and 1994/95 (both Division 1*).
Most defeats in a season: 20 in 1963/64 (Division 3, 23 matches).
Most draws in a season: 14 in 2001/02 (Division 2*, 23 matches).
Fewest draws in a season: 0 in 1888/89 (Football League, 11 matches). In 23-match programme: 1 in 1963/64 (Division 3).
Most goals scored in a season: 41 in 1959/60 (Division 4); and 1997/98 (Division 3*, both 23 matches).
Most goals conceded in a season: 72 in 1926/27 (Division 2, 21 matches).
Fewest goals scored in a season: 7 in 1901/02 (Division 1, 17 matches); 9 in 1912/13 (Division 1, 19 matches). In programme of 21 and 23 matches: 13 in 1921/22 (Division 2, 21); 1924/25 (Division 1, 21); and 1996/97 (Division 2*, 23).
Fewest goals conceded in a season: 17 in 1893/94 (Division 2, 14 matches). In programme of 23 matches: 18 in 1995/96 (Division 2*).
Longest unbeaten run: 10 matches from April 24th 1971 (Division 4) to October 30th 1971 (Division 3).
Longest winning run: 7 matches from December 3rd 1997 to February 14th 1998 (Division 3*).
Longest run of drawn matches: 5 matches from March 11th to April 8th 1969 (Division 4).
Longest run of defeats: 11 matches from December 27th 1902 to September 5th 1903 (Division 1); and from February 15th 1964 (Division 3) to August 31st 1964 (Division 4).
Longest run without a win: 29 matches from September 19th 1992 to November 13th 1993 (Division 1*).
Longest run without a drawn match: 19 matches from October 9th 1948 to September 24th 1949 (Division 3S); and from September 8th 1951 to April 12th 1952 (Division 2). In 1951/52 the Magpies drew their first and last matches with the 19 intervening ones all producing a result.
Longest scoring run: 17 matches from October 17th 1959 (Division 4) to August 20th 1960 (Division 3).
Longest run without scoring: 7 matches from October 19th to December 26th 1996 (Division 2*).
Longest run of clean sheets: 4 matches from August 31st to September 28th 1935 (Division 3S); from March 11th to March 29th 1969 (Division 4); and from September 20th to October 21st 1980 (Division 2). The 1935 instance comprised the first four matches of the 1935/36 season.
Longest run without a clean sheet: 39 matches from April 7th 1939 to January 31st 1948 (Division 3S). This sequence included the final six games of 1938/39 and the first 33 post-war matches from September 7th 1946. A total of 33 was also registered between December 27th 1890 (Football League) and April 22nd 1893 (Division 1), this final game being a test match on a neutral ground.
Longest sequence with the same result and scoreline is four times which has occurred twice, 0-0 in both cases; from August 31st to September 28th 1935 (Division 3S); and from March 11th to March 29th 1969 (Division 4).

Scored in every away match
The Magpies have achieved this feat only once, in 1896/97 (Division 2) when they scored in all 15 away matches, though they failed in one of their two away test matches.

Failed to keep clean sheet in any away match
The last time the Magpies failed to keep a clean sheet in any away Football League match in a season was 1946/47 when they were in Division 3S, playing 21 away matches. Previous occasions were: 1888/89 (Football League, 11 matches); 1891/92 (Football League, 13 matches); 1892/93 (Division 1, 16 matches including a test match).

See under **Goalscoring** for biggest away victories and defeats.

BASS CHARITY VASE

This invitation charity tournament dates from the 1880s and still continues with Notts County Reserves taking part in some recent seasons. In its early years it was a much more high-profile event with the leading Football League teams from the Midlands competing, including the Magpies. Results of these first team games are as follows:

1890/91: 3-4 v Burton Swifts (a). April 8th 1891; 1891/92: 5-0 v Burton Swifts (a), March 12th 1892, 2-1 v Wolverhampton Wanderers (a), April 5th 1892, 0-5 v Derby County (a), April 27th 1892; 1892/93: 0-2 v Stoke (a), March 23rd 1893; 1893/94: 2-0 v Wolverhampton Wanderers (h), April 5th 1894, 0-2 v Stoke (a), April 12th 1894.

BOOKS ON NOTTS COUNTY

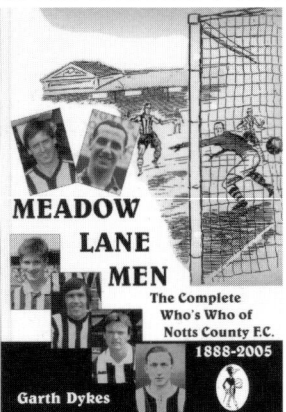

This list is restricted to books dealing mainly with the history of Notts County and therefore omits club yearbooks, promotion souvenirs, biographies and memoirs as well as Notts County sections of general football histories.

Centenary Handbook 1862-1962, from Notts County Football Club. Pyramid Press, London, 1962 (52 pages).

Legends of Notts County, The, by Dave Bracegirdle. Breedon Books, Derby, 2005 (208 pages).

Magpies, The. The Story of Notts County Football Club, by Keith Warsop assisted by Paul Wain. Sporting and Leisure Press, Buckingham, 1984 (192 pages).

Meadow Lane Men. The Complete Who's Who of Notts County Football Club, by Garth Dykes (includes Notts County managers compiled by Keith Warsop). Yore Publications, Harefield, Middlesex, 2004 (304 pages).

Notts County. A Pictorial History. The highs and lows of the world's oldest professional football club, by Paul Wain with additional material from Colin Slater. Yore Publications, Harefield, Middlesex, 2004 (112 pages).

Notts County Football Club, by Dave McVay. Archive, Manchester, 1988 (128 pages, paperback).

Notts County Football Club on old picture postcards and cigarette cards, by Grenville Jennings ('Yesterday's Nottingham' series No.44) . Reflections of a Bygone Age, Keyworth, Nottingham, 2004 (40 pages not numbered, paperback).

Official History of Notts County 1862-1995, The, by Tony Brown assisted by Paul Wain and Keith Warsop. Yore Publications, Harefield, Middlesex, 1996 (272 pages).

Story of Notts County Association Football Club, The, by Jimmy Cantrell. Ports & Cities Publishing, Liverpool, 1927 (16 pages). This is a really scarce publication seen by very few collectors.

CARLING CUP: see Football League Cup

CLOSURE

Notts County have been forced to close down only once in their history. This was for the wartime season of 1941/42 when German air raids over Nottingham on the night of May 8th/9th 1941 caused heavy bomb damage to the Meadow Lane ground at the Spion Kop end. It was not in playing order in time for the Magpies to compete in the 1941/42 Football League war competitions though they were able to play a friendly match during that season. They resumed full operations in 1942/43.

CLUB NAMES

Notts County has never been the company name though, of course, that is the name they trade under. In the early days they were usually known as "Notts.", with the full stop or "the Notts. Club". Sometimes early reports show them as Nottingham or Nottinghamshire but by the 1880s with the growth of other local clubs it became necessary to distinguish Notts from the others. Also, when the Nottinghamshire F.A. were formed on November 16th 1882 there was a need to separate the club side from the county representative team.

In 1890 on the formation of the limited company, the Magpies applied to the F.A. for a change of name from "Notts FC" to "Notts Incorporated FC" as this was the registered company name. Thankfully this never caught on (imagine "Notts Inc." in League tables!) and Notts Incorporated FC itself went into liquidation when Blenheim 1862 Ltd took over in December 2003 (see also under **Limited Company**).

Some of the clubs met by Notts in the Football League later changed their names though in this compilation the ones used at the time the matches were played are retained. These changes include:

Accrington FC were founder members of the League and became defunct in 1895. They had no connection with Accrington Stanley (formed 1893), despite many claims that the latter were League founders.

Ardwick became Manchester City in 1894.

Burslem Port Vale became simply Port Vale in 1913 when they moved from Burslem to Hanley.

Burton Swifts and Burton Wanderers merged in 1901 as Burton United.

Chester added City to their name in 1983.

Clapton Orient became Leyton Orient in 1946, Orient from 1966 to 1987 and then Leyton Orient again.

Hartlepools United became Hartlepool in 1968 and Hartlepool United (without the "s") in 1977.

Leeds City were closed for financial irregularities in 1919 and had no connection with Leeds United.

Leicester Fosse became City in 1919.

Newton Heath became Manchester United in 1902.

Rotherham Town's successor club, also Town, merged with Rotherham County in 1925 to become United.

Small Heath became Birmingham in 1905 and added City to their name in 1945.

South Shields became Gateshead in 1930 when they moved to the latter town.
Stoke added City to their name in 1925.
Swansea Town switched to City in 1970 following the town's elevation to that status.
Walsall Swifts and Walsall Town merged in 1888 as Town Swifts, becoming simply Walsall in 1895.
Wigan Borough resigned from the League in 1931 and became defunct. They had no connection with Wigan Athletic.
Wimbledon became Milton Keynes Dons when they moved to that town in 2004.
Woolwich Arsenal became Arsenal soon after they left Woolwich for Highbury in 1913.
Workington were always simply that. Workington Town are the Rugby League club.

COACHES

The role of coach is a fairly modern one since his duties in former times would have been the responsibility of the manager and perhaps the trainer. Indeed the post is sometimes called assistant manager rather than coach while the first coaches appointed by the Magpies in the inter-war years had the title of team manager though that did not imply any control over team selection. The first of these "team managers", though really a coach, was Charlie Bell in 1922/23, then came Harold Wightman 1930/31 and Will Jennings 1931-34. Next was Eric Tomkin in 1939/40 though by this time he was called coach.

Post-war Frank Broome was coach to George Poyser and assistant manager to Tommy Lawton in 1956 and 1957 while Stuart Imlach was coach in 1968 and 1969. Ronnie Fenton began as youth coach in 1971 before stepping up as senior coach and when he became manager Colin Addison was appointed his assistant 1975/76. Mick Jones was coach in 1976/77 while Jimmy Sirrel had Colin Murphy as his coach and assistant manager 1977/78.

Howard Wilkinson was coach 1979-82, Mick Walker had various spells from 1983, Dick Bate took over 1985-87, Paul Hart was player-coach 1987-88 and John Newman had the job for 1988-90. Mick Jones returned as assistant-manager 1990-93 with Mick Walker as coach, Russell Slade was Mick's assistant-manager 1993/94 with Wayne Jones the coach, then in 1994 Wayne stepped up as assistant-manager. By 1996 Mark Smith was the coach and Gary Brazil filled the post from 1998 separated by stints as full manager. John Gaunt was assistant manager to Gary Mills and then became coach when Darren Gee took over as assistant. Gaunt was then assistant to Ian Richardson and Ross Maclaren to Gudjon Thordarson while John Gannon filled the role under Steve Thompson in 2006. In more recent years the coaching staff has increased to include a specialist goalkeeping coach (Steve Cherry in 2006/07) and Mike Whitlow as player coach in 2005/06.

Although Howard Wilkinson and Larry Lloyd became team managers with Jimmy Sirrel as their general manager the two former were to all practical purposes the day-to-day managers. Later in 1995/96 and the first half of 1996/97 Steve Thompson was team manager with Colin Murphy general manager.

COCA COLA CUP: see Football League Cup

COLOURS

The club colours were originally amber and black hoops and at first the players also wore blue caps. Amber and black stayed until 1880 when chocolate and Cambridge blue halves were paraded for the first time on December 11th that year. From the formation of the limited company in summer 1890, black and white stripes have been the norm, though with variations. When County won promotion to Division 1 in 1922/23 the board decided on July 4th 1923 to switch to white shirts with a black V and a Magpie badge on the breast. After relegation in 1925/26 it was agreed on June 29th 1926 to revert to black and white stripes.

When Charlie Jones was appointed manager for 1934/35 he undertook a thorough overhaul of the club including changing the colours back to chocolate and Cambridge blue halves but instant relegation saw a quick return to black and white stripes for 1935/36. On occasions during the war years black and white hoops were preferred but for 1946/47 white shirts with black collars and cuffs came in. Black and white stripes made yet another return for 1952/53 after the departure of Tommy Lawton who therefore never played in this traditional strip.

The final big change was for 1962/63 when the design was white shirts with a black circle round the neck and the club badge on the breast. This lasted for just the one season and since then the Magpies have stood by black and white stripes though from 1977/78 there have been an increasing number of variations on this basic design, often prompted by commercial and sponsorship considerations. The number and thickness of the stripes have varied, including a black pin stripe on a white shirt, a white-breasted shirt with stripes around it and a gold trim with the black stripes while, of course, sponsors' names came and went. The traditional black shorts were also discarded for white ones for a period in the 1990s but it seems that County will now forever be faithful to black and white. The colours for away change strips to avoid a shirts clash with the opposition have been varied many times.

Since 1984, the shirts have included the name of the club sponsors as follows: 1984 (February) Monarch; 1984/85 to 1986/87 Wrangler; 1987/88 to 1988/89 Home Ales; 1989/90 to 1993/94 Home Bitter (from 1990/91 McEwans Lager on some away and change strips); 1994/95 to 1995/96 Harp Lager; 1996/97 to 1999/2000 SAPA Aluminium; 2000/01 SportsLogic; 2001/02 Logitog; 2002/03 Paragon Interiors; 2003/04 Fascia Mania; 2004/05 to 2005/06 Paragon Interiors; 2006/07 Medoc.

When the Magpies met Huddersfield Town (a), Division 3, November 25th 1989, they started the game wearing their usual black and white stripes while the home side were in blue and white stripes but at half-time referee A.B.Wilkie ordered County to change so they came out for the second half in Huddersfield's away strip of yellow and black check. This did not prevent the Magpies from clocking up a 2-1 victory.

CORINTHIANS

The most famous club in the history of amateur football were formed in 1882 and relied mainly on university and public school players for their strength. Two years later Notts County played the first of a series of matches against the Corinthians, on November 13th 1884 (h) when they thrashed the amateurs 7-1. Yet only a month later the Corinthians beat F.A.Cup holders Blackburn Rovers 8-1. The series ended on February 16th 1907 when Notts lost 4-1 (a) and shortly after this match the breakaway Amateur Football Association which included the Corinthians split with the F.A. Consequently matches with A.F.A. clubs were banned so ending these games with Notts County. Complete record from County's viewpoint: P.20 W.9 D.3 L.8 F.48 A.46. Notts County's biggest win was the first match detailed above while the heaviest defeat was 7-0 (a) on March 6th 1886. In 1939 the Corinthians amalgamated with the Casuals and now play as Corinthian-Casuals in one of the lower leagues.

COUNTY CUP

This competition was instituted by the Nottinghamshire F.A. in 1936/37 for the county's senior clubs and continued until the outbreak of war. It was restarted in 1960/61 when it was restricted to the three Football League clubs in Nottinghamshire, Notts County, Nottingham Forest and Mansfield Town. Pre-war Newark Town of the Midland League also took part though they never met the Magpies. After being in abeyance since 2002 the County Cup was revived in 2006/07.

The Magpies' first match in the County Cup was v Mansfield Town (a), October 14th 1936 and they won 5-1. This is still their record win in the tournament and Harry Mardon's hat-trick remains one of only two for Notts in the County Cup, the other being by David Reeves v Mansfield Town (h), April 20th 1993. Notts went on to beat Forest in the final 1-0 after extra time to become the first holders of the trophy. Their record defeat is 7-1 v Forest (a), May 18th 1982.

Notts made a notable fight-back v Forest (a), May 8th 1961 when they were 3-0 down with 23 minutes left. Goals by Chris Joyce (71 and 84 minutes) and Alan Withers (87) levelled it at 3-3 but Forest scored the decider in extra time.

Tony Flower was not only County's first substitute in the competition when he replaced Stan Marshall after 64 minutes v Mansfield Town (h), October 25th 1966, but also became the first substitute to score, a feat he achieved only one minute after coming into the game.

The first penalty tie-breaker in the County Cup was also the first time the Magpies had been involved in one. This was v Mansfield Town (a), May 1st 1975 after a 0-0 draw. Notts won the shoot-out 5-4 and their first scorer was Eric Probert.

The record Meadow Lane attendance in the County Cup is 14,442 v Forest, April 14th 1964 but when the two sides met at the City Ground on May 9th 1967 a crowd of 22,851 set up the overall competition record.

The Magpies have won the County Cup six times in all; in 1936/37, 1962/63, 1974/75, 1975/76, 1984/85 and 1994/95. Complete record: P.66 W.21 D.11 L.34 F.93 A.122, with 8 of the draws won on penalties and 3 lost.

CRICKET

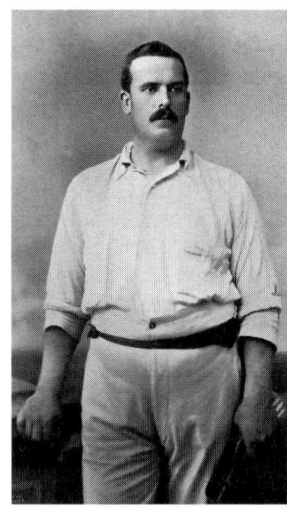

William Gunn   *Johnny Dixon*   *Harry Daft*   *Mordecai Sherwin*

Many first-class cricketers have played for Notts County in League and Cup games, the last one being Dennis Oakes who represented Warwickshire five times in 1965 and made his last appearance for the Magpies v Exeter City (h) on May 1st 1971.

During the 1880s a large number of Nottinghamshire cricketers were associated with County and in 1883/84 as many as six played together in seven F.A. Cup ties. They were Mordecai Sherwin, Herbert Emmitt, William Gunn, Arthur Cursham, Johnny Dixon and Harry Cursham. In addition both Harry Moore and Stuart Macrae, who also played in these Cup games, had appeared for Nottinghamshire Colts while Moore went on to play for South Australia when engaged as a cricket professional in Adelaide.

Following is a list of Notts County footballers known to have appeared in first-class cricket with the date of their debut for County: James Burns (Essex; Notts debut 1891/92); Ian Buxton (Derbyshire; Notts 1969/70); Arthur Cursham (Nottinghamshire and Derbyshire; Notts 1872/73); Harry Cursham (Nottinghamshire; Notts 1877/78); Harry Daft (Nottinghamshire; Notts 1885/86); Johnny Dixon (Nottinghamshire; Notts 1883/84); Herbert Emmitt (Nottinghamshire; Notts 1882/83); Billy Flint (Nottinghamshire; Notts 1908/09); William Gunn (Nottinghamshire plus 11 Tests for England;

Notts 1882/83); Frank Guttridge (Nottinghamshire and Sussex; Notts 1888/89); Arthur Henfrey (Cambridge University; Notts 1893/94); Eric Houghton (Warwickshire; Notts 1946/47); Albert Iremonger (Nottinghamshire; Notts 1904/05); Garnet Lee (Nottinghamshire and Derbyshire; Notts 1910/11); Tinsley Lindley (Cambridge University and Nottinghamshire; Notts 1885/86); Billy Locker (Derbyshire; Notts 1890/91); Harry Moore (South Australia; Notts 1881/82); Dennis Oakes (Warwickshire; Notts 1967/68); Hugh Owen (Cambridge University and Essex; Notts 1888/89); Harry Pennington (Lancashire; Notts 1900/01); Jack Sharpe (Surrey and Nottinghamshire plus 3 Tests for England; Notts 1889/90); Mordecai Sherwin (Nottinghamshire plus 3 Tests for England; Notts 1883/84); Tom Simpson (Nottinghamshire; Notts 1899/1900); Sam Widdowson (Nottinghamshire; Notts 1872/73).

Many other cricketers played for County in the early days of non-competitive matches and later there were several who appeared in Minor County cricket such as Alfred Harrisson (Lincolnshire) and Haydn Morley who played for Derbyshire in non first-class games.

Double international
William Gunn played for England v Scotland and Wales at football in 1883/84 and then played in 11 Test matches against Australia between 1886 and 1899.

Test cricket
Mordecai Sherwin and Jack Sharpe are the only other Notts County players to win Test cricket caps, Sherwin playing three times against Australia in 1886/87 and 1888 while Sharpe also faced Australia three times in 1890 and 1891/92.

International football
Cricketers Arthur Cursham, Harry Cursham, Harry Daft, Johnny Dixon, William Gunn and Harry Moore all played for England at football while with Notts County. Four more cricketers who played for Notts County, Arthur Henfrey (Corinthians), Eric Houghton (Aston Villa), Tinsley Lindley (Nottingham Forest) and Sam Widdowson (Nottingham Forest), also played football for England while with the clubs named.

CRISES

1872: In 1867 Notts decided to stage athletic sports so a band was hired, prizes were awarded and a big crowd turned up but the deficit was nearly £30, a large sum in those days. Members' subscriptions were increased from 5s to 10s but the 1869 sports also produced a financial loss so that the club were by now £60 in debt. Members then took out £1 debentures but in February 1872 the *Nottingham Daily Guardian* announced "Imminent Demise of the Notts Club" after only four players turned up for an away match at Lincoln. Of course it wasn't but it took Notts more than ten years to clear the debt.

1881: Several seasons of poor results by Notts climaxed early in 1881/82 when both Blackburn Rovers and Queen's Park handed out 10-1 thrashings. With membership below 40 and the athletics debt still not paid off there was talk of winding up the club. A crisis meeting was held at the Lion Hotel when committee member Arthur Ashwell took the chair to make a fighting speech and encourage the club to continue. Those great forwards Arthur and Harry Cursham gave their backing and Notts lived to fight on to such effect that they reached the F.A.Cup semi-finals in 1882/83 and 1883/84.

1893: In 1890/91 the Magpies were losing F.A.Cup finalists and finished third in the Football League with their reserves as champions of the Midland Alliance. Boosted by such success, grandiose plans were laid for a billiards room and clubhouse on Thurland Street, while the paying out of more and higher wages to the growing army of Scottish professionals and a deficiency of £248 13s 4d caused by the need to set up a limited company in 1890 combined with a lack of discipline both on and off the field to bring Notts close to financial disaster. By the end of 1892/93 Notts had been relegated to Division 2, the finances worsened, the club chairman and four other directors quit and the annual meeting was told that only drastic economies would enable the club to survive. So serious was the position that at one stage Notts considered declining to compete in Division 2 and to opt for the Midland League with the chance of more local derbies. Sanity prevailed, however, and the F.A.Cup success of 1893/94 turned things round.

1928: The directors decided that the club's financial burden was too great so plans were made to wind up the old company of Notts Incorporated FC and launch a new one, Notts County Football Club Limited with a share capital of £20,000. For the plan to succeed the supporters had to buy the £20,000 shares but support was poor so that the new company was put into voluntary liquidation and the old company reinstated.

1965: From 1955 to 1965 the Magpies had been a struggling club, lifted only by two excellent seasons under manager Frank Hill. Early in December 1965 the directors decided that the financial position was hopeless and Notts could not continue. Local journalist Colin Slater took an important role in persuading experienced managers Andy Beattie and Peter Doherty to act as unpaid advisers to the club and, encouraged by this, Nottingham businessman Bill Hopcroft rescued the Magpies with a £10,000 cash injection. Four years later Jimmy Sirrel arrived as manager and the lean years were over ... for a time.

1986: Before the start of 1986/87 Magpies chairman Jack Dunnett stated that the club had a deficit of £1.8m and County could soon be facing liquidation. As part of a recovery plan, the Lifeline fund-raising scheme was introduced and to this day continues to help Notts. It was launched with a hugely successful and profitable evening at the Astoria night club which pulled in 1,500 fans and a Lifeline friendly against Forest was also staged which raised £14,899

2003: In November 2000 Notts chairman Derek Pavis signed a deal to sell his share holding to American Albert Scardino. Though the payments to Pavis were to be in instalments which later stalled, Scardino took control and appointed Peter Storrie as deputy chief executive with responsibility for the day-to-day running of County. New signings at large salaries were made in a gamble to achieve immediate promotion and when results failed to materialise the club were facing debts of around £6 million. On June 17th 2002 the Magpies were put into administration and their future looked bleak. After various failed attempts by prospective new owners to complete a satisfactory deal, the Football League lost patience and set a deadline for Notts to find acceptable owners or be expelled from the League. Happily, the League was persuaded to extend the deadline and agreed to transfer the Notts County share in the Football League to the Blenheim Consortium on December 3rd 2003 just before the new deadline was due to expire.
See also **Limited Company**.

DEBUTS
Most debutants in a match
The highest number of players to make their Football League debuts in a single match for Notts County are, of course, the eleven who took part in the club's first-ever League encounter in September 1888. Discounting this exceptional occasion, the record is nine v Bournemouth (h) on August 31st 1946, Division 3S, the debutants being Reg Beresford, Cyril Brown, Harry Brown, Horace Cumner, Eddie Gannon, Jack Hubbard, Albert Parks, George Robinson and Fred Whittaker. As this was the first League match after the seven-season break for the Second World War, it perhaps should not be counted. Three of the nine had played for the Magpies already in the 1945/46 F.A.Cup.

Nine was also the total number of debutants v Lincoln City (a) on August 5th 2006, League 2*, but three of the players involved came on as substitutes. The six who started the match were Lawrie Dudfield, Jason Lee, Austin McCann, Ian Ross, Gary Silk and Alan White with the addition of substitutes Tom Curtis, Junior Mendes and Tcham N'Toya.

The next highest number is seven v Aston Villa (h) on December 8th 1888, Football League, when the players were Tom Cooke, Charlie Dobson, Haydn Morley, Arthur Shaw, Herbert Snook, Fred Weightman and Tom Widdowson. Again, there were special circumstances surrounding this game as it took place while County's first team were away playing an F.A.Cup tie the same afternoon. Of the seven, two were veterans who had previously played F.A.Cup games for Notts and two were borrowed from local club Notts Rangers.

In pre-substitute days six debutants were fielded on two occasions, as follows: v Wolverhampton Wanderers (a) on September 7th 1889, Football League (Sandy Ferguson, James Macmillan, Jimmy Oswald, Johnny Oswald, William "Tich" Smith and George Toone); and v Swindon Town (a), August 27th 1938, Division 3S (Tom Flower, Benny Gaughran, Sid Protheroe, Charles "Chick" Read, Jimmy Watson and Archie Young).

Unlucky debut
Jimmy Jackson was injured during his debut v Bristol City (h) on April 15th 1949. Because he was then called up for National Service his next match for the Magpies was delayed until October 13th 1951 or two-and-a-half years later.

Walter Coulston made his debut, also v Bristol City (h), on May 6th 1939 shortly after being signed from Barnsley. Because of the outbreak of war at the start of the following season, this remained his only official League outing for Notts though he did play in the two 1939/40 matches which were scrubbed from the records after the outbreak of war forced the League to abandon its programme.

See under **Goalscoring** for goals on debut.

DISCIPLINARY
Sent off
In the early years of the Football League referees were reluctant to impose the ultimate sanction of dismissing a player from the field. Fouls or bad tackles tended to be regarded as "all part of the game" so that a misplaced shoulder charge could result in serious injury to the recipient but would be viewed by the referee as an accident. However, one sure way to get sent off then as now would be to insult or swear at the official.

For instance, when the referee abandoned County's match at Tottenham in 1912/13 because of fog with just eight minutes left and the Magpies leading 3-1, goalkeeper Albert Iremonger's outburst of "offensive remarks" at the official led to a three-match ban and the end of Albert's club record run of successive appearances.

This relaxed state of affairs lasted for some three-quarters of a century and as recently as 1967 Nottingham Forest were commended by the League for not having a player sent off in 28 years! In this context it is worth noting that Notts skipper Jack Montgomery was sent off twice in 1906/07, first v Liverpool and then v Birmingham; an unusual if unwanted feat at that time. From the early 1970s, though, referees were increasingly instructed to clamp down on foul or violent play and the red card system was introduced in October 1976 though it was discontinued in 1981 before being reinstated in 1987.

As far as the Magpies were concerned we have records of only eight players being sent off during the 20-year inter-war period so that players holding the club's sending-off records date from more recent times with its less lenient refereeing. The highest number of sendings off for Notts in a single season is eight in 2001/02 when Danny Allsopp, Ian Baraclough, Nicky Fenton, Stuart Garden, Simon Grayson, Richard Liburd (twice) and Lee Wilkie all had to take the traditional early bath. Next comes 1994/95 with six and the "naughty boys" were Paul Devlin (twice), Martin Kuhl, John Williams and Dean Yates (twice) with both Devlin and Yates getting one of their red cards in Anglo-Italian Cup games. Dean Yates is the most sent-off Magpie with six dismissals followed by Ian Richardson with four.

The Tinsley Lindley affair
Notts County drew 1-1 v Aston Villa (h), Football League, November 9th 1889, when they included Tinsley Lindley, the England and Nottingham Forest striker. Lindley had been signed specifically for this game and Villa made an official protest at a time when rules governing a player's qualification were stricter than they became later. County were found guilty and fined £5 plus the deduction of a League point. The club, as they were entitled to do under the then regulations, called a special meeting of all 12 League clubs and Lindley, a barrister by profession, presented his own defence. He argued that Notts had been subjected to two punishments for one offence, the fine and the deduction. The League agreed and reinstated the point but upped the fine to £25.

Special match
Notts lost 6-0 in a League match v Preston North End (a) on December 12th 1891. Heavy snow and extreme cold led to five Notts players walking off when the score was 4-0 and Preston added two more goals against a five-man Magpie side which had earlier lost Archie Osborne who left the field following a scuffle with Preston's Drummond and did not return. Preston protested about the behaviour of the County players; however the League ordered that the result should stand but that the clubs should play a second game on January 25th 1892 with Preston receiving half the gate money and the other half being split between the League and Notts. Preston won that 6-2 but Notts pocketed £10 8s, their share of the gate.

Ford Sporting League
In 1970/71 the Ford Motor Company sponsored a League-approved competition in which points were awarded or deducted based on goals scored and disciplinary records. All 92 League clubs were grouped in one large table using actual results from all four divisions with the first 42 games being used for Division 3 and 4 clubs. Clubs won a point for each home goal, two points for each away goal while five were deducted for each booking and ten for each sending off. The Magpies, who were Division 4 champions that season, finished 13th of the 92, earning 109 goalscoring points and losing 55 disciplinary ones. So they ended up with 54 points compared with top club Oldham Athletic's 97 and bottom outfit Bolton Wanderers with minus 57. This was the only season of this competition.

The Charlton Athletic postponement
On December 8th 1990 the Magpies were due to play Charlton Athletic in a Division 2 match at Selhurst Park but a heavy snowstorm in the midlands and the north led to 29 League and Cup games being called off. However, London was not affected by the weather and Selhurst Park was perfectly playable but Notts had planned to travel on the Saturday morning. As a result they were unable to get clear of Nottingham and so their game was postponed. The Football League fined County heavily for not turning up as scheduled. According to the League, Notts should have noted the weather forecast and travelled to London on the Friday. The club were also warned as to their future conduct in this matter. They lost the rearranged game 3-1 on January 22nd 1991.

FAMILIES
Twins
Teddy and Billy May played together in two League matches for Notts during 1888/89, v Blackburn Rovers on December 15th and v Derby County on December 22nd 1888 (both away).

Brothers
Apart from the May twins, there have been many instances of brothers appearing for the club. These are the instances in the Football League when brothers appeared together:

Two sets of brothers in the same Notts team, 1961/62. From left, Peter and John Butler, Tony and Peter Bircumshaw

In 1888/89 two sets of brothers appeared together v Derby County (a) on December 22nd 1888, the May twins (see above) and Alf and Charlie Shelton. This feat was repeated in 1961/62 when Peter and Tony Bircumshaw together with John and Peter Butler turned out against Portsmouth (a) on February 24th 1962 and again v Barnsley (h) on March 3rd.

In total the Mays played together in two matches in 1888/89 and the Sheltons in 15. The latter pair also made four appearances together in 1890/91. In 1961/62 the Bircumshaws lined up together 13 times and the Butlers six. The Bircumshaws had earlier achieved the feat in two matches in 1960/61.

Jimmy and Johnny Oswald appeared together in 19 matches in 1889/90, then Ike and Albert Waterall lined up together in five matches in 1910/11, three in 1911/12 and six in 1912/13. A third brother, Tom, played in 1906/07 when Ike also appeared but the two never turned out together. Percy and Bertie "Paddy" Mills played together in two matches in 1927/28 and 15 in 1928/29. Finally, Craig and Chris Short were teammates 16 times in 1990/91, 25 in 1991/92 and once in 1992/93.

Although brothers Chris and Wayne Fairclough both played for the Magpies, their spells at Meadow Lane did not coincide so they never played together for the club. Wayne left in 1990 whereas Chris did not make his Notts debut until 1998 towards the end of his distinguished career.

Similarly, brothers Harry and Garnet Walkerdine spent different periods with Notts. Harry played 1890-93 and Garnet appeared once in 1903/04.

In early F.A.Cup ties there were several instances of multiple sets of brothers appearing together. Ernest, Harold and Richard Greenhalgh appeared v Sheffield FC (h) on November 3rd 1877 while Charles and Harry Cursham were also in this Notts team. The same three Greenhalghs plus brothers Erasmus and St.John Keely appeared together in the replay (a) on December 1st 1877.

The three Greenhalghs plus three Curshams, Arthur, Charles and Harry, teamed up together v Nottingham Forest (h) on November 15th 1878. The three Curshams along with Ernest and Harold Greenhalgh were together in three F.A.Cup ties in 1880/81. Then the Curshams went on to play together in five F.A.Cup matches in 1881/82 along with Alf and Charlie Dobson. In 1882/83 and 1883/84 Arthur and Harry Cursham and Alf and Charlie Dobson appeared together in 12 F.A.Cup ties. There are many other occasions where single pairs of brothers appeared together in the F.A.Cup.

Four brothers Snook appeared for County in the 1880s though none of them played together in a competitive match, only in friendlies. Fred had five F.A.Cup outings, Herbert one in the League and three in the Cup, James one in the Cup and Percy two in the Cup.

In the 1860s and 1870s various members of the Rothera family were involved with Notts County. Brothers Charles and Fred were players together and both later had a spell as club secretary. Charles was the scorer of the first Notts hat-trick, v South Derbyshire (a), November 18th 1869.

Father and son
Goalkeeper George Toone played between 1889/90 and 1901/02 while his son, George junior, played once in 1913/14 before going on to become a Watford regular. Harry Daft played between 1884/85 and 1894/95 while his father, Richard, captained Notts in the late 1860s before the institution of competitive football. Both Dafts also played cricket for Nottinghamshire.

General
For seven seasons brothers Albert and Jimmy Iremonger were on County's staff. Ex-Forester Jimmy was appointed trainer in 1919/20 and Albert ended his 21-year playing career with the Magpies at the close of 1925/26.

FLOODLIGHTS

The first game under floodlights in England took place at Bramall Lane, Sheffield, on October 14th 1878 and was considered to be a great success so such matches were quickly arranged elsewhere. The first one involving Notts County was v Derbyshire at Trent Bridge on November 30th the same year. An estimated attendance of 4,000 saw County win 1-0 with a 47th minute goal from Tom Oliver but the *Nottingham Daily Express* summed up: "Financially the match was a marked success but regarded as an exhibition of the electric light it was scarcely so successful as could have been desired."

The power was generated on the ground by two portable engines, one behind each goal driving Siemens dynamos. The *Express* report gave some details, saying that the machines were "capable of producing equal to 6,000 and 3,000 candles respectively. Each lamp was suspended on a pole about 15ft in altitude, about 20ft in front of each of the goal posts which were about 110yds apart. Behind each lamp was a reflector so as to cast the light over the space occupied by the players. The current was conveyed to each lamp by cables of copper wire insulated by gutta percha, the positive wire being about one-eighth of an inch in diameter and the negative wire about a quarter of an inch thick."

Problems were caused because it was a foggy night which meant that more lights should have been used. One light went out when the belt of one of the driving engines flew off and while repairs were being carried out the crowd was left in darkness. At other times the lights flickered but the engineers soon had things working again.

Floodlight matches under more modern conditions were held back for many years because of an F.A. prohibition and progress did not come until a resolution of January 1951 which lifted the ban for friendly and exhibition games. Among the pioneers of floodlights at this period were Notts County who installed them for an opening match at Meadow Lane against Derby County on March 23rd 1953. The match was a 1-1 draw and attracted a crowd of 20,193.

Within three years the F.A. lifted the ban on lights for League and Cup games but improved and higher standards of lighting meant that the Meadow Lane set soon had to be replaced. New lights were therefore installed at a cost of £22,500 and they were officially opened v Port Vale, Division 3, October 11th 1962.

A further new and improved set was in place for the start of 1977/78 and these were in their turn replaced when the ground was upgraded in 1992.

F.A.CUP

The plan for a Football Association Challenge Cup was proposed on July 20th 1871 and approved on October 15th, the competition getting under way later that same year.

First match
Notts County first entered for 1877/78, their opening match was v Sheffield at Trent Bridge on November 3rd 1877 and it was drawn 1-1. Harry Cursham scored for Notts who lined up: Harold Greenhalgh; Ernest Greenhalgh, Henry Jessop; George Seals, Sam Widdowson; Alfred Pearson, Richard Greenhalgh, Charles Cursham, Erasmus Keely, Harry Cursham, Tom Oliver. The replay at Sheffield on December 1st was lost 3-0.

Winners
On March 31st 1894 the Magpies beat Bolton Wanderers 4-1 at Goodison Park in the 1893/94 Cup final to become the first Division 2 side to win the trophy. Logan (3) and Watson scored for Notts whose team was: George Toone; Theo "Fay" Harper, Jack Hendry; Charlie Bramley, Davey Calderhead, Alf Shelton; Arthur Watson, Sam Donnelly, Jimmy Logan, Dan Bruce, Harry Daft. Att. 37,000; receipts £1,189.

Runners-up
Notts lost 3-1 to Blackburn Rovers at Kennington Oval on March 21st 1891. Jimmy Oswald scored for Notts before a crowd of 23,000. Receipts were £1,454.

Semi-finalists
The club reached the semi-finals on three other occasions as follows:
March 17th 1883 v Old Etonians at Kennington Oval. Lost 2-1; scorer Harry Cursham. Notts led 1-0 at half-time.
March 1st 1884 v Blackburn Rovers at Aston Lower Grounds, Birmingham. Lost 1-0.
March 25th 1922 v Huddersfield Town at Turf Moor, Burnley. Lost 3-1; scorer Harold Hill.

The Cup
The trophy which the Magpies won in 1893/94 is not the present one but was the first of four. It was much smaller than the existing one, cost about £20 and was made early in 1872 by Messrs Martin, Hall & Co. Only a year after Notts let the Cup go on show in a shop window in Arkwright Street, it was stolen from another shop window display, this time in Birmingham, and the holders, Aston Villa, were fined £25 by the F.A. It was never recovered.

Extra time
The first occasion Notts were involved in extra time was on November 27th 1880 for a first round replay against Derbyshire (a). The score after 90 minutes was 2-2 but County went on to win 4-2.

Meadow Lane
Although the ground was opened at the start of 1910/11, the first F.A. Cup tie played there was not until January 10th 1920 when Millwall were beaten 2-0 in a first round game. In the intervening years the Magpies had been drawn away for five successive seasons and then the First World War extended the gap.

Replays
In 1923/24 Crystal Palace beat Notts 2-1 in the second round after three 0-0 draws. So only three goals were scored in seven hours of play inclusive of extra time.

Substitutes
The first substitute used by the Magpies in an F.A. Cup game was Paddy McGovern v Runcorn (a), first round on December 9th 1967. He came on for Ron Farmer.

Scotland
The last season in which Scottish clubs competed was 1886/87. Up to that point Queen's Park were the only Scottish opponents of Notts in the Cup. The Scots drew 2-2 at Trent Bridge in the sixth round in 1884/85 and won the replay 2-1 at Derby Cricket Ground.

Sold ground rights
When the Magpies were drawn at home to Bradford City in the first round on January 15th 1910 they sold the ground rights to their opponents for £1,000. The match therefore took place at Valley Parade and Bradford won 4-2.

Qualifying Competition
In 1888/89, Notts had to enter the qualifying competition for the only time in their history. They won four such matches and went on to reach the second round proper. The extra Cup games clashed with the Football League programme so that Notts played League and Cup games on the same day three times as follows:

October 6th 1888 v Blackburn Rovers (h) 3-3 (League); v Eckington (h) 4-1 (Cup). Both were played at Trent Bridge successively, starting at lunch-time.

October 27th 1888 v Burnley (h) 6-1 (League); v Beeston St John's (h) 4-2 (Cup). Again, both at Trent Bridge.

December 8th 1888 v Aston Villa (h) 2-4 (League); v Staveley (a) 3-1 (Cup).

In the first two matches the Cup side was mainly made up of reserves but in the third one, it was the League game which featured the reserves.

Two-legged ties
In 1945/46 only, the Cup used two-legged ties for the rounds proper, except for the semi-finals and final. In the first round the Magpies beat Bradford City 4-3 on aggregate but lost 3-2 to Northampton Town in the next round.

Walkovers
Twice Notts have been given walkovers in the Cup when their opponents scratched. On November 5th 1881 Birmingham Calthorpe conceded and on November 5th 1887 Basford Rovers did the same.

Best and worst sequences
Winning run: 5 matches October 6th 1888 to February 2nd 1889; unbeaten run: 9 matches (4 won, 5 drawn) January 7th to March 8th 1922; losing run: 6 matches December 5th 1964 to November 15th 1969; winless run: 6 matches (5 lost, 1 drawn) January 24th 1931 to January 12th 1935.

Complete record
County's complete record: P.313 W.135 D.59 L.119 F.581 A.461, which divides into Home: P.152 W.79 D.33 L.40 F.346 A.177; and Away: P.161 W.56 D.26 L.79 F.235 A.284. In addition there were four early ties declared void after protests, as follows: P.4 W.2 L.2 F.8 A.13.
See also under **PROTESTS**.

FOOTBALL LEAGUE

Notts County were founder members of the Football League which was formed on April 17th 1888 at a meeting held at the Royal Hotel, Manchester, following preliminary meetings at Anderton's Hotel, Fleet Street, London, during March.

First matches
The club's first match in the League was on September 15th v Everton at Anfield, losing 2-1 with Moore as County's scorer. Team: Jack Holland; Frank Guttridge, Tom McLean; George Brown, Ben Warburton, Alf Shelton; Billy Hodder, Ted Harker, Bob Jardine, Albert Moore, Edwin Wardle.

The first home match followed on October 6th 1888 at Trent Bridge v Blackburn Rovers and was drawn 3-3. County scorers were Daft, Jardine and Moore. Team: Holland; Warburton, Guttridge; Brown, Charlie Shelton, Alf Shelton; Hodder, Moore, Tom Allin, Harry Daft, Jardine.

County's first match in Division 2 was on September 2nd 1893 v Crewe Alexandra at the Alexandra Ground and resulted in a 2-0 win with goals from Bruce and Watson. Team: George Toone; Theo "Fay" Harper, Jack Hendry; Archie Osborne, Davey Calderhead, Alf Shelton; Arthur Watson, Sam Donnelly, Dan Bruce, George Kerr, Harry Dixon.

The first match in Division 3S came on August 30th 1930 v Coventry City at Highfield Road which was won 2-1. Watson (own goal) and Keetley scored for the Magpies. Team: Jimmy Ferguson; Percy Mills, Charlie Bisby; Jack Dowsey, Frank Froggatt, Haydn Kemp; George Taylor, Tom Fenner, Tom Keetley, Harold Andrews, Sam Haden.

When the two third divisions were split into Division 3 and 4 in 1958, County's first game in the new Division 3 was on August 23rd 1958 v Accrington Stanley at Meadow Lane which was a 1-1 draw. Newsham scored for Notts. Team: Jimmy Linton; Ray Chatham, Frank Cruickshank; Bert Loxley, Peter Russell, Gerry Carver; Don Roby, Ron Wylie, Jackie Lane, Stan Newsham, Johnny Langford.

Immediate relegation saw Notts play their first Division 4 match on August 22nd 1959 v Chester at Meadow Lane and win 2-1. Roby and Newsham were the scorers for County. Team: George Smith; John Butler, Cruickshank; John Sheridan, Ken Rawson, Carver; Roby, Chris Joyce, Bob Forrest, Roy Horobin, Alan Withers.

The Magpies played their 1,000th League match on February 25th 1922 v West Ham United (a) when they lost 2-1; their 2,000th came on December 13th 1952 v Blackburn Rovers (h), marked with a 5-0 victory and four goals from Ken McPherson; with No.3,000 Notts were the first League club to reach this figure and fittingly the game on March 25th 1975 was v Nottingham Forest (h) for a 2-2 draw; and finally the 4,000th game was on January 10th 1998 v Rochdale (a) resulting in a 2-1 win. This came in the middle of their club record sequence of ten successive victories, six of them away.

By the close of 2006/07 County had clocked up 4,434 League games. These figures exclude the two games of the abandoned 1939/40 season as well as test matches and play-offs.

Top of the pile
The Magpies headed the Football League on December 20th 1890 with only five games left to play in a 22-match campaign but they took only four more points and finished third. They briefly topped the League a few more times during their early seasons, the last occasion being on November 29th 1924. This ignores the more modern case of August 30th 1983 when only two games had been completed.

Bottom spot
Notts County were bottom of the entire Football League on September 21st 1968 and again on September 18th 2004.

Oddities
Although the Magpies won the Division 2 title in 1922/23 they finished with more points than goals! They gained 53 points from 42 matches but scored only 46 goals.

When Notts were relegated from Division 1 at the end of the 1991/92 season they dropped down into Division 1! This was because the new F.A. Premier League began operations in 1992/93, leaving the Football League with three divisions instead of four. Hence the old Division 2 was retitled Division 1.

Records
Most wins in a season: 30 in 1970/71 (Division 4, 46 matches).
Fewest defeats in a season: 5 in 1997/98 (Division 3*, 46 matches).
Fewest wins in a season: 5 in 1888/89 (League, 22 matches); 1904/05 (Division 1, 34 matches). In programme of 38 matches: 7 in 1912/13 (Division 1); In programme of 46 matches: 7 in 1996/97 (Division 2*).
Most defeats in a season: 28 in 1963/64 (Division 3, 46 matches).
Most draws in a season: 18 in 1968/69 (Division 4, 46 matches).
Fewest draws in a season: 2 in 1888/89 (League, 22 matches); 1895/96 (Division 2, 30 matches). In programme of 34 matches: 4 in 1900/01 (Division 1); 1901/02 (Division 1). In programme of 42 matches: 5 in 1926/27 (Division 2); 1948/49 (Division 3S). In programme of 46 matches: 8 in 1959/60 (Division 4); 1969/70 (Division 4).
Most goals scored in a season: 107 in 1959/60 (Division 4, 46 matches); 102 in 1948/49 (Division 3S, 42 matches).
Most goals conceded in a season: 97 in 1934/35 (Division 2, 42 matches).
Fewest goals scored in a season: 28 in 1912/13 (Division 1, 38 matches). In programme of 46 matches: 33 in 1996/97 (Division 2*, 46 matches).
Fewest goals conceded in a season: 31 in 1893/94 (Division 2, 28 matches); 1924/25 (Division 1, 42 matches). In programme of 46 matches: 36 in 1970/71 (Division 4).
Most games scored in during season: 43 in 1959/60 (Division 4, 46 matches) and 1971/72 (Division 3, 46 matches); in 42-match season 39 in 1930/31 (Division 3S). In 1896/97 Notts scored in all 30 Division 2 matches.
Fewest games scored in during season: 24 in 1996/97 (Division 2*, 46 matches).
Most clean sheets during season: 23 in 1922/23 (Division 2, 42 matches).
Most matches without a clean sheet during season: 37 in 1934/35 (Division 2, 42 matches), 1955/56 (Division 2, 42 matches) and 1981/82 (Division 1, 42 matches).
Longest unbeaten run: 19 matches from April 26th 1930 (Division 2) to December 6th 1930 (Division 3S).
Longest winning run: 10 matches from December 3rd 1997 to January 31st 1998 (Division 3*).
Longest run of drawn matches: 5 matches from December 2nd to December 26th 1978 (Division 2).
Longest run of defeats: 7 matches from September 4th to November 2nd 1912 (Division 1); and from April 8th to May 6th 1933 (Division 2, the last 7 matches of the season).
Longest run without a win: 18 matches from November 26th 1904 to April 8th 1905 (Division 1).
Longest run without a drawn match: 22 matches from February 14th 1903 to November 7th 1903 (Division 1); and from September 12th 1959 to January 9th 1960 (Division 4).
Best start to a season before first defeat: 1930/31 (Division 3S) P.18 W.12 D.6 F.51 A.20 Pts.30; then lost 2-1 to Southend United (a) on December 17th 1930.
Worst start to a season before first win: 1977/78 (Division 2) P.11 D.5 L.6 F.12 A.24 Pts.5; then beat Charlton Athletic (h) 2-0 on October 22nd 1977.
Best winning start to a season: 1893/94 (Division 2) P.4 W.4 F.8 A.2 Pts.8; and 1928/29 (Division 2) P.4 W.4 F.10 A.2 Pts.8.
Worst losing start to a season: 1963/64 (Division 3) P.5 L.5 F.1 A.12 Pts.0.
Longest match scoring sequence: 35 matches from April 26th 1930 (Division 2) to March 21st 1931 (Division 3S). This sequence included scoring in the first 34 matches of 1930/31; and from October 10th 1959 (Division 4) to August 27th 1960 (Division 3). This sequence included scoring in the last 32 matches of 1959/60.
Longest match sequence without keeping a clean sheet: 45 matches from December 24th 1955 to December 29th 1956 (Division 2). These were the last 20 matches of 1955/56 and the first 25 of 1956/57. Strangely, the last clean sheet before the sequence began was a 5-0 win over Middlesbrough (h) and the first afterwards was ... a 5-0 win over Stoke City (h)!
Longest sequence of recording same result: Four successive 1920/21 matches ended 1-1, from October 30th to November 20th 1920, v Cardiff City (a), Coventry City (h & a), and Leicester City (h), so all four matches were against "citys". In 1909/10 between October 23rd and November 27th 1909 three consecutive matches ended in 3-1 victories, then came a 2-1 win which was followed by two more 3-1 successes so that of six wins in a row, five were by 3-1.
See also under **Away Records**; **Goalscoring (team)**; **Home Records**; **Play-offs**; **Points**; **Promotion**; **Re-election**; **Relegation**; **Test Matches**.

FOOTBALL LEAGUE CUP

At the annual meeting of the Football League in May 1960 a proposal that they should introduce their own Cup competition was approved by 31 votes to 16. Whereas entry to the tournament was originally optional it has been compulsory since 1971. Initially unpopular with the leading clubs, the F.L.Cup grew in stature once the decision was made to play the final at Wembley Stadium. The competition has been known by various sponsors' names since 1981: Milk Cup 1981/82 to 1985/86; Littlewoods Challenge Cup 1986/87 to 1989/90; Rumbelows League Cup 1990/91 and 1991/92; Coca Cola Cup 1992/93 to 1997/98; Worthington Cup 1998/99 to 2002/03; Carling Cup 2003/04 to date.

Notts County's first F.L.Cup game was on October 20th 1960 v Brighton and Hove Albion (h) which resulted in a 3-1 defeat with Noon scoring for the Magpies. A crowd of 10,449 saw the following represent Notts: George Smith; John Butler, Harry Noon; John Sheridan, Bert Loxley, Gerry Carver; Don Roby, Chris Joyce, Tony Hateley, Bob Forrest, Alan Withers. The first F.L.Cup game at Meadow Lane was the following season on September 14th 1961 v Derby County, 2-2.

The club's best seasons were in 1963/64, 1972/73 and 1975/76 when they reached the fifth round. The biggest victory was 6-1 v Bolton Wanderers (h), 3rd round, October 30th 1984; the biggest defeat 7-1 v Newcastle United (h), 2nd round 2nd leg, October 5th 1993 and v Manchester City (a), 1st round 2nd leg, August 19th 1998.

Best and worst sequences

Winning run: 4 matches August 16th to October 31st 1972; unbeaten run: 5 matches (2 won, 3 drawn) October 3rd to November 29th 1983; losing run: 5 matches October 8th 1985 to August 25th 1987; winless run: 11 matches (7 lost, 4 drawn) October 26th 1964 to August 17th 1971.

Home service

In 1963/64 Notts County's run to the 5th round was aided by the luck of the draw for in all four ties (plus a bye in the 1st round) the Magpies came out of the hat first and consequently played entirely at Meadow Lane.

Complete playing record: P.135 W.56 D.23 L.56 F.202 A.212, divided as follows: Home P.65 W.36 D.9 L.20 F.127 A.87; Away P.70 W.20 D.14 L.36 F.75 A.125.

See also **Giant-killing**.

FOOTBALL LEAGUE GROUP CUP: see Anglo-Scottish Cup

FOOTBALL LEAGUE TROPHY: see Associate Members Cup

FOREIGN TEAMS

Although the Magpies have never taken part in any of the major European competitions they have played many matches against overseas teams. The first such match was on October 4th 1888 when a Canadian touring team were beaten 2-0 at Trent Bridge.

The first match against a European team was on County's first tour abroad, to Denmark in 1910 where the opening match against a Danish XI was on June 1st, producing a 2-2 draw. Since then there have been many tours to Europe as well as East Africa, the Far East and brief trips to Gibraltar.

The first home European match was on May 10th 1951 as part of the Festival of Britain celebrations when a 1-1 draw was played against FC Austria of Vienna before a crowd of 17,362. A similar celebratory match was against Minsk Dynamo (h) on May 9th 1975 to mark the 30th anniversary of VE Day. It was drawn 4-4 but Minsk won a penalty shoot-out 4-3. In 1993/94 and 1994/95 Notts competed in the Anglo-Italian Cup, the first time they met overseas opposition competitively.

See also **Tours**.

FORMATION

In 1862 young men who worked mainly in Nottingham's banks and law offices used their Thursday half-holiday to play football in The Park, the estate between Nottingham Castle and Derby Road which was not built up then to anywhere near today's extent. As one contemporary report said: "For the first year or two, [Notts] confined itself principally to friendly games among the members", and another: "These gentlemen with others met in The Park Hollow and kicked the ball about with such satisfaction to themselves that they decided to form a club".

A meeting was therefore called at the George Hotel on the corner of George Street on December 7th 1864 where it was agreed that "A Foot Ball Club be established for this County, and that it shall be named the Notts. Foot Ball Club". The following day Notts played their first game against outside opposition, v Trent Valley on the Meadows Cricket Ground and on January 2nd 1865 came their debut against a major side when they lost 1-0 to Sheffield, also on the Meadows Ground.

The major problem in discussing Notts County's formation is reconciling the date of December 7th 1864 with the traditional formation year of 1862 but it seems clear that the pioneers, some of whom were still around in 1912 when the Magpies held a 50th anniversary banquet, regarded the continuity of play from 1862 as more important than the formalisation in 1864. Since the members played only friendly matches among themselves before this date there was no need for a formal organisation until outside opponents were sought.

Pedantically speaking, the correct Notts County formation entry ought to be a qualified one: "Established 1864 after informal play since 1862", but the latter tradition has had too long a life to be challenged now, especially when we have documentary evidence for continuous play from 1862.

Incidentally, in the various sources the club appears as Nottinghamshire, Nottingham, Nottm., Notts., Notts (with and without the full-stop), Notts Club and Notts County but continuity of officials makes it clear that only one club is involved.

The entry in some recent editions of the *SkySports Football Yearbook* (formerly *Rothmans*) about an 1862 match at Cremorne Gardens can safely be ignored for neither the players mentioned in the quoted report nor the venue appear in any of the early sources on Notts County though it does show that football was already popular in Nottingham by that year.

FREIGHT ROVER TROPHY: see Associate Members Cup

FULL MEMBERS CUP
Full members of the Football League were those in the old Divisions 1 and 2. Each club had a vote whereas Division 3 and 4 clubs, who were associate members, had four votes between them. The Full Members Cup ran from 1985/86 to 1991/92 and the Magpies competed in 1990/91 and 1991/92 when it was sponsored as the Zenith Data Systems Cup. In the latter season Notts reached the semi-finals where they lost 2-1 (after extra time) at Meadow Lane to Leicester City before 11,559 fans. County's complete record: P.5 W.2 D.2 L.1 F.8 A.7.

GATE RECEIPTS
As with transfer fees, this section is particularly vulnerable to inflation as will be seen from the following progressive table of the gate receipts record at Magpies home matches (TB indicates Trent Bridge home match):

£564 11s 4d	v Nottingham Forest (TB), Division 1, October 8th 1898. Described as "record for a League game in Nottingham"	
£565	v Nottingham Forest (TB), Division 1, December 26th 1900.	
£681	v Nottingham Forest (TB), Division 1, December 26th 1902.	
£1,335	v Tottenham Hotspur (TB), F.A.Cup 3rd round, February 23rd 1907. 1s gate, double the normal 6d admission	
£755	v Nottingham Forest, Division 1, September 3rd 1910. Meadow Lane opening match	
£1,038 17s 6d	Barnsley v Swindon Town, F.A.Cup semi-final replay, April 3rd 1912, staged at Meadow Lane	
£906 11s 3d	v Derby County, Division 1, October 5th 1912.	
£2,103 1s 8d	v Sheffield Wednesday, Division 2, December 27th 1920.	
£4,129	v Aston Villa, F.A.Cup 2nd round, January 29th 1921.	
£3,600	v Swansea Town, Division 3S, December 26th 1947. Meadow Lane League record	
£5,631 14s 6d	v Portsmouth, F.A.Cup 4th round, February 2nd 1952.	
£6,425 5s 6d	v York City, F.A.Cup 6th round, March 12th 1955.	
£9,611	v Aston Villa, Division 3, March 4th 1972.	
£14,022 76p	v Nottingham Forest, Division 2, December 26th 1973.	
£14,328 11p	v Everton, F.L.Cup 4th round replay, November 25th 1975.	
£23,215 62p	v Leeds United, F.A.Cup 3rd round, January 3rd 1976.	
£22,660 35p	v Nottingham Forest, Division 2, April 9th 1977. Meadow Lane League record	
£30,654 15p	v Aston Villa, F.A.Cup 3rd round, January 5th 1982.	
£63,505	v Everton, F.A.Cup 6th round, March 10th 1984.	
£124,539	v Manchester City, F.A.Cup 5th round, February 16th 1991.	

These details must be read in relation to the minimum admission charges which used to be laid down by the Football League. This is how they rose until the end of the 1970s: Pre-First World War, 6d; 1919/20, 1s; 1942/43, 1s 3d; 1951/52, 1s 5d; 1955/56 2s; 1960/61, 2s 6d; 1965/66, 4s; 1968/69, 5s; 1970/71, 6s; 1972/73, 40p (8s); 1975/76, 65p; 1976/77, 80p; 1977/78, 90p. County's share of the F.A.Cup final receipts in 1893/94 was £199 6s 8d.

GIANT-KILLING
The Magpies seem to have been specialists in falling victim to Cup giant-killers but perhaps they can claim to have pulled off one of the finest pieces of giant-killing of all. That, of course, was to beat Division 1 Bolton Wanderers 4-1 in the F.A.Cup final at Goodison Park in 1893/94, the first Division 2 club to achieve this feat.

Other good performances as a Division 2 side against Division 1 opponents came in 1920/21 when the reigning League champions West Bromwich Albion were beaten 3-0 in the F.A.Cup 1st round; and in 1954/55 when Chelsea, who went on to win the League title that season, were defeated 1-0 in the 5th round.

In more recent times, Notts have achieved some fine results in the F.L.Cup. As a Division 3 side they beat two Division 1 sides, Southampton and Stoke City, in 1972/73 and then in 1975/76, when in Division 2, they knocked out top division giants Leeds United and Everton, the former especially under manager Don Revie being one of the most successful and feared teams in the country.

Since the formation of the Premier League in 1992 the Magpies have gained shocked F.L.Cup victories against two of the elite, Tottenham Hotspur in 1994/95 and Middlesbrough in 2006/07. In the former case Notts were only one tier below in Division 1* but in the second they were in League 2* (the latest manifestation of the old Division 4). On the other hand, in 2002/03, non-Leaguers Southport, who were in the Nationwide Conference, beat Notts 4-2 in the F.A.Cup.

The list which follows shows all occasions when Notts, in a lower division, have beaten a team from the top division and all other wins with more than one division difference between the sides:

4-1 v Bolton Wanderers (Goodison Park), F.A.Cup final, March 31st 1894 (Notts Division 2, opponents Division 1).
3-0 v West Bromwich Albion (h), F.A.Cup 1st round, January 8th 1921 (Notts Division 2, opponents Division 1).
3-1 v Southampton (a), F.L.Cup 3rd round, October 3rd 1972 (Notts Division 3, opponents Division 1).
3-1 v Stoke City (h), F.L.Cup 4th round, October 31st 1972 (Notts Division 3, opponents Division 1).
1-0 v Leeds United (a), F.L.Cup 3rd round, October 8th 1975 (Notts Division 2, opponents Division 1).
2-0 v Everton (h), F.L.Cup 4th round replay, November 25th 1975 (Notts Division 2, opponents Division 1).
1-0 v Manchester City (h), F.A.Cup 5th round, February 16th 1991 (Notts Division 2, opponents Division 1).
3-0 v Tottenham Hotspur (h), F.L.Cup 3rd round, October 26th 1994 (Notts Division 1*, opponents Premier League).
2-1 v Crystal Palace (a), F.L.Cup 1st round, August 22nd 2006 (Notts League 2*, opponents Championship*).
1-0 v Middlesbrough (a), F.L.Cup 2nd round, September 20th 2006 (Notts League 2*, opponents Premier League).
2-1 v Southampton (h), F.L.Cup 3rd round, October 24th 2006 (Notts League 2*, opponents Championship*).

Now come the times when Notts have lost to teams from lower divisions or non-League sides. This includes all occasions when Notts were in the top division but otherwise omits those with just one division difference:

    2-1 v South Shore (a), F.A.Cup 5th round, January 23rd 1886 (Notts among top clubs, opponents almost unknown).
    3-2 v Middlesbrough Ironopolis (a), F.A.Cup 2nd round, February 4th 1893 (Notts Division 1, opponents non-League).
    1-0 v Southampton (h), F.A.Cup 2nd round, February 11th 1899 (Notts Division 1, opponents Southern League).
    2-1 v Reading (h), F.A.Cup 1st round, January 25th 1902 (Notts Division 1, opponents Southern League).
    3-1 v Swindon Town (a), F.A.Cup 1st round, January 14th 1911 (Notts Division 1, opponents Southern League).
    2-0 v Swindon Town (a), F.A.Cup 2nd round, February 3rd 1912 (Notts Division 1, opponents Southern League).
    2-0 v Bristol Rovers (a), F.A.Cup 1st round, January 11th 1913 (Notts Division 1, opponents Southern League).
    (the above five Southern League victors could possibly be excluded as giant-killers because they were of equal strength to all but the very strongest Football League clubs)
    1-0 v York City (h), F.A.Cup 6th round, March 12th 1955 (Notts Division 2, opponents Division 3N).
    3-1 v Rhyl (h), F.A.Cup 3rd round, January 5th 1957 (Notts Division 2, opponents Cheshire League).
    1-0 v Bath City (h), F.A.Cup 2nd round, December 5th 1959 (Notts Division 4, opponents Southern League).
    1-0 v Runcorn (a), F.A.Cup 1st round, December 9th 1967 (Notts Division 4, opponents Cheshire League).
    4-3 v Doncaster Rovers (h), F.L.Cup 1st round, August 28th 1973 (Notts Division 2, opponents Division 4).
    2-0 v Crewe Alexandra (a), F.L.Cup 2nd round, August 30th 1978 (Notts Division 2, opponents Division 4).
    1-0 v Peterborough United (h), F.A.Cup 4th round, January 24th 1981 (Notts Division 2, opponents Division 4).
    3-2 v Lincoln City (h), F.L.Cup 2nd round 2nd leg, October 27th 1981 (Notts Division 1, opponents Division 3).
        (Lincoln won this two-legged tie 4-3 on aggregate)
    2-0 v Middlesbrough (h), F.A.Cup 4th round, January 29th 1983 (Notts Division 1, opponents Division 2).
    4-2 v Southport (a), F.A.Cup 1st round, November 16th 2002 (Notts Division 2*, opponents Nationwide Conference).

GOAL AVERAGE/DIFFERENCE

Notts County have been saved from possible relegation by a superior goal average once and also avoided having to apply for re-election for this reason. In 1897/98 the five bottom teams in Division 1 all had 24 points with the Magpies fourth from bottom on a goal average of 0.782, putting them 0.060 above a relegation place. However, the League was extended after that season so the two bottom clubs, Blackburn Rovers and Stoke, were re-elected to the top division. In 1966/67 Notts were fifth from bottom of Division 4 with a superior goal average to Rochdale who thus had to apply for re-election. County's average was 0.736 compared to Rochdale's 0.704, a difference of 0.032 of a goal. In 1888/89 a better goal average kept County next to bottom above last-placed Stoke in the original League but they still had to apply for re-election. On June 4th 1976 goal difference rather than goal average was introduced by the League but this has not so far affected Notts in a critical way though it could have done on the final day of 2005/06 if results had gone differently for there was a definite threat of relegation to the Nationwide Conference.

    The biggest goal difference in favour of Notts came in the Division 4 championship campaign of 1970/71 with plus 53 while the worst was in the relegation season of 1934/35 with minus 51 though it should be pointed out that, as mentioned above, goal difference did not replace goal average until 1976.

    In order to encourage more attacking play the League scrapped goal difference on June 5th 1992 and opted for more goals scored to decide placings for clubs level on points. This move made only a minimal difference in attacking play and so on June 12th 1999 the League returned to goal difference.

GOAL NETS

These were devised and patented by Mr. John Alexander Brodie of Liverpool who sent his designs to the F.A. after testing them in local matches. The F.A. were sufficiently impressed to use them in the North v South international trial match which was staged at Nottingham Forest's Town Ground in the Meadows on January 12th 1891. Former County player Fred Geary, born in Hyson Green, Nottingham, but then with Everton, opened the scoring for the North in the 12th minute and so can claim to have been the first player to "drive the ball into the net" and give all sports reporters a vital phrase in their armoury. After interviewing Mr. Brodie on February 4th 1891 about payment, the F.A. decided on March 11th to use the nets in that season's Cup final at Kennington Oval on March 21st, where the holders, Blackburn Rovers, beat Notts 3-1. So Jimmy Oswald, who scored for County, became the first Magpie to "put the ball into the back of the net". There is a well-known drawing of one of Blackburn's goals being scored with the net clearly seen behind the goalposts. So Nottingham and Notts County were deeply involved in the pioneering use of this essential part of modern football.

    The F.A. were now convinced about the value of goal nets and recommended their use whenever possible, finance permitting. The Football League followed suit on September 18th 1891 and four days later the Notts directors agreed "that goal nets be procured". They were obtained in time to be used at Trent Bridge in the match v Stoke on September 26th so that the ball "was driven into the back of the net" from then on in County's home games and Harry Walkerdine was the first Notts player to do it before a home crowd. A few weeks later the League made the use of nets compulsory.

GOALSCORING (individual)

Aggregate record for a single season: Tom Keetley with 39 in 34 matches, Division 3S, 1930/31. The record for Division 1 is 22 in 29 matches by Jimmy Cantrell in 1909/10, in Division 2, 28 by Jack Peart in 30 matches in 1913/14 and by Tom Keetley in 29 matches in 1931/32, in Division 3 (from 1958/59) 27 in 45 matches by Tony Hateley in 1960/61 and in Division 4 (from 1959/60, including the renamed Division 3* from 1997/98 and League 2* from 2004/05) 28 by Gary Jones in 44 matches in 1997/98. The club's leading goalscorer in Football League matches each season (including play-offs) is:

Season	Player	Goals	Games	Season	Player	Goals	Games
1888/89	Bob Jardine	9	18	1951/52	Bobby Crookes	15	38
1889/90	Jimmy Oswald	15	19	1952/53	Cecil McCormack	13	25
1890/91	Jimmy Oswald	14	22	1953/54	Tom Johnston	16	38
1891/92	Jimmy Oswald	15	24	1954/55	Jimmy Jackson	17	20
1892/93	Dan Bruce	12	26	1955/56	Jimmy Jackson	8	24
1893/94	Jimmy Logan	21	21	1956/57	Gordon Wills	19	41
1894/95	Elijah Allsopp	16	25	1957/58	Jackie Lane	11	26
1895/96	Walter Bull	15	30	1958/59	Don Roby	13	43
1896/97	Tom Boucher	23	34	1959/60	Stan Newsham	23	34
1897/98	Tom Boucher	7	26	1960/61	Tony Hateley	27	45
1898/99	Alex Maconnachie	14	33	1961/62	Tony Hateley	19	40
1899/00	Joe McMain	13	26	1962/63	Tony Hateley	22	32
1900/01	Jack Morris	16	33	1963/64	Jeff Astle	11	41
1901/02	Percy Humphreys	14	31	1964/65	Jimmy Rayner	13	32
1902/03	Arthur Green	14	32	1965/66	Ronnie Still	13	34
	Percy Humphreys	14	33	1966/67	Stan Marshall	12	25
1903/04	Arthur Green	19	30	1967/68	Les Bradd	10	28
1904/05	Jerry Dean	8	30	1968/69	Don Masson	13	38
	Arthur Green	8	27	1969/70	Don Masson	23	43
1905/06	Arthur Green	13	34	1970/71	Tony Hateley	22	29
	Walter Tarplin	13	36	1971/72	Les Bradd	21	46
1906/07	Percy Humphreys	13	29	1972/73	Kevin Randall	19	45
1907/08	Fred Jones	6	22	1973/74	Kevin Randall	13	42
1908/09	Jimmy Cantrell	18	38	1974/75	Ian Scanlon	14	32
1909/10	Jimmy Cantrell	22	29	1975/76	Les Bradd	16	42
1910/11	Jimmy Cantrell	13	28	1976/77	Les Bradd	12	30
1911/12	Sam Richards	13	31		Mick Vinter	12	36
1912/13	Jack Peart	7	11	1977/78	Mick Vinter	19	39
1913/14	Jack Peart	28	30	1978/79	Mick Vinter	12	41
1914/15	Jack Peart	11	32	1979/80	Ray O'Brien	10	41
1919/20	Harold Hill	12	33	1980/81	Trevor Christie	14	39
1920/21	Harold Hill	11	22	1981/82	Iain McCulloch	16	40
1921/22	David Brown	7	14	1982/83	Iain McCulloch	10	34
1922/23	Donald Cock	13	33	1983/84	Trevor Christie	19	39
1923/24	Donald Cock	11	32	1984/85	Rachid Harkouk	15	35
1924/25	Arthur Davis	10	41	1985/86	Ian McParland	15	44
	Alf Widdowson	10	39	1986/87	Ian McParland	24	45
1925/26	Arthur Davis	14	36	1987/88	Ian McParland	21	43
1926/27	Arthur Davis	16	32	1988/89	Gary Lund	8	42
	Neil Harris	16	27	1989/90	Tommy Johnson	20	43
1927/28	Bertie Mills	20	31	1990/91	Tommy Johnson	18	40
1928/29	Harold Andrews	20	39	1991/92	Tommy Johnson	9	31
1929/30	Harold Andrews	17	38	1992/93	Mark Draper	11	44
1930/31	Tom Keetley	39	34	1993/94	Gary McSwegan	15	37
1931/32	Tom Keetley	28	29	1994/95	Paul Devlin	9	40
1932/33	Tom Keetley	15	20	1995/96	Gary Martindale	8	19
1933/34	Charlie Macartney	15	34		Devon White	8	20
1934/35	Fred Shaw	11	20	1996/97	Gary Martindale	6	28
1935/36	Wilf Notley	9	20	1997/98	Gary Jones	28	44
	Tom Rickards	9	33	1998/99	Ian Richardson	7	23
1936/37	Hughie Gallacher	25	32	1999/00	Mark Stallard	13	36
1937/38	Willie Chalmers	8	27	2000/01	Mark Stallard	17	42
	Bill Fallon	8	29	2001/02	Danny Allsopp	19	43
1938/39	David Martin	16	26	2002/03	Mark Stallard	24	45
1946/47	Jackie Sewell	21	37	2003/04	Paul Heffernan	20	38
1947/48	Tommy Lawton	18	19	2004/05	Glynn Hurst	14	41
1948/49	Jackie Sewell	26	42	2005/06	Glynn Hurst	9	18
1949/50	Tommy Lawton	31	37	2006/07	Jason Lee	15	34
1950/51	Tom Johnston	14	37				
	Jackie Sewell	14	26				

Jason Lee, leading scorer 2006/07

Harry Cursham in an England shirt. He is the all-time leading scorer in the F.A.Cup, with 49 goals

Fast scoring

The fastest goal recorded for the Magpies is by Barrie Jones v Torquay United (h), Division 3, March 31st 1962 when it was timed as only six seconds after kick-off. For many years it remained the second joint quickest League goal on record.

A hat-trick in just two minutes 45 seconds was netted by Ian Scanlon v Sheffield Wednesday (h), Division 2, November 16th 1974, including a penalty. Despite Scanlon's hat-trick, Notts were held to a 3-3 draw.

Rachid Harkouk netted three goals in six minutes as the Magpies made it five in eight minutes v Bolton Wanderers (h), F.L.Cup 3rd round, October 30th 1984. At the time these were both stated to be records for the competition.

Danny Allsopp's hat-trick v Mansfield Town (a), F.L.Cup 1st round, August 21st 2001, came in exactly 10 minutes.

Consecutive games

The record Football League individual match scoring sequence for the Magpies is six consecutive games with a total of eight occasions shared by seven players. The record for the most goals scored in this sequence is ten by Stan Newsham in six Division 4 games between October 10th and November 7th 1959, then comes Tom Keetley with nine Division 3S goals between February 7th and March 14th 1931. Four players have scored seven goals in their six-match sequence: Jimmy Cantrell in Division 1 between December 18th 1909 and January 22nd 1910; Jack Peart in Division 2 between February 7th and March 14th 1914; Tony Hateley in the last Division 4 game of 1970/71 and the first five of the 1971/72 Division 3 campaign, between May 1st and September 4th 1971; and Mark Stallard in Division 2* between August 14th and September 18th 1999. In achieving the feat for a second time Keetley scored six Division 2 goals between August 29th and September 19th 1931 and finally Mick Vinter also hit six in Division 2 between March 21st and April 8th 1978. Vinter was the only Notts player to find the net in these six matches nor were there any own goals!

F.A.Cup

The record individual score in an F.A.Cup tie is six goals by Harry Cursham v Wednesbury Strollers (at Derby), 2nd round replay, December 10th 1881.

The joint holder of the individual F.A.Cup final goalscoring record is Jimmy Logan with a hat-trick for Notts v Bolton Wanderers (Goodison Park), March 31st 1894.

The record for the number of Notts County goals in a single season's F.A.Cup games is ten by Harry Cursham in 1886/87. The club played six ties and Cursham scored in every one.

Debuts, goal-scoring

The record number of goals scored on a Football League debut for Notts County is three, shared by three players: Tom Keetley v Bristol City (h), Division 2, August 31st 1929; Fred Shaw v Swansea Town (h), Division 2, December 29th 1934; and Brett Angell v Bournemouth (h), Division 2*, December 11th 1999 (he netted his first inside one minute!).

Ten players have scored two goals on League debut. They are: Jimmy Logan v Grimsby Town (h), Division 2, October 5th 1893; Peter Logan v Blackburn Rovers (h), Division 1, November 5th 1898; Arthur Davis v Chelsea (a), Division 1, February 9th 1924; Arnold Bramham v Nottingham Forest (a), Division 2, February 9th 1935; Wilf Notley v Queens Park Rangers (h), Division 3S, October 19th 1935; Charlie Ferguson v Exeter City (h), Division 3S, August 29th 1936; Sedley Cooper v Swindon Town (h), Division 3S, March 13th 1937; Iain McCulloch v West Ham United (a), Division 2, August 19th 1978; Garry Birtles and Geoff Pike in the same match v Wigan Athletic (h), Division 3, August 15th 1987.

A large number of players have scored one goal on debut. The most noteworthy was probably John Brearley v Burnley (a), test match, April 26th 1897, as this gave the Magpies a 1-0 victory which ensured promotion to Division 1. Tommy Lawton not only scored on debut v Northampton Town (a), Division 3S, November 15th 1947, but then netted two on his home debut v Bristol Rovers, November 22nd 1947. Other famous goalscoring debutants include Jackie Sewell, Tony Hateley and Don Masson.

Scoreless

The outfield player who has made the most League appearances for the Magpies without scoring a single goal is right-back Bert Morley who remained scoreless in 258 games between 1906/07 and 1914/15. Two others, also full-backs, who have exceeded 200 without a goal are Tommy Deans in 239 games between 1949/50 and 1955/56, and John "Bill" Brindley in 223 games (2 being as substitute) between 1970/71 and 1975/76.

Hat-tricks

The individual goalscoring record for a single game was set up by Harry Jackson who scored eight v Wellingborough Grammar School (a) on February 4th 1886. That, however, was a friendly and the record for a first-class competitive match is held by Harry Cursham with six v Wednesbury Strollers (at Derby) on December 10th 1881, an F.A.Cup 2nd round replay. Next to Cursham, the top scoring feats are as follows:

Five goals
- Harry Daft v Basford Rovers (h), F.A.Cup 1st round, October 30th 1886
- Bob Jardine v Burnley (h), Football League, October 27th 1888
- Dan Bruce v Burslem Port Vale (h), Division 2, February 26th 1895
- Bertie "Paddy" Mills v Barnsley (h), Division 2, November 19th 1927

Four goals
- Harry Cursham v Rotherham Town (h), F.A.Cup 1st round, October 24th 1885
- Frank Burton v Basford Rovers (h), F.A.Cup 1st round, October 30th 1886
- Andrew McGregor v Sheffield United (a), F.A.Cup 1st round, January 17th 1891
- Arthur Watson v Crewe Alexandra (h), Division 2, February 17th 1894
- Arthur Green (2 pen.) v Blackburn Rovers (h), Division 1, March 19th 1904
- Jimmy Cantrell v Manchester City (h), Division 1, February 20th 1909
- Neil Harris v Arsenal (h), Division 1, December 26th 1925
- Arthur Davis v Barnsley (a), Division 2, October 30th 1926
- Tom Keetley v Fulham (h), Division 3S, September 6th 1930
- Tom Fenner v Burnley (h), Division 2, December 10th 1932
- Tommy Lawton v Ipswich Town (h), Division 3S, September 9th 1948
- Tommy Lawton v Exeter City (h), Division 3S, October 16th 1948
- Jackie Sewell v Exeter City (h), Division 3S, October 16th 1948
- Tommy Lawton v Newport County (h), Division 3S, January 15th 1949
- Jackie Sewell v Newport County (h), Division 3S, January 15th 1949
- Jimmy Jackson v Everton (a), Division 2, October 20th 1951
- Ron Wylie v Birmingham City (h), Division 2, April 19th 1952
- Ken McPherson v Blackburn Rovers (h), Division 2, December 13th 1952
- Jimmy Jackson v West Ham United (h), Division 2, January 1st 1955
- Paul Heffernan v Stockport County (h), Division 2*, February 21st 2004

Tommy Lawton; four goals in a game three times and three hat-tricks

Three goals
- Arthur Cursham v Sheffield FC (h), F.A.Cup 1st round, November 4th 1882
- Harry Cursham v Aston Villa (h), F.A.Cup 5th round, March 3rd 1883
- Harry Cursham v Sheffield Heeley (h), F.A.Cup 1st round, November 10th 1883
- Harry Jackson v Rotherham Town (h), F.A.Cup 1st round, October 24th 1885
- William Gunn v Sheffield FC (h), F.A.Cup 2nd round, November 21st 1885
- Harry Jackson v Sheffield FC (h), F.A.Cup 2nd round, November 21st 1885
- Harry Cursham v Notts Rangers (a), F.A.Cup 3rd round, December 12th 1885
- Harry Cursham v Notts Rangers (h), F.A.Cup 2nd round replay, November 20th 1886
- Harry Cursham v Great Marlow (h), F.A.Cup 5th round, January 29th 1887
- Harry Daft v Lincoln Ramblers (h), F.A.Cup 1st round, October 15th 1887
- Albert Moore v Lincoln Ramblers (h), F.A.Cup 1st round, October 15th 1887
- Harry Daft v Accrington FC (a), Football League, October 12th 1889
- Jimmy Oswald v Accrington FC (a), Football League, October 12th 1889
- Teddy May v Aston Villa (h), F.A.Cup 2nd round, February 1st 1890
- Jimmy Oswald v Accrington FC (h), Football League, September 20th 1890
- Billy Locker v Aston Villa (h), Football League, November 29th 1890
- Jimmy Oswald v Aston Villa (h), Football League, November 29th 1890
- Harry Walkerdine v Accrington FC (h), Football League, November 28th 1891
- Harry Daft v Aston Villa (h), Football League, January 2nd 1892
- Jimmy Oswald v Burnley (h), Football League, March 1st 1892
- Harry Daft v West Bromwich Albion (h), Division 1, November 19th 1892
- Jimmy Oswald v West Bromwich Albion (h), Division 1, November 19th 1892
- Jimmy Oswald v Shankhouse (h), F.A.Cup 1st round, January 21st 1893
- Jimmy Logan v Burslem Port Vale (h), Division 2, October 26th 1893
- Jimmy Logan v Northwich Victoria (h), Division 2, November 23rd 1893
- George Kerr v Burton Swifts (h), Division 2, November 30th 1893
- Dan Bruce v Rotherham Town (h), Division 2, January 11th 1894
- Jimmy Logan v Bolton Wanderers (at Everton), F.A.Cup final, March 31st 1894
- Jimmy Logan v Walsall Town Swifts (h), Division 2, December 25th 1894
- Walter Bull v Rotherham Town (h), Division 2, March 16th 1895
- Walter Bull v Woolwich Arsenal (h), Division 2, November 7th 1896
- Tom Boucher v Burton Swifts (a), Division 2, January 2nd 1897
- Walter Bull v Lincoln City (h), Division 2, January 23rd 1897
- Arthur Hadley v Blackburn Rovers (h), Division 1, December 23rd 1899
- Alf Warner v Wolverhampton Wanderers (h), Division 1, October 6th 1900
- Jack Morris v Sheffield Wednesday (h), Division 1, September 14th 1901
- Jack Morris (1 pen.) v Small Heath (h), Division 1, December 28th 1901
- Percy Humphreys v Wolverhampton Wanderers (h), Division 1, March 28th 1902
- Percy Humphreys v Derby County (h), Division 1, March 23rd 1907
- Jimmy Cantrell v Woolwich Arsenal (h), Division 1, October 7th 1909
- Jack Peart v Liverpool (h), Division 1, March 22nd 1913
- Jack Peart v Fulham (h), Division 2, November 1st 1913
- Jack Peart v Grimsby Town (h), Division 2, December 27th 1913
- Billy Flint v Leeds City (a), Division 2, January 24th 1914
- Billy Death v Wolverhampton Wanderers (h), Division 2, September 5th 1921
- Jimmy Sullivan v West Bromwich Albion (a), Division 1, November 7th 1925
- Arthur Davis v Tottenham Hotspur (h), Division 1, November 28th 1925
- Arthur Davis v Huddersfield Town (h), Division 1, May 1st 1926

Chris Staniforth v Barnsley (h), Division 2, November 19th 1927
George Taylor v Preston North End (h), Division 2, April 7th 1928
Harry Andrews v West Bromwich Albion (a), Division 2, September 3rd 1928
Bertie "Paddy" Mills v Hull City (h), Division 2, January 19th 1929
Tom Keetley v Bristol City (h), Division 2, August 31st 1929
Tom Keetley v Clapton Orient (h), Division 3S, October 11th 1930
Tom Keetley v Newport County (a), Division 3S, October 18th 1930
Tom Keetley v Torquay United (a), Division 3S, November 15th 1930
Harold Andrews v Walsall (h), Division 3S, April 3rd 1931
Tom Keetley v Plymouth Argyle (a), Division 2, October 10th 1931
Tom Keetley v Manchester United (a), Division 2, October 24th 1931
Tom Keetley v Chesterfield (a), Division 2, November 7th 1931
(Keetley's three hat-tricks above came in successive away games)
Tom Keetley (1 pen.) v Southampton (h), Division 2, November 28th 1931
Tom Fenner v Burnley (h), Division 2, December 12th 1931
Tom Keetley v Port Vale (h), Division 2, December 25th 1931
Sid Elliott v Bradford Park Avenue (a), Division 2, December 17th 1932
Fred Shaw v Swansea Town (h), Division 2, December 29th 1934
Fred Shaw v Southampton (h), Division 2, February 2nd 1935
Hughie Gallacher (1 pen.) v Northampton Town (h), Division 3S, October 17th 1936
Willie Chalmers v Bournemouth (h), Division 3S, February 6th 1937
Hughie Gallacher v Bristol Rovers (h), Division 3S, February 27th 1937
David Martin v Aldershot (a), Division 3S, February 11th 1939
Tommy Lawton v Horsham (h), F.A.Cup 1st round, November 29th 1947
Jackie Sewell v Horsham (h), F.A.Cup 1st round, November 29th 1947
Tommy Lawton v Stockton (at Middlesbrough), F.A.Cup 2nd round replay, December 20th 1947
Jackie Sewell v Reading (h), Division 3S, January 17th 1948
Tom Johnston v Crystal Palace (a), Division 3S, February 19th 1949
Tom Johnston v Watford (h), Division 3S, February 26th 1949
Tommy Lawton (2 pen.) v Swindon Town (h), Division 3S, November 12th 1949
Jackie Sewell v Newport County (h), Division 3S, February 25th 1950
Cecil McCormack v Leeds United (h), Division 2, October 4th 1952
Jimmy Jackson v Doncaster Rovers (h), Division 2, April 11th 1955
Ron Wylie v Bristol Rovers (h), Division 2, December 3rd 1955
Gordon Wills v Barnsley (h), Division 2, December 1st 1956
Bob Forrest v Gateshead (h), Division 4, September 17th 1959
Stan Newsham v Doncaster Rovers (a), Division 4, October 17th 1959
Chris Joyce v Crystal Palace (h), Division 4, January 2nd 1960
Tony Hateley v Barnsley (h), Division 3, September 10th 1960
Roy Horobin v Bournemouth (a), Division 3, December 31st 1960
Alan Withers v Newport County (h), Division 3, February 4th 1961
Peter Bircumshaw v Port Vale (a), Division 3, March 11th 1961
Peter Bircumshaw v Newport County (h), Division 3, September 30th 1961
Tony Hateley v Bournemouth (a), Division 3, October 12th 1961
Tony Hateley v Bradford Park Avenue (h), Division 3, December 23rd 1961
Tony Hateley (2 pens.) v Queens Park Rangers (h), Division 3, February 23rd 1963
Tony Hateley v Halifax Town (h), Division 3, March 23rd 1963
Jeff Astle v Oldham Athletic (h), Division 3, December 28th 1963
Jimmy Rayner v Chesterfield (h), Division 4, September 26th 1964
Derek Pace v Doncaster Rovers (h), Division 4, January 23rd 1965
Tony Hateley v Peterborough United (h), Division 4, January 30th 1971
Tony Hateley v Colchester United (h), Division 4, April 12th 1971
Ian Scanlon (1 pen.) v Sheffield Wednesday (h), Division 2, November 16th 1974
Mick Vinter v Millwall (a), Division 2, January 22nd 1977
Mick Vinter v Sheffield United (h), Division 2, March 13th 1979
Iain McCulloch v West Bromwich Albion (a), Division 1, March 24th 1982
Trevor Christie v Brighton & Hove Albion (h), Division 1, April 17th 1982
Trevor Christie v Leicester City (a), Division 1, August 27th 1983
Rachid Harkouk v Bolton Wanderers (h), F.L.Cup 3rd round, October 30th 1984
David Hunt v Bristol City (h), Division 3, October 12th 1985
Rachid Harkouk v Scarborough (h), F.A.Cup 1st round, November 17th 1985
Mick Waitt v Gillingham (h), Division 3, January 3rd 1987
Ian McParland v Port Vale (h), Division 3, February 7th 1987
Geoff Pike v Southend United (h), Division 3, September 5th 1987
Ian McParland (1 pen.) v Fulham (h), Division 3, January 30th 1988
Gary Lund v Rotherham United (h), Division 3, April 23rd 1988
Ian McParland v Mansfield Town (h), F.L.Cup 1st round 1st leg, August 30th 1988
Paul Barnes v Reading (a), Division 3, March 4th 1989
Tommy Johnson v Blackburn Rovers (h), Division 2, March 30th 1991
Dave Regis v Plymouth Argyle (h), Division 2, April 27th 1991
Gary McSwegan v Derby County (h), Division 1*, September 25th 1993
Brett Angell v Bournemouth (h), Division 2*, December 11th 1999
Danny Allsopp v Mansfield Town (a), F.L.Cup 1st round, August 21st 2001
Danny Allsopp v Tranmere Rovers (h), Division 2*, March 2nd 2002
Paul Heffernan v Queens Park Rangers (h), Division 2*, December 26th 2003

A goalkeeper's view of Tom Keetley.

Tony Hateley, scorer of seven hat-tricks for Notts.

Glynn Hurst, scorer of County's most recent hat-trick.

Glynn Hurst v Rochdale (a), League 2*, September 25th 2004
Glynn Hurst v Bury (a), League 2*, October 29th 2005

Leading hat-trick specialists are Tom Keetley 10, Harry Cursham and Tony Hateley 7, Tommy Lawton and Jimmy Oswald 6, Harry Daft and Jackie Sewell 5, Jimmy Logan 4, Walter Bull, Arthur Davis, Jimmy Jackson, Ian McParland and Jack Peart 3, Danny Allsopp, Harold Andrews, Peter Bircumshaw, Dan Bruce, Jimmy Cantrell, Trevor Christie, Tom Fenner, Hughie Gallacher, Rachid Harkouk, Paul Heffernan, Percy Humphreys, Glynn Hurst, Harry Jackson, Tom Johnston, Bertie "Paddy" Mills, Jack Morris, Fred Shaw, Mick Vinter and Ron Wylie 2. A further 46 players each scored one hat-trick.

Four goals or more in a match are counted as simple hat-tricks in these totals. This list includes Football League, F.A.Cup and F.L.Cup and no Notts player has scored a hat-trick in any of the various other competitive games such as the Associate Members Cup or the Anglo-Scottish Cup.

Tom Keetley's ten hat-tricks were all scored in League matches so this is the Notts record for this competition. A number of high-profile goalscorers such as Les Bradd and Mark Stallard never achieved the feat for the Magpies though Bradd later netted hat-tricks for both Stockport County and Wigan Athletic.

The first Notts County hat-trick of all was by Charles Rothera v South Derbyshire (a), November 18th 1869 in the days before competitive football was introduced.

Record aggregates

Record in Football League career: Les Bradd 125 in 442 matches, 1967/68 to 1977/78. Aggregate record in F.A.Cup ties: Harry Cursham 49 in 43 matches (plus two in a match ruled void), 1877/78 to 1890/91. This is the all-time record total in F,A.Cup history. The F.L.Cup record is 10 in 21 matches by Trevor Christie. Harry Cursham (1877/78 to 1890/91) scored at least 208 goals, all but 53 of them in non-competitive games.

Aggregate record in all competitions

The following have scored 60 or more goals in their Notts County competitive career:

	Career	*Total*	*League*	*F.A.Cup*	*F.L.Cup*	*Others*
Les Bradd	1967/68 to 1977/78	137	125	4	7	1
Tony Hateley	1958/59 to 1971/72	114	109	4	1	–
Jackie Sewell	1946/47 to 1950/51	104	97	7	–	–
Tommy Lawton	1947/48 to 1951/52	103	90	13	–	–
Tom Keetley	1929/30 to 1932/33	98	94	4	–	–
Don Masson	1968/69 to 1981/82	97	92	3	1	1
Tom Johnston	1948/49 to 1956/57	92	88	4	–	–
Ian McParland	1980/81 to 1988/89	90	69	9	5	7
Harry Daft	1885/86 to 1894/95	81	58	20	–	3
Mark Stallard	1998/99 to 2004/05	79	69	3	7	–
Trevor Christie	1979/80 to 1983/84	79	63	3	10	3
Gary Lund	1987/88 to 1994/95	79	63	4	5	7
Percy Humphreys	1901/02 to 1906/07	73	66	7	–	–
Sam Richards	1910/11 to 1921/22	71	69	2	–	–
Tom Fenner	1927/28 to 1933/34	70	69	1	–	–
Jimmy Cantrell	1907/08 to 1912/13	65	64	1	–	–
Jimmy Oswald	1889/90 to 1892/93	65	55	10	–	–
Mick Vinter	1972/73 to 1978/79	63	54	5	1	3

(Gary Lund's League total includes play-off goal)

Les Bradd, Notts County's leading scorer

Others with 50 or more are: Arthur Green 1902/03 to 1906/07 59 (56 in Football League); Harold Andrews 1927/28 to 1931/32 58 (55); Walter Bull 1894/95 to 1903/04 58 (53); Tommy Johnson 1988/89 to 1991/92 57 (51, including 4 in play-offs); Harold Hill 1919/20 to 1924/25 56 (50); Arthur Davis 1923/24 to 1927/28 54 (51); Iain McCulloch 1978/79 to 1983/84 54 (51); Danny Allsopp 1999/2000 to 2002/03 53 (42); Harry Cursham 1877/78 to 1890/91 53 (2); Dan Bruce 1892/93 to 1895/96 52 (48, including 1 in test match); Jerry Dean 1904/05 to 1911/12 52 (49); Rachid Harkouk 1980/81 to 1985/86 52 (39); Jack Peart 1912/13 to 1919/20 52 (51); Mark Draper 1988/89 to 1993/94 50 (41); Jimmy Jackson 1948/49 to 1957/58 50 (47).

In their entire League careers, County's leading scorers ended up with the following aggregates: Tom Keetley 284; Tommy Lawton 231 (which excludes wartime competitions); Jackie Sewell 228, Tony Hateley 211 and Les Bradd 182.

GOALSCORING (team)
Double figures
The matches in which Notts County have scored double figures are as follows:

Football League
- 11-1 v Newport County (h), Division 3S, January 15th 1949.
- 10-0 v Burslem Port Vale (h), Division 2, February 26th 1895.

F.A.Cup
- 15-0 v Rotherham Town (h), 1st round, October 24th 1885.
- 13-0 v Basford Rovers (h), 1st round, October 30th 1886.
- 11-1 v Wednesbury Strollers (Derby), 2nd round replay, December 10th 1881.

Friendlies
- 15-1 v Newark (h), January 8th 1881.
- 15-1 v Newquay (a), July 26th 2002.
- 13-3 v Dumfries (h), December 28th 1889.
- 11-0 v Lockwood Bros. (h), January 15th 1887.
- 10-0 v Mitchell's St. George's (h), February 17th 1883.
- 10-1 v Cambridge University (h), October 27th 1892.
- 10-1 v Local Clubs XI (h), October 5th 1882.

Notts County have never conceded double figures except in wartime and friendly matches. These occasions were as follows:
- 14-0 v Preston North End (a), November 6th 1886.
- 11-4 v Walsall (a), League South, November 9th 1940.
- 10-0 v Mitchell's St. George's (a), December 12th 1887.
- 10-1 v Southwell (a), December 6th 1877.
- 10-1 v Blackburn Rovers (a), October 22nd 1881.
- 10-1 v Queen's Park (a), November 26th 1881.
- 10-1 v Aston Villa (a), April 11 1887.

Highest scores
Highest home scores by Notts County (division titles at the time of the match are shown)
- Football League: 9-0 v Accrington FC, November 29th 1891.
- Division 2: 10-0 v Burslem Port Vale, February 26th 1895.
- Division 3S: 11-1 v Newport County, January 15th 1949.
- Division 3: 8-1 v Newport County, September 30th 1961.
- Division 4: 7-1 v Crystal Palace, January 2nd 1960.
- F.A.Cup: 15-0 v Rotherham Town, 1st round, October 24th 1885.
- F.L.Cup: 6-1 v Bolton Wanderers, 3rd round, October 30th 1984.

Against
- Football League: 7-0 v Preston North End, November 3rd 1888.
- Division 2: 6-1 v Manchester United, February 10th 1923.
- Division 3S: 4-1 v Leyton Orient, February 7th 1948.
- Division 3: 5-1 v Shrewsbury Town, September 29th 1962.
- Division 3*: 5-0 v Macclesfield Town, January 25th 2005.
- F.A.Cup: 6-0 v Aston Villa, 3rd round, January 5th 1982.
- F.L.Cup: 7-1 v Newcastle United, 2nd round 2nd leg, October 5th 1993.

Highest away scores
- Football League: 8-1 v Accrington FC, October 12th 1889.
- Division 2: 5-1 v Everton, October 20th 1951; v Doncaster Rovers, March 1st 1952; v Fulham, November 20th 1976.
- Division 3S: 5-0 v Gillingham, February 28th 1931
- Division 3/Division 2*: 5-3 v York City, August 22nd 1987. Arguably of equal merit: 4-0 v Bristol City, March 18th 1989; 4-0 v Bury, March 9th 2002.
- Division 3*: 5-2 v Exeter City, March 3rd 1998.
- F.A.Cup: 11-1 v Wednesbury Strollers (Derby), 2nd round replay, December 10th 1881. This was on a neutral ground. On opponents home ground the record victory is 9-1 v Sheffield United, 1st round, January 17th 1891.
- F.L.Cup: 4-2 v Aldershot, 2nd round 1st leg, October 3rd 1983.

Against
- Football League 9-1 v Aston Villa, September 29th 1888; v Blackburn Rovers, November 16th 1889.
- Division 2: 9-1 v Portsmouth, April 9th 1927.
- Division 3S: 5-0 v Millwall, January 24th 1938.
- Division 3: 7-0 v Bury, November 12th 1960.
- Division 4: 6-0 v Brighton and Hove Albion, October 10th 1964.
- F.A.Cup: 8-1 v Newcastle United, 3rd round, January 8th 1927.
- F.L.Cup: 7-1 v Manchester City, 1st round 2nd leg, August 19th 1998.

High scoring draws
Notts County's highest scoring draw is 4-4, achieved in five Football League matches and two F.A.Cup ties as follows:
- v Derbyshire (h), F.A.Cup 1st round, November 4th 1880.
- v Birmingham St.George's (a), F.A.Cup 1st round, January 18th 1890.
- v West Bromwich Albion (a), Division 1, November 7th 1925.
- v Barnsley (a), Division 2, October 30th 1926 (Arthur Davis scored all four for Notts).
- v Halifax Town (h), Division 3, January 3rd 1959.
- v Wigan Athletic (h), Division 3, August 15th 1987 (Garry Birtles and Geoff Pike scored two goals apiece on Notts debut).
- v Bristol City (h), Division 2*, November 27th 1999.

One hundred goals or more in a season
The Magpies have twice topped the 100 goals in a Football League season with 107 in 1959/60 when they were Division 4 champions and 102 in 1948/49 in Division 3S. In 1987/88 Notts reached 103 goals in League and Cup games combined, made up of 82 League, 2 play-offs and 19 cups. Including friendlies, they have scored 100 or more goals in a season on 22 occasions, the first being 1882/83 with 107 in 23 games and the last 1997/98 when they totalled 101 in 59. The record is 1893/94 with 147 in 66 matches. Notts County have never conceded 100 goals in a League season with 97 in 1934/35 ranking as the worst. In all matches the goals against have reached the century 14 times with a record 125 in 40 games in 1944/45 while 102 in 35 in 1886/87 was their first century against and 105 in 67 in 1993/94 the last time this happened. The club reached a century in both the for and against columns in four seasons, 1889/90 (121-124), 1891/92 (137-104), 1892/93 (130-115) and 1993/94 (103-105).

Scored in every match
When Notts County were Division 2 champions in 1896/97 they scored in all 30 matches, home and away, though not in one of their four test matches.

Failed to score (season)
In 1996/97 Notts County failed to score in 24 of their 46 Division 2* matches, the highest number of League blank scoresheets in their history.

Successive clean sheets
From March 11th to April 5th 1969 the Magpies, who had Mick Rose in goal, kept six clean sheets in successive matches in Division 4, a club record which was equalled from October 21st to November 14th 1970, also Division 4. This time the goalkeeping honours were shared with Roy Brown being on duty for the first two games and Barry Watling coming in for the others.

Failed to score in successive matches
From December 29th 1984 to January 26th 1985 Notts played five successive Division 2 matches without scoring a goal and so equalling the previous longest blank spells from January 25th to February 22nd 1964 in Division 3 and from November 30th to December 25th 1912 in Division 1. During 1906/07 the Magpies had two spells of four matches without scoring separated only by a 2-2 draw which meant that from September 29th to November 24th 1906 the club had a run of nine matches, in eight of which they had been goalless.

See also **Away Records**, **Football League**, **Home Records**, and **War-time Football**.

GOALKEEPERS

Notts County Football League goalkeeping averages 1888/89 to 2006/07
Averages are not normally associated with footballers but they are used here to see how Notts County's goalkeepers compare during their Football League careers. The figure given is the average number of goals conceded per match. The percentage figure relates to the proportion of "clean sheets" per matches played.

In judging the relative merits of the players, remember that cover for goalkeepers today is better organised than in the past and the laws of the game also afford the goalkeeper more protection now.

Test matches and play-offs are included but not the 1939/40 abandoned season. Matches involving goalkeepers selected as outfield players are not included in their totals.

On four occasions since 2001 goalkeepers were replaced by their cover on the substitutes bench. These count as separate appearances for each of the goalkeepers involved but only goals conceded while they were on the field of play have been counted in their record.

Player	First and last matches	Games	Goals	Avge	Clean Sheets	%
Barry Watling	10-1-1970 to 18-3-1972	65	68	1.04	21	32.30
Roy Brown	17-10-1970 to 5-4-1975	113	125	1.10	41	36.28
Darren Ward	12-8-1995 to 5-5-2001	254	283	1.11	74	29.13
Tom Flower	27-8-1938 to 10-4-1939	36	41	1.13	14	38.88
Saul Deeney	29-3-2003 to 17-3-2007	49	58	1.18	14	28.57
George Blyth	31-8-1935 to 7-5-1938	99	120	1.21	37	37.37
Kevin Pilkington	6-8-2005 to 5-5-2007	84	106	1.26	22	26.19
Eric McManus	7-11-1972 to 5-5-1979	229	298	1.30	66	28.82
Albert Iremonger	1-4-1905 to 1-5-1926	564	739	1.31	183	32.44
Mick Leonard	15-9-1979 to 11-2-1989	206	272	1.32	54	26.21
Steve Cherry	18-2-1989 to 8-4-1995	272	360	1.32	75	27.57
Raddy Avramovic	18-8-1979 to 14-5-1983	149	205	1.37	36	24.16
Mick Rose	18-3-1966 to 2-3-1970	109	152	1.39	34	31.19
Roy Smith	18-12-1948 to 1-11-1952	110	160	1.45	33	30.00
Harry Brown	31-8-1946 to 6-11-1948	93	138	1.48	18	19.35
Harry Pennington	8-9-1900 to 21-4-1905	126	187	1.48	39	30.95
Jimmy Ferguson	17-3-1928 to 28-3-1932	158	237	1.50	44	27.84
George Streets	13-9-1919 to 7-1-1928	133	201	1.51	43	32.33
Stuart Garden	15-12-2001 to 17-4-2004	52	81	1.55	13	25.00
George Smith	26-11-1955 to 29-4-1967	323	520	1.60	78	24.14
Steve Mildenhall	11-8-2001 to 7-8-2004	76	123	1.61	18	23.68
Bob Suter	18-2-1899 to 26-1-1907	42	69	1.64	14	33.33
George Toone	7-9-1889 to 11-1-1902	272	455	1.67	63	23.16
Tommy Knox	3-2-1934 to 4-4-1936	72	122	1.69	15	20.83
Gordon Bradley	9-9-1950 to 19-4-1958	192	335	1.74	38	19.79
Len Hammond	26-8-1933 to 20-1-1934	26	46	1.76	4	15.38

Peter Butler	25-9-1961 to 26-3-1966	44	79	1.79	11	25.00
Seamus McDonagh	27-8-1983 to 2-2-1985	35	64	1.82	7	20.00
Jimmy Maidment	17-10-1931 to 29-4-1933	44	82	1.86	12	27.27
Jimmy Linton	8-11-1952 to 28-3-1959	114	220	1.92	20	17.54
Harry Earle	3-9-1904 to 15-4-1905	23	47	2.04	4	17.39
George Hopkins	15-1-1927 to 10-3-1928	28	58	2.07	3	10.71
The following goalkeepers played between 2 and 20 games:						
*Fred Whittaker	3-5-1947 to 29-5-1947	2	1	0.50	1	50.00
Jimmy Thraves	10-2-1891 to 17-10-1891	4	3	0.75	2	50.00
Paul Crichton	21-10-1986 to 8-11-1986	5	4	0.80	1	25.00
John Davies	29-3-1986 to 6-5-1986	10	11	1.10	4	40.00
Billy Soutar	26-12-1930 to 7-2-1931	7	8	1.14	3	37.50
Wayne Henderson	10-8-2004 to 11-12-2004	11	13	1.18	3	27.27
Mick Gadsby	16-12-1967 to 2-3-1968	11	14	1.27	4	36.66
Paul Reece	23-10-1994 to 7-5-1995	11	14	1.27	3	27.27
Iain Hesford	30-11-1985 to 8-2-1986	10	13	1.30	2	20.00
Pegguy Arphexad	13-3-2004 to 20-3-2004	3	4	1.33	0	0.00
Mick Brannon	29-1-1938 to 16-4-1938	3	4	1.33	0	0.00
Jason Kearton	21-1-1995 to 14-3-1995	10	15	1.50	1	10.00
Bobby Mimms	15-3-1986 to 22-3-1986	2	3	1.50	1	50.00
Harry Orgill	3-9-1947 to 27-12-1947	2	3	1.50	0	0.00
Mike Pollitt	22-2-1997 to 3-3-1998	10	15	1.50	0	0.00
Paul Gibson	8-5-1999 to 2-12-2000	11	17	1.54	2	18.18
Kenneth Tewkesbury	27-8-1932 to 19-12-1932	7	11	1.57	0	0.00
Bobby Catlin	29-8-1992 to 21-8-1993	3	5	1.66	0	0.00
Joe Donaldson	18-3-1899 to 25-3-1899	3	5	1.66	0	0.00
Graham Smith	31-8-1968 to 7-3-1969	10	17	1.70	2	20.00
Jimmy Cargill	10-9-1966 to 10-3-1967	10	18	1.80	2	20.00
Frank Lane	13-3-1976 to 20-3-1976	2	4	2.00	0	0.00
John Nugent	18-2-1905 to 24-4-1905	3	6	2.00	1	16.66
George Taylor	15-4-1939 to 6-5-1939	6	13	2.16	1	7.69
Matt Reilly	2-9-1905 to 26-12-1905	16	36	2.25	0	0.00
Sam McCappin	28-10-1899 to 3-2-1900	7	16	2.28	1	6.25
Mark Mellors	10-4-1903 to 28-11-1903	9	21	2.33	1	4.76
Jack Mowl	13-11-1948 to 4-12-1948	3	7	2.33	0	0.00
Murrey Steele	26-10-1912 to 1-3-1913	3	7	2.33	0	0.00
Tom Wall	17-4-1933 to 6-5-1933	3	7	2.33	0	0.00
Mick Stone	30-3-1959 to 29-4-1959	7	17	2.42	1	5.88
Dick Twigg	14-3-1959 to 16-3-1959	2	5	2.50	0	0.00
Tom Poskett	13-10-1934 to 27-4-1935	10	26	2.60	1	10.00
Rob Elliot	12-3-2005 to 26-3-2005	4	11	2.75	0	0.00
J Sharman	15-1-1898 to 14-10-1899	2	6	3.00	0	0.00
Bernard Wright	23-1-1947 to 22-3-1947	2	6	3.00	0	0.00
Tom Widdowson	8-12-1888 to 16-3-1889	12	37	3.08	1	8.33
Jack Holland	15-9-1888 to 24-11-1888	8	26	3.25	0	0.00
Jimmy Lindley	30-9-2000 to 6-10-2000	2	8	4.00	0	0.00
The following played in one match only:						
Bill Burrows	16-12-1893	1	0	0.00	1	100.00
Abe West	4-11-1912	1	0	0.00	1	100.00
Bill Brown	10-11-1894	1	1	1.00	0	0.00
Andy Goram	5-9-1998	1	1	1.00	0	0.00
Alfred Harrisson	24-11-1894	1	1	1.00	0	0.00
Shaun Marshall	15-4-2006	1	1	1.00	0	0.00
*Bill Corkhill	21-12-1946	1	2	2.00	0	0.00
*Ben Craythorne	26-12-1906	1	2	2.00	0	0.00
Tim Dalton	22-4-1986	1	2	2.00	0	0.00
Jack Dewick	2-11-1946	1	2	2.00	0	0.00
Charlie Watson	1-5-1968	1	2	2.00	0	0.00
Dale Belford	22-8-1987	1	3	3.00	0	0.00
Aidan Davison	15-4-1989	1	3	3.00	0	0.00
Tommy Hampson	15-2-1930	1	3	3.00	0	0.00
Brian Parkin	10-10-1998	1	3	3.00	0	0.00
Mordecai Sherwin	10-11-1888	1	3	3.00	0	0.00
*Jack Hendry	31-3-1893	1	4	4.00	0	0.00
Hugh Owen	3-11-1888	1	7	7.00	0	0.00
Grand total	**15-9-1888 to 5-5-2007**	**4452**	**6554**	**1.47**	**1187**	**26.66**

*Denotes regular outfield players who were selected as goalkeeper.

Stand-in goalkeepers
Gordon Bradley was injured in the 42nd minute of the match v Leicester City (a), Division 2, September 22nd 1956, after conceding three goals. He was replaced in goal by Gordon Wills who conceded three more (In the above table Bradley's record includes only the three goals he let in but the grand total adds the other three; the same applies to the following cases).

Centre-half and captain Alex Gibson replaced the injured Mick Rose in goal in the 32nd minute v Crewe Alexandra (h), Division 4, October 4th 1967 when Notts won 1-0 for what was also Les Bradd's debut for the Magpies.

Mick Leonard suffered an ankle injury in the 28th minute v Blackpool (a), Division 3, October 18th 1986, and had to be replaced. At that point he had conceded one goal then Darren Davis took over and conceded one more.

Albert Iremonger was sent off when Notts were 2-0 down v Derby County (a), Division 1, October 11th 1919 and Jack Foster went in goal to concede one more in a 3-1 defeat. Also getting marching orders was Iain Hesford v Doncaster Rovers (a), Division 3, December 28th 1985 when the Magpies were at 1-1. David Hunt went between the posts as Notts lost 2-1. Since substitute goalkeepers were allowed on the bench from 1993 outfielders no longer have to face the task of deputising in the event of injuries or dismissals such as the above.

Stand-in goalkeepers who started the match include full-back Jack Hendry v Preston North End (a), Division 1, March 31st 1893, after George Toone missed the train. Notts had to play with 10 men. Next was half-back Ben Craythorne v Sheffield United (a), Division 1, December 26th 1906, when Bob Suter's train was delayed. Finally came three cases in the bad winter of 1946-47 when Harry Brown, who had to travel from Aldershot camp, was held up by railway delays. Half-back Bill Corkhill deputised v Walsall (a), Division 3S, December 21st 1946, then centre-forward Fred Whittaker filled in on the two other occasions, v Bristol City (a), May 3rd 1947 and v Reading (h), May 29th 1947.

The reverse procedure was the case v Newport County (a), Division 4, February 28th 1970 when the club's nominated substitute missed the coach and reserve goalkeeper Barry Watling had to fill the role. During the match Don Masson came off injured and Watling went on to replace him.

Clean sheets
The most achieved by a Magpies goalkeeper in a single League season is 19 (one in a play-off) in 46 appearances (plus three play-offs) by Darren Ward in 1995/96. Roy Brown achieved 18 (43 matches) in 1971/72 and repeated the feat in 1972/73 (42). Including two in play-offs Steve Cherry also notched up 18 in 1989/90 (46 plus three play-offs). In a career, as the table above shows, Albert Iremonger is way out ahead with 183, more than 100 in front of his nearest rival, but he did have 564 appearances to help him along the way.

Goalscoring
Steve Mildenhall is the only Notts County goalkeeper to get on the scoresheet from that position. He achieved the feat v Mansfield Town (a), F.L.Cup 1st round, August 21st 2001, when he took a free-kick 25 yards out in the 34th minute. The ball bounced close to a melee of players and flew over Stags goalkeeper Kevin Pilkington into the net, having travelled 85 yards. Notts won 4-3.

Gordon Bradley scored in the 89th minute v Leicester City (a), Division 2, September 22nd 1956, after being injured in the 42nd minute. He received treatment up to the end of half-time then resumed limping on the wing to get his name on the scoresheet but too late to save the Magpies from a 6-3 defeat.

Darren Ward: 19 clean sheets in 1995/96

Odd spot
When Notts beat Sheffield Wednesday 6-1 (h), Division 1, September 14th 1901, visiting goalkeeper Frank Stubbs gave a superb first-half display as Wednesday led 1-0. However, Stubbs was kicked on the head shortly before the break and began to behave strangely in the dressing room. A doctor examined him and suggested he was suffering from hysteria. Whatever the cause, Stubbs gifted County their second-half goals by helping the ball on its way several times, perhaps because of memory lapses. Luckily, Stubbs suffered no after-effects and in later life he became mayor of Loughborough.

GOLDEN GOAL
This "sudden death" method of deciding a drawn game was briefly popular in the late 1990s and it meant that play continued in extra time only until a goal was scored. Sadly, teams were disinclined to risk anything and usually concentrated on defence until they came to the penalty shoot-out decider. The Magpies have played and won one match decided by a golden goal. This was when they won 3-2 v Bury (a), Associate Members Cup 2nd round, October 30th 2001. Danny Allsopp scored the "golden" decider in the 115th minute.

GREATEST XI?
The invitation to the opening night of the "Shoot!" exhibition in 2000, organised by the Notts County Football in the Community scheme to celebrate their tenth anniversary, selected the following eleven players as the greatest County team of all time. In the old 2-3-5 line-up, they are:

Albert Iremonger; Pedro Richards, Tommy Deans; Don Masson, David Needham, Mark Draper; John Chiedozie, Jackie Sewell, Tommy Lawton, Les Bradd, Tommy Johnson.

GROUNDS

The founders of Notts County played originally in the Hollow, a patch of open ground close to the cavalry barracks by Barrack Lane in Nottingham's Park estate but when they became good enough to meet outside opposition in 1864/65, the ground of the Meadows Cricket Club was used (this ground survives today as a children's recreation area). Occasionally Trent Bridge cricket ground was hired for a major match but this did not become the club's regular home until 1883. In addition, Nottingham Forest's then home ground on the Forest was used once in 1869-70 for a match against Lincoln.

The site of the Castle Cricket Club ground (the small rectangle under the "t" of Cricket and the "nd" of Ground). The Meadows Ground can be seen top left.

For season 1877/78 the Meadows ground was vacated in favour of the Beeston Cricket Club ground adjacent to Beeston railway station (the ground is today covered by a car park). They remained there for three seasons before another move, in 1880/81, to the Castle Cricket Club ground in the Meadows, later covered by railway sheds and now by housing development. After three seasons here, County then became regular tenants of Trent Bridge cricket ground in 1883/84 following Nottingham Forest's move from this venue. Because Trent Bridge was also needed for cricket, Notts County sometimes played matches early or late in the season at other locations including the Meadows and Castle grounds. Later they also used Forest's Town Ground and then the City Ground. After representations from the Football League in the early 1900s about playing all their home matches at one venue the club began to search for a new site including a plot of land on Meadow Lane. However no action was taken and the City Ground continued to be used for end-of-season fixtures. Then, in 1908, the trustees of Trent Bridge decided not to renew the club's lease when it expired in 1910.

Forced now to move rapidly, Notts rented the Meadow Lane site from Nottingham City Council and the new ground was ready for the start of the 1910/11 season. The stand at Trent Bridge was dismantled and erected at the Meadow Lane end of the new ground. It survived until 1978 when offices and a squash court were built on the site. A covered County Road side area was replaced in 1925 with a new stand, the one with the familiar gable carrying the club's formation date. In 1949 10-12ft. in height was added to the Kop to help accommodate the huge post-war crowds. The pitch had to be shortened by 6ft. in 1985 as spectators in the sponsors' boxes at the Meadow Lane end could not see the goalmouth directly beneath them. Between 1992 and 1994 the stadium was completely transformed with new all-seater stands surrounding the playing area. The new main stand was named after the then chairman Derek Pavis who was responsible for the new-look ground and the County Road stand named after former manager Jimmy Sirrel. First and last matches at the various grounds:

Park Hollow: Only games among club members were involved.

Meadows Cricket Ground: v Trent Valley, December 8th 1864, 0-0; v Nottingham Forest (Notts F.A. Senior Cup semi-final), March 19th 1887, 1-1.

The Forest: v Lincoln, March 12th 1870, 1-0 (only home match here).

Trent Bridge Cricket Ground: v Sheffield F.C., December 3rd 1870, 0-0; v Walsall Swifts, September 29th 1883, 4-2 (first match after becoming regular tenants); v Aston Villa (Division 1), April 16th 1910, 2-3.

Beeston Cricket Ground: v Stoke, October 13th 1877, 4-1; v Derby Grammar School, March 12th 1880, 2-2.

Castle Ground: v Queen's Park (Glasgow), November 6th 1880, 3-4; v Loughborough Town (friendly), September 2nd 1895, 3-1.

Town Ground: v (Glasgow) Rangers (friendly), April 15th 1895, 1-0; v Aston Villa (friendly), April 29th 1897, 1-2.

City Ground: v Stoke (Division 1), April 15th 1899, 2-0; v Blackburn Rovers (Division 1), April 18th 1908, 0-2.

Meadow Lane: v Nottingham Forest (Division 1), September 3rd 1910, 1-1.

(Dates for Town and City Ground matches do not include Notts featuring as the away team to Forest; only when used as County's home ground).

International

The only full international to be staged at a Notts County ground was England v Ireland at Trent Bridge on February 20th 1897. England won 6-0. Attendance 14,000.

F.A.Cup semi-finals

The following F.A.Cup semi-finals have been staged on a Notts County ground:

March 1st 1884 at Trent Bridge, Queen's Park (Glasgow) 4 Blackburn Olympic 0.
March 7th 1885 at Trent Bridge, Blackburn Rovers 5 Old Carthusians 1.
March 5th 1887 at Trent Bridge, West Bromwich Albion 3 Preston North End 1.
April 3rd 1912 at Meadow Lane, Barnsley 1 Swindon Town 0 (replay).
March 28th 1925 at Meadow Lane, Cardiff City 3 Blackburn Rovers 1.

Representative matches

An England international trial match between Amateurs and Professionals was played at Trent Bridge on March 28th 1895 when the Professionals won 7-0. The attendance was 1,200.

Meadow Lane staged the then annual F.A.XI v RAF match on October 9th 1957 when 7,000 saw a 5-2 win for the F.A.XI. This match took place during the National Service years and many good players turned out. Stan Newsham was the only Magpie involved and he lined up alongside Brian Clough (then of Middlesbrough) for the F.A. XI who also included Forest's Jack Burkitt. The RAF featured Doug Baird, then with Partick Thistle but later to spend a spell with Forest.

See under **Home Records** for total competitive playing record on each ground.

The County Ground in 1927, by Surrey Flying Services/Picture the Past. Meadow Lane is to the right and note there is no County Road at this time.

HEIGHT

Albert Iremonger meets the Prince of Wales, April 1921

Shortest

The shortest player to appear in a Football League match for Notts is probably Steve Holder whose only appearance was as substitute v Northampton Town (h) on April 24th 1970. Football annuals show his height as 5ft. 3in. Next comes Tony Freeman (1946/47 to 1949/50), Willie Carlin (1971/72 to 1973/74) and John Gissing (19578-58 to 1960/61). All three were recorded as 5ft. 4in. However Henry Sissons, whose only Notts outing was in the 1894/95 test match v Derby County (at Filbert Street) on April 27th 1895, was exactly 5ft. tall. These were all forwards or midfield players. The shortest full-backs appear to have been Tom Prescott (1896/97 to 1904/05) and Andrew Mosley (1908/09 and 1909/10), both of whom were 5ft. 7½in.

Tallest

Goalkeeper Albert Iremonger (1904/05 to 1925/26) is on record as the tallest Notts County player and until recent years the tallest in any League match. His height was given as 6ft. 5½in. For many years, next came winger William Gunn who played in League matches between 1888/89 and 1892/93 but was a regular member of the side earlier in the 1880s. He was 6ft. 3in. However, more recently the Magpies have fielded a number of players 6ft. 4in. tall. They include Colin Foster (1993/94), Steve Mildenhall (2001/02 to 2003/04), Brian Parkin (1998/99), Clive Platt (2003/04), Mike Pollitt (1996/97), Mick Waitt (1984/85 to 1986/87) and Lee Wilkie (2001/02). In 1906/07, in addition to first choice goalkeeper Iremonger, reserve 'keeper Bob Suter was 6ft. 1in. This was all but matched while Mildenhall was with the Magpies as reserve goalkeeper Saul Deeney was 6ft. 1in.

HOME RECORDS (Football League matches only)
Best home seasons:
Two points for a win

	P	W	D	L	F	A	Pts	
1970/71	23	19	4	0	59	12	42	Div.4
1959/60	23	19	1	3	66	27	39	Div.4
1972/73	23	17	4	2	40	12	38	Div.3
1949/50	21	17	3	1	60	12	37	Div.3S
1930/31	21	16	4	1	58	13	36	Div.3S
1971/72	23	16	3	4	42	19	35	Div.3
1960/61	23	16	3	4	52	24	35	Div.3
1913/14	19	16	2	1	55	13	34	Div.2

In Division 1

	P	W	D	L	F	A	Pts
1900/01	17	13	2	2	39	18	28
1924/25	21	11	6	4	29	12	28

Three points for a win

	P	W	D	L	F	A	Pts	
1989/90	23	17	4	2	40	18	55	Div.3
1993/94	23	16	3	4	43	26	51	Div.1*
1997/98	23	14	7	2	41	20	49	Div.3*
1986/87	23	14	6	3	52	24	48	Div.3
1995/96	23	14	6	3	42	21	48	Div.2*

In Division 1

	P	W	D	L	F	A	Pts
1982/83	21	12	4	5	37	25	40

Worst home seasons:
Two points for a win

	P	W	D	L	F	A	Pts	
1904/05	17	1	7	9	16	33	8	Div.1
1888/89	11	4	2	5	24	32	10	League
1889/90	11	4	3	4	20	19	11	League
1897/98	15	4	6	5	23	23	14	Div.1
1912/13	19	6	4	9	19	20	16	Div.1
1899/00	17	5	7	5	29	22	17	Div.1
1895/96	15	8	1	6	41	22	17	Div.2
1958/59	23	5	9	9	33	39	19	Div.3
1934/35	21	8	3	10	29	33	19	Div.2
1979/80	21	4	11	6	24	22	19	Div.2

In Division 3S

	P	W	D	L	F	A	Pts
1935/36	21	10	5	6	40	25	25

In Division 4

	P	W	D	L	F	A	Pts
1965/66	23	9	8	6	32	25	26

Three points for a win

	P	W	D	L	F	A	Pts	
1996/97	23	4	9	10	20	25	21	Div.2*
1984/85	21	6	5	10	25	32	23	Div.2
1983/84	21	6	7	8	31	36	25	Div.1
2004/05	23	6	7	10	21	27	25	League 2*
1991/92	21	7	5	9	24	29	26	Div.1
2003/04	23	6	9	8	32	27	27	Div.2*

Most wins in a season: 19 in 1959/60; and 1970/71 (both Division 4, 23 matches).
Fewest defeats in a season: 0 in 1970/71 (Division 4).
Fewest wins in a season: 1 in 1904/05 (Division 1, 17 matches). In programme of 21 and 23 matches: 4 in 1979/80 (Division 2, 21); and 1996/97 (Division 2*, 23).
Most defeats in a season: 10 in 1934/35; 1984-85 (both Division 2, 21 matches); 1996/97 (Division 2*, 23 matches); and 2004/05 (League 2*, 23 matches).
Most draws in a season: 11 in 1974/75; 1979/80 (both Division 2, 21 matches); and 2005/06 (League 2*, 23 matches).
Fewest draws in a season: 1 in 1890/91 (Football League, 11 matches); 1893/94 (Division 2, 14 matches); 1895/96; 1896/97 (both Division 2, 15 matches); 1922/23 (Division 2, 21 matches); and 1959/60 (Division 4, 23 matches).
Most goals scored in a season: 68 in 1948/49 (Division 3S, 21 matches).
Most goals conceded in a season: 39 in 1958/59 (Division 3, 23 matches).
Fewest goals scored in a season: 16 in 1904/05 (Division 1, 17 matches); 19 in 1912/13 (Division 1, 19 matches); 20 in 1996/97 (Division 2*, 23 matches).
Fewest goals conceded in a season: 12 in 1924/25 (Division 1, 21 matches); 1949/50 (Division 3S, 21 matches); 1970/71 (Division 4); and 1972/73 (Division 3, both 23 matches).
Longest unbeaten run: 25 matches from April 24th 1970 (Division 4) to August 14th 1971 (Division 3).
Longest winning run: 14 matches from September 17th 1959 to February 13th 1960 (Division 4).
Longest run of drawn matches: 7 from March 4th to August 8th 2006 (League 2*). The last 6 home matches of 2005/06 plus the first of 2006/07.
Longest run of defeats: 5 on three occasions in 1953/54; 1957/58 (both Division 2); and 1958/59 (Division 3).
Longest run without a win: 13 matches from November 26th 1904 to September 23rd 1905 (Division 1).
Longest run without a drawn match: 23 matches from March 14th 1959 (Division 3) to March 12th 1960 (Division 4).
Longest scoring run: 38 matches from January 26th 1893 (Division 1) to November 9th 1895 (Division 2). At Meadow Lane: 34 matches from September 17th 1959 (Division 4) to February 4th 1961 (Division 3).
Longest run without scoring: 4 matches from January 11th to March 22nd 1958 (Division 2) and March 4th to April 5th 1986 (Division 3).

Longest run of clean sheets: 12 matches from December 16th 1972 to April 23rd 1973 (Division 3).
Longest run without a clean sheet: 23 matches from December 27th 1955 to December 24th 1956 (Division 2). The last clean sheet before the sequence began was 5-0 v Middlesbrough and the first to end the sequence was ... 5-0 v Stoke City!
Longest sequence with the same result and scoreline is three times which has occurred on ten occasions; 0-0 in 1984/85 (Division 2); 1-1 in 1958/59 (Division 3), 1977/78 twice (Division 2) and 2005/06 (League 2*); 1-0 in 1910/11 (Division 1), 1922/23 (Division 2) and 1930/31 (Division 3S); 2-1 in 1959/60 (Division 4); and 0-1 in 1994/95 (Division 1*).

Scored in every home match

The last time the Magpies scored in every home Football League match in a season was 1977/78 when they were in Division 2, playing 21 home matches. Previous occasions were: 1890/91 (Football League, 11 matches); 1891/92 (Football League, 13 matches); 1893/94 (Division 2, 14 matches); 1894/95 (Division 2, 15 matches); 1896/97 (Division 2, 15 matches); 1913/14 (Division 2, 19 matches); and 1930/31 (Division 3S, 21 matches).

Failed to keep clean sheet in any home match

The only time Notts County failed to keep a clean sheet in any home Football League match in a season was 1889/90 when they played 11 home matches.

Notts County's competitive home record on their various grounds is as follows:

	P	W	D	L	F	A	Pts 2 win	Pts 3 win
At Meadow Lane								
Football League	1868	918	485	465	3155	2062	1643	938
Play-offs	4	3	0	1	5	3		
F.A.Cup	100	47	22	31	177	119		
F.L.Cup	65	36	9	20	127	87		
Full Members Cup	4	2	1	1	5	4		
Assoc. Members Cup	18	5	5	8	15	20		
Division 3S Cup	4	2	1	1	6	6		
Anglo-Italian Cup	8	5	3	0	16	10		
Anglo-Scottish Cup	12	7	3	2	19	10		
Watney Cup	1	0	0	1	0	3		
Total	2084	1025	529	530	2436	1930		
At Trent Bridge								
Football League	312	163	78	71	689	393	404	
Test match	1	1	0	0	1	0	2	
F.A.Cup	46	28	8	10	147	48		
United Counties Lge	3	0	1	2	0	4	1	
Total	362	192	87	83	837	445		
At the Castle Ground								
Football League	13	7	1	5	24	18	15	
F.A.Cup	5	4	1	0	21	10		
United Counties Lge	2	1	0	1	2	5	2	
Total	20	12	2	6	47	33		
At the City Ground								
Football League	21	9	6	6	35	28	24	
At the Town Ground								
Football League	3	2	0	1	8	5	4	
Test match	1	0	1	0	1	1	1	
United Counties Lge	2	0	0	2	3	5	0	
Total	6	2	1	3	12	11		
At Beeston Cricket Ground								
F.A.Cup	1	0	0	1	1	3		

See under **Goalscoring** for biggest home victories and defeats.

INTERNATIONAL PLAYERS

Most capped players

The record is held by Kevin Wilson who won 16 Northern Ireland caps while with the Magpies. Harry Cursham has the most for England (8 appearances) and Martin O'Neill (Northern Ireland) is the only other Notts player to clock up 8 caps.

England

Following five unofficial "England v Scotland" matches, all played at Kennington Oval cricket ground in London with both sides selected by the F.A., official internationals began with the England v Scotland match at Glasgow on November 30th 1872. Ernest Greenhalgh, who played at full-back in this match, was therefore Notts County's first international player. To date, the last Magpie to turn out for England was Tommy Lawton v Denmark at Copenhagen on September 26th 1948. Here is a complete list of the club's England internationals:

    Bill Ashurst (5): Sweden (2) 1922/23; Scotland, Wales and Belgium 1924/25.
    Arthur Cursham (6): Scotland 1875/76, 1876/77 and 1877/78; Wales 1878/79; Scotland and Wales 1882/83.
    Harry Cursham (8): Wales 1879/80; Scotland, Wales and Ireland 1881/82 and 1882/83; Ireland 1883/84.
    Harry Daft (5): Ireland 1888/89; Scotland and Wales 1889/90; Ireland 1890/91 and 1891/92.
    Johnny Dixon (1): Wales 1884/85.
    Alf Dobson (4): Ireland 1881/82; Scotland, Wales and Ireland 1883/84.
    Charlie Dobson (1): Ireland 1885/86.
    Ernest Greenhalgh (2): Scotland 1872-73 (2).
    William Gunn (2): Scotland and Wales 1883/84.
    Percy Humphreys (1): Scotland 1902-03.
    Tommy Lawton (4): Scotland, Sweden and Italy 1947/48; Denmark 1948/49.
    Stuart Macrae (6): Scotland, Wales and Ireland 1882/83 and 1883/84.

Harry Moore (2): Ireland 1882/83; Wales 1884/85.
Bert Morley (1): Ireland 1909/10.
Harold Morse (1): Scotland 1878/79.
Alf Shelton (6): Ireland 1888/89; Scotland and Wales 1889/90 and 1890/91; Scotland 1891/92.
Charlie Shelton (1): Ireland 1888/89.
George Toone (2): Scotland and Wales 1891/92.

Near miss: Horace Cope was selected for England v Ireland at Belfast in 1925/26 but had to withdraw because of injury. He was never chosen again. The most Notts County players in one England team are three as follows:

1882/83 v Scotland at Sheffield and v Wales at Kennington Oval: Arthur and Harry Cursham and Stuart Macrae;
v Ireland at Liverpool: Harry Cursham, Stuart Macrae and Harry Moore.
1883/84 v Scotland at Glasgow and v Wales at Wrexham: Alf Dobson, William Gunn and Stuart Macrae;
v Ireland at Belfast: Harry Cursham, Alf Dobson and Stuart Macrae.
1888/89 v Ireland at Liverpool: Harry Daft, Alf and Charlie Shelton.

Brothers

The above appearances by the Curshams and the Sheltons are the only times Notts County brothers played together for England.

Goalscoring

Harry Cursham scored five goals including a hat-trick v Ireland at Belfast in 1883/84. Others to score are: Harry Daft 3, Arthur Cursham and Tommy Lawton 2, William Gunn 1.

Unofficial

Frank Broome played twice for the F.A. XI v Australia on the 1951 tour there and scored a hat-trick in the match at Sydney. Jesse Pye played for England v Belgium at Wembley in a 1945/46 Victory international and scored a goal.

Scotland

There have been no Notts County players capped by Scotland. When the Magpies had their strongest contingent of Scots in the 1890s the Scottish F.A. was ignoring Anglo-Scots in its international sides. For instance, though Jimmy Oswald spent four seasons with County, he was only selected for Scotland while with Scottish clubs, both before and after his stay in Nottingham. None of Don Masson's 17 caps were won while with Notts though Iain McCulloch did achieve two Scottish Under-21 selections.

Wales

Willie Davies (6): England, Scotland and Ireland 1928/29 and 1929/30.
Arthur Green (5): England 1902/03; Scotland and Ireland 1903/04; Ireland and England 1905/06.
Eddie Lawrence (1): Scotland 1931/32.
John Morgan (2): England and Scotland 1879/80.
Darren Ward: Portugal 1999/2000.

Goalscoring

Arthur Green scored a hat-trick v Ireland at Wrexham in 1905/06 and Willie Davies scored twice v Scotland at Glasgow in 1928/29

Northern Ireland

Martin O'Neill (8): Austria, Turkey, West Germany, England, Wales and Finland 1983/84; Romania and Finland 1984/85.
Kevin Wilson (16): Lithuania and Germany 1991/92; Albania, Spain (2), Denmark, Lithuania and Latvia 1992/93; Latvia, Denmark (2), Republic of Ireland, Romania, Liechtenstein, Colombia and Mexico 1993/94.

Goalscoring

Kevin Wilson scored three goals in total and Martin O'Neill two.

Republic of Ireland

Bill Fallon (5): Hungary 1934/35 and 1935/36 (2); Switzerland and France 1936/37.
Eddie Gannon (1): Switzerland 1948/49.
Jim "Seamus" McDonagh (5): Holland 1983/84; USSR, Norway, Denmark and Switzerland 1984/85.
Con Moulson (2): Switzerland and France 1936/37.
Ray O'Brien (4): Norway and Poland 1975/76; Spain and Poland 1976/77.

Others

John Chiedozie (Nigeria), Rachid Harkouk (Algeria) and Aki Lahtinen (Finland) were all capped by their countries while with the Magpies.

See also **Under-21 Caps**.

INTER-LEAGUE MATCHES

The first Football League representative side which drew 1-1 with the Football Alliance at Olive Grove, Sheffield, on April 20th 1891 included two Notts County players, Harry Daft and Tommy McInnes. Although Scottish, McInnes was selected because he was playing for a Football League club.

The complete list of the club's inter-league players until the Football League ended such regular fixtures in 1977 are as follows:

Bill Ashurst (1) Irish League 1923/24.
Walter Bull (1) Scottish League 1900/01.
Reuben Craythorne (1) Irish League 1906/07.
Harry Daft (2) Football Alliance 1890/91; Scottish League 1891/92.
Harry Fletcher (1) Irish League 1898/99.
Percy Humphreys (1) Scottish League 1902/03.
Albert Iremonger (2) Irish League and Southern League 1911/12.
Ted McDonald (1) Irish League 1902/03.
Tommy McInnes (2) Football Alliance 1890/91; Scottish League 1891/92.
Jack Peart (1) Scottish League 1913/14.
Tom Prescott (1) Scottish League 1898/99.

Goalscorers: McInnes scored once v the Scottish League in 1891/92 and Fletcher once v the Irish League in 1898/99.

JOHNSTONE'S PAINT TROPHY: see Associate Members Cup

KICK-OFF
Under the early rules of the game, teams would change ends every time a goal was scored and the team conceding the goal was allowed the kick to restart the game. Ever since half-time was introduced in 1875, the team which kicks off the first half of a game concedes that privilege to the opposition at the start of the second half.

However, when the Magpies met Chesterfield at Saltergate, Division 4, October 11th 1969, they kicked off in both halves, courtesy of referee R.E.Raby of Leeds, who seemed oblivious to shouts from the crowd pointing out his error. Nor did either of his linesmen notice what had happened but Notts gained no advantage from the event, crashing 5-0 after David Needham had been sent off in the 37th minute.

LDV VANS TROPHY: see Associate Members Cup

LEGENDS MATCH
On October 5th 2003 a crowd of 8,500 saw Notts County Legends beat Nottingham Forest Legends 3-2 at Meadow Lane in a special match to boost County's Supporters Trust funds in their attempt to save the Magpies from extinction during the period in administration. Former stars from both clubs turned out as Tommy Johnson, Kevin Bartlett and Phil Stant (penalty) netted for County while Garry Birtles and Ian McParland replied for Forest. The day was a huge success with around £40,000 going into the kitty.

One hundred years earlier a similar match took place at the City Ground on April 10th 1903 when Forest Veterans beat Notts Veterans 1-0 and raised £150 for the Nottingham Sick and Hospital Society Co. Fund. The attendance was 6,500 and Teddy May, who had played for both clubs, scored the winner.

LEYLAND DAF CUP: see Associate Members Cup

LIMITED COMPANY
Notts County became a limited company during the summer of 1890. The moves were initiated by Arthur Williams who proposed a resolution to that effect at the general spring meeting at the Albert Hall on April 28th 1890. The resolution was "to register the club under Section 23 of the Companies Act 1867 with Limited Liability." This was carried and further meetings were held to establish the new company. The original share capital was £2,500 in 500 shares of £5 each and the club was registered under the title of The Notts Incorporated Football Club. Twelve directors were elected as follows: A.T.Ashwell, A.Barlow, B.F.Blackburn, A.J.Chamberlain, T.Cooper, W.Gunn, R.Halford, A.Lofthouse, F.P.Norris, W.B.Scottorn, H.Vickers and A.Williams. The first board meeting was on August 19th 1890 at the Lion Hotel when Mr.Williams was elected chairman.

In 1928 County's financial position was described by the chairman, Alderman Henry Heath, as "the worst in the club's history." After taking advice from financial experts it was decided to put Notts Incorporated into liquidation and to float a new limited liability company, Notts County Football Club Ltd. Attempts were made to float the new company during summer 1928 but public response was poor and at a board meeting on October 10th that year it was resolved "that the Notts County Football Club Ltd. go into voluntary liquidation and that the Board of Directors revert to the Articles of Association originally published by the Notts Incorporated Football Club." The proposed new club was officially wound up at a meeting on November 14th 1928.

Notts Incorporated survived until 2003. When the club entered administration on June 17th 2002 Notts Incorporated was run by the administrators until the offer of the Blenheim Consortium was accepted and, with the approval of the Football League, Notts County came out of administration on December 3rd 2003. At that point the old company went into liquidation and the new company, Blenheim 1862 Ltd, was registered at Companies House.

In March 2003 more than 400 fans attended meetings at which the Supporters Trust was formed. Its purpose was to raise funds to help the club to survive and it set a target of £250,000. This was achieved in December 2003 as the Magpies came out of administration and the Trust were able to have a representative on the new board of directors. Early in 2007 the Trust gained a majority shareholding in the club and therefore in effect had boardroom control.

The following have been chairmen of the board: A.Williams 1890-92; R.Deplidge 1892-95; Ald.H.Heath 1895-1930; Lord Belper 1930-35; C.G.Barnes 1935-56; L.Machin 1956-64; C.F.Williamson 1964-66; W.A.Hopcroft 1966-69; J.J.Dunnett 1969-87; D.Pavis 1987-2002; A.Scardino 2002-03; Administrators 2003; S.Thompson 2005-06; J.Moore 2006-date.

LITTLEWOODS CUP: see Football League Cup

LONG SERVICE
Directors
Alderman Henry Heath was elected to the board on June 5th 1893, was chairman from 1895-1931 and relinquished his seat in 1934/35. He was then elected an honorary director and so, at his death in 1943, had kept up a 50-year connection with Notts County.

William Gunn was elected to the new limited company's first board in 1890 and retained his seat, latterly as club president, until his death in 1921, a spell of 31 years. He first appeared as a player in 1881/82, thus giving 40 years service on and off the field. Gunn is the only director to turn out as a player while a board member. He made two League and one Cup appearances in such a role.

Charles Barnes was a director for 35 years, from his election on August 24th 1921 until his resignation on October 31st 1956, a span of 35 years. He succeeded Lord Belper as chairman in 1935 and was in addition club president from 22nd April 1952, retaining both positions until he left the club.

General
Horace Henshall was a Notts County player from 1912/13 to 1921/22, then became secretary-manager 1927-34, staying on as secretary only for another season, so that his club links covered 23 years, though not unbroken.

Managers
Albert Fisher was Notts County secretary-manager from 1913-27, a period of 14 years. Jimmy Sirrel's reign stretched over 18 years, 1969-87 but he was away in charge of Sheffield United 1975-77 and was also general manager during 1982-85 when Howard Wilkinson, Larry Lloyd and Richie Barker had managerial control of the playing side.

Players
Albert Iremonger made his Notts County debut on April 1st 1905 and played his last match on May 1st 1926, a period of 21 years as a player. Next comes Billy Flint with 17 years, stretching from April 3rd 1909 to April 10th 1926. Bill Corkhill had a period of more than 19 years between his debut on February 6th 1932 and his last outing on September 12th 1951 but this was broken by a seven-year spell with Cardiff City, 1938-45.

Secretaries
Tom Harris was appointed secretary December 27th 1893 and resigned on June 9th 1913 because of ill health. He was elected a director on June 4th 1892 and stepped down on May 29th 1902 but continued as secretary. Altogether he had an unbroken association of 21 years with the Magpies.

Trainers
Jack Wheeler came to Meadow Lane as trainer in summer 1957 along with new manager Tommy Lawton. The pair had been team-mates at Kettering Town where Tommy was player-manager. Jack stayed as trainer until the close of 1982/83 and so gave 26 years of service to the Magpies which also included a couple of stints as caretaker-manager.

Groundsmen
Peter Thompson retired as groundsman in 1998 after caring for the Meadow Lane pitch for 37 years.

MANAGERS
It is difficult to compile a complete record of managers as in the old days men who were managers were not accorded that title and there is some confusion between men who would now be regarded simply as secretaries and those who had anything at all to do with team management.

Before the formation of the limited company in 1890 the committee or one of its sub-committees were responsible for team selection and this practice continued during the time of the early board of directors. For instance, at the inaugural board meeting on August 19th 1890 it was resolved "that Messrs. A.Barlow, W.Gunn, A.Lofthouse, F.P.Norris and W.B.Scottorn be, and they are hereby appointed, a committee to be called 'The Team Management Committee' with power on behalf of the Board of Directors to manage the League team during the next football season, subject to the Board of Directors – such committee in cases of emergency also to have power to select the players for such team." This arrangement lasted for a few seasons but generally the team was selected at board meetings.

It was on May 30th 1913 that the board decided to advertise for a team manager following the resignation through illness of the secretary, Tom Harris. In the event, the post became one of secretary-manager and on July 6th 1913 Albert Fisher was appointed the club's first real manager in the modern sense, duties to start on August 1st. However, at this stage the team was still selected at board meetings and although Mr. Fisher soon began to decide on the line-up himself, his choice had to be approved by the board.

In 1923/24 Charles Bell was appointed team manager under Mr. Fisher but he was what would now be regarded as coach and had little or no say in team selection. In 1930/31 there was also a team manager, Harold Wightman, under secretary-manager Horace Henshall while Will Jennings was team manager from October 31st 1931 to May 5th 1934, also under Mr. Henshall.

Charlie Jones was appointed manager on May 5th 1934 in succession to Mr. Henshall and he was County's first manager to have complete control over team selection. The club's complete list of managers from the appointment of Albert Fisher is as follows:

Albert Fisher secretary-manager August 1st 1913 to May 31st 1927; Bob White secretary-manager July 17th 1917 to January 29th 1919 (during Albert Fisher's absence in the Armed Forces); Horace Henshall secretary-manager June 1st 1927 to May 5th 1934 (continued as secretary to April 17th 1935); Charlie Jones May 5th 1934 to December 6th 1934; Directors sub-committee December 6th 1934 to April 29th 1935; David Pratt secretary-manager April 29th 1935 to June 28th 1935; Percy Smith secretary-manager July 19th 1935 to October 31st 1936; Jimmy McMullan secretary-manager November 10th 1936 to December 29th 1937; Harry Parkes secretary-manager January 11th 1938 to July 13th 1939;

James "Tony" Towers secretary-manager July 13th 1939 to July 14th 1942 (he was a Notts County director 1927-1943); Frank Womack July 14th 1942 to November 4th 1943; Major Frank Buckley March 1st 1944 to May 11th 1946; Arthur Stollery June 12th 1946 to February 15th 1949; Wilf Fisher secretary-manager February 15th 1949 to May 25th

1949 (he was club secretary July 14th 1942 to November 4th 1956); Eric Houghton May 25th 1949 to September 1st 1953; George Poyser October 22nd 1953 to January 7th 1957; Frank Broome acting manager January 7th 1957 to May 7th 1957 then assistant-manager to December 27th 1957; Tommy Lawton May 7th 1957 to July 1st 1958; Ernest "Tim" Coleman and Jack Wheeler joint-caretaker managers July 1st 1958 to October 17th 1958; Frank Hill October 17th 1958 to October 31st 1961; "Tim" Coleman team manager October 31st 1961 to June 31st 1963; Eddie Lowe player-manager July 1st 1963 to April 12th 1965; "Tim" Coleman team manager April 12th 1965 to December 10th 1965;

Andy Beattie and Peter Doherty managerial advisers with "Tim" Coleman as assistant December 10th 1965 to March 18th 1966; Jack Burkitt March 18th 1966 to February 23rd 1967 after taking leave of absence through ill-health (nervous exhaustion caused by overwork) from December 6th 1966; Andy Beattie acting manager December 6th 1966, then general manager February 23rd 1967 to September 28th 1967 (during this time he undertook team selection duties except from March 13th 1967 to end of 1966/67 season); Billy Gray March 13th 1967 to September 23rd 1968 (relinquished team selection duties to Andy Beattie August 1st 1967 to September 28th 1967); Jack Wheeler caretaker-manager September 23rd 1968 to November 19th 1969; Jimmy Sirrel November 19th 1969 to October 16th 1975; Ron Fenton October 16th 1975 to October 6th 1977; Jimmy Sirrel October 6th 1977 to August 28th 1982 when he became general manager; Howard Wilkinson team manager August 28th 1982 to June 24th 1983; Larry Lloyd July 7th 1983 to October 21st 1984; Jimmy Sirrel caretaker-manager October 21st 1984 to November 5th 1984; Richie Barker November 5th 1984 to April 19th 1985; Jimmy Sirrel April 20th 1985 to June 2nd 1987; John Barnwell June 7th 1987 to December 2nd 1988; John Newman acting-manager December 2nd 1988 to January 5th 1989; Neil Warnock January 5th 1989 to January 14th 1993; Mick Walker January 14th 1993 to September 14th 1994; Russell Slade September 14th 1994 to January 12th 1995; Howard Kendall January 12th 1995 to April 1st 1995; Wayne Jones, Steve Nicol and Dean Thomas caretaker-managers April 1st 1995 to June 5th 1995; Colin Murphy general manager and Steve Thompson team manager June 5th 1995 to December 23rd 1996; Sam Allardyce January 16th 1997 to October 14th 1999; Gary Brazil caretaker-manager October 14th 1999 then manager 26th October 1999 to June 28th 2000; John "Jocky" Scott June 28th 2000 to October 10th 2001; Gary Brazil again October 10th 2001 to January 7th 2002; Billy Dearden January 7th 2002 to January 7th 2004; Gary Mills January 9th 2004 to November 4th 2004; Ian Richardson player-caretaker-manager then full player-manager November 4th 2004 to May 17th 2005; Gudjon Thordarson May 17th 2005 to May 25th 2006; Steve Thompson June 12th 2006 to date.

The following table shows the record of Notts County while various managers were in charge. Because of the change to three points for a win in 1981, the order is based on the difference between matches won and lost.

	P	W	D	L	F	A	Pts	+/-
Jimmy Sirrel	561	236	166	159	810	680	694	+77
Jimmy McMullan	49	29	10	10	83	45	68	+19
Neil Warnock	183	75	46	62	254	242	271	+13
Sam Allardyce	123	51	32	40	167	144	185	+11
John Barnwell	62	25	20	17	98	68	95	+8
Frank Hill	140	59	27	54	260	246	145	+5
Ron Fenton	82	32	22	28	124	113	86	+4
Eric Houghton	173	70	37	66	296	281	177	+4
Jocky Scott	57	23	15	19	76	83	84	+4
Arthur Stollery	112	47	22	43	209	167	116	+4
Steve Thompson	115	42	35	38	133	118	161	+4
*Frank Broome	17	6	8	3	28	18	20	+3
Albert Fisher	412	155	104	153	532	542	414	+2
Tim Coleman	113	41	32	40	153	174	114	+1
*John Newman	5	3	0	2	7	7	9	+1
Percy Smith	55	20	16	19	81	77	56	+1
Mick Walker	75	29	18	28	104	106	105	+1
*Wilf Fisher	14	6	1	7	24	23	13	-1
David Pratt	1	0	0	1	1	5	0	-1
*Jones,Nicol,Thomas	7	1	3	3	3	9	6	-2
Howard Kendall	14	4	4	6	20	21	16	-2
Jack Burkitt	35	12	8	15	53	57	32	-3
Andy Beattie	33	10	9	14	33	41	29	-4
Horace Henshall	294	105	80	109	492	470	290	-4
Ian Richardson	30	9	8	13	29	40	35	-4
Harry Parkes	62	22	13	27	67	88	57	-5
*Jack Wheeler	70	20	25	25	75	85	65	-5
Howard Wilkinson	42	15	7	20	55	71	52	-5
Gudjon Thordarson	46	12	16	18	46	63	52	-6
Directors (1934/35)	25	8	3	14	31	55	19	-6
Gary Mills	37	9	11	17	43	56	39	-8
Russell Slade	18	3	4	11	14	25	13	-8
Richie Barker	24	5	5	14	22	36	20	-9
Billy Gray	61	19	14	28	69	100	52	-9
Gary Brazil	50	13	14	23	61	71	53	-10
Charlie Jones	17	1	4	12	15	42	6	-11
Tommy Lawton	42	12	6	24	44	80	30	-12
Billy Dearden	92	26	25	41	115	142	103	-15
George Poyser	137	46	30	61	200	257	122	-15
Larry Lloyd	53	12	11	30	61	100	47	-18
Eddie Lowe	87	22	21	44	99	162	65	-22

* denotes caretaker-manager. (Jimmy Sirrel's points total comprises 489 at 2 for a win and 205 at 3)

Jimmy Sirrel, with Don Masson

Long service

Albert Fisher was secretary-manager for 14 years 1913-1927 though he was absent for 18 months in the Armed Forces. Jimmy Sirrel totalled 12 years as manager in three separate spells, his first period lasting one month under six years. Horace Henshall was secretary-manager for six years 11 months and then continued as secretary for another year.

Quick service

The manager with the shortest spell in office is David Pratt who was appointed on April 29th 1935 and resigned on June 28th of the same year – a reign in office of just two months! He took charge of just one Magpies League match. Howard Kendall lasted just over two-and-a-half months from January 12th to April 1st 1995.

Player-manager

The Magpies have had only two player-managers in their history. The first was Eddie Lowe who made nine League appearances while in charge. More recently Ian Richardson became the second with a single League outing as player-manager. But note that William Gunn, while a director and member of the team management sub-committee played twice in League games, in 1890/91 and 1892/93 as well as an F.A. Cup tie in the former season.

Former players

Apart from the player-managers, only five players with Notts County have also filled the manager's post. They are Horace Henshall, Eric Houghton, Tommy Lawton, Richie Barker and Gary Mills. This ignores caretaker-managers such as Frank Broome.

Nottingham Forest

Andy Beattie is the only man to have been manager of both Nottingham Forest and Notts County though Forest's first manager of all, Harold Wightman, was team manager at Meadow Lane in 1930/31 but this was in reality the club coach position. The following Forest players subsequently managed the Magpies: John Barnwell, Jack Burkitt, Billy Gray, Charlie Jones, Larry Lloyd and Gary Mills. In addition Ron Fenton was on Forest's coaching staff after leaving Meadow Lane.

MANSFIELD TOWN

The present club were formed as Mansfield Wesleyans in 1897, became Mansfield Wesley in 1906 when their link with Bridge Street Methodist Church ended, and changed their name to Mansfield Town in 1910. An earlier Town club who were defunct by the turn of the 19th century had played friendlies against Notts County but encounters with the current outfit date from 1907/08 when County Reserves and Wesley met in the Notts and District League. The first teams had to wait until 1936/37 for their first match when the Magpies won 5-1 (h) in the newly-established County Cup. The following season saw their first League meeting when both were in Division 3S. Notts won 2-0 (h), October 7th 1937, before 13,632 spectators.

Record win for the Magpies is 5-0 (h), F.L.Cup 1st round 1st leg, August 30th 1988 when Ian McParland notched a hat-trick and, in the League, 5-1 (h), Division 3S, March 29th 1947. Mansfield's biggest victory is 4-0 (Field Mill), September 16th 1963, Division 3, with a hat-trick from Roy Chapman. The record attendances are: Meadow Lane, 16,905, Division 3, November 6th 1971; Field Mill: 16,784, February 26th 1972, so both records were set in 1971/72.

In addition to McParland's hat-trick, another one for the Magpies was scored by Danny Allsopp in 10 minutes (a), F.L.Cup 1st round, August 21st 2001, a match also notable for goalkeeper Steve Mildenhall's 85-yard free-kick which went into the Stags goal to give County a 4-3 success.

Complete competitive record, from the Magpies' point of view:

	P	W	D	L	F	A
Division 2	2	2	0	0	4	1
Division 3S	6	3	1	2	10	6
Division 3/2*	16	6	6	4	25	25
Division 4/3*/League 2*	8	3	3	2	11	10
Football League	32	14	10	8	50	42
F.L.Cup	6	2	1	3	11	11
Associate Members Cup	3	0	1	2	1	3
Division 3S Cup	1	0	0	1	0	3
Anglo-Scottish Cup	2	1	0	1	1	1
Total	44	17	12	15	63	60

(The clubs have never met in the F.A.Cup)

Other first-team matches:

	P	W	D	L	F	A
World War 2	19	9	1	9	35	39
County Cup	33	15	7*	11	59	48

(*Notts won five and lost two of the penalty shoot-outs)

In the 1890s Notts met an earlier Mansfield Town club as follows:

	P	W	D	L	F	A
Friendlies	6	5	0	1	17	8

MATCHES

Until modern times, County's busiest season was their F.A.Cup-winning campaign of 1893/94 when they took part in 66 matches inclusive of friendlies. This was not beaten until nearly a century later when 68 games were notched up in 1985/86, 1987/88 and 1990/91. This last season produced 38 victories, the largest achieved by the Magpies in any one season. Most defeats stand at 32, shared between 1944/45 and 1963/64. From 1864/65 to the close of 2006/07, Notts have played 6,332 known first-team matches, counting friendlies, benefits, testimonials, overseas tours and wartime seasons, with the following outcome: W. 2431, D. 1451, L. 2450, F. 10030, A. 9911. Fittingly, they registered their 10,000th goal in a match at Meadow Lane when Jason Lee scored in the 2-1 win over Wrexham on November 18th 2006.

MILK CUP: see Football League Cup

NICKNAMES

Notts County have been nicknamed "the Magpies" ever since they changed their colours from chocolate and blue to black and white stripes at the time of the conversion to a limited company in 1890. Before this they were known as "the Lambs" and the two nicknames ran in harness for a few years. For instance, the *Nottingham Daily Express* of April 11th 1893, reporting a friendly at Kettering, said: "The first appearance of the Magpies in Northamptonshire had been sufficiently advertised, consequently a large number of spectators assembled to see the famous "Lambs".

The origin of the name "Lambs" is more obscure than "Magpies". Even in the 18th century the mob of roughs from the Narrow Marsh area of Nottingham were known as the Lambs because of their un-lamblike behaviour, especially during elections. A crowd invasion during an England v Nottinghamshire cricket match on the Forest in 1817 referred to the "Lambs". In their early days Notts County were notorious for rough tactics and this seems to be the reason the title was appropriated for the football club.

NOTTINGHAM FOREST

Horace Gager and Tommy Lawton, captains of Forest and County

The Reds were formed in 1865, probably in December, and their first outside match was against Notts County on the Forest, March 22nd 1866. The Nottingham Daily Guardian reported a 0-0 draw though Forest written histories claim a 1-0 victory. This difference can possibly be reconciled because under the Nottingham rules at the time goals took precedence in deciding a result but if they were equal then "touchdowns" (tries in modern parlance) came into play. It seems likely that the result was 0-0 but Forest made a touchdown and so claimed the match.

The two sides met regularly after that with honours about even but in 1877 with Notts aspiring to be the top team in the area they began cutting back on local games and dropped Forest from their fixture list. Matches were resumed in dramatic circumstances in 1878/79 when Forest first entered for the F.A.Cup. The two rivals were drawn together in the 1st round and Notts had home advantage at their Beeston Cricket Ground headquarters but it was Forest who won 3-1 and went on to reach the semi-finals at the first attempt.

Cup ties and friendlies kept the two foes busy until 1892 when Forest, as Football Alliance champions, applied to join Division 1 of the Football League. This was by no means a certainty as the League were not keen on two clubs from the same town being members so Forest sent a deputation to the Magpies to plead for support. They did indeed get it for the Notts board minutes state that the club "shall then support by its vote the admission of the Forest club to the First Division of the Football League." The first League clash followed with Notts 3-0 victors at Trent Bridge on October 8th 1892. The firsts in other divisions are: Division 2: 2-2 (h), December 25th 1913; Division 3S: 2-1 (a), November 3rd 1949; plus in the F.L.Cup: 0-4 (a), October 25th 1977.

County's record win is 5-0 in friendlies (1881/82 and 1886/87) but in League and Cup it is 4-1 (h), Division 1, January 8th 1910 and 4-1 again (h), Division 2, February 12th 1955. Their record defeat is 7-1 (friendly 1879/80 and County Cup 1981/82) but in League and Cup 6-2 (h), Division 2, February 13th 1932 and 5-0 (a), Division 1, November 24th 1900.

League doubles were achieved by Notts in 1949/50 (Division 3S, 2-0 & 2-1) and 1954/55 (Division 2, 4-1 & 1-0) while Forest's doubles were in 1904/05 (Division 1, 2-1 & 2-1), 1926/27 (Division 2, 2-1 & 2-0), 1927/28 (Division 2, 2-1 & 2-1), 1931/32 (Division 2, 6-2 & 2-1) and 1932/33 (Division 2, 4-2 & 3-0). Trent Bridge/Meadow Lane scores shown first in this list.

Complete record in major competitive matches (from Notts County's point of view):

	P	W	D	L	F	A
Division 1	40	13	11	16	48	50
Division 2/1*	44	13	12	19	55	69
Division 3S	2	2	0	0	4	1
Football League	86	28	23	35	107	120
F.A.Cup	6	2	1	3	10	11
F.L.Cup	1	0	0	1	0	4
Anglo-Italian Cup	1	0	1	0	1	1
Anglo-Scottish Cup	1	0	1	0	0	0
Utd Counties League	4	0	0	4	3	9
Total	99	30	26	43	121	145
Other first-team matches:						
World War 1	16	5	5	6	29	28
World War 2	21	9	2	10	40	47
League Jubilee Fund	2	0	1	1	2	5
County Cup	33	6	4*	23	34	74
(*Notts won all four penalty shoot-outs)						
Notts Senior Cup	6	1	1	4	5	14
Friendlies	69	20	19	30	91	108
(Friendlies include testimonial and charity matches)						
Grand total	246	71	58	117	322	421

Played for both clubs
The following 53 footballers played for both Notts County and Nottingham Forest in the Football League (inclusive of Forest in the F.A. Premier League): Tony "Tanner" Allen, Geoff Ball, Len Barry, Bill Baxter, Garry Birtles, John "Bill" Brindley, Matt Broughton, Bill Brown, Kenny Burns, Barry Butlin, Colin Calderwood, David Campbell, Jimmy Cargill, Bob "Sammy" Chapman, Trevor Christie, Gordon Coles, Harry Daft, Jack Edwards, Chris Fairclough, Ron Farmer, Justin Fashanu, Gary Fleming, Colin Foster, Tom Gibson, George Goucher, Arthur Green, Paul Hart, Bill Hooper, Bob Innes, Nigel Jemson, Tom Johnston, Albert Jones, Chris Joyce, Johnny Langford, Ron "Tot" Leverton, Colin Lyman, Neil McCallum, Prestwood Machin, David "Boy" Martin, Gary Mills, David Needham, Martin O'Neill, Harry Orgill, Arthur Shaw, Ken Simcoe, Albert Smith, William "Tich" Smith, Fred Spencer, Alec Stewart, Geoff Thomas (the 1990s and not the 1950s player), Bob Vasey, Tom Wall and Darren Ward. There is also Steve Burke who played for Notts in the League and came on once as a Forest substitute in the Anglo-Scottish Cup.

In addition, before Forest joined the Football League in 1892, a further 19 players appeared for County in the League and/or F.A.Cup and for Forest in the Football Alliance (1889/90-1891/92) and/or F.A.Cup. They were: Tom Bausor, George Brown, Frank Burton, Herbert Fletcher, William Gunn, Frank Guttridge, Bill Hodder, Jack Holland, Harry Jackson, Bob Jardine, Tinsley Lindley, John Mabbott, Teddy May, Dave Russell, George Shepperson, Fred Weightman, Sam Widdowson, Tom Widdowson and Albert Williamson. These lists of 73 players exclude those who were on the books of both clubs at some time but did not turn out in the first team for one or the other.

It should be noted that in 1892/93 both clubs had a Scottish forward called Tom McInnes but these were two different players and in fact faced each other when the sides met that season.

Forest at Meadow Lane
Apart from matches where the Magpies were the home team, Forest have appeared at Meadow Lane in an F.A.Cup 1st round 2nd replay, v Sheffield United, January 22nd 1923 when the result was 1-1. Forest used Meadow Lane as their home venue when the City Ground was flooded v Manchester City, Division 2, November 23rd 1946, losing 1-0. The attendance was 32,194. Again, following the City Ground fire in 1968 Forest played five home games at Meadow Lane between September 3rd and November 2nd 1968 in Division 1 with the following playing record: P.5 W.0 D.3 L.2 F.6 A.9 Pts.3.

Notts and Forest Combined XIs
The two clubs have fielded a combined XI on a number of charity or testimonial occasions. These include:
  February 2nd 1892 (Trent Bridge): Combined XI 3 Press and Panto 4 (comic match for charity).
  May 3rd 1902 (City Ground): Combined XI 4 Derby County 1 (Ibrox Disaster Fund).
  December 10th 1913 (Meadow Lane): Combined XI 1 Football League XI 1 (testimonial for Notts secretary Tom Harris).
  April 29th 1929 (Meadow Lane): Combined XI 2 International XI 5 (testimonial for former Notts manager Albert Fisher).
  April 18th 1977 (Meadow Lane): Combined XI 2 Midlands XI 1 (David Needham testimonial).

The players and officials at the testimonial match for Tom Harris, December 10th 1913. Back: A Adams (referee), ET Vizard, J Moore, M Hamill, FP Emberton, F Womack, H Hodgson. Next to back: S Fazackerley, H Morley, S Hardy, A Iremonger, W Meredith, J McCall, J Mercer, R Norris, T McLean. Seated: T Gibson, G Needham, J Bell, TE Harris, R Crompton, JG Peart, W Campbell, CE Sutcliffe (linesman). Front: HV Henshall, R Firth, SR Richards, Alderman J Houston.

PENALTIES

The penalty kick was introduced into the Football League for 1891/92. Among the incidents which influenced its adoption was one during the F.A.Cup tie between Notts County and Stoke at Trent Bridge on February 14th 1891 when Stoke, a goal down, were in a scoring position with home goalkeeper George Toone well beaten but left-back Jack Hendry fisted the ball away. Stoke were awarded a free-kick but Notts managed to clear the ball and went on to win 1-0.

The first recorded penalty scorer for the Magpies was Jimmy Logan v Burton Wanderers (a), F.A.Cup 2nd round, February 10th 1894 while in the League the first on record was by Elijah Allsopp v Bury (h), Division 2, November 24th 1894.

The most penalties converted in a season for Notts is seven by Arthur Green in 1903/04, Kevin Randall in 1972/73 and Ray O'Brien in 1979/80.

A penalty goal which was vital to the Magpies' fight against relegation in 1907/08 came from George Dodd v Chelsea (a), Division 1, April 29th 1908 to produce a 2-1 win. If Notts had lost or drawn they would have dropped into Division 2 instead of Bolton Wanderers.

During the 1972/73 season Kevin Randall scored from the penalty spot in six successive matches, four in Division 3 and two in the F.A.Cup as follows: November 11th 1972 v Charlton Athletic (h), Division 3; November 18th v Altrincham (a), F.A.Cup 1st round; November 25th v Oldham Athletic (h), Division 3; December 2nd v Grimsby Town (a), Division 3; December 9th v Lancaster City (h), F.A.Cup 2nd round; and December 16th v Chesterfield (h), Division 3.

In the match v Portsmouth (a), Division 2, September 22nd, 1973, three Magpies players all missed the same penalty. Kevin Randall and Don Masson took the first two, each of which had to be retaken because of encroachments, then Brian Stubbs missed with the third attempt!

The leading all-time penalty scorer for the Magpies is Don Masson with 18 in League matches (none in Cups) while Ray O'Brien takes over as record holder for all competitive games with 19 (14 League and 5 in Cups). Close behind comes Percy Mills with 16 (League only) and then Jerry Dean with 15 (14 League and 1 Cup).

PENALTY SHOOT-OUTS

The penalty shoot-out was introduced into major English football during the pre-season Watney Cup tournament in the early 1970s to replace the toss of a coin to decide the result of drawn matches in knock-out competitions where replays were undesirable. The Magpies' first experience was in the County Cup semi-final v Mansfield Town on May 1st 1975 when they won 5-4 on penalties after a 0-0 draw but it was some time before the system replaced replays in first-class competitions. The following are the known occasions involving Notts:

- 4-3 v Hereford United (a), Associate Members Cup southern quarter-final, February 21st 1990, after 1-1 draw.
  (Notts scorers: Phil Robinson, Dean Yates, Paul Barnes and Tommy Johnson. Phil Turner missed).
- 1-3 v Sunderland (h), Full Members Cup 2nd round, December 11th 1990, after 2-2 draw.
  (Notts scorer: Mark Draper. Tommy Johnson, Dean Thomas and Paul Harding missed).
- 4-3 v Southend United (h), Anglo-Italian Cup semi-final 2nd leg, February 16th 1994, after 1-1 aggregate draw.
  (Notts scorers: Phil Turner, Gary Lund, Gary McSwegan and Mark Draper. Meindert Dijkstra missed).
- 3-2 v Stoke City (a), Anglo-Italian Cup semi-final 2nd leg, January 31st 1995, after 0-0 aggregate draw.
  (Notts scorers: Gary Mills, Andy Legg and Steve Nicol. Phil Turner missed).
- 2-4 v Scunthorpe United (a), Associate Members Cup 2nd round, January 28th 1997, after 1-1 draw.
  (Notts scorers: James Hunt and Tim Wilkes. Gary Martindale and Peter Kennedy missed).
- 4-2 v Wigan Athletic (a), F.A.Cup 2nd round replay, December 15th 1998, after 0-0 draw.
  (Notts scorers: Ian Hendon, Shaun Murray, Fran Tierney and Tony Garcia).
- 7-6 v Preston North End (a), F.L.Cup 1st round, August 12th 2003, after 0-0 draw.
  (Notts scorers: Mark Stallard, Tony Hackworth, Nicky Fenton, Ian Baraclough, Kevin Nicholson, Paul Heffernan and Tony Barrass).
- 2-4 v Barnsley (h), Associate Members Cup 1st round, October 15th 2003, after 0-0 draw.
  (Notts scorers: Darren Caskey and Paul Heffernan. Tony Hackworth and Ian Baraclough missed).

PHYSIOS: see TRAINERS

PLAY-OFFS

These were introduced in 1986/87 to settle some League promotion and relegation issues. Four teams take part in each of the three competitions with two semi-finals over two legs followed by a final. These were also originally over two legs but since 1990 have been a single game at first Wembley Stadium and more recently at Cardiff's Millennium Stadium before returning to the new Wembley in 2007.

Notts have qualified for four play-offs, being successful twice and failing twice. In 1987/88 they lost in the Division 3 semi-finals, then won Wembley finals in successive years, 1989/90 for promotion to Division 2, and 1990/91 for promotion to Division 1. In 1995/96 they were beaten Division 2* finalists.

The record play-off victory was 3-1 v Brighton and Hove Albion, Division 2 final, June 2nd 1991 and record defeat was by the same score v Walsall (h), Division 3 semi-final 1st leg, May 15th 1988. The leading scorer was Tommy Johnson (pictured left, with the play-off trophy) with four goals in six games while most appearances of six were shared among six players, Steve Cherry, Tommy Johnson, Charlie Palmer, Dean Thomas, Phil Turner and Dean Yates. Complete record: P.11 W.5 D.4 L.2 F.15 A.11.

See also **Test Matches** and **Wembley Stadium**.

PLAYER OF THE YEAR

This award was approved by the directors on November 2nd 1964 and the trophy was presented in 1965 by the Supporters' Club to the footballer voted Notts County Player of the Year. Don Masson was Player of the Year three times while Ian Richardson was twice the outright winner plus a shared title. Shaun Murphy, Mark Stallard and Phil Turner won it twice. Complete list of winners:

1964/65 George Smith	1986/87 Dean Yates
1965/66 Brian Bates	1987/88 Geoff Pike
1966/67 Alex Gibson	1988/89 Chris Withe
1967/68 Keith Smith	1989/90 Phil Turner
1968/69 Don Masson	1990/91 Craig Short
1969/70 David Needham	1991/92 Steve Cherry
1970/71 Brian Stubbs	1992/93 Dave Smith
1971/72 Les Bradd	1993/94 Phil Turner
1972/73 Roy Brown	1994/95 Shaun Murphy
1973/74 Don Masson	1995/96 Shaun Murphy
1974/75 John "Bill" Brindley	1996/97 Matt Redmile
1975/76 Ray O'Brien	1997/98 Gary Jones
1976/77 Arthur Mann	1998/99 Ian Richardson, Darren Ward (joint)
1977/78 Mick Vinter	1999/00 Alex Dyer
1978/79 Eric McManus	2000/01 Mark Stallard
1979/80 David Hunt	2001/02 Danny Allsopp
1980/81 Don Masson	2002/03 Mark Stallard
1981/82 Iain McCulloch	2003/04 Ian Richardson
1982/83 Raddy Avramovic	2004/05 Ian Richardson
1983/84 John Chiedozie, Trevor Christie (joint)	2005/06 David Pipe
1984/85 Pedro Richards	2006/07 Mike Edwards
1985/86 Tristan Benjamin	

Mark Stallard, Player of the Year 2002/03 *David Pipe, Player of the Year 2005/06* *Mike Edwards, Player of the Year 2006/07*

PLAYERS

Most in season
The first-ever season of the Football League in 1888/89 consisted of a programme of 22 matches in which 33 players represented Notts County and this remained the most players ever used by the club until recent seasons. The record was beaten in 1994/95 when 36 players made League appearances in the 46 games. This was exceeded in the relegation season of 1996/97 with 37 players turning out for the Magpies, a figure equalled in both 1998/99 and 2003/04 which was another relegation campaign. In fact, since 1994/95 the number of players used has dropped below 30 only three times, during the Division 3* championship term of 1997/98 with 28 then in 2002/03 with 27 and in 2006/07 with 25. Part of the increase in the last decade or so is certainly caused by the larger number of substitutes allowed and their growing use in the final minutes of matches but also by the use of more short-term loan players.

Fewest in season
The lowest number of players to turn out for the club in a League season is 17 during the 46-match Division 4 title winning campaign of 1970/71. This equalled the record set up in Division 1 in 1908/09 but then the programme was restricted to 38 matches.

1,000 League players
By the close of 2006/07, Notts County had fielded 1,003 players in Football League matches excluding six who appeared only in the two games of the abandoned 1939/40 season and one whose sole outing was in the 1894/95 test match. Player number 1,000 was Jay Smith when he came on as substitute v Wrexham (h), League 2*, November 18th 2006.

Overseas-born players
A total of 44 overseas-born players from 24 countries are known to have worn the Notts County colours in League and Cup games, ignoring those born in Ireland who are usually considered part of the British Isles soccer set-up. Englishmen who were born in India because their fathers were serving overseas in the Armed Forces or being employed there constitute the earliest two, Walter Hills (debut 1924/25) and Bertie "Paddy" Mills (debut 1925/26). Continuing this tradition in recent times, Declan Edge (1985/86) was born in Malaysia, Chris Short (debut 1990/91) and Steve Scoffham (debut 2003/04) both in Germany. The first genuine foreign player to appear for Notts was Canadian Fred Whittaker (1946/47), then came Chilean Ted Robledo (1957/58). Raddy Avramovic (debut 1979/80) from Yugoslavia was the first European-born Magpies player while Tristan Benjamin (debut 1974/75) from St. Kitts was the first from the Caribbean. In recent years Africans, Australians and Scandinavians have been added to the mix but to date the most exotic birth location must belong to Didier Rabat (1998/99) who hails from New Caledonia in the South Seas, though his one outing was limited to an Associate Members Cup tie.

POINTS
Highest
Notts County's record season for point scoring must be shared between the bottom division championship seasons of 1970/71 and 1997/98. In the former, with two points for a win, they totalled 69 points from 46 matches while in the latter, with three points for a win, they reached 99, also from 46 matches. If one allocates three points for a win to the 1970/71 record the total is 99 points while two points for a win applied to 1997/98 equals 70 points so honours are just about even.
(a) Two points for a win
The 1970/71 record of 69 points was from 46 games. In a 42-match season the record is 59 obtained in winning the Division 3S title in 1930/31 while in a 38-match season the best is 53 points in 1913/14 when the Magpies were Division 2 champions.
Other highests are: 1900/01, 40 points from 34 matches in Division 1; 1896/97, 42 from 30 when Division 2 champions; 1893/94, 39 from 28 in Division 2; 1890/91, 26 from 22 in the Football League.
Altogether the Magpies have reached the 50-point mark 14 times as follows: 69 in 1970/71 (Division 4, 46 games); 62 in 1971/72 (Division 3, 46); 60 in 1959/60 (Division 4, 46); 59 in 1930/31 (Division 3S, 42); 58 in 1949/50 (Division 3S, 42); 57 in 1972/73 (Division 3, 46); 56 in 1936/37 (Division 3S, 42); 53 in 1913/14 (Division 2, 38), 1922/23 (Division 2, 42) and 1980/81 (Division 2, 42); 52 in 1969/70 (Division 4, 46); 51 in 1960/61 (Division 3, 46) and 1962/63 (Division 3, 46); and 50 in 1965/66 (Division 4, 46).
The record number of points for each division is as follows: Division 1: 45 in 42 matches, 1924/25; Division 2: 53 in 38, 1913/14, 53 in 42, 1922/23 and 1980/81; Division 3S: 59 in 42, 1930/31; Division 3: 62 in 46, 1971/72; Division 4, 69 in 46, 1970/71.
(b) Three points for a win
The 1997/98 record of 99 points in Division 3* is obviously the best for a 46-match campaign. With 42 matches the record is 52 in Division 1, 1982/83. Notts have topped the 70-mark seven times as follows: 99 in 1997/98 (Division 3*, 46 games); 87 in 1989/90 (Division 3, 46); 81 in 1987/88 (Division 3, 46); 80 in 1990/91 (Division 2, 46); 78 in 1995/96 (Division 2*, 46); 76 in 1986/87 (Division 3, 46); and 71 in 1985/86 (Division 3, 46).
The record number of points for each division is as follows: Division 1: 52 in 42 matches, 1982/83; Division 2/1*: 80 in 46, 1990/91; Division 3/2*: 87 in 46, 1989/90; Division 4/3*/League 2*: 99 in 46, 1997/98.
Lowest
(a) Two points for a win
The worst-ever season for point-scoring was the first Football League campaign of 1888/89 with only 12 gained. However, only 22 matches were played. Next comes 1904/05 with only 18 from 34 games in Division 1. When the fixture list grew to 38 matches, the record low was in Division 1 in 1912/13 with 23 points and since the extension to 42 the worst total was in Division 2 in 1934/35 with 25. The worst 46-match season was in Division 3 in 1963/64 with 27 points.
Since the fixture list was extended to 34 games for 1898/99 the Magpies have totalled fewer than 30 points as follows: 18 in 1904/05 (Division 1, 34 games); 23 in 1912/13 (Division 1, 38); 25 in 1934/35 (Division 2, 42); 27 in 1963/64 (Division 3, 46); 29 in 1958/59 (Division 3, 46); 29 in 1903/04 (Division 1, 34); and 29 in 1899/1900 (Division 1, 34).
Lowest points total in each division is as follows: Division 1: 12 in 22 matches, 1888/89; 18 in 34, 1904/05, 23 in 38, 1912/13; and 33 in 42, 1925/26. Division 2: 25 in 42, 1934/35. Division 3S: 40 in 42, 1946/47; Division 3: 27 in 46, 1963/64; and Division 4: 37 in 46, 1966/67.
(b) Three points for a win
The worst season for points was 1996/97 in Division 2* with 35 from the 46 games while in a 42-match campaign the lowest was in 1984/85 with 37 in Division 2. The seasons in which Notts have notched below 50 points are as follows: 35 in 1996/97 (Division 2*, 46 games); 37 in 1984/85 (Division 2, 42); 40 in 1991/92 (Division 1, 42); 40 in 1994/95 (Division 1*, 46); 41 in 1983/84 (Division 1, 42); 42 in 2003/04 (Division 2*, 46); and 47 in 1981/82 (Division 1, 42).
Lowest points total in each division is as follows: Division 1: 40 in 42 matches, 1991/92; Division 2/1*: 37 in 42, 1984/85; Division 3/2*: 35 in 46, 1996/97; Division 4/3*/League 2*: 52 in 46, 2004/05 and 2005/06.

PROFESSIONALISM
The F.A. legalised professionalism on July 20th 1885 and Notts County then registered six of their footballers as paid players for 1885/86: Herbert Emmitt, William Gunn, Ted Harker, Harry Moore, Albert Peters and Mordecai Sherwin. Previously, the six would have had to appear as amateurs.

PROGRAMMES

When Notts County became tenants at Trent Bridge cricket ground in 1883 there was already a printer established there providing scorecards for Nottinghamshire cricket matches. This was the firm of George Richards of Greyhound Street, Nottingham, whose business was continued after his death by his son, Charles Henry Richards.

Consequently Richards printed match cards for Notts County matches and they were just that, a single card sheet with a stylised drawing of the players on one side and advertisements on the back. By the 1890s there were more pages though the players' names still appeared on the front in the classic 1-2-3-5 formation and advertisements filled most of remainder along with a short editorial. A good reason for buying the Richards card was the introduction of a results board in 1898. The card provided the key to the letter on the board to show which game was which. The board was scheduled to be used for the first time during a match on November 19th but it was not completed in time and so at half-time the scores were carried round the ground chalked on a board attached to a post. The board came into use on December 3rd 1898 and such half-time scoreboards survived the move to Meadow Lane and remained a feature until quite modern times.

This match card followed the same style until the First World War and the next three styles also lasted a long time, from 1920-34, 1934-51 and 1951-61. The covers had a black and white masthead with a County logo plus an advertisement (the Home Brewery and the Co-op were regulars here) which meant that the general style remained unaltered throughout this time. The years since 1961 have seen the programme contract and expand in physical dimensions and contents; centenary year programmes were a handy pocket size 11cm by 14cm and a newspaper style format was adopted for *The Magpie* from 1975/76 to 1977/78. The use of colour makes today's programmes more attractive but regrettably indistinguishable from those of most other League clubs.

The price was not shown on early match cards but was held at 2d from 1919 to 1948/49. By 1970 this had risen to 1s, 1975 to 10p, 1980 to 25p and by 1990 the first £1 programme was on sale. Later in the 1990s this had risen to £2 while £2 50p arrived in the early 2000s.

PROMOTION

The Magpies have won promotion 12 times, three of them via play-offs. Some facts from the seasons involved are given here:

1896/97: Although champions of Division 2 after spending four seasons in that section, they still had to compete in the test matches (the play-offs of that era) where they won back their Division 1 status. The regular players usually lined up: George Toone; Tom Prescott, Bill Gibson; Charlie Bramley, Davey Calderhead, Elijah Allsopp or Bob Crone; Billy Langham, John Allan, Tom Boucher, John Murphy, Walter Bull. Season's record:

	P	W	D	L	F	A	Pts
Home	15	12	1	2	60	18	25
Away	15	7	3	5	32	25	17
Total	30	19	4	7	92	43	42
Test matches	4	2	2	0	3	1	6

1913/14: Notts were champions of Division 2 immediately after relegation in 1912/13. The regular players were: Albert Iremonger; Bert Morley, Alf West; Teddy Emberton, Arthur Clamp or Will Jennings, Dick Allsebrook; Ted Bassett, Billy Flint, Jack Peart, Sam Richards, Horace Henshall. Season's record:

	P	W	D	L	F	A	Pts
Home	19	16	2	1	55	13	34
Away	19	7	5	7	22	23	19
Total	38	23	7	8	77	36	53

1922/23: Again Division 2 champions, three years after relegation. Among the home defeats were a 6-1 thrashing by Manchester United and 4-0 by Crystal Palace! They conceded only five more goals in their remaining 19 home games. The regular squad was: Albert Iremonger or George Streets; Bill Ashurst, Horace Cope or Frank Marriott; Billy Flint, Norman Dinsdale, Jack Wren or Haydn Kemp; Joe Daly, Jack Cook or Lachlan McPherson, Donald Cock, Harold Hill, Llew Price. Season's record:

	P	W	D	L	F	A	Pts
Home	21	16	1	4	29	15	33
Away	21	7	6	8	17	19	20
Total	42	23	7	12	46	34	53

1930/31: The Magpies were Division 3S champions in their first season in that section. This was the campaign in which Tom Keetley notched the club's individual seasonal scoring record with 39 goals. Regular players: Jimmy Ferguson; Percy Mills, Charlie Bisby; Jack Dowsey, Frank Froggatt or Harold Smith, Haydn Kemp; George Taylor, Tom Fenner, Tom Keetley, Harold Andrews, Sam Haden. Season's record:

	P	W	D	L	F	A	Pts
Home	21	16	4	1	58	13	36
Away	21	8	7	6	39	33	23
Total	42	24	11	7	97	46	59

1949/50: After eight consecutive seasons in Division 3S, the Magpies took the championship fired by the scoring power of Tommy Lawton, Jackie Sewell and Tom Johnston. Regulars: Roy Smith; Tommy Deans or Aubrey Southwell, Norman Rigby; Harry Chapman, Bill Baxter, Harry Adamson; Frank Broome or Fred Evans, Jackie Sewell, Tommy Lawton, Billy Evans, Tom Johnston. Season's record:

Home	21	17	3	1	60	12	37
Away	21	8	5	8	35	38	21
Total	42	25	8	9	95	50	58

1959/60: In their first season in Division 4, Notts were runners-up and so gained promotion to Division 3 at the first attempt. Regular players: George Smith; John Butler, Harry Noon or Oliver Beeby; John Sheridan or Alex Gibson, Bert Loxley, Gerry Carver; Don Roby, Roy Horobin, Stan Newsham or Tony Hateley, Bob Forrest, Alan Withers or Peter Bircumshaw. Season's record:

Home	23	19	1	3	66	27	39
Away	23	7	7	9	41	42	21
Total	46	26	8	12	107	69	60

1970/71: Seven seasons in Division 4 ended as the Magpies took the Division 4 title with 69 points, at the time a record for that division. They were also unbeaten at Meadow Lane. Regular line-up: Barry Watling; Bill Brindley, Bob Worthington; Mick Jones or Dennis Oakes, David Needham, Brian Stubbs; Jon Nixon, Les Bradd or Richie Barker, Tony Hateley, Don Masson, Charlie Crickmore. Season's record:

Home	23	19	4	0	59	12	42
Away	23	11	5	7	30	24	27
Total	46	30	9	7	89	36	69

1972/73: Only two seasons after returning to Division 3 the Magpies finished runners-up to gain promotion to Division 2 though in December they were as low as 18th but after Christmas lost only twice in a magnificent late climb up the table into the promotion spot. Regulars: Roy Brown; Bill Brindley, Bob Worthington; Don Masson, David Needham, Brian Stubbs; Jon Nixon, Kevin Randall, Les Bradd, Willie Carlin or Arthur Mann, Steve Carter. Season's record:

Home	23	17	4	2	40	12	38
Away	23	6	7	10	27	35	19
Total	46	23	11	12	67	47	57

1980/81: Notts regained Division 1 status after eight seasons in Division 2 by finishing runners-up to West Ham United. Don Masson notched up a hat-trick of promotion captaincies following 1970/71 and 1972/73. Regulars: Raddy Avramovic; Tristan Benjamin, Ray O'Brien, Eddie Kelly or Mark Goodwin, Brian Kilcline, Pedro Richards, Iain McCulloch, Don Masson, Trevor Christie, David Hunt, Paul Hooks. Sub: Rachid Harkouk. Season's Record:

Home	21	10	8	3	26	15	28
Away	21	8	9	4	23	23	25
Total	42	18	17	7	49	38	53

1989/90: Notts achieved promotion from Division 3 via the play-offs where they brushed aside Bolton Wanderers on aggregate before conquering Tranmere Rovers at Wembley Stadium in the final. As the Magpies were 18 points clear of Bolton and 7 ahead of Tranmere in the final table, justice was done at Wembley. Regular players: Steve Cherry; Charlie Palmer or David Norton, Nicky Platnauer, Craig Short, Dean Yates, Phil Robinson, Mark Draper, Phil Turner, Gary Lund or Kevin Bartlett, Phil Stant or Dean Thomas, Tommy Johnson or Gary Chapman. Season's record:

Home	23	17	4	2	40	18	55
Away	23	8	8	7	33	35	32
Total	46	25	12	9	73	53	87
Play-offs	3	2	1	0	5	1	

1990/91: A triumphant Notts County leapt from Division 3 to Division 1 in successive seasons, and again their promotion from Division 2 came via a Wembley play-off success. Again, they were at least ten points ahead of their two play-off opponents in the final table. Middlesbrough were their semi-final victims before Brighton and Hove Albion were thrashed 3-1 in the final. Regular squad: Steve Cherry; Charlie Palmer, Paul Harding or Alan Paris or Nicky Platnauer, Craig Short, Dean Yates, Don O'Riordan, Dean Thomas, Phil Turner, Kevin Bartlett, Dave Regis or Mark Draper, Tommy Johnson. Season's record:

Home	23	14	4	5	45	28	46
Away	23	9	7	7	31	27	34
Total	46	23	11	12	76	55	80
Play-offs	3	2	1	0	5	2	

1997/98: A Division 3* promotion season in which many club records were broken and various entries in this compilation list them. Most remarkable detail is that the home and away records were almost identical, in fact the away one just marginally superior, a really unusual feature in football statistics. Promotion was secured on 28th March 1998 with six games remaining. Press reports at the time said this was the record for the earliest post-war promotion, but in fact Middlesbrough had done it with seven left to play on March 23rd 1974. Regular squad: Darren Ward; Ian Hendon, Dennis Pearce, Matt Redmile or Ian Richardson, Gary Strodder, Ian Baraclough, Steve Finnan, Phil Robinson or Shaun Derry, Sean Farrell, Gary Jones, Mark Robson. Season's results:

Home	23	14	7	2	41	20	49
Away	23	15	5	3	41	23	50
Total	46	29	12	5	82	43	99

PROTESTS

During the early years of competitive football, protests were almost as much part of the game as bookings and sendings off are now. The F.A. eventually clamped down on this situation by ruling that protests must be made before the game was played and not afterwards. But in the 1880s and 1890s it was very different and Notts were involved in a number of notorious protests.

1881/82: Notts beat Wednesbury Strollers 5-3 (h), F.A.Cup 2nd round, November 24th 1881. Strollers protested that the result should have been 3-3 and they were therefore entitled to a replay. They claimed two disputed goals had been allowed by referee Leonard Lindley who was a Nottingham man; that Notts defender Harry Moore was not properly qualified and had played under the name "Wheeler"; that the crowd had encroached on the pitch and threatened the Wednesbury players and umpire. The F.A. upheld the protest and decreed a replay on a neutral ground. This went ahead on Derbyshire county cricket ground on December 10th 1881 and Strollers must have wished they had not bothered to protest as they were thrashed 11-1.

1889/90: Notts lost 5-0 away to Sheffield Wednesday at Olive Grove, F.A.Cup 3rd round, February 15th 1890 and protested about the state of the pitch plus the weather conditions. The game would never have started under today's rules as rain and snow fell in sheets before and during play. The F.A. ordered a replay at the same venue on February 22nd and this time County won 3-2 but now it was Wednesday's turn to protest, claiming that three ineligible players had been included in County's team. Again, this was upheld and the third game was at Derbyshire county cricket ground on March 3rd when Notts lost 3-2.

1891/92: The Magpies lost 3-0 to Sunderland at Newcastle Road, F.A.Cup 1st round, January 16th 1892 but protested about the state of the pitch and the weather. The protest was upheld and the match replayed at the same venue on January 23rd, resulting in another defeat for Notts, this time by 4-0.

RED CARDS: see Disciplinary

RE-ELECTION

Although Notts County were never forced to apply for re-election to Divisions 3 or 4, they did have to submit to this indignity in the days when the Football League consisted of just 12 clubs. In fact the seasons involved were the very first two of the League, 1888/89 and 1889/90. At that time the four bottom clubs had to apply for re-election and in 1888/89 Notts finished 11th of 12. All four re-applying clubs regained their places but County finished bottom of the four in the voting, just two votes ahead of Birmingham St. George's. The poll was Stoke 10, Burnley 9, Derby County 8, Notts County 7, St. George's 5, Sheffield Wednesday 4, Bootle 2, Sunderland 2, Newton Heath 1, Grimsby Town 0, South Shore (Blackpool) 0, Sunderland Albion 0, Nelson 0.

In 1889/90 Notts were 10th but this time it was agreed that neither Aston Villa nor Bolton Wanderers should be included in the re-election process as there was a dispute over which of the two finished fourth from bottom. Then Notts and Burnley were voted back in and Sunderland were elected in place of Stoke.

There was a struggle to avoid having to apply for re-election to Division 4 in 1966/67, 1967/68 and 1968/69. In the first of these seasons County were 20th out of 24, missing one of the re-election places on goal average ahead of Rochdale. Both teams had 37 points but Rochdale's goal average was 0.032 worse. In 1967/68 Notts finished 17th, five points ahead of a re-election place but it needed victories in the two final matches to achieve this. Early in 1968/69 Notts were bottom of Division 4 after taking only eight points from the first 16 matches but they revived to finish 19th, three points ahead of York City who did have to apply for re-election. York, in fact, beat Notts 2-0 on April 23rd but County then took three points from their two remaining matches.

Since the Football League instituted automatic promotion and relegation with the Conference in 1986 the fear of having to apply for re-election has been removed though the threat of relegation to the Conference has replaced it, the most recent being in 2005/06 when only the results on the season's final day meant that Notts were safe.

RELEGATION

Notts County have suffered 15 relegations as well as having to apply for re-election twice in the first two seasons of the Football League when there were just 12 clubs in one section. Details of these 17 seasons are:

1888/89: County finished next to bottom, level on 12 points with Stoke but with a superior goal average. They were re-elected in a close vote. Season's record:

	P	W	D	L	F	A	Pts
Home	11	4	2	5	25	32	10
Away	11	1	0	10	15	41	2
Total	22	5	2	15	40	73	12

1889/90: The club climbed to third from bottom but as four clubs were up for re-election, this did not signify. This time they were comfortably re-elected and never had to submit to this process again. Season's record:

	P	W	D	L	F	A	Pts
Home	11	4	3	4	20	19	11
Away	11	2	2	7	23	32	6
Total	22	6	5	11	43	51	17

1892/93: The Magpies were third from bottom of Division 1 in the very first season of promotion and relegation. Despite their position Notts beat League champions Sunderland, runners-up Preston North End, F.A.Cup holders West Bromwich Albion (by 8-1!) and that season's subsequent F.A.Cup winners Wolverhampton Wanderers but these were all home successes and the away record was a poor one. Under the rules then operating the Magpies had to play a test match against the third place team in Division 2 to decide who took the Division 1 spot for 1893/94. This took place on Manchester City's then ground, Hyde Road, v Darwen and after only 15 minutes Notts were 2-0 up before slipping to a 3-2 defeat.

1892/93 season's record:

Home	15	8	3	4	34	15	19
Away	15	2	1	12	19	46	5
Total	30	10	4	16	53	61	24
Test match	1	0	0	1	2	3	

1912/13: Sixteen unbroken seasons in Division 1 ended with the Magpies next to bottom though they did beat League champions Sunderland at Meadow Lane. Season's record:

Home	19	6	4	9	19	20	16
Away	19	1	5	13	9	36	7
Total	38	7	9	22	28	56	23

1919/20: Again Notts were next to bottom and again they beat the League champions, this time it was West Bromwich Albion who were the victims as were runners-up Burnley and F.A.Cup winners Aston Villa. In fact the first home defeat was not inflicted until February 7th. Season's record:

Home	21	9	8	4	38	25	26
Away	21	3	4	14	18	49	10
Total	42	12	12	18	56	74	36

1925/26: For the first time the Magpies ended up in bottom spot though they kept up their habit of beating the League champions. They met title-holders Huddersfield Town at Meadow Lane for the last match of the season when all issues had been settled and were 4-2 winners. Other home victims were Arsenal (runners-up), Sunderland (3rd), Bury (4th), Sheffield United (5th and Cup holders), Aston Villa (6th) and Bolton Wanderers (eventual Cup winners). Yet **SIX** home matches were lost. The Huddersfield game was the last played by the Magpies in Division 1 for 55 years. Season's record:

Home	21	11	4	6	37	26	26
Away	21	2	3	16	17	48	7
Total	42	13	7	22	54	74	33

1929/30: Notts were bottom in Division 2 in a campaign which brought only one away success yet, typically, that was against divisional champions Blackpool. So the Magpies had to face life in Division 3S for the first time. Season's record:

Home	21	8	7	6	33	26	23
Away	21	1	8	12	21	44	10
Total	42	9	15	18	54	70	33

1934/35: After winning their opening home match, County drew one and lost six out of the next seven at Meadow Lane, a start from which they never recovered to finish bottom and return to Division 3S. The only away success was at the City Ground, 3-2 v Nottingham Forest. Season's record:

Home	21	8	3	10	29	33	19
Away	21	1	4	16	17	64	6
Total	42	9	7	26	46	97	25

1957/58: County were next to bottom in Division 2, ending eight successive seasons at this level. It took five home matches for the Magpies to register their first Meadow Lane victory but later they beat Division 2 champions West Ham United. Ironically, Doncaster Rovers, who finished three points behind Notts in bottom place, won 5-0 at Meadow Lane and 4-0 at Doncaster. Season's record:

Home	21	9	3	9	24	31	21
Away	21	3	3	15	20	49	9
Total	42	12	6	24	44	80	30

1958/59: Relegation in successive seasons ensued with Notts again next to bottom and so they had to face Division 4 for the first time. They did not win a home match after February 21st and only one away. Doncaster Rovers, who accompanied the Magpies down from Division 2, were again their partners in the descent to Division 4. Season's record:

Home	23	5	9	9	33	39	19
Away	23	3	4	16	22	57	10
Total	46	8	13	25	55	96	29

1963/64: A dreadful season saw Notts bottom of Division 3. After victory at Port Vale on January 18th they won only one more match in their remaining 19 fixtures. Season's record:

Home	23	7	8	8	29	26	22
Away	23	2	1	20	16	66	5
Total	46	9	9	28	45	92	27

1983/84: New manager Larry Lloyd's reign got off to a good start with two wins in two games which put Notts top of the whole Football League but then things went rapidly downhill as the Magpies slumped to seven consecutive defeats. Despite an impressive 5-2 triumph against Aston Villa, there was no real consistency so it was back to Division 2 after only three seasons at the elite level. Season's record:

Home	21	6	7	8	31	36	25
Away	21	4	4	13	19	36	16
Total	42	10	11	21	50	72	41

1984/85: The gloom of the previous season worsened in Division 2 as both Larry Lloyd and his successor Richie Barker left Meadow Lane and Jimmy Sirrel took the reins late on for the third time. The old magician only just failed to conjure up a great escape and it was not until the last day of the season that Notts were doomed to face life back in Division 3. Season's record:

Home	21	6	5	10	25	32	23
Away	21	4	2	15	20	41	14
Total	42	10	7	25	45	73	37

1991/92: Successive promotions via the play-offs from Divisions 3 and 2 saw the Magpies back in the top flight under manager Neil Warnock but scarce resources meant the club were unable to retain Division 1 status at the first attempt and so missed out on being founder-members of the F.A. Premier League. Season's record:

Home	21	7	5	9	24	29	26
Away	21	3	5	13	16	33	14
Total	42	10	10	22	40	62	40

1994/95: After being just outside the play-offs the previous season, County's fortunes went into decline. Managerial comings and goings did not help stability with Messrs. Mick Walker, Russell Slade and Howard Kendall all departing before the caretaker triumvirate of Wayne Jones, Steve Nicol and Dean Thomas took the helm for the final few matches. However, they were unable to prevent a return to Division 2*. Winning the Anglo-Italian Cup at Wembley was small consolation. Season's record:

Home	23	7	8	8	26	28	29
Away	23	2	5	16	19	38	11
Total	46	9	13	24	45	66	40

1996/97: After losing in the 1995/96 play-off final at Wembley, probably the worst season in the history of Notts County followed which saw them drop back into the bottom division of the League for the first time since 1971. Only twice did they score three goals in a match while in 24 games they failed to find the net at all. Season's record:

Home	23	4	9	10	20	25	21
Away	23	3	5	15	13	34	14
Total	46	7	14	25	33	59	35

2003/04: A disastrous season started with four straight defeats and ended with just one win in the final 12 games. This sequence was prefaced by three consecutive victories which briefly raised hopes of escaping the drop. But instead of finding themselves going into Division 3* for the coming campaign, the Magpies went into League 2* as the division was renamed by the League during summer 2004. Season's record:

Home	23	6	9	8	32	27	27
Away	23	4	3	16	18	51	15
Total	46	10	12	24	50	78	42

REPRESENTATIVE MATCHES
The club

Notts County's first match against a representative side was at Trent Bridge on March 17th 1873 when a side chosen by F.A. secretary Charles Alcock to represent London drew 0-0. To date the last such match was the club's centenary game v An England XI at Meadow Lane on May 2nd 1962. Notts lost 3-1 (Hateley the scorer) and the attendance was 11,022.

Altogether Notts have played ten matches against representative sides, four of them during war-time. Complete results:

- March 17th 1873 (Trent Bridge) v London 0-0.
- November 29th 1873 (Trent Bridge) v London 2-0.
- February 16th 1874 (Kennington Oval) v London 0-4.
- February 18th 1874 (Crystal Palace) v London 1-1.
- October 4th 1888 (Trent Bridge) v Canadian touring team 2-0.
- September 21st 1940 (Meadow Lane) v Army XI 1-1.
- December 14th 1940 (Meadow Lane) v F.A. XI 2-1.
- March 8th 1941 (Meadow Lane) v Services XI 3-1.
- December 13th 1941 (Meadow Lane) v Polish XI 1-3.
- May 2nd 1962 (Meadow Lane) v England XI 1-3.

Note: Notts played the South of England twice (1883/84 won 6-1, and 1889/90 won 6-3) and a Midlands XI (1894/95 drew 4-4) but these were scratch teams.

The Players

Until the start of the Second World War, official trial matches were staged by the England selectors. Notts County players in these were as follows:

- Bill Ashurst (1) England v Rest 1924/25.
- Len Barry (2) Amateurs v Professionals 1923/24; England v Rest 1925/26.
- Walter Bull (2) North v South 1899/1900 and 1900/01.
- Henry Chapman (1) North v South 1882/83.
- Harry Cursham (2) North v South 1882/83 and 1883/84.
- Alf Dobson (3) North v South 1881/82, 1882/83 and 1883/84.
- Fred "Teddy" Emberton (1) Stripes v Whites 1910/11.
- Ernest Greenhalgh (1) North v South 1870/71.
- William Gunn (2) North v South 1883/84 and 1885/86.
- Albert Iremonger (1) Whites v Stripes 1910/11.
- Stuart Macrae (1) North v South 1883/84.
- Harry Moore (1) North v South 1882/83.
- Bert Morley (1) Whites v Stripes 1909/10.
- Tom Prescott (1) North v South 1898/99.
- Charles Rothera (1) North v South 1870/71.
- Alf Shelton (2) Whites v Stripes 1889/90; North v South 1890/91.
- George Toone (2) North v South 1890/91; Whites v Stripes 1891/92.
- Harry Walkerdine (1) Whites v Stripes 1891/92.

Tours: Two Notts County players appeared on F.A. Commonwealth tours. Jackie Sewell toured Canada in May-June 1950, scoring seven goals, and Frank Broome went to Australia in summer 1951, scoring 16 goals.

RESERVE TEAM

Matches by a Notts County Second XI developed during the 1870s and by the 1880s a full reserve team operation was active. For a few years at the beginning of the 1890s the reserves played under the title of Notts County Rovers but the use of independent titles for reserve teams was outlawed by the F.A. It was as the Rovers that they entered the Midland Alliance in 1890/91 and they were the champions in their first season of league football. Until 1935/36 they entered the Notts Senior Cup and won it as follows: 1884/85, 1899/1900, 1900/01, 1910/11, 1911/12, 1924/25, 1928/29, 1933/34, 1934/35 (the first XI played in the final v Forest) and 1935/36. They have been champions of the following leagues: Midland Alliance 1890/91; Notts and District League 1903/04 and 1907/08; Central Alliance 1914/15; Midland League 1954/55; Midlands Midweek League 1957/58; North Midlands League 1973/74.

At the close of 2004/05 the Magpies dispensed with a reserve team but continued to run a youth team in 2005/06 though this too was closed down for 2006/07. The record of Notts County Reserves in the main competitions in which they played each season is as follows:

	P	W	D	L	F	A	Pts	Position
Midland Alliance								
1890/91	14	9	4	1	33	17	22	1st
1891/92	18	10	2	6	45	33	22	3rd
1892/93	20	9	2	9	41	43	20	6th
Notts & District League								
1894/95	22	10	4	8	61	35	24	6th
1895/96	23	7	4	12	34	51	16*	11th
(* 2 points deducted)								
1896/97	26	13	3	10	48	41	29	5th
1897/98	26	15	3	8	66	37	33	5th
1898/99	25	15	3	7	59	39	33	4th
1899/00	22	11	1	10	45	39	23	8th
1900/01	20	13	3	4	45	17	29	3rd
1901/02	18	11	4	3	45	21	26	2nd
1902/03 1st series	12	8	1	3	35	16	17	1st
1902/03 2nd series	12	8	1	3	26	11	17	2nd
(lost 3-0 to Forest Reserves in championship play-off)								
1903/04	21	16	2	3	62	19	34	1st
Midland League								
1904/05	32	17	5	10	79	48	39	7th
1905/06	34	9	9	16	53	73	27	13th
1906/07	38	7	6	25	44	89	20	20th
Notts & District League								
1907/08	24	21	0	3	107	20	42	1st
Midland League								
1908/09	38	12	6	20	63	74	30	16th
1909/10	42	17	8	17	78	72	42	12th
1910/11	38	18	2	18	88	81	38	9th
1911/12	36	15	6	15	63	58	36	11th
1912/13	38	10	6	22	67	85	26	18th
Central Alliance								
1913/14	30	12	3	15	51	54	27	9th
1914/15	30	21	4	5	75	32	46	1st
Midland League								
1919/20	34	10	11	13	50	56	31	13th
1920/21	38	22	9	7	80	45	53	2nd
1921/22	42	15	7	20	63	57	37	16th
1922/23	42	16	12	14	76	55	44	8th
1923/24	42	21	8	13	83	51	50	5th
Midland Combination								
1924/25	22	8	7	7	33	29	23	5th
1924/25 Cup Grp	10	2	5	3	11	12	9	4th
1925/26	24	13	0	11	50	45	26	6th
1925/26 Cup Grp	12	5	2	5	23	27	12	5th
1926/27	24	7	1	16	43	81	15	12th
1926/27 Cup Grp	12	4	2	6	25	30	10	5th
Midland League								
1927/28	44	24	5	15	141	83	53	4th
1928/29	50	21	15	14	91	75	57	8th
1929/30	50	22	9	19	136	114	53	11th
1930/31	46	17	6	23	120	121	40	17th
1931/32	46	24	11	11	115	81	59	4th
1932/33	44	20	10	14	104	76	50	9th
1933/34	32	13	2	17	64	64	28	11th
1934/35	38	17	11	10	71	59	45	6th
1935/36	40	14	11	15	68	68	39	12th
1936/37	42	17	5	20	92	106	39	15th
1937/38	42	16	9	17	70	72	41	12th
1938/39	42	11	6	25	60	121	28	20th

Midlands Senior League

Season	P	W	D	L	F	A	Pts	Pos
1944/45	24	10	2	12	56	92	22	—

Midland League

Season	P	W	D	L	F	A	Pts	Pos
1945/46	36	6	11	19	59	110	23	18th
1946/47	42	16	4	22	90	113	36	16th
1947/48	42	16	6	20	72	95	38	15th
1948/49	42	18	14	10	79	60	50	6th
1949/50	46	15	10	21	84	82	40	16th
1950/51	42	15	10	17	59	58	40	14th
1951/52	42	30	3	9	108	54	63	2nd
1952/53	46	22	10	14	92	64	54	7th
1953/54	46	23	7	16	104	74	53	7th
1954/55	46	27	11	8	135	60	65	1st
1955/56	46	21	12	13	106	72	54	8th
1956/57	46	15	14	17	86	87	44	14th
1957/58	46	20	3	23	97	95	43	15th

Football Combination

Season	P	W	D	L	F	A	Pts	Pos
1958/59 Div.2	32	6	8	18	47	78	20	16th
1959/60 Div.2	38	16	8	14	86	76	40	10th
1960/61 Div.2	38	20	5	13	81	73	45	4th
1961/62 Sat. Div.	34	13	5	16	67	81	31	12th
1962/63 Sat. Div.	34	7	4	23	38	99	18	18th
1963/64 Div.1	34	7	4	23	35	86	18	18th
1964/65 Div.2	36	7	10	19	53	89	24	17th
1965/66 Div.2	38	7	11	20	46	81	25	17th
1966/67 Div.2	24	7	1	16	30	48	15	11th
1966/67 Cup Grp	8	3	1	4	15	13	7	3rd

North Midlands League

Season	P	W	D	L	F	A	Pts	Pos
1967/68	16	5	2	9	29	40	12	8th
1967/68 Cup Grp	16	5	2	9	17	29	12	6th
1968/69	26	5	9	12	31	59	19	12th
1969/70	28	15	7	6	58	34	37	4th
1970/71	26	13	7	6	59	35	33	3rd
1971/72	28	18	5	5	66	31	41	2nd
1972/73	28	13	8	7	58	36	34	5th
1973/74	28	18	7	3	77	27	43	1st
1974/75	28	21	5	2	74	15	47	2nd
1975/76	24	13	2	9	55	30	28	4th
1976/77	22	13	4	5	47	21	30	2nd
1977/78	28	10	8	10	42	36	28	7th
1978/79	30	12	7	11	50	34	31	6th
1979/80	28	8	13	7	36	39	29	8th
1980/81	28	10	3	15	41	50	23	11th
1981/82	24	10	4	10	43	36	24	6th

Central League (later known as Pontins Reserve League)

Season	P	W	D	L	F	A	Pts	Pos
1982/83 Div.2	30	9	6	15	45	73	24	14th
1983/84 Div.2	30	15	4	11	61	40	49	5th
1984/85 Div.1	34	8	6	20	40	78	30	18th
1985/86 Div.2	34	18	3	13	82	58	57	6th
1986/87 Div.2	32	8	5	19	42	69	29	17th
1987/88 Div.2	34	12	6	16	39	46	42	12th
1988/89 Div.2	34	20	8	6	77	48	68	2nd
1989/90 Div.1	34	8	9	17	44	90	33	15th
1990/91 Div.2	34	16	6	12	56	46	54	6th
1991/92 Div.2	34	18	7	9	53	37	61	4th
1992/93 Div.1	34	12	8	14	56	52	44	11th
1993/94 Div.1	34	12	8	14	43	50	44	12th
1994/95 Div.1	34	15	6	13	46	48	51	7th
1995/96 Div.1	34	9	7	18	48	64	34	17th

(from 1996/97 Premier Division created and Division 2 renumbered as Division 1)

Season	P	W	D	L	F	A	Pts	Pos
1996/97 Div.1	24	12	5	7	38	35	41	3rd
1997/98 Div.1	24	3	7	14	23	56	16	13th
1998/99 Div.2	24	7	6	11	31	48	27	11th
1999/00 Div.2	22	6	6	10	32	37	24	11th
2000/01 Div.2	20	9	6	5	42	32	33	4th
2001/02 Div.2	20	9	6	5	36	22	33	4th
2002/03 Div.1 E	20	8	3	9	29	17	27	6th
2003/04 Div.1 E	18	6	4	8	25	26	22	6th
2004/05 Div.1 E	18	4	3	11	17	36	15	9th

The class of 1990. Chairman Pavis and Manager Warnock welcome young players to the County Ground. From left, Richard Walker, Mark Wells, Shaun Browne, Craig Finch, Anthony Thompson, Stephen Aldridge

Additional competitions played in by Notts County Reserves, usually with a mix of reserve and youth players, include Midland Midweek League 1933/34 to 1934/35 and 1950/51 to 1959/60; and North Midlands Combination 1957/58 to 1959/60. In 1893/94 the Reserves played only friendly matches because of financial problems.

RUGBY FOOTBALL
League
The Notts County directors gave permission for a Rugby League test match to be staged at Meadow Lane during 1911/12. The match was played on December 6th 1911 when England beat the Australian touring team by 5 points to 3 and attracted a crowd of 3,000. Rugby League returned in 1986 when Mansfield Marksmen met Fulham before 950 spectators.
Union
Rugby Union made its Meadow Lane debut on March 3rd 1945 with a match between the Notts, Lincs and Derby XV and a RAF XV. A crowd of 2,500 saw an RAF victory by 10-9. In 2006 the Union code made a longer term return when Nottingham Rugby Club signed a deal to use Meadow Lane for their home matches and the first was the pre-season friendly v Leicester Tigers on Bank Holiday Monday, August 28th, which was marked with a 26-13 victory and a crowd of 2,500. The National Division 1 Meadow Lane programme began on September 3rd 2006 when Exeter were 24-19 winners before just under 2,000 fans.

On October 6th 1917 things went in the reverse direction when the Magpies played a Local XI on the then Notts RFC ground at Ireland Avenue, Beeston. Jimmy Cantrell scored in a 1-0 victory.

RUMBELOWS CUP: see Football League Cup

SEASON
In the early days of the club the length of the football season was extremely short, running from early November until the middle of March. With the expansion of the fixture list the season began to expand too and from 1876/77 Notts usually began their programme early in October and finished by the end of March. By 1883/84 the opening match was played on September 22nd and the final one on April 3rd. The next season the last match took place as late as April 25th.

The next major expansion of the season occurred after the formation of the Football League in 1888 and was directly caused by the large number of Scottish professionals signed by County. To enable the wage bill to be met it became necessary to play a number of away friendly matches with a guaranteed cash payment from the home club who were hoping to make a profit from hosting such a galaxy of famous players. Almost the whole of April 1890 was taken up with 14 such matches, the final one being played on May 1st.

At this stage the season settled down to run from September 1st until the last Saturday in April and this remained the norm until football restarted after the First World War. In 1919/20 the season ran from August 30th until May 1st and throughout the inter-war years the last Saturday in August until the first Saturday in May remained the standard, except for charity games which could be played later in May if permission was granted by the F.A.

The big freeze-up of 1946/47 saw that season extended so that County's last match was on May 29th, still the latest date on which they have fulfilled a League fixture with the exception of play-offs. In 1947/48 the season began a week earlier on August 23rd and this was the rule until the late 1960s. Meanwhile both 1962/63 (May 20th) and 1965/66 (May 21st) were extended because of bad weather causing fixture congestion. In 1968/69 the start of the season was brought forward to August 10th and it has generally remained around this date.

Nowadays seasons are stretched by pre-season matches and the end of season play-offs so that Notts can claim to have played competitive football in every month of the year! They met Brighton and Hove Albion in the 1991 play-off final on June 2nd and in the 1970s played a Watney Cup and Anglo-Scottish Cup tie in late July.

SECRETARIES
In the early days of the club, players also filled the various official posts. The first non-player secretary was Edwin Browne, who was also assistant secretary of Nottinghamshire CCC. He took office for the 1882/83 season and perhaps his cricket links helped to pave the way for County to become tenants of Trent Bridge Cricket Ground from 1883/84.

Another type of secretary developed just before the First World War and continued to be popular during the inter-war period. This was the secretary-manager whose duties included running the team as well as undertaking secretarial work. They were generally retired footballers with little experience of such office duties and usually had to have clerical assistance. The first such secretary-manager appointed by the Magpies was Albert Fisher who took over on August 1st 1913. On July 14th 1942 Wilf Fisher became full-time secretary after working in the office since 1934 and being assistant secretary from August 23rd 1939, handling much of the secretarial work for the so-called secretary-managers. More recently the secretary for a time acquired the more grandiose and lengthier title of chief executive officer.

Complete list of Notts County secretaries is as follows (*denotes secretary-manager):
1864-66 John Patterson; 1866-68 Edward Steegmann; 1868-70 Charles Rothera; 1870-72 Fred Rothera; 1872-79 Ernest Greenhalgh; 1879-80 Tom Oliver; 1880-81 Harold Morse; 1881-82 Harry Cursham; 1882-93 Edwin Browne; 1893 Thomas Featherstone (also a director); 1893-1913 Tom Harris (also a director to 1902); 1913 George Osborne (also a director) during illness of Mr Harris; 1913-27 *Albert Fisher; 1927-35 Horace Henshall (secretary-manager to May 5th 1934, then secretary only); 1935 *David Pratt; 1935-36 *Percy Smith; 1936-37 *Jimmy McMullan; 1938-39 *Harry Parkes; 1939-42 *Tony Towers (also a director); 1942-56 Wilf Fisher; 1956-73 Charles "Chick" Heath; 1973-81 Dennis Marshall; 1981-83 Lance Hayward; 1983-85 Ken Mott; 1985-1996 Neal Hook (as chief executive and for a time managing director); 1996-99 Ian Moat; 1999-date Tony Cuthbert.

SENDINGS-OFF: see Disciplinary

SHERPA VAN TROPHY: see Associate Members Cup

SPONSORED COMPETITIONS
These are shown under the generic name of the competition; e.g., F.L.Cup and not Carling Cup but all sponsored titles are shown and cross-referred.

SPONSORSHIP: see **Colours** for club sponsors' names on playing strip.

STRESS LEAGUE
This "league table" was issued in January 2007 by Littlewoods Pools and showed Notts County as the most stressful team to support in the country post-war out of the 92 Premier and Football League clubs. The survey took into account a number of different factors such as frequent switching of divisions, narrowly missing out on promotion and relegation, regular failure to win at home, losing matches from a winning position, losing in play-offs, financial problems leading to uncertainty over the club's future, changes in ownership and frequent changes of manager.

The top ten most stressful clubs to support were listed as: 1. Notts County; 2. MK Dons; 3. Carlisle United; 4. Darlington; 5. Swindon Town; 6. Bury; 7. Crewe Alexandra; 8. Portsmouth; 9. Stockport County; 10. Grimsby Town. Nottingham Forest were ranked 47th, Mansfield Town 59th and least stressful of all were Liverpool at 92nd.

SUBSTITUTES
From 1965/66 the Football League allowed one substitute per game in place of an injured player, then from the next season of 1966/67 the F.A.Cup and the F.L.Cup followed suit. From 1967/68 one substitute per game was allowed without the need for the withdrawn player to be injured. This recognition that substitutes could be used tactically led to an increase of two per game and, in 1994/95, to two outfield players plus a goalkeeper. For 1999/2000 the Football League fell into line with the Premier League by the introduction of five substitutes though the manager could introduce only three of the five.

The first Notts County substitute called on was Dennis Shiels who replaced injured right winger Brian Bates after 75 minutes v Lincoln City (h), Division 4, February 5th 1966. The Magpies were reported to be the last club to use a substitute in League games. The first substitute to score for Notts was Richie Barker v Southport (h), Division 4, March 13th 1971, after he had replaced Les Bradd.

The first substitute used by Notts in the F.A.Cup was Paddy McGovern v Runcorn (a), 1st round, December 9th 1967, and in the F.L.Cup, Stan Marshall v Mansfield Town (a), 1st round replay, August 29th 1966.

Goalkeeper Barry Watling was an outfield substitute for the injured Don Masson v Newport County (a), Division 4, February 28th 1970, as he was the only player available apart from the 11 selected for the game because the nominated substitute had missed the coach.

Geoff Ball went on as substitute as early as the 7th minute v Scunthorpe United, Division 4, January 4th 1969, following an injury to Bob Worthington.

Before the substitute rule was introduced for competitive matches they had sometimes been allowed in friendlies by mutual consent. The earliest Notts County one on record is v Leek, December 17th 1887, when Harold Brown hurt his shoulder and an unnamed substitute was allowed. Another was v Rangers (a), January 2nd 1902, when Walter Bull replaced Ellis Gee after half-time.

The following have made 30 or more Football League substitute appearances for Notts: Tony Hackworth 37, Wayne Fairclough 32, Gary Martindale 32, Tony Agana 31, Ian McParland 31, Kevin Rapley 31, Mick Vinter 31, Sean Farrell 30.

SUDDEN DEATH: see GOLDEN GOAL

SUNDAY GAMES
During the power emergency of 1974 the Football League sanctioned Sunday matches for the first time. Notts County's first was v Crystal Palace (h) on January 20th 1974 when a crowd of 14,478 saw Palace win 3-1. The match against Nottingham Forest (a) was also on a Sunday, March 3rd 1974 when the attendance was 29,657 and the result 0-0. Since then Sunday games have become standard fare, especially since television deals in recent times.

However, County's first Sunday game of all dates back to their third match of their continental tour to Denmark in 1910 when they beat a Danish XI 2-1 at Copenhagen on Sunday June 5th. Other early tours abroad also saw Sunday play.

SUPPORTERS TRUST: see Limited Company

TELEVISION
When the Notts County directors met on November 30th 1959 secretary Chick Heath read out a letter from the BBC regarding plans to televise the Magpies' 2nd round F.A.Cup tie v Bath City at Meadow Lane on December 5th. This was the first time a Notts game had been televised live and the viewers' were treated to one of the giant-killing feats of the season as Southern League Bath won by the only goal. Despite the attraction of the small screen, 25,889 fans turned out to watch

TEST MATCHES

These were the forerunners of the modern play-offs and were devised to decide promotion and relegation after the Football League first formed a Division 2 in 1892. For three seasons the arrangement was that the top team in Division 2 met the bottom team in Division 1 on a neutral ground, the second top playing the second bottom and the third top meeting the third bottom. Drawn games were replayed and the winners were promoted or, in the case of Division 1 clubs, retained their status. From 1895/96 the bottom two in Division 1 and the top two in Division 2 formed a mini-league, each meeting the two teams from the other division but not the one from their own division.

Notts played test matches in 1892/93, 1893/94, 1894/95 and 1896-7 as follows:

1892/93 (third from bottom in Division 1) v Darwen (Hyde Road, Manchester) 2-3 on April 22nd 1893 despite being 2-0 up in 13 minutes. Notts relegated.
1893/94 (third in Division 2) v Preston North End (Olive Grove, Sheffield) 0-4 on April 28th 1894. Not promoted.
1894/95 (second in Division 2) v Derby County (Filbert Street, Leicester) 1-2 on April 27th 1895. Not promoted.
1896/97 (Division 2 champions) v Sunderland (h) 1-0 and (a) 0-0; v Burnley (h) 1-1 and (a) 1-0. Promoted after Notts topped the mini-league with six points. The winner v Burnley which saw Notts promoted was scored by left-winger John Brearley in his only match of the season.

THIRD DIVISION CUP

At the 1933 annual meeting of the Football League the Southern and Northern sections of Division 3 were given permission to run their own knock-out cup competitions and these continued from 1933/34 to the outbreak of war in September 1939. After the club were relegated from Division 2 in 1934/35 they took part in the Southern Section Cup from 1935/36 to 1938/39 inclusive.

Their best season was 1936/37 when they reached the semi-finals where they drew 1-1 with Watford. Because of fixture congestion the replay was held over to the start of 1937/38 when the Magpies lost 8-3, their record defeat in this competition. Immediately afterwards they were drawn against Watford in the 1937/38 competition, losing 2-0. Watford had also provided the opposition for the Magpies' debut in the Southern Section Cup in 1935/36 though this time County won 2-1.

Most goals in total aggregate were scored by Harry Mardon with five in four appearances, 1936/37 and 1937/38 while Percy Mills claimed the most appearances, playing in seven games over the four seasons.

Notts County's complete record: P.8 W.3 D.1 L.4 F.16 A.23

TOURS

Invitations to play matches in Germany in 1907 and 1910 were declined so the Magpies first overseas tour was to Denmark in June 1910 as guests of the Akadezuisk Boldklub of Copenhagen. Notts drew 1-1 with a Danish XI on June 1st to inaugurate their first match on foreign soil. The next tour, to Barcelona in 1914, saw a hat-trick of victories over Barcelona including one by 10-3.

There was a further tour to Barcelona in 1922 when Notts met Scottish League side St Mirren, who were also on tour, in a special match for a cup and medals which the Magpies lost 2-1, their first overseas defeat. There was a second visit to Denmark in 1923 and a tour of Central Europe in 1925 which brought their first losses against continental teams with a 1-0 defeat to Prague and 3-1 to Ostrau. This tour produced a considerable financial loss, mainly because the guarantee offered by the continental promoters was never paid. After this disaster, the Magpies gave up such tours until after the Second World War.

In 1945 they visited Cologne for a single match against a British Army XI and in 1954 went to Holland. Then came a 17-year gap until 1971 when two matches were played in Italy and this heralded a busy touring period over the next 35 years. The 1975 and 1977 trips to Gibraltar were for games against Fulham and St Mirren respectively.

Complete tour record:		P	W	D	L	F	A
1910	Denmark	3	2	1	0	8	5
1914	Spain	3	3	0	0	17	6
1922	Spain	3	1	1	1	6	5
1923	Denmark	3	3	0	0	7	2
1925	Central Europe	4	1	1	2	3	5
1945/46	Germany	1	1	0	0	5	2
1954	Holland	3	0	2	1	5	6
1971	Italy	2	2	0	0	6	3
1972/73	Gibraltar	1	1	0	0	7	0
1975	Gibraltar	2	1	1	0	5	4
1976	Kenya	4	2	0	2	6	5
1977	Gibraltar	2	1	1	0	4	3
1981/82	Gibraltar	1	1	0	0	1	0
1983	Spain	2	0	1	1	2	4
1983/84	Spain	1	0	0	1	0	1
1984	Kenya	3	2	0	1	9	9
1992/93	Gibraltar	1	1	0	0	4	0
1994	Slovakia	2	1	0	1	1	1
1999	Far East	4	2	1	1	6	5
2003	Italy	2	0	1	1	0	1
1910-2003	*Total*	47	25	10	12	102	67

TRAINERS

The position of trainer evolved during the 1880s along with professionalism. As with many other traditional football occupations it is difficult to define just who the first trainer was. However by 1890 the position was filled by Henry Kirk, although during the club's F.A.Cup run in 1890/91 former goalkeeper and Nottinghamshire wicket-keeper Mordecai Sherwin was called in to take charge.

It is clear the directors were not completely satisfied with Kirk for in 1891/92 former half-back Herbert Emmitt was offered the job but he declined. The players themselves put in a petition to retain Kirk and he stayed until the Magpies were relegated at the end of the 1892/93 season; perhaps the reason why he was so popular with the players may have something to do with lax discipline.

Nowadays trainers prefer the name of physio and spend more time in the dressing room with potions, sprays and exercise machines than they used to in the old days when a bucket of cold water and a sponge was considered sufficient. Since Kirk departed in 1893, the Notts trainers/physios have been:

1893-1903	Joe Goode	1948-1956	Bill Moore
1903-1905	George Swift	1956-1957	Vic Potts
1905-1917	Tom Prescott	1957-1983	Jack Wheeler
1919-1927	Jimmy Iremonger	1983-1986	John Short
1927-1929	Tom Ratcliffe	1986-1989	Wayne Jones
1929-1934	Fred Banks	1989-1992	David Wilson
1934-1936	Bill Seddon	1992-1994	David Lawson
1936-1938	Tom Ratcliffe	1994-1996	Dennis Pettit
1938-1940	Ernie England	1996-2004	Roger Cleary
1945-1948	Tom Ratcliffe	2004-date	John Haselden
1948	Bill Corkhill (acting)		

Long service

Jack Wheeler spent 26 years as trainer in which he never missed a first-team match, being on duty in 1,292 League and cup games as well as more than 80 County Cup, friendlies and tour matches. His total was made up of 1,152 League games, 49 F.A.Cup, 61 F.L.Cup, 29 Anglo-Scottish Cup and 1 Watney Cup. Tom Ratcliffe had three spells as trainer. He was first appointed in 1927 and ended his connection with Notts in 1948, a spell of 21 years but only seven of them as Magpies trainer.

Old players

George Swift and Tom Prescott were former Notts County players while Bill Corkhill, who was acting trainer in 1948 before the appointment of Bill Moore, was still on the playing staff at the time. Jimmy Iremonger and Fred Banks were former Nottingham Forest players.

Miscellaneous

Trainer Joe Goode appeared in the first team v Sheffield Wednesday (a), United Counties League, March 4th 1895.

TRANSFERS

In 1922 the Football League passed a regulation that all transfer fees should be treated as private and confidential so that sums as stated in the media and in record books are only estimates, though often aided by informed "leaks".

The first four-figure transfer in which the Magpies were involved was the sale of centre-forward Jimmy Cantrell to Tottenham Hotspur in October 1912. It was stated to be £1,500. The record fee paid by Notts between the wars was the £3,000 St Mirren received for the transfer of centre-half George Walker in the 1933 close season.

The first five-figure fee involving Notts made national headlines as it was the £20,000 paid to Chelsea in November 1947 for England centre-forward Tommy Lawton which was also the then British record. However, this figure was only reached with some financial manoeuvring as wing-half Bill Dickson left Meadow Lane for Stamford Bridge at an evaluation of £2,500. The cash actually paid by Notts was £17,500 but in order to reach the £20,000 record separate cheques changed hands for the two players. Notts topped this sum in September 1950 when they paid Bradford Park Avenue £25,000 for centre-half Leon Leuty.

The British record was again broken by the Magpies, this time an outward bound one when they sold inside-right Jackie Sewell to Sheffield Wednesday for £34,500 in March 1951.

As transfer fees gradually and then swiftly rose into the thousands and then the millions, Notts could no longer afford to be among the front-runners in this area. To date the club's record signing remains striker Tony Agana who cost £750,000 from Sheffield United in November 1991 to top the £600,000 Orient received for winger John Chiedozie in August 1981.

The record fee received by Notts was £2,500,000 from Derby County for central defender Craig Short in September 1992 and £1,300,000 from the same club for striker Tommy Johnson in March 1992. Mark Draper's fee of £1,250,000 when he moved to Leicester City in the 1994 close season had to be settled by a tribunal after the clubs failed to agree. These sums are a vast increase on the £150,000 Notts were paid by Wrexham for Mick Vinter in June 1979 just 13 years or so earlier.

UNDER-21 CAPS
The following ten Notts County players have won U-21 international caps for the four home countries while with the club:
England
    Mark Draper (3): 1990/91 v Eire (sub); 1991/92 v Germany, Poland.
    Tommy Johnson (5): 1990/91 v Hungary (sub), Eire (sub); 1991/92 v Germany, Turkey, Poland.
    Brian Kilcline (2): 1982/83 v Denmark, Greece.
    Dean Yates (5): 1988/89 v Denmark (sub), Bulgaria, Senegal, Eire, USA.
Scotland
    Iain McCulloch (2): 1981/82 v England (2).
Wales
    Michael Brough (3): 2002/03 v Azerbaijan (sub); 2003/04 v Italy, Finland.
    Dan Martin (1): 2005/06 v Malta (sub).
    David Pipe (6): 2004/05 v Latvia, Azerbaijan, England, Poland, Germany, Austria.
    Darren Ward (2): 1995/96 v Moldova, Germany.
Northern Ireland
    Emmet Friars (7): 2004/05: v Sweden, Scotland; 2005/06: v Eire (sub), Israel, Wales (sub), Liechtenstein (sub), Scotland.

UNITED COUNTIES LEAGUE
This league for clubs' first teams was formed during the summer of 1893 and comprised two sections based on the East and West Midlands. Its aim was to fill up some of the dates between cup-ties in the latter part of the season which until then had been mainly given over to friendlies. It lasted for two seasons and in 1894/95 only East Midlands clubs participated. The Magpies finished in bottom spot in both seasons and in fact won only one match and drew one out of 13.

The leading scorer was Harry Daft with three goals in five games while George Toone made the record number of appearances with 11. County's biggest and only victory was 2-1 v Sheffield Wednesday (h) on March 17th 1894 while their heaviest defeat came from Derby County (a) who were 8-1 victors on January 13th 1894. The Magpies complete record was P.13 W.1 D.1 L.11 F.9 A.37.

WAR-TIME FOOTBALL
During both world wars the Football League competition was suspended though in the First World War not until after the close of the 1914/15 season. Wartime regional tournaments were introduced in 1915 and the Magpies took part in the Midland Section which divided into a Principal Tournament and a Subsidiary Tournament which was played towards the end of the season on a mini-league basis.

Here are Notts County's season by season records during the First World War:

Principal Tournament

	P	W	D	L	F	A	Pts	Position
1915/16	26	10	6	10	39	36	26	8
1916/17	30	13	6	11	47	52	32	7
1917/18	28	7	9	12	43	54	23	10
1918/19	30	16	9	5	65	38	41	3

Subsidiary Tournament

	P	W	D	L	F	A	Pts	Position
1915/16	10	5	3	2	16	12	13	2
1916/17	6	1	2	3	9	12	4	4
1917/18	6	4	0	2	19	8	8	1
1918/19	6	2	0	4	13	13	4	3

A system of regional league football was also adopted during the Second World War. The F.A. Cup was suspended until 1945/46 when it was resumed on a two-leg basis for the only season in its history. However, a League Cup competition was organised, being split into north and south sections from 1942/43.

Here are County's season-by-season records in the various wartime leagues:

East Midlands Regional

	P	W	D	L	F	A	Pts	Position
1939/40	20	6	2	12	40	57	14	11/out of 11

South Regional

1940/41	21	8	3	10	42	66	0.64	30/34

(goal average and not points decided positions)
1941/42 Did not compete because of bomb damage to Meadow Lane.

North Regional (first and second championships)

1942/43 (1)	18	7	2	9	34	57	16	29/48
(2)	20	9	6	5	37	34	24	12/54
1943/44 (1)	18	4	3	11	26	53	11	47/50
(2)	20	3	0	17	23	68	6	54/56
1944/45 (1)	18	2	1	15	19	62	5	54/54
(2)	21	4	0	17	29	62	8	59/60

(in these seasons the first championship ended on December 25th and the second started on December 26th)

Division 3 South (Northern Section)

1945/46	20	8	4	8	39	47	20	6/11

Division 3 South Cup Group (Northern Section)

1945/46	16	5	0	11	17	31	10	11/11

The League Cup qualifying competition from 1942/43 included 10 matches which counted towards the League second championship. The Magpies' results in the League Cup knock-out stages were as follows:

1939/40 Preliminary round v Mansfield Town (a) 5-3; first round v Arsenal (a) 0-4, (h) 1-5 (aggregate 1-9).

1940/41 First round v West Bromwich Albion (h) 4-0, (a) 0-5 (aggregate 4-5).
1941/42 Did not compete because of bomb damage to Meadow Lane.
1942/43 First round v Derby County (a) 3-1, (h) 2-2 (aggregate 5-3); second round v Sheffield United (a) 1-4, (h) 2-1 (aggregate 3-5).
1943/44 Failed to qualify.
1944/45 Failed to qualify.
Division 3 South (Northern Section) Cup
1945/46 Failed to qualify.

Goal-scoring: individual

Jimmy Cantrell was the Magpies leading scorer in the Midland Section matches for every season during the First World War. He totalled 63 goals with a best of 22 in 1918/19. He also scored 13 in the Subsidiary Tournaments plus two in friendlies, to bring his wartime aggregate to 78.

Because of the large number of players called on, few goalscoring records of the Second World War can match Cantrell. Leading aggregate scorer was Colin Collindridge with 20 (12 League and eight Cup).

Four or more goals in a match
    5 Jimmy Cantrell v Grimsby Town (h) December 22nd 1917.
    4 Jimmy Cantrell v Huddersfield Town (a) February 15th 1919.
    4 Horace Henshall v Nottingham Forest (a) September 11th 1915.
    (including two penalties)

Goal-scoring: team

Biggest win
    8-0 v Grimsby Town (h) December 22nd 1917.
Biggest defeats
    11-4 v Walsall (a) November 9th 1940.
    9-1 v Leicester City (h) October 30th 1943.
    8-0 v Chesterfield (a) December 23rd 1944.
    8-1 v Lincoln City (a) October 31st 1942.
    8-1 v Lincoln City (a) December 25th 1942.
    8-1 v West Bromwich Albion January 11th 1941.
    8-2 v Coventry City (a) May 6th 1944.
    8-5 v Lincoln City (a) December 18th 1943.

Appearances

As well as topping the scoring chart, Jimmy Cantrell also clocked up the most wartime appearances for the Magpies with 127 in both Principal and Subsidiary Tournaments. Billy Flint with 101 was the only other player to reach a century.

WATNEY CUP

This was the Football League's first sponsored tournament, was played pre-season between 1970 and 1973 and introduced the penalty shoot-out to English soccer. Entry was for the four top scoring clubs, one per division, aside from the title, promotion and European qualification teams. Notts qualified in 1972 by virtue of their 74 Division 3 goals in 1971/72. A Meadow Lane crowd of 14,405 saw them beaten 3-0 by Sheffield United of Division 1.

WEMBLEY STADIUM

The Magpies have played five matches at the old Wembley Stadium, three times in League play-off finals and twice in the Anglo-Italian Cup final which produced overall three victories and two defeats. Details:
    Division 3 play-off final: May 27th 1990 v Tranmere Rovers, won 2-0. County scorers Tommy Johnson, Craig Short. Attendance 29,252.
    Division 2 play-off final: June 2nd 1991 v Brighton and Hove Albion, won 3-1. County scorers Tommy Johnson 2, Dave Regis. Attendance 59,940.
    Anglo-Italian Cup final: March 20th 1994 v Brescia, lost 1-0. Attendance 17,185.
    Anglo-Italian Cup final: March 19th 1995 v Ascoli, won 2-1. County scorers Tony Agana, Devon White. Attendance 11,704.
    Division 2* play-off final: May 26th 1996 v Bradford City, lost 2-0. Attendance 39,972.

Two County players appeared in four Wembley games, skipper Phil Turner and goalkeeper Steve Cherry, while defender Charlie Palmer and striker Tony Agana turned out three times.

WHEELBARROW SONG

The anthem of Notts County fans emerged in modern times in comparison to some long-established ones such as West Ham United whose "I'm forever blowing bubbles" dates back to the 1920s. The story goes that some Notts supporters were on their way to a match and were walking past an allotment on which a gardener was pushing a wheelbarrow when suddenly a wheel came off. Shortly afterwards the Magpies were away at Shrewsbury Town in a F.L.Cup tie, August 22nd 1989 and "the wheels came off" as they crashed 3-0 with Wayne Fairclough receiving his marching orders. As the match progressed the misery-struck fans began to sing "I had a wheelbarrow; the wheel came off."

It just took off from there and began to be sung even when it was the opponents of Notts whose wheels were coming off. Chants of "County, County, County!" were added and by the time of the televised F.A.Cup game at Tottenham in 1990/91, radio stations were besieged with phone calls asking about the Wheelbarrow Song. Meadow Lane chief executive Neal Hook even went on to Radio One to explain what it was all about. So tradition does not have to go back decades; it can be made almost overnight.

WORTHINGTON CUP: see Football League Cup

ZENITH DATA SYSTEMS CUP: see Full Members Cup

INTRODUCTION TO THE STATISTICS PAGES

The season-by-season grids show the results of games in all major competitions, including the Football League, F.A. Cup, Football League Cup, Third Division (South) Cup, the Full Members' Cup and the Associate Members' Cup. The latter competition has been played under a number of sponsor's names and is currently the Johnstone's Paint Trophy.

Home games are identified by the opponent's name in upper case, away games by the use of lower case. County's score is always given first. Attendances for League games are taken from the official Football League records for seasons 1925/26 to 2000/01; for other seasons attendances based on newspaper reports have been used. The official Football League figures are sometimes at variance with contemporary newspaper reports.

We have not attempted to specify line-up formations for the early seasons. When numbers are used, they reflect traditional positions as follows: 1, goalkeeper; 2 and 3, full backs; 4, 5 and 6, half backs, 7 and 11, outside right and left; 8 and 10, inside right and left; 9, centre forward. It is almost impossible to follow such strict numbering in recent seasons; the numbers chosen hopefully give an indication of where the player played.

Substitutes, from season 1965/66 onwards, have the numbers 12, 13 and 14. Number 12 is used if only one substitute was used (no matter what number was on the player's shirt). The players replaced are underlined. Unused substitutes are not included.

The identification of goal scorers in early seasons is somewhat problematic. Reports often say that the ball "was forced over the line in a scrimmage". Also, with no shirt numbers (until 1939) and with reporters often enduring difficult physical conditions while they made their match notes, it is not surprising that mistakes could occur.

A full player list is provided for every player who has made a Football League appearance. Date and place of birth are shown, where known, and the year of death. The next two columns, "seasons played", act as an index to the season-by-season grids. The years shown are the "first year" of the season; for example, 1971 is season 1971/72. The two columns show the season in which the player made his first team debut; and the final season that he played. However, if he only played in one season, the second column is blank. An entry of "2006" in the second column does not imply that the player has left the club, but means that he appeared in the "final season" (2006/07) of the book.

Note that some players also made F.A. Cup appearances before 1888/89 and in 1945/46. If a player also made a League appearance his F.A. Cup appearances for those seasons are included in the list; his "seasons played" columns include his F.A. Cup appearances. Previous and next clubs show where he was transferred from, and the club he moved to. Non-league and junior club information is included when known. Full international caps (not necessarily won whilst at Notts) are as follows: al (Algeria), au (Australia), bm (Bermuda), e (England), fi (Finland), gh (Ghana), i (Ireland), ja (Jamaica), mn (Montserrat), n (Northern Ireland), ng (Nigeria), no (Norway), nz (New Zealand), r (Republic of Ireland), s (Scotland), sk (St Kitts), w (Wales) and yu (Yugoslavia).

The appearance columns have separate totals for the League, F.A. Cup, Football League Cup, League test matches and play-offs, and the other major tournaments (such as the current Johnstone's Paint Trophy). Goals scored are also shown under the five headings. If a player has had more than one spell at the club playing first team football, a consolidated set of appearance and goals are shown on the first line. Subsequent lines show the seasons involved on his return to the club, and his new pair of previous and next clubs.

A full record of meetings against all other League clubs (in the Football League) is included. Some clubs have played under different names, but the totals are consolidated under the present day name in this table. Final League tables are also included.

A list of friendly games after the start of the Football League are included. The Nottinghamshire County Cup has provided regular fixtures with Mansfield Town and Nottingham Forest; these games are indicated by a "CC" after the result. Pre-season games are included when the first team is known to have been used.

The book was printed in June 2007. All statistics, including player appearances and goal totals, are calculated up to and including the final game of the 2006/07 season.

Jay Smith became County's 1000th Football League player in 2006/07

1864/65

#	Date		Opponent	Score		Players
1	Dec	8	TRENT VALLEY	0-0		
2	Jan	2	SHEFFIELD	0-1		J Patterson (capt.), T Elliott, W Elliott, R Fountain, H Moody, R Daft, CF Daft, G Parr, John Parr, H Parr, JW Thackery, JB Gibson, EB Steegman, A Scrimshaw, W Goddard, H Simons, JS Wright, W Wright
3	Mar	9	Lincoln	0-0		J Patterson (capt.), H Simons, JB Gibson, E Steegman, W Wright, F Wright, B Bradley, CF Daft, S Scrimshaw, E Bradley, H Moody, W Elliott, J Hack, J Hodges, WA Hodges
4		23	Sheffield	0-1		J Patterson (capt.), H Simons, CF Daft, T Bignall, W Elliott, J Wright, H Moody, J Hack, J Hodges, T Elliott, FB Gibson, Allott, B Bradley

Home games at the Meadows Cricket Ground

1865/66

#	Date		Opponent	Score		Players
1	Jan	25	SHEFFIELD	1-2	Packer	J Patterson, FC Smith, A Deedes, JS Wright, JB Gibson, AB Baillon, G Packer, H Browne, W Elliott, S Scrimshaw, H Rastall, WA Hodges, JC Hodges, J Hack, C Steegman
2	Mar	15	Sheffield	0-1		J Patterson (capt.), AB Baillon, H Moody, G Packer, W Elliott, J Hack, W Birkin, J Shaw, W Lymbery, H Browne, CF Daft, HH Herbert, G Steegman, JM Astill, J Wilkinson
3		22	Nottm. Forest	0-0		EB Steegman, J Hack (capt.), AB Baillon, W Elliott, T Elliott, W Ward, JC Hodges, H Browne, W Goddard, B Bradley, J Wilkinson
4	Apr	19	NOTTM. FOREST	0-0		EB Steegman, J Hack, AB Baillon, W Elliott, W Ward, CS Wardle, Lees, J Wilkinson, Wright, S Scrimshaw, Stranger

Home games at the Meadows Cricket Ground

1866/67

#	Date		Opponent	Score		Players
1	Dec	13	Practice			FC Smith with A Deedes, G Pym, WA Hodges, JC Hodges, W Ward, W Bury, G Fellows. EB Steegman with H Simons, W Goddard, R Daft, J Hack, AB Baillon, HW Chambers
2		20	NOTTM. FOREST	1-1	Hack	A Deedes (capt), WA Birkin, AB Baillon, J Hack, TP Keely, JC Hodges, FC Smith, WA Hodges, W Ward, W Goddard, EB Steegman, CS Wardle, A Waring, G Baillon, W. Browne
3	Feb	7	PUBLIC SCHOOLS	1-0	WA Hodges	AB Baillon, WS Birkin, W Goddard, J Hack, WA Hodges, JC Hodges, F Newsome, EB Steegman, H Simons, W Ward, CS Wardle
4		14	Sheffield	1-0	Rothera (and a rouge)	A Deedes (capt.), EB Steegman, JC Hodges, John Lambert, C Rothera, CS Wardle, W Goddard, J Hack, AB Baillon, W Lymbery, TP Keely
5		28	Nottm. Forest	1-0	WA Hodges	FC Smith (capt.), AB Baillon, T Keely, JC Hodges, WA Hodges, T Elliott, J Lambert, J Hack, W Ward (2 short)
6	Mar	14	SHEFFIELD	1-0	JC Hodges	A Deedes (capt.), WA Hodges, JC Hodges, J Hack, W Goddard, T Keeley, J Lambert, C Rothera, FC Smith, CS Wardle, AB Baillon

Game 1 at Bramcote, 2 and 3 at the Meadows, game 6 at Trent Bridge

1867/68

#	Date		Opponent	Score		Players
1	Nov	21	Robin Hood Rifles	1-0	JC Hodges	AB Baillon, F Baillon, B Richard, CF Elliott, JS Shaw, CS Wardle, C Rothera, G Hine, WA Hodges (capt), JC Hodges, W Ward (absent)
2		28	Sheffield			No details available
3	Dec	12	Practice Match			11 of the Town (capt. A Deedes) v. 11 of the County (capt. R Daft)
4		26	Nottm. Forest (Practice)			No details available
5	Jan	23	ROBIN HOOD RIFLES	0-0		JC Hodges, WA Hodges, AB Baillon, RF Baillon, C Rothera, J Rothera, L Melville, A Lambert, W Bell, W Ward, JH Stafford, CS Wardle
6	Feb	6	PUBLIC SCHOOLS	0-0		No details available
7		20	PUBLIC SCHOOLS	1-0	WA Hodges	WA Hodges (capt.), JC Hodges, J Hack, CH Stafford, CS Wardle, W Ward, AB Baillon, F Baillon, R Rothera, H Simons

Home games at the Meadows Cricket Ground

1868/69

#	Date		Opponent	Score	Scorers
1	Jan	28	ROBIN HOOD RIFLES	0-0	
2	Feb	26	Newark	0-2	
3	Mar	4	NEWARK	2-1	Unknown
4		11	ROBIN HOOD RIFLES		
5		18	SOUTH DERBYSHIRE		

Home games at the Meadows

Players: Baillon AB, Barks A, Beckett E, Daft R, Elliott W, Forman A, Greenhalgh EH, Hack J, Hine A, Hodges JC, Hodges WA, Lambert J, Morse H, Rothera CL, Rothera FW, Stafford CH, Steegman EB, Wardle CS, Wilde C, Williams H

1869/70

#	Date		Opponent	Score	Scorers
1	Nov	6	Nottm. Forest	0-0	
2		11	NEWARK	3-0	AB Baillon, Daft, CL Rothera
3		18	South Derbyshire	3-2	CL Rothera 3
4	Dec	2	ROBIN HOOD RIFLES	4-0	AB Baillon, Daft, CL Rothera, EH Greenhalgh
5		16	Sheffield	0-1	
6	Jan	20	Lincoln	1-0	Daft
7		29	SHEFFIELD	0-0	
8	Feb	3	Newark	1-0	Daft
9		26	SOUTH DERBYSHIRE	0-0	
10	Mar	12	LINCOLN	1-0	EM Keely
11		17	Chesterfield	3-1	CH Stafford 2, unknown

Home games at the Meadows except 10 (on the Forest)
Played in game 5: Palethorpe

1870/71

#	Date		Opponent	Score	Scorers
1	Nov	17	NEWARK	0-0	
2		24	Nottm. Law Club	0-1	
3	Dec	3	SHEFFIELD	0-0	
4		15	Lincoln	2-0	Wardle, FW Rothera
5	Feb	9	NOTTM. LAW CLUB	1-1	Unknown
6		16	Newark	1-0	J Lambert
7		23	Chesterfield	0-0	
8	Mar	4	LINCOLN	1-0	Unknown
9		9	Sheffield	0-0	
10		11	Nottm Forest	1-1	Unknown

All home games at the Meadows Cricket Ground except 3, Trent Bridge
Played in game 8: Fisher, J Rothera, CH Stafford.
Played in game 10: Diamond, A Hine, CH Stafford

1871/72

#	Date		Opponent	Score	Scorers
1	Oct	28	LINCOLN	1-0	Baillon
2	Nov	9	NOTTM. LAW CLUB	1-0	CL Rothera
3		16	South Derbyshire	1-4	
4		25	NEWARK	1-0	AW Lambert
5	Dec	28	Newark	2-1	Wardle, S Morse
6	Jan	4	PUBLIC SCHOOLS	0-0	
7		11	NOTTM LAW CLUB	0-0	
8		25	Sheffield	0-1	
9	Feb	8	Lincoln	0-1	
10		13	NOTTM. FOREST	0-1	
11		24	Nottm. Forest	1-2	J Parr
12	Mar	16	SHEFFIELD		

All home games at the Meadows Cricket Ground
Played in game 5: H Williams. In game 6: H Morse, S Smith, S Windley.
Played in game 7: Jones. In game 8: C Browne, JW Rothera.
Played in game 9: Browne, Carlisle, Muir, Padley, JH Richardson, Riggall, H Wyles (all of Lincoln). In game 10: MJ Ellison, Wake.

1872/73

				Ashwell AT	Baillon AB	Bright A	Bright J	Cursham AW	Davies H	Forman A	Greenhalgh A	Greenhalgh EH	Hack J	Hayes G	Johnson WG	Jones E	Keely EM	Kirk JP	Marriott F	Mason W	Owen JRB	Parr J	Pearson AH	Revis WH	Robinson WM	Seals CJ	Spencer CJ	Stafford CH	Tomlinson J	Wake J	Ward J	Wardle CS	Whiteley W	Widdowson SW
1	Oct 31	NOTTM. LAW CLUB	1-0 EH Greenhalgh		x					x	x	x			x	x					x	x	x			x				x		x	
2	Nov 14	SOUTH DERBYSHIRE	1-0 Revis				x		x		x	x		x		x		x				x	x		x							x		
3	28	Lincoln	1-1	x			x			x		x									x	x	x	x	x							x		
4	Dec 7	Nottm. Forest	0-1	x		x	x		x	x	x										x	x		x					x			x	x	
5	12	OCKBROOK	4-0 Owen 2, Cursham, unknown	x		x	x	x		x	x			x				x		x		x			x			x			x			
6	Jan 4	NOTTM. FOREST	0-0		x		x			x					x							x	x	x				x				x			
7	16	Sheffield	2-3 Widdowson 2	x	x	x	x								x	x					x		x	x	x									x
8	Feb 15	SHEFFIELD	1-0 Owen			x	x			x							x	x			x	x	x	x	x		x							x
9	22	LINCOLN	4-0 Cursham, Revis, Widdowson 2				x			x			x		x	x					x	x	x	x	x	x								x
10	Mar 17	LONDON	0-0			x	x			x		x							x	x		x	x	x										x
11	27	NOTTM. LAW CLUB	0-0					x	x		x	x	x							x		x	x							x	x			

All home games at Meadows Cricket Ground except 9, Trent Bridge
Played in game 3: JP Johnson
Played in game 6: S Morse, E Morse, H Greenhalgh, F Rayner

1873/74

				Allen	Ashwell HG	Ashwell F	Baillon AB	Bates AJ	Bright A	Bright J	Cursham AW	Cursham FC	Greenhalgh A	Greenhalgh EH	Hodges JC	Johnson J	Johnson WG	Marriott F	Morse E	Morse S	Owen JRB	Parr J	Pearson AH	Revis WH	Robinson WM	Rothera CL	Rothera FW	Seals G	Spencer CJ	Stafford CH	Steegman EB	Wake RG	Wardle CS	Widdowson SW
1	Oct 25	STOKE	2-0 Widdowson 2				x				x		x	x			x						x	x		x			x	x				x
2	Nov 1	Lincoln	0-0	x							x			x	x	x			x			x			x				x			x	x	
3	6	South Derbyshire	3-4 AW Cursham 2, Spencer			x	x	x	x				x								x		x	x	x				x					
4	20	NOTTM. LAW CLUB	0-2		x	x	x						x			x						x			x							x	x	
5	29	LONDON	2-0 Spencer, Robinson			x		x	x	x			x					x	x			x			x				x	x				
6	Dec 18	SAWLEY ATHLETIC	0-0			x		x	x			x	x								x	x			x	x		x						x
7	20	Newark	2-0 Spencer, one og	x	x	x																x				x	x	x						x
8	27	Nottm. Forest	1-1 EH Greenhalgh		x	x						x			x	x	x	x	x			x	x											
9	Jan 15	Sheffield	0-2			x		x	x			x			x				x			x			x	x	x							
10	Feb 7	NOTTM. FOREST	0-0			x		x	x	x		x						x	x		x	x			x									
11	16	London	0-4			x		x	x			x										x			x	x	x	x						x
12	18	London	1-1 Widdowson			x		x				x										x			x	x	x	x						x

Home games at Trent Bridge except 4, 6 at the Meadows
Played in game 4: Norris. In game 6, Forman. In game 7: J Forman, JR Forman.
Played in game 8: J Lambert. In game 11: T Lambert. In game 12: W Mason, H Davies.

1874/75

				Baillon AB	Bethel	Bright J	Chapman W	Cursham AW	Freeman	Goodyer AC	Greenhalgh EH	Greenhalgh H	Hadden JH	Hadden WJ	Jessop H	Johnson WG	Parr J	Power GE	Revis WH	Roberts	Robinson WM	Rothera CL	Rothera FW	Seals G	Smith JH	Spencer CJ	Wake RG	Widdowson SW
1	Nov 14	NOTTM. FOREST	0-0		x	x	x	x	x		x	x				x				x		x		x		x			
2	21	SHEFFIELD	0-3	x		x		x			x						x		x		x		x		x			x	x
3	Jan 14	Sheffield	2-1 EH Greenhalgh, Cursham				x	x			x				x		x		x				x		x		x		
4	21	Newark	7-0 EH Greenhalgh 2, Widdowson 2, Revis, Spencer, H Greenhalgh	x							x	x	x	x			x		x				x		x			x	x
5	30	Queen's Park	0-6					x			x	x	x				x		x	x			x			x		x	x
6	Feb 6	SHEFFIELD	1-0 og	x		x		x			x						x		x				x				x	x	x
7	9	Nottm. Forest	1-5 Parr	x						x	x	x	x	x		x	x				x	x	x						
8	Mar 8	QUEEN'S PARK	1-1 Widdowson				x	x			x				x				x				x			x	x		

Home games at Trent Bridge except 1, Meadows
Played in game 3: B Ashwell, T Lambert, J Whyat, AW Winfield.

1875/76

				Ashwell AT	Ashwell HG	Bates AJ	Caborn CJ	Chapman W	Cursham AW	Dobson WH	Dodson AT	Ellis D	Greenhalgh EH	Greenhalgh H	Greenhalgh RJ	Hadden WJ	Jessop H	Keely A	Keely EM	Lambert J	Lambert T	Parr J	Power GE	Revis WH	Rothera FW	Seals G	Steegman EB	Widdowson SW
1	Nov 13	Nottm. Forest	0-2																										
2	27	SHEFFIELD	0-0		x				x			x	x	x			x		x			x		x	x	x		x	
3	Dec 11	Derbyshire	1-1 Hadden		x		x					x	x	x	x									x	x	x			
4	16	Grantham	0-0		x								x	x										x	x				
5	Jan 6	GRANTHAM	2-0 Revis, HG Ashwell		x				x			x	x	x	x									x	x	x			
6	Feb 10	Sheffield	2-7 Ellis 2	x			x		x	x	x	x	x	x	x	x								x					
7	17	Derby Grammar School	1-0 Cursham						x	x			x	x	x							x							
8	24	Cambridge University	0-0							x		x	x	x	x		x							x	x				
9	29	NOTTM. FOREST	1-0 Cursham						x			x	x	x	x							x			x	x			

Home games at Trent Bridge except 5, Meadows
One player unknown in game 7

65

1876/77

						Ashwell F	Baillon AB	Cursham AW	Cursham CL	Davies W	Dobson AT	Dobson WH	Greenhalgh EH	Greenhalgh H	Greenhalgh RJ	Hadden WJ	Jessop H	Keely EM	Keely ER	Keely SW	Oliver TA	Parr G	Pearson WA	Potter S	Rothera FW	Seals G	Wake WR	Widdowson SW
1	Oct	7	Queen's Park	1-5	og			x					x	x	x	x	x	x	x	x		x		x		x		x	
2	Nov	18	Nottm. Forest	2-0	AW Cursham, one og		x	x					x	x	x	x	x	x	x		x				x	x		
3	Dec	16	NEWARK	4-1	Unknown		x	x	x	x	x	x		x	x		x		x				x			x		
4	Jan	27	MANCHESTER	2-0	RJ Greenhalgh, AW Cursham		x	x					x	x	x	x		x			x					x		x
5	Feb	1	Sheffield	3-7	AW Cursham 2, Oliver	x		x	x		x		x	x		x		x			x		x			x		
6		8	NOTTM. FOREST	1-1	Oliver		x	x					x	x	x	x	x	x			x	x				x		
7		24	Derby Grammar School	0-2			x	x	x	x			x	x	x	x	x	x			x					x		
8	Mar	17	SHEFFIELD	2-0	Hadden, H Greenhalgh	x		x					x	x	x	x		x			x					x		x

Home games at Trent Bridge except 6, Meadows

1877/78

						Baillon AB	Butler H	Corfield HA	Cursham AW	Cursham CL	Cursham HA	Dobson AT	Greenhalgh EH	Greenhalgh H	Greenhalgh RJ	Jessop H	Keely EM	Keely ER	Keely SW	Oliver TA	Pearson AH	Reckless S	Seals G	Widdowson SW
1	Oct	13	STOKE	4-1	HA Cursham 3, RJ Greenhalgh				x		x		x	x	x		x		x	x	x			x	x
2		25	NOTTM. LAW CLUB	5-6	Unknown	x							x	x	x		x		x	x	x		x	x	x
3	Nov	17	Queen's Park	1-6	EM Keely				x		x		x	x	x	x	x		x	x			x		
4	Dec	6	Soutwell	1-10	Reckless						x		x		x		x					x			
5		15	Manchester	6-0	HA Cursham 5, EM Keely	x			x	x	x	x	x		x		x	x		x		x			
6		20	Sheffield	1-2	HA Cursham				x	x	x	x			x		x	x	x	x					
7		22	Derbyshire	4-0	Unknown				x	x	x	x	x		x	x	x	x					x		
8	Jan	12	SOUTHWELL	4-0	Unknown				x		x	x	x	x	x	x	x	x							x
9		19	QUEEN'S PARK	1-2	AW Cursham				x	x	x	x	x	x	x	x	x	x							x
10	Feb	2	Stoke	1-0	Corfield		x	x	x	x	x	x	x	x	x			x							x
11		9	Manchester	4-1	CL Cursham. RJ Greenhalgh, HA Cursham, H Greenhalgh	x			x	x	x	x	x		x		x						x	x	
12		20	DERBY GRAMMAR SCHOOL	8-2	HA Cursham 4, Oliver, Seals, CL Cursham, AW Cursham	x			x	x	x		x		x						x			x	x
13		23	SHEFFIELD	7-0	CL Cursham 3, AW Cursham 2, HA Cursham, RJ Greenhalgh	x			x	x	x		x		x						x			x	x
14		28	NOTTM LAW CLUB	2-8	Dobson, Corfield			x				x	x									x	x		

Home games at Beeston except 9 (Trent Bridge).
Played in game 2: AH Pearson. In game 3: FW Rothera
Played in game 4: Hill, Jones, Warner, B Oldini, Johnson
Played in game 12: WH Scotton. In game 14: Harrison, Haughton, Neale, Russell, Smith

F.A. Cup

R1	Nov	3	SHEFFIELD	1-1	HA Cursham	1500			x	x		x	x	x	x	x						x	x		x	x
rep	Dec	1	Sheffield	0-3		1500				x	x	x	x	x	x	x	x			x			x			x

Home game at Trent Bridge.
Played in the replay: E Jessop

1878/79

						Ashwell F	Britten TJ	Cursham AW	Cursham CL	Cursham HA	Dobson AT	Grace GF	Greenhalgh EH	Greenhalgh H	Greenhalgh RJ	Jarrett RJ	Jessop E	Jessop H	Morse H	Owen Rev. JRB	Pearson AH	Seals G	Smythe A	Widdowson SW	Woodcock A
1	Oct	5	Stoke	0-1				x	x	x	x		x	x	x			x	x		x				
2		19	SHEFFIELD	8-0	RJ Greenhalgh 3, CL Cursham 2. HA Cursham 2, Seals				x	x	x		x	x	x			x	x		x		x		
3	Nov	9	Queen's Park	0-4				x	x	x	x		x	x	x			x	x		x		x		
4		23	Derby Grammar School	8-0	Unknown			x	x	x	x		x	x	x			x	x		x		x		
5		30	DERBYSHIRE	1-0	Oliver		x	x	x	x	x		x	x	x			x						x	
6	Dec	5	DERBYSHIRE	6-1	AW Cursham 2, HA Cursham 2, CL Cursham, E Jessop			x	x	x	x		x	x	x	x		x							
7		7	NEWARK	4-1	RJ Greenhalgh 2, Corfield 2	x		x					x		x			x			x				
8	Feb	1	QUEEN'S PARK	0-2		x		x	x		x		x		x			x			x				
9		8	GREY FRIARS	2-3	CL Cursham, Rev. JRB Owen				x		x	x	x		x	x		x		x	x		x		
10		20	Sheffield	4-2	Britten, Woodcock, unknown 2		x	x		x	x		x		x			x							x
11	Mar	8	STOKE	1-0	AW Cursham			x	x	x			x	x	x		x	x			x	x			

Games 2, 5, 8 and 9 at Trent Bridge. Games 6 and 11 at the Meadows. Game 7 at Beeston Cricket Ground. Game 5 played under floodlights.
Played in game 7: H Corfield, CJ Lewis, R Baillon, W Davies. In game 3: J. Lindon.

F.A. Cup

R1	Nov	16	NOTTM FOREST	1-3	Rev. JRB Owen	500		x	x	x	x		x	x	x			x	x		x		x		

Played at Beeston Cricket Ground

1879/80

#	Date		Opponent	Score	Scorers	Baillon JC	Bennett FT	Butler H	Chapman H	Cursham AW	Cursham CL	Cursham HA	Dobson AT	Dobson CF	Everall J	Greenhalgh EH	Greenhalgh H	Greenhalgh RJ	Horsley A	Jessop E	Jessop H	Lounds J	Morgan JR	Morse H	Oliver TA	Pearson D	Pearson WA	Seals G	Smythe EM
1	Oct	11	Derby Grammar School	2-0	Unknown						8	10	4								7			6	11	3	2	9	
2		25	Derbyshire	3-4	Unknown					8		10				2	1	9		7	3			6			4	9	
3	Nov	1	Sheffield	0-5						8		10				2	1		9	7	3			6	11			9	
4		15	Queen's Park	1-4	HA Cursham					8		10	4			9				7	3		2	6	11				5
5	Jan	17	Nottm. Forest	1-7	CL Cursham						8	10	4		9	2				7	3			6	11			1	
6	Feb	28	SHEFFIELD	2-3	CL Cursham, unknown				4	8	9					2	1			11	7			6		3		9	
7	Mar	6	GREY FRIARS	3-3	E Jessop 2, CL Cursham		7				9		4	8		2		9			11		10	3	6			1	
8		12	DERBY GRAMMAR SC.	2-2	RJ Greenhalgh, Bennett	4	7			6	5	2		3				10	9										

The players' positions were still somewhat flexible; thus two number 9s will be found in some of the games.
Home games at Trent Bridge except number 6, Beeston.
Played in game 1: Richards. One unknown player in game 3. Goalkeeper in game 4: SG Smith.
Played in game 5: V. Smith. Played in game 6: J Smith. Goalkeeper unknown in game 8. Played in game 8: A Orton (8), CL Maltby (11).

F.A. Cup

#	Date		Opponent	Score		Att					Cursham CL		Dobson AT		Everall J	Greenhalgh EH	Greenhalgh H			Jessop E	Jessop H		Morgan JR	Morse H	Oliver TA		Pearson WA	Seals G	Smythe EM
R1	Nov	8	Nottm. Forest	0-4		2000						10			9	1				7	3		2	6	11			9	4

Played at Trent Bridge. Played at no. 5: S Macrae.

1880/81

#	Date		Opponent	Score	Scorers	Bourne A	Chapman H	Cursham AW	Cursham CL	Cursham HA	Dobson AT	Dobson CF	Ellis D	Everall J	Greenhalgh EH	Greenhalgh H	Greenhalgh RJ	Jessop E	Jessop H	Lewis CJ	Macrae S	Maltby CL	Morse H	Oliver TA	Palmer S	Pearson WA	Stacey WH	Standing W	Willis W
1	Oct	16	Nottm. Forest	0-4				7	10	11					3				5	3	6		4		8	1			
2	Nov	6	QUEEN'S PARK	3-4	AW Cursham 2, HA Cursham		6	7	8	10	2		3			1					5		9	11	4				
3	Dec	11	SHEFFIELD	8-1	HA Cursham 5, Morse 3		6	7	8	10	2				4	1			3				9		5				11
4		18	STAVELEY	3-2	CL Cursham, HA Cursham, Morse		6	7	8	10	2				11	1			3		5		9		4				
5	Jan	8	NEWARK	15-1	* See below		6	7	8	10	2				11	1	4		3				9		5				
6		15	Blackburn Rovers	1-3	Morse		6	7	8	10	2				11	1			3				9		5		4		
7	Feb	5	BLACKBURN ROVERS	3-7	CL Cursham, HA Cursham 2		6	7	8	10	2	3			11	1					5		9		4				
8		19	Sheffield	4-2	AW Cursham, CL Cursham, Morse, one og		6	7	8	10	2	4		5	11				3				9				1		
9	Mar	5	NOTTM. FOREST	1-0	AW Cursham		6	7	8	10	2				11				3		5		9		4				
10		14	Staveley	1-1	CF Dobson	9	6	7	8	10	2	4			11				3	1					5				

Home games at the Castle Cricket Ground
Scorers in game 5: HA Cursham 5, EH Greenhalgh 3, Morse 2, CL Cursham, 2 og, 2 unknown
Played in game 1: Rev. AC Ratcliffe (at 9). In game 9, W Sorby (in goal)

F.A. Cup

#	Date		Opponent	Score	Scorers	Att	Bourne A	Chapman H	Cursham AW	Cursham CL	Cursham HA	Dobson AT	Dobson CF	Ellis D	Everall J	Greenhalgh EH	Greenhalgh H	Greenhalgh RJ	Jessop E	Jessop H	Lewis CJ	Macrae S	Maltby CL	Morse H	Oliver TA	Palmer S	Pearson WA	Stacey WH	Standing W	Willis W
R1	Nov	4	DERBYSHIRE	4-4	AW Cursham, HA Cursham 2, one unknown	500		6	7	8	11	2				4	1					5	10	9		9				
rep.		27	Derbyshire	4-2	HA Cursham 2, EH Greenhalgh, Morse	1700		6	7	8	10	2				11	1			3		5		9		4				
R3	Feb	12	ASTON VILLA	1-3	CL Cursham	4000		6	7	8	10	2				11	1			3		5		9		4				

Home games at Trent Bridge.
R1 replay after extra time. Notts had a bye in round 2.

1881/82

						Bausor T	Bourne B	Chapman H	Cursham AW	Cursham CL	Cursham HA	Danks T	Dobson AT	Dobson CF	Emmitt HW	Fletcher H	Greenhalgh EH	Gunn W	Jessop H	Maltby CL	Moore HT	Morse H	Oliver TA	Wilks J
1	Oct	1	Derby Midland	1-1	AW Cursham				8	7	11		2	6										10
2		8	Stoke	4-1	Unknown																			
3		22	Blackburn Rovers	1-10	Bausor			5	8	7	11		2	6			9					10	4	
4	Nov	10	GRANTHAM	13-0	Unknown	9		5	8	7	11		2	6		4	10		1		3			
5		12	STAVELEY	7-0	HA Cursham 4, CL Cursham 2, Bausor	9		5	8	7	11		2	6		4	10		1		3			
6		26	Queen's Park	1-10	CL Cursham	9		5	8	7	11		2			4	10		1	6	3			
7	Dec	3	Aston Villa	2-2	HA Cursham, unknown	9		5	8	7	11		2	6			10		1		3		4	
8		17	Nottm. Forest	5-0	Bausor 2, HA Cursham 2, Greenhalgh	9		5	8	7	11		2	6		4	10		1		3			
9	Jan	5	OLD CARTHUSIANS	5-1	Bausor 3, HA Cursham 2	9		5	8	7	11		2		4		10		1	6	3			
10		26	SHEFFIELD	5-1	HA Cursham 2, Bausor 2, Greenhalgh	9		5	8	7	11		2				10		1	6	3			
11		28	DERBY MIDLAND	7-2	HA Cursham 4, AW Cursham, Bausor, Greenhalgh	9	4	5	8	7	11	2					10		1		3			
12	Feb	4	Pilgrims	5-1	HA Cursham 4, Bausor	9		5	8	7	11		2				10		1		3	4		
13		6	Old Carthusians	0-4		9		5	8	7	11		2				10		1	6	3			
14		11	NOTTM. FOREST	1-2	CL Cursham	9		5	8	7	11		2	6			10		1		3	4		
15		18	STOKE	4-3	Bausor 2, Emmitt, Danks	9	1	5	8			11			6	4	10	2			3			7
16		21	Sheffield	5-0	Bausor, HA Cursham, 3 unknown	9	7	5	8		11				6	2	10		1		3			
17		25	QUEEN'S PARK	5-1	HA Cursham	9		5			11		2	6	4		10	7	1		3			

Home games at the Castle Cricket Ground
Played in game 1: Biddell (at 1), R Cursham (3), Dexter (4), Gawthorne (5), Simpkin (9). In game 3, CL Lewis (1), C Beardshaw (3). In game 10: W Sherlock (4).
Played in game 11: C Matthews (6). In game 12: ED Ellis (6). In game 13: JG Thompson (4). In game 16: H Shelton (4). In game 17: E Jessop (8).
Team details unknown for match 2.

F.A. Cup

							Bausor T	Bourne B	Chapman H	Cursham AW	Cursham CL	Cursham HA	Danks T	Dobson AT	Dobson CF	Emmitt HW	Fletcher H	Greenhalgh EH	Gunn W	Jessop H	Maltby CL	Moore HT	Morse H	Oliver TA	Wilks J
R2	Nov	24	WEDNESBURY STROLLERS	5-3	AW Cursham 2, HA Cursham 2, Knowles (og)		9		5	8	7	11		2	6		4	10		1		3			
rep	Dec	10	Wednesbury Strollers	11-1	HA Cursham 6, AW Cursham 2, CF Dobson, CL Cursham, Bausor		9		5	8	7	11		2	6	4		10		1		3			
R3		31	Aston Villa	2-2	Bausor 2	7000	9		5	8	7	11		2	6		4	10		1		3			
rep	Jan	7	ASTON VILLA	2-2	Chapman, AW Cursham	7000	9		5	8	7	11		2	6		4	10		1		3			
rep2		14	Aston Villa	1-4	HA Cursham	12000	9		5	8	7	11		2	6		4	10		1		3			

Round 1: Drawn v. Calthorpe; walk over.
Round 2 at the Castle Ground. Void game (not included in players' records) after protest. Replayed at Derby Cricket Ground
First game with Aston Villa after extra time (at 90 mins, 2-2)
R3 first replay at the Castle Ground, also after extra time (at 90 mins, 1-1)

1882/83

FA Cup Semi-finalists

						Bausor T	Billyeald H	Chapman H	Cursham AW	Cursham CL	Cursham HA	Dobson AT	Dobson CF	Emmitt HW	Gillet LF	Greenhalgh EH	Gunn W	Harker E	Jessop H	Macrae S	Moore AE	Moore HT	Seals G	Smith SG
1	Oct	5	LOCAL CLUBS XI	10-1	HA Cursham 6, Bausor 2, Gunn	11		6			9	2	4	5		10	7		1			3		
2		7	Aston Villa	2-1	HA Cursham 2	11		6	8		9	2	4			5	7		1			3		10
3		14	SHEFFIELD	8-1	Smith 2, HA Cursham 2, Gunn 2, AW Cursham	11		6	8		9	2	4			5	10		1			3		7
4		21	STOKE	5-0	HA Cursham 4, CF Dobson	11		6	8		9	2	4			5	10					3		7
5		28	LIVERPOOL RAMBLERS	3-1	HA Cursham 2, AW Cursham			6	8		9	2	4			11	10		1	5		3		7
6	Nov	11	BLACKBURN ROVERS	7-1	AW Cursham 3, Smith 2, Gunn, Greenhalgh			6	8		9	2	4			11	10			5		3		7
7		18	WALSALL	7-2	HA Cursham 2, Gunn 2, Smith, AW Cursham, CF Dobson			6	8		9	2	4			11	10		1	5		3		7
8		25	QUEEN'S PARK	1-3	Gunn			6	8		9	2	4				10	11	1	5		3		7
9	Dec	2	Wednesbury Old Athletic	1-5	Unknown			6	8	10	9	2	4					11		5		3		7
10		23	OLD CARTHUSIANS	2-0	Smith, HA Cursham			6	8		9	2	4		1	11	10			5		3		7
11		30	POLLOKSHIELDS ATH.	5-2	AW Cursham 2, Greenhalgh 2, E Jessop		1	6	8			2	4			11	10	5				3		7
12	Jan	13	WEDNESBURY OLD ATH.	6-1	HA Cursham 2, Gunn, AW Cursham, Smith, HT Moore			6	8		9	2	4		1	11	10			5		3		7
13		20	Nottm. Forest	1-1	HA Cursham			6	8		9	2	4			11	10			5		3	1	7
14		27	Queen's Park	4-5	AW Cursham 3, unknown			6	8		9	2	4	5	1	11	10					3		7
15	Feb	6	Sheffield	8-2	HA Cursham 4, Gunn, Beardshaw(og), Marsden(og), Wake(og)			6	8		9	2	4		1	11	10	7			5	3		
16		17	MITCHELL'S ST. GEORGE'S	10-0	HA Cursham 3, Gunn 2, Greenhalgh, CF Dobson, Smith, AW Cursham			6	8		9	2	4			11	10			5		3		7
17		24	DERBY MIDLAND	3-0	AE Moore, Smith, Snook			6				2	4	5		11	10		1		8			7
18	Mar	24	Stoke	5-1	Unknown			9			11					3	10				8			7

Home games at the Castle Ground except 5 (Meadows), 6, 8 and 11 (Trent Bridge). Game 13 also at Trent Bridge (Forest home match).
Team details incomplete for game 18. Unknown scorers in games 1, 3, 9 and 16.
Played in game 1: W Walker (8). In game 4: H Morse (1). In game 9, J Handford (1). In game 11: E Jessop(9). In game 17: JB Snook (9), T Fiddler (3).
Played in game 6: J Everall (1). In game 16: T Bloom (1).

F.A. Cup

							Bausor T	Billyeald H	Chapman H	Cursham AW	Cursham CL	Cursham HA	Dobson AT	Dobson CF	Emmitt HW	Gillet LF	Greenhalgh EH	Gunn W	Harker E	Jessop H	Macrae S	Moore AE	Moore HT	Seals G	Smith SG
R1	Nov	4	SHEFFIELD	6-1	AW Cursham 3, HA Cursham 2, Smith	3000			6	8		9	2	4			11	10		1	5		3		7
R3	Dec	27	PHOENIX BESSEMER	4-1	Gunn 2, AW Cursham, HA Cursham	3000			6	8		9	2	4			11	10			5		3	1	7
R4	Feb	12	Sheffield Wednesday	4-1	AW Cursham 2, HA Cursham, Smith	4000			6	8		9	2	4		1	11	10			5		3		7
R5	Mar	3	ASTON VILLA	4-3	HA Cursham 3, Gunn	10000			6	8		9	2	4		1	11	10			5		3		7
SF		17	Old Etonians	1-2	HA Cursham				6	8		9	2	4	3	1	11	10			5				7

Bye in round 2
Semi final played at Kennington Oval
R1 and R5 at Castle ground, R3 at the Meadows (Castle Ground flooded).

68

1883/84

FA Cup Semi-finalists

					Brown H	Chapman H	Cursham AW	Cursham HA	Dixon JA	Dobson AT	Dobson CF	Emmitt HW	Fidler A	Gunn W	Harker E	Jessop H	Macrae S	Moore AE	Moore HT	Scotton WH	Shelton C	Sherwin M	Smith SG	Snook FW	Snook JB	Woolley E
1	Sep	22	Stoke	1-1	Gunn		6	7	10		2	9	4		11			5			3				1	8		
2		29	WALSALL SWIFTS	4-2	AW Cursham, Gunn, CF Dobson, HA Cursham			7	9	10	2	4	3		11	6		5							1	8		
3	Oct	4	ATTERCLIFFE	6-2	HA Cursham 3, AT Dobson, AW Cursham, Gunn			7	9		2	4	3		11	8		5						1				6
4		6	WEDNESBURY OLD ATH.	3-0	Gunn, HA Cursham, Smith		6	7	9		2	4	3		11	10		5						1	8			
5		13	Blackburn Rovers	0-4			6		7		2	4	3		11	9		5		10				1	8			
6		20	Nottm. Forest	0-0				7	9		2	4	3		11	6		5	10					1	8			
7		27	SOUTH OF ENGLAND	6-1	Dixon 2, CF Dobson, HA Cursham 2, JB Snook		6		11	10	2	4	3		7	8		5						1			9	
8	Nov	3	BLACKBURN OLYMPIC	3-2	AW Cursham 2, Gunn		6	9	11	10	2	4			7		3	5						1	8			
9		5	Aston Villa	1-2	CF Dobson		6	9	11	10	2	4			7		3	5						1				
10		17	BRENTWOOD	3-2	HA Cursham 3			8	11	10	2	9	4		7	6		5			3			1				
11		24	SHEFFIELD	4-1	AW Cursham, CF Dobson, HA Cursham, one og		6	8	11	10	2	9	4		7			5			3			1				
12	Dec	15	PADIHAM	5-1	HA Cursham 4, CF Dobson		6	8	11		2	9	5		7	4					3			1				10
13		17	Sheffield	1-1	HA Cursham		6	8	11				5	2	7						3	4		1				10
14		22	LOCKWOOD BROS.	1-1	CF Dobson	6		8	11	10	2	9	5		7		1				3	4						
15		26	NOTTM. FOREST	5-1	CF Dobson 2, Dixon, HA Cursham, Hancock (og)		6	8	11	10	2	9	4		7						3		5	1				
16	Jan	5	DERBY MIDLAND	3-3	AW Cursham 2, CF Dobson		6	8	11	10	2	9	3		7			5			1							4
17		12	BOLTON ASSOC.	7-1	AW Cursham 2, Gunn 2, Macrae, Dixon, HA Cursham		6	8	11	10	2	9	4		7			5			3			1				
18		14	WEDNESBURY TOWN	4-0	Emmitt 2, Dixon, HA Cursham		6	8	11	10	2	9	5		7	4					3			1				
19		26	Sheffield Wednesday	0-0			6			10		9	5			8			7	3						2		11
20	Feb	16	STOKE	4-1	AW Cursham, Gunn, Dixon, HA Cursham	4	6	8	11	10		9	5		7		1				3					2		
21		23	ASTON VILLA	2-0	Emmitt, Chapman		6	8		10		9	4		11						3		5	1		2		
22		26	GREAT LEVER	4-1	HA Cursham 2, Gunn, CF Dobson		6	8	11	10	2	9			7	4					3		5	1				
23	Mar	8	Walsall Swifts	1-2	Unknown		6					5	2	7	4				8	3								11
24		26	Attercliffe	0-2			6					4	3		7					8									
25	Apr	3	QUEEN'S PARK	0-3			6	8	11	10		9	4		7			5			3			1		2		

All games at Trent Bridge except 25, Castle Ground (AW Cursham's benefit)
Played in game 3: Wilson (10)
Played in game 9: OG Wall (no. 8). In game 13: EH Greenhalgh (9)
Played in game 19: A Malpas (1), J Smith (4)
Played in game 21: E Jessop (7). In game 23: G Turner (1)
Played in games 23 and 24: H Jackson (9), JA Brown (10). Played in game 24: A Huskinson (1), J Everall (2), T Charles (5), H Matthews (11)

	Apps	2	20	20	21	16	18	23	22	2	24	12	4	14	4	16	3	3	19	6	3	2	6
	Goals		1	10	20	4	1	11	3		10			1					1				

F.A. Cup

							Brown H	Chapman H	Cursham AW	Cursham HA	Dixon JA	Dobson AT	Dobson CF	Emmitt HW	Fidler A	Gunn W	Harker E	Jessop H	Macrae S	Moore AE	Moore HT	Scotton WH	Shelton C	Sherwin M	Smith SG	Snook FW	Snook JB	Woolley E
R1	Nov	10	SHEFFIELD HEELEY	3-1	HA Cursham 3	4000		6	9	11	10	2	4	3					5						1	8		7
R2	Dec	1	NOTTM. FOREST	3-0	Dixon, AW Cursham, CF Dobson	10000		6	8	11	10	2	9	4		7			5			3			1			
R3		20	Grantham	4-1	HA Cursham 2, Macrae, AW Cursham	600		6	8	11	10	2		4		7			5			3			1		9	
R4	Jan	19	BOLTON WANDERERS	2-2	Macrae, AW Cursham	12000		6	8	11	10	2	9	4		7			5			3			1			
rep	Feb	2	Bolton Wanderers	2-1	CF Dobson 2	14496		6	8	11	10	2	9	4		7			5			3			1			
R5		9	SWIFTS	1-1	HA Cursham	11000		6	8	11	10	2	9	4		7			5			3			1			
rep		14	Swifts	1-0	HA Cursham	2500		6	8	11	10	2	9	4		7			5			3			1			
SF	Mar	1	Blackburn Rovers	0-1		15000		6	7	9	10	2	8	4		11			5			3			1			

Home games at Trent Bridge. Semi-final at Aston Lower Grounds, Birmingham. Round 4 and round 5 ties after extra time.

The team that played Blackburn Rovers in the FA Cup semi-final. Back: Ashwell (umpire), Dixon, Emmitt, Gunn, Harry Moore, Alf Dobson. Centre: Sherwin, Arthur Cursham, Macrae. Front: Charlie Dobson, Harry Cursham, Chapman

1884/85

#	Date		Opponent	Score	Scorers	Att	Brown HH	Brown JA	Chapman H	Cotterill WH	Coulby GA	Cursham HA	Daft HB	Danks T	Dixon JA	Dobson AT	Dobson CF	Emmitt HW	Fidler T	Gunn W	Harker E	Jackson H	Macrae S	Marshall AT	Moore AE	Moore HT	Shelton C	Sherwin M	Snook FW	Woolley E
1	Oct	2	DERBY COUNTY	3-1	Gunn, Dixon, Cursham	1500			6			11		8	10			5		7	4	9				3		1	2	
2		4	SHEFFIELD	6-2	Jackson 3, Cursham 2, Gunn	1500			6			11		8				5		7		9				3	4	1	2	
3		11	Blackburn Olympic	0-3		4000	11		6						10			5		7		9			8	3	4	1	2	
4		18	SHEFFIELD WEDNESDAY	0-0		2000			6					8	10	2	4	5		7	11	9				3		1		
5		25	DARWEN	2-0	Jackson, Danks	3000			6			11		8	10	2	4	5		7		9				3		1		
6	Nov	1	Sheffied Wednesday	1-0	AE Moore	2000	11		5		9	3	7		10		4								8	2				
7		13	CORINTHIANS	7-1	Marshall 3, Gunn 2, Jackson, Cursham				6			11			10	2	4	5		7		9		8		3		1		
8		15	BRENTWOOD	3-0	Jackson, Cursham, Marshall	2000			6			11			10	2	4	5		7		9		8		3		1		
9		22	NOTTS RANGERS	6-2	AE Moore 2, Cursham 2, Jackson, Marshall	2000			6			11				2	4	5		7		9		8	10	3				
10		27	Oxford University	2-1	Gunn 2				6			11			10	2		4		7		9		8		3	5	1		
11		29	BLACKBURN ROVERS	2-3	Gunn, Dixon	8000						11			10	2	4	6		7		9	5	8		3		1		
12	Dec	20	DERBY MIDLAND	8-0	Cursham 4, Jackson 2, Marshall 2	1000			6			11					4	5		7		9		8	10	3		1	2	
13		22	CORINTHIANS	3-2	Cursham 2, Jackson	2000			6			11					4	5		7		9		8		3		1	2	
14		26	NOTTM. FOREST	0-3		10000						11			10		4	6		7		9	5	8		3		1	2	
15		27	ACTON	5-0	Jackson 2, AE Moore, Cursham, Fidler	1000			6			11			10				5	7		9			8	3		1	2	
16		29	HENDON	8-2	* See below	1000		11	6			5			10		4	2	7					9	8	3		1		
17	Jan	10	WEDNESBURY OLD ATH.	5-0	JA Brown 2, Gunn, AE Moore, Cursham	1000		11				9			10		4	5		7					8	3		1	2	
18		17	BLACKBURN OLYMPIC	1-1	Gunn	6000		11	6						10		4	5		2		9		7	8	3		1		
19		31	Preston North End	2-3	Hay (og), Dixon	8000			6	2	1				10		4	5		7		9		11	8	3				
20	Feb	7	PRESTON NORTH END	2-1	AE Moore, Dixon	8000				1	11				10	2	4	6		7		9	5		8	3				
21		14	SWIFTS	3-1	Jackson, Dixon, Cursham	3000				1	11				10	2	4	6		7		9	5		8	3				
22	Mar	7	Sheffield	3-0	HH Brown, E Woolley, HB Daft		11	10	6	2			9				5		3						7					8
23		14	Bolton Wanderers	2-4	Jackson, E Woolley	8000	11		6	3		7					4	5		8		9				3				10
24		21	Blackburn Rovers	0-2		2000	11	10			1	5	9			2	4	6		7					8	3				
25		28	Notts Rangers	2-1	Gunn, Cursham	3000		11	6		1	9			10		4	5		7					8	3			2	
26	Apr	11	PRESTON NORTH END	1-2	Jackson	3000		8			1	11			10		4	6				9	5		7	3	2			
27		18	NOTTM. FOREST	3-2	Cursham 2, Gunn	6000					1	11			10		4	2		7		9	5		8	3	6			
28		25	Derby County	0-2				11							10		4	2	6						7	3	5			
					Apps		3	10	19	3	8	22	2	5	22	10	22	25	4	24	2	21	6	10	18	26	6	16	9	2
					Goals		1	3				19	1	1	7			1	11			15		8	6					2

Home games at Trent Bridge except 26 and 27 at the Castle Ground.
Game 25 was a Notts F.A. Cup semi final
(Forest scratched from final, so Notts won on a walk-over).
Scorers in game 16: AE Moore 3, Dixon 2, Gunn, Marshall, JA Brown
Played in game 2: B Wright of Glasgow Rangers (10). In game 6: WV Machin (1), J Stennet (6). In games 15 (at 6) and 22 (4): AE Scott. In 22, 23 and 28: J Woolley (1).
In game 9, R Simpkin (1). Only 10 men in game 17 (AT Marshall did not arrive). Played in game 23, W Topham (2). In game 28, JB Snook (9), CF Daft (8).

F.A. Cup

#	Date		Opponent	Score	Scorers	Att	Brown HH	Brown JA	Chapman H	Cotterill WH	Coulby GA	Cursham HA	Daft HB	Danks T	Dixon JA	Dobson AT	Dobson CF	Emmitt HW	Fidler T	Gunn W	Harker E	Jackson H	Macrae S	Marshall AT	Moore AE	Moore HT	Shelton C	Sherwin M	Snook FW	Woolley E
R1	Nov	8	NOTTS OLYMPIC	2-0	Dixon, Emmitt	2000			6			11			10	2	4	5		7	8	9				3		1		
R2	Dec	6	Staveley	2-0	Gunn, Cursham	2500						11			10	2	4	6		7		9	5	8		3		1		
R3	Jan	3	SHEFFIELD	5-0	*see below	5000						11			10		4	6		7		9	5	8		3		1	2	
R4		24	Walsall Swifts	4-1	Jackson 2, Gunn, JA Brown	5000		11	6						10		4	5		7		9			8	3		1		
R6	Feb	21	QUEEN'S PARK	2-2	Gunn, Cursham	17000				1	11				10	2	4	6		7		9	5		8	3				
rep		28	Queen's Park	1-2	Jackson	10000				1	11				10	2	4	6		7		9	5		8	3				

R6 replay at Derby Cricket Ground. Home games at Trent Bridge. Scorers in R3: CF Dobson, Gunn, Jackson, Cursham, Marshall. Played in R4: F Johnson (2). Bye in R5.

1885/86

#	Date		Opponent	Score	Scorers	Att	Brown HH	Brown JA	Butler F	Chapman H	Cotterill WH	Coulby GA	Cursham HA	Daft HB	Dobson CF	Emmitt HW	Gunn W	Harker E	Huskinson CJ	Jackson H	Lindley T	Macrae S	Marshall AT	Moore AE	Moore HT	Peters A	Shelton C	Shelton G	Sherwin M	Snook FW	Turner G	Wilson J
1	Sep	19	Lincoln	4-0	Cursham 2, Daft, Gunn								1	10	9	6	4	7		11	5			8	3					2		
2		26	Derby County	3-0	Jackson 2, Gunn	5000							1	10	11	6	4	7		9	5			8	3					2		
3	Oct	1	SHEFFIELD WEDNESDAY	6-1	AE Moore 3, Jackson 2, Daft	4000							1	10	11	6	4	7		9	5			8	3					2		
4		3	BRENTWOOD	3-0	AE Moore, Daft, Jackson	4000							1	10	11	6	4	7		9	5			8	3					2		
5		10	Queen's Park	1-5	Daft	5000	11	10			6	5	7	3	8				4	9										2		
6		10	WALSALL SWIFTS	0-1		1500										2	5	7		9				8	3			1				
7		17	PRESTON NORTH END	0-4		5000							1	10	11	6	4	7		9	5			8	3					2		
8		31	Blackburn Rovers	3-1	Jackson, Turner (og), Gunn	600					6	4		10	11		5	7		9				8	3	2		1				
9	Nov	7	BLACKBURN OLYMPIC	4-0	Cursham, AE Moore, Jackson 2	4000					6			10	11	4	5	7		9				8	3					1	2	
10		14	WEST BROMWICH ALB.	4-3	Cursham 3, Gunn	2000					6			10	11	4	5	7		9				8	3					1	2	
11		28	Nottm. Forest	4-1	Daft 2, Cursham, Jackson	8000								10	11	4	5	7		9	5			8	3					1	2	
12	Dec	5	OXFORD UNIVERSITY	6-0	Jackson 2, Daft 2, Cursham, Gunn	2000								10	11	4	5	7		9	5			8	3					1	2	
13		19	Sheffield	6-1	Jackson 3, JA Brown, Robinson (og)		11	10								4	6		7	9							5		8	1		
14		26	BOLTON WANDERERS	3-3	Cursham 2, Gunn	10000		9				4		10	11	6	5	7						8	3					1	2	
15		28	GREAT LEVER	1-3	Gunn	8000		9				4		10	11	6	5	7						8	3					1	2	
16	Jan	2	Preston North End	2-8	Jackson 2	7000						4				6	5	7		9				8	3					1	2	
17		9	BLACKBURN ROVERS	4-0	Daft 2, Jackson	4000								10	11		4	7		9	5			8	3	6				1	2	
18		16	NOTTM. FOREST	5-0	Cursham 3, Jackson, AE Moore	9000								10	11	6	4	7		9	5			8	3					1	2	
19		30	DERBY COUNTY	7-3	*See below	2000						4			11	6	5		7	9				8	3	2			10	1		
20	Feb	4	Wellingborough GS	11-3	Jackson 8, unknown 3			11				5	2			4	6		8	9					3		11					
21		6	Blackburn Olympic	0-0		2000						4			11	6	5	7		9				8	3	2			10			
22		13	ASTON VILLA	3-5	Gunn, Jackson, Jones (og)							4	6		11		5	7		9				8	3	2			10			
23		20	QUEEN'S PARK	1-0	Jackson						6			3	11	4		7		9	10	5	2	8							1	
24		20	Walsall Swifts	0-5						8		4					5	2							3							9
25		27	ACCRINGTON	3-2	Cursham 2, Jackson	2000								11			4		7	10	9		5	8	3	3	6				1	
26	Mar	6	Corinthians	0-7		2000								10	11	6	5	7		9			2	8	3	4				1		
27		9	Aston Villa	2-3	Dawson (og), one unknown									2	11	8	5		7	10	9				3	4						
28		13	Accrington	1-2	Jackson	2000			11	6	2						5			9					3	4						8
29		20	West Bromwich Alb.	0-3										2	11	6	5		7	10	9			8	3	4						
30		27	Sheffield Wednesday	1-1	Wilson (og)							2			11	6	5		7	9					3							
31	Apr	3	Bolton Wanderers	1-6	Jackson					8			1	2	7	6	5			11	9				3			10			
32		15	Derby County	1-4	Jackson								1	10	7	6	5		4	9	11		2	8	3							

Home games at Trent Bridge. Game 32 for the Derby County Charity Cup
Scorers in game 19: AE Moore 2, Jackson 2, Daft, Harker, G Shelton.
Played in games 5, 21, 22 and 24: J Woolley (at 1)
Played in game 6: T Danks (10), AE Scott (4), PH Richards (6), E Woolley (11)
Played in game 13: C West (2), J Bentley (3)
Played in game 20: GN Brown (10), JR Sands (1)
Played in games 27 to 30 inclusive: J Slater (at 1).
Played in game 24: Rose (11), Thompson (10), HJ Moore (6), CF Daft (7). In game 27: HA Morley (6)
Played in game 28: Dicks (7), Maltby (10). In game 30: J Housley (4). In game 31: Hibbert (4)

	Apps	2	5	3	6	11	10	24	26	24	30	20	10	6	28	2	11	3	24	29	11	2	5	13	15	3	2
	Goals		1					15	11			8	1		34				8					1			

Five own goals, four unknown

F.A. Cup

			Opponent	Score	Scorers	Att							Cursham HA	Daft HB	Dobson CF	Emmitt HW	Gunn W	Harker E		Jackson H	Lindley T			Moore AE	Moore HT					Snook FW	Turner G	
R1	Oct	24	ROTHERHAM TOWN	15-0	* See below	1500					6			10	11	4	5	7		9				8	3					1	2	
R2	Nov	21	SHEFFIELD	8-0	Gunn 3, Jackson 3, Cursham, Daft	3000					6			10	11	4	5	7		9				8	3					1	2	
R3	Dec	12	Notts Rangers	3-1	Cursham 3	3000								10	11	6	4	7		9	5			8	3					1	2	
R5	Jan	23	South Shore	1-2	Emmitt	3000								10	11	6	4	7		9	5			8	3					1	2	

Scorers in R1: Cursham 4, Jackson 3, AE Moore 2, Daft 2, Dobson, Emmitt, Gunn, Brown (og)
Bye in R4

1886/87

#	Date		Opponent	Score	Scorers	Att	Brown GH	Brown JA	Burton FE	Cotterill WH	Cursham HA	Daft HB	Dixon JA	Dobson CF	Emmitt HW	Harker E	Holland JH	Jackson H	Macrae S	Marshall AT	May E	May W	Moore AE	Morley HA	Morley W	Peters A	Spibey G	Spibey J
1	Oct	2	BRENTWOOD	2-0	Jackson, Harker	1000	6				4	3	11		5	7	1	9		2			8					
2		7	WALSALL TOWN	4-4	Moore, Jackson, Daft, W May				7	6	3		11		5		1	9		2		10	8			4		
3		9	STOKE	1-2	W May	1500	6		7		5		11		4		1	9		2		10	8	3				
4		16	SHEFFIELD	9-1	Jackson 4, Harker 2, Moore 2, Daft	1000				4	10	11		6	5	7	1	9		2			8	3				
5		23	DERBY COUNTY	3-6	Harker, Jackson, Daft	3000					10	11		6	4	7	1	9	5	2			8	3				
6		25	Blackburn Olympic	3-4	Cursham 2, one unknown		6				10				5		1	9					8	3		4	11	
7	Nov	6	Preston North End	0-14					11	7	6	10			5		1	9		2			8	3		4		
8		27	Accrington	0-8		2000	6			7	4				5		1									3	11	
9	Dec	4	DERBY MIDLAND	3-2	Cursham, Daft, Burton				7		10	11		6	5	4	1	9		2			8	3				
10		16	CORINTHIANS	1-1	Emmitt	2000			9		10	11		6	4	7	1		5				8	3	2			
11		18	WOLVES	3-1	Daft 2, Jackson	3000					10	11		6	5	7	1	9		2			8	3				4
12		27	NOTTM. FOREST	0-2							10	11		6	4	7	1	9	5	2			8	3				
13	Jan	15	LOCKWOOD BROS.	11-0	* See below	1500					10	11		6	5	7	1	9		2			8	3				4
14		22	WEST BROMWICH ALB.	3-1	Jackson 2, Emmitt	4000					10	11		6	5	7	1	9		2			8	3				4
15	Feb	5	MITCHELLS ST. GEORGES	5-0	Cursham 3, Harker, Morley	2000					10	11		6	5	7	1	9		2			8	3				4
16		12	Nottm. Forest	2-1	Cursham 2	10000					10	11		6	4	7	1	9	5	2			8	3				
17		22	BLACKBURN ROVERS	2-2	Moore, Jackson	2000					10	11		6	5	7	1	9					8	3	2			4
18		26	ASTON VILLA	1-3	Moore	3000					11	9		6	5	4	1			2		7	10	3				
19	Mar	7	Derby County	3-3	Cursham, Daft, W May						11	9			5	4	1				8	7		2			3	6
20		12	Stoke	1-4	W May					10	11	9			5	4	1				8	7		2			3	6
21		19	NOTTM. FOREST	1-1	Cursham	3000				8	10	9		6	5	7	1			2				3				4
22		21	Sheffield	4-1	Burton, W May, GN Brown, one unknown		4	11	9		3				5		1				8	7		2				
23		26	Queen's Park	2-5	Cursham, Daft		6				10	9			5	4	1			2	8	7		3				
24		28	Hibernian	0-6			6					9			5	4	1			2	8	7		3				
25		31	PRESTON NORTH END	2-3	Burton, Bakewell				9				8	6	4		1		5		10	11		3	2			
26	Apr	2	Wolverhampton Wan.	0-2				9						6	4		1			2	7					3		
27		9	Derby County	0-3									11		5		1				8	9		3			6	4
28		11	Aston Villa	1-10	Maltby					11	10				4		1			3		7				2		6
29		16	Nottm. Forest	1-3	Daft	2000				8		11		6	5	7	1		9	2			10	3		4		
					Apps		7	3	12	5	23	21	2	16	29	19	29	15	6	20	8	11	18	24	3	7	5	10
					Goals		1		3		15	11			2	6		14			5	5	5	1				

Scorers in game 13: Jackson 3, Cursham 2, Daft 2, Dobson, Harker, Spibey and Salkeld (og)
All games at Trent Bridge except game 21, Castle Ground.
Games 21 and 29 were the Notts F.A. Cup semi-final.
One own goal, two unknown, three by players in footnote

Played in game 6: J Carlin (2).
Played in games 8 and 24: Reddish (at 10).
Played in game 1: Wilson (3). In game 6, Warrell (7). In game 8: Oliver (2), Spencer (8), Webb (9).
Played in game 18, A Gill (8). In game 20: F Geary (10). In game 21, C Huskinson (11).
Played in game 22: A Shepherd (6), GN Brown (10). In game 25: GH Bakewell (7). In game 26, Stevens (10), Thorpe (11), Rouse (8).
Played in game 27: A Shaw (10), ES Wardle (7), L Wright (2). In games 23 and 24: A Shulcer (at 11).
Played in game 28: A Shepherd (5), JT Marshall (8), Maltby (9).

F.A. Cup

Rd	Date		Opponent	Score	Scorers	Att	Brown GH	Brown JA	Burton FE	Cotterill WH	Cursham HA	Daft HB	Dixon JA	Dobson CF	Emmitt HW	Harker E	Holland JH	Jackson H	Macrae S	Marshall AT	May E	May W	Moore AE	Morley HA	Morley W	Peters A	Spibey G	Spibey J
R1	Oct	30	BASFORD ROVERS	13-0	Daft 5, Burton 5, Jackson, Cursham, Slater(og)	800	3		7		10	11		6	5	4	1	9		2			8					
R2	Nov	13	NOTTS RANGERS	3-3	Jackson, Cursham, Burton				7	4	10	11			5	6	1	9		2			8	3				
rep		20	NOTTS RANGERS	5-0	Cursham 3, Jackson, Burton	5000			7		10	11		6	5	4	1	9		2			8	3				
R3	Dec	11	Staveley	3-0	Jackson 2, Cursham	3000					10	11		6	4	7	1	9	5	2			8	3				
R5	Jan	29	GREAT MARLOW	5-2	Cursham 3, Jackson, Speller (og)	8000					10	11		6	4	7	1	9	5	2			8	3				
R6	Feb	19	WEST BROMWICH ALB.	1-4	Cursham	15067					10	11		6	4	7	1	9	5	2			8	3				

Bye in Round 4

1887/88

#	Date		Opponent	Score	Scorers	Att	Brown GH	Brown GN	Brown HH	Brown JA	Clements JE	Cursham HA	Daft HB	Dixon JA	Dobson CF	Emmitt HW	Gunn W	Harker E	Holland JH	Jackson H	Lovegrave WF	Marshall IT	May W	Moore AE	Moore HT	Morley HA	Shepherd A	Snook HD	Stevens H	Warburton BF	Wardle ES
1	Sep	17	Walsall Town	0-4					11	10						5			1	9			4	8	3						7
2		24	Stoke	1-3	Dixon							10	11	8	6	4	7		1	9					3	2					
3	Oct	1	LEEK	8-1	JA Brown 4, Jackson 2, Gunn, Daft	good				10			11		6	5	7	4	1	9				8	3	2					
4		3	West Bromwich Albion	1-5	Jackson		6			10						5	7		1	9		11	8		3	2					
5		6	MITCHELL'S ST GEORGE	5-2	Jackson 3, Gunn, Daft	fair	6						11			5	7	4	1	9		10			3	2					
6		8	EVERTON	1-1	Jackson	1500	6		11	10						5	7	4	1	9				8	3						
7		22	ASTON VILLA	8-2	JA Brown 4, Jackson 2, Gunn, Emmitt	3000	6			10			8		11	5	7	4	1	9					3	2					
8		29	Blackburn Rovers	4-4	Wilkinson 2, Jackson, Daft		6						11			4	7	8	1	10					3	2	5				
9	Nov	5	PRESTON NORTH END	2-3	Jackson, JA Brown	7000	6			10			11	8		5	7	4	1	9					3	2					
10		19	GRIMSBY TOWN	4-0	Cursham 2, Gunn, Daft	2000	6			10		8	11		4	5	7		1	9					3	2					
11	Dec	3	Nottm. Forest	1-0	Daft	good	6			10		2	11	8		5	7	4	1	9					3						
12		10	BLACKBURN ROVERS	4-2	Jackson 3, Gunn	2000	6			10	5	3	11			4	7	8	1	9						2					
13		12	Mitchell's St George	0-10						10	3	2	11			5	7		1	9								6		8	
14		17	Preston North End	2-5	Daft, JA Brown	4000	6	8		10	5	2	11			4	7			9					3						
15		17	Leek	1-2	Marshall				11												9				3		5		10		
16		22	CORINTHIANS	1-4	Daft	fair	6			10		2	11	8			7	4	1	9					3						
17		26	NOTTM. FOREST	0-0		12000	6			10		2	11	8			7	4	1	9					3						
18		31	WALSALL SWIFTS	4-0	Daft 2, Ackroyd, Sheriston	1000	6					2	11			4	7		1	9	8				3						
19	Jan	7	Grimsby Town	3-4	Daft 2, Lovegrove	4000	6						11			4	7		1	9	8				3	2					
20		14	WEST BROMWICH ALB.	3-3	Daft 2, Jackson		6					3	11	7				4	1	9	8										
21		21	NOTTS RANGERS	0-8		2000	6	7				3	11					4	1	9	8										
22		28	CHURCH	6-0	Jackson 3, Gunn 2, Dixon			7				3		10		5	7		1	9	8							2		4	
23	Feb	4	STOKE	2-1	Jackson, Daft		6					3	11			5			1	9	10	8						2	7	4	
24		11	HALLIWELL	1-4	Wardle	small		8	11											9								3				7
25		11	Queen's Park	2-2	Harker, Gunn	1000	6						2	11			7	8	1	9		8			3				5		
26		14	BOLTON WANDERERS	0-3		4000	6									5	10	7	1	9		8			3			2	11	4	
27		18	DERBY COUNTY	2-3	Emmitt, Marshall	good	6			10			3			5	7		1	9		8						2	11	4	
28	Mar	5	Sheffield Wednesday	4-3	Geary 2, Daft, Hodder	1500					3		11			4	7		1	8				2	6			5			
29		10	Everton	1-3	Gunn							10	6			4	7		1	9					3		5	8			
30		17	Long Eaton Rangers	1-5	Harker	1000						2	11			6	7	10	1	9					3	5				4	8
31		24	Halliwell	0-7		3500			10				11			5	7		1	9					3				8	6	
32		31	Derby County	0-3		2000	5					2	11			6	7	10	1	9					3					4	8
33	Apr	7	Aston Villa	3-3	Wardle 2, Weightman							2				4	10		1	9							5			6	7
			Apps				21	4	6	14	5	19	24	7	3	26	27	16	30	30	3	10	3	4	20	13	7	5	7	10	5
			Goals							10		2	15	2		2	9	2		19	1	2									3

All home games at Trent Bridge.

Played in game 1: Maltby (6). In game 2, H Knight (5)
Played in games 1 and 6 (at 2) and 4 (at 4): A Peters.
Played in game 5, FE Burton (8). In game 8: Wilkinson (9). In game 13, EC Princip (4). In game 14: M Sherwin (1)
Played in game 15: JR Sands (1), G Spibey (2), J Spibey (3), C Hibbert (4), WH Cotterill (6), Neal (7), A Shelton (8)
Played in 16: W Sadler (5). In game 17: C Shelton (5). In games 20 and 21: AT Marshall (2). In game 22, J Plackett (6).
Played in games 18 to 21 inclusive: W Sheriston (at 5), J Ackroyd (at 10).
Played in game 24: W Sadler (5), M Sherwin (1), WH Cotterill (4), A Shelton (6), W Topham (2), Oliver (10).
Played in game 25: T Robertson, of Cowlairs (4). In game 28, F Geary (9), W Hodder (10). In game 29; Oliver (2).
Played in game 31: F Spibey(2), J Spibey(4). In game 33, EC Princip (8), FH Guttridge (3), Weightman (11)

Six goals scored by players listed in footnote

F.A. Cup

#	Date		Opponent	Score	Scorers	Att																									
R1	Oct	15	LINCOLN RAMBLERS	9-0	AE Moore 3, Daft 3, Jackson 2, Gunn					10			11		6	5	7	4	1	9				8	3	2					
R2			Basford Rovers	wo																											
R3	Nov	26	Nottm. Forest	1-2	Gunn	11500	5			10			8	11		4	7	6	1	9					3	2					

R1 played at Trent Bridge by arrangement

1888/89

11th in The Football League

#	Date		Opponent	Score	Scorers	Att	Allin T	Brown GH	Clements JE	Cursham HA	Daft HB	Dobson CF	Emmitt HW	Galbraith	Guttridge FH	Harker E	Hodder W	Holland JH	Jackson H	Jardine R	May E	May W	McLean T	Moore AE	Shaw AF	Shelton A	Shelton C	Sherwin M	Snook HD	Warburton BF	Wardle ES	Widdowson TH
1	Sep	15	Everton	1-2	Moore	7000		4							2	8	7	1		9			3	10		6				5	11	
2		22	Stoke	0-3		3000		4			8				3		7	1	11	9			2	10		6	5					
3		29	Aston Villa	1-9	Coulton(og)	4000					8				2		10	1					3	9		6	5					
4	Oct	6	BLACKBURN ROVERS	3-3	Daft, Jardine, Moore	4000	9	4		2	10				3		7	1		11				8		6	5					
5		13	EVERTON	3-1	Daft, Jardine, Moore	3000	9	4		2	10				3		7	1		11				8		6	5					
6		20	West Bromwich Alb.	2-4	Allin 2	2000	9	4		2	10				3		7	1		11				8		6				5		
7		27	BURNLEY	6-1	Jardine 5, Daft	4000	9	4	3		10				2		7	1		11				8		6	5					
8	Nov	3	PRESTON NORTH END	0-7		7000	9	4	3		10				2		7			11				8		6	5					
9		10	ACCRINGTON	3-3	Daft, Jardine, C Shelton	8000				2	10				3	4	7			11			9	8		6	5	1				
10		24	STOKE	0-3		2000		4		2	10				3		7	1		11			9	8		6	5					
11	Dec	8	ASTON VILLA	2-4	Jardine, Weightman	2000	9	4				5								11				6	8			3				1
12		15	Blackburn Rovers	2-5	Brown, Hodder	4000		4	3		11			9	2		7						10	8	5	6						1
13		22	Derby County	2-3	Daft, Hodder	2500		4	3	9	10				2		7						11	8		6	5					1
14		29	Burnley	0-1							10	4		3			7		9	8	11		5			6						1
15	Jan	5	Preston North End	1-4	Daft	4000			3		10	4		9			7						8	11	2	6	5					1
16		12	WEST BROMWICH ALB.	2-1	Cursham, Hodder	2000		4	3	9	10						7						8	11	2	6	5					1
17		19	WOLVERHAMPTON W.	3-0	May 2, Cursham	3000		4	3	9	10						7						8	11	2	6	5					1
18		26	Accrington	2-1	Daft, McLennan(og)	5000		4	3		10				9		7						8	11	2	6	5					1
19	Feb	23	Wolverhampton Wand.	1-2	Jackson	4000		4	3					5			7	10	9	8	11		2			6						1
20	Mar	5	BOLTON WANDERERS	0-4		3000		4	3		9				2		7			8	11					10	6	5				1
21		9	Bolton Wanderers	3-7	Jackson, May, one unknown	3000		4	3		9		5		2		7		10	8	11					6						1
22		16	DERBY COUNTY	3-5	Bailey, Daft, Jackson	5000		4	3		11						8		10		2					6	5				7	1
			Apps				6	19	12	8	19	1	4	1	17	2	20	9	5	18	11	4	12	10	2	21	15	1	1	2	2	12
			Goals				2	1			2	8					3		3	9	3			3			1						

Games 20 and 22 played at the Castle Ground.

Two own goals, one unknown, two by players in footnote

Played in game 3: W Gunn (no. 7), JA Brown (11). Played in game 8: HG Owen (1).
Played in game 11: T Cooke (7), F Weightman (10, one goal). In game 22: F Bailey (9, one goal).
Played in games 11 and 14: HA Morley (2).

F.A. Cup

#	Date		Opponent	Score	Scorers	Att	Allin T	Brown GH	Clements JE	Cursham HA	Daft HB	Dobson CF	Emmitt HW	Galbraith	Guttridge FH	Harker E	Hodder W	Holland JH	Jackson H	Jardine R	May E	May W	McLean T	Moore AE	Shaw AF	Shelton A	Shelton C	Sherwin M	Snook HD	Warburton BF	Wardle ES	Widdowson TH
Q1	Oct	6	ECKINGTON	4-1	Jackson, Emmitt, Marshall 2	2000						6	5		4				9							1	3	2	7			
Q2		27	BEESTON ST. JOHN'S	4-2	Harker, HH Brown 2, Marshall	2000						6			10											1	2	5	7			
Q3	Nov	17	DERBY MIDLAND	2-1	Daft, Harker	1500		4		2	10	5			11		1	9					8	6			3		7			
Q4	Dec	8	Staveley	3-1	Cursham, Daft, Wardle	2000		3	9	10	4	2					11			8			6	5					7			
R1	Feb	2	OLD BRIGHTONIANS	2-0	C Shelton, Moore	3000		4	3		10				7					11	2		8			6	5					1
R2		16	Sheffield Wednesday	2-3	A Shelton, FW Snook	10000		4	3		10						7		9	11	2					6	5					1

Played in game Q1: JT Marshall (no. 8, 2 goals), H Stevens (10), HH Brown (11).
Played in game Q2: H Stevens (3), WH Cotterill (4), JT Marshall (8, 1goal), GN Brown (9), HH Brown (11, 2 goals).
Q1 and Q2 games played by the reserve team before the League game on the same day.
FW Snook played in Round 1 (at 9) and Round 2 (at 8).

		p	w	d	l	f	a	pts
1	Preston North End	22	18	4	0	74	15	40
2	Aston Villa	22	12	5	5	61	43	29
3	Wolverhampton Wan.	22	12	4	6	51	37	28
4	Blackburn Rovers	22	10	6	6	66	45	26
5	Bolton Wanderers	22	10	2	10	63	59	22
6	West Bromwich Alb.	22	10	2	10	40	46	22
7	Accrington	22	6	8	8	48	48	20
8	Everton	22	9	2	11	35	47	20
9	Burnley	22	7	3	12	42	62	17
10	Derby County	22	7	2	13	41	61	16
11	NOTTS COUNTY	22	5	2	15	40	73	12
12	Stoke	22	4	4	14	26	51	12

William Britain, well-known for its range of toy soldiers, also produced sets of model footballers for each of the twelve founder members of the Football League. This is the Notts set, placed in front of a modern Subbuteo goal.

1889/90

10th in The Football League

							Calderhead D	Clements JE	Daft HB	Ferguson A	Lindley T	May E	McInnes T	McLean T	McMillan G	Oswald, James	Oswald, John	Sharpe JW	Shaw AF	Shelton A	Smith AW	Smith, William	Toone G	Walkerdine H	Wilkinson F
1	Sep	7	Wolverhampton Wand.	0-2		4000		2	11	4		10		5	3	9	8			6		7	1		
2		14	Aston Villa	1-1	James Oswald	6500	5		11	4		10		2	3	9	8			6		7	1		
3		21	WEST BROMWICH ALB.	1-2	W Smith	4000	5		11	4		10		2	3	9	8			6		7	1		
4		28	Derby County	0-2		4000	5		11	4				2	3	9	8	10		6		7	1		
5	Oct	5	STOKE	3-1	James Oswald 2, Daft	3000	5		11	4		8		2	3	9	10			6		7	1		
6		12	Accrington	8-1	* see below	1500	5		11	4		8		2	3	9	10			6		7	1		
7		19	EVERTON	4-3	W Smith 2, May, James Oswald	6000	5		11	4		8		2	3	9	10			6		7	1		
8		26	Bolton Wanderers	4-0	James Oswald 2, John Oswald, OG	5000	5		11	4		8		2	3	9	10			6		7	1		
9	Nov	2	BURNLEY	1-1	James Oswald	1000	5		11	4		8		2	3	9	10			6		7	1		
10		9	ASTON VILLA	1-1	Daft	4000	5		11	4	9	8		2	3		10			6		7	1		
11		16	Blackburn Rovers	1-9	John Oswald	6000	5	9	11	4		8		2	3		10			6		7	1		
12	Dec	7	Everton	3-5	Daft, James Oswald, W Smith	5000	5		11	4		8		2	3	9	10			6		7	1		
13		14	WOLVERHAMPTON W.	0-2		3000	5		11	4			8	2	3	9	10		7	6			1		
14		21	DERBY COUNTY	3-1	James Oswald 2, John Oswald	3000	5		11	4			8	2	3	9	10		7	6			1		
15	Jan	4	West Bromwich Alb.	1-5	Daft, McInnes	1500	5		11	4		9	8	2	3		10			6			1	7	
16		11	BOLTON WANDERERS	3-5	Daft 2, James Oswald	4000			11	4			8	2	3	9	10			6			1	7	5
17	Feb	18	BLACKBURN ROVERS	1-1	John Oswald	4000	5		11		9	7		2	3	8	10			6	4		1		
18	Mar	1	Preston North End	3-4	Calderhead 2, James Oswald	3000	5		11	4		7		2	3	9	10			6		8	1		
19		13	ACCRINGTON	3-1	Daft, W Smith 2	2000	5		11			8		2	3	9	10			6	4	7	1		
20		15	Burnley	0-3			5			6		8	7	2	3	9	10	11			4		1		
21		24	Stoke	1-1	James Oswald	2500	5			6		8	7	2	3	9	10	11			4		1		
22		27	PRESTON NORTH END	0-1		3000	5			4		11	8	2	3	9	10			6		7	1		

*Scorers in game 6: James Oswald 2, Daft 3, John Oswald 2, W Smith
Games 3, 19, 22 at the Castle Ground

	Apps	20	2	19	20	2	18	7	22	22	19	22	3	2	20	4	15	22	2	1
	Goals	2		10			1	1			15	6					7			

One own goal

F.A. Cup

							Calderhead D	Clements JE	Daft HB	Ferguson A	Lindley T	May E	McInnes T	McLean T	McMillan G	Oswald, James	Oswald, John	Sharpe JW	Shaw AF	Shelton A	Smith AW	Smith, William	Toone G	Walkerdine H	Wilkinson F
R1	Jan	18	Birmingham St. George's	4-4	John Oswald 2, Daft, McInnes	12000	5	3	11	4		8	7	2		9	10			6			1		
rep		25	BIRM. ST. GEORGE'S	6-2	McInnes 2, May 2, Daft, John Oswald	large	5		11	4		8	7	2	3	9	10			6			1		
R2	Feb	1	ASTON VILLA	4-1	May 3, James Oswald	3000	5		11	4		8	7	2	3	9	10			6			1		
R3		15	Sheffield Wednesday	0-5		6500	5		11	4		8	7	2	3	9	10			6			1		
rep		22	Sheffield Wednesday	3-2	Daft, John Oswald, W Smith	14000	5		11	4		8		2	3	9	10			6		7	1		
rep2	Mar	3	Sheffield Wednesday	1-2	McInnes	8000			11	4	9	8	7	2	3					6		10	1		

Played in R3 rep. 2: C Hibbert (no. 5)
R3 and R3 replay both replayed after protest. R3 rep. 2 at Derbyshire Cricket Ground.

		p	w	d	l	f	a	pts
1	Preston North End	22	15	3	4	71	30	33
2	Everton	22	14	3	5	65	40	31
3	Blackburn Rovers	22	12	3	7	78	41	27
4	Wolverhampton Wan.	22	10	5	7	51	38	25
5	West Bromwich Alb.	22	11	3	8	47	50	25
6	Accrington	22	9	6	7	53	56	24
7	Derby County	22	9	3	10	43	55	21
8	Aston Villa	22	7	5	10	43	51	19
9	Bolton Wanderers	22	9	1	12	54	65	19
10	NOTTS COUNTY	22	6	5	11	43	51	17
11	Burnley	22	4	5	13	36	65	13
12	Stoke	22	3	4	15	27	69	10

1890/91

3rd in The Football League, FA Cup Finalists

#		Date	Opponent	Score	Scorers	Att	Calderhead D	Cursham HA	Daft HB	Ferguson A	Gunn W	Hendry J	Locker W	Lyle D	McGregor AC	McInnes T	McLean T	Osborne AW	Oswald, James	Shelton A	Shelton C	Thraves J	Toone G
1	Sep	6	Bolton Wanderers	2-4	McInnes, ANO	6000	5		11			3	10		7	8	2	4	9	6			1
2		13	Aston Villa	2-3	Locker, McGregor	6000	5		11			3	10		7	8	2	4	9	6			1
3		20	ACCRINGTON	5-0	Oswald 3, Locker, A Shelton		5		11			3	10		7	8	2	4	9	6			1
4		22	Wolverhampton Wand.	1-1	Osborne	4000	5		11			3	10		7	8	2	4	9	6			1
5		27	DERBY COUNTY	2-1	McGregor, McInnes	6000	5		11			3	10		7	8	2	4	9	6			1
6	Oct	2	BOLTON WANDERERS	3-1	Calderhead, McInnes, Oswald	6000	5		11			3	10		7	8	2	4	9	6			1
7		11	WEST BROMWICH ALB.	3-2	Daft, McGregor, Oswald	8000	5		11			3	10		7	8	2	4	9	6			1
8		18	West Bromwich Alb.	1-1	McInnes	7367	5		11			3	10		7	8		4	9	6	2		1
9		25	Accrington	2-3	Locker, Daft	4000	5		11			3	10		7	8		4	9	6	2		1
10	Nov	1	EVERTON	3-1	Daft, McGregor, McInnes	13000	5		11			3	10		7	8	2	4	9	6			1
11		8	Preston North End	0-0		4000	5		11			3	10		7	8	2	4	9	6			1
12		15	BLACKBURN ROVERS	1-2	Oswald	11000	5		11			3	10		7	8	2	4	9	6			1
13		22	WOLVERHAMPTON W.	1-1	Locker	3000	5		11	6		3	10		7	8	2	4	9				1
14		29	ASTON VILLA	7-1	Locker 3, Oswald 3, McInnes	4000			11			3	10		7	8	2	4	9	6	5		1
15	Dec	6	PRESTON NORTH END	2-1	Locker, Oswald	10000	5		11			3	10		7	8	2	4	9	6			1
16		15	SUNDERLAND	2-1	Daft, Locker	8000	5		11			3	10		7	8	2	4	9	6			1
17		20	Burnley	1-0	Oswald	5000	5		11			3	10		7	8	2	4	9	6			1
18		27	Derby County	1-3	Locker	1000	5		11			3	10		7	8	2	4	9	6			1
19	Jan	3	Everton	2-4	Locker, one og	13000	5		11		2	3	10		7	8		4	9	6			1
20		24	Sunderland	0-4		5000	2					3	11	10	7	8		4	9	6	5		1
21	Feb	10	BURNLEY	4-0	McGregor 2, McInnes, Oswald	4000	5	2	11			3			10	7	8	4	9	6		1	
22	Mar	14	Blackburn Rovers	7-1	Daft 2, McGregor 2, Oswald 2, Locker	6000	5		11	2		3	10		7	8		4	9	6		1	
			Apps				21	1	21	2	1	22	21	2	22	22	16	22	22	21	4	2	20
			Goals				1		6				12		8	7		1	14	1			

Game 3 at the Castle Ground

One own goal, one unknown

F.A. Cup

		Date	Opponent	Score	Scorers	Att	Calderhead D	Cursham HA	Daft HB	Ferguson A	Gunn W	Hendry J	Locker W	Lyle D	McGregor AC	McInnes T	McLean T	Osborne AW	Oswald, James	Shelton A	Shelton C	Thraves J	Toone G
R1	Jan	17	Sheffield United	9-1	McGregor 4, Oswald 2, Daft, Locker, McInnes	9000	5		11			3	10		7	8	2	4	9	6			1
R2		31	BURNLEY	2-1	Daft 2	8000	5		11		2	3	10		7	8		4	9	6		1	
R3	Feb	14	STOKE	1-0	Locker	12000	5		11			3	10		7	8	2	4	9	6		1	
SF		28	Sunderland	3-3	McGregor, McInnes, Oswald	25000	5	2	11			3	10		7	8		4	9	6		1	
rep	Mar	11	Sunderland	2-0	Oswald 2	16000	5		11			3	10		7	8	2	4	9	6		1	
F		21	Blackburn Rovers	1-3	Oswald	23000	5		11	2		3	10		7	8		4	9	6		1	

SF and replay at Bramall Lane, Final at Kennington Oval

		p	w	d	l	f	a	pts
1	Everton	22	14	1	7	63	29	29
2	Preston North End	22	12	3	7	44	23	27
3	NOTTS COUNTY	22	11	4	7	52	35	26
4	Wolverhampton Wan.	22	12	2	8	39	50	26
5	Bolton Wanderers	22	12	1	9	47	34	25
6	Blackburn Rovers	22	11	2	9	52	43	24
7	Sunderland	22	10	5	7	51	31	23
8	Burnley	22	9	3	10	52	63	21
9	Aston Villa	22	7	4	11	45	58	18
10	Accrington	22	6	4	12	28	50	16
11	Derby County	22	7	1	14	47	81	15
12	West Bromwich Alb.	22	5	2	15	34	57	12

1891/92

8th in The Football League

#		Date	Opponent	Result	Scorers	Att	Abrahams J	Bakewell GH	Bell E	Bramley C	Burns J	Calderhead D	Daft HB	Elleman AR	Hendry J	Hooley A	McInnes T	McLean T	Osborne AW	Oswald, James	Shelton A	Shelton C	Thraves J	Toone G	Walker JA	Walkerdine H	Whitelaw A	Widdowson, Albert	Wilkinson F	Williamson A
1	Sep	5	PRESTON NORTH END	2-0	Daft 2	10000	7					5	11		3		8		4	9	6			1		10	2			
2		12	Blackburn Rovers	4-5	Oswald 2, Walkerdine, Forbes(og)	7000	7					5	11		3		8		4	9	6			1		10	2			
3		19	Derby County	0-3		10000	7					5	11		3		8		4	9	6			1		10	2			
4		26	STOKE	1-1	Walkerdine	6000	7			4		5	11		3		8	2		9	6			1		10				
5	Oct	1	BOLTON WANDERERS	2-0	Daft, Bakewell	3000	7	4		4		5	11		3		8	2		9	6			1		10				
6		10	WEST BROMWICH ALB.	4-0	McInnes 2, Elleman, Walkerdine	2000				4		5	11	7	3		8	2		9	6	1				10				
7		17	Wolverhampton Wand.	1-2	Elleman	900				4		5	11	7	3		8	2		9	6	1				10				
8		24	DARWEN	5-0	Daft 2, Oswald 2, Walkerdine	4000				4		5	11	7	3		8	2		9	6			1		10				
9		31	West Bromwich Alb.	2-2	McInnes 2	3000				4		5	11	7	3		8	2		9	6			1		10				
10	Nov	7	Aston Villa	1-5	Walkerdine	3000				4	8	5	11		3		7	2		9	6			1		10				
11		14	WOLVERHAMPTON W.	2-2	Daft, Walkerdine	6000				4		5	11	7	3		8	2		9	6			1		10				
12		21	Accrington	0-2		1000			9	4		5	11	7	3		8	2			6			1		10				
13		28	ACCRINGTON	9-0	* See below	3000				4		5	11		3		8	2		9	6			1		10				7
14	Dec	5	Sunderland	0-4			7		8	4		5	11		3			2		9	6			1		10				
15		12	Preston North End	0-6		700	7			4		5	11		3		8	2		9	6			1		10				
16		19	BLACKBURN ROVERS	2-2	Abrahams, Walkerdine	7000	7			4		5	11		3		8	2		9	6			1		10				
17	Jan	2	ASTON VILLA	5-2	Daft 3, Oswald 2	7000				4		5	11		3		8	2		9	6			1	10	7				
18		9	EVERTON	1-3	Walkerdine	4000				4		5	11		3		8	2			6			1	10	9				7
19	Feb	6	Stoke	3-1	Daft 2, Walkerdine	4000		10		4		5	11		3		8			9	6			1		7	2			
20		20	DERBY COUNTY	2-1	Oswald 2	5000		10		4		5	11		3		8			9	6			1		7	2			
21		27	Darwen	3-2	Oswald 2, McInnes	3000	7	10				5			3		8	4		9			6	1		11	2			
22	Mar	1	BURNLEY	5-1	Oswald 3, Hooley, Walkerdine	2000						5	11		3	7	8			9	6			1		10	2	4		
23		26	Bolton Wanderers	0-2		6000				4		5			3	7	8			9	6			1		10	2	11		
24	Apr	9	SUNDERLAND	1-0	Oswald	10000						5	11		3	7	8		4	9	6			1	10		2			
25		15	Burnley	0-1		10000						5	11		3		8		4	9	6			1		10	2		7	
26		16	Everton	0-4		10000				4		5	11		3		8			9	6			1		10	2		7	

* Scorers in game 13: Walkerdine 3, Daft 2, Calderhead, McInnes, Oswald, one unknown
Games 1, 24 at the Castle Ground

Apps	4	5	5	19	1	26	24	6	26	3	25	16	5	24	25	1	2	24	3	25	11	3	1	2
Goals	1	1				1	13	2			1	6		15						13				

One own goal, one unknown

F.A. Cup

		Date	Opponent	Result		Att	Abrahams J	Bakewell GH	Bell E	Bramley C	Burns J	Calderhead D	Daft HB	Elleman AR	Hendry J	Hooley A	McInnes T	McLean T	Osborne AW	Oswald, James	Shelton A	Shelton C	Thraves J	Toone G	Walker JA	Walkerdine H	Whitelaw A	Widdowson, Albert	Wilkinson F	Williamson A
R1	Jan	16	Sunderland	0-3		16000						5	11		3		8		4		6	10		1		9	2			
rep		23	Sunderland	0-4		12000		7	10			5	11		3		8	4			6			1		9	2			

First game declared void after protest. Played in first game: W Locker (no. 7).

		p	w	d	l	f	a	pts
1	Sunderland	26	21	0	5	93	36	42
2	Preston North End	26	18	1	7	61	31	37
3	Bolton Wanderers	26	17	2	7	51	37	36
4	Aston Villa	26	15	0	11	89	56	30
5	Everton	26	12	4	10	49	49	28
6	Wolverhampton Wan.	26	11	4	11	59	46	26
7	Burnley	26	11	4	11	49	45	26
8	NOTTS COUNTY	26	11	4	11	55	51	26
9	Blackburn Rovers	26	10	6	10	58	65	26
10	Derby County	26	10	4	12	46	52	24
11	Accrington	26	8	4	14	40	78	20
12	West Bromwich Alb.	26	6	6	14	51	58	18
13	Stoke	26	5	4	17	38	61	14
14	Darwen	26	4	3	19	38	112	11

Back: Kirk (trainer), Bramley, Calderhead, Toone, Hendry, A Shelton, Gilbert (linesman). Front: McLean, Burns, McInnes, Oswald, Walkerdine, Daft

1892/93

14th in Division One (Relegated)

#		Date	Opponent	Score	Scorers	Att	Bramley C	Bruce D	Burke J	Calderhead D	Daft HB	Docherty E	Gunn W	Harper T	Hendry J	King LH	Mabbott J	McGregor AC	McInnes T	Oswald, James	Parke J	Shelton A	Toone G	Walker JA	Walkerdine H	Whitelaw A	Wilkinson F
1	Sep	3	SHEFFIELD WEDNESDAY	0-1		10000				5	11	8			3			7		9	4	6	1		10	2	
2		10	Sunderland	2-2	Bramley, Walkerdine	10000	4			5	11	8			3			7		9		6	1		10	2	
3		17	DERBY COUNTY	1-1	Walkerdine	8000	4			5	11	8			3			7		9		6	1		10	2	
4		24	Wolverhampton Wand.	0-3		4000	4			5	11				3			7		9		6	1	8	10	2	
5	Oct	1	PRESTON NORTH END	3-1	Daft, Docherty, McGregor	8000	4			5	11	8			3			7		9		6	1		10	2	
6		6	BOLTON WANDERERS	2-2	Bramley, Daft	8000	4	9		5	11				3			7		8		6	1		10	2	
7		8	NOTTM. FOREST	3-0	Walkerdine, Daft, Bruce	15000	4	9		5	11				3			7		8		6	1		10	2	
8		19	Derby County	5-4	Bruce 2, Daft 2, McGregor	5000	4	9		5	11				3			7		8		6	1		10	2	
9		22	Burnley	0-3		7000		9		5	11	10			3			7	8	4		6	1			2	
10		29	West Bromwich Alb.	2-4	Burke, Bruce	3000		9	10	5	11				3			7	8	4		6	1			2	
11	Nov	5	STOKE	0-1		10000		9	10	5	11				3			7	8	4		6	1			2	
12		12	Newton Heath	3-1	Burke, McInnes, Oswald	8000	4		11	10	5				3				7	8	9	6	1			2	
13		19	WEST BROMWICH ALB.	8-1	Daft 3, Oswald 3, Bruce 2	1000	4	10		5	11				3				7	8	9	6	1			2	
14		26	SUNDERLAND	3-1	Daft, McGregor, McInnes	8000	4	10		5	11				3				7	8	9	6	1			2	
15	Dec	8	BURNLEY	3-1	McInnes, Oswald, Hillman(og)	4000	4	10		5	11				3				7	8	9	6	1			2	
16		10	Accrington	2-4	Daft, Oswald	1500	4	10		5	11				3				7	8	9	6	1			2	
17		17	EVERTON	1-2	Oswald	10000	4	10		5	11				3				7	8	9	6	1			2	
18		24	Blackburn Rovers	0-1		3000		9		5	11	4			3				7	10	8	6	1			2	
19		31	ASTON VILLA	1-4	Bruce	3000	4	9	10	5	11				3				7		8	6	1			2	
20	Jan	7	Everton	0-6		8000		10	11					4	3	8			7		9	6	1			2	5
21		14	BLACKBURN ROVERS	0-0		3000	4	10	11						3	7					9	6	1		8	2	5
22		26	NEWTON HEATH	4-0	Bruce, Oswald, Gunn, Burke	7000	4	10	11	5			7		3					8	9	6	1			2	
23	Feb	11	ACCRINGTON	2-0	Bruce, McInnes	4000		11	10	5					3					8	9	6	1		7	2	4
24		25	Nottm. Forest	1-3	Bruce	15000	4	11	10						3			7	8		9	6	1			2	5
25	Mar	11	Stoke	0-1		6000	4	11	10	5					3					8	9	6	1		7	2	
26		18	Aston Villa	1-3	McInnes	7000	4	11	10	5					3		7			8	9	6	1			2	
27		25	Bolton Wanderers	1-4	McInnes	4000	4	11	10	5					3			7		8	9	6	1			2	
28		31	Preston North End	0-4		6000	4	11	10	5				3						8	7	6				2	
29	Apr	3	Sheffield Wednesday	2-3	Oswald 2	1000	4	9	10	5				6	3					8	7	11	1			2	
30		8	WOLVERHAMPTON W.	3-0	Bruce, Burke, Oswald	5000	4	9	10	5				6	3					8	7	11	1			2	
			Apps				23	25	15	27	18	6	1	4	30	2	1	22	19	30	1	30	29	1	11	30	4
			Goals				2	11	4		10	1	1					3	6	11							

Games 1, 3 annd 30 at Castle Ground
Game 28: Only 10 men.

One own goal

Test Match

	Date	Opponent	Score	Scorers	Att																					
Apr	22	Darwen	2-3	Kenyon (og), Bruce	3000	4	11	10	5					3					8	9	6	1		7	2	

Played at Hyde Road, Manchester

F.A. Cup

		Date	Opponent	Score	Scorers	Att																					
R1	Jan	21	SHANKHOUSE	4-0	Oswald 3, McInnes	5000	4		11	10					3			7	8	9		6	1			2	5
R2	Feb	4	Middlesbro' Ironopolis	2-3	Burke, Walkerdine	10000	4		11	10	5				3				8	9		6	1		7	2	

		p	w	d	l	f	a	pts
1	Sunderland	30	22	4	4	100	36	48
2	Preston North End	30	17	3	10	57	39	37
3	Everton	30	16	4	10	74	51	36
4	Aston Villa	30	16	3	11	73	62	35
5	Bolton Wanderers	30	13	6	11	56	55	32
6	Burnley	30	13	4	13	51	44	30
7	Stoke	30	12	5	13	58	48	29
8	West Bromwich Alb.	30	12	5	13	58	69	29
9	Blackburn Rovers	30	8	13	9	47	56	29
10	Nottingham Forest	30	10	8	12	48	52	28
11	Wolverhampton Wan.	30	12	4	14	47	68	28
12	Sheffield Wed.	30	12	3	15	55	65	27
13	Derby County	30	9	9	12	52	64	27
14	NOTTS COUNTY	30	10	4	16	53	61	24
15	Accrington	30	6	11	13	57	81	23
16	Newton Heath	30	6	6	18	50	85	18

1893/94

3rd in Division Two, FA Cup Winners

#	Date		Opponent	Score	Scorers	Att	Allsopp E	Bramley C	Bruce D	Burrows W	Calderhead D	Daft HB	Dixon H	Donnelly S	Harper T	Hendry J	Kerr G	King LH	Logan J	Mabbott J	McLachlan J	Osborne AW	Shelton A	Shepperson G	Toone G	Watson AE	Wilkinson F
1	Sep	2	Crewe Alexandra	2-0	Bruce, Watson	2000			9		5		11	8	2	3	10						4	6		1	7	
2		9	WOOLWICH ARSENAL	3-2	Bruce 2, Watson	6000			9		5		11	8	2	3	10						4	6		1	7	
3		11	Northwich Victoria	1-0	Bruce	1000			9		5		11	8	2	3	10						4	6		1	7	
4		16	Rotherham Town	2-0	Bramley, Daft	1200	8	9			5	11			2	3	10						4	6		1	7	
5		30	LIVERPOOL	1-1	Watson	4000			9		5	11			2	3	10			8			4	6		1	7	
6	Oct	5	GRIMSBY TOWN	3-0	Logan 2, Bruce	4000		8			5	11			2	3	10		9				4	6		1	7	
7		14	NEWCASTLE UNITED	3-1	Daft, Logan, Watson	5000					5	11	10	2		3			9		8	4	6		1	7	
8		21	Grimsby Town	2-5	Logan, Higgins(og)	3000		10			5	11			2	3	8		9				4	6		1	7	
9		26	PORT VALE	6-1	Logan 3, Daft, Kerr, Watson	3000	4	10			5	11			2	3	8		9					6		1	7	
10		28	Ardwick	0-0		4000	4	10			5	11			2	3	8		9					6		1	7	
11	Nov	4	MIDDLESBRO' IRON.	3-0	Watson, Logan, Daft	5000	4	10			6	11			2	3	8		9			5				1	7	
12		16	LINCOLN CITY	1-2	Bruce	2000	4	10			5	11			2	3	7		9	8				6	1			
13		18	Liverpool	1-2	Bruce	6000		10			5	11			2	3	8		9				4	6		1	7	
14		23	NORTHWICH VIC.	6-1	Logan 3, Bruce 2, Watson	1500		10			5	11			2	3	8		9				4	6		1	7	
15		25	Port Vale	0-1		1000		10			5	11			2	3	8		9				4	6		1	7	
16		30	BURTON SWIFTS	6-2	Kerr 3, Logan, Daft, Watson	2000	4	10			2	11				3	8		9				5	6		1	7	
17	Dec	9	Newcastle United	0-3		3000	4	8			5	11		7	2	3	10		9					6		1		
18		16	Middlesbro' Ironopolis	0-0		2000	11		1	5				8	2	3	10	7	9					6				4
19		30	Burton Swifts	2-0	Logan 2		4	10				11		7	2	3	8		9			5				1		6
20	Jan	11	ROTHERHAM TOWN	4-2	Bruce 3, Kerr	1500	4	10				11		7		3	8		9			5	2			1		6
21		20	WALSALL	2-0	Bruce, Shelton	2000	4	9			2	11		8		3	10						5	6		1	7	
22	Feb	3	SMALL HEATH	3-1	Logan, Watson, Jenkyns(og)	5000	4	10			2	11		8		3			9				5	6		1	7	
23		17	CREWE ALEXANDRA	9-1	Watson 4, Bruce 2, Logan 2, Daft	200	4	10			3	11		8	2				9				5	6		1	7	
24	Mar	12	Walsall	1-2	Logan	2000	4	10			6	11		8	2	3	7		9				5			1		
25		15	ARDWICK	5-0	Logan 2, Allsopp, Bruce, Kerr	2500	7	4	10		5	11			2	3	8		9					6		1		
26		23	Lincoln City	2-0	Bruce, Daft	6000		4	10		5	11		8	2	3			9					6		1	7	
27		24	Woolwich Arsenal	2-1	Bruce, Logan	13000		4	10		5	11		8	2	3			9					6	7	1		
28	Apr	7	Small Heath	0-3		6000		4	9		5	11		8	2	3	10							6		1	7	
			Apps				1	18	26	1	26	24	3	15	24	27	23	1	21	1	2	19	25	1	27	20	3
			Goals				1	1	18			7					6		21				1			13	

Game 2 at Castle Ground

Two own goals

Test match

| | Apr | 28 | Preston North End | 0-4 | | 8000 | | 4 | 10 | | 3 | 11 | | 8 | 2 | | | | 9 | | | | 6 | | 1 | 7 | 5 |

Played at Olive Grove, Sheffield

F.A. Cup

R1	Jan	27	BURNLEY	1-0	Logan	8000		4	10		5	11			2	3			9					6		1	7	
R2	Feb	10	Burton Wanderers	2-1	Donnelly, Logan(p)	6000		4	10		5	11		8	2	3	7		9					6		1		
R3		24	Nottm. Forest	1-1	Bruce	15000		4	10		5	11		8	2	3			9					6		1	7	
rep	Mar	3	NOTTM. FOREST	4-1	Logan, Bruce 2, Donnelly	12000		4	10		5	11		8	2	3			9					6		1	7	
SF		10	BLACKBURN ROVERS	1-0	Daft	20000		4	10		5	11		8	2	3			9					6		1	7	
F		31	BOLTON WANDERERS	4-1	Logan 3, Watson	37000		4	10		5	11		8	2	3			9					6		1	7	

Round 3 first game after extra time.
SF at Bramall Lane, Final at Goodison Park

Played in Round 1: AG Henfrey (at no. 8). Calderhead sent off.

United Counties League (East Midlands Division)

#	Date		Opponent	Score	Scorers	Att																						
1	Dec	2	SHEFFIELD UNITED	0-0		good		4	10		5	11		8	2	3	7		9					6		1		
2	Jan	6	Nottm. Forest	0-1		4000		4	10			11		7	2	3	8		9			5				1		6
3		13	Derby County	1-8	Kerr			4	10			11		7		3	8		9			5	2			1		6
4	Mar	17	SHEFFIELD WEDNESDAY	2-1	Daft, Shepperson	3000		4	10		5	11		7	2	3			9					6	8	1		
5		26	DERBY COUNTY	0-4		4000				1								6	7			4			8			5
6	Apr	9	Sheffield Wednesday	0-4		1000		4	11		2			8		3	10		9			5				1		6
7		19	NOTTM. FOREST	3-4	Bruce, Daft 2	3000		4	10			11		8	2	3			9			5	6			1	7	

Games 4 and 5 at Castle Ground, game 7 at Town Ground. Return game with Sheffield United not played.
Played in game 5: Askew (3), Dean (10), Murray (2), H Sissons (9), J Burke (11).
Played in game 6: Gadsby (7).

		p	w	d	l	f	a	pts
1	Liverpool	28	22	6	0	77	18	50
2	Small Heath	28	21	0	7	103	44	42
3	NOTTS COUNTY	28	18	3	7	70	31	39
4	Newcastle United	28	15	6	7	66	39	36
5	Grimsby Town	28	15	2	11	71	58	32
6	Burton Swifts	28	14	3	11	79	61	31
7	Burslem Port Vale	28	13	4	11	66	64	30
8	Lincoln City	28	11	6	11	59	58	28
9	Woolwich Arsenal	28	12	4	12	52	55	28
10	Walsall Town Swfts	28	10	3	15	51	61	23
11	Middlesbro Ironopolis	28	8	4	16	37	72	20
12	Crewe Alexandra	28	6	7	15	42	73	19
13	Ardwick	28	8	2	18	47	71	18
14	Rotherham Town	28	6	3	19	44	91	15
15	Northwich Victoria	28	3	3	22	30	98	9

The Cup Winners. Back: Bramley, Harper, Calderhead, Toone, Hendry, Shelton, Goode (trainer). Front: Watson, Donnelly, Logan, Bruce, Daft

1894/95

2nd in Division Two

		Date	Opponent	Score	Scorers	Att	Allan J	Allsopp E	Arnott W	Bramley C	Brealey H	Brown W	Bruce D	Bull W	Calderhead D	Chadburn J	Daft HB	Donnelly S	Ferrier J	Fletcher F	Guttridge FH	Hall WH	Harper T	Harrisson AE	Hendry J	Logan J	Shelton A	Shepperson G	Stothert J	Toone G	Watson AE
1	Sep	15	DARWEN	2-1	Calderhead, Chadburn	10000		8	4				10		5	7	11						2		3	9	6		1		
2		17	Burslem Port Vale	3-0	Allsopp 2, Bramley	1000		8	4				10		5	7	11						2		3	9	6		1		
3		22	Newcastle United	2-2	Daft, Chadburn	3000		8	4				10		5	7	11						2		3	9	6		1		
4		29	LINCOLN CITY	3-0	Bruce, Daft, Logan	7000		8	4				10		5	7	11						2		3	9	6		1		
5	Oct	4	GRIMSBY TOWN	3-2	Chadburn, Daft, Logan	5000		8	4				10		5	7	11						2		3	9	6		1		
6		6	LEICESTER FOSSE	3-0	Allsopp 2, Daft	10000		8	4				10		5	7	11						2		3	9	6		1		
7		13	MANCHESTER CITY	1-3	Logan	3000		8	4				10		5	7	11						2		3	9	6		1		
8		27	WOOLWICH ARSENAL	2-2	Chadburn, Logan	2000			4				10		5	7	11	8					2		3	9	6		1		
9	Nov	3	Woolwich Arsenal	1-2	Logan	11000			4				10	8	5	7	11						2		3	9	6		1		
10		5	Rotherham Town	2-1	Allsopp, Bruce			9	4				10	2	5	7	11								3		6	8	1		
11		10	CREWE ALEXANDRA	5-1	Bruce 2, Allsopp, Donnelly, Shelton	3500		10	4		1		9	2	5	7	11	8								3		6				
12		24	BURY	2-1	Allsopp 2(1p)	10000		10	4				9		5	7		8					11		2	1	3	6		1		
13	Dec	1	Leicester Fosse	1-5	Fletcher	5000			4				9	10	5		11			7			2		3	8	6		1		
14		8	Burton Wanderers	0-1		3000		10	4				9		5			8					11		3		6			2	1	7
15		15	NEWTON HEATH	1-1	Bruce	3000		10	4				11		5			8						2		3	9	6			1	7
16		22	Burton Swifts	2-2	Allsopp 2			10	4				11		5	7		8						2		3	9	6		1		
17		25	WALSALL	5-0	Logan 3, Calderhead, Donnelly	4000	10		4				11		5	7		8						2		3	9	6		1		
18	Jan	1	Bury	1-2	Allsopp	9838	10	7	4				11		5			8						2		3	9	6		1		
19		5	BURTON WANDERERS	2-0	Bramley, Hendry	3000	10	7	4				11					8						2		3	9	5		6	1	
20		12	BURTON SWIFTS	5-1	Allsopp 2, Donnelly 2, Allan	1500	10	7	4						5			8					11	2		3	9	6		1		
21		16	Crewe Alexandra	3-0	Logan 2, Allan	100	10	7	4				11		5			8						2		3	9			6	1	
22		26	Darwen	1-2	Bramley	4000	10		4				11			7		8			2					3	9	5		6	1	
23	Feb	5	Grimsby Town	1-0	Allsopp	4000	10	11	4				2		5	7		8								3	9	6		1		
24		26	BURSLEM PORT VALE	10-0	* See below	1500	10	7	4				9	11				8						2		3		5	6	1		
25	Mar	9	Manchester City	1-7	Bruce	7000	10	7	4				9	11	5			8						2		3		6		1		
26		16	ROTHERHAM TOWN	4-2	Bull 3, Donnelly	2000	10	7	4	2			9	11	5			8								3			6	1		
27		23	NEWCASTLE UNITED	2-1	Bruce, Bull	4000	10	7	4				9	11	5			8	2							3		6		1		
28		25	Walsall	1-2	Bruce	1500	10	7	4				9	11	5					2							6	8	3	1		
29	Apr	12	Lincoln City	3-1	Allsopp, Bruce, Bull	5000	7	8		4		11	9	10	5											3		6	2	1		
30		20	Newton Heath	3-3	Chadburn 2, Bruce	12000	9	8	4				10		5	7						11				3		6	2	1		

Game 1 at the Castle Ground
*Scorers in game 24: Bruce 5, Donnelly 2, Allsopp, Bull, Allan

	Apps	14	25	1	30	1	1	29	10	27	17	12	17	2	5	1	2	18	1	29	20	27	2	9	28	2
	Goals	3	16		3			15	6	2	6	4	7		1					1	10	1				

Test Match

	Date	Opponent	Score	Scorer	Att																								
Apr	27	Derby County	1-2	Fletcher	8000	9	8	4						5	7				11						3		6		2	1	

Played at Filbert Street, Leicester. Played at no. 10: H Sissons

F.A. Cup

		Date	Opponent	Score	Scorer	Att																								
R1	Feb	2	Sheffield Wednesday	1-5	Allsopp(p)	7000	10	7	2	4			11		5			8								3	9	6		1		

United Counties League

		Date	Opponent	Score	Scorers	Att																								
1	Feb	9	SHEFFIELD WEDNESDAY	0-2		1000	10		4				2	11	5	7		8								3	9			6	1	
2	Mar	4	Sheffield Wednesday	2-5	Allsopp, Chadburn	fair		11				1	9		5	10		8						2			6	3				
3		14	LEICESTER FOSSE	0-2		700			4				9	5	7			10		11								8		1		
4		30	Nottm. Forest	0-3		3000	10						9	11	5	7											6	8	3	1		
5	Apr	13	Leicester Fosse	1-2	Garrett	4500						7			5			11									4		2	1		
6		29	NOTTM. FOREST	0-1		1000	9		4						5	7			6							3				2	1		

Game 6 played at the Town Ground. Played in game 2: J Goode (7) Only 10 men. In game 3: J McGinn (2), J Mounteney (6), T McLean (3).
Played in game 4: T McLean (2), F Coles (4). In game 5: Broughton (9), Garrett (8), Haslam (3), Howkins (6), Oldershaw (5). F Coles(10).
Played in game 6: Dugard (10), Garrett(8), R Jardine (11).

Back: Harris (secretary), Chadburn, Donnelly, W Gunn (director), Fletcher, Allsopp, Goode (trainer). Front: Hendry, Shelton, Bramley, Calderhead, Bruce, Harrisson, Stothert

		p	w	d	l	f	a	pts
1	Bury	30	23	2	5	78	33	48
2	NOTTS COUNTY	30	17	5	8	75	45	39
3	Newton Heath	30	15	8	7	78	44	38
4	Leicester Fosse	30	15	8	7	72	53	38
5	Grimsby Town	30	18	1	11	79	52	37
6	Darwen	30	16	4	10	74	43	36
7	Burton Wanderers	30	14	7	9	67	39	35
8	Woolwich Arsenal	30	14	6	10	75	58	34
9	Manchester City	30	14	3	13	82	72	31
10	Newcastle United	30	12	3	15	72	84	27
11	Burton Swifts	30	11	3	16	52	74	25
12	Rotherham Town	30	11	2	17	55	62	24
13	Lincoln City	30	10	0	20	52	92	20
14	Walsall Town Swfts	30	10	0	20	47	92	20
15	Burslem Port Vale	30	7	4	19	39	77	18
16	Crewe Alexandra	30	3	4	23	26	103	10

1895/96

10th in Division Two

#		Date	Opponent	Score	Scorers	Att	Allan J	Allsopp E	Bramley C	Brealey H	Bruce D	Bull W	Calderhead D	Cale F	Chadburn J	Coles F	Connor JH	Fletcher F	Handley G	Hendry J	Kiddier JF	McCallum N	Russell D	Shelton A	Shepperson G	Stothert J	Toone G
1	Sep	7	LIVERPOOL	2-3	Allsopp, Calderhead	8000	9	8	4		10	11	5		7					3				6		2	1
2		14	Burslem Port Vale	4-0	Allan 2, Bruce, Allsopp	2000	9	8	4		10	11	5		7					3				6		2	1
3		21	Newcastle United	1-5	Bruce	7000	9	7	4		10	11	5							3			8	6		2	1
4		28	DARWEN	4-1	Bull 2, Allan, Brealey	5000	9			11		10	5		7					3		8	4	6		2	1
5	Oct	3	GRIMSBY TOWN	5-3	Allan 2, Bruce, Bull, Brealey	3500	9			11	8	10	5		7					3			4	6		2	1
6		5	Crewe Alexandra	1-5	Chadburn	500	9			11	8	10	5		7					3			4	6		2	1
7		19	LINCOLN CITY	2-0	Allan, Bull	3000	9	11				10	4		7		3					8	5	6		2	1
8		26	Liverpool	0-3		6000	9	11	4			8	10		7					3			5	6		2	1
9	Nov	2	WOOLWICH ARSENAL	3-4	Chadburn, Shelton, Calderhead	4000	8			11	9	10	4		7					3			5	6		2	1
10		9	BURTON WANDERERS	1-4	Chadburn	3000	9				10	11	4		7					3		8	5	6		2	1
11		16	Rotherham Town	0-1		500	8		4	11	10	9	5		7					3				6		2	1
12		23	NEWTON HEATH	0-2		3000	8	11	4			9	5	10	7					3				6		2	1
13		30	ROTHERHAM TOWN	0-0		1500		6	4			9	5		7					3	10			11	8	2	1
14	Dec	7	BURSLEM PORT VALE	7-2	Bull 2, Fletcher 2, Allan, Calderhead, Kiddier	1000	8	6	4			11	5		7		2	9		3	10						1
15		14	Newton Heath	0-3		3000	9	8	4			11	5		7		2			3	10		6				1
16		25	LOUGHBOROUGH	2-0	Bull, Chadburn	3000	8		4	11		10	5		7		2			3	9			6			1
17		28	Loughborough	3-1	Brealey, Calderhead, Chadburn	1500	8	4		11		10	5		7		2			3	9			6			1
18	Jan	1	Darwen	0-2			10	4				11	5		7		2	9	8	3				6			1
19		11	Leicester Fosse	1-2	Bull	6000	8	6	4			10	5		7		2	11		3	9						1
20		18	Burton Swifts	0-0		2000	8	4				10	5		7		2	11		3	9			6			1
21	Feb	8	LEICESTER FOSSE	1-2	Bull	4000	10	9	4			11	5		7		2			3		8		6			1
22		22	BURTON SWIFTS	5-0	Allan 2, McCallum 2, Bramley	2000	10		4			11	5		7	6	2			3	9	8					1
23		29	MANCHESTER CITY	3-0	Bull, Kiddier, Allan	3000	10		4			11	5		7		2			3	9	8		6			1
24	Mar	7	Woolwich Arsenal	0-2		5000	10		4			11	5		7		2			3	9	8		6			1
25		14	NEWCASTLE UNITED	0-1		2000	10		4			11	5		7		2			3		8		6	9		1
26		21	Grimsby Town	0-3		3000	10		4			11	5		7					3	9	8		6		2	1
27	Apr	3	Lincoln City	3-2	Bull, Kiddier, Allan	4000	10		4			11	5		7		2			3	9	8		6			1
28		4	CREWE ALEXANDRA	6-0	Bull 2, Chadburn, Kiddier, McCallum, Shelton	1000	10		4			11	5		7		2			3	9	8		6			1
29		6	Burton Wanderers	3-1	Chadburn, Bull 2	3000	10		4			11	5		7		2			3	9	8		6			1
30		8	Manchester City	0-2		6000	10		4			11	5		7		2			3	9	8		6			1
			Apps				29	14	21	7	9	30	29	1	29	1	17	4	1	29	15	13	9	26	2	14	30
			Goals				11	2	1	3	3	15	4		7			2			4	3		2			

Game 1 at the Town Ground

F.A.Cup

		Date	Opponent	Score	Scorers	Att	Allan J	Allsopp E	Bramley C	Brealey H	Bruce D	Bull W	Calderhead D	Cale F	Chadburn J	Coles F	Connor JH	Fletcher F	Handley G	Hendry J	Kiddier JF	McCallum N	Russell D	Shelton A	Shepperson G	Stothert J	Toone G
R1	Feb	1	Wolverhampton Wand.	2-2	Bull 2	9300	10	9	4			11	5		7		2			3		8		6			1
rep		5	WOLVERHAMPTON W.	3-4	Allan, Allsopp, Bull	8000	10	9	4			11	5		7		2			3		8		6			1

		p	w	d	l	f	a	pts
1	Liverpool	30	22	2	6	106	32	46
2	Manchester City	30	21	4	5	63	38	46
3	Grimsby Town	30	20	2	8	82	38	42
4	Burton Wanderers	30	19	4	7	69	40	42
5	Newcastle United	30	16	2	12	73	50	34
6	Newton Heath	30	15	3	12	66	57	33
7	Woolwich Arsenal	30	14	4	12	58	42	32
8	Leicester Fosse	30	14	4	12	57	44	32
9	Darwen	30	12	6	12	72	67	30
10	NOTTS COUNTY	30	12	2	16	57	54	26
11	Burton Swifts	30	10	4	16	39	69	24
12	Loughborough	30	9	5	16	40	66	23
13	Lincoln City	30	9	4	17	53	75	22
14	Burslem Port Vale	30	7	4	19	43	78	18
15	Rotherham Town	30	7	3	20	34	97	17
16	Crewe Alexandra	30	5	3	22	30	95	13

1896/97

Top of Division Two: Promoted after Test Matches

#		Date	Opponent	Score	Scorers	Att	Allan J	Allsopp E	Boucher T	Bramley C	Bull W	Calderhead D	Carter AB	Chadburn J	Cookson AE	Crank J	Crone R	Devey W	Gibson W	Henrys A	Kinsey G	Langham W	Murphy, John	Prescott TG	Smith, William	Stewart A	Toone G
1	Sep	5	LOUGHBOROUGH	3-1	Chadburn 2, Smith	1000		4	9		11	5		7					3	6			10	2	8		1
2		12	Leicester Fosse	3-2	Murphy, Smith, Bull	6000		4	9		11	5		7					3	6			10	2	8		1
3		19	NEWCASTLE UNITED	3-1	Murphy, Bull, Langham	6000		4	9		11	5							3	6		7	10	2	8		1
4		26	Woolwich Arsenal	3-2	Smith, Boucher 2	9000		4	9		11	5							3	6		7	10	2	8		1
5	Oct	1	GRIMSBY TOWN	1-3	Murphy	10000		4	9		11	5							3	6		7	10	2	8		1
6		3	Burton Wanderers	3-0	Murphy 2, Boucher	1000		4	9		11	5							3	6		7	10	2	8		1
7		10	MANCHESTER CITY	3-3	Murphy, Bull, Calderhead	5000	8	4	9		11	5							3	6		7	10	2			1
8		17	LEICESTER FOSSE	6-0	Allan 2, Murphy 2, Bull, Calderhead	5000	8	6	9	4	11	5							3			7	10	2			1
9		24	Loughborough	1-0	Boucher	2000	8	6	9	4	11	5							3			7	10	2			1
10		31	Manchester City	4-1	Murphy 2, Bramley, Langham	8000	8	6	9	4	11	5							3			7	10	2			1
11	Nov	7	WOOLWICH ARSENAL	7-4	Bull 3, Allan, Allsopp, Langham, Murphy	4000	8	6	9	4	11	5							3			7	10	2			1
12		14	WALSALL	5-2	Boucher 2, Murphy 2, Bull	5000	8	6	9	4	11	5							3			7	10	2			1
13		21	Grimsby Town	1-3	Boucher	7000		6	9	4	11	5			8				3			7	10	2			1
14		28	Blackpool	2-3	Boucher, Bull	2500	8	6	9	4	11	5							3			7	10	2			1
15	Dec	5	BURTON SWIFTS	6-1	Boucher 2, Langham 2, Murphy, Allan	4000	8		9	4	11	5							3			7	10	2	6		1
16		12	Newcastle United	2-2	Allan, Bull	14000	8		9	4	11	5			6				3			7	10	2			1
17		19	NEWTON HEATH	3-0	Allan, Langham, Murphy	8000	8		9	4	11	5			6				3			7	10	2			1
18	Jan	2	Burton Swifts	4-1	Boucher 3, Langham	2000	8		9	4	11	5						6	3			7	10	2			1
19		9	GAINSBORO' TRINITY	2-0	Allan, Boucher	1000	8	6	9	4	11	5						3				7	10	2			1
20		16	Walsall	3-1	Murphy 2, Bull	3000	8		9	4	11	5						6	3			7	10	2			1
21		23	LINCOLN CITY	8-0	Bull 3, Boucher 2, Murphy 2, Allan	2000	8	4	9		11	5						6	3			7	10	2			1
22	Feb	6	DARWEN	4-0	Boucher 2, Allan, Langham	4000	8	6	9	4	10	5		11			2		3			7					1
23		27	Darwen	1-2	Bull	4000	8	4	9		11	5						6	3			7	10	2			1
24	Mar	6	Gainsborough Trinity	2-3	Boucher, Murphy	3000		4	9		11	5	8					6	3			7	10	2			1
25		13	BURTON WANDERERS	5-0	Bull 2, Boucher, Carter, Smith	6000			9		11	5	8		4			6	3				10	2	7		1
26		20	BLACKPOOL	3-1	Boucher, Langham, Murphy	7000			9		11	5	8					6	3			7	10	2		4	1
27		27	Newton Heath	1-1	Devey	10000	8		9		11	5						7	3		6		10	2		4	1
28		31	Lincoln City	1-1	Murphy		8		9		11						5	7	3		6		10	2		4	1
29	Apr	3	SMALL HEATH	1-2	Boucher	5000			9		11	5						8	3		6	7	10	2		4	1
30		10	Small Heath	1-3	Langham	7000	8		9		11					2	6	10	3		5	7				4	1

Games 1 and 3 at the Town Ground

Apps	19	19	30	14	30	28	3	4	3	1	11	4	29	7	4	25	28	28	8	5	30
Goals	9	1	22	1	17	2	1	2				1				10	22		4		

Test matches

#		Date	Opponent	Score	Scorers	Att	Allan J	Allsopp E	Boucher T	Bramley C	Bull W	Calderhead D	Carter AB	Chadburn J	Cookson AE	Crank J	Crone R	Devey W	Gibson W	Henrys A	Kinsey G	Langham W	Murphy, John	Prescott TG	Smith, William	Stewart A	Toone G
1	Apr	17	SUNDERLAND	1-0	Langham	7000	8		9		11	5					4		3			7	10	2		6	1
2		19	Sunderland	0-0		10000	8		9		11	5					4		3			7	10	2		6	1
3		24	BURNLEY	1-1	Boucher (p)	15000	8		9		11	5					4		3			7	10	2		6	1
4		26	Burnley	1-0	Brearley	11000	8		9			5					4		3			7	10	2		6	1

Game 3 at the Town Ground   Played in game 4: J Brearley (at no. 11)

F.A. Cup

		Date	Opponent	Score	Scorers	Att	Allan J	Allsopp E	Boucher T	Bramley C	Bull W	Calderhead D	Carter AB	Chadburn J	Cookson AE	Crank J	Crone R	Devey W	Gibson W	Henrys A	Kinsey G	Langham W	Murphy, John	Prescott TG	Smith, William	Stewart A	Toone G
R1	Jan	30	Small Heath	2-1	Allan, Boucher	10000	8		9	4	11	5						6	3			7	10	2			1
R2	Feb	13	Aston Villa	1-2	Bull	4000	8		9	4	11	5						6	3			7	10	2			1

Players only; Back: Bramley, Smith, Prescott, Toone, Allsopp, Gibson. Sitting: Langham, Allan, Calderhead (in a suit), Murphy, Bull. Front: Boucher

		p	w	d	l	f	a	pts
1	NOTTS COUNTY	30	19	4	7	92	43	42
2	Newton Heath	30	17	5	8	56	34	39
3	Grimsby Town	30	17	4	9	66	45	38
4	Small Heath	30	16	5	9	69	47	37
5	Newcastle United	30	17	1	12	56	52	35
6	Manchester City	30	12	8	10	58	50	32
7	Gainsborough Trin.	30	12	7	11	50	47	31
8	Blackpool	30	13	5	12	59	56	31
9	Leicester Fosse	30	13	4	13	59	57	30
10	Woolwich Arsenal	30	13	4	13	68	70	30
11	Darwen	30	14	0	16	67	61	28
12	Walsall	30	11	4	15	54	69	26
13	Loughborough	30	12	1	17	50	64	25
14	Burton Swifts	30	9	6	15	46	61	24
15	Burton Wanderers	30	9	2	19	31	67	20
16	Lincoln City	30	5	2	23	27	85	12

Test Matches

		p	w	d	l	f	a	pts
1	NOTTS COUNTY	4	2	2	0	3	1	6
2	Sunderland	4	1	2	1	3	2	4
3	Burnley	4	1	1	2	3	4	3
4	Newton Heath	4	1	1	2	3	5	3

1897/98

13th in Division One

#		Date	Opponent	Score	Scorers	Att	Allan J	Boucher T	Brailsford JR	Bramley C	Brearley J	Bull W	Calderhead D	Carter AB	Crone R	Deighton AD	Devey W	Fletcher H	Fraser J	Gibson W	Hendry R	Langham W	Leonard J	Lewis G	Murphy, John	Potter A	Prescott TG	Sanderson E	Sharman J	Stewart A	Toone G
1	Sep	2	Stoke	0-2		3500	8	9				11	5		4		10			3		7					2			6	1
2		4	Nottm. Forest	1-1	Bull	15000	8	9				11	5		4		7			3					10		2			6	1
3		11	ASTON VILLA	2-3	Langham, Murphy	15000	8	9					5		4		11			3		7			10		2			6	1
4		18	Bolton Wanderers	0-1		9000	8	9					5		4		11			3		7			10		2			6	1
5		25	DERBY COUNTY	1-1	Bull	12000	8	9				11	5		4		7			3					10		2			6	1
6	Oct	2	Sheffield Wednesday	1-3	Boucher	12000	8	9	4			11	5		3		7								10		2			6	1
7		7	PRESTON NORTH END	1-1	Langham	11000	8	9				11	5		4	10				3		7					2			6	1
8		9	NOTTM. FOREST	1-3	Allan	15000	10					11	5	8	4		9			3		7					2			6	1
9		16	Aston Villa	2-4	Carter, Stewart(p)	20000	10	9				6	5	8	4		11					7					2			3	1
10		23	STOKE	4-0	Devey 2, Allan, Stewart	6000	10	9				4	5	8	3		11					7					2			6	1
11		30	Wolverhampton Wand.	1-3	Carter	4000	10			11		3	5	8	4						9	7					2			6	1
12	Nov	6	BOLTON WANDERERS	1-2	Langham	8000	10			4		3		8	5		11				9	7					2			6	1
13		27	Bury	0-0		2000		10				3	5	8	4	11					9	7					2			6	1
14	Dec	4	SHEFFIELD WEDNESDAY	0-0		3000		10				11	5	8	4					3	9	7					2			6	1
15		11	Everton	0-1		5000		10					5	8	4	11				3	9	7					2			6	1
16		18	WOLVERHAMPTON W.	2-2	Carter, Deighton	7000		10				9	5	8	4	11				3		7					2			6	1
17		25	Derby County	2-1	Bull, Langham	12000		10				9	5	8	4	11				3		7					2			6	1
18	Jan	1	SHEFFIELD UNITED	1-3	Stewart(p)	10000		10				9	5	8	4	11						7	3				2			6	1
19		3	Sunderland	0-2		3000		10				9	5	8		11				3		7	4				2			6	1
20		15	EVERTON	3-2	Boucher 2, Langham	8000		10				9	5	8	4	11						7	3				2		1	6	
21	Feb	5	SUNDERLAND	0-1		7000		10				9	5		4			11				7	3			8	2			6	1
22		19	Sheffield United	1-0	Murphy	7000		10				4	5	8				11				7	3		9		2			6	1
23		26	BURY	2-1	Fraser, Carter	7000		10				4	5	8				11				7	3		9		2			6	1
24	Mar	5	BLACKBURN ROVERS	0-0		6000		10					5	8	4			11				7	3		9		2			6	1
25		12	Liverpool	0-2		9000		8					5			10		11					3		9	7	2	4		6	1
26		19	WEST BROMWICH ALB.	2-2	Boucher, Fraser	6000	8	9					5			10		11	7				3				2	4		6	1
27	Apr	2	LIVERPOOL	3-2	Boucher 2, Leonard	8000	8	9					5					11					3	7			2	4		6	1
28		4	West Bromwich Alb.	3-0	Allan, Boucher, Fletcher	4000	8	9				7	5					10	11				3				2	4		6	1
29		8	Preston North End	1-3	Allan	9000	8	9				7	5					10	11				3				2	4		6	1
30		9	Blackburn Rovers	1-0	Fletcher	5000	8					4	5					10	11		9	7	3				2			6	1
					Apps		17	26	1	1	1	23	29	16	21	10	10	4	10	12	7	22	1	13	9	2	30	5	1	30	29
					Goals		4	7				3		4		1	2	2	2			5	1		2					3	

F.A. Cup

		Date	Opponent	Score		Att	Allan J	Boucher T	Brailsford JR	Bramley C	Brearley J	Bull W	Calderhead D	Carter AB	Crone R	Deighton AD	Devey W	Fletcher H	Fraser J	Gibson W	Hendry R	Langham W	Leonard J	Lewis G	Murphy, John	Potter A	Prescott TG	Sanderson E	Sharman J	Stewart A	Toone G
R1	Jan	29	WOLVERHAMPTON W.	0-1		15000		10				9	5	8	4	11				3		7					2			6	1

		p	w	d	l	f	a	pts
1	Sheffield United	30	17	8	5	56	31	42
2	Sunderland	30	16	5	9	43	30	37
3	Wolverhampton Wan.	30	14	7	9	57	41	35
4	Everton	30	13	9	8	48	39	35
5	Sheffield Wed.	30	15	3	12	51	42	33
6	Aston Villa	30	14	5	11	61	51	33
7	West Bromwich Alb.	30	11	10	9	44	45	32
8	Nottingham Forest	30	11	9	10	47	49	31
9	Liverpool	30	11	6	13	48	45	28
10	Derby County	30	11	6	13	57	61	28
11	Bolton Wanderers	30	11	4	15	28	41	26
12	Preston North End	30	8	8	14	35	43	24
13	NOTTS COUNTY	30	8	8	14	36	46	24
14	Bury	30	8	8	14	39	51	24
15	Blackburn Rovers	30	7	10	13	39	54	24
16	Stoke	30	8	8	14	35	55	24

1898/99

5th in Division One

#		Date	Opponent	Score	Scorers	Att	Boucher T	Bull W	Calderhead D	Carter AB	Donaldson J	Fletcher H	Fraser J	Hadley A	Hannigan R	Lewis G	Logan P	Maconnachie A	Montgomery J	Prescott TG	Sanderson E	Suter ER	Thurman AJ	Toone G	Watts A
1	Sep	3	Burnley	1-1	Maconnachie	6000	9	4	5			10	11		7	3		8		2	6			1	
2		10	SHEFFIELD UNITED	2-2	Fletcher 2	15000	9	4	5			10	11		7	3		8		2	6			1	
3		17	Newcastle United	2-1	Hadley, Maconnachie	25000	9	4	5			10	11	7		3		8		2	6			1	
4		24	PRESTON NORTH END	1-0	Fraser	12000	9	4	5			10	11	7		3		8		2	6			1	
5	Oct	1	Liverpool	0-0		15000	9	4	5			10	11	7		3		8		2	6			1	
6		8	NOTTM. FOREST	2-2	Hadley, Maconnachie(p)	20000	9	4	5			10	11	7		3		8		2	6			1	
7		15	Bolton Wanderers	1-0	Maconnachie	5000	9	4	5			10	11	7		3		8		2	6			1	
8		22	DERBY COUNTY	2-2	Hadley, Maconnachie	16000	9	4	5			10	11	7		3		8		2	6			1	
9		29	West Bromwich Alb.	0-2		4000	9	4	5			10	11		7	3		8		2	6			1	
10	Nov	5	BLACKBURN ROVERS	5-3	*See below	6000	10	4	5				11		7		9	8	3	2	6			1	
11		12	Sheffield Wednesday	1-1	Fraser	10000	10	4	5				11		7	3	9	8		2	6			1	
12		19	SUNDERLAND	5-2	Fletcher 2, Logan 2, Maconnachie	17000	10	4	5			7	11			3	9	8		2	6			1	
13		26	Wolverhampton Wand.	0-1		6000	10	4	5			7	11			3	9	8		2	6			1	
14	Dec	3	EVERTON	0-1		10000	10	4	5			7	11				9	8	3	2	6			1	
15		10	BURY	4-1	Boucher, Fletcher, Fraser, Logan	8000	10		5	4		7	11			3	9	8		2	6			1	
16		17	Stoke	1-1	Fletcher	5000	8		5			10	11	7		3	9			2	6		4	1	
17		24	ASTON VILLA	1-0	Maconnachie	16000			5			10	11	7		3	9	8		2	6		4	1	
18		27	LIVERPOOL	1-1	Fletcher(p)	16000	9		5			10	11	7		3		8		2	6			1	4
19		31	BURNLEY	2-2	Maconnachie 2	12000			5			10	11		7	3	9	8		2	6			1	4
20	Jan	2	Blackburn Rovers	0-6		4000	9		5			10	11		7	3		8		2	6			1	4
21		7	Sheffield United	2-2	Hannigan, Maconnachie	6000			5			10	11		7	3	9	8		2	6			1	4
22		14	NEWCASTLE UNITED	3-1	Fletcher, Logan, Maconnachie	7000			5			10	11		7	3	9	8		2	6			1	4
23	Feb	4	Nottm. Forest	0-0		12000			5			10	11	7		3	9	8		2	6			1	4
24		18	Derby County	2-4	Fletcher, Hadley	8000		4	5			10	11	7		3		9		2	8	1			6
25	Mar	9	WEST BROMWICH ALB.	0-0		2488		4	5			9	11	7				8	3	2	10	1			6
26		11	SHEFFIELD WEDNESDAY	1-0	Fletcher	8000		4	5			10	11		7		9	8	3	2		1			6
27		18	Sunderland	1-1	Maconnachie	7000		4	5		1	10		11	7		9	8	3	2					6
28		20	Preston North End	0-2		3000		4	5		1	10		11	7		9	8	3	2					6
29		25	WOLVERHAMPTON W.	0-2		3000		4	5		1	10		11	7	2	9	8	3						6
30	Apr	1	Everton	2-1	Boucher, Fletcher	12000	9	2	5			10	11	7		3		8			6	1			4
31		3	BOLTON WANDERERS	2-1	Fletcher, Hadley	8000	9	2	5			10	11	7		3		8			6	1			4
32		8	Bury	0-2		5000	9	2	5			10	11	7		3		8			6	1			4
33		15	STOKE	2-0	Maconnachie, Fletcher	5000	9	2	5			10	11	7		3		8			6	1			4
34		22	Aston Villa	1-6	Bull	18900	9	2	5			10	11	7	4	3		8				1			6

Game 33 at the City Ground
Scorers in game 10: Logan 2, Boucher, Hannigan, Maconnachie

	Boucher T	Bull W	Calderhead D	Carter AB	Donaldson J	Fletcher H	Fraser J	Hadley A	Hannigan R	Lewis G	Logan P	Maconnachie A	Montgomery J	Prescott TG	Sanderson E	Suter ER	Thurman AJ	Toone G	Watts A
Apps	23	25	34	1	3	32	31	19	15	28	16	33	7	28	29	8	2	23	17
Goals	3	1				13	3	5	2		6	14							

F.A. Cup

		Date	Opponent	Score	Scorers	Att	Boucher T	Bull W	Calderhead D	Carter AB	Donaldson J	Fletcher H	Fraser J	Hadley A	Hannigan R	Lewis G	Logan P	Maconnachie A	Montgomery J	Prescott TG	Sanderson E	Suter ER	Thurman AJ	Toone G	Watts A
R1	Jan	28	KETTERING	2-0	Fletcher, Maconnachie	7000			4	5			10	11		7	3	9	8		2	6			1	
R2	Feb	11	SOUTHAMPTON	0-1		18000	9		5			10	11	7		3		8		2	6			1	4

Back: Callan (director), Prescott, Bull, Calderhead, Sanderson, Lewis, Goode (trainer). Centre: Harris (secretary), Hannigan, Maconnachie, Fletcher, Fraser, Toone. Front: Boucher.

		p	w	d	l	f	a	pts
1	Aston Villa	34	19	7	8	76	40	45
2	Liverpool	34	19	5	10	49	33	43
3	Burnley	34	15	9	10	45	47	39
4	Everton	34	15	8	11	48	41	38
5	NOTTS COUNTY	34	12	13	9	47	51	37
6	Blackburn Rovers	34	14	8	12	60	52	36
7	Sunderland	34	15	6	13	41	41	36
8	Wolverhampton Wan.	34	14	7	13	54	48	35
9	Derby County	34	12	11	11	62	57	35
10	Bury	34	14	7	13	48	49	35
11	Nottingham Forest	34	11	11	12	42	42	33
12	Stoke	34	13	7	14	47	52	33
13	Newcastle United	34	11	8	15	49	48	30
14	West Bromwich Alb.	34	12	6	16	42	57	30
15	Preston North End	34	10	9	15	44	47	29
16	Sheffield United	34	9	11	14	45	51	29
17	Bolton Wanderers	34	9	7	18	37	51	25
18	Sheffield Wed.	34	8	8	18	32	61	24

1899/1900

15th in Division One

#		Date	Opponent	Score	Scorers	Att	Ball WH	Bull W	Calderhead D	Chalmers J	Fletcher H	Goss W	Hadley A	Lewis G	Maconnachie A	Marsh I	McCairns T	McCappin S	McDonald E	McMain J	Montgomery J	Prescott TG	Sharman J	Simpson T	Smith, Walter	Suter ER	Warner A
1	Sep	2	Derby County	1-0	Maconnachie	12000	6	4	5	11	10		7	3	8							9	2			1	
2		9	BURY	2-2	Bull, Maconnachie	10000	6	4	5	11	10		7	3	8							9	2			1	
3		16	WOLVERHAMPTON W.	0-0		12000	6	4	5	11	10		7	3	8							9	2			1	
4		23	Manchester City	1-5	Maconnachie	20000	6	4	5		10	11	7	3	9							8	2			1	
5		30	SHEFFIELD UNITED	1-2	Fletcher	8000	6	4	5		10	11	7	2	8		9						3			1	
6	Oct	5	LIVERPOOL	2-1	Maconnachie(p), Hadley	10000	6	4	5		10	11	7	2	8		9						3			1	
7		7	Newcastle United	0-6		20000	6	4	5		10	11	7		8		9					7	3			1	
8		14	ASTON VILLA	1-4	Ball	10000	6	4	5		10	11	7	3	8		9						2	1			
9		21	Liverpool	1-3	Ball	10000	6	4	5		10	11	7	3	8							9	2			1	
10		28	BURNLEY	6-1	Maconnachie 2, McMain 2, Bull, Hadley	10000	6	4	5	11	10		7	3	8							9	2				
11	Nov	4	Preston North End	3-4	Maconnachie 2, Hadley	4000	6	4	5	11	10		7	3	8			1		9			2				
12		11	NOTTM. FOREST	1-2	McMain	12000		4	5	11	10		7	3	8			1	6	9			2				
13		18	Glossop	0-0		4000		4	5		11		7	3	8			1	6	9			2				10
14		25	STOKE	1-3	Fletcher	12000		4	5	11	10		7	3	8			1	6	9			2				
15	Dec	2	Sunderland	0-5		6000		4	6	11	10		7		8	5		1		9	3		2				
16		9	WEST BROMWICH ALB.	1-2	Maconnachie(p)	8000	6		5			7		11	2	8				10	9	3	4			1	
17		16	Everton	2-0	Hadley, McMain	4000		4	5	11		10	7	2	8				6	9	3					1	
18		23	BLACKBURN ROVERS	5-1	Hadley 3, McMain 2	5000		4	5	11		10	7	2	8				6	9	3					1	
19		30	DERBY COUNTY	0-0		8000		4	5	11		10	7	2	8				6	9	3					1	
20	Jan	6	Bury	1-0	McMain	912		4	5	11		10	7	2	8				6	9	3					1	
21		13	Wolverhampton Wand.	2-2	Chalmers, Goss	5000		4	5	11		10	7	2	8				6	9	3					1	
22		20	MANCHESTER CITY	1-1	Bull	10000		4	5	11		10	7	2	8				6	9	3					1	
23	Feb	3	Sheffield United	1-1	McMain	5000		4	5	11		10	7	2	8			1	6	9	3						
24		17	Aston Villa	2-6	Hadley 2	16000		4	5	11	10		7	2	8				6	9	3					1	
25	Mar	3	Burnley	0-3		5000		4	5		9	10	7	2	8				6		3			11		1	
26		10	PRESTON NORTH END	3-0	McMain 2, Warner	10000		4	5	11			7	2	8				6	9	3					1	10
27		17	Nottm. Forest	3-0	Maconnachie(p), Hadley, Chalmers	8000		4	5	11			7	2	8				6	9	3					1	10
28		24	GLOSSOP	0-0		5000		4	5	11			7	2	8	6					3				9	1	10
29		31	Stoke	0-1		7000		4	5	11	10		7	2	8	6					3					1	9
30	Apr	7	SUNDERLAND	3-1	McMain 2, Maconnachie	6000		4	5	11	7			2	8				6	9	3					1	10
31		14	West Bromwich Alb.	0-0		5000		4	5	11	7	10		2	8				6		3					1	9
32		16	NEWCASTLE UNITED	0-0		10000		4	5	11	7			2	8				6	9	3					1	10
33		21	EVERTON	2-2	Maconnachie, McMain	6000		4	5	11	7			2	8				6	9	3					1	10
34		28	Blackburn Rovers	0-2		6000		4	5	11	7	10								6	3	2			9	1	8
			Apps				34	34	11	25	24	16	28	32	33	3	4	7	20	26	23	14	1	1	2	26	10
			Goals				2	3		2	2	1	10		12					13							1

Games 32,33 at the City Ground

F.A. Cup

		Date	Opponent	Score	Scorers	Att	Ball WH	Bull W	Calderhead D	Chalmers J	Fletcher H	Goss W	Hadley A	Lewis G	Maconnachie A	Marsh I	McCairns T	McCappin S	McDonald E	McMain J	Montgomery J	Prescott TG	Sharman J	Simpson T	Smith, Walter	Suter ER	Warner A
R1	Jan	27	CHORLEY	6-0	McMain 2, Bull, Chalmers, Goss, Maconnachie	6000		4	5	11		10	7	2	8				6	9	3					1	
R2	Feb	10	BURY	0-0		10000		4	5	11		10	7	2	8				6	9	3					1	
rep		14	Bury	0-2		3000		4	5	11		10	7	2	8				6	9	3					1	

Back: Bramley (treasurer), Harris (secretary), Prescott, Suter, Lewis, Ball, Shelton (director), Goode (trainer). Centre: Hadley, Maconnachie, Calderhead, Fletcher, Chalmers, Thomas (director). Front: Bull, McMain.

		p	w	d	l	f	a	pts
1	Aston Villa	34	22	6	6	77	35	50
2	Sheffield United	34	18	12	4	63	33	48
3	Sunderland	34	19	3	12	50	35	41
4	Wolverhampton Wan.	34	15	9	10	48	37	39
5	Newcastle United	34	13	10	11	53	43	36
6	Derby County	34	14	8	12	45	43	36
7	Manchester City	34	13	8	13	50	44	34
8	Nottingham Forest	34	13	8	13	56	55	34
9	Stoke	34	13	8	13	37	45	34
10	Liverpool	34	14	5	15	49	45	33
11	Everton	34	13	7	14	47	49	33
12	Bury	34	13	6	15	40	44	32
13	West Bromwich Alb.	34	11	8	15	43	51	30
14	Blackburn Rovers	34	13	4	17	49	61	30
15	NOTTS COUNTY	34	9	11	14	46	60	29
16	Preston North End	34	12	4	18	38	48	28
17	Burnley	34	11	5	18	34	54	27
18	Glossop	34	4	10	20	31	74	18

1900/01

3rd in Division One

#		Date	Opponent	Score	Scorers	Att	Ball WH	Brearley J	Bull W	Gee E	Hadley A	Lewis G	Maconnachie A	McDonald E	Montgomery J	Morris JJ	Pennington H	Prescott TG	Ross W	Simpson T	Smith DW	Spencer F	Suter ER	Warner A
1	Sep	1	SUNDERLAND	2-2	Bull, Warner	10000			5	11		2	8	6	3	7			9		4		1	10
2		3	Wolverhampton Wand.	2-3	Ross 2	5000			5	11		2	8	6	3	7			9		4		1	10
3		8	Derby County	1-2	Hadley	10000	4	10	5	11	7	2	8	6	3		1		9					
4		10	Stoke	1-1	Morris	5000	4		5	11	7	3	8	6		10	1	2	9					
5		15	BOLTON WANDERERS	3-1	Gee, Morris, Hadley	10000	4		5	11	7	3	8	6		10	1	2	9					
6		22	Sheffield Wednesday	1-4	Hadley	12000	4		5	11	7	3	8	6		10	1	2	9					
7		29	Preston North End	1-0	Morris	6000	4		5	11	7	3		6		10	1	2	9					8
8	Oct	6	WOLVERHAMPTON W.	4-1	Warner 3, Ross	14000	4		5		7	3		6		10	1	2	9	11				8
9		13	Aston Villa	2-1	Gee, Morris	16000	4		5	11	7	3		6		10	1	2	9					8
10		20	LIVERPOOL	3-0	Ross, Morris, Bull	18000	4		5	11	7	3		6		10	1	2	9					8
11		27	Newcastle United	0-2		16000	4		5	11	7	3		6		10	1	2	9					8
12	Nov	3	SHEFFIELD UNITED	2-4	Morris, Ross	12000	4		5	11	7	2		6	3	10	1		9					8
13		5	West Bromwich Alb.	0-1		3000	4		2		7	3	8	6		10	1		9	11	5			
14		10	Manchester City	0-2		16000	5	4		11		3	8	6		10	1		9		2	7		
15		17	BURY	1-0	Ross	7000	4	11	5			3	8	6		10	1	2	9			7		
16		24	Nottm. Forest	0-5		15000	4	11	5			3	7	6		10	1	2	9					8
17	Dec	1	BLACKBURN ROVERS	2-1	Ross, Morris	6000	4		5	11	7			6		10	1	2	9		3			8
18		15	WEST BROMWICH ALB.	1-0	Warner	4000	4		5	11	7	3		6		10	1	2	9					8
19		22	Everton	1-0	Spencer	7000	4		5	11		3		6		10	1	2	9			7		8
20		26	NOTTM. FOREST	1-0	Ross	20000	4		5	11		3		6		10	1	2	9			7		8
21		29	Sunderland	1-1	Warner	7000	4		5	11		3		6		10	1	2	9			7		8
22	Jan	5	DERBY COUNTY	2-1	Gee, Ross	15000	4	6	5	11		3				10	1	2	9			7		8
23		19	SHEFFIELD WEDNESDAY	2-0	Warner, Morris	4000	4		5	11		3		6		10	1	2	9			7		8
24	Feb	16	ASTON VILLA	2-0	Warner, Ross	14000		4	5	11	7	3		6		10	1	2	9					8
25	Mar	2	NEWCASTLE UNITED	3-1	Gee, Morris, Warner	4000	4	6	5	11	7	3				10	1	2	9					8
26		9	Sheffield United	2-4	Warner 2	12000	4		5	11	7	3		6		10	1	2	9					8
27		16	MANCHESTER CITY	0-0		6000	4	5		11	7	3		6		10	1	2	9					8
28		23	Bury	0-1		7000			5	11	7	3		6		10	1	2	9					8
29		27	PRESTON NORTH END	6-1	Ross, Warner, Morris 2, Gee, Hadley	1500	4		5	11	7	3		6		10	1	2	9					8
30	Apr	5	Bolton Wanderers	1-0	Hadley	15617	4		5	11	7	3		6		10	1	2	9					8
31		6	Blackburn Rovers	2-0	Morris, Hadley	7000	4		5	11	7	2		6	3	10	1		9					8
32		8	Liverpool	0-1		20000	4		5	11	7	2		6	3	10	1		9					8
33		9	EVERTON	3-2	Morris 2, Ross	9000	4		5	11	7	2		6	3	10	1		9					8
34		13	STOKE	2-4	Morris 2	6000	4		5	11	7	2		6	3	10	1		9					8
			Apps				31	8	32	30	24	33	10	32	8	33	32	24	34	2	5	7	2	27
			Goals						2	5	6					16			12			1		12

Games 1, 33, 34 at the City Ground

F.A. Cup

		Date	Opponent	Score	Scorers	Att	Ball WH	Brearley J	Bull W	Gee E	Hadley A	Lewis G	Maconnachie A	McDonald E	Montgomery J	Morris JJ	Pennington H	Prescott TG	Ross W	Simpson T	Smith DW	Spencer F	Suter ER	Warner A
R1	Feb	9	LIVERPOOL	2-0	Morris 2	18000	4		5	11	7	3		6		10	1	2	9					8
R2		23	WOLVERHAMPTON W.	2-3	Morris, Warner	17000	4		5	11	7	3		6		10	1	2	9					8

		p	w	d	l	f	a	pts
1	Liverpool	34	19	7	8	59	35	45
2	Sunderland	34	15	13	6	57	26	43
3	NOTTS COUNTY	34	18	4	12	54	46	40
4	Nottingham Forest	34	16	7	11	53	36	39
5	Bury	34	16	7	11	53	37	39
6	Newcastle United	34	14	10	10	42	37	38
7	Everton	34	16	5	13	55	42	37
8	Sheffield Wed.	34	13	10	11	52	42	36
9	Blackburn Rovers	34	12	9	13	39	47	33
10	Bolton Wanderers	34	13	7	14	39	55	33
11	Manchester City	34	13	6	15	48	58	32
12	Derby County	34	12	7	15	55	42	31
13	Wolverhampton Wan.	34	9	13	12	39	55	31
14	Sheffield United	34	12	7	15	35	52	31
15	Aston Villa	34	10	10	14	45	51	30
16	Stoke	34	11	5	18	46	57	27
17	Preston North End	34	9	7	18	49	75	25
18	West Bromwich Alb.	34	7	8	19	35	62	22

1901/02

13th in Division One

#		Date	Opponent	Score	Scorers	Att	Bull W	Gee E	Hadley A	Humphreys P	Innes R	Joynes R	Lewis G	Mainman HL	McDonald E	Montgomery J	Morris JJ	Pennington H	Prescott TG	Ross W	Simpson T	Spencer F	Suter ER	Toone G	Warner A
1	Sep	7	Derby County	0-2		11000	5	11	7		4		3		6		10	1	2	9					8
2		9	Aston Villa	0-2		15000	5	11	7		4		3		6		10	1	2	9					8
3		14	SHEFFIELD WEDNESDAY	6-1	Morris 3, Gee 2, Humphreys	12000	5	11		9	4		3		6		10	1	2	7					8
4		21	GRIMSBY TOWN	3-0	Morris, McDonald, Humphreys	7000	5	11		8	4		3		6		10	1	2	9					7
5		28	Bolton Wanderers	1-1	Morris	9047	5	11		8	4		3		6		10	1	2	9					7
6	Oct	3	NEWCASTLE UNITED	0-2		10000	5	11		8			3	4	6		10	1	2	9					7
7		5	MANCHESTER CITY	2-0	Ross, Warner	12000	5	11					3	4	6		10	1	2	9		7			8
8		12	Wolverhampton Wand.	1-3	Morris	10000	5	11		9			3	4	6		10	1	2		7				8
9		19	LIVERPOOL	2-2	Humphreys 2	8000	5	11		9			3	4	6		10	1	2		7				8
10		26	Newcastle United	0-8		16000	5	11		9			3	4	6		10	1	2			7			8
11	Nov	2	ASTON VILLA	0-3		12000	5	11		8	4		3		6		10		2			7	1		9
12		9	Sheffield United	0-3		7000	3	11		9	4			5	6		10		2		8	7	1		
13		16	NOTTM. FOREST	3-0	Ross 2, McDonald	12000	5	11		8	4		3		6		10	1	2	9		7			
14		23	Bury	0-3		6000	5	11		8	4		3		6		10	1	2	9		7			
15		30	BLACKBURN ROVERS	3-0	Gee, Humphreys, Hadley	8000	5	11	7	8	4		3		6		10	1	2	9					
16	Dec	7	Stoke	0-3		8000	5	11	7	8	4		3		6		10	1	2	9					
17		14	EVERTON	0-2		5000	5	11	7	10	4		2		6	3		1		9					8
18		21	Sunderland	1-2	Spencer	5000	9	11		8	4		2	5	6	3	10	1				7			
19		26	Nottm. Forest	0-1		20000	5	11		8	4		2	5	6	3	10	1				7			
20		28	SMALL HEATH	6-1	Morris 3(1p), Humphreys, Lewis, Bull	8000	9	11		8	4	7	2	5	6	3	10							1	
21	Jan	4	DERBY COUNTY	3-2	Joynes, Bull, Humphreys	5000	9			8	4	7	2	5	6	3	10				11			1	
22		11	Sheffield Wednesday	0-4		7000	9	11		8	4	7	2	5	6	3	10							1	
23		18	Grimsby Town	0-1		8000	9	11		8	4	7	2	5	6	3	10	1							
24	Feb	1	Manchester City	0-1		14000	5	11		8	4	7	2		6	3	10	1		9					
25		15	Liverpool	1-0	Ross	10000	5	11		8	4	7			6	3	10	1	2	9					
26	Mar	8	SHEFFIELD UNITED	4-0	Morris 2, Ross, Joynes	6000	5	11		8	4	7			6	3	10	1	2	9					
27		22	BURY	2-1	Ross 2	8000	5	11		8	4	7			6	3	10	1	2	9					
28		28	WOLVERHAMPTON W.	5-3	Humphreys 3, Ross 2	10000	5	11		8	4	7			6	3	10	1	2	9					
29		29	Blackburn Rovers	2-4	McDonald, Bull	6000	5	11		8	4	7			6	3	10	1	2	9					
30		31	BOLTON WANDERERS	2-1	Humphreys, Morris	18000	5	11		8	4	7			6	3	10	1	2	9					
31	Apr	5	STOKE	1-1	Bull	4000	5	11		8	4	7			6	3	10	1	2	9					
32		12	Everton	1-0	Humphreys	10000	5	11		8	4	7			6	3	10	1	2	9					
33		19	SUNDERLAND	2-0	Humphreys 2	10000	5	11		8	4	7			6	3	10	1	2	9					
34		26	Small Heath	0-0		4000	5	11		8	4	7			6	3	10	1	2	9					
			Apps				34	33	5	31	29	15	23	12	34	18	33	29	26	23	4	8	2	3	12
			Goals				4	3	1	14		2	1		3		12			9		1			1

Game 33 at the City Ground

F.A. Cup

R1	Jan	25	READING	1-2	Lewis	10000	9	11			4		2	5	6	3	10	1			7				8

	p	w	d	l	f	a	pts
1 Sunderland	34	19	6	9	50	35	44
2 Everton	34	17	7	10	53	35	41
3 Newcastle United	34	14	9	11	48	34	37
4 Blackburn Rovers	34	15	6	13	52	48	36
5 Nottingham Forest	34	13	9	12	43	43	35
6 Derby County	34	13	9	12	39	41	35
7 Bury	34	13	8	13	44	38	34
8 Aston Villa	34	13	8	13	42	40	34
9 Sheffield Wed.	34	13	8	13	48	52	34
10 Sheffield United	34	13	7	14	53	48	33
11 Liverpool	34	10	12	12	42	38	32
12 Bolton Wanderers	34	12	8	14	51	56	32
13 NOTTS COUNTY	34	14	4	16	51	57	32
14 Wolverhampton Wan.	34	13	6	15	46	57	32
15 Grimsby Town	34	13	6	15	44	60	32
16 Stoke	34	11	9	14	45	55	31
17 Small Heath	34	11	8	15	47	45	30
18 Manchester City	34	11	6	17	42	58	28

Back: Bramley (treasurer), Prescott, Suter, Harris (secretary), Pennington, Lewis, Montgomery, H Spencer (director).
Centre: F Spencer, Innes, Bull, Pollock, Mainman, Goode (trainer). Front: Warner, Humphreys, Ross, Morris, Gee.

1902/03

15th in Division One

#		Date	Opponent	Score	Scorers	Att	Bull W	Gee E	Green AW	Humphreys P	Innes R	Joynes R	Kirk JJ	Mainman HL	McDonald E	McIntyre JA	Mellors M	Montgomery J	Morris JJ	Pennington H	Prescott TG	Ross W	Swift G	Whyte P
1	Sep	6	WEST BROMWICH ALB.	3-1	Ross, Joynes, Gee	10000	5	11		8	4	7			6			3	10	1	2	9		
2		13	Derby County	1-4	Humphreys	12000	5			8	4	7			6	11		3	10	1	2	9		
3		15	Stoke	2-0	Humphreys, Green	8000	5		9	8	4	7			6			3	10	1	2	11		
4		20	Bolton Wanderers	1-0	Bull	10000	5		9	8	4	7			6			3	10	1	2	11		
5		27	MIDDLESBROUGH	2-0	Humphreys, Ross	10000	5		9	8	4	7			6			3	10	1		11	2	
6	Oct	3	SHEFFIELD WEDNESDAY	0-3		6000	5		9	8	4	7			6			3	10	1	2	11		
7		4	Newcastle United	1-6	Green	10000	5	11	9	8		7		4	6			3		1	2	10		
8		11	WOLVERHAMPTON W.	0-0		9000	5	11	9	8	4	7			6			3		1	2	10		
9		18	Liverpool	2-0	Ross, Green	15000	5	11	9	8		7		4	6			3		1	2	10		
10		25	SHEFFIELD UNITED	1-1	Green	10000	5	11	9	8		7		4	6			3		1	2	10		
11	Nov	1	Grimsby Town	1-1	Humphreys	6000	5	11	9	8		7		4	6			3		1	2	10		
12		8	ASTON VILLA	2-1	Green 2	8000	5	11	9	8	4	7			6			3		1	2	10		
13		15	Nottm. Forest	0-0		15000	5	11	9	8		7		4	6			3		1	2	10		
14		22	BURY	1-0	Green(p)	8000	5	11	9	8		7		4	6					1	2	10	3	
15		29	Blackburn Rovers	2-1	Humphreys, Green(p)	6000	5	11	9	8	4	7			6					1	2	10	3	
16	Dec	6	SUNDERLAND	0-0		10000	5	11	9	8	4	7			6					1	2	10	3	
17		20	EVERTON	2-0	Humphreys, Green	8000		11	9	8	4	7		5	6					1	2	10	3	
18		26	NOTTM. FOREST	1-1	Green	20000	5	11	9	8		7		4	6					1	2	10	3	
19		27	Sheffield Wednesday	0-2		25000	5	11	9	8	4	7			6					1	2	10	3	
20	Jan	3	West Bromwich Alb.	2-3	Green 2	15000	5		9	8		7		4	6				10	1	2	11	3	
21		10	DERBY COUNTY	2-1	Humphreys, Morris	16000	2		9	8	4	7		5	6				10	1		11	3	
22		17	BOLTON WANDERERS	1-3	Ross	5000	2		9	8	4	7		5	6				10	1		11	3	
23		24	Middlesbrough	1-2	Morris	10000	5	11	9	8				4	6				10	1	2		3	7
24		31	NEWCASTLE UNITED	2-2	Humphreys 2	10000	5		9	8				4	6			3	10	1	2	11		7
25	Feb	14	LIVERPOOL	1-2	Bull	8000	5	11	9	8				4	6			3		1	2	10		7
26		28	GRIMSBY TOWN	0-1		8000	5	11	9	8	4	7	6					3		1		10	2	
27	Mar	26	Bury	1-3	Humphreys	1782	11		9	8	4	7		5	6	10		3		1	2			
28		28	BLACKBURN ROVERS	4-0	McIntyre, Humphreys 2, Green	5000	5	11	9	8		7		4	6	10		3		1	2			
29	Apr	4	Sunderland	1-2	McIntyre	12000	5	11	9		4	7			6	10		3		1		8	2	
30		10	Sheffield United	0-3		7000	5	11	9	8		7		4	6	10	1	3			2			
31		11	STOKE	3-0	Humphreys 2, Green(p)	6000	5	11	9	8		7		4	6	10		3		1	2			
32		13	Wolverhampton Wand.	0-2		3000	5	11	9	8		7		4	6	10	1				2		3	
33		15	Aston Villa	1-2	McIntyre	7000	2	11	9	8	4	7		5	6	10				1			3	
34		18	Everton	0-2		8000	5	11	9	8	4	7			6	10				1		2	3	
			Apps				33	24	32	33	19	31	1	25	28	9	2	21	11	32	27	27	16	3
			Goals				2	1	14	14		1				3			2			4		

Game 1 at the City Ground

F.A. Cup

		Date	Opponent	Score	Scorers	Att	Bull W	Gee E	Green AW	Humphreys P	Innes R	Joynes R	Kirk JJ	Mainman HL	McDonald E	McIntyre JA	Mellors M	Montgomery J	Morris JJ	Pennington H	Prescott TG	Ross W	Swift G	Whyte P
R1	Feb	7	SOUTHAMPTON	0-0		15000	5	11	9	8		7		4	6			3	10	1	2			
rep		11	Southampton	2-2	Gee 2	16734	5	11	9	8				4	6			3		1	2	10		7
rep2		16	Southampton	2-1	Humphreys, Green	18000		11	9	8	4			5	6			3		1	2	10		7
R2		21	Grimsby Town	2-0	Green, Humphreys	9000	5	11	9	8	4				6			3		1	2	10		7
R3	Mar	7	Bury	0-1		20000	5	11	9					4	6			3	8	1	2	10		7

R1 replay and replay 2 after extra time. Replay 2 at Villa Park.

	p	w	d	l	f	a	pts
1 Sheffield Wed.	34	19	4	11	54	36	42
2 Aston Villa	34	19	3	12	61	40	41
3 Sunderland	34	16	9	9	51	36	41
4 Sheffield United	34	17	5	12	58	44	39
5 Liverpool	34	17	4	13	68	49	38
6 Stoke	34	15	7	12	46	38	37
7 West Bromwich Alb.	34	16	4	14	54	53	36
8 Bury	34	16	3	15	54	43	35
9 Derby County	34	16	3	15	50	47	35
10 Nottingham Forest	34	14	7	13	49	47	35
11 Wolverhampton Wan.	34	14	5	15	48	57	33
12 Everton	34	13	6	15	45	47	32
13 Middlesbrough	34	14	4	16	41	50	32
14 Newcastle United	34	14	4	16	41	51	32
15 NOTTS COUNTY	34	12	7	15	41	49	31
16 Blackburn Rovers	34	12	5	17	44	63	29
17 Grimsby Town	34	8	9	17	43	62	25
18 Bolton Wanderers	34	8	3	23	37	73	19

Back: Spencer (director), Prescott, Montgomery, Pennington, Harris (secretary), Swift, Gee, Bramley (director).
Centre: Thomas (director), Joynes, Innes, Bull, McDonald, Ross, Goode (trainer). Front: Humphreys, Green, Morris

1903/04

13th in Division One

#		Date	Opponent	Score	Scorers	Att	Bull W	Chapman HG	Clare WE	Dainty HC	Gee E	Glen A	Green AW	Griffiths A	Humphreys P	Kelly W	Mainman HL	McCall J	McDonald E	Mellors M	Montgomery J	Pennington H	Prescott TG	Reid J	Ross W	Sands J	Tarplin W	Walkerdine G	Ward A
1	Sep	1	Sunderland	1-4	Glen	15000	5					11	10	9	8		4	7	6		3	1	2						
2		5	Everton	1-3	Humphreys	22000	5					11	10	9	8		4	7	6		3	1	2						
3		12	STOKE	1-0	Green	10000	5					11		9	8		4	7	6		3	1	2	10					
4		19	Derby County	1-0	Humphreys	12000	3			5	11		9		8		4		6			1	2	10	7				
5		26	MANCHESTER CITY	0-3		15000	3			5	11		9		8		4		6			1	2	10	7				
6	Oct	1	LIVERPOOL	4-2	Green 2, Humphreys, Chapman	10000		7		5	11		9		8		4		6		3	1	2	10					
7		3	WOLVERHAMPTON W.	0-2		12000		7		5	11		9		8		4		6		3	1	2	10					
8		10	Sheffield United	1-3	Green(p)	15000				5	11	10	9	3	8		4		6			1	2		7				
9		17	NEWCASTLE UNITED	3-2	Prescott, Green, Ross	9000	3	10		6	11		9		8	4	5			1			2		7				
10		24	Aston Villa	0-4		20000	3	7		4	11		9		8		5		6	1			2		10				
11		31	MIDDLESBROUGH	3-2	Humphreys, Green 2	10000	3			4	11		9		8		5		6	1			2		10				7
12	Nov	7	Liverpool	1-2	Humphreys	10000	3			4	11		9		8		5		6	1			2		10				7
13		14	BURY	0-0		8000	3			4	11		9		8		5		6	1			2		10				7
14		21	Blackburn Rovers	0-3		7000	3			4	11	10	9	6	8		5			1			2		7				
15		28	NOTTM. FOREST	1-3	Green	5000	5	8		6	11		9		7		4				1	3	2		10				
16	Dec	12	SUNDERLAND	2-1	Montgomery, Green(p)	7000	5	0		6	11	10	9		7		4				3	1	2						
17		19	West Bromwich Alb.	0-0		6000	5			6	11	10	8		7		4				3	1	2		9				
18		25	Nottm. Forest	1-0	Ross	15000	5			6	11	10	8		7		4				3	1	2		9				
19		26	SMALL HEATH	2-0	Humphreys, Green	12000	5			6	11	10	8		7		4				3	1	2		9				
20	Jan	1	Bury	0-3		12000	5				11	10	8		7		4		6		3	1	2		9				
21		2	EVERTON	0-3		7000	5				11	10	8	4	7				6		3	1	2		9				
22		9	Stoke	2-0	Green 2(1p)	5000	5				11		9	4	8				6		3	1	2		10				7
23		16	DERBY COUNTY	2-2	Green(p), Humphreys	15000	5				11		9	4	8				6		3	1	2		10				7
24		23	Manchester City	0-3		12000	5				11			4	8				6		3	1	2		9			10	7
25		30	Wolverhampton Wand.	1-1	Glen	5000	5				11	10		4	8				6		3	1	2		9				7
26	Feb	13	Newcastle United	1-4	Humphreys	5000	5			4	11	10	9	3	8				6			1	2		7				
27		20	WEST BROMWICH ALB.	2-3	Glen, Green(p)	5000	5			4	11	10	9	3	8				6			1	2		7				
28		22	Sheffield Wednesday	0-2		7000	3			4	7	10			8	5			6			1	2		9	11			
29		27	Middlesbrough	0-1		5000	5			4	7	10		3	8				6			1	2		9	11			
30	Mar	19	BLACKBURN ROVERS	4-2	Green 4(2p)	6000	5	7			11	10	9	4	8				6		3	1	2						
31	Apr	1	ASTON VILLA	0-0		15000	5				11	10	9	4	8		6				3	1	2		7				
32		2	SHEFFIELD WEDNESDAY	1-0	Humphreys	13000	5				11	10	9	4	8		6				3	1	2		7				
33		4	SHEFFIELD UNITED	2-1	Ross, Green	15000	5				11	10	9		8		4		6		3	1	2		7				
34		23	Small Heath	0-2		8000	5		2		11	10	9		8		4		6		3	1				7			
					Apps		31	7	1	20	34	20	30	13	34	2	24	3	25	7	21	27	33	5	26	2	1	1	7
					Goals			1				3	19		9								1		1	3			

F.A. Cup

		Date	Opponent	Score	Scorers	Att	Bull W	Chapman HG	Clare WE	Dainty HC	Gee E	Glen A	Green AW	Griffiths A	Humphreys P	Kelly W	Mainman HL	McCall J	McDonald E	Mellors M	Montgomery J	Pennington H	Prescott TG	Reid J	Ross W	Sands J	Tarplin W	Walkerdine G	Ward A
R1	Feb	6	MANCHESTER UTD.	3-3	Ross, Humphreys 2	12000	5				11		9	4	8				6		3	1	2		10				7
rep		10	Manchester Utd.	1-2	Green (p)	15000	3			5	11	10	9	4	8				6			1	2		7				

		p	w	d	l	f	a	pts
1	Sheffield Wed.	34	20	7	7	48	28	47
2	Manchester City	34	19	6	9	71	45	44
3	Everton	34	19	5	10	59	32	43
4	Newcastle United	34	18	6	10	58	45	42
5	Aston Villa	34	17	7	10	70	48	41
6	Sunderland	34	17	5	12	63	49	39
7	Sheffield United	34	15	8	11	62	57	38
8	Wolverhampton Wan.	34	14	8	12	44	66	36
9	Nottingham Forest	34	11	9	14	57	57	31
10	Middlesbrough	34	9	12	13	46	47	30
11	Small Heath	34	11	8	15	39	52	30
12	Bury	34	7	15	12	40	53	29
13	NOTTS COUNTY	34	12	5	17	37	61	29
14	Derby County	34	9	10	15	58	60	28
15	Blackburn Rovers	34	11	6	17	48	60	28
16	Stoke	34	10	7	17	54	57	27
17	Liverpool	34	9	8	17	49	62	26
18	West Bromwich Alb.	34	7	10	17	36	60	24

Back: Swift (trainer), Prescott, Pennington, Montgomery, T Harris (secretary). Centre: Chapman, Mainman, Dainty, McDonald, Gee. Front: Humphreys, Green, Reid.

1904/05

Bottom of Division One (not relegated, division expanded)

#		Date	Opponent	Score	Scorers	Att	Anderson J	Broughton M	Clare WE	Clinch T	Craythorne R	Dean RJ	Earle HT	Emberton FP	Gee E	Green AW	Griffiths A	Humphreys P	Iremonger A	Mainman HL	Montgomery J	Muir R	Nugent J	Pennington H	Prescott TG	Reid J	Shufflebottom J	Tarplin W	Wainwright T	Wilkinson JW
1	Sep	3	EVERTON	1-2	Reid	12000	4						1		11	9	6	8		5	3	7			2	10			
2		5	Sunderland	0-5		8000	4								11	9	6	8		5	3	7		1	2	10			
3		10	Small Heath	2-1	Dean, Craythorne	15000	4		2		10	8	1		11	9	6			5	3	7							
4		17	MANCHESTER CITY	1-1	Dean	10000	4		2	3	10	8	1		11	9	6			5		7							
5		24	Stoke	2-0	Green, Dean	6000	4			2	10	8	1		11	9	6			5	3	7							
6	Oct	1	Sheffield United	1-2	Green	14000	4			2	10	8	1		11	9	6			5	3	7							
7		8	NEWCASTLE UNITED	0-3		12000	4				10	8	1		11	9	6			5	3	7							2
8		15	Preston North End	1-3	Green	10000			2		10	11	1	4		9	6	8		5	3	7							
9		22	MIDDLESBROUGH	0-0		7000			2			11	1	4		9	6	8		5	3	7				10			
10		29	Wolverhampton Wand.	1-3	Craythorne	7000	6		2		10		1	4	11	9		8		5	3	7							
11	Nov	5	BURY	0-1		7000				2	10		1	4		9	6	8			3	7				11	5		
12		12	Aston Villa	2-4	Griffiths, Green	20000					10	7	1	4	11	9	2	8		6	3							5	
13		19	BLACKBURN ROVERS	2-1	Dean, Crompton(og)	7000					10	8	1	4	11	9	2	5		6	3	7							
14		26	Nottm. Forest	1-2	Craythorne	10000					10	8	1	4	11	9	2	5		6	3	7							
15	Dec	3	SHEFFIELD WEDNESDAY	2-2	Dean, Broughton	8000		7		2	10	8	1	4	11	9		5		6	3								
16		17	WOOLWICH ARSENAL	1-5	Green	14000		7		2	10	8	1	4	11	9		5		6	3								
17		24	Derby County	1-1	Gee	8000					10	8		4	11	7	2	5		6	3		1				9		
18		31	Everton	1-5	Humphreys	14000						6		4	11	7	2	5			3				10		9		
19	Jan	2	Newcastle United	0-1		20000					6	7	1	4	11	8	2	5			3				10		9		
20		7	SMALL HEATH	0-0		8000					6	8	1	4	11	10	2			5	3	7					9		
21		14	Manchester City	1-2	Tarplin	10000					10	8	1	4	11		2	5		6	3	7					9		
22		21	STOKE	0-0		8000					10	8	1	4	11		2	5		6	3	7					9		
23		28	SHEFFIELD UNITED	1-5	Humphreys(p)	8000	6				10	7	1	4	11	9	2	8		5	3								
24	Feb	11	PRESTON NORTH END	1-3	Dean	6000					6	8	1	4	11		2	5			3	7				10	9		
25		18	DERBY COUNTY	0-0		10000					6	8		4	11	10	2	5			3	7	1				9		
26		25	WOLVERHAMPTON W.	3-4	Dean(p), Tarplin, Craythorne	5000					6	8		4	11		2	5			3	7	1			10	9		
27	Mar	11	ASTON VILLA	1-2	Tarplin	4000					10	7		4	11	9	2	5		6	3						8		
28		18	Blackburn Rovers	0-1		8000					11	7		4		9	2	5			3			1		10	8	6		
29		25	NOTTM. FOREST	1-2	Reid	8000					6	7		4	11		2	9			3			1		10	8	5		
30	Apr	1	Sheffield Wednesday	0-1		5000					6	7			11		2	9	1	4	3					10	8	5		
31		8	SUNDERLAND	2-2	Humphreys, Tarplin	3000					6	7				11	2	8	1	4	3					10	9	5		
32		15	Woolwich Arsenal	2-1	Green, Humphreys	12000					6	7	1	4	11	9	2	8		5	3						10		
33		21	Bury	0-2		10000					6	7		4	11	9	2	8		5	3			1			10		
34		24	Middlesbrough	5-2	Humphreys 2, Dean, Green 2	10000					6	7		4	11	9	2	8		5	3		1				10		
			Apps				9	2	5	6	31	30	23	25	30	27	31	28	2	26	33	19	3	6	2	11	18	5	1
			Goals					1			4	8			1	8		6								2	4		

Games 1 and 31 at the City Ground

One own goal

F.A. Cup

		Date	Opponent	Score		Att				Clinch T	Craythorne R	Dean RJ	Earle HT	Emberton FP	Gee E		Griffiths A	Humphreys P		Mainman HL	Montgomery J	Muir R				Reid J		Tarplin W		
R1	Feb	4	Bury	0-1		12000					8	1	4	11			2	5		6	3	7				10		9		

		p	w	d	l	f	a	pts
1	Newcastle United	34	23	2	9	72	33	48
2	Everton	34	21	5	8	63	36	47
3	Manchester City	34	20	6	8	66	37	46
4	Aston Villa	34	19	4	11	63	43	42
5	Sunderland	34	16	8	10	60	44	40
6	Sheffield United	34	19	2	13	64	56	40
7	Small Heath	34	17	5	12	54	38	39
8	Preston North End	34	13	10	11	42	37	36
9	Sheffield Wed.	34	14	5	15	61	57	33
10	Woolwich Arsenal	34	12	9	13	36	40	33
11	Derby County	34	12	8	14	37	48	32
12	Stoke	34	13	4	17	40	58	30
13	Blackburn Rovers	34	11	5	18	40	51	27
14	Wolverhampton Wan.	34	11	4	19	47	73	26
15	Middlesbrough	34	9	8	17	36	56	26
16	Nottingham Forest	34	9	7	18	40	61	25
17	Bury	34	10	4	20	47	67	24
18	NOTTS COUNTY	34	5	8	21	36	69	18

1905/06

16th in Division One

#		Date	Opponent	Score	Scorers	Att	Chalmers T	Craythorne R	Dean RJ	Emberton FP	Fountain R	Gee E	Green AW	Griffiths A	Harrison A	Humphreys P	Iremonger A	Jones AT	Mainman HL	Montgomery J	Poppitt J	Reilly M	Robertson S	Tarplin W	Wainwright T	Waterall T	Wilkinson JW
1	Sep	2	Stoke	0-3		7000		6	7	4	10	11	9			8			5	3		1	2				
2		9	BOLTON WANDERERS	3-3	Humphreys, Tarplin, Dean	4000		6	7	4		11	9			8			5	3		1	2	10			
3		16	Woolwich Arsenal	1-1	Gee	18000		6	7	4		11	9	2		8			5	3		1		10			
4		23	BLACKBURN ROVERS	1-1	Dean(p)	8000		6	7	4		11	9	2		8			5	3		1		10			
5		30	Sunderland	3-1	Craythorne, Dean(p), Green	6000		6	7	4		11	9	2		8			5	3		1		10			
6	Oct	5	WOLVERHAMPTON W.	5-2	Green, Tarplin 2, Humphreys 2	4500		6	7	4		11	9	2		8	1		5	3				10			
7		7	BIRMINGHAM	0-0		15000		6	7	4		11	9	2		8	1		5	3				10			
8		14	Everton	2-6	Gee, Dean	14000		6	8	4		11	9	2	7		1			3				10	5		
9		21	DERBY COUNTY	1-0	Green	8000		6	7	4		11	9	2		8	1		5	3				10			
10		28	Sheffield Wednesday	1-3	Gee	12000		6	7	4		11		2		8			5		10	1		9			3
11	Nov	4	NOTTM. FOREST	1-1	Tarplin	15000		6	7	4		11		2		8			5		10	1		9			3
12		11	Manchester City	1-5	Dean(p)	7000		6	7	4		11		2		8					10	1		9	5		3
13		18	BURY	2-2	Dean, Humphreys	8000		6	7	4		11		2		8			5	3	10	1		9			
14		25	Middlesbrough	1-4	Green	8000		6	7	4		11	9	2		5					10	1		8			3
15	Dec	2	PRESTON NORTH END	2-2	Tarplin, Gee	8000		6	7	4		11	9	2		5					8	1		10			3
16		9	Newcastle United	1-3	Tarplin	18000		6	8	4		11	9		7	5		2		3		1		10			
17		16	ASTON VILLA	2-1	Dean, Green	9000		6	7	4		11	9			8		2	5	3		1		10			
18		23	Liverpool	0-2		15000		6	7	4		11	9			8		2	5	3		1		10			
19		25	Nottm. Forest	2-1	Dean(p), Green	17000		6	7	4		11	9			8		2	5	3		1		10			
20		26	SHEFFIELD UNITED	2-3	Gee, Green	16000		6	7	4		11	9	2		8			5	3		1		10			
21		27	SUNDERLAND	4-1	Tarplin 2, Poppitt, Green	8000		6	7			11	9	2			1		5	3	8			10	4		
22		30	STOKE	1-1	Dean(p)	10000		6	7	4		11	9				1	2	5	3	8			10			
23	Jan	1	Sheffield United	0-1		18500		6	7	4		11	9				1	2	5		8			10			3
24		20	WOOLWICH ARSENAL	1-0	Tarplin	10000		6	7	4		11	9	3		8	1	2	5					10			
25		27	Blackburn Rovers	3-1	Tarplin 2, Humphreys	12000		6	7	4		11	9	3		8	1	2	5					10			
26	Feb	3	Bolton Wanderers	0-2		10000		6	7	4		11	9	3		8	1	2	5					10			
27		10	Birmingham	2-4	Tarplin 2	8000		6	7	4		11	9			8	1	2	5	3				10			
28		17	EVERTON	0-0		10000		6	7	4		11	9			8	1	2	5	3				10			
29		24	Derby County	1-1	Humphreys	7000		6	7	4		11	9			8	1	2	5	3				10			
30	Mar	3	SHEFFIELD WEDNESDAY	1-3	Humphreys	10000		6	7	4		11	9	5		8	1	2		3				10			
31		17	MANCHESTER CITY	3-0	Green(p), Dean, Humphreys	10000		6	7	4		11	9			8	1	2	5	3				10			
32		21	LIVERPOOL	3-0	Dean, Green, Humphreys	6000		6	7	4		11	9	2		8	1		5	3				10			
33		24	Bury	0-0		6000	5	6	7	4		11	9	2		8	1			3				10			
34		31	MIDDLESBROUGH	1-1	Humphreys	15000	5	6	7	4		11	9	2		8	1			3				10			
35	Apr	7	Preston North End	1-4	Chalmers	7000	5	6	7	4		11	9	2		8	1			3				10			
36		14	NEWCASTLE UNITED	1-0	Green	16000		6	7	4		11	9	2		8	1		5	3				10			
37		16	Wolverhampton Wand.	1-6	Green	8000		6	7	4			9	2		8	1		5	3				10		11	
38		21	Aston Villa	1-2	Green	12000	5	6	7	4		11	9	2	10	8	1			3							
			Apps				4	38	38	37	1	37	34	26	3	34	22	14	28	29	9	16	2	36	3	1	6
			Goals				1	1	11			5	13			10					1			13			

Game 36 at the City Ground

F.A. Cup

		Date	Opponent	Score		Att		Craythorne R	Dean RJ	Emberton FP		Gee E	Green AW			Humphreys P	Iremonger A	Jones AT	Mainman HL	Montgomery J				Tarplin W			
R1	Jan	13	Sunderland	0-1		20000		6	7	4		11	9			8	1	2	5	3				10			

Back: Robertson, Wright, Emberton, Reilly, Montgomery, Harris (secretary). Front: Dean, Humphreys, Mainman, Fountain, Gee, Craythorne.

		p	w	d	l	f	a	pts
1	Liverpool	38	23	5	10	79	46	51
2	Preston North End	38	17	13	8	54	39	47
3	Sheffield Wed.	38	18	8	12	63	52	44
4	Newcastle United	38	18	7	13	74	48	43
5	Manchester City	38	19	5	14	73	54	43
6	Bolton Wanderers	38	17	7	14	81	67	41
7	Birmingham	38	17	7	14	65	59	41
8	Aston Villa	38	17	6	15	72	56	40
9	Blackburn Rovers	38	16	8	14	54	52	40
10	Stoke	38	16	7	15	54	55	39
11	Everton	38	15	7	16	70	66	37
12	Woolwich Arsenal	38	15	7	16	62	64	37
13	Sheffield United	38	15	6	17	57	62	36
14	Sunderland	38	15	5	18	61	70	35
15	Derby County	38	14	7	17	39	58	35
16	NOTTS COUNTY	38	11	12	15	55	71	34
17	Bury	38	11	10	17	57	74	32
18	Middlesbrough	38	10	11	17	56	71	31
19	Nottingham Forest	38	13	5	20	58	79	31
20	Wolverhampton Wan.	38	8	7	23	58	99	23

1906/07　　18th in Division One

							Chalmers T	Clamp A	Craythorne R	Dean RJ	Emberton FP	Gee E	Green AW	Griffiths A	Humphreys P	Iremonger A	Jones AT	Jones, Aaron	Mainman HL	Matthews W	Montgomery J	Morley H	Mosley A	Pope FH	Poppitt J	Suter ER	Tarplin W	Waterall I	Waterall T	Watts TH
1	Sep	1	BOLTON WANDERERS	0-0		5000			6	7	4	11	9		8	1	2		5	3							10			
2		8	Manchester Utd.	0-0		35000			6	7	4	11	9		8	1	2		5	3							10			
3		15	STOKE	2-2	Humphreys, Poppitt	11000			6	7	4	11			8	1	2		5	3					9		10			
4		17	Everton	2-2	Tarplin, Humphreys	10000	5		6	7	4	11	9		8	1	2			3							10			
5		22	Blackburn Rovers	2-0	Gee, Green	10000	5		6	7	4	11	9		8	1	2			3							10			
6		29	SUNDERLAND	0-0		15000			6	7	4	11		2	8	1			5	3					9		10			
7	Oct	6	Birmingham	0-2		10000			6	7	4		9		8	1	2		5	3							10		11	
8		13	EVERTON	0-1		10000	6			7	4	11			8	1	2		5	3		9					10			
9		20	Woolwich Arsenal	0-1		25000			6	7	4	11		2	8	1			5	3		9					10			
10		27	SHEFFIELD WEDNESDAY	2-2	Dean, Gee	14000			6	7	4	11		2	8	1			5	3							10			9
11	Nov	3	Bury	0-3		7000			6	7	4	11		2	8	1			5	3					9		10			
12		10	MANCHESTER CITY	0-0		10000			6	7	4	11	9	2	8	1			5	3										10
13		17	Middlesbrough	0-2		12000				8	4	11	9	6		1	2		5	3							10	7		
14		24	PRESTON NORTH END	0-0		8000			6	8	4	11	9	2		1			5	3							10	7		
15	Dec	1	Newcastle United	3-4	Dean, Green, Gee	28000			10	7	4	11	9	6		1	2		5	3							8			
16		8	ASTON VILLA	1-1	Dean(p)	10000				7	4	11	9	6	8	1	2		5	3							10			
17		15	Liverpool	1-5	Waterall	10000			10	7	4		9	6	8	1	2		5	3									11	
18		22	BRISTOL CITY	2-3	Jones, Gee	10000			6	7	4	11		2	8	1		9		10	3									5
19		24	Derby County	0-3		10000	6			7	4	11		2	5	1		9		8	3										
20		26	Sheffield United	1-2	Humphreys	15000	5		1		4	11		6	9		2		8	3							10	7		
21		29	Bolton Wanderers	0-0		6000	5	6			4	11		3	9		2		8						1		10	7		
22	Jan	5	MANCHESTER UTD.	3-0	Gee(p), Matthews, Humphreys	10000	5		6		4	11		2	9				8	3					1		10	7		
23		19	Stoke	1-1	Craythorne	4000	5		6	7	4	11		3	9		2		8						1		10			
24		26	BLACKBURN ROVERS	1-2	Gee	10000	5		6	10	4	11		3			2	9	8						1			7		
25	Feb	9	BIRMINGHAM	2-2	Matthews, Jones	10000		5	6	7	4			2	9	1		10		8	3								11	
26	Mar	2	Sheffield Wednesday	3-1	Humphreys, Matthews 2	10000		5	6	7	4			2	9	1		10		8	3								11	
27		13	BURY	1-2	Humphreys	7000		5	6					3	9	1	2	10						11		8				
28		16	Manchester City	1-2	Craythorne	18000	5	6	10	7	4			3	8	1		9				2		11						
29		29	DERBY COUNTY	4-0	Humphreys 3, Waterall	20000		5	6	7	4			3	9	1		10		8		2							11	
30		30	Preston North End	0-0		8000		5	6	7	4				9	1		10		8		2	3						11	
31	Apr	1	SHEFFIELD UNITED	4-0	Humphreys 2, Dean, Matthews	18000	5		6	7	4			3	9	1				8		2					10		11	
32		6	NEWCASTLE UNITED	1-0	Jones	12000	5		6	7	4	11		3	9	1		10		8		2								
33		10	MIDDLESBROUGH	2-2	Tarplin, Matthews	7000		5	6	7	4	11		3		1		10		8		2					9			
34		13	Aston Villa	0-0		15000		5	6	7	4					1		10		8	3	2					9		11	
35		17	WOOLWICH ARSENAL	4-1	Clamp, Humphreys 2, Waterall	3000		5	6	7	4			3	9	1		10		8		2							11	
36		20	LIVERPOOL	2-0	Tarplin, Jones	10000		5	6	7	4			3		1		9				2					8		11	
37		24	Sunderland	1-3	Jones	3000		5	6	7	4	10		3		1		9				2					8		11	
38		27	Bristol City	0-1		10000		5	6	7	4			3		1		9				2			10		8		11	
				Apps			12	13	33	35	38	26	11	29	29	33	16	16	15	16	24	10	2	2	6	4	27	6	12	3
				Goals				1	2	4		6	2		13		5		6						1		3		3	

Games 1, 32, 33, 35 and 36 at the City Ground

F.A. Cup

R1	Jan	12	PRESTON NORTH END	1-0	Matthews	15000	5		6	7	4	11		2	9				8	3					1	10			
R2	Feb	2	Burslem Port Vale	2-2	Humphreys, Matthews	9000		5	6	7	4			2	9		10		8	3					1			11		
rep		6	BURSLEM PORT VALE	5-0	*see below	10000		5	6	7	4			2	9	1		10	8	3								11		
R3		23	TOTTENHAM HOTSPUR	4-0	Dean 2, Humphreys, Matthews	25000		5	6	7	4			2	9	1		10	8	3								11		
R4	Mar	9	West Bromwich Albion	1-3	Jones	27474		5	6	7	4	11		2	9	1		10	8	3										

*Scorers in R2 replay: Matthews 2, Jones, Humphreys, Emberton

		p	w	d	l	f	a	pts
1	Newcastle United	38	22	7	9	74	46	51
2	Bristol City	38	20	8	10	66	47	48
3	Everton	38	20	5	13	70	46	45
4	Sheffield United	38	17	11	10	57	55	45
5	Aston Villa	38	19	6	13	78	52	44
6	Bolton Wanderers	38	18	8	12	59	47	44
7	Woolwich Arsenal	38	20	4	14	66	59	44
8	Manchester United	38	17	8	13	53	56	42
9	Birmingham	38	15	8	15	52	52	38
10	Sunderland	38	14	9	15	65	66	37
11	Middlesbrough	38	15	6	17	56	63	36
12	Blackburn Rovers	38	14	7	17	56	59	35
13	Sheffield Wed.	38	12	11	15	49	60	35
14	Preston North End	38	14	7	17	44	57	35
15	Liverpool	38	13	7	18	64	65	33
16	Bury	38	13	6	19	58	68	32
17	Manchester City	38	10	12	16	53	77	32
18	NOTTS COUNTY	38	8	15	15	46	50	31
19	Derby County	38	9	9	20	41	59	27
20	Stoke	38	8	10	20	41	64	26

Bramley (treasurer), Emberton, AT Jones, Iremonger, Montgomery, Harris (secretary), Green, Prescott (trainer). Front: Dean, Humphreys, Tarplin, Mainman, Poppitt, Craythorne, Gee.

1907/08

18th in Division One

#		Date	Opponent	Score	Scorers	Att	Bemment F	Calladine CF	Cantrell J	Chalmers T	Clamp A	Craythorne R	Dean RJ	Dodd GF	Emberton FP	Gooch PG	Griffiths A	Harper R	Iremonger A	Jones AF	Jones, Aaron	Matthews W	Montgomery J	Moore GW	Morley H	Munro D	O'Donnell D	Tarplin W	Warner A	Waterall T
1	Sep	2	Woolwich Arsenal	1-1	Munro	10000					5	6	7		4		3		1			10	8			2	11	9		
2		4	Newcastle United	1-1	Aaron Jones	25000					5	6	7		4		3		1			10	8			2	11	9		
3		7	Sunderland	3-4	O'Donnell 2, Waterall	25000					5	6	7		4		3		1			10	8			2		9		11
4		14	WOOLWICH ARSENAL	2-0	Matthews, Waterall	12000					5	6	7		4		3		1			10	8			2		9		11
5		21	Sheffield Wednesday	0-2		16000	5					6	7		4		3		1			10	8			2		9		11
6		28	BRISTOL CITY	3-1	Dean(p), O'Donnell, Craythorne	12000	5					6	7		4		3		1			10	8			2		9		11
7	Oct	3	BURY	2-1	Matthews, Emberton	10000	5					6	7		4		3		1	10			8			2		9		11
8		5	NEWCASTLE UNITED	0-1		16000	5					6	7		4		3		1	10			8			2		9		11
9		12	Manchester City	1-2	Tarplin	13000	5					6	7		4		3		1				8			2	10	9		11
10		19	PRESTON NORTH END	0-1		8000					5	6	7		4		3		1			9				2		10	8	11
11		26	Bury	0-0		8000	6				5	9	7		4		3		1			8				2			10	11
12	Nov	2	ASTON VILLA	0-3		12000					5	6	7		4		3		1			8				2		9	10	11
13		9	Liverpool	0-6		8000	4				5	6	7		8		3		1	10						2		9		11
14		16	MIDDLESBROUGH	2-0	AF Jones 2	9000					5	6	7		4				1	10			8	3		2	11	9		
15		23	Sheffield United	1-0	O'Donnell	7000					5	6	7		4				1	10				3		2	11	9	8	
16		30	CHELSEA	2-0	Warner, AF Jones	10000					5	6	7		4				1	10				3		2		9	8	11
17	Dec	7	Nottm. Forest	0-2		18000					5	6	7		4				1	11			8	3		2		9	10	
18		14	MANCHESTER UTD.	1-1	AF Jones	7000					5	6	7		4				1	10			8	3		2	11	9		
19		21	Blackburn Rovers	1-1	AF Jones	30000					5	6	7		4				1	10			8	3		2	11	9		
20		25	EVERTON	2-1	Tarplin 2	14000					5	6	7		4				1	10				3		2	11	9		
21		26	Birmingham	0-0		20000					5	6	7	8	4				1	10				3		2	11	9		
22		27	BIRMINGHAM	0-0		12000					5	6	7	8	4				1	10				3		2	11	9		
23		28	BOLTON WANDERERS	0-1		6000		7			5	6		10	4				1					3	8	2		9		11
24	Jan	4	SUNDERLAND	4-0	Dean(p), Tarplin 2, Dodd	8000					5	6	7	8	4				1	10				3		2	11	9		
25		18	SHEFFIELD WEDNESDAY	1-2	AF Jones	10000					5	6	7		4				1	10				3		2	11	9	8	
26		25	Bristol City	1-2	Dean(p)	7000					5	6	7		4				1	10			8	3		2	11	9		
27	Feb	8	MANCHESTER CITY	1-0	Clamp	8000					5	6	7	10	4				1	11			8	3		2		9		
28		15	Preston North End	0-1		8000					5	6	7	10	4				1	11			8	3		2		9		
29	Mar	2	Aston Villa	1-5	Dean	6000					5	6	7	9	4				1	10			8	3		2				11
30		7	LIVERPOOL	2-2	Dodd(p), Matthews	8000		7			5	6		10	4				1				8	3		2	11	9		
31		14	Middlesbrough	1-3	Dodd	15000	6	7		5	4			9					1	10				3		2	11	8		
32		21	SHEFFIELD UNITED	0-3		10000	6		10		5			11	4	9		7	1				8	3		2				
33	Apr	4	NOTTM. FOREST	2-0	Cantrell, Gooch	16000			10		5	6		11		9	4	7	1				8	3		2				
34		11	Manchester Utd.	1-0	Dodd	14000			10		5	6		11		9	4	7	1				8	3		2				
35		18	BLACKBURN ROVERS	0-2		12000			10		5	6		11			4	7	1				8	3		2		9		
36		20	Everton	0-1		10000			9		5	6					4	7	1	10			8	3		2				11
37		25	Bolton Wanderers	1-0	Cantrell	15000			9		5			11	4		6	7	1	10			8	3		2				
38		29	Chelsea	2-1	Harper, Dodd(p)	10000			9		5			11	4		6	7	1	10			8	3		2				

Game 35 at the City Ground

	Bemment F	Calladine CF	Cantrell J	Chalmers T	Clamp A	Craythorne R	Dean RJ	Dodd GF	Emberton FP	Gooch PG	Griffiths A	Harper R	Iremonger A	Jones AF	Jones, Aaron	Matthews W	Montgomery J	Moore GW	Morley H	Munro D	O'Donnell D	Tarplin W	Warner A	Waterall T
Apps	9	3	7	1	33	34	28	16	34	3	18	7	38	22	6	28	25	1	38	12	18	15	7	15
Goals			2		1	1	4	5	1	1		1		6	1	3				1	4	5	1	2

F.A. Cup

		Date	Opponent	Score	Scorers	Att	Clamp A	Craythorne R	Dean RJ	Emberton FP	Iremonger A	Jones AF	Matthews W	Montgomery J	Morley H	Munro D	O'Donnell D	Tarplin W	Waterall T
R1	Jan	11	MIDDLESBROUGH	2-0	AF Jones 2	16000	5	6	7	4	1	10		3	2	11	8	9	
R2	Feb	1	BOLTON WANDERERS	1-1	Tarplin	18000	5	6	7	4	1	10	8	3	2	11		9	
rep		5	Bolton Wanderers	1-2	Tarplin	17441	5	6	7	4	1	10	8	3	2			9	11

R2 replay after extra time

		p	w	d	l	f	a	pts
1	Manchester United	38	23	6	9	81	48	52
2	Aston Villa	38	17	9	12	77	59	43
3	Manchester City	38	16	11	11	62	54	43
4	Newcastle United	38	15	12	11	65	54	42
5	Sheffield Wed.	38	19	4	15	73	64	42
6	Middlesbrough	38	17	7	14	54	45	41
7	Bury	38	14	11	13	58	61	39
8	Liverpool	38	16	6	16	68	61	38
9	Nottingham Forest	38	13	11	14	59	62	37
10	Bristol City	38	12	12	14	58	61	36
11	Everton	38	15	6	17	58	64	36
12	Preston North End	38	12	12	14	47	53	36
13	Chelsea	38	14	8	16	53	62	36
14	Blackburn Rovers	38	12	12	14	51	63	36
14	Woolwich Arsenal	38	12	12	14	51	63	36
16	Sunderland	38	16	3	19	78	75	35
17	Sheffield United	38	12	11	15	52	58	35
18	NOTTS COUNTY	38	13	8	17	39	51	34
19	Bolton Wanderers	38	14	5	19	52	58	33
20	Birmingham	38	9	12	17	40	60	30

1908/09

15th in Division One

#		Date	Opponent	Score	Scorers	Att	Cantrell J	Chalmers T	Clamp A	Craythorne R	Dean RI	Dodd GF	Emberton FP	Flint WA	Griffiths A	Harper R	Iremonger A	Jones AF	Matthews W	Montgomery J	Morley H	Mosley A	Walker A
1	Sep	5	WOOLWICH ARSENAL	2-1	Cantrell, Matthews	15000	10		5	6		11	4			7	1		8	3	2		9
2		12	Sheffield Wednesday	0-2		20000	10		5	6		11	4			7	1		8	3	2		9
3		19	Newcastle United	0-1		35000	10		5	6		11	4			7	1		8	3	2		9
4		26	BRISTOL CITY	0-1		12000	10		5	6	7	11	4				1		8	3	2		9
5	Oct	3	Preston North End	0-0		9000	9		5	6	7	11	4				1	10	8	3		2	
6		10	MIDDLESBROUGH	3-2	Cantrell 2, Matthews	10000	9		5	6	7	11	4				1	10	8	3	2		
7		17	Manchester City	0-1		20000	9		5	6	7	11	4				1	10	8	3		2	
8		24	LIVERPOOL	1-2	Walker	8000	9		5	6	7	11	4				1		8	3		2	10
9		31	Bury	1-3	Walker	7000	9		5	6	7	11	4				1		8	3		2	10
10	Nov	7	SHEFFIELD UNITED	3-1	Cantrell, Dodd, Walker	8000	9		5	6	7	10	4				1		8		2	3	11
11		14	Aston Villa	1-1	Dodd	12000	9		5	6	7	10	4				1		8	3		2	11
12		21	NOTTM. FOREST	3-0	Dodd 2(1p), Dean	16000	9		5	6	7	10	4				1		8	3	2		11
13		28	Sunderland	1-0	Dean	12000	9		5	6	7	10	4				1		8	3	2		11
14	Dec	5	CHELSEA	3-0	Cantrell, Craythorne, Dean	14000	9		5	6	7	10	4				1		8	3	2		11
15		12	Blackburn Rovers	2-0	Dodd, Walker	10000	9		5	6	7	10	4				1		8	3	2		11
16		19	BRADFORD CITY	1-1	Matthews	9000	9		5	6	7	10	4				1		8	3	2		11
17		25	Everton	1-0	Walker	35000	9		5	6	7	10	4				1		8	3	2		11
18		26	EVERTON	0-0		25000	9		5		7	10	4		6		1		8	3	2		11
19	Jan	1	Manchester Utd.	3-4	Dodd 2, Dean	20000	9		5	6	7	10	4				1		8	3	2		11
20		2	Woolwich Arsenal	0-1		12000	9		5	6	7	10	4				1		8	3	2		11
21		9	SHEFFIELD WEDNESDAY	1-0	Walker	12000	9		5	6	7	10	4				1		8	3	2		11
22		23	NEWCASTLE UNITED	0-4		12000	9		5	6	7	10	4				1		8	3	2		11
23		30	Bristol City	0-1		10000	9		5	6	7	10	4				1		8	3	2		11
24	Feb	13	Middlesbrough	2-1	Cantrell 2	12000	9		5	6	7	10	4				1		8	3	2		11
25		20	MANCHESTER CITY	5-1	Cantrell 4, Walker	4000	9		5	6	7	10	4				1		8	3	2		11
26		27	Liverpool	1-1	Matthews	10000	9		5	6	7	10	4				1		8	3	2		11
27	Mar	10	PRESTON NORTH END	1-0	Matthews	4500	9		5	6	7	10	4				1		8	3	2		11
28		13	Sheffield United	2-3	Matthews, Cantrell	15000	9		5	6	7	10	4				1		8	3	2		11
29		20	ASTON VILLA	1-1	Dodd	6000	9		5	6	7	10	4				1		8	3	2		11
30		24	BURY	3-2	Dean(p), Cantrell 2	2000	9		5	6	7	10	4				1		8	3	2		11
31		27	Nottm. Forest	0-1		14000	9		5	6	7	10	4				1		8	3	2		11
32	Apr	3	SUNDERLAND	0-0		8000	9		5	6		7	4	10	2		1		8	3			11
33		9	LEICESTER FOSSE	2-3	Cantrell 2	16000	9		5		7		4	10	6		1		8	3	2		11
34		10	Chelsea	2-3	Matthews, Birnie (og)	30000	9		5		7	10	4		6		1		8	3	2		11
35		12	Leicester Fosse	2-0	Dodd, Cantrell	8000	9		5	6	7	10	4		2		1		8	3			11
36		13	MANCHESTER UTD.			7000	9	6	5	6	7	10	4				1		8	3	2		11
37		17	BLACKBURN ROVERS	2-3	Cantrell, Jones	6000	9		5	6	7	11	4				1	10	8	3			
38		24	Bradford City	2-2	Dean 2(1p)	18000	9		5	6	7		4				1	10	8	3	2		11
			Apps				38	1	38	34	35	35	38	2	5	3	38	5	38	37	31	6	34
			Goals				18			1	7	9						1	7				7

Games 1, 33, 36 and 37 at the City Ground
Game 32: Joint benefit for Montgomery and Griffiths

One own goal

F.A. Cup

		Date	Opponent	Score		Att	Cantrell J		Clamp A	Craythorne R	Dean RI	Dodd GF	Emberton FP				Iremonger A		Matthews W	Montgomery J	Morley H		Walker A
R1	Jan	16	BLACKBURN ROVERS	0-1		13700	9		5	6	7	10	4				1		8	3	2		11

		p	w	d	l	f	a	pts
1	Newcastle United	38	24	5	9	65	41	53
2	Everton	38	18	10	10	82	57	46
3	Sunderland	38	21	2	15	78	63	44
4	Blackburn Rovers	38	14	13	11	61	50	41
5	Sheffield Wed.	38	17	6	15	67	61	40
6	Woolwich Arsenal	38	14	10	14	52	49	38
7	Aston Villa	38	14	10	14	58	56	38
8	Bristol City	38	13	12	13	45	58	38
9	Middlesbrough	38	14	9	15	59	53	37
10	Preston North End	38	13	11	14	48	44	37
11	Chelsea	38	14	9	15	56	61	37
12	Sheffield United	38	14	9	15	51	59	37
13	Manchester United	38	15	7	16	58	68	37
14	Nottingham Forest	38	14	8	16	66	57	36
15	NOTTS COUNTY	38	14	8	16	51	48	36
16	Liverpool	38	15	6	17	57	65	36
17	Bury	38	14	8	16	63	77	36
18	Bradford City	38	12	10	16	47	47	34
19	Manchester City	38	15	4	19	67	69	34
20	Leicester Fosse	38	8	9	21	54	102	25

1909/10

9th in Division One

#		Date	Opponent	Score	Scorers	Att	Cantrell J	Clamp A	Craythorne R	Dean RJ	Dodd GF	Emberton FP	Flint WA	Garrett FH	Griffiths A	Iremonger A	Jones AF	Matthews W	Montgomery J	Morley H	Mosley A	Pepper FW	Walker A	Waterall I
1	Sep	1	Chelsea	2-2	Dean(p), Cantrell	10000	9	5	6	7	10	4				1		8	3	2			11	
2		4	Nottm. Forest	1-2	Walker	16000	9	5	6	7	10	4				1		8	3	2			11	
3		6	Manchester Utd.	1-2	Jones	5000		5		7	9	4			6	1	10	8	3	2			11	
4		11	SUNDERLAND	1-1	Jones	6000	9	5			7	11	4		6	1	10	8	3	2				
5		18	Everton	0-2		25000	9	5	6			11	4			1	10	8	3	2				7
6		25	MANCHESTER UTD.	3-2	Jones, Waterall, Matthews	9000	9	5	6			11	4			1	10	8	3	2				7
7	Oct	2	Bradford City	1-2	Cantrell	24000	9	5	6			11	4			1	10	8	3	2				7
8		7	WOOLWICH ARSENAL	5-1	Cantrell 3, Jones, Clamp	10000	9	5	6	7		11	4			1	10	8	3	2				
9		9	SHEFFIELD WEDNESDAY	0-0		16000	9	5	6	7		11	4			1	10	8	3	2				
10		16	Bristol City	1-3	Cantrell	7000	9	5				11	4		6	1	10		3	2			8	7
11		18	Sheffield United	2-2	Cantrell, Dodd	10000	9	5		7	11	4			6	1	10	8	3	2				
12		23	BURY	3-1	Jones, Cantrell, Dean	7000	9	5		7	11	4			6	1	10	8	3	2				
13		30	Tottenham Hotspur	3-1	Cantrell 2, Matthews	25000	9	5		7	11	4			6	1	10	8	3	2				
14	Nov	6	PRESTON NORTH END	3-1	Dodd(p), Dean, Jones	10000	9	5		7	11	4			6	1	10	8	3	2				
15		13	MIDDLESBROUGH	2-1	Matthews, Cantrell	9000	9	5	6	7		4				1	10	8	3	2			11	
16		20	Newcastle United	3-1	Jones, Cantrell, Dean	20000	9	5	6	7		4			3	1	10	8		2			11	
17		27	LIVERPOOL	3-1	Jones 2, Cantrell	6000	9	5	6	7	11	4			3	1	10	8		2				
18	Dec	4	Aston Villa	1-1	Matthews	6000	9	5	6	7	11	4			3	1	10	8		2				
19		11	SHEFFIELD UNITED	1-2	Dean(p)	10000	9	5	6	7	11	4				1	10	8	3	2				
20		18	Woolwich Arsenal	2-1	Jones, Cantrell	8000	9	5	6	7	11	4				1	10	8	3	2				
21		25	CHELSEA	2-1	Jones, Cantrell	14000	9	5	6	7	11	4				1	10	8	3	2				
22		28	BLACKBURN ROVERS	2-2	Matthews, Cantrell	18000	9	5	6	7	11	4				1	10	8	3	2				
23	Jan	1	Bolton Wanderers	4-3	Flint 2, Dean, Cantrell	20000	9	5	6	7	11	4	8			1	10		3	2				
24		8	NOTTM. FOREST	4-1	Cantrell 2, Jones, Walker	10000	9	5	6	7		4				1	10	8	3	2			11	
25		22	Sunderland	3-0	Matthews, Cantrell, Jones	7000	9	5	6	7		4				1	10	8	3	2			11	
26	Feb	12	BRADFORD CITY	3-2	Matthews, Jones 2	15000		5	6	7	11	4				1	10	8	3		2		9	
27		19	Sheffield Wednesday	0-0		8000	9	5	6	7		4				1	10	8	3	2			11	
28		26	BRISTOL CITY	0-2		9000	9	5	6	7			9			1	10	8	3	2	4		11	
29	Mar	5	Bury	1-1	Dodd	10000		5	6		9				4	1	10	8	3	2			11	7
30		12	TOTTENHAM HOTSPUR	3-0	Dodd, Flint, Jones	8000		5	6		9		8		4	1	10		3	2			11	7
31		19	Preston North End	0-4		7000		5	6		11		8		4	1	10	9	3	2				7
32		25	Blackburn Rovers	0-2		12000		5	6	7	9	4			2	1	10	8	3					11
33		26	Middlesbrough	0-2		12000		5	6		9			4	2	1	10	8	3				11	7
34		28	BOLTON WANDERERS	0-0		9000		5	6			4	9		2	1	10	8	3				11	
35	Apr	2	NEWCASTLE UNITED	2-2	Dodd(p), Matthews	9000	9	5	6		11	4			2	1	10	8	3					7
36		9	Liverpool	1-2	Cantrell	8000	9	5			11	4			6	1	10	8	3					7
37		13	EVERTON	2-3	Matthews, Cantrell	3000	9	5			11	4			6	1	10	8	3		2			7
38		16	ASTON VILLA	2-3	Waterall, Jones	11000	9	5	3		11	4			2	1	10	8				6		7
			Apps				29	38	29	25	31	33	5	1	20	38	36	35	34	31	3	1	15	14
			Goals				22	1		6	5		3				17	9					2	2

Last season at Trent Bridge

F.A. Cup

		Date	Opponent	Score	Scorers	Att	Cantrell J	Clamp A	Craythorne R	Dean RJ	Dodd GF	Emberton FP	Flint WA	Garrett FH	Griffiths A	Iremonger A	Jones AF	Matthews W	Montgomery J	Morley H	Mosley A	Pepper FW	Walker A	Waterall I
R1	Jan	15	Bradford City	2-4	Jones 2	17000	9	5	6	7		4				1	10	8	3	2			11	

Notts sold ground rights for £1000

	p	w	d	l	f	a	pts
1 Aston Villa	38	23	7	8	84	42	53
2 Liverpool	38	21	6	11	78	57	48
3 Blackburn Rovers	38	18	9	11	73	55	45
4 Newcastle United	38	19	7	12	70	56	45
5 Manchester United	38	19	7	12	69	61	45
6 Sheffield United	38	16	10	12	62	41	42
7 Bradford City	38	17	8	13	64	47	42
8 Sunderland	38	18	5	15	66	51	41
9 NOTTS COUNTY	38	15	10	13	67	59	40
10 Everton	38	16	8	14	51	56	40
11 Sheffield Wed.	38	15	9	14	60	63	39
12 Preston North End	38	15	5	18	52	58	35
13 Bury	38	12	9	17	62	66	33
14 Nottingham Forest	38	11	11	16	54	72	33
15 Tottenham Hotspur	38	11	10	17	53	69	32
16 Bristol City	38	12	8	18	45	60	32
17 Middlesbrough	38	11	9	18	56	73	31
18 Woolwich Arsenal	38	11	9	18	37	67	31
19 Chelsea	38	11	7	20	47	70	29
20 Bolton Wanderers	38	9	6	23	44	71	24

Pre-season practice match, Whites v Stripes. Back: Clark, Taylor, Craythorne, Morley, Emberton, Iremonger, Cantrell, Garrett, Martin, TJ Rowbotham (referee). Centre: Dean, Matthews, Montgomery, Dodd, Walker. Front: Freestone, Birch, Mosley, Griffiths, I Waterall, Jones, A Waterall, Keeling

1910/11

11th in Division One

#		Date		Opponent	Score	Scorers	Att	Bettison F	Bradley H	Cantrell J	Clamp A	Craythorne R	Dean RJ	Dodd GF	Emberton FP	Flint WA	Garrett FH	Grice R	Griffiths A	Iremonger A	James L	Jones AF	Lee GM	Matthews W	Montgomery J	Morley H	Pacey H	Richards S	Walker A	Waterall A	Waterall I
1	Sep	1		Blackburn Rovers	1-1	Dean	17000		11	9	5	6	7		4				2	1		10		8	3						
2		3		NOTTM. FOREST	1-1	Matthews	25000			9	5	6	7	11	4				2	1		10		8	3						
3		10		Manchester City	1-0	Richards	30000				5	6	7		4	9			2	1				8	3			10			11
4		17		EVERTON	0-0		15000			9	5	6	7		4				2	1				8	3			10			11
5		24		Sheffield Wednesday	3-1	Richards 2, Flint	12000				5	6	7		4	9			2	1				8	3			10			11
6	Oct	1		BRISTOL CITY	2-0	Richards, Waterall	15000				5	6	7		4	9			2	1				8	3			10			11
7		8		Newcastle United	0-2		30000				5	6	7		4	9			2	1				8	3			10			11
8		15		TOTTENHAM HOTSPUR	1-0	Matthews	14000			9	5	6	7		4				2	1				8	3			10			11
9		22		Middlesbrough	1-4	Cantrell	15000			9	5	6	7		4				2	1				8	3			10			11
10		29		PRESTON NORTH END	3-3	Matthews, Waterall, Cantrell	10000			9	5		7		4		6		2	1				8	3			10			11
11	Nov	5		Oldham Athletic	1-2	Cantrell	8000	2		9	5		7		4		6			1				8	3			10			11
12		12		Manchester Utd.	0-0		7000		11		5	6		10	4	9				1			2	8	3						7
13		19		LIVERPOOL	1-0	Richards	12000		11		5				4	9		6		1			2	8	3			10			7
14		26		Bury	0-0		5000				5			11	4	9				1			2	8	3		6	10			7
15	Dec	3		SHEFFIELD UNITED	0-3		6000				5	4	7	9						1			2	8	3		6	10			11
16		10		Aston Villa	1-3	Cantrell	12000			9	5	6	7		4	8				1		10			3	2					11
17		17		SUNDERLAND	1-1	Richards	7000			9	5	6	7		4	8				1					3	2		10			11
18		24		Woolwich Arsenal	1-2	Cantrell	8000			9	5	6	7		4	8			2	1					3			10			11
19		26		BRADFORD CITY	1-1	Dean(p)	25000			9	5	6	7		4	10			2	1				8	3						11
20		31		Nottm. Forest	2-0	Cantrell 2	16000			9	5	6	7		4	10				1				8	3	2					11
21	Jan	7		MANCHESTER CITY	0-1		10000				5	6	7		4	9			2	1				8	3			10			11
22		21		Everton	0-5		14000			9	5	6	7		4	8				1					3	2		10			11
23		28		SHEFFIELD WEDNESDAY	2-0	Dodd, Matthews	12000			9	5	6	7	11	4	10				1				8	3	2					
24	Feb	4		Bristol City	0-1		5000			9		6		11	4	10	5			1				8	3	2					7
25		11		NEWCASTLE UNITED	2-2	Cantrell 2	12000			9		6		11	4		5			1				8	3	2			10		7
26		18		Tottenham Hotspur	0-3		25000			9	5	6		11	4					1				8	3	2			10		7
27	Mar	4		Preston North End	0-2		5000			9	5	6	7		4	10				1				8	3	2					11
28		11		OLDHAM ATHLETIC	1-0	Matthews	10000			9	5	6	7		4	10				1				8	3	2					11
29		18		MANCHESTER UTD.	1-0	Cantrell	8000			9	5	6	7		4	10				1				8	3	2					11
30		25		Liverpool	1-2	Waterall	7000			9	5	6	7		4	10				1				8	3	2					11
31	Apr	1		BURY	1-0	Craythorne	6000			9	5	6	7		4	10			2	1				8	3						11
32		8		Sheffield United	2-0	Craythorne, Cantrell	3000			9	5	6			4	10			2	1				8	3						11
33		14		BLACKBURN ROVERS	2-0	Montgomery(p), Dean	20000			9	5	6	7		4	10				1				8	3	2					11
34		15		ASTON VILLA	1-2	Dean(p)	18000			9	5	6	7		4	10			2	1					3					8	11
35		17		Bradford City	1-0	Cantrell	15000			9	5	6			4		11	3	1		2							10		8	7
36		18		MIDDLESBROUGH	1-0	Richards	8000			9	5	6	7		4				1		2				3			10		8	11
37		22		Sunderland	1-1	Cantrell	10000			9	5		7		4				2	1					3			10	6	8	11
38		29		WOOLWICH ARSENAL	0-2		8000				5	6	7		4	9			3	1						2		10		8	11

First season at Meadow Lane

| | | | | | | | | Apps | 1 | 3 | 28 | 36 | 33 | 30 | 9 | 37 | 25 | 4 | 1 | 20 | 38 | 2 | 3 | 4 | 29 | 36 | 14 | 2 | 20 | 3 | 5 | 35 |
| | | | | | | | | Goals | | | 13 | | 2 | 4 | 1 | | 1 | | | | | | | | 5 | 1 | | | 7 | | | 3 |

F.A. Cup

| R1 | Jan | 14 | Swindon Town | 1-3 | Dean(p) | 12332 | | | 9 | 5 | 6 | 7 | | 4 | 8 | | | | 1 | | | | 3 | 2 | | | 10 | | | 11 |

		p	w	d	l	f	a	pts
1	Manchester United	38	22	8	8	72	40	52
2	Aston Villa	38	22	7	9	69	41	51
3	Sunderland	38	15	15	8	67	48	45
4	Everton	38	19	7	12	50	36	45
5	Bradford City	38	20	5	13	51	42	45
6	Sheffield Wed.	38	17	8	13	47	48	42
7	Oldham Athletic	38	16	9	13	44	41	41
8	Newcastle United	38	15	10	13	61	43	40
9	Sheffield United	38	15	8	15	49	43	38
10	Woolwich Arsenal	38	13	12	13	41	49	38
11	NOTTS COUNTY	38	14	10	14	37	45	38
12	Blackburn Rovers	38	13	11	14	62	54	37
13	Liverpool	38	15	7	16	53	53	37
14	Preston North End	38	12	11	15	40	49	35
15	Tottenham Hotspur	38	13	6	19	52	63	32
16	Middlesbrough	38	11	10	17	49	63	32
17	Manchester City	38	9	13	16	43	58	31
18	Bury	38	9	11	18	43	71	29
19	Bristol City	38	11	5	22	43	66	27
20	Nottingham Forest	38	9	7	22	55	75	25

1911/12

16th in Division One

#		Date	Opponent	Score	Scorers	Att	Cantrell J	Clamp A	Craythorne R	Dean RI	Emberton FP	Flint WA	Garrett FH	Grice R	Griffiths A	Iremonger A	Matthews W	McCulloch G	Morley H	Pacey H	Pepper FW	Richards S	Walker A	Waterall A	Waterall I	West, Alf
1	Sep	2	West Bromwich Alb.	1-2	Richards	25000	9	5	6	7	4					1	8		2			10			11	3
2		9	SUNDERLAND	3-1	Craythorne, Matthews, Richards	12000	9	5	6	7	4					1	8		2			10			11	3
3		16	Blackburn Rovers	0-0		15000	9	5	6	7	4					1	8		2			10			11	3
4		23	SHEFFIELD WEDNESDAY	1-0	Matthews	12000	9	5	6	7	4					1	8		2			10			11	3
5		30	Bury	1-0	Richards	8000	9	5	6	7	4					1	8		2			10			11	3
6	Oct	5	BRADFORD CITY	0-0		11000	9	5	6	7	4	10				1	8		2						11	3
7		7	MIDDLESBROUGH	2-1	Cantrell, Matthews	18000	9	5	6	7	4	10				1	8		2						11	3
8		14	PRESTON NORTH END	1-2	Flint	10000		5	6	7	4	9				1	8		2					10	11	3
9		21	Tottenham Hotspur	2-2	Matthews, Cantrell	25000	9	5	6	7	4					1	8		2			10			11	3
10		28	MANCHESTER UTD.	0-1		14000	9	5	6	7	4					1	8		2			10			11	3
11	Nov	4	Liverpool	0-3		14000		5	6	7	4	9				1	8		2			10			11	3
12		18	Newcastle United	2-3	Dean 2	20000		5	6	7	4	9				1	8		2			10			11	3
13		25	SHEFFIELD UNITED	2-0	Cantrell, Richards	14000	9	5	6	7	4					1	8		2			10			11	3
14	Dec	2	Oldham Athletic	2-1	Richards 2	10000		5	6	7	4	9				1	8		2			10			11	3
15		9	BOLTON WANDERERS	3-2	Flint 2, Matthews	12000		5	6	7	4	9				1	8		2			10			11	3
16		16	Bradford City	3-2	Flint, Richards, Dean	10000		5	6	7	4	9				1	8		2			10			11	3
17		23	WOOLWICH ARSENAL	3-1	Flint, Matthews, Richards	12000		5	6	7	4	9				1	8		2			10			11	3
18		25	MANCHESTER CITY	0-1		20000		5	6	7	4					1	8		2			10	9		11	3
19		26	Manchester City	0-4		30000				7	4	9	5		6	1	8		2			10			11	3
20		30	WEST BROMWICH ALB.	2-0	Richards, Waterall	12000		5		7	4	9	6			1	8		2			10			11	3
21	Jan	6	Sunderland	0-5		10000		5		7	4	9				1	8		2	6		10			11	3
22		20	BLACKBURN ROVERS	1-3	Cantrell	3000	9	5	6		4	7				1	8		2			10			11	3
23		27	Sheffield Wednesday	0-3		8000	9	5	6		4	7				1	8		2			10			11	3
24	Feb	10	Middlesbrough	0-4		10000	9	5	6	7		8				1	4		2			10			11	3
25		14	BURY	2-0	Flint 2	4000	11	5	6		4	9				1	8		2			10			7	3
26		17	Preston North End	1-2	Waterall	5000	8	5		7	4	9				1	6		2			10			11	3
27		24	TOTTENHAM HOTSPUR	2-2	Cantrell, West(p)	12000	10	5	6		4	9	11			1	8		2						7	3
28	Mar	2	Manchester Utd.	0-2		7000	9	5	6	7	4	8	11			1			2			10				3
29		9	LIVERPOOL	0-0		5000		5			9	6	11			1	8		2		4	10			7	3
30		13	ASTON VILLA	2-0	Flint, Matthews	8000	9	5	6	7		10				1	8		2		4				11	3
31		16	Aston Villa	1-5	Cantrell	15000	9	5	6	7		10				1	8		2		4				11	3
32		23	NEWCASTLE UNITED	1-4	Cantrell	8000	9	5	6	7		10				1	8		2		4				11	3
33		30	Sheffield United	3-1	Richards 2, Dean	10000	9	5	6	7	4	8				1			2			10			11	3
34	Apr	5	EVERTON	0-1		15000	9	5	6	7	4	8				1			2			10			11	3
35		6	OLDHAM ATHLETIC	1-1	Flint	6000		5	6	7	4	8				1		9	2			10			11	3
36		8	Everton	1-1	Richards	16000		5	6	7	4	9				1			2			10		8	11	3
37		13	Bolton Wanderers	0-3		12735		5	6	7	4	9				1			2			10		8	11	3
38		27	Woolwich Arsenal	3-0	Cantrell, Dean, Richards	8000	9	5	6	7	4	8				1			2			10			11	3
					Apps		23	37	33	33	33	29	3	3	1	38	31	1	38	1	4	31	1	3	37	38
					Goals		8		1	5		9					7					13		2	1	1

F.A. Cup

		Date	Opponent	Score	Scorers	Att	Cantrell J	Clamp A	Craythorne R	Dean RI	Emberton FP	Flint WA	Garrett FH	Grice R	Griffiths A	Iremonger A	Matthews W	McCulloch G	Morley H	Pacey H	Pepper FW	Richards S	Walker A	Waterall A	Waterall I	West, Alf
R1	Jan	13	Luton Town	4-2	Cantrell, Matthews, Richards, I Waterall	8000	9	5	6		4	7				1	8		2			10			11	3
R2	Feb	3	Swindon Town	0-2		13780	10	5	6	7	4	9				1	8		2						11	3

		p	w	d	l	f	a	pts
1	Blackburn Rovers	38	20	9	9	60	43	49
2	Everton	38	20	6	12	46	42	46
3	Newcastle United	38	18	8	12	64	50	44
4	Bolton Wanderers	38	20	3	15	54	43	43
5	Sheffield Wed.	38	16	9	13	69	49	41
6	Aston Villa	38	17	7	14	76	63	41
7	Middlesbrough	38	16	8	14	56	45	40
8	Sunderland	38	14	11	13	58	51	39
9	West Bromwich Alb.	38	15	9	14	43	47	39
10	Woolwich Arsenal	38	15	8	15	55	59	38
11	Bradford City	38	15	8	15	46	50	38
12	Tottenham Hotspur	38	14	9	15	53	53	37
13	Manchester United	38	13	11	14	45	60	37
14	Sheffield United	38	13	10	15	63	56	36
15	Manchester City	38	13	9	16	56	58	35
16	NOTTS COUNTY	38	14	7	17	46	63	35
17	Liverpool	38	12	10	16	49	55	34
18	Oldham Athletic	38	12	10	16	46	54	34
19	Preston North End	38	13	7	18	40	57	33
20	Bury	38	6	9	23	32	59	21

1912/13

19th in Division One (Relegated)

#		Date	Opponent	Score	Scorers	Att	Allsebrook R	Bird W	Cantrell J	Clamp A	Craythorne R	Emberton FP	Flint WA	Henshall HV	Hooper W	Iremonger A	James L	Jones AF	Morley H	Peart JG	Richards S	Steele MA	Tomlinson T	Waterall A	Waterall I	Wathey F	West, Abe	West, Alf	Williams D	Woolley J
1	Sep	2	MANCHESTER CITY	0-1		6000			9	5	6	4	8			1		10	2				11		7		3			
2		7	WEST BROMWICH ALB.	1-1	Flint	13000			9	5	6	4	8			1		10	2				11		7		3			
3		14	Everton	0-4		25000			9	5	6	4	8			1		10	2				11		7		3			
4		21	SHEFFIELD WEDNESDAY	1-2	Cantrell	12000			9	5	6	4	8			1			2	10				11	7		3			
5		28	Blackburn Rovers	1-2	West(p)	20000			11	5	6	4	9			1		10	2				8	7			3			
6	Oct	5	DERBY COUNTY	0-1		30000			11	5	6	4	9			1		10	2				8	7			3			
7		19	MIDDLESBROUGH	1-3	Richards	12000				5	6	4	9	7		1			2		8			10	11			3			
8		26	Sunderland	0-4		8000				5	6	4	9	8					2		10	1	11		7			3			
9	Nov	2	Manchester Utd.	1-2	West(p)	12000				5	6	4	8	7				10	2					11			3	9		
10		4	Tottenham Hotspur	3-0	West(p), Flint, I Waterall	12000				5	6	4	8	7				10	2					11		1	3	9		
11		9	ASTON VILLA	1-1	Williams	18000				5	6	4	8	11		1		10	2					7			3	9		
12		16	Liverpool	0-0		15000				5	6	4	8	11		1		10	2					7			3	9		
13		23	BOLTON WANDERERS	1-0	Henshall	8000				5	6	4	8	11		1		10	2					7			3	9		
14		30	Sheffield United	0-2		8000				5		4	6	11	7	1		10	2		8						3	9		
15	Dec	7	NEWCASTLE UNITED	0-1		10000				5		4	6	11	7	1		10	2		8						3	9		
16		14	Oldham Athletic	0-4		7000				5		4	6	11	7	1			2		10			8				3	9		
17		21	CHELSEA	0-0		12000	6			5		4	9	11	7	1			2		10							3	8		
18		25	Woolwich Arsenal	0-0		10000	6			5		4	10	11		1			2					8	7			3	9		
19		26	WOOLWICH ARSENAL	2-1	Jones 2	16000	6			5			4	11	7	1		10	2					8				3	9		
20		28	West Bromwich Alb.	0-2		20000	6			5			4	11	7	1	2	10						8				3	9		
21	Jan	2	Manchester City	0-4		17000	6			5			4	11	7	1		10			8							3	9		2
22		4	EVERTON	0-1		5000	6			5			4	9	7	1		10	2						11			3	8		
23		18	Sheffield Wednesday	1-3	Williams	15000	6			5			4	11		1		10	2					8		7		3	9		
24		25	BLACKBURN ROVERS	3-1	Williams, Jones, Henshall	15000	6			5			4	11		1		10	2					8	7			3	9		
25	Feb	8	Derby County	0-1		12000	6			5			4	11		1		10	2					8	7			3	9		
26		15	TOTTENHAM HOTSPUR	0-1		10000	6			5			4		7	1		10	2	9			11					3	8		
27	Mar	1	SUNDERLAND	2-1	Flint, Peart	10000	6			5			4	11	7				2	9		1		10				3	8		
28		8	MANCHESTER UTD.	1-2	Flint(p)	10000	6			5			4	11	7	1			2	9				10				3	8		
29		15	Aston Villa	0-1		20000	6			5			4	11		1			2		10			8		7		3	9		
30		21	Bradford City	0-1		12000	6			5			4	11		1			2	9	10					7		3	8		
31		22	LIVERPOOL	3-0	Peart 3	7000	6			5		4		11		1			2	9	10			8		7		3			
32		24	BRADFORD CITY	1-1	Richards	15000	6			5		4		11		1			2	9	10			8		7		3			
33		29	Bolton Wanderers	0-0		16580	6			5		4				1			2		10		11	8		7		3	9		
34	Apr	2	Middlesbrough	1-1	Peart	8000	6			5		4	7	11		1			2	9	10			8				3			
35		5	SHEFFIELD UNITED	0-1		12000	6			5		4	8	11		1			2	9	10				7			3			
36		12	Newcastle United	0-0		10000	6			5		4	7	11		1			2	9	10							3	8		
37		19	OLDHAM ATHLETIC	2-1	A Waterall, Peart(p)	8000	6			5		4	7			1			2	9	10		11	8				3			
38		26	Chelsea	2-5	Hooper, Peart	15000		8		5		4	6		7	1				9	10				11			3			2
			Apps				21	1	6	38	13	26	35	24	16	34	1	20	35	11	18	3	7	18	19	7	1	38	24	2
			Goals						1				4	2	1			3		7	2			1	1			3	3		

F.A. Cup

R1	Jan	11	Bristol Rovers	0-2		11000	6			5			4	11	7	1		10	2					8				3	9		

		p	w	d	l	f	a	pts
1	Sunderland	38	25	4	9	86	43	54
2	Aston Villa	38	19	12	7	86	52	50
3	Sheffield Wed.	38	21	7	10	75	55	49
4	Manchester United	38	19	8	11	69	43	46
5	Blackburn Rovers	38	16	13	9	79	43	45
6	Manchester City	38	18	8	12	53	37	44
7	Derby County	38	17	8	13	69	66	42
8	Bolton Wanderers	38	16	10	12	62	63	42
9	Oldham Athletic	38	14	14	10	50	55	42
10	West Bromwich Alb.	38	13	12	13	57	50	38
11	Everton	38	15	7	16	48	54	37
12	Liverpool	38	16	5	17	61	71	37
13	Bradford City	38	12	11	15	50	60	35
14	Newcastle United	38	13	8	17	47	47	34
15	Sheffield United	38	14	6	18	56	70	34
16	Middlesbrough	38	11	10	17	55	69	32
17	Tottenham Hotspur	38	12	6	20	45	72	30
18	Chelsea	38	11	6	21	51	73	28
19	NOTTS COUNTY	38	7	9	22	28	56	23
20	Woolwich Arsenal	38	3	12	23	26	74	18

Back: Bramley (treasurer), A Waterall, Harris (secretary), Morley, Iremonger, Emberton, Steele, Montgomery, McLean (assistant trainer). Centre: Wathey, Bird, Clamp, Richards, Alf West. Front: I Waterall, Craythorne, Cantrell, F Jones, Tomlinson, Prescott (trainer)

1913/14
Top of Division Two (Promoted)

							Allsebrook R	Bassett E	Bird W	Clamp A	Craythorne R	Emberton FP	Flint WA	Haig P	Henshall HV	Iremonger A	James L	Jennings W	Lamb J	Machin P	Morley H	Peart JG	Richards S	Toone G Jr	Waterall I	West, Alf	Williams D
1	Sep	6	Grimsby Town	0-0		7000	6			5		4	8			1					2	9	10		7	3	11
2		13	BIRMINGHAM	5-1	Waterall 2, Flint 2, Williams	12000	6			5		4	8			1					2	9	10		7	3	11
3		15	Woolwich Arsenal	0-3		20000	6		9	5		4	8			1					2		10		7	3	11
4		20	Bristol City	1-1	Bassett	12000		7		5	6	4	8	11		1				2			10			3	9
5		24	BLACKPOOL	2-0	Richards, Williams	5000		7		5	6	4	8			1					2		10		11	3	9
6		27	LEEDS CITY	4-0	Richards 2, Flint, Bassett	12000	6	7		5		4	8		11	1					2		10			3	9
7	Oct	2	LINCOLN CITY	2-1	Richards, Henshall	12000	6	7		5		4	8		11	1					2		10			3	9
8		4	Clapton Orient	0-1		12000		7	10		6	4	8			1		9			2				5	11	3	
9		11	GLOSSOP	2-2	Richards 2	10000	6	7		5		4	8		11	1					2	9	10			3	
10		18	Stockport County	2-1	Peart, Richards	8000	6	7				4	8		11	1		5			2	9	10			3	
11		25	BRADFORD PARK AVE.	2-3	Peart 2	10000	6	7				4	8		11	1		5			2	9	10			3	
12	Nov	1	FULHAM	4-0	Peart 3, Flint	12000	6	7				4	8		11	1		5			2	9	10			3	
13		8	Leicester Fosse	2-0	Peart, Richards	12000	6	7				4	8		11	1		5			2	9	10			3	
14		15	WOLVERHAMPTON W.	2-0	Henshall, Richards	7000	6	7				4	8		11	1		5			2	9	10			3	
15		22	Hull City	0-2		10000	6	7				4	8		11	1		5			2	9	10			3	
16		29	BARNSLEY	3-1	Richards, Flint, Peart	10000	6	7				4	8		11	1		5			2	9	10			3	
17	Dec	6	Bury	3-3	Richards, Peart, Flint	5000	6	7				4	8		11	1		5			2	9	10			3	
18		13	HUDDERSFIELD T	3-0	Peart 2, Richards	10000	6	7				4	8		11	1		5			2	9	10			3	
19		20	Lincoln City	0-0		5000	6	7				4	8		11	1		5			2	9	10			3	
20		25	NOTTM. FOREST	2-2	Peart 2	20000	6	7				4	8		11	1		5			2	9	10			3	
21		26	Nottm. Forest	0-1		20000	6	7				4	8		11	1		5			2	9	10			3	
22		27	GRIMSBY TOWN	4-0	Peart 3, Flint	14000		7		5	6	4	8		11	1					2	9	10			3	
23	Jan	1	WOOLWICH ARSENAL	1-0	Flint	10000	6	7				4	8		11	1					2	9	10			3	
24		3	Birmingham	1-2	Richards	10000	6	7	9	5		4	8		11	1					2		10			3	
25		17	BRISTOL CITY	4-0	Richards 2, Peart, Bassett	9000		7		5		4	8			1					2	9	10		11	3	
26		24	Leeds City	4-2	Flint 3, Richards	28000	6	7		5		4	8		11	1					2	9	10			3	
27	Feb	7	CLAPTON ORIENT	3-0	Richards, Henshall, Peart	9000	6	7		5		4	8		11	1					2	9	10			3	
28		14	Glossop	1-1	Peart	2000	6	7				4	8		11	1		5			2	9	10			3	
29		21	STOCKPORT COUNTY	2-1	Peart, Bassett	12000	6	7				4	8		11	1		5			2	9	10			3	
30		28	Bradford Park Ave.	3-0	Richards 2, Peart	26000	6	7		5		4	8		11	1					2	9	10			3	
31	Mar	7	Fulham	2-1	Henshall, Peart	18000	6	7		5		4	8		11	1					2	9	10			3	
32		14	LEICESTER FOSSE	4-1	Peart 2, Flint, Richards	14000	6	7		5		4	8		11	1					2	9	10			3	
33		21	Wolverhampton Wand.	1-4	Flint	13000	6	7		5		4	9		11	1			8		2		10			3	
34		28	HULL CITY	4-1	Peart 2, Allsebrook, Bassett	26000	6	7				4	8		11	1		5	10		2	9				3	
35	Apr	4	Barnsley	1-0	Flint	13000	6	7				4	8		11	1	3	5			2	9	10				
36		11	BURY	2-0	Richards, Peart	10000	6	7				4	8		11	1	3	5			2	9	10				
37		13	Blackpool	0-0		8000	6	7				4	8			1	2	5				9	10		11	3	
38		18	Huddersfield T	1-2	Peart	11000	6	7				4	8		11	1		5			2	9	10			3	
						Apps	34	35	3	18	4	38	38	1	30	38	3	20	2	1	36	30	36	1	7	36	7
						Goals		1	5				14		4							28	21		2		2

F.A. Cup

R1	Jan	10	Sheffield Wednesday	2-3	Flint, Peart(p)	27600	6	7		5		4	8		11	1					2	9	10			3	

Back: Emberton, Clamp, Morley, Iremonger, Steele, Jennings, Craythorne, Henshall. Front: Waterall, Flint, Williams, Bird, Peart, Richards, Allsebrook, West

		p	w	d	l	f	a	pts
1	NOTTS COUNTY	38	23	7	8	77	36	53
2	Bradford Park Ave.	38	23	3	12	71	47	49
3	Woolwich Arsenal	38	20	9	9	54	38	49
4	Leeds City	38	20	7	11	76	46	47
5	Barnsley	38	19	7	12	51	45	45
6	Clapton Orient	38	16	11	11	47	35	43
7	Hull City	38	16	9	13	53	37	41
8	Bristol City	38	16	9	13	52	50	41
9	Wolverhampton Wan.	38	18	5	15	51	52	41
10	Bury	38	15	10	13	39	40	40
11	Fulham	38	16	6	16	46	43	38
12	Stockport County	38	13	10	15	55	57	36
13	Huddersfield Town	38	13	8	17	47	53	34
14	Birmingham	38	12	10	16	48	60	34
15	Grimsby Town	38	13	8	17	42	58	34
16	Blackpool	38	9	14	15	33	44	32
17	Glossop	38	11	6	21	51	67	28
18	Leicester Fosse	38	11	4	23	45	61	26
19	Lincoln City	38	10	6	22	36	66	26
20	Nottingham Forest	38	7	9	22	37	76	23

1914/15   16th in Division One

						Allsebrook R	Bassett E	Bird W	Clamp A	Dale G	Emberton FP	Flint WA	Henshall HV	Iremonger A	Jennings W	Lamb J	Morley H	Peart JG	Perry J	Richards S	Sisson T	Waterall I	West, Alf	Woolley J
1	Sep	2	Aston Villa	1-2	Lamb	10000	6						4	8	1	5	11	2	9		10		7	3	
2		5	Liverpool	1-1	Lamb	20000	6			8			4	7	1	5	10	2	9				11	3	
3		12	BRADFORD PARK AVE.	1-2	Allsebrook	10000	6			8			4	7	1	5	10	2	9				11	3	
4		19	Oldham Athletic	0-2		6000	6	7		5	8		9		1	4		2					10	11	3	
5		26	MANCHESTER UTD.	4-2	Peart 2(1p), Flint, Richards	10000	6			5			4	8	11	1			2	9		10		7	3	
6	Oct	3	Bolton Wanderers	2-1	Peart 2	14113	6			5			4	8	11	1			2	9		10		7	3	
7		10	BLACKBURN ROVERS	1-1	Flint	12000	6			5			4	8	11	1			9	2		10		7	3	
8		17	MANCHESTER CITY	0-2		14000	6			5			4	8	11	1			9	2		10		7	3	
9		24	Sunderland	1-3	Peart	9000	6	7		5			4	8		1			9	2		10		11	3	
10		31	SHEFFIELD WEDNESDAY	1-2	Waterall	10000	6	7	8	5			4	9		1				2		10		11	3	
11	Nov	7	West Bromwich Alb.	1-4	Flint	12000	6			5			4	8	11	1			2	9		10		7	3	
12		14	EVERTON	0-0		10000	6			5			4	8	11	1			2	9		10	3	7		
13		21	Chelsea	1-4	Emberton	15000	6			5		4	8	11	1				2	9		10	3	7		
14		28	BRADFORD CITY	0-0		7000	6						4	11	1	5	8		2	9		10	3	7		
15	Dec	5	Burnley	0-0		9000	6	8					4	11	1	5			2	9		10		7		3
16		12	TOTTENHAM HOTSPUR	1-2	Richards	5000	6			5			8	11	1	4		2	9	3	10		7			
17		19	Newcastle United	1-1	Lamb	10000	6					3	4	11	1	5	8	2	9		10		7			
18		25	Middlesbrough	0-1		10000	6					3	4	11	1	5	8	2	9		10		7			
19		26	MIDDLESBROUGH	5-1	Dale 2, Richards 2, Henshall	12000	6				8	3	4	11	1	5		2	9		10		7			
20		28	Sheffield United	0-1		15000	6				8	3	4	11	1	5		2	9		10		7			
21	Jan	2	LIVERPOOL	3-1	Peart, Richards, Dale	6000	6				8	3	4	11	1	5			9	2	10		7			
22		16	Bradford Park Ave.	1-3	Dale	9000	6				8	5	4	11	1	9		2			10		7	3	
23		23	OLDHAM ATHLETIC	2-1	Bird, Richards	5000	6	7	9		8		4	11	1	5		2			10			3	
24		30	Manchester Utd.	2-2	Dale, Bird	8000	6	7	9		8		4	11	1	5		2			10			3	
25	Feb	13	Blackburn Rovers	1-5	Henshall	3000	6		9		8		4	11	1	5		2			10		7	3	
26		20	Tottenham Hotspur	0-2		10000	6		10	5	8	2	4	11	1				9				7	3	
27		22	Manchester City	0-0		20000	6		10	5	8	3		11	1	4			9	2			7		
28		27	SUNDERLAND	2-1	Richards, Scott(og)	7000	6			5	8		4	11	1				9	2	10		7	3	
29	Mar	6	Sheffield Wednesday	0-0		11000	6			5	8	3		11	1	4			9	2	10		7		
30		13	WEST BROMWICH ALB.	1-1	Peart	9000	6			5	8	3	4	11	1				9	2	10		7		
31		17	BOLTON WANDERERS	0-0		5000	6			5	8	3	4	11	1				9	2	10		7		
32		20	Everton	0-4		16000	6			5	8	3	4	11	1				9	2	10		7		
33	Apr	2	SHEFFIELD UNITED	3-1	Henshall, Flint, Peart	9000	6			5			4	8	11	1			2	9	3	10		7		
34		3	Bradford City	1-3	Peart	8000	6	7		5			4	8		1			2	9	3	10		11		
35		5	ASTON VILLA	1-1	Peart	12000	6	7		5				8	11	1	4		9	3	10			2	
36		10	BURNLEY	0-0		9000	6			5	7		8	11	1	4		2	9	3	10				
37		24	NEWCASTLE UNITED	1-0	Henshall	11000	6	7		5			8	11	1	4		2	9	3	10				
38		28	CHELSEA	2-0	Peart, Richards	9000	6			5			8	11	1	4		2	9	3	10		7		
			Apps				38	9	6	24	18	26	36	31	38	22	6	25	32	18	34	3	33	18	1
			Goals					1		2		5	1	4	4			3		11	8		1		

One own goal

F.A. Cup

| R1 | Jan | 9 | Bolton Wanderers | 1-2 | Richards | 17870 | 6 | | | 8 | 3 | | 4 | 11 | 1 | 5 | | 2 | 9 | | 10 | | 7 | | |

		p	w	d	l	f	a	pts
1	Everton	38	19	8	11	76	47	46
2	Oldham Athletic	38	17	11	10	70	56	45
3	Blackburn Rovers	38	18	7	13	83	61	43
4	Burnley	38	18	7	13	61	47	43
5	Manchester City	38	15	13	10	49	39	43
6	Sheffield United	38	15	13	10	49	41	43
7	Sheffield Wed.	38	15	13	10	61	54	43
8	Sunderland	38	18	5	15	81	72	41
9	Bradford Park Ave.	38	17	7	14	69	65	41
10	West Bromwich Alb.	38	15	10	13	49	43	40
11	Bradford City	38	13	14	11	55	49	40
12	Middlesbrough	38	13	12	13	62	74	38
13	Liverpool	38	14	9	15	65	75	37
14	Aston Villa	38	13	11	14	62	72	37
15	Newcastle United	38	11	10	17	46	48	32
16	NOTTS COUNTY	38	9	13	16	41	57	31
17	Bolton Wanderers	38	11	8	19	68	84	30
18	Manchester United	38	9	12	17	46	62	30
19	Chelsea	38	8	13	17	51	65	29
20	Tottenham Hotspur	38	8	12	18	57	90	28

Back: McLean (assistant trainer), I Waterall, Emberton, Clamp, Craythorne. Standing: Fisher (sec/manager), Goddard (director), Morley, Jennings, Iremonger, Allsebrook, West, Prescott (trainer), Bramley (director). Sitting: Newton (director), Bird, Flint, Peart, Richards, Henshall, Godfrey (director). Front: Bassett, Williams

1915/16

#	Date		Opponent	Score	Scorers	Att	1	2	3	4	5	6	7	8	9	10	11
1	Sep	4	HULL CITY	2-0	Cantrell, Henshall	6000	Iremonger A	Morley H	Perry J	Jennings W	Clamp A	Allsebrook	Waterall I	Flint WA	Cantrell J	Lilley B	Henshall HV
2		11	Nottm. Forest	5-3	Henshall 4 (2p), Flint	12000	Iremonger A	Morley H	Perry J	Bird W	Jennings W	Allsebrook	Waterall I	Flint WA	Cantrell J	Parrish J	Henshall HV
3		18	BARNSLEY	1-0	Flint	4000	Iremonger A	Morley H	Perry J	Jennings W	Clamp A	Allsebrook	Waterall I	Flint WA	Bird W	Parrish J	Henshall HV
4	Oct	2	SHEFFIELD UNITED	3-0	Flint 2, Cantrell	3000	Iremonger A	Morley H	Perry J	Jennings W	Clamp A	Allsebrook	Waterall I	Flint WA	Cantrell J	Richards S	Henshall HV
5		9	Bradford City	2-1	Cantrell, Parrish	5000	Iremonger A	Morley H	Perry J	Bagshaw JJ	Clamp A	Allsebrook	Waterall I	Flint WA	Cantrell J	Parrish J	Henshall HV
6		16	HUDDERSFIELD T	1-1	Parrish	6000	Iremonger A	Morley H	Perry J	Toone G (Jr)	Jennings W	Allsebrook	Waterall I	Flint WA	Cantrell J	Parrish J	Henshall HV
7		23	Grimsby Town	2-2	Cantrell, Flint	4000	Iremonger A	Morley H	Perry J	Jennings W	Toone G (Jr)	Allsebrook	Waterall I	Flint WA	Cantrell J	Richards S	Henshall HV
8		30	Lincoln City	0-3		4000	Iremonger A	Morley H	Perry J	Bagshaw JJ	Clamp A	Allsebrook	Waterall I	Flint WA	Cantrell J	Bache JW	Dunn R
9	Nov	6	DERBY COUNTY	5-0	Cantrell 3, Bache, Flint	7000	Iremonger A	Morley H	Perry J	Bagshaw JJ	Clamp A	Allsebrook	Waterall I	Flint WA	Cantrell J	Bache JW	Henshall HV
10		13	Sheffield Wednesday	1-4	Cantrell	5000	Iremonger A	Morley H	Perry J	Jennings W	Toone G (Jr)	Bagshaw JJ	Plant	Flint WA	Cantrell J	Bache JW	Henshall HV
11		20	BRADFORD PARK AVE.	3-0	Bache, Cantrell, Henshall (p)	4000	Iremonger A	Morley H	Perry J	Jennings W	Bowser S	Bagshaw JJ	Wright H	Flint WA	Cantrell J	Bache JW	Henshall HV
12		27	Leeds City	4-0	Bache 2, Bagshaw, Cantrell	4000	Iremonger A	Morley H	Perry J	Jennings W	Clamp A	Bagshaw JJ	Wright H	Flint WA	Cantrell J	Bache JW	Henshall HV
13	Dec	4	Hull City	0-3		1000	Iremonger A	Morley H	Perry J	Jennings W	Clamp A	Bagshaw JJ	Wright H	Flint WA	Cantrell J	Bache JW	Leatherland J
14		11	NOTTM. FOREST	0-0		7000	Iremonger A	Morley H	Perry J	Jennings W	Bowser S	Bagshaw JJ	Waterall I	Flint WA	Cantrell J	Bache JW	Henshall HV
15		18	Barnsley	0-1		5000	Iremonger A	Morley H	Perry J	Flint WA	Jennings W	Bagshaw JJ	Waterall I	Richards S	Cantrell J	Bache JW	Henshall HV
16		25	LEICESTER FOSSE	1-2	Henshall	4000	Iremonger A	Morley H	Johnson J	Jennings W	Clamp A	Bagshaw JJ	Waterall I	Richards S	Cantrell J	Bache JW	Henshall HV
17		27	Leicester Fosse	1-2	Henshall (p)	3000	Iremonger A	Sissons W	Perry J	Jennings W	Clamp A	Bagshaw JJ	Waterall I	Flint WA	Cantrell J	Bache JW	Henshall HV
18	Jan	1	Sheffield United	1-1	Flint	5500	Steele MA	Morley H	Perry J	Bagshaw JJ	Clamp A	Allsebrook	Waterall I	Flint WA	Cantrell J	Bache JW	Henshall HV
19		8	BRADFORD CITY	1-0	Cantrell	5000	Iremonger A	Morley H	Perry J	Bagshaw JJ	Bowser S	Allsebrook	Waterall I	Flint WA	Cantrell J	Bache JW	Henshall HV
20		15	Huddersfield Town	1-2	Henshall (p)	4000	Iremonger A	Morley H	Perry J	Bagshaw JJ	Bowser S	Allsebrook	Waterall I	Flint WA	Cantrell J	Bache JW	Henshall HV
21		22	GRIMSBY TOWN	1-2	Bache	3000	Steele MA	Perry J	Feebery J	Bagshaw JJ	Clamp A	Allsebrook	Waterall I	Flint WA	Cantrell J	Bache JW	Henshall HV
22		29	LINCOLN CITY	2-1	Bache, Ward (og)	4000	Steele MA	Morley H	Feebery J	Robson M	Jennings W	Allsebrook	Waterall I	Thurman M	Cantrell J	Bache JW	Henshall HV
23	Feb	5	Derby County	0-2		2000	Iremonger A	Morley H	Feebery J	Robson M	Bagshaw JJ	Allsebrook	Richards S	Sankey T	Cantrell J	Bache JW	Henshall HV
24		12	SHEFFIELD WEDNESDAY	1-1	Allsebrook	4000	Iremonger A	Morley H	Perry J	Flint WA	Jennings W	Allsebrook	Waterall I	Bird W	Cantrell J	Bache JW	Henshall HV
25		19	Bradford Park Avenue	0-4		4000	Steele MA	Morley H	Johnson J	Flint WA	Jennings W	Allsebrook	Waterall I	Bird W	Cantrell J	Bache JW	Henshall HV
26	Apr	21	LEEDS CITY	1-1	Foster	3000	Iremonger A	Morley H	Johnson J	Flint WA	Foster JH	Bagshaw JJ	Waterall I	Bird W	Cantrell J	Richards S	Henshall HV
27	Mar	4	Leicester Fosse	0-0		3000	Iremonger A	Morley H	Johnson J	Bagshaw JJ	Jennings W	Allsebrook	Waterall I	Flint WA	Flint WA	Bache JW	Henshall HV
28		11	CHESTERFIELD	1-1	Bird	1500	Iremonger A	Johnson J	Bagshaw JJ	Jennings W	Bowser S	Allsebrook	Waterall I	Bird W	Flint WA	Richards S	Henshall HV
29		18	DERBY COUNTY	3-1	Henshall, Richards, Waterall (p)	2000	Iremonger A	Morley H	Johnson J	Jennings W	Bowser S	Allsebrook	Waterall I	Bird W	Flint WA	Richards S	Henshall HV
30		25	Stoke	0-3		4000	Iremonger A	Morley H	Perry J	Flint WA	Bowser S	Jennings W	Waterall I	Bird W	Cantrell J	Richards S	Henshall HV
31	Apr	1	NOTTM. FOREST	2-0	Cantrell, Richards	6000	Iremonger A	Morley H	Johnson J	Flint WA	Foster JH	Bagshaw JJ	Waterall I	Bird W	Cantrell J	Richards S	Henshall HV
32		8	LEICESTER FOSSE	1-1	Bird	3000	Iremonger A	Morley H	Johnson J	Bagshaw JJ	Foster JH	Allsebrook	Waterall I	Bird W	Cantrell J	Flint WA	Henshall HV
33		15	Chesterfield	1-0	Henshall	4000	Iremonger A	Morley H	Johnson J	Jennings W	Foster JH	Bagshaw JJ	Flint WA	Bird W	Cantrell J	Richards S	Henshall HV
34		22	Derby County	3-2	Bird, Cantrell, Waterall(p)	4000	Iremonger A	Jennings W	Johnson J	Flint WA	Foster JH	Bagshaw JJ	Waterall I	Bird W	Cantrell J	Richards S	Henshall HV
35		24	Nottm. Forest	2-4	Cantrell, Richards	9000	Iremonger A	Morley H	Johnson J	Flint WA	Foster JH	Bagshaw JJ	Jennings W	Bird W	Cantrell J	Richards S	Henshall HV
36		29	STOKE	3-0	Richards 2, Bird	3000	Iremonger A	Morley H	Johnson J	Blackburn G	Foster JH	Bagshaw JJ	Wright H	Bird W	Cantrell J	Richards S	Henshall HV

Games 1 - 26: League, Midland Section
Games 27 - 36: Subsidiary Competition

1916/17

			Opponent	Score	Scorers	Att										
1	Sep	2	Nottm. Forest	3-4	Cantrell, Henshall, Walker		Iremonger A	Morley H	Pennington J	Flint WA	Foster JH	Bagshaw JJ	Pykett B	Bird W	Cantrell J	Walker JH	Henshall HV
2		9	BARNSLEY	1-1	Walker		Iremonger A	Perry J	Pennington J	Bowser S	Foster JH	Bagshaw JJ	Bartrop W	Bird W	Cantrell J	Walker JH	Henshall HV
3		16	Leeds City	0-5		3000	Neal G	Jennings W	Pennington J	Walker JH	Foster JH	Bagshaw JJ	Laxton LE	Flint WA	Cantrell J	Housley H	Henshall HV
4		23	SHEFFIELD UNITED	2-0	Cantrell, Mann	3000	Iremonger A	Morley H	Pennington J	Flint WA	Foster JH	Jennings W	Laxton LE	Mann J	Cantrell J	Housley H	Henshall HV
5		30	Bradford City	2-1	Cantrell 2	2000	Iremonger A	Morley H	Pennington J	Flint WA	Foster JH	Jennings W	Tattershall W	Walker JH	Cantrell J	Housley H	Henshall HV
6	Oct	7	LEICESTER FOSSE	5-1	Cantrell 3, Housley 2	3000	Iremonger A	Morley H	Pennington J	Flint WA	Foster JH	Bagshaw JJ	Tattershall W	Walker JH	Cantrell J	Housley H	Henshall HV
7		14	Grimsby Town	3-3	Flint, Housley, Jennings	2000	Neal G	Bagshaw JJ	Dexter G	Flint WA	Jennings W	Graham DC	Laxton LE	Walker JH	Pykett B	Housley H	Henshall HV
8		21	CHESTERFIELD	1-4	Walker	4000	Neal G	Morley H	Pennington J	Flint WA	Foster JH	Jennings W	Walker JH	Pykett B	Cantrell J	Housley H	Walker JH
9		28	ROTHERHAM COUNTY	2-2	Dunn, Housley	2000	Iremonger A	Morley H	Pennington J	Flint WA	Bowser S	Woodlands A	Scrimshaw A	Turner H	Housley H	Walker JH	Dunn R
10	Nov	4	Huddersfield T	0-1		3000	Iremonger A	Morley H	Pennington J	Flint WA	Bowser S	Woodlands A	Scrimshaw A	Walker JH	Cantrell J	Housley H	Brownlow W
11		11	LINCOLN CITY	0-4		2500	Iremonger A	Charlesworth G	Dexter G	Flint WA	Foster JH	Bagshaw JJ	Foster WH	Clarke	Cantrell J	Walker JH	Dunn R
12		18	Sheffield Wednesday	0-2		2000	Iremonger A	Perry J	Pennington J	Flint WA	Bowser S	Bagshaw JJ	Scrimshaw A	Walker JH	Cantrell J	Richards S	Reider
13		25	BRADFORD PARK AVE.	2-1	Cantrell, Cooke	3000	Iremonger A	Perry J	Pennington J	Flint WA	Bowser S	Walker JH	Cooke JR	Cantrell J	Sambrooke C	Richards S	Henshall HV
14	Dec	2	Birmingham	0-4			Neal G	Perry J	Pennington J	Flint WA	Bowser S	Walker JH	Cooke JR	Cantrell J	Sambrooke C	Richards S	Hayes J
15		9	NOTTM. FOREST	2-2	Cantrell, Richards	3000	Neal G	Perry J	Pennington J	Flint WA	Bird W	Walker JH	Cooke JR	Housley H	Sambrooke C	Richards S	Hayes J
16		16	Barnsley	0-4			Neal G	Perry J	Kay H	Walker JH	Flint WA	Bird W	James W	Housley H	Cantrell J	Richards S	Foster WH
17		23	LEEDS CITY	1-0	Housley	500	Iremonger A	Morley H	Perry J	Flint WA	Woodlands A	Walker JH	James W	Housley H	Cantrell J	Richards S	Henshall HV
18		25	Hull City	0-2		2000	Edleston	Bagshaw JJ	Woolley J	Flint WA	Woodlands A	Walker JH	Cooke JR	Housley H	Cantrell J	Richards S	Foster WH
19		26	HULL CITY	7-1	Richards 3, Cantrell 2, Dunn, Walker	5000	Iremonger A	Clay T	Woolley J	Flint WA	Bagshaw JJ	Walker JH	James W	Walker JH	Cantrell J	Richards S	Dunn R
20		30	Sheffield United	1-0	James	7000	Iremonger A	Wilson J	Walker JH	Flint WA	Woodlands A	Charles F	Johnson H (Jr)	James W	Cantrell J	Bird W	Dunn R
21	Jan	6	BRADFORD CITY	1-0	Richards	2000	Iremonger A	Morley H	Pennington J	Flint WA	Woodlands A	Walker JH	Bird W	Cantrell J	Sambrooke C	Richards S	Dunn R
22		13	Leicester Fosse	1-0	Walker (p)	1600	Neal G	White T	Pennington J	Flint WA	Woodlands A	Walker JH	James W	Bird W	Cantrell J	Richards S	Dunn R
23		20	GRIMSBY TOWN	2-3	Dunn, Walker	1200	Neal G	Morley H	White T	Flint WA	Bird W	Walker JH	James W	Cantrell J	Sambrooke C	Richards S	Dunn R
24		27	Chesterfield	1-3	Housley	2500	Branston JT	White T	Pennington J	Flint WA	Bird W	Walker JH	Scrimshaw A	Davis F	Cantrell J	Housley H	Dunn R
25	Feb	3	Rotherham County	3-0	Cantrell, Richards, Scrimshaw	4500	Branston JT	White T	Pennington J	Flint WA	Jennings W	Walker JH	Scrimshaw A	Bird W	Cantrell J	Richards S	Dunn R
26		10	HUDDERSFIELD T	2-1	Flint, Richards	1500	Branston JT	White T	Pennington J	Dexter F	Jennings W	Walker JH	Scrimshaw A	Flint WA	Cantrell J	Richards S	Dunn R
27		17	Lincoln City	2-1	Flint, Richards		Branston JT	White T	Pennington J	Flint WA	Jennings W	Walker JH	Scrimshaw A	Bird W	Cantrell J	Richards S	Dunn R
28		24	SHEFFIELD WEDNESDAY	1-0	Richards	3000	Branston JT	White T	Dexter F	Flint WA	Jennings W	Walker JH	Scrimshaw A	Bird W	Cantrell J	Richards S	Dunn R
29	Mar	3	Bradford Park Avenue	1-1	Fearnley	2500	Branston JT	White T	Walker JH	Barraclough	Woodlands A	Jennings W	Scrimshaw A	Flint WA	Cantrell J	Fearnley	Dunn R
30		10	BIRMINGHAM	1-1	Woods	2000	Branston JT	White T	Pennington J	Flint WA	Woodlands A	Walker JH	Scrimshaw A	Woods J	Cantrell J	Richards S	Dunn R
31	Mar	24	NOTTM. FOREST	2-2	Flint, Walker (p)	4000	Branston JT	White T	Pennington J	Flint WA	Woodlands A	Walker JH	Scrimshaw A	Woods J	Cantrell J	Richards S	Dunn R
32		31	Birmingham	1-1	Walker (p)		Branston JT	White T	Pennington J	Flint WA	Jennings W	Walker JH	Scrimshaw A	Bird W	Cantrell J	Driver T	Dunn R
33	Apr	7	Leicester Fosse	1-2	Cantrell		Branston JT	White T	Walker JH	Starkey G	Flint WA	Walker JH	Scrimshaw A	Bird W	Cantrell J	Richards S	Dunn R
34		9	LEICESTER FOSSE	2-3	Cantrell, Richards	3000	Branston JT	White T	Walker JH	Flint WA	Hawley F	Jennings W	Scrimshaw A	Bird W	Cantrell J	Richards S	Dunn R
35		14	Nottm. Forest	3-2	Flint 2, Cantrell		Iremonger A	Morley H	Pennington J	White T	Woodlands A	Jennings W	Scrimshaw A	Bird W	Flint WA	Walker JH	Cantrell J
36		21	BIRMINGHAM	0-2			Iremonger A	White T	Pennington J	Flint WA	Woodlands A	Walker JH	Scrimshaw A	Bird W	Cantrell J	Richards S	Dunn R

Games 1 - 30: League, Midland Section
Games 31 - 36: Subsidiary Competition

1917/18

1 Sep	1	LEICESTER FOSSE	2-1	Richards, Tremelling		Iremonger A	Smith J	Smith G	Bryan J	Tremelling S	McNeal R	Waterall I	Flint WA	Cantrell J	Richards S	Jones B
2	8	Leicester Fosse	0-1			Iremonger A	Bagshaw JJ	Smith G	Bryan J	Tremelling S	McNeal R	Scrimshaw H	Flint WA	Cantrell J	Richards S	Waterall I
3	15	HULL CITY	2-2	Cantrell, Richards		Branston JT	Clay T	Charlesworth G	Flint WA	Hawley F	McNeal R	Scrimshaw H	Pykett B	Cantrell J	Richards S	Waterall I
4	22	Hull City	2-1	Cumming, Hawley		Branston JT	Charlesworth G	Loversuch A	Flint WA	Hawley F	Bagshaw JJ	Scrimshaw H	Cumming J	Cantrell J	Richards S	Waterall I
5 Oct	13	Barnsley	0-0			Branston JT	Clay T	Charlesworth G	Bryan J	Hawley F	McNeal R	Sheldon L	Cumming J	Cantrell J	Richards S	Waterall I
6	20	BARNSLEY	4-2	Cantrell 2, Sheldon, Day(og)		Branston JT	Smith G	Charlesworth G	Bryan J	Hawley F	McNeal R	Sheldon L	Cumming J	Cantrell J	Richards S	Waterall I
7	27	Bradford Park Avenue	0-1		3000	Branston JT	Smith G	Charlesworth G	Bryan J	Hawley F	McNeal R	Sheldon L	Cumming J	Cantrell J	Richards S	Jennings W
8 Nov	3	BRADFORD PARK AVE.	0-1		2000	Iremonger A	Charlesworth G	Smith G	Bryan J	Hawley F	Bagshaw JJ	Laxton LE	Cumming J	Cantrell J	Richards S	Waterall I
9	10	Sheffield United	1-6	Cantrell	6000	Iremonger A	Smith J	Charlesworth G	Bryan J	Hawley F	McNeal R	Sheldon L	Cumming J	Boyne R	Richards S	Cantrell J
10	17	SHEFFIELD UNITED	0-6			Iremonger A	Smith J	Charlesworth G	Bryan J	Hawley F	McNeal R	Sheldon L	Cumming J	Cantrell J	Richards S	Dunn R
11	24	Leeds City	0-2		2000	Branston JT	Charlesworth G	Yates A	Cumming J	Hawley F	McNeal R	Sheldon L	Leafe D	Cantrell J	Richards S	Dunn R
12 Dec	1	LEEDS CITY	2-4	Cumming, Richards	3000	Branston JT	Charlesworth G	Marriott F	Bryan J	Hawley F	McNeal R	Sheldon L	Cumming J	Cantrell J	Richards S	Waterall I
13	8	LINCOLN CITY	1-1	Cantrell		Branston JT	Smith J	Charlesworth G	Bryan J	Hawley F	Cumming J	Sheldon L	Goodman T	Cantrell J	Richards S	Dunn R
14	15	Lincoln City	2-1	Richards 2		Branston JT	Charlesworth G	Marriott F	Bryan J	Bagshaw JJ	Wield T	Cumming J	Sheldon L	Cantrell J	Richards S	Waterall I
15	22	GRIMSBY TOWN	8-0	Cantrell 5, Richards 2, Henshall (p)		Branston JT	Charlesworth G	Marriott F	Bryan J	Bagshaw JJ	Wield T	Waterall I	Cumming J	Cantrell J	Richards S	Henshall HV
16	25	NOTTM. FOREST	0-1			Branston JT	Clay T	Charlesworth G	Flint WA	Bagshaw JJ	Waterall A	Sheldon L	Cumming J	Cantrell J	Richards S	Waterall I
17	26	Nottm. Forest	0-0			Iremonger A	Clay T	Charlesworth G	Bryan J	Bagshaw JJ	Waterall A	Sheldon L	Flint WA	Cantrell J	Richards S	Waterall I
18	29	Grimsby Town	0-2			Iremonger A	Charlesworth G	White J	Bryan J	Flint WA	Graham DC	Sheldon L	Short J	Cantrell J	Richards S	Waterall I
19 Jan	5	BIRMINGHAM	3-3	Cantrell, Richards, Short		Branston JT	Charlesworth G	Atkin J	Bryan J	Bagshaw JJ	Marriott F	Sheldon L	Short J	Cantrell J	Richards S	Waterall I
20	12	Birmingham	2-7	Richards 2		Branston JT	Perry J	Charlesworth G	Bell JJ	Bagshaw JJ	Bryan J	Sheldon L	Short J	Cantrell J	Richards S	Crossley CH
21	19	BRADFORD CITY	2-2	Cantrell, Richards		Iremonger A	Charlesworth G	Marriott F	Bryan J	Bagshaw JJ	Cumming J	Sheldon L	Short J	Cantrell J	Richards S	Willis AS
22	26	Bradford City	0-0			Iremonger A	Charlesworth G	Marriott F	Bryan J	Bagshaw JJ	Cumming J	Sheldon L	Short J	Cantrell J	Poole WS	Timmins W
23 Feb	2	HUDDERSFIELD T	3-2	Cantrell 2, Richards	2000	Branston JT	Charlesworth G	Marriott F	Bryan J	Bagshaw JJ	Cumming J	Sheldon L	Short J	Cantrell J	Richards S	Timmins W
24	16	SHEFFIELD WEDNESDAY	3-0	Waterall 2, Short		Iremonger A	Charlesworth G	Marriott F	Timmins W	Bagshaw JJ	Bryan J	Sheldon L	Short J	Cantrell J	Richards S	Waterall I
25	23	Sheffield Wednesday	1-2	Richards		Iremonger A	Charlesworth G	Marriott F	Bryan J	Bagshaw JJ	Timmins W	Sheldon L	Short J	Cantrell J	Richards S	Mee GW
26 Mar	2	ROTHERHAM COUNTY	2-2	Cantrell, Richards		Iremonger A	Charlesworth G	Marriott F	Bryan J	Bagshaw JJ	Timmins W	Sheldon L	Short J	Cantrell J	Richards S	Mee GW
27	9	Rotherham County	2-2	Cantrell 2	4000	Iremonger A	Charlesworth G	Marriott F	Bryan J	Bagshaw JJ	Timmins W	Sheldon L	Short J	Cantrell J	Richards S	Waterall I
28 Apr	2	Huddersfield Town	1-2	Cantrell		Keeling S	Clay T	Charlesworth G	Bryan J	Bagshaw JJ	Timmins W	Waterall I	Short J	Cantrell J	Richards S	Mee GW
29 Mar	16	LEICESTER FOSSE	5-0	Short 2, Cantrell, Charlesworth(p), Richards		Iremonger A	Charlesworth G	Marriott F	Bryan J	Bagshaw JJ	Timmins W	Sheldon L	Short J	Cantrell J	Richards S	Brooks
30	23	Leicester Fosse	1-3	Cantrell		Iremonger A	Charlesworth G	Pennington J	Bryan J	Bagshaw JJ	Timmins W	Sheldon L	Short J	Cantrell J	Richards S	Mee GW
31	29	NOTTM. FOREST	3-1	Flint, Short, Waterall		Iremonger A	Clay T	Charlesworth G	Flint WA	Bagshaw JJ	Timmins W	Scrimshaw H	Short J	Cantrell J	Richards S	Waterall I
32	30	BIRMINGHAM	5-1	Cantrell 2, Richards 2, Mee		Iremonger A	Clay T	Charlesworth G	Bryan J	Bagshaw JJ	Timmins W	Sheldon L	Short J	Cantrell J	Richards S	Mee GW
33 Apr	1	Nottm. Forest	3-0	Richards 2, Cantrell		Iremonger A	Clay T	Charlesworth G	Flint WA	Bagshaw JJ	Timmins W	Waterall I	Short J	Cantrell J	Richards S	Mee GW
34	6	Birmingham	2-3	Cantrell 2		Iremonger A	Charlesworth G	Keeling S	Short J	Bagshaw JJ	Timmins W	Sheldon L	Scrimshaw H	Cantrell J	Richards S	Mee GW

Games 1 - 28: League, Midland Section
Games 29 - 34: Subsidiary Competition

1918/19

	Date	Opponent	Score	Scorers	Att	1	2	3	4	5	6	7	8	9	10	11
1	Sep 7	Leeds City	1-4	Short	5000	Johnson J	Clay T	Marriott F	Waterall A	Bagshaw JJ	Timmins W	Sheldon L	Cumming J	Short J	Richards S	Waterall I
2	14	LEEDS CITY	5-2	Cantrell 2, Clay (p), Richards, Short	7000	Johnson J	Clay T	Marriott F	Waterall A	Bagshaw JJ	Timmins W	Sheldon L	Short J	Cantrell J	Richards S	Waterall I
3	21	Sheffield United	2-2	Cantrell, Richards	10000	Johnson J	Clay T	Marriott F	Waterall A	Bagshaw JJ	Timmins W	Sheldon L	Short J	Cantrell J	Richards S	Waterall I
4	28	SHEFFIELD UNITED	5-2	Short 3, Cantrell 2	6000	Johnson J	Clay T	Marriott F	Waterall A	Bagshaw JJ	Timmins W	Sheldon L	Short J	Cantrell J	Walker JH	Mee GW
5	Oct 5	Bradford Park Avenue	0-0		3000	Johnson J	Charlesworth G	Marriott F	Flint WA	Bagshaw JJ	Timmins W	Walker JH	Short J	Cantrell J	Richards S	Waterall I
6	12	BRADFORD PARK AVE.	4-1	Cantrell 2, Richards 2	7000	Johnson J	Clay T	Marriott F	Flint WA	Bagshaw JJ	Timmins W	Sheldon L	Short J	Cantrell J	Richards S	Waterall I
7	19	HULL CITY	1-0	Cantrell		Iremonger A	Charlesworth G	Marriott F	Bryan J	Bagshaw JJ	Timmins W	Sheldon L	Hill H	Cantrell J	White	Waterall I
8	26	Hull City	1-1	Cantrell		Iremonger A	Charlesworth G	Marriott F	Bryan J	Bagshaw JJ	Waterall A	Sheldon L	Short J	Cantrell J	Tinsley W	Waterall T
9	Nov 2	COVENTRY CITY	4-0	Bagshaw, Charlesworth(p), Short, Tinsley		Iremonger A	Charlesworth G	Marriott F	Bryan J	Bagshaw JJ	Timmins W	Waterall I	Storer H	Cantrell J	Richards S	Waterall T
10	9	Coventry City	1-5	Storer		Iremonger A	Clay T	Marriott F	Kemp H	Bagshaw JJ	Timmins W	Waterall I	Storey	Cantrell J	Richards S	Waterall T
11	16	BARNSLEY	4-4	Clay 2 (2p), Kemp, Short		Iremonger A	Clay T	Marriott F	Cumming J	Bagshaw JJ	Waterall T	Waterall I	Storey	Price W	Richards S	Timmins W
12	23	Barnsley	0-1			Iremonger A	Clay T	Marriott F	Flint WA	Bagshaw JJ	Waterall T	Waterall I	Short J	Cumming J	Richards S	Kemp H
13	30	LEICESTER FOSSE	1-0	Short		Iremonger A	Charlesworth G	Marriott F	Waterall A	Bagshaw JJ	Waterall T	Cooke JR	Kemp H	Kemp H	Richards S	Waterall I
14	Dec 7	Leicester Fosse	0-3			Orme JH	Charlesworth G	Marriott F	Flint WA	Bagshaw JJ	Jennings W	Waterall I	Short J	Cantrell J	Richards S	Waterall T
15	14	Lincoln City	1-0	Short		Iremonger A	Clay T	Marriott F	Flint WA	Bagshaw JJ	Waterall T	Waterall I	Short J	Cantrell J	Richards S	Henshall HV
16	21	LINCOLN CITY	2-1	Cantrell 2		Iremonger A	Clay T	Marriott F	Flint WA	Bagshaw JJ	Waterall T	Waterall I	Short J	Cantrell J	Richards S	Henshall HV
17	25	Nottm. Forest	0-2			Iremonger A	Clay T	Marriott F	Flint WA	Bagshaw JJ	Waterall T	Waterall I	Short J	Cantrell J	Richards S	Henshall HV
18	26	NOTTM. FOREST	1-1	Richards		Hasell AA	Clay T	Marriott F	Flint WA	Bagshaw JJ	Waterall T	Waterall I	Short J	Cantrell J	Richards S	Mee GW
19	28	Rotherham County	1-0	Cantrell		Hasell AA	Bagshaw JJ	Marriott F	Flint WA	Jennings W	Waterall T	Waterall I	Short J	Cantrell J	Richards S	Mee GW
20	Jan 4	ROTHERHAM COUNTY	2-0	Richards, Cantrell		Iremonger A	Bagshaw JJ	Marriott F	Flint WA	Jennings W	Waterall T	Waterall I	Short J	Cantrell J	Richards S	Henshall HV
21	11	Birmingham	7-0	Cantrell 3, Richards 2, Short 2		Iremonger A	Charlesworth G	Marriott F	Flint WA	Bagshaw JJ	Waterall T	Waterall I	Short J	Cantrell J	Richards S	Henshall HV
22	18	BIRMINGHAM	2-0	Cantrell, Richards		Iremonger A	Charlesworth G	Marriott F	Flint WA	Bagshaw JJ	Waterall T	Waterall I	Short J	Cantrell J	Richards S	Henshall HV
23	25	Bradford City	6-3	Short 3, Leonard 2, Richards		Iremonger A	Charlesworth G	Marriott F	Flint WA	Bagshaw JJ	Waterall T	Waterall I	Short J	Leonard H	Richards S	Henshall HV
24	Feb 1	BRADFORD CITY	2-0	Richards 2		Iremonger A	Charlesworth G	Marriott F	Flint WA	Bagshaw JJ	Waterall T	Waterall I	Short J	Cantrell J	Richards S	Henshall HV
25	8	Huddersfield T	1-1	Jennings		Iremonger A	Charlesworth G	Marriott F	Flint WA	Bagshaw JJ	Waterall T	Waterall I	Jennings W	Cantrell J	Richards S	Henshall HV
26	15	HUDDERSFIELD T	6-2	Cantrell 4, Bagshaw, Charlesworth(p)		Iremonger A	Charlesworth G	Marriott F	Flint WA	Bagshaw JJ	Morris W	Waterall I	Short J	Cantrell J	Richards S	Henshall HV
27	22	Sheffield Wednesday	2-2	Waterall, Newman		Iremonger A	Charlesworth G	Marriott F	Flint WA	Bagshaw JJ	Short J	Waterall I	Bell	Newman GW	Richards S	Henshall HV
28	Mar 1	SHEFFIELD WEDNESDAY	0-0			Iremonger A	Charlesworth G	Marriott F	Flint WA	Bagshaw JJ	Johnson J	Waterall I	Short J	Cantrell J	Richards S	Henshall HV
29	8	Grimsby Town	0-0			Iremonger A	Charlesworth G	Marriott F	Flint WA	Jennings W	Walker JH	Sheldon L	Newman GW	Cantrell J	Richards S	Henshall HV
30	15	GRIMSBY TOWN	3-1	Cantrell, Cook, Newman		Iremonger A	Charlesworth G	Marriott F	Flint WA	Bagshaw JJ	Jennings W	Cook J	Newman GW	Cantrell J	Richards S	Henshall HV
31	Mar 22	Leicester Fosse	1-5	Cook		Iremonger A	Bacon T	Walkerdine	Flint WA	Foster JH	Allsebrook R	Cook J	Jennings W	Davis	Richards S	Henshall HV
32	29	LEICESTER FOSSE	5-0	Richards 2, Cantrell, Dale, Henshall		Iremonger A	West, Alf	Marriott F	Flint WA	Foster JH	Allsebrook R	Cook J	Dale G	Cantrell J	Richards S	Henshall HV
33	Apr 5	Birmingham	3-0	Dale, Henshall, Richards		Iremonger A	West, Alf	Marriott F	Flint WA	Foster JH	Allsebrook R	Cook J	Dale G	Cantrell J	Richards S	Henshall HV
34	12	BIRMINGHAM	1-2	Short		Iremonger A	West, Alf	Marriott F	Flint WA	Foster JH	Allsebrook R	Cook J	Short J	Cantrell J	Richards S	Henshall HV
35	18	Nottm. Forest	2-3	Cantrell, Cook		Steele MA	Charlesworth G	West, Alf	Flint WA	Foster JH	Allsebrook R	Cook J	Thompson	Cantrell J	Richards S	Henshall HV
36	21	NOTTM. FOREST	1-3	Richards		Steele MA	Charlesworth G	West, Alf	Flint WA	Jennings W	Allsebrook R	Cook J	Dale G	Peart JG	Richards S	Mee GW

Games 1 - 30: League, Midland Section
Games 31 - 36: Subsidiary Competition

Standing: Fisher (secretary/manager), Newton (director), White (director), Bagshaw, A Iremonger, unknown, J Iremonger (trainer), Charlesworth, I Waterall, Bramley (director), Godfrey (director). Sitting: RJ Cooke, Newman, Cantrell, Richards, Henshall. On ground: Jennings, Flint, Marriott.

1919/20

21st in Division One (Relegated)

#	Date		Opponent	Score	Scorers	Att	Allsebrook R	Bagshaw JJ	Charlesworth G	Cook J	Cooke JR	Currie JB	Flint WA	Foster JH	Gibson T	Henshall HV	Hill H	Hoten RV	Iremonger A	Johnson J	Jones JW	Marriott F	McLeod W	Pearl JG	Pembleton A	Richards S	Stoakes JH	Streets GH	Tasker E	Waterall J	Widdowson, Alf	Woodland A
1	Aug	30	BURNLEY	2-0	Richards, Henshall	10000	6		2	8			4			11			1	3			9	5	10				7		
2	Sep	1	Sheffield United	0-3		8500	6		2	10	8		4			11			1	3			9	5					7		
3		6	Burnley	1-2	Peart	15000			2	10		8	4	6		11			1	3			9	5					7		
4		13	Sheffield Wednesday	0-0		5000			2	10	7	8	4	6		11						3	9	5		1					
5		20	SHEFFIELD WEDNESDAY	3-1	Henshall, Charlesworth(p), Peart	12000			2	10	7	8	4	6		11						3	9	5		1					
6		27	Manchester City	1-4	Currie	7000			2	10	7	8	4	6		11	9		1			3		5							
7	Oct	2	SHEFFIELD UNITED	2-2	Henshall, Peart	8000	6		2			10	8	4		11			1			3	9	5					7		
8		4	MANCHESTER CITY	4-1	Charlesworth(p), Cook 2, Peart	14000			2	8			4	6		11	10		1			3	9	5					7		
9		11	Derby County	1-3	Peart	15000			2	8			4	6		11	10		1			3	9	5					7		
10		18	DERBY COUNTY	2-2	Henshall, Charlesworth(p)	25000			2	8			4	6		11			1			3	9	5	10				7		
11		25	West Bromwich Alb.	0-8		30000				8	7		4	6		11	10		1			3	9	5			2				
12	Nov	1	WEST BROMWICH ALB.	2-0	Hill 2	14000			2	8	7		4	6			10					3	9	5		1			11		
13		8	Sunderland	1-3	Cook	15000			2	8	7		4	6			10					3	9	5		1			11		
14		15	SUNDERLAND	2-2	Hill, Richards	15000			2				4	6		11	8					3	9	5	10	1			7		
15		22	Arsenal	1-3	Hill	25000			2		7		4	6		11	8					3	9	5	10	1					
16		29	ARSENAL	2-2	Richards, McLeod	7000							4	5		11	8			2		3	9		6	10	1		7		
17	Dec	6	Everton	2-1	Hill, McLeod	18000			2				4	5		11	8					3	9		6	10	1		7		
18		13	EVERTON	1-1	Charlesworth(p)	16000			2				4	5		11	8			3			9		6	10	1		7		
19		20	Bradford City	4-3	Henshall, Hill 2, McLeod	12000				8			4	5	2	11	10			3			9		6		1		7		
20		25	BLACKBURN ROVERS	5-0	McLeod 2, Foster, Richards 2	15000							4	5	2	11	10					3	9		6	8	1		7		
21		27	BRADFORD CITY	5-2	Hill, Richards 2, Henshall, Gibson(p)	35000	6						4		2	11	8					3	9		5	10	1		7		
22	Jan	1	Blackburn Rovers	1-1	Cook	30000				8		10	4	5	2	11						3	9		6		1		7		
23		3	Bolton Wanderers	0-1		18471				8		7	4	5	2	11	10					3	9		6		1				
24		17	BOLTON WANDERERS	2-2	McLeod, Hill	20000							4	5	2	11	8					3	9		6	10	1		7		
25		24	PRESTON NORTH END	1-2	McLeod	15000			2				4	5	3	11	8						9		6	10	1		7		
26	Feb	7	BRADFORD PARK AVE.	0-2		20000				10			4		2	11	8					3	9		6		1		7		5
27		14	Bradford Park Ave.	1-0	Cook	20000		5		8	7		4		2	11		10	1			3	9								6
28		26	LIVERPOOL	1-0	Hill	10000		5		8	7		4		2	11	10					3	9				1				6
29		28	Liverpool	0-3		30000		5	2	8	7			6		10						3	9				1		11		4
30	Mar	4	Preston North End	0-2		12000		5	9		7			2		8			3			6	10				1		11		4
31		13	CHELSEA	0-1		16000		5	2	8			4	3		10		1				6				9		7	11		
32		17	Chelsea	0-2		23000		5	2	8		10	6	3		9		1		11	4								7		
33		20	Newcastle United	1-2	Hill	35000		5	2					3		8	10			11	4		9				1		7		6
34		27	NEWCASTLE UNITED	0-0		16000		5	2				6	3		8			1	11			10						7	9	4
35	Apr	2	MIDDLESBROUGH	1-1	Hill	20000		5	2				3	11	8			1	10			9		6				7		4
36		3	Aston Villa	1-3	Waterall	35000		5	2					3	8			1	10	11		9		6				7		4
37		5	Middlesbrough	2-5	McLeod, Holmes(og)	22000		5						3		10		1	2	11		9		6	7					4
38		10	ASTON VILLA	2-1	Henshall, McLeod	18000		5	2				4	3	10	8		1		11		9		6				7		
39		17	Oldham Athletic	0-0		18000		5	2				4	3	10	8		1		11		9		6				7		
40		24	OLDHAM ATHLETIC	2-1	Henshall 2	17000		5	2				4	3	10	8		1		11		9		6				7		
41		26	Manchester Utd.	0-0		20000		5	2				4	3	10	8		1		11		9		6				7		
42	May	1	MANCHESTER UTD.	0-2		23000		5	2				4	3	10	8		1		11		9		6				7		
			Apps				4	16	30	21	12	8	27	32	23	32	33	2	21	10	10	27	30	9	35	11	2	21	1	33	1	10
			Goals						4	5		1		1	1	9	12						9	5		7			1			

Played in game 37: W Poole (8).
Game 9: Iremonger sent off after 65 mins; Foster went in goal

One own goal

F.A. Cup

R		Date		Opponent	Score	Scorers	Att																									
R1	Jan	10		MILLWALL	2-0	Hill, McLeod	30000			8			4	5	2	11	10					3	9		6			1		7		
R2		31		MIDDLESBROUGH	1-0	John Cook	28000				10			4	5	2	11	8					3	9		6			1		7		
R3	Feb	21		BRADFORD PARK AVE.	3-4	Gibson(p), Henshall, McLeod	36246				8			4	5	2	11	10					3	9					1		7		6

		p	w	d	l	f	a	pts
1	West Bromwich Alb.	42	28	4	10	104	47	60
2	Burnley	42	21	9	12	65	59	51
3	Chelsea	42	22	5	15	56	51	49
4	Liverpool	42	19	10	13	59	44	48
5	Sunderland	42	22	4	16	72	59	48
6	Bolton Wanderers	42	19	9	14	72	65	47
7	Manchester City	42	18	9	15	71	62	45
8	Newcastle United	42	17	9	16	44	39	43
9	Aston Villa	42	18	6	18	75	73	42
10	Arsenal	42	15	12	15	56	58	42
11	Bradford Park Ave.	42	15	12	15	60	63	42
12	Manchester United	42	13	14	15	54	50	40
13	Middlesbrough	42	15	10	17	61	65	40
14	Sheffield United	42	16	8	18	59	69	40
15	Bradford City	42	14	11	17	54	63	39
16	Everton	42	12	14	16	69	68	38
17	Oldham Athletic	42	15	8	19	49	52	38
18	Derby County	42	13	12	17	47	57	38
19	Preston North End	42	14	10	18	57	73	38
20	Blackburn Rovers	42	13	11	18	64	77	37
21	NOTTS COUNTY	42	12	12	18	56	74	36
22	Sheffield Wed.	42	7	9	26	28	64	23

Back: Gibson, Flint, Foster, Pembleton, Iremonger, Streets, Woodland, Bagshaw, Marriott. Front: Waterall, Hill, McLeod, Cook, Henshall

1920/21

6th in Division Two

#		Date	Opponent	Score	Scorers	Att	Ashurst W	Bagshaw JJ	Barry LJ	Boreham RW	Cook J	Cooper E	Cope HW	Daly J	Death WG	Dinsdale N	Dolphin A	Flint WA	Gibson T	Henshall HV	Hill H	Hoten RV	Iremonger A	Kemp H	Marriott F	McLeod W	Pembleton A	Richards S	Stevens S	Walker JH	Widdowson, Alf	Woodland A
1	Aug	28	Bristol City	1-0	Woodland	30000	2										7	4	3	11	8		1			10			9	6		5
2		30	BARNSLEY	1-0	Stevens	18000	2										7	4	3	11	8		1			10			9	6		5
3	Sep	4	BRISTOL CITY	2-2	Stevens, Flint	18000	2				8	10	7					4		11			1		3			6	9			5
4		6	Barnsley	2-2	Henshall, Stevens	10000	2	5				10	7					4		11			1	8	3				9		6	
5		11	Nottm. Forest	0-1		20000	2	5			10	8	7					4	3	11			1						9		6	
6		18	NOTT. FOREST	2-0	Stevens 2	20000	2	6					7					4		11	10		1	8	3				9			5
7		25	Fulham	1-3	Hill	18000	2	6									7	4		11	10		1	8	3				9			5
8	Oct	2	FULHAM	2-1	Kemp, Dolphin	14000	2	6			10						7	4		11			1	8	3				9			5
9		9	Stoke	0-1		10000	2	6			10						7	4		11			1	8	3				9			5
10		16	STOKE	3-0	Stevens 2, Dolphin	14000	2				10					5	7	4		11			1	8	3				9			6
11		23	CARDIFF CITY	1-2	Henshall	22000	2									5	7	4		11			1	8	3			10	9			6
12		30	Cardiff City	1-1	Stevens	30000	2				8					5	7	4		11			1		3	10			9			6
13	Nov	6	COVENTRY CITY	1-1	McLeod	19000	2				8					5	7			11			1		3	10			9	4		6
14		13	Coventry City	1-1	Richards	20000	2									5	7				8		1		3	4	10	9			6
15		20	LEICESTER CITY	1-1	Richards	20000	2									5	7			11	8		1		3	4	10	9			6
16		27	Leicester City	3-0	Richards, Henshall, Hill	22000	2									5	7	4		11	8		1		3	9	6				6
17	Dec	4	LEEDS UNITED	1-2	Dinsdale	9000	2									5	7	4		11	8		1		3		6	10	9			
18		11	Leeds United	0-3		18000	2									5	7	9	3	11			1	8		6	10					4
19		18	Blackpool	2-0	Dolphin, Widdowson	7000	2				8					5	7	4	3	11			1			6	10				9	
20		25	Sheffield Wednesday	1-1	Richards	25000	2				8					5	7	4	3	11			1			6	10				9	
21		27	SHEFFIELD WEDNESDAY	3-0	Cook, Richards 2	24000	2				8					5	7	4	3	11			1				10				9	6
22	Jan	1	BLACKPOOL	1-2	Gibson(p)	15000	2				8					5	7	4	3	11							10		1		9	6
23		15	Rotherham County	0-0		12000					8					5		4	2	11				7	3			10	9	1		6
24		22	ROTHERHAM COUNTY	1-0	Stevens	12000					8					5		4	2	11				7	3	6	10		9	1		
25	Feb	5	Birmingham	1-2	Barton(og)	40000									11		7	4	2					8	3	10	6		9	1		5
26		12	Port Vale	2-1	Hill 2	16000									11	5	7	4	2		8				3	9	6	10		1		
27		16	BIRMINGHAM	0-0		14000								2	11	5	7	4			8				3	10	6		9	1		
28		19	PORT VALE	0-1		11000							11	2		5	7	4			8				3	10	6		9	1		
29		26	South Shields	0-1		16000										5	7	4	2	11	8	10	1		3	9						6
30	Mar	5	SOUTH SHIELDS	2-0	Gibson 2(2p)	10000					8				11	5	7	4	2		9		1		3		10					6
31		12	Hull City	1-1	Gibson(p)	8000								7	11	5		4	2		8		1		3		10	9				6
32		19	HULL CITY	4-1	Hill 2, Henshall, Richards	12000					8			7		5		4	2	11	9		1		3	6	10					
33		25	West Ham United	2-0	Hill, Richards	25000					8			7		5		4	2	11	9		1		3	6	10					
34		26	WOLVERHAMPTON W.	2-1	Hill 2	16000			11		8			7		5		4	2		9		1		3	6	10					
35		28	WEST HAM UNITED	1-1	Hoten	22000	2				8			7		5		4		11	9	10			3	6				1		
36	Apr	2	Wolverhampton Wand.	0-1		25000			11		8			7		5		4	2		9		1		3	6	10					
37		9	STOCKPORT COUNTY	3-0	Henshall, Hill 2	10000	2				8			7		5		4	3	11	9		1			6	10					
38		16	Stockport County	0-1		8000	2				8			7		5		4	3	11	9		1			6	10					
39		23	CLAPTON ORIENT	3-1	Flint, Cook, Richards	9000	2				8			3	7			4		11						6	10		1		9	5
40		30	Clapton Orient	0-3		19000					8			7		5		4	2	11	9		1		3	6	10					6
41	May	2	BURY	2-1	Henshall, Widdowson	12000	2	5			8			7	11			4	3	10						6				1	9	
42		7	Bury	1-0	Widdowson	6000	2	6			8				11	5		3	10			1							9	4		

Played in game 14: JW Jones (11). In game 42: R Platts (7).

Apps	28	8	2	3	26	4	3	11	7	30	24	38	24	33	22	2	32	11	29	10	23	23	22	10	5	7	23
Goals					2					1	3	2	4	6	11	1		1		1		9	9			3	1

One own goal

F.A. Cup

		Date	Opponent	Score	Scorers	Att																										
R1	Jan	8	WEST BROMWICH ALB.	3-0	Stevens 2, Cook	32995					8					5		4	2	11				7	3	6	10	9	1			
R2		29	ASTON VILLA	0-0		45014	2				8					5		4		11				7	3	6	10	9	1			
rep	Feb	2	Aston Villa	0-1		49491	2				8					5		4		11				7	3	6	10	9	1			

		p	w	d	l	f	a	pts
1	Birmingham	42	24	10	8	79	38	58
2	Cardiff City	42	24	10	8	59	32	58
3	Bristol City	42	19	13	10	49	29	51
4	Blackpool	42	20	10	12	54	42	50
5	West Ham United	42	19	10	13	51	30	48
6	NOTTS COUNTY	42	18	11	13	55	40	47
7	Clapton Orient	42	16	13	13	43	42	45
8	South Shields	42	17	10	15	61	46	44
9	Fulham	42	16	10	16	43	47	42
10	Sheffield Wed.	42	15	11	16	48	48	41
11	Bury	42	15	10	17	45	49	40
12	Leicester City	42	12	16	14	39	46	40
13	Hull City	42	10	20	12	43	53	40
14	Leeds United	42	14	10	18	40	45	38
15	Wolverhampton Wan.	42	16	6	20	49	66	38
16	Barnsley	42	10	16	16	48	50	36
17	Port Vale	42	11	14	17	43	49	36
18	Nottingham Forest	42	12	12	18	48	55	36
19	Rotherham County	42	12	12	18	37	53	36
20	Stoke	42	12	11	19	46	56	35
21	Coventry City	42	12	11	19	39	70	35
22	Stockport County	42	9	12	21	42	75	30

Back: Flint, Streets, Walker, Foster, Ashurst, Iremonger. Next to back: McLeod, Cook, Marriott, Hill, Henshall, Stevens, Bagshaw. Next to front: Charlesworth, Cooper, Widdowson, Kemp, Jones, Cope. Front: Pembleton, Woodland, Dolphin

1921/22

13th in Division Two

						Ashurst W	Brown D	Cashmore AA	Chipperfield JJ	Cook J	Cope HW	Crapper J	Daly J	Death WG	Dinsdale N	Flint WA	Gibson T	Henshall HV	Hill H	Iremonger A	Kemp H	Marriott F	McPherson L	Moore H	Pembleton A	Platts R	Richards S	Streets GH	Widdowson, Alf	Woodland A
1	Aug	27	BRISTOL CITY	0-2		16000		10			8	2		7	11		4	3		9	1					6					5
2		29	Wolverhampton Wand.	2-1	Hill, Death	20000	2	9			8			7	11	5	4	3		10								1			6
3	Sep	3	Bristol City	2-2	Daly, McPherson	25000	2	9						7	11	5	4			10	1		3	8							6
4		5	WOLVERHAMPTON W.	4-0	Death 3, Hill	12000	2	9						7	11	5	4			10	1		3	8							6
5		10	SHEFFIELD WEDNESDAY	2-0	Brown 2	15000	2	9						7	11	5	4			10	1		3	8							6
6		17	Sheffield Wednesday	0-0		15000	2	9						7	11	5	4			10	1		3	8							6
7		24	FULHAM	3-0	Brown, Flint, McPherson	17000	2	9							11	5	4			10	1		3	8		7					6
8	Oct	1	Fulham	0-4		20000	2	9							11	5	4			10	1		3	8		7					6
9		6	BARNSLEY	1-4	Daly	12000	2	9						7	11	5	4				1		3	8	6				10		
10		8	BLACKPOOL	2-1	Brown, Dinsdale	15000		9						7		5		2			1		3	8	6	11			10	4
11		15	Blackpool	2-1	Widdowson, Brown	8000	2	9								5		3	11		1			8	6	7			10	4
12		22	CLAPTON ORIENT	0-0		10000	2	9						7		5		3	11		1			8	6	4			10	
13		29	Clapton Orient	1-2	Widdowson	15000	2	8						7		5	4	3	11		1				6			10	9	
14	Nov	5	NOTTM. FOREST	1-1	Widdowson	25000	2		9		8			7		5	4				1		3		6	11			10	
15		14	Nottm. Forest	0-0		15000	2		9		8								11		1		3		6	7			10	5
16		19	Stoke	0-0		8000	2		9						11					8	1		3		6	4	7			10	5
17		26	STOKE	0-0		14000	2		9					7		5				8	1	4	3		6					10	
18	Dec	3	LEEDS UNITED	4-1	Henshall, Cashmore 2, Marriott(p)	14000	2		9		8			7		5			11		1	4	3		6		10				
19		10	Leeds United	1-1	Henshall	16000		9	9		8			7		5		2	11		1	4	3		6		10				
20		17	Hull City	0-2		13000					8	2				5			11	9	1	4	3		6		7	10			
21		24	HULL CITY	2-0	Richards 2	10000	2		9	11	8					5	4		7		1	6	3				10				
22		26	Crystal Palace	0-1		20000	2		9	11	8					5	4		7		1		3							10	6
23		27	CRYSTAL PALACE	3-2	Cashmore 2, Dinsdale(p)	20000	2		9	11	8					5	4		7	10	1		3		6						
24		31	BRADFORD PARK AVE.	3-0	Cook, Brown 2	12000	2	9		11	8					5	4		7	10	1		3		6						
25	Jan	21	SOUTH SHIELDS	2-0	Cashmore 2	9000	2		9	11	8					5	4		7	10	1		3		6						
26	Feb	4	PORT VALE	1-2	Dinsdale	6000	2		9		8					5	4		11		1	6	3			7	10				
27		11	Port Vale	0-0		10000	2									5	4		11	10	1	6	3	8		7				9	
28		25	West Ham United	0-0		20000			11	8			7				4	2		10	1	6	3		5					9	
29		28	Bradford Park Ave.	1-2	McPherson	7000			8	11			7					2		1	6	3	10	5					9	4
30	Mar	11	Bury	0-1		8000			8	11		2		7		5		3		10	1	6			4				9	
31		15	South Shields	0-0		10000	2		10	11	8			7		5	4				1	6	3						9	
32		18	Leicester City	0-3		14000	2			11	8			7		5	4			10	1	6	3						9	
33		29	WEST HAM UNITED	1-1	Cook	7000	2				8			7		5	4		11	10	1	6	3					1	9	
34	Apr	1	Derby County	1-1	Chipperfield	10000	2			11	8			7			4			10	1	6	3		5			1	9	
35		5	BURY	1-1	Hill	5000	2			11	8			7		5	4			10	1	6	3					1	9	
36		8	DERBY COUNTY	1-2	Hill	5000	2			11	8	3		7		5	4			10	1	6						1	9	
37		14	ROTHERHAM COUNTY	2-0	Widdowson, Chipperfield	12000				11	8	3				5	4	2		10	1				6	7			9	
38		15	COVENTRY CITY	1-1	Widdowson	7000				11	8	3				5	4	2		10					6	7		1	9	
39		17	Rotherham County	0-3		12000	2				8	3			11	5				10					6	7		1	9	4
40		22	Coventry City	2-4	Hill 2	14000	2			11	8	3	7			5	4			10	1				6				9	
41		26	LEICESTER CITY	0-0		5000	2			11	8	3	7			5	4			10	1				6				9	
42		29	Barnsley	0-3		13000	2				11	3				5				10	1			8	6	4	7		9	

Played in game 17: H Oldershaw (11)

	Apps	33	14	14	18	25	10	2	23	12	36	30	12	14	28	35	16	29	13	16	13	14	6	7	26	15
	Goals		7	6	2	3			2	4	3	1		2	6			1	3				2		5	

F.A. Cup

							Ashurst	Brown	Cashmore	Chipperfield	Cook	Cope	Crapper	Daly	Death	Dinsdale	Flint	Gibson	Henshall	Hill	Iremonger	Kemp	Marriott	McPherson	Moore	Pembleton	Platts	Richards	Streets	Widdowson	Woodland
R1	Jan	7	Grimsby Town	1-1	Hill	12000	2		9	11	8					5	4		7	10	1		3		6						
rep		12	GRIMSBY TOWN	3-0	Cook, Henshall, Hill	16381	2		9		8		7			5	4		11	10	1		3		6						
R2		28	Bradford City	1-1	Widdowson	18752	2		8	11						5	4		7	10	1		3		6					9	
rep	Feb	1	BRADFORD CITY	0-0		20108	2		9	11	8					5	4		7	10	1		3		6						
rep2		6	Bradford City	1-0	Widdowson	29882	2				8					5	4		11	10	1	6	3			7				9	
R3		18	West Bromwich Albion	1-1	Widdowson	43853	2				8		7			5	4		11	10	1	6	3							9	
rep		22	WEST BROMWICH ALB.	2-0	Cook, Hill	24278				11	8		7			5	4	2		10	1	6	3							9	
R4	Mar	4	ASTON VILLA	2-2	Chipperfield 2	35551	2			11	8		7			5	4			10	1	6	3							9	
rep		8	Aston Villa	4-3	Chipperfield, Hill, Widdowson, Cook	40161	2			11	8		7			5	4	3		10	1	6								9	
SF		25	Huddersfield T	1-3	Hill	46323	2				8		7			5	4		11	10	1	6	3							9	

R2 replay after extra time. R2 replay 2 at Bramall Lane.   R4 replay after extra time. Semi-final at Turf Moor, Burnley

Back: Brown, Little, Fisher, Ashurst, Woodland, Flint. Standing: McLean (assistant trainer), J Iremonger (trainer), Henshall, Cope, Dinsdale, A Iremonger, Pembleton, McPherson, Gibson, Fisher (secretary manager). Next to front: Widdowson, Platts, Hill, Kemp, Death. Front: Richards, Cook, Daly, Marriott

		p	w	d	l	f	a	pts
1	Nottingham Forest	42	22	12	8	51	30	56
2	Stoke	42	18	16	8	60	44	52
3	Barnsley	42	22	8	12	67	52	52
4	West Ham United	42	20	8	14	52	39	48
5	Hull City	42	19	10	13	51	41	48
6	South Shields	42	17	12	13	43	38	46
7	Fulham	42	18	9	15	57	38	45
8	Leeds United	42	16	13	13	48	38	45
9	Leicester City	42	14	17	11	39	34	45
10	Sheffield Wed.	42	15	14	13	47	50	44
11	Bury	42	15	10	17	54	55	40
12	Derby County	42	15	9	18	60	64	39
13	NOTTS COUNTY	42	12	15	15	47	51	39
14	Crystal Palace	42	13	13	16	45	51	39
15	Clapton Orient	42	15	9	18	43	50	39
16	Rotherham County	42	14	11	17	32	43	39
17	Wolverhampton Wan.	42	13	11	18	44	49	37
18	Port Vale	42	14	8	20	43	57	36
19	Blackpool	42	15	5	22	44	57	35
20	Coventry City	42	12	10	20	51	60	34
21	Bradford Park Ave.	42	12	9	21	46	62	33
22	Bristol City	42	12	9	21	37	58	33

1922/23

Champions of Division Two (Promoted)

#	Date		Opponent	Score	Scorers	Att	Ashurst W	Barry LJ	Brodie G	Cock DJ	Cook J	Cooper J	Cope HW	Daly J	Death WG	Dinsdale N	Fenwick R	Flint WA	Gibson T	Harris G	Heathcote J	Hill H	Iremonger A	Kemp H	Marriott F	McPherson L	Platts R	Price LP	Streets GH	Widdowson, Alf	Wren JE
1	Aug	26	Coventry City	2-1	Hill 2	16000	2				8		3	7	4						10	9	1	6			11				5
2		28	SOUTH SHIELDS	2-0	Hill 2	12000	2				8		3	7	4						10	9	1	6			11				5
3	Sep	2	COVENTRY CITY	2-0	Cope, Cook	14000	2				8		3	7	4						10	9	1	6			11				5
4		4	South Shields	0-1		10000	2				8		3	7	4						10	9	1	6			11				5
5		9	HULL CITY	0-1		12000	2		8					7	4						10	9	1	6	3		11				5
6		16	Hull City	2-0	Price, Daly	10000	2				8		3	7	5		4				10	9	1				11				6
7		23	Sheffield Wednesday	1-0	Cook	17000	2				8		3	7	5		4				10	9	1				11				6
8		30	SHEFFIELD WEDNESDAY	1-0	Heathcote	15000	2				8		3	7	5		4				10	9	1				11				6
9	Oct	7	Barnsley	0-1		15000				9	8		3	7	5		4				10		1		2		11				6
10		14	BARNSLEY	1-0	Daly	15000	2			9	8		3	7	5		4				10						11	1			6
11		21	Port Vale	0-0		14000	2			9	8		3	7	5		4					10					11	1			6
12		28	PORT VALE	1-0	Hill	10000	2			9			3	7	5		4					10			8		11	1			6
13	Nov	4	BLACKPOOL	2-0	Hill, Daly	12000	2			9			3	7	5		4					10			8		11	1			6
14		11	Blackpool	1-1	Cock	10000	2			9			3	7	5		4					10			8		11	1			6
15		18	WOLVERHAMPTON W.	4-1	Cock 2, McPherson, Daly	12000	2			9			3	7	5		4					10			8		11	1			6
16		25	Wolverhampton Wand.	0-1		17000	2			9			3	7	5		4					10			8		11				6
17	Dec	2	BRADFORD CITY	0-0		10000	2			9			3		5		4					10	1		8	7	11				6
18		9	Bradford City	2-1	Cock 2	10000	2			9			3	7	5		4				10		1	6	8		11				6
19		16	SOUTHAMPTON	1-0	Cock	9000	2			9		10	3	7	5		4						1	6	8		11				6
20		23	Southampton	1-0	Hill	9000	2			9				7	5		4					10	1	11	3	8					6
21		25	FULHAM	1-0	McPherson	14000	2	11		9				7	5		4					10			3	8					6
22		26	Fulham	1-2	Cock	25000	2	11		9				7	5		4					10	1		3	8					6
23		30	Derby County	0-0		18000	2	11						7	5		4					10			3	8			1	9	6
24	Jan	6	DERBY COUNTY	1-2	Dinsdale (p)	22000	2	11		9				7	5		4					10			3				1	8	6
25		20	Leicester City	1-2	Daly	25000	2			9	8			7	5			3	10					4			11	1			6
26		27	LEICESTER CITY	1-0	Dinsdale	25000	2	11		9	8			7	5			3					1	4		10					6
27	Feb	10	MANCHESTER UTD.	1-6	Cock	10000	2	11		9	8		3	7	5		4						1			10					6
28		17	Bury	2-2	Price, Cock	10000	2			10	8		3		5		4				7			6			11	1	9		
29		21	Manchester Utd.	1-1	Widdowson	17000	2			10				7		5	4				8			6	3		11	1	9		
30	Mar	3	Rotherham County	0-1		10000	2			10	8				5		4				7			6	3		11	1	9		
31		10	ROTHERHAM COUNTY	2-0	Cook, Cock	2000	2			9	8		3	7		5			6			10		4			11	1			
32		17	CLAPTON ORIENT	3-1	Hill, Platts, Cooper	14000	2			9		8	3		5							10		4			7	11	1		6
33		21	BURY	1-0	Hill	9000	2	11		9		8	3		5	4						10		6			7	1			
34		24	Clapton Orient	1-2	Cock	17000	2			9		8	3	7	5							10		4			11	1			6
35		30	Crystal Palace	1-0	Hill	17000	2			9		8	3		5		4					10		6			7	11	1		
36		31	STOCKPORT COUNTY	2-0	Hill, Dinsdale	14000	2			9	8				5	4						10				3	7	11	1		6
37	Apr	2	CRYSTAL PALACE	0-4		18000	2			9	8				5	4						10		6	3		7	11	1		
38		7	Stockport County	0-0		12000	2	11		9		8			5	4	3					10		6			7		1		
39		14	LEEDS UNITED	1-0	Dinsdale	12000	2	11		9	8				5	4	3					10		6			7		1		
40		18	WEST HAM UNITED	2-0	Cock 2	15000	2			9	8		3		5	11	4					10		6			7		1		
41		21	Leeds United	0-3		8000	2			9	8		3		5	11	4					10		6			7		1		
42	May	5	West Ham United	1-0	Hill	26000	2			9		8	3		5		4					10	1				7	11			6
					Apps		41	9	1	33	22	6	28	29	2	40	3	31	4	1	12	35	19	23	11	14	10	31	23	5	29
					Goals					13	3	1	1	5		4					1	12				2	1	2			1

F.A. Cup

	Date		Opponent	Score		Att	Ashurst			Cock	Cook		Cope	Daly	Death							Hill	Iremonger								Wren
R1	Jan	13	Plymouth Argyle	0-0		27000	2			9	8		3	7	11	5		4				10	1								6
rep		17	PLYMOUTH ARGYLE	0-1		16000	2			9	8			7	11	5		4					1	10	3							6

		p	w	d	l	f	a	pts
1	NOTTS COUNTY	42	23	7	12	46	34	53
2	West Ham United	42	20	11	11	63	38	51
3	Leicester City	42	21	9	12	65	44	51
4	Manchester United	42	17	14	11	51	36	48
5	Blackpool	42	18	11	13	60	43	47
6	Bury	42	18	11	13	55	46	47
7	Leeds United	42	18	11	13	43	36	47
8	Sheffield Wed.	42	17	12	13	54	47	46
9	Barnsley	42	17	11	14	62	51	45
10	Fulham	42	16	12	14	43	32	44
11	Southampton	42	14	14	14	40	40	42
12	Hull City	42	14	14	14	43	45	42
13	South Shields	42	15	10	17	35	44	40
14	Derby County	42	14	11	17	46	50	39
15	Bradford City	42	12	13	17	41	45	37
16	Crystal Palace	42	13	11	18	54	62	37
17	Port Vale	42	14	9	19	39	51	37
18	Coventry City	42	15	7	20	46	63	37
19	Clapton Orient	42	12	12	18	40	50	36
20	Stockport County	42	14	8	20	43	58	36
21	Rotherham County	42	13	9	20	44	63	35
22	Wolverhampton Wan.	42	9	9	24	42	77	27

Back: McPherson, Bell (coach), Cope, J Iremonger (trainer), Platts, Marriott, Cook, Heathcote, A Iremonger, Ashurst, McLean (assistant trainer), Death. Centre: Daly, Widdowson, Flint, Hill, Dinsdale, Wren, Gibson, Ashford, Harris. Front: Shepherd, Kirkwood

1923/24

10th in Division One

#	Date		Opponent	Score	Scorers	Att	Allen H	Ashurst W	Barry LJ	Cock DJ	Cook J	Cooper J	Cope HW	Cornwell R	Daly J	Davis AG	Dinsdale N	Fenwick R	Flint WA	Harris G	Hill H	Iremonger A	Kemp H	Mackay JA	McPherson L	Pape A	Platts R	Price LP	Smith WA	Streets GH	Widdowson, Alf	Wren JE
1	Aug	25	BURNLEY	2-1	Hill 2	20000		2		9		8	3				5		4		10	1	6	7				11				
2		29	Middlesbrough	3-2	Cooper, Cock, Mackay	10000		2		9		8		3			5		4		10	1	6	7				11				
3	Sep	1	Burnley	1-1	Cock	18000		2		9		8	3				5				10	1	6	7	4			11				
4		8	HUDDERSFIELD T	1-0	Hill	20000		2		9		8	3		7		5		4		10	1	6					11				
5		15	Huddersfield T	0-0		15000		2	11	9		8	3		7		5		4		10	1	6									
6		22	NOTTM. FOREST	2-1	Cock 2	30000		2	11	9		8	3		7		5		4		10	1	6									
7		29	Nottm. Forest	0-1		32000			11	9		8	2	3	7		5		4		10	1										6
8	Oct	4	MIDDLESBROUGH	1-0	Hill	12000		2	11	9		8	3		7		5		4		10	1	6									
9		6	TOTTENHAM HOTSPUR	0-0		25000		2	11	9		8		3	7		5		4		10	1	6									
10		13	Tottenham Hotspur	3-1	Cock, Cooper, Hill	35000		2		9		8		3	7		5				10	1	6		4			11				
11		20	EVERTON	1-1	Cock	18000		2		9		8	3		7		5				10	1	6		4			11				
12		27	Everton	0-3		30000		2		9		8	3		7		5				10	1	6		4			11				
13	Nov	3	Aston Villa	0-0		25000		2	11	9		8	3				5				10	1	6					7				4
14		10	ASTON VILLA	0-1		15000		2		9	8		3		7		5		4		10	1	6					11				
15		17	Birmingham	0-0		15000		2		9		8	3				5		4		7	1	6					11			10	
16		24	BIRMINGHAM	1-1	Pape	14000		2		9		8	3				5		4		7	1	6			10		11				
17	Dec	1	Manchester City	0-1		24000		2		10	8			3			5		4		7	1	6			9		11				
18		8	MANCHESTER CITY	2-0	Cock, Pape	10000		2		9				3			5		4		10					8	7	11	1			6
19		15	Bolton Wanderers	1-7	Cock	16272		2		9				3				5	4		10					8	7	11	1			6
20		22	BOLTON WANDERERS	1-1	Cock	10000		2		9			3					5			10	1	6			8	7	11				4
21		26	ARSENAL	1-2	Cock	14000			11	9		2	3		5						10	1	6			8	7					4
22		27	Arsenal	0-0		16000				9	8		2	3	7		5				10	1	6					11				4
23		29	Sunderland	1-1	Cope	8000				9	8		2	3	7		5				10	1	6					11				4
24	Jan	1	Blackburn Rovers	1-4	Daly	20000				9	8		2	3	7		5				10	1	6					11				4
25		5	SUNDERLAND	1-2	Cooper	16000		2		9		8	3		7		5				10	1	6					11				4
26		19	PRESTON NORTH END	0-0		12000	10	2		9		8	3		7		5		4				6					11	1			
27		26	Preston North End	1-2	Hill	16000		2		9		8	3		7		5		4		10		6					11	1			
28	Feb	9	Chelsea	6-0	Widdowson 2, Price 2, Davis 2	15000		2			8			3	7	10	5		4				1	6				11			9	
29		16	NEWCASTLE UNITED	1-0	Platts	14000		2			8			3		10	5		4				1	6			7	11			9	
30	Mar	1	WEST HAM UNITED	1-1	Widdowson	10000					8		3			10	5		4				1	6			7	11	2		9	
31		5	CHELSEA	0-0		8000		2	11		8		3			10	5		4				1	6			7				9	
32		8	West Ham United	1-1	Widdowson	20000					8	3				10	5		4				1	6			7	11	2		9	
33		15	Cardiff City	2-0	Davis, Blair(og)	18000				9			3	2	7	10	5		4				1	6				11			8	
34		19	Newcastle United	2-1	Cock, Davis	10000				9					7	10	5		4				1					11			8	6
35		22	CARDIFF CITY	1-0	Davis	20000		2	11	9			3		7	10	5		4				1	6							8	
36	Apr	5	SHEFFIELD UNITED	0-2		15000		2		9			3		7	10	5		4				1	6				11			8	
37		7	Sheffield United	1-3	Davis	7000		2	11	9				3	7	10	5		4				1	6							8	
38		12	West Bromwich Alb.	0-5		7000		2				8	3		7	10	5						1	6	4			11			9	
39		18	BLACKBURN ROVERS	3-0	Hill 2, Widdowson	16000		2					3		7	10	5				8			6				11		1	9	4
40		19	WEST BROMWICH ALB.	1-0	Davis	15000		2	11				3		7	10	5				8			6						1	9	4
41		26	Liverpool	0-1		15000		2					3		7	10	5				8			6				11		1	9	4
42	May	3	LIVERPOOL	1-2	Widdowson	8000		2					3			10	5		4		8			6			7	11		1	9	
					Apps		1	33	11	32	4	25	32	17	26	15	40	2	26	1	30	34	38	3	5	6	17	24	2	8	16	14
					Goals					11		3	1		1	7					8					1	2	1	2		6		

F.A. Cup

	Date		Opponent	Score	Scorers	Att	Ashurst	Barry	Cock	Cook	Cooper	Cope	Cornwell	Daly	Davis	Dinsdale	Fenwick	Flint	Harris	Hill	Iremonger	Kemp	Mackay	McPherson	Pape	Platts	Price	Smith	Streets	Widdowson	Wren
R1	Jan	12	Queens Park Rangers	2-1	Pape, Price	13000	2			8		3		7		5				10	1	6			9		11				4
R2	Feb	2	Crystal Palace	0-0		19500	2		9	8			3	7		5		4		11	1	6			10						
rep		6	CRYSTAL PALACE	0-0		20600	2			8			2	7		5		4		10	1	6					11			9	
r2		11	Crystal Palace	0-0		16440	2			8			2	7		5		4		10	1	6					11			9	
r3		18	Crystal Palace	1-2	Widdowson	10259	2		9				2			5		4		10	1	6			7		11			8	

R2 replay and replay 2 after extra time. Replays 2 and 3 at Villa Park

		p	w	d	l	f	a	pts
1	Huddersfield Town	42	23	11	8	60	33	57
2	Cardiff City	42	22	13	7	61	34	57
3	Sunderland	42	22	9	11	71	54	53
4	Bolton Wanderers	42	18	14	10	68	34	50
5	Sheffield United	42	19	12	11	69	49	50
6	Aston Villa	42	18	13	11	52	37	49
7	Everton	42	18	13	11	62	53	49
8	Blackburn Rovers	42	17	11	14	54	50	45
9	Newcastle United	42	17	10	15	60	54	44
10	NOTTS COUNTY	42	14	14	14	44	49	42
11	Manchester City	42	15	12	15	54	71	42
12	Liverpool	42	15	11	16	49	48	41
13	West Ham United	42	13	15	14	40	43	41
14	Birmingham	42	13	13	16	41	49	39
15	Tottenham Hotspur	42	12	14	16	50	56	38
16	West Bromwich Alb.	42	12	14	16	51	62	38
17	Burnley	42	12	12	18	55	60	36
18	Preston North End	42	12	10	20	52	67	34
19	Arsenal	42	12	9	21	40	63	33
20	Nottingham Forest	42	10	12	20	42	64	32
21	Chelsea	42	9	14	19	31	53	32
22	Middlesbrough	42	7	8	27	37	60	22

1924/25

9th in Division One

#	Date		Opponent	Score	Scorers	Att	Ashurst W	Barry LJ	Cock DJ	Cope HW	Cornwell R	Daly J	Davis AG	Dinsdale N	Fenwick R	Flint WA	Greatorex L	Hill H	Hills WJ	Hilton F	Iremonger A	Keeling P	Kemp H	Mitchell M	Platts R	Smith G	Smith WA	Staniforth C	Streets GH	Widdowson, Alf	Wren JE
1	Aug	30	West Bromwich Alb.	2-1	Daly, Davis	20000	2	11	9	3		7	10	5		4					1		6							8	
2	Sep	1	LEEDS UNITED	1-0	Widdowson	16000	2	11	9	3		7	10	5		4					1		6							8	
3		6	TOTTENHAM HOTSPUR	0-0		20000	2	11		3		7	10	5		4		8			1									9	6
4		10	Leeds United	1-1	Cope	18000	2	11		3		7	10	5		4	9				1									8	6
5		13	Bolton Wanderers	0-1		15393		11		3	2	7	10	5		4	9				1									8	6
6		15	Birmingham	0-1		12000		11	9	3	2	7	10	5		4							6						1	8	
7		20	NOTTM. FOREST	0-0		25000	2	11		3		7	10	5		4		8			1		6						1	9	
8		27	EVERTON	3-1	Hill, Barry, Davis	12000	2	11		3		7	10	5		4		8			1		6							9	
9	Oct	4	Sunderland	1-0	Davis	25000	2	11	9	3		7	10	5		4					1		6							8	
10		11	CARDIFF CITY	3-0	Cope(p), Cock, Widdowson	20000	2	11	9	3		7	10	5							1		6	4						8	
11		18	Preston North End	1-0	Barry	16810	2	11	9		3	7	10	5							1		6	4						8	
12		25	Bury	1-2	Cock	20000	2	11	9		3	7	10	5		4					1		6							8	
13	Nov	1	MANCHESTER CITY	2-0	Cock, Barry	10000	2	11	9		3	7	10	5		4							6						1	8	
14		8	Arsenal	1-0	Cock	35000	2	11	9		3	7	10	5		4							6						1	8	
15		15	ASTON VILLA	0-0		24000	2	11	9	3		7	10	5		4							6						1	8	
16		22	Huddersfield T	0-0		10000	2	11	9			3	7	10	5								6						1	8	4
17		29	BLACKBURN ROVERS	0-0		16000	2	11				3	7	10	5								6		9				1	8	4
18	Dec	6	West Ham United	0-3		18000	2	11				3	7	10	5		4				1				8					9	6
19		13	SHEFFIELD UNITED	2-0	Cock 2	10000	2	11	9	3				5		4	10				1				7					8	6
20		20	Newcastle United	0-1		20000	2	11	9			3		10	5	4					1		6		7					8	
21		25	LIVERPOOL	1-2	Davis	18000	2	11	9			3		10	5	4					1		6		7					8	
22		26	Liverpool	0-1		30000	2	11	9			3		10	5	4		8				7	6						1		
23		27	WEST BROMWICH ALB.	0-2		6000		11	9			3		10	5		8				1		6	4	7		2				
24	Jan	3	Tottenham Hotspur	1-1	Platts	30000	2	11	9			3		10	5						1		6	4	7		8				
25		17	BOLTON WANDERERS	0-1		14000	2	11	9	3				10	5						1		6		7		8			4	
26		24	Nottm. Forest	0-0		15000	2	11	9	3		7		10	5						1		6				8			4	
27	Feb	7	SUNDERLAND	4-1	Widdowson, Cock 2, Davis	16000	2	11	9	3		7	10	5		4					1		6							8	
28		14	Cardiff City	1-1	Davis	20000	2	11			3	7	10	5		4					1		6							8	
29		28	BURY	1-1	Dinsdale	9000		11		3		7	10	5		4					1					2	9			8	6
30	Mar	7	Manchester City	1-2	Barry	18000		11		3			10	5		4					1	7	6			2	9			8	
31		14	ARSENAL	2-1	Staniforth, Widdowson	12000	2	11		3			9	5		4					1	7	6				10			8	
32		18	Everton	0-1		25000	2	11		3			10							5		7	4				8	1	9	6
33		21	Aston Villa	0-0		15000		11			3		9	5							1	7	6			2	10		8	4	
34	Apr	1	PRESTON NORTH END	1-0	Widdowson	4000		11		3			9	5		4					1	7	6			2	10			8	
35		4	Blackburn Rovers	2-0	Widdowson, Davis	8000		11		3			10	5		4					1		6			2	8			9	
36		10	Burnley	1-1	Staniforth	17000		11		3		7	10			4			5		1		6			2	8			9	
37		11	WEST HAM UNITED	4-1	Widdowson 2, Davis, Flint	10000		11		3		7	10	5		4							6			2	8		1	9	
38		13	BURNLEY	2-0	Widdowson, Davis	8000		11		3		7	10	5		4					1		6			2	8			9	
39		18	Sheffield United	0-2		8000		11		3		7	10	5		4					1		6			2	8			9	
40		25	NEWCASTLE UNITED	2-0	Davis, Widdowson	7000	2	11		3		7	10	5		4					1		6				8			9	
41		29	HUDDERSFIELD T	1-1	Kemp	8000	2	11		3		7	10	5		4					1		6				8			9	
42	May	2	BIRMINGHAM	0-1		8000	2	11		3		7	10	5							1		6				8			9	4
					Apps		30	42	20	28	16	30	41	39	1	31	4	3	1	2	32	6	35	5	8	9	1	18	10	39	11
					Goals			4	8	2		1	10	1		1	1						1		1		2			10	

F.A. Cup

			Opponent	Score	Scorers	Att																									
R1	Jan	10	Coventry City	2-0	Cock, Davis	21736	2	11	9	3			10	5									6	7					1	8	4
R2		31	NORWICH CITY	4-0	Davis 2, Cock, Barry	21061	2	11	9	3		7	10	5		4					1		6							8	
R3	Feb	21	CARDIFF CITY	0-2		39000	2	11	9	3		7	10	5		4					1		6							8	

		p	w	d	l	f	a	pts
1	Huddersfield Town	42	21	16	5	69	28	58
2	West Bromwich Alb.	42	23	10	9	58	34	56
3	Bolton Wanderers	42	22	11	9	76	34	55
4	Liverpool	42	20	10	12	63	55	50
5	Bury	42	17	15	10	54	51	49
6	Newcastle United	42	16	16	10	61	42	48
7	Sunderland	42	19	10	13	64	51	48
8	Birmingham	42	17	12	13	49	53	46
9	NOTTS COUNTY	42	16	13	13	42	31	45
10	Manchester City	42	17	9	16	76	68	43
11	Cardiff City	42	16	11	15	56	51	43
12	Tottenham Hotspur	42	15	12	15	52	43	42
13	West Ham United	42	15	12	15	62	60	42
14	Sheffield United	42	13	13	16	55	63	39
15	Aston Villa	42	13	13	16	58	71	39
16	Blackburn Rovers	42	11	13	18	53	66	35
17	Everton	42	12	11	19	40	60	35
18	Leeds United	42	11	12	19	46	59	34
19	Burnley	42	11	12	19	46	75	34
20	Arsenal	42	14	5	23	46	58	33
21	Preston North End	42	10	6	26	37	74	26
22	Nottingham Forest	42	6	12	24	29	65	24

Back: W Smith, Wren, Ashurst, Albert Iremonger, Streets, Jimmy Iremonger (trainer), Dinsdale, Cope, unknown, McLean (assistant trainer). Centre: Hills, Daly, Staniforth, Hill, Kemp, Widdowson, G Smith, unknown. Front: Cornwell, Davis, Barry, Cock, Flint, Mitchell, Price

1925/26

22nd in Division One (Relegated)

#		Date	Opponent	Score	Scorers	Att	Ashurst W	Barry LJ	Cope HW	Cornwell R	Daly J	Davis AG	Dinsdale N	Flint WA	Harris N	Hilton F	Iremonger A	Kelly P	Kemp H	Mills BR	Price LP	Smith G	Smith WA	Staniforth C	Streets GH	Sullivan JA	Taylor GT	Widdowson, Alf	Wren JE
1	Aug	29	LEEDS UNITED	1-0	Davis	18155		11	3	2	7	10	5	4			1		6					8				9	
2	Sep	2	Liverpool	0-2		19616		11	3	2	7	10	5	4					6					8	1			9	
3		5	Newcastle United	3-6	Widdowson, Staniforth 2	33264		11	3	2		10	5	4			1		6					8			7	9	
4		7	Burnley	0-0		13561		11	3	2		10	5	4	6	1								9			7	8	
5		12	BOLTON WANDERERS	3-0	Staniforth 2, Widdowson	18587	2	11	3			10	5		4	1								9			7	8	6
6		19	Birmingham	1-0	Staniforth	3977	2	11	3			10	5		6	1								9			7	8	4
7		21	BURNLEY	0-1		8363	2	11			3	10	5		6	1								9			7	8	4
8		26	Aston Villa	1-2	Widdowson	22382		11	3			10	5		6	1			4				2	9			7	8	
9	Oct	1	LIVERPOOL	1-2	Widdowson	9802	2	11	3			10	5		6	1			4					9			7	8	
10		3	LEICESTER CITY	2-2	Davis, Newton(og)	34508	2	11	3			10	5	4	6				8						1		7	9	
11		10	West Ham United	0-1		21401	2	11	3			10	5		6	1			4					9			7	8	
12		17	BURY	4-1	Widdowson 2, Davis, Cope(p)	15312	2	11	3			10	5		6	1			4							9	7	8	
13		24	Blackburn Rovers	1-4	Davis	10096	2	11			3	10	5		6	1			4							9	7	8	
14		31	SHEFFIELD UNITED	2-0	Sullivan 2	13343	2	11			3	10	5	4	6	1								8		9	7		
15	Nov	7	West Bromwich Alb.	4-4	Sullivan 3, Davis	17186	2	11			3	10	5	4	6	1								8		9	7		
16		14	EVERTON	0-3		14962	2	11			3	10	5	4											1	9	7		
17		21	Manchester City	1-1	Davis	16837	2	11				10	5	4	8	6							3	9	1		7		
18		28	TOTTENHAM HOTSPUR	4-2	Davis 3, Harris	12191	2	11				10	5	4	8	6	1						3	9			7		
19	Dec	5	Cardiff City	1-2	Davis	17856	2					10	5	4	8	6	1				11		3	9			7		
20		12	SUNDERLAND	2-0	Widdowson, Dinsdale	20583	2	11	3			10	5	4	8	6	1										7	9	
21		19	Huddersfield T	0-2		7972	2	11	3			10	5	4	8	6	1										7	9	
22		25	Arsenal	0-3		33398	2	11	3			10	5	4	8	6	1										7	9	
23		26	ARSENAL	4-1	Harris 4	32045	2	11	3			10	5	4	8	6	1										7	9	
24	Jan	2	Leeds United	1-2	Harris	14615	2	11	3			10	5		8	6	1		4								9	7	
25		16	NEWCASTLE UNITED	1-3	Sullivan	10700		11			7		5		8	6	1		4			2	3	10		9			
26		23	Bolton Wanderers	1-2	Sullivan	15507		11					5	4	8	6	1					2	3	10		9	7		
27	Feb	6	ASTON VILLA	1-0	Flint	18426		11						10	5	4	8		1	6			2	3			9	7		
28		13	Leicester City	0-1		30938		11						10	5	4	8		1	6			2	3			7	9		
29		27	Bury	1-3	Kelly	14480		11	3						5	4	9		8	6			2			1	7	10	
30	Mar	3	BIRMINGHAM	3-0	Barry, Harris, Kelly	8131		11						10	5	4	9		8	6			2	3			1	7		
31		6	BLACKBURN ROVERS	1-1	Cope	10658		11	3					10	5	4	9		8	6			2			1	7		
32		13	Sheffield United	0-3		16507		11	3					10	5	4	9		8	6			2			1	7		
33		20	WEST BROMWICH ALB.	0-0		14888		11	3				10	5				1	8	6	9		2				7		4
34		22	WEST HAM UNITED	1-1	Mills	4278		11	3				10	5				1	8	6	9		2				7		4
35		27	Everton	0-3		20517		11	3					5		9		1	8	6	10		2				7		4
36	Apr	2	MANCHESTER UTD.	0-3		18453		11	3					5		8	6	1	10	4			2					9	
37		3	MANCHESTER CITY	1-0	Daly	16266		11			7	10			8	5	1	9	4			2	3						6
38		5	Manchester Utd.	1-0	Smith W(p)	19606		11			7	10			8	5	1	9	4			2	3						6
39		10	Tottenham Hotspur	0-4		17892		11				10		4	5	1		8	6			2	3	9			7		
40		17	CARDIFF CITY	2-4	Staniforth, Davis	8712		11				10	4		5	1		8	6			2	3	9			7		
41		24	Sunderland	1-3	Taylor	8262		11						5	8		1	10	6			2	3	9			7		4
42	May	1	HUDDERSFIELD T	4-2	Davis 3, Daly	4715		11			7	10	5			6	1	8	4			2	3	9					
					Apps		19	41	23	9	7	36	39	23	22	29	34	14	27	3	1	16	17	21	8	9	35	20	9
					Goals			1	2			14	1	1	7			2	1					6		7	1	7	

One own goal

F.A. Cup

R3	Jan	9	LEICESTER CITY	2-0	Widdowson, Taylor	33495	2	11				10	5		8	6	1		4					3			7	9	
R4		30	NEW BRIGHTON	2-0	Harris 2	18944		11				10	5	4	8		1		6					3			9	7	
R5	Feb	20	FULHAM	0-1		33000		11				10	5	4	8	6	1					2	3				9	7	

Played in game 2: WJ Hills (at no. 2)

	p	w	d	l	f	a	pts
1 Huddersfield Town	42	23	11	8	92	60	57
2 Arsenal	42	22	8	12	87	63	52
3 Sunderland	42	21	6	15	96	80	48
4 Bury	42	20	7	15	85	77	47
5 Sheffield United	42	19	8	15	102	82	46
6 Aston Villa	42	16	12	14	86	76	44
7 Liverpool	42	14	16	12	70	63	44
8 Bolton Wanderers	42	17	10	15	75	76	44
9 Manchester United	42	19	6	17	66	73	44
10 Newcastle United	42	16	10	16	84	75	42
11 Everton	42	12	18	12	72	70	42
12 Blackburn Rovers	42	15	11	16	91	80	41
13 West Bromwich Alb.	42	16	8	18	79	78	40
14 Birmingham	42	16	8	18	66	81	40
15 Tottenham Hotspur	42	15	9	18	66	79	39
16 Cardiff City	42	16	7	19	61	76	39
17 Leicester City	42	14	10	18	70	80	38
18 West Ham United	42	15	7	20	63	76	37
19 Leeds United	42	14	8	20	64	76	36
20 Burnley	42	13	10	19	85	108	36
21 Manchester City	42	12	11	19	89	100	35
22 NOTTS COUNTY	42	13	7	22	54	74	33

Back: Cope, Cornwell, W Smith, Wren, Price, Dinsdale, Davis, Allen. Centre: Taylor, Mitchell, Flint, Dukes, Crapper, Kemp, Barry, Staniforth. Front: Hills

1926/27

16th in Division Two

#		Date	Opponent	Score	Scorers	Att	Ashurst W	Barry LJ	Bisby CC	Cope HW	Daly J	Davis AG	Dinsdale N	Goucher GH	Harris N	Hillhouse JT	Hills WJ	Hilton F	Hopkins GH	Kelly P	Kemp H	Mills BR	Plackett S	Price LP	Smith G	Smith WA	Stevenson AE	Stokes A	Streets GH	Sullivan IA	Taylor GT	Widdowson, Alf
1	Aug	28	South Shields	0-5		6835	2	11			7	10	5					6				8				3			1	9		4
2		30	Preston North End	1-4	Mills	15289	2	11			7	10	5					6				8				3			1	9		4
3	Sep	4	HULL CITY	1-0	W Smith	9629	2	11			7	10	5		4					8	6	9				3			1			
4		6	Chelsea	0-2		15572	2	11			7	10	5		4					8	6	9				3			1			
5		11	Wolverhampton Wand.	1-0	Harris	14390	2	11				10	5		9			4		7	6	8				3			1			
6		13	CHELSEA	5-0	Barry, W Smith(p), Harris, Mills, Davis	9094	2	11				10	5		9			4		7	6	8				3			1			
7		18	NOTTM. FOREST	1-2	Harris	18539	2	11				10	5		9			4		7	6	8				3			1			
8		25	CLAPTON ORIENT	3-1	Harris, Davis 2	8804	2	11				10	5		9					7	6	8			4	3			1			
9	Oct	2	Middlesbrough	2-4	Davis, W Smith	15386	2	11				10	5		9					7	6	8			4	3			1			
10		9	PORT VALE	2-1	Kelly, Harris	11838	2	11				10	5		9					7	6	8			4	3			1			
11		16	Reading	1-7	Dinsdale	12936	2	11	3			10	5		9					7	6	8							1			4
12		23	SWANSEA TOWN	1-3	Davis	11634	2	11				6	5		9			4			8		7			3			1	10		
13		30	Barnsley	4-4	Davis 4	4671	2	11	3		7	10	5							8	6	4							1			9
14	Nov	6	MANCHESTER CITY	1-0	Sullivan(p)	5953	2	11	3		7	10	5							8	6	4							1	9		
15		13	Darlington	2-4	Davis, Barry	5038	2	11	3		7	10	5							8	6	4							1	9		
16		20	PORTSMOUTH	2-3	Harris, Kelly	7974	2	11	3			10	5		8	6				7		4							1			9
17		27	Oldham Athletic	2-5	Harris, Davis	11886		11	3			10	5		8	6				7		4		2					1			9
18	Dec	4	FULHAM	4-0	Harris 2, Kelly 2	9486		11	3	2	7	10	5		9			6		8		4							1			
19		18	BLACKPOOL	2-3	Davis, Harris	8108		11	3		7	10	5		9			6		8		4		2					1			
20		25	SOUTHAMPTON	0-1		11373		11	3			10	5		8					7	6	4				2			1	9		
21		27	Southampton	0-2		19120					7		5		9					8	6	4	11	2	3	10			1			
22	Jan	1	PRESTON NORTH END	1-1	Widdowson	10006							5		8		6			7	4	10	11	2	3				1			9
23		15	SOUTH SHIELDS	4-1	Harris 2, Mills, Kelly	8717		11	3			10	5		8		6		1	7	4	9			2							
24		22	Hull City	0-2		8891		11	3			10	5		8		6		1	7	4	9		2	3							
25		29	Grimsby Town	4-1	Widdowson 2, Kelly, Harris	9347		11	3			10	5		8		6		1	7				2			4					9
26	Feb	5	Nottm. Forest	0-2		25578		11	3			10	5		8		4		1	7	6			2								9
27		9	WOLVERHAMPTON W.	2-2	Kelly, Harris	5106		11	3			10			8		5		1	7	6			2			4					9
28		12	Clapton Orient	1-2	Davis	10846		11	3			10			9		5		1	8	4			2							7	
29		23	MIDDLESBROUGH	2-2	Harris, Barry	12042		11	3			10			9	4	5			8		6		2					1		7	
30		26	Port Vale	2-6	Davis, Barry	9638		11	3			10			9		5			8	4	6		2					1		7	
31	Mar	12	Swansea Town	1-0	Taylor	13026		11	3				5				4			8	9	6		2					1	10	7	
32		16	READING	2-0	Kelly, Sullivan	8880		11	3				5				4			8	9	6		2					1	10	7	
33		19	BARNSLEY	1-1	Sullivan	15327		11	3			10	5				4			8		6		2					1	9	7	
34		26	Manchester City	1-4	Widdowson	17242		11	3				5	10			4			8		6		2					1		7	9
35	Apr	2	DARLINGTON	3-1	Davis 2, Kelly	8138		11	3			10	5				4			8		6		2					1		7	9
36		9	Portsmouth	1-9	Kelly	15768			3			10	5		4					8		6	11	2		9			1		7	
37		16	OLDHAM ATHLETIC	1-2	Price(p)	8497			3			10	5		9		4			8		6	11	2					1		7	
38		18	BRADFORD CITY	4-0	Kelly 2, Daly, Harris	7988			3		7		5		9		4			8		6	11	2					1			10
39		19	Bradford City	2-1	Kelly, Price(p)	13046			3		7		5		9	4				8		6	11	2					1			10
40		23	Fulham	0-3		12643			3		7		5			4				8		6	11	2		9			1			10
41		30	GRIMSBY TOWN	3-0	Barry, Kelly, Widdowson	9196		11	3				5				4	1		8	6			2						9	7	10
42	May	7	Blackpool	0-5		5651		11	3			5	2				1			8	6		6							9	7	10
					Apps		16	35	28	1	13	32	38	1	27	4	2	26	8	40	22	27	14	8	20	21	3	2	34	11	12	17
					Goals			5			1	16	1		16					14		3		2		3				3	1	5

F.A. Cup

		Date	Opponent	Score	Scorers	Att																										
R3	Jan	8	Newcastle United	1-8	Widdowson	32564		11			7		5				6		8	4	10		2	3				1			9

Back: W Smith, Ashurst, Hilton, Streets, Price, Lowe, Dinsdale, Hyde. Centre: Kemp, Widdowson, Green, Hills, Stevenson, Bisby, G Smith, Daly. Front: Rhodes, Barry, Davis, Harris, BR Mills, Kelly

		p	w	d	l	f	a	pts
1	Middlesbrough	42	27	8	7	122	60	62
2	Portsmouth	42	23	8	11	87	49	54
3	Manchester City	42	22	10	10	108	61	54
4	Chelsea	42	20	12	10	62	52	52
5	Nottingham Forest	42	18	14	10	80	55	50
6	Preston North End	42	20	9	13	74	72	49
7	Hull City	42	20	7	15	63	52	47
8	Port Vale	42	16	13	13	88	78	45
9	Blackpool	42	18	8	16	95	80	44
10	Oldham Athletic	42	19	6	17	74	84	44
11	Barnsley	42	17	9	16	88	87	43
12	Swansea Town	42	16	11	15	68	72	43
13	Southampton	42	15	12	15	60	62	42
14	Reading	42	16	8	18	64	72	40
15	Wolverhampton Wan.	42	14	7	21	73	75	35
16	NOTTS COUNTY	42	15	5	22	70	96	35
17	Grimsby Town	42	11	12	19	74	91	34
18	Fulham	42	13	8	21	58	92	34
19	South Shields	42	11	11	20	71	96	33
20	Clapton Orient	42	12	7	23	60	96	31
21	Darlington	42	12	6	24	79	98	30
22	Bradford City	42	7	9	26	50	88	23

1927/28

15th in Division Two

	Date	Opponent	Score	Scorers	Att	Andrews H	Barry LJ	Bisby CC	Connell A	Davies W	Davis AG	Dinsdale N	Fenner T	Ferguson JS	Froggatt F	Gibbon H	Haden S	Hilton F	Hopkins GH	Kelly P	Kemp H	Matthews CH	Mills BR	Mills PC	Plackett S	Smith G	Staniforth C	Stokes A	Streets GH	Taylor GT	Widdowson, Alf
1	Aug 27	BRISTOL CITY	1-2	Staniforth	15302	11	3				10	5						4	1	7			8		6	2	9				
2	Sep 3	Stoke City	0-3		22236	11	3											5	1	8			4		6	2	9			7	10
3	7	Chelsea	0-5		18416	11	3											5	1	8			4		6	2	9			7	10
4	10	SOUTHAMPTON	0-0		9673	11	3								7			5	1						6	2	8	4			10
5	17	Nottm. Forest	1-2	BR Mills	21957	11	3											5	1	8	4		9		6	2	10			7	
6	24	Oldham Athletic	0-0		12417	11	3											5	1		4		9		6	2	10			7	
7	Oct 1	GRIMSBY TOWN	3-2	Davis 2, Staniforth	7174		3				8							5	1		4		9		6	2	10			7	
8	6	CHELSEA	0-1		9127		3				10						11	5	1		4		8		6	2	9			7	
9	8	Reading	2-2	BR Mills, Staniforth	11978		3				10						11	5	1		4		8		6	2	9			7	
10	15	BLACKPOOL	3-1	Taylor, Davis, Staniforth	11885		3				10						11	5	1		4		8		6	2	9			7	
11	22	PORT VALE	2-4	Connell, Staniforth	9053		3	8			10						11	5	1		4				6	2	9			7	
12	29	South Shields	3-2	Staniforth 2, Kelly	6379		3				10	5					11	6		8	4				2		9			1	7
13	Nov 5	LEEDS UNITED	2-2	Staniforth, Hilton(p)	9866		3				10	5					11	6		8	4				2		9			1	7
14	12	Wolverhampton Wand.	2-2	Davis, Kelly	16100		3				10	5					11	6		8	4				2		9			1	7
15	19	BARNSLEY	9-0	BR Mills 5, Staniforth 3, Haden	9382		3				10			5			11	6			4		9		2		8			1	7
16	26	Preston North End	0-4		16041		3				10			5			11	6			4		9		2		8			1	7
17	Dec 3	SWANSEA TOWN	2-0	Taylor, BR Mills	11618		3				10			5			11	6			4		9		2		8			1	7
18	10	Fulham	1-2	Staniforth	11562		3				10			5			11	6					9		2		8	4		1	7
19	17	HULL CITY	1-1	BR Mills	8758		3				10			5			11	6			4		9		2		8			1	7
20	24	Manchester City	1-3	BR Mills	18362		3	8						5			11	6			4		9		2					1	7	10
21	26	West Bromwich Alb.	2-2	BR Mills, Kemp	14642		3	8						5			11	6	1		4		9		2					7	10
22	27	WEST BROMWICH ALB.	3-0	Widdowson 2, BR Mills	17755		3	8						5			11	6					9	4	2					1	7	10
23	31	Bristol City	2-1	BR Mills 2	6476		3							5			11	6			4		9		2		8			1	7	10
24	Jan 7	STOKE CITY	1-2	Haden	13365		3							5			11	6			4		9		2		8			1	7	10
25	21	Southampton	1-5	BR Mills	10002		3					5					11	6	1		4		9		2						7	8
26	Feb 4	OLDHAM ATHLETIC	2-1	Kemp, Kelly	8678		3							5			11	6	1	8	4		9		2						7	10
27	11	Grimsby Town	0-1		7666		3				10			5			11	6	1	8	4		9		2						7	
28	18	READING	1-1	Fenner	8034		3						8	5	7		11	6	1		4		9		2		10					
29	22	NOTTM. FOREST	1-2	BR Mills	13241		3						8	5			11	6	1		4		9		2		10				7	
30	25	Blackpool	3-3	BR Mills, Staniforth 2	9423		3						8	5	7		11	6	1		4		9		2		10					
31	Mar 3	Port Vale	0-3		9644		3						8					7	5	1		4		9			6	2	10				
32	10	SOUTH SHIELDS	4-1	BR Mills 2, Hilton(p), Taylor	8117		3						7	5			11	6	1		4		9		2		10				8	
33	17	Leeds United	0-6		17643		3		7					1	5		11	6			4	8	9		2		10					
34	24	WOLVERHAMPTON W.	1-2	Haden	13617		3		11					1	5		10	6			4	7	9		2						8	
35	31	Barnsley	0-0		5619	10	3		7					1			11	5		8			9	2	6			4				
36	Apr 6	CLAPTON ORIENT	3-0	BR Mills, Haden, Hilton(p)	13924	10	3		7					1			11	5		8			9	2	6			4				
37	7	PRESTON NORTH END	6-2	Davies 2, Taylor 3, Haden	16226	10	3		7					1	5		11			8				2	6			4			9	
38	9	Clapton Orient	1-0	Taylor	10166	10	3							1	5		11			8		7			6	2		4			9	
39	14	Swansea Town	1-1	Taylor	11566	10	3		7					1	5		11			8					6	2		4			9	
40	21	FULHAM	0-1		7655	10	3		7					1	5		11			8					6	2		4			9	
41	28	Hull City	1-1	Wilson(og)	5284	10	3		7				8	1	5		11	4							6	2					9	
42	May 5	MANCHESTER CITY	2-1	Fenner, Taylor	9907	10	3		7				8	1	5		11	4						2	6						9	

LP Price played in games 7 (at 11) and 31 (11).
JA Sullivan played in games 4 (at 9) and 25 (10).

| | | | | | | Apps | 8 | 42 | 4 | 9 | 16 | 5 | 7 | 10 | 24 | 3 | 2 | 35 | 38 | 20 | 15 | 28 | 3 | 31 | 4 | 21 | 38 | 27 | 8 | 12 | 34 | 10 |
| | | | | | | Goals | | | | 1 | 2 | 4 | | 2 | | | | 5 | 3 | | 3 | 2 | | 20 | | | | 14 | | | 9 | 2 |

One own goal

F.A. Cup

	Date	Opponent	Score	Scorers	Att		Barry LJ											Hilton F			Kelly P			Mills BR		Plackett S		Staniforth C		Streets GH	Taylor GT	Widdowson, Alf
R3	Jan 14	SHEFFIELD UNITED	2-3	BR Mills, Taylor	28232		3							5				11	6		4			9		2		8		1	7	10

		p	w	d	l	f	a	pts
1	Manchester City	42	25	9	8	100	59	59
2	Leeds United	42	25	7	10	98	49	57
3	Chelsea	42	23	8	11	75	45	54
4	Preston North End	42	22	9	11	100	66	53
5	Stoke City	42	22	8	12	78	59	52
6	Swansea Town	42	18	12	12	75	63	48
7	Oldham Athletic	42	19	8	15	75	51	46
8	West Bromwich Alb.	42	17	12	13	90	70	46
9	Port Vale	42	18	8	16	68	57	44
10	Nottingham Forest	42	15	10	17	83	84	40
11	Grimsby Town	42	14	12	16	69	83	40
12	Bristol City	42	15	9	18	76	79	39
13	Barnsley	42	14	11	17	65	85	39
14	Hull City	42	12	15	15	41	54	39
15	NOTTS COUNTY	42	13	12	17	68	74	38
16	Wolverhampton Wan.	42	13	10	19	63	91	36
17	Southampton	42	14	7	21	68	77	35
18	Reading	42	11	13	18	53	75	35
19	Blackpool	42	13	8	21	83	101	34
20	Clapton Orient	42	11	12	19	55	85	34
21	Fulham	42	13	7	22	68	89	33
22	South Shields	42	7	9	26	56	111	23

1928/29

5th in Division Two

#		Date	Opponent	Result	Scorers	Att	Andrews H	Astley J	Bisby CC	Childs H	Davies W	Dowsey J	Fenner T	Ferguson JS	Froggatt F	Haden S	Hilton F	James W	Kemp H	Matthews CH	Maw AW	McGorian IM	Mills BR	Mills PC	Plackett S	Stokes A	Taylor GT	Wright F
1	Aug	25	Millwall	1-0	Fenner	27221	10		3		7		8	1	5	11	4							2	6		9	
2		27	WEST BROMWICH ALB.	3-1	Taylor, Andrews, Haden	10395	10		3		7		8	1	5	11	4							2	6		9	
3	Sep	1	PORT VALE	3-0	Haden 2, Fenner	15314	10		3		7		8	1	5	11	4							2	6		9	
4		3	West Bromwich Alb.	3-1	Andrews 3	9541	10		3		7		8	1	5	11	4							2	6		9	
5		8	Hull City	1-1	Andrews	14790	10		3		7		8	1	5	11	4							2	6		9	
6		15	TOTTENHAM HOTSPUR	2-0	Fenner 2	23304	10		3		7		8	1	5	11	4							2	6		9	
7		22	Reading	2-1	Taylor, Davis	12165	10		3		7		8	1	5	11	4							2	6		9	
8		29	PRESTON NORTH END	0-1		19380	10		3		7		8	1	5	11	4							2	6		9	
9	Oct	6	Middlesbrough	1-3	Davis	16984	10		3		7		8	1	5	11	4							2	6		9	
10		13	OLDHAM ATHLETIC	2-0	Haden, Andrews	11957	10		3		7		8	1	5	11	4							2	6		9	
11		20	NOTTM. FOREST	1-1	Fenner	22249	10		3		7		8	1	5	11			4					2	6		9	
12		27	Bristol City	4-0	Andrews 2, BR Mills 2	8496	10		3				8	1	5	11			4	7			9	2	6			
13	Nov	3	BARNSLEY	4-1	BR Mills, Andrews 2, Fenner	16917	10		3		7		8	1	5	11			4				9	2	6			
14		10	Clapton Orient	2-2	Andrews, PC Mills	9746	10		3		7		8	1	5	11							9	2	6	4		
15		17	BLACKPOOL	3-1	BR Mills 2, Fenner	13987	10		3				8	1	5	11			4	7			9	2	6			
16		24	Swansea Town	0-1		10498	10		3		7		8	1	5	11			4				9	2	6			
17	Dec	1	BRADFORD PARK AVE.	3-3	Davis, Fenner, BR Mills	14875	10		3		7		8	1	5	11			4				9	2	6			
18		8	Grimsby Town	2-2	Haden, Fenner	12381	10		3		7		8	1	5	11			4				9	2	6			
19		15	STOKE CITY	1-0	BR Mills	10166	10		3		7		8	1	5	11			4				9	2	6			
20		22	Chelsea	1-1	BR Mills	19560	10		3		7		8	1	5	11			4				9	2	6			
21		25	SOUTHAMPTON	1-1	Andrews	21865	10		3		7		8	1	5	11			4				9	2	6			
22		26	Southampton	0-4		20441	10		3				8	1	5	11	6			7				2		4	9	
23		29	MILLWALL	4-5	Fenner 2, Andrews, Froggatt	12727	10		3				8	1	5	11			4				9	2	6			
24	Jan	5	Port Vale	0-3		7475	10	3			7		8	1	5	11	4						9	2	6			
25		19	HULL CITY	6-0	Andrews, BR Mills 3, Fenner 2	13271	10		3		7		8	1		11	5		4				9	2	6			
26		26	Tottenham Hotspur	0-3		16946	10		3		7		8	1		11	5		4				9	2	6			
27	Feb	2	READING	1-1	Andrews	9807	10		3		7		8	1	5	11			4	7			9	2	6			
28		9	Preston North End	1-0	Taylor	15666	10		3		7		8	1	5	11			4					2	6		9	
29		16	MIDDLESBROUGH	0-3		11534			3		7	10	8	1	5	11			4					2	6		9	
30		23	Oldham Athletic	2-3	Andrews, Fenner	10947	10		3		7	9	8	1	5	11			4			6		2				
31	Mar	2	Nottm. Forest	2-1	Dowsey, Fenner	18438	10		3		7	8	8	1	5	11			4					2	6			
32		9	BRISTOL CITY	2-0	Fenner, PC Mills	13001	10		3		7	8	8	1	5	11			4					2	6			
33		13	CHELSEA	4-3	Fenner 2, Andrews, Haden(p)	11235	10		3		7	8	8	1	5	11			4					2	6			
34		16	Barnsley	0-2		7518	10		3		7	8	8	1	5	11			4					2	6			
35		23	CLAPTON ORIENT	2-0	Haden, Andrews	10965	10	3			7	8	8	1	5	11			4					2	6			
36		30	Blackpool	2-3	Taylor 2	16049	10		3		7	8		1	5	11			4					2	6		9	
37	Apr	1	WOLVERHAMPTON W.	3-0	Bisby, Davis, James	16373			3		7		8	1	5	11	10	4						2	6		9	
38		2	Wolverhampton Wand.	1-3	Kemp	12060								1	5	11	10	6	7	8				2		4	9	
39		6	SWANSEA TOWN	5-1	Dowsey 2, James, Andrews, Haden(p)	9429	9	3	2			8		1	5	11	10	4	7						6			
40		13	Bradford Park Ave.	2-2	Andrews, Haden	15104	9	3	2		7	8		1	5	11	10	4							6			
41		20	GRIMSBY TOWN	1-2	James	28139	9		3		7	8		1	5	11	10	4						2	6			
42		27	Stoke City	0-5		8165	9			2	7	8		1	5	11	10	4							6			3
					Apps		39	4	39	1	36	12	36	42	40	42	14	6	29	6		1	15	39	39	3	17	1
					Goals		20		1		4	3	18		1	9		3	1				11		2		5	

F.A. Cup

R3	Jan	12	Derby County	3-4	Haden 2, Andrews	21318	10		3		7		8	1	5	11	4						9	2	6			

Back: Andrews, Astley, Hilton, C Smith, Hamilton, B Mills. Standing: Fenner, Ratcliffe (trainer), Holdsworth, Robertson, Wilson, Ferguson, P Mills, Henshall (sec/mgr), Plackett. Seated: Davies, Kemp, Childs, Bisby, Taylor, Haden. Front: Stokes, Keeling, Kerry, Matthews

		p	w	d	l	f	a	pts
1	Middlesbrough	42	22	11	9	92	57	55
2	Grimsby Town	42	24	5	13	82	61	53
3	Bradford Park Ave.	42	22	4	16	88	70	48
4	Southampton	42	17	14	11	74	60	48
5	NOTTS COUNTY	42	19	9	14	78	65	47
6	Stoke City	42	17	12	13	74	51	46
7	West Bromwich Alb.	42	19	8	15	80	79	46
8	Blackpool	42	19	7	16	92	76	45
9	Chelsea	42	17	10	15	64	65	44
10	Tottenham Hotspur	42	17	9	16	75	81	43
11	Nottingham Forest	42	15	12	15	71	70	42
12	Hull City	42	13	14	15	58	63	40
13	Preston North End	42	15	9	18	78	79	39
14	Millwall	42	16	7	19	71	86	39
15	Reading	42	15	9	18	63	86	39
16	Barnsley	42	16	6	20	69	66	38
17	Wolverhampton Wan.	42	15	7	20	77	81	37
18	Oldham Athletic	42	16	5	21	54	75	37
19	Swansea Town	42	13	10	19	62	75	36
20	Bristol City	42	13	10	19	58	72	36
21	Port Vale	42	15	4	23	71	86	34
22	Clapton Orient	42	12	8	22	45	72	32

1929/30

22nd in Division Two (Relegated)

							Andrews H	Bisby CC	Davies W	Dowsey J	Feebery A	Fenner T	Ferguson JS	Fisher F	Froggatt F	Haden S	Hampson T	Jakeman GW	James W	Keetley T	Kemp H	Lawless H	Matthews CH	Maw AW	Mays AW	Merritt R	Mills PC	Plackett S	Taylor GT	Vallance R
1	Aug	31	BRISTOL CITY	3-1	Keetley 3	12259	10	3	7	8		1			5	11		2		9	4							6		
2	Sep	2	Bradford City	0-2		20366	10	3	7	8		1			5	11		4		9						2		6		
3		7	Nottm. Forest	1-1	Keetley	18230	10	3	7	4	8	1			5	11		2		9	6									
4		9	BRADFORD CITY	2-0	Keetley 2	8890		3	7	4	8	1			5	11		2	10	9	6									
5		14	Reading	0-2		13957	10	3	7	4	8	1			5	11		2		9	6									
6		16	Cardiff City	1-3	Maw	11533	11	3	7			1			5			2	10		4			8					9	6
7		21	CHARLTON ATHLETIC	4-0	Andrews 2, Keetley 2(1p)	12213	10	3	7	4		1			5	11		2		9				8						6
8		25	CARDIFF CITY	2-1	Fenner 2	7778	10	3	7	4	8	1			5	11		2		9										6
9		28	Hull City	0-0		8680	10	3	7	4	8	1			5	11				9							2	6		
10	Oct	5	STOKE CITY	3-3	Andrews 2, Fenner	18129	10	3	7	4	8	1			5	11		2		9										6
11		12	Wolverhampton Wand.	1-5	Andrews	19937	10	3	7	4	9	1			5	11		2			6			8						
12		19	CHELSEA	2-2	Davies, Fenner	13878	10	3	7	4	9	1			5	11		2			6			8						
13		26	Bury	0-2		8691	10			4		1			5	11		2			6	7	8				3		9	
14	Nov	2	BLACKPOOL	0-2		13282			7	8		1			5	11		2	10	9	4						3			6
15		9	Barnsley	2-2	Keetley, Andrews	5116	10		7	8		1			5	11			2	9	4						3			6
16		16	BRADFORD PARK AVE.	1-1	Haden	8034	10	3	7	4		1			5	11				9	6			8			2			
17		23	West Bromwich Alb.	2-4	Fisher, Taylor	10801	10	3	7	5			1	8		11					4						2		9	6
18		30	TOTTENHAM HOTSPUR	0-1		10294	10	3	7	8		1		5							4					11	2	6	9	
19	Dec	7	Southampton	2-2	Davies, Keetley	9153		3	7	5		1	8			11			10	9	4						2	6		
20		14	MILLWALL	1-1	Keetley	8776		3	7	5		1	8			11			10	9	4						2	6		
21		21	Oldham Athletic	2-2	Andrews, Keetley	13172	10	3	7	4		1			5	11				9							2	6	8	
22		25	Swansea Town	2-3	Andrews, Taylor	7148	10	3	7	4		1			5	11								8			2	6	9	
23		26	SWANSEA TOWN	0-0		19284	10	3	7	4		1			5	11				9							2	6	8	
24		28	Bristol City	0-0		8520	10	3	7	4		1			5	11				9	6						2		8	
25	Jan	4	NOTTM. FOREST	0-0		20917	10	3	7	4		1			5	11				9	6						2		8	
26		18	READING	3-0	James, Andrews, Davies	10614	10	3	7	4		1			5	11			9		6						2		8	
27	Feb	1	HULL CITY	4-1	Andrews 2, James, Haden	11747	9	3		4		1			5	11			10		6		7				2		8	
28		8	Stoke City	1-1	Andrews	8689	9	3	7	4		1			5	11			10		6						2		8	
29		15	WOLVERHAMPTON W.	0-3		11268	9	3		4					5	11	1		10		6		7				2		8	
30		22	Chelsea	1-3	Taylor	27103	9			4	3	1				11					6	5	7	10			2		8	
31	Mar	1	BURY	1-3	Andrews	7016	10			4	3	1				11					6	5	7	8			2		9	
32		8	Blackpool	2-1	Andrews, Maw	13233	10	3		4		1			5	11					6			8	9		2		7	
33		15	BARNSLEY	3-0	Mays, Henderson(og), Maw	6006	10	3		4		1			5	11					6			8	9		2		7	
34		22	Bradford Park Ave.	3-3	Andrews 2, Maw	10497	10	3		4		1			5	11					6			8	9		2		7	
35		29	WEST BROMWICH ALB.	2-1	Mays 2	10026	10	3		4		1			5	11					6			8	9		2		7	
36	Apr	5	Tottenham Hotspur	0-2		17848	10	3		4		1			5	11					6			8	9		2		7	
37		7	Charlton Athletic	0-1		3801	10	3		4		1			5	11					6		7		9		2			
38		12	SOUTHAMPTON	1-2	Andrews	7632	10	3		4		1			5	11			9		6			8			2		7	
39		18	Preston North End	1-3	Mays	10592	10	3		8		1			5	11					6				9		2	4	7	
40		19	Millwall	0-2		10029	10	3		4	8	1			5	11						9	6				2		7	
41		22	PRESTON NORTH END	0-3		10002	10	3		4	8	1			5	11						9					2		7	6
42		26	OLDHAM ATHLETIC	1-1	Mills	9945	10			4	3	8	1		5	11					6				9		2		7	
						Apps	38	36	26	41	3	12	41	3	37	40	1	14	10	20	33	2	6	15	8	1	32	10	25	8
						Goals	17		3			4		1		2			2	12				4	4		1		3	

One own goal

F.A. Cup

R3	Jan	11	West Ham United	0-4		28384	10	3	7	4		1			5	11				9	6						2		8	

		p	w	d	l	f	a	pts
1	Blackpool	42	27	4	11	98	67	58
2	Chelsea	42	22	11	9	74	46	55
3	Oldham Athletic	42	21	11	10	90	51	53
4	Bradford Park Ave.	42	19	12	11	91	70	50
5	Bury	42	22	5	15	78	67	49
6	West Bromwich Alb.	42	21	5	16	105	73	47
7	Southampton	42	17	11	14	77	76	45
8	Cardiff City	42	18	8	16	61	59	44
9	Wolverhampton Wan.	42	16	9	17	77	79	41
10	Nottingham Forest	42	13	15	14	55	69	41
11	Stoke City	42	16	8	18	74	72	40
12	Tottenham Hotspur	42	15	9	18	59	61	39
13	Charlton Athletic	42	14	11	17	59	63	39
14	Millwall	42	12	15	15	57	73	39
15	Swansea Town	42	14	9	19	57	61	37
16	Preston North End	42	13	11	18	65	80	37
17	Barnsley	42	14	8	20	56	71	36
18	Bradford City	42	12	12	18	60	77	36
19	Reading	42	12	11	19	54	67	35
20	Bristol City	42	13	9	20	61	83	35
21	Hull City	42	14	7	21	51	78	35
22	NOTTS COUNTY	42	9	15	18	54	70	33

Back: Fisher, Plackett, Mills, Hilton, Robinson, James. Standing: Banks (assistant trainer), Fenner, McGorian, Ferguson, Robertson, Hampson, Froggatt, Feebery, Ratcliffe (trainer). Seated: Dowsey, Davies, Maw, Merritt, Keetley, Taylor, Andrews, Matthews. Front: Bisby, Haden, Kemp

1930/31

Champions of Division Three (South) - Promoted

			Opponent	Score	Scorers	Att	Andrews H	Bisby CC	Dowsey J	Feebery A	Fenner T	Ferguson JS	Froggatt F	Haden S	Hall GW	Hamilton W	Jakeman GW	Keetley T	Kemp H	Lovatt HA	Maw AW	Mills PC	Shooter A	Smith HR	Soutar HW	Stimpson GH	Taylor GT	Turner GW	Whitcombe GC
1	Aug	30	Coventry City	2-1	Watson(og), Keetley	17915	10	3	4		8	1	5	11				9	6			2					7		
2	Sep	3	THAMES	4-0	Andrews, Taylor, Keetley 2	10125	10	3	4		8	1	5	11				9	6			2					7		
3		6	FULHAM	6-1	Keetley 4, Andrews, Fenner	10167	10	3	4		8	1	5	11				9	6			2					7		
4		8	Norwich City	2-2	Fenner, Taylor	10985	10		4	3	8	1	5	11				9	6			2					7		
5		13	Swindon Town	2-1	Andrews, Taylor	6797	10		4	3	8	1	5	11				9	6			2					7		
6		20	BOURNEMOUTH	2-0	Fenner 2	9579	10		4	3	8	1	5	11				9	6			2					7		
7		24	Brentford	2-2	Keetley 2	9999	10		4	3	8	1		11			5	9	6			2					7		
8		27	Watford	1-0	Fenner	1939	10		4	3	8	1	5	11				9	6			2					7		
9	Oct	2	NORWICH CITY	4-0	Keetley 2, Mills(p), Fenner	6987		3	4		8	1	5	11				9	6	10		2					7		
10		4	BRISTOL ROVERS	3-0	Fenner 2, Maw	11929		3	4		8	1	5	11				9	6	10		2					7		
11		11	CLAPTON ORIENT	5-0	Keetley 3, Fenner 2	11106	10	3	4		8	1	5	11			6	9				2					7		
12		18	Newport County	3-2	Keetley 3	5245	10	3	4		8	1	5	11				9	6			2					7		
13		25	GILLINGHAM	2-1	Andrews, Fenner	11740	10	3			8	1	5	11			4	9	6			2					7		
14	Nov	1	Exeter City	3-3	Maw 2, Andrews	7315	9	3			8	1	5	11			4		6		10	2					7		
15		8	BRIGHTON & HOVE ALB.	2-2	Keetley, Andrews	12362	10	3			8	1	5	11			4	9	6			2					7		
16		15	Torquay United	4-1	Andrews, Keetley 3	6730	10	3	4		8	1		11			5	9	6			2					7		
17		22	NORTHAMPTON T	2-2	Andrews, Keetley	21329	10	3	4		8	1		11			5	9	6			2					7		
18	Dec	6	CRYSTAL PALACE	2-2	Fenner, Keetley	11935		3	4		8	1		11				9	6			2					7		
19		17	Southend United	1-2	Kemp	4827	9		4	3	8	1		11					6		10	2		5			7		
20		20	LUTON TOWN	1-0	Fenner	11307		3	4		8	1		11			6				10	2	9	5			7		
21		25	Queens Park Rangers	1-4	Maw	14501	10	3	4			1		11					6		8	2	9				7		5
22		26	QUEENS PARK RANGERS	2-0	Keetley 2	13696	10	3	4					11				9	6			2				1	7		5
23		27	COVENTRY CITY	4-1	Keetley 2, Andrews, Lovatt	16803	10	3	4					11				9	6	8		2				1	7		5
24	Jan	3	Fulham	1-3	Andrews	11606	10	3	4					11				9		8		2		6	1		7		5
25		17	SWINDON TOWN	2-0	Keetley, Haden	11448	10	3	4					11				9		8		2		6	1		7		5
26		28	Bournemouth	1-2	Turner	4778	10		4	3	8							9				2		6	1		7	11	5
27		31	WATFORD	1-0	Andrews	11705	10		4	3	8							9				2		6	1		7	11	5
28	Feb	7	Bristol Rovers	2-2	Fenner, Keetley	11552	10		4	3	8							9				2		5	1	6	7	11	
29		14	Clapton Orient	4-1	Fenner, Keetley 2, Taylor	6245	10	3	4		8	1		11				9				2		5		6	7		
30		21	NEWPORT COUNTY	5-0	Fenner, Keetley 2, Dowsey	11913	10	3	4		8	1		11				9				2		5		6	7		
31		28	Gillingham	5-0	Andrews 2, Haden(p), Keetley, Fenner	8264	10	3	4		8	1		11		7		9	6					5		2			
32	Mar	7	EXETER CITY	1-2	Keetley	12781	10	3	4		8	1		11				9	6					5		2	7		
33		14	Brighton & Hove Alb.	3-1	Keetley 2, Andrews	14037	10	3	4		8	1		11				9				2		5		6	7		
34		21	TORQUAY UNITED	2-0	Haden(p), Fenner	11951	10	3	4		8	1		11				9				2		5		6	7		
35		28	Northampton T	0-0		14284	10	3	4		8	1		11				9				2		5		6	7		
36	Apr	3	WALSALL	6-1	Andrews 3, Fenner 2, Keetley	11858	10	3	4		8	1		11				9				2		5		6	7		
37		4	BRENTFORD	1-0	Keetley	14759	10	3	4		8	1		11				9				2		5		6	7		
38		6	Walsall	1-2	Maw	5187		3	5		8	1		11				9	4		10	2				6	7		
39		11	Crystal Palace	1-1	Taylor	19638		3	4		8	1		11		6				9	10	2		5			7		
40		18	SOUTHEND UNITED	1-1	Haden	11919		3	4		8	1		11		6		9			10	2		5			7		
41		25	Luton Town	0-3		7312		3	4			1		11	8	6				9	10	2		5			7		
42	May	2	Thames	0-0		3731		3	4			1		11	10	6				9	8	2		5			7		
					Apps		33	33	39	9	35	35	14	39	1	2	12	34	24	7	13	40	2	21	7	11	41	3	7
					Goals		17		1		21			4				39	1	1	5	1					5	1	

One own goal

F.A. Cup

			Opponent	Score	Scorers	Att	Andrews H	Bisby CC	Dowsey J	Feebery A	Fenner T	Ferguson JS	Froggatt F	Haden S	Hall GW	Hamilton W	Jakeman GW	Keetley T	Kemp H	Lovatt HA	Maw AW	Mills PC	Shooter A	Smith HR	Soutar HW	Stimpson GH	Taylor GT	Turner GW	Whitcombe GC
R1	Nov	29	Chesterfield	2-1	Fenner, Taylor	13401	10	3	4		8	1		11				9	6			2		5			7		
R2	Dec	13	Doncaster Rovers	1-0	Bowman(og)	17763		3	4		8	1		11				9	6	10		2		5			7		
R3	Jan	10	SWANSEA TOWN	3-1	Andrews 2, Keetley	23802	10	3	4					11				9		8		2		6	1		7		5
R4		24	Sheffield United	1-4	Keetley	42178	10	3	4					11				9	6	8		2		5	1		7		

		p	w	d	l	f	a	pts
1	NOTTS COUNTY	42	24	11	7	97	46	59
2	Crystal Palace	42	22	7	13	107	71	51
3	Brentford	42	22	6	14	90	64	50
4	Brighton & Hove A.	42	17	15	10	68	53	49
5	Southend United	42	22	5	15	76	60	49
6	Northampton Town	42	18	12	12	77	59	48
7	Luton Town	42	19	8	15	76	51	46
8	Queen's Park Rgs.	42	20	3	19	82	75	43
9	Fulham	42	18	7	17	77	75	43
10	Bournemouth	42	15	13	14	72	73	43
11	Torquay United	42	17	9	16	80	84	43
12	Swindon Town	42	18	6	18	89	94	42
13	Exeter City	42	17	8	17	84	90	42
14	Coventry City	42	16	9	17	75	65	41
15	Bristol Rovers	42	16	8	18	75	92	40
16	Gillingham	42	14	10	18	61	76	38
17	Walsall	42	14	9	19	78	95	37
18	Watford	42	14	7	21	72	75	35
19	Clapton Orient	42	14	7	21	63	91	35
20	Thames	42	13	8	21	54	93	34
21	Newport County	42	11	6	25	69	111	28
22	Norwich City	42	10	8	24	47	76	28

Back: Henshall (secretary-manager), Dowsey, Jakeman, Hamilton, Warren, Ferguson, Palmer, Soutar, Mills, HR Smith, Stimpson, Fenner, Wightman (coach). Standing: Banks (trainer), *Barnes, *Towers, *HS Hobson, *WN Hobson, Turner, *Tunnicliffe, Feebery, *Halford, Alderman, Godfrey (treasurer), *Thraves, *Harper, Mellors (assistant trainer). Seated: *Wright, Sheldon, Hall, Taylor, Bisby, Kemp, Lord Belper (president & chairman), Keetley, Maw, Andrews, Haden, Lovett, *Irving. Front: Thorpe, Nelson, Froggatt, Shooter. (*directors)

A photographer from Overends (a Bradford company) called at Meadow Lane on a training day early in season 1931/32. A rather misty County Ground is pictured above. As well as the team group (on page 3 of this book) he also photographed many of the players.

Willie Hall, Jack Wright and Bill Jones

Jim Ferguson

Harry Lovatt, Jimmy Maidment and Steve Coglin

1931/32

16th in Division Two

#		Date	Opponent	Score	Scorers	Att	Andrews H	Bisby CC	Coglin S	Corkhill WG	Dowsey J	Elliott S	Feebery A	Fenner T	Ferguson JS	Grice F	Haden S	Hall GW	Jakeman GW	Keetley T	Lawrence E	Lovatt HA	Maidment JHC	Maw AW	Mills PC	Molloy W	Smith HR	Stimpson GH	Taylor GT	Thorpe AE	Wright JE
1	Aug	29	MILLWALL	2-0	Haden, Keetley	15464	10	3			4			8	1		11		6	9					2		5		7		
2	Sep	2	Bristol City	2-3	Keetley, Mills	8552	10	3			4			8	1		11		6	9					2		5		7		
3		5	Bradford City	2-0	Taylor, Keetley	13731	10							8	1		11		6	9	4				2		5	3	7		
4		12	LEEDS UNITED	1-1	Keetley	12630	10								1		11		6	9	4	8			2		5	3	7		
5		14	Oldham Athletic	2-5	Andrews, Keetley	7117	10	3			4				1		11			9	6			8	2			5	7		
6		19	Swansea Town	1-5	Keetley	10933	10	3			4				1		11		5	9	6			8	2				7		
7		23	OLDHAM ATHLETIC	1-0	Wright	7068		3	10		4				1	5	11	8		6					2				7		9
8		26	BARNSLEY	2-3	Lovatt 2	11700	10				4		3		1	5	11	8		6	9				2				7		
9	Oct	3	Nottm. Forest	1-2	Haden	20703	9		10				3	8	1		11		5	6					2			4	7		
10		10	Plymouth Argyle	4-3	Keetley 3, Fenner	22655							3	8	1		11	10	4	9	6				2		5		7		
11		17	TOTTENHAM HOTSPUR	3-1	Keetley, Fenner, Taylor	13397							3	8			11	10	4	9	6		1		2		5		7		
12		24	Manchester Utd.	3-3	Keetley 3	6694		2					3	8	1		11	10	4	9	6						5		7		
13		31	BRADFORD PARK AVE.	0-2		12687	6	3						8	1		11	10	4	9							5	2	7		
14	Nov	7	Chesterfield	4-1	Keetley 3, Fenner	10303		3						8			11	10	4	9	6		1				5	2	7		
15		14	CHARLTON ATHLETIC	2-2	Keetley, Haden	11681		3						8			11		4	9	6		1	10			5	2	7		
16		21	Stoke City	2-2	Hall, Keetley	10816		3						8		5	11	10	4	9	6		1					2	7		
17		28	SOUTHAMPTON	5-0	Keetley 3(1p), Fenner 2	10307	11	3	10					8	1	5			4	9	6							2	7		
18	Dec	5	Preston North End	0-0		6320	9	3	10					8	1	5	11		4		6							2	7		
19		12	BURNLEY	5-0	Fenner 3, Grice, Haden	13198	9	3	10					8	1	5	11		4		6							2	7		
20		19	Wolverhampton Wand.	0-0		16305		3	10					8	1	5	11		4	9	6							2	7		
21		25	PORT VALE	4-2	Keetley 3, Coglin	21367		3	10					8	1	5	11		4	9	6							2	7		
22		26	Port Vale	0-2		13463		3	10					8	1	5	11		4	9	6							2	7		
23	Jan	2	Millwall	3-4	Keetley 2, Coglin	13752		3	10					8	1	5	11		4	9	6				2				7		
24		16	BRADFORD CITY	1-1	Taylor	10693			10						1	5	11	8		9	6				2			4	3	7	
25		23	Leeds United	2-2	Taylor, Maw	14562	10	3							1	5	11			9	6				2			4	7		
26		30	SWANSEA TOWN	1-2	Maw	10628	10	3							1	5	11			9	6			8	2			4	7		
27	Feb	6	Barnsley	1-1	Fenner	5188		3		4				8			11	10		9	6		1		2		5		7		
28		13	NOTTM. FOREST	2-6	Haden, Taylor	17199		3		4				8			11	10		9	6		1		2		5		7		
29		20	PLYMOUTH ARGYLE	3-0	Hall 2, Fenner	11434							3	8	1	5	11	10	4	9	6								2	7	
30		27	Tottenham Hotspur	0-2		20481							3	8	1	5	11	10	4	9	6								2	7	
31	Mar	5	MANCHESTER UTD.	1-2	Mellor (og)	10817	9						3	8	1	5	11	10	4		6								2	7	
32		12	Bradford Park Ave.	1-1	Grice	12015		3						8	1	9	11		4		6				2		5		7		
33		19	CHESTERFIELD	1-1	Elliott	14507		3				9		8	1		11	10	4		6				2		5		7		
34		25	Bury	1-2	Haden	7482		3				9		8	1		11	10	4		6						5	2	7		
35		26	Charlton Athletic	1-3	Mills(p)	15356	10	3				9			1		11		4		6				8	2	5	3	7		
36		28	BURY	0-1		11706		3				9		8	1		11	10	4		6					2	5		7		
37	Apr	2	STOKE CITY	2-1	Haden, Taylor	10839		3						8		5	11	10			6	1				9	4	2	7		
38		9	Southampton	1-3	Molloy	7332		3						8		5	11	10			6	1				9	4	2	7		
39		16	PRESTON NORTH END	1-4	Keetley	5872		3						8		5	11	10		9	6	1					4	2	7		
40		23	Burnley	1-1	Keetley	5604			10		8	3					11		4	9	6	1			2		5		7		
41		30	WOLVERHAMPTON W.	3-1	Taylor, Haden, Fenner	12289			10					3	8		11		4	9	6	1			2		5		7		
42	May	7	BRISTOL CITY	3-0	Fenner, Coglin, Mills(p)	5773			10					3	8		11			9	6	1			2		5		7	4	
					Apps		16	28	13	2	6	5	11	32	30	20	41	21	30	29	39	2	12	6	24	2	26	23	42	1	1
					Goals		1		3			1		12		2	8	3		28			2		2	3	1		7		1

One own goal

F.A. Cup

		Date	Opponent	Score	Scorers	Att																									
R3	Jan	9	BRISTOL CITY	2-2	Keetley 2	22761		3	10					8	1	5	11		4	9	6							2	7		
rep		13	Bristol City	2-3	Hall, Grice	16065	10	3							1	5	11	8		9	6				2			4	7		

		p	w	d	l	f	a	pts
1	Wolverhampton Wan.	42	24	8	10	115	49	56
2	Leeds United	42	22	10	10	78	54	54
3	Stoke City	42	19	14	9	69	48	52
4	Plymouth Argyle	42	20	9	13	100	66	49
5	Bury	42	21	7	14	70	58	49
6	Bradford Park Ave.	42	21	7	14	72	63	49
7	Bradford City	42	16	13	13	80	61	45
8	Tottenham Hotspur	42	16	11	15	87	78	43
9	Millwall	42	17	9	16	61	61	43
10	Charlton Athletic	42	17	9	16	61	66	43
11	Nottingham Forest	42	16	10	16	77	72	42
12	Manchester United	42	17	8	17	71	72	42
13	Preston North End	42	16	10	16	75	77	42
14	Southampton	42	17	7	18	66	77	41
15	Swansea Town	42	16	7	19	73	75	39
16	NOTTS COUNTY	42	13	12	17	75	75	38
17	Chesterfield	42	13	11	18	64	86	37
18	Oldham Athletic	42	13	10	19	62	84	36
19	Burnley	42	13	9	20	59	87	35
20	Port Vale	42	13	7	22	58	89	33
21	Barnsley	42	12	9	21	55	91	33
22	Bristol City	42	6	11	25	39	78	23

Back: Dowsey, Bycroft, Corkhill, HR Smith, Grice, Raven, M Smith. Standing: Andrews, Taylor, Stimpson, Thorpe, Feebery, Jones, Wright. Seated: Murphy, Sheldon, Lawrence, Ferguson, Bisby, Maidment, Lovatt, Coglin, Haden. Front: Mills, Jakeman, Fenner, Keetley, Maw, Hall

1932/33

15th in Division Two

#	Date		Opponent	Score	Scorers	Att	Burgon A	Corkhill WG	Elliott S	Feebery A	Feeney TW	Fenner T	Grice F	Haden S	Hall GW	Jakeman GW	Keetley T	Lawrence E	MacCartney CW	Maidment JHC	Mills PC	Proudfoot J	Rickards T	Smith HR	Smith JW	Stimpson GH	Taylor GT	Tewkesbury KC	Wall TH	Watson J	Watson N
1	Aug	27	LINCOLN CITY	1-1	Mills(p)	20987							8		11	4	9	6			2	10				3	7	1			5
2		29	Bury	1-3	Keetley	8871							5	11	10	2	9	6				8				3	7	1			4
3	Sep	3	West Ham United	1-1	Keetley	10656			8				6	11		2	9				3	10		5			7	1			4
4		10	FULHAM	1-2	Keetley	10168			8				6	11		2	9	4			3	10		5			7	1			
5		17	Chesterfield	0-0		11049			8	3	10		6	11		4	9			1	2			5			7				
6		24	BRADFORD CITY	2-0	Haden, Elliott	13400			8	3	10		6	11		4			9	1	2			5			7				
7	Oct	1	Swansea Town	0-2		9636			8	3	10		6	11		4			9	1	2			5			7				
8		6	BURY	2-2	MacCartney, Feeney	8044	11		8		10			6		4			9	1	2			5		3	7				
9		8	NOTTM. FOREST	2-4	Keetley, Taylor	16732	11							6		10	9			1	2	8		5	4	3	7				
10		15	PORT VALE	5-0	Keetley 2, Feeney, Hall, Haden	9217				8				11	10		9	6		1	2			5	4	3	7				
11		22	Charlton Athletic	3-3	Haden, Fenner, Taylor	10398					8			11	10		9	6		1	2			5	4	3	7				
12		29	STOKE CITY	3-4	Fenner, Keetley, Taylor	11358					8			11	10		9	6		1	2			5	4	3	7				
13	Nov	5	Manchester Utd.	0-2		24178					8			11	10		9	6		1	2			5	4	3	7				
14		12	PLYMOUTH ARGYLE	4-1	Elliott 2, Taylor, Hall	10479			9		8			11	10	3		6		1	2			5			7				4
15		19	Preston North End	0-3		7298			9		8			11	10	3		6		1	2			4			7				5
16		26	OLDHAM ATHLETIC	2-1	Taylor, Hall	8971			9		8	5		11	10			6			3			4	2		7	1			
17	Dec	3	Grimsby Town	1-1	Elliott	6065			9		8	5		11	10			6			3			4	2		7	1			
18		10	BURNLEY	4-2	Fenner 4	8216			9		8	5		11	10			6			3			4	2		7				
19		17	Bradford Park Ave.	4-3	Elliott 3, Hall	8678			9		8			11	10			6		1	3			5	4		7				
20		24	TOTTENHAM HOTSPUR	3-0	Taylor 2, Elliott	16355			9		10	8		11				6		1	3			5	4		7				
21		26	MILLWALL	1-0	Elliott	17627			9		10	8	6	11						1	3			5	4		7				
22		27	Millwall	1-1	Keetley	19958		8			10		6	11			9			1	3			5	4		7				
23		31	Lincoln City	1-1	Haden	9260			9		10	8	6	11						1	3			5	4		7				
24	Jan	7	WEST HAM UNITED	2-0	Smith JW, Haden	11437		10	9			8	6	11						1	3			5	4		7				
25		21	Fulham	4-3	Taylor 2, Keetley, Mills(p)	14795			10			8	6	11			9			1	3			5	4		7				
26	Feb	1	CHESTERFIELD	1-1	Keetley	4799			10			8	6	11			9			1	3			5	4		7				
27		4	Bradford City	2-1	MacCartney, Corkhill	12755		8							10			6	4	9	1	3		5			2	7			
28		11	SWANSEA TOWN	1-2	Haden	12352		8			10			6	11				4	9	1	3		5			2	7			
29		18	Nottm. Forest	0-3		19014			9				8	6	11			10			1	3		5	4		2	7			
30	Mar	4	CHARLTON ATHLETIC	3-2	Pugsley(og), Burgon 2	8696	9		8					6	11			10			1	3		5	4		2	7			
31		11	Stoke City	2-0	MacCartney, Haden	14376					8			6	11				4	9	1	3	10	5			2	7			
32		18	MANCHESTER UTD.	1-0	Keetley	13016					8			6	11		9	4		1	3	10		5			2	7			
33		20	Port Vale	0-4		5682					8			6	11		9	6		1		10		5	4		2	7	3		
34		25	Plymouth Argyle	2-0	Keetley 2	11609		8			10			6	11	6	9	4		1				5			2	7	3		
35	Apr	1	PRESTON NORTH END	0-0		9346		8	10					6	11	4	9	6		1				5			2	7	3		
36		8	Oldham Athletic	0-5		7257			10		8			6	11	4	9	6		1				5			2	7	3		
37		14	Southampton	2-6	Fenner, Taylor	8108						10	8	6	11				9	1	3	4		5			2	7			
38		15	GRIMSBY TOWN	1-3	Keetley	9230			10				8	6	11		4	9		1	3			5			2	7			
39		17	SOUTHAMPTON	1-2	Burgon	7588	10							6	11				9		2	8		5		4	7		1	3	
40		22	Burnley	1-2	Elliott	7665		4	9				8	6	11						3		10	5			2	7		1	
41		29	BRADFORD PARK AVE.	1-4	Keetley	3306		4					8	6	11		9			1	3		10	5			2	7			
42	May	6	Tottenham Hotspur	1-3	Grice	28015		4	9	3			8	6	11								10	5			2	7		1	

	Burgon A	Corkhill WG	Elliott S	Feebery A	Feeney TW	Fenner T	Grice F	Haden S	Hall GW	Jakeman GW	Keetley T	Lawrence E	MacCartney CW	Maidment JHC	Mills PC	Proudfoot J	Rickards T	Smith HR	Smith JW	Stimpson GH	Taylor GT	Tewkesbury KC	Wall TH	Watson J	Watson N
Apps	4	8	26	4	17	22	28	41	12	14	20	24	8	32	36	10	3	33	23	35	42	7	3	5	5
Goals	3	1	11		2	6	1	7	4		15		3		2				1		10				

One own goal

F.A. Cup

			Opponent	Score	Scorer	Att	Burgon A	Corkhill WG	Elliott S	Feebery A	Feeney TW	Fenner T	Grice F	Haden S	Hall GW	Jakeman GW	Keetley T	Lawrence E	MacCartney CW	Maidment JHC	Mills PC	Proudfoot J	Rickards T	Smith HR	Smith JW	Stimpson GH	Taylor GT	Tewkesbury KC	Wall TH	Watson J	Watson N
R3	Jan	14	Tranmere Rovers	1-2	Corkhill	12420		10	9			8	6	11						1	3			5	4		2	7			

		p	w	d	l	f	a	pts
1	Stoke City	42	25	6	11	78	39	56
2	Tottenham Hotspur	42	20	15	7	96	51	55
3	Fulham	42	20	10	12	78	65	50
4	Bury	42	20	9	13	84	59	49
5	Nottingham Forest	42	17	15	10	67	59	49
6	Manchester United	42	15	13	14	71	68	43
7	Millwall	42	16	11	15	59	57	43
8	Bradford Park Ave.	42	17	8	17	77	71	42
9	Preston North End	42	16	10	16	74	70	42
10	Swansea Town	42	19	4	19	50	54	42
11	Bradford City	42	14	13	15	65	61	41
12	Southampton	42	18	5	19	66	66	41
13	Grimsby Town	42	14	13	15	79	84	41
14	Plymouth Argyle	42	16	9	17	63	67	41
15	NOTTS COUNTY	42	15	10	17	67	78	40
16	Oldham Athletic	42	15	8	19	67	80	38
17	Port Vale	42	14	10	18	66	79	38
18	Lincoln City	42	12	13	17	72	87	37
19	Burnley	42	11	14	17	67	79	36
20	West Ham United	42	13	9	20	75	93	35
21	Chesterfield	42	12	10	20	61	84	34
22	Charlton Athletic	42	12	7	23	60	91	31

Back: Feebery, Affleck, Maidment, Mills, JW Smith, Wall, HR Smith, J Watson. Standing: Henshall (sec-manager), A Burgon, Stimpson, Brough, Grice, N Watson, Corkhill, Raven, Mellors (asst-trainer), Banks (trainer). Seated: H Burgon, Lawrence, Proudfoot, Jakeman, Keetley, MacCartney, Elliott, Hall, Haden. Front: Taylor, Fenner, Day, Feeney

1933/34

18th in Division Two

#	Date		Opponent	Score	Scorers	Att
1	Aug	26	Hull City	1-0	Taylor	13441
2	Sep	2	FULHAM	4-1	MacCartney 2, Feebery(p), Fenner	14715
3		4	Lincoln City	1-0	Taylor	8647
4		9	Southampton	2-3	Fenner, MacCartney	12237
5		13	LINCOLN CITY	2-0	Taylor, MacCartney	13709
6		16	BLACKPOOL	1-1	Fenner	18957
7		23	Bradford City	1-3	Fenner	11726
8		30	PORT VALE	3-2	Fenner 2, MacCartney	15364
9	Oct	7	Nottm. Forest	0-2		23828
10		14	Swansea Town	1-1	MacCartney	7715
11		21	GRIMSBY TOWN	1-2	MacCartney	16890
12		28	Bradford Park Ave.	2-3	MacCartney, Taylor	8628
13	Nov	4	PRESTON NORTH END	2-2	Tremelling(og), Mills(p)	11445
14		11	Oldham Athletic	0-2		6578
15		18	BURNLEY	3-1	Lewis 2, Burgon	7938
16		25	Brentford	2-2	MacCartney, Taylor	12110
17	Dec	2	BOLTON WANDERERS	1-2	MacCartney	11279
18		9	Manchester Utd.	2-1	Lewis, Haden	15564
19		16	PLYMOUTH ARGYLE	2-1	Elliott, MacCartney	7590
20		23	West Ham United	3-5	Burgon 2, Elliott	16370
21		25	MILLWALL	0-1		17298
22		26	Millwall	2-3	MacCartney, Hancock(og)	10172
23		30	HULL CITY	0-0		9248
24	Jan	1	Bury	1-3	Lewis	9886
25		6	Fulham	0-3		15023
26		20	SOUTHAMPTON	2-2	Cresswell, Lawrence	10942
27	Feb	3	BRADFORD CITY	3-0	Riley 2, Burgon	10773
28		7	Blackpool	1-2	Barley	10188
29		10	Port Vale	0-0		10645
30		17	NOTTM. FOREST	1-0	Cresswell	19643
31		24	SWANSEA TOWN	1-1	Cresswell	10828
32	Mar	3	Grimsby Town	2-2	Elliott, Riley	10918
33		17	Preston North End	0-2		10797
34		24	OLDHAM ATHLETIC	1-1	Cresswell	7897
35		30	BURY	2-1	MacCartney 2	13382
36		31	Burnley	0-1		13971
37	Apr	7	BRENTFORD	1-2	MacCartney	11657
38		14	Bolton Wanderers	0-1		11652
39		16	BRADFORD PARK AVE.	1-0	Elliott	9141
40		21	MANCHESTER UTD.	0-0		9645
41		28	Plymouth Argyle	0-1		7465
42	May	5	WEST HAM UNITED	1-2	Lewis	4436

Game 37: Benefit for Haden

F.A. Cup

R3	Jan	13	Swansea Town	0-1		13000

Back: Mellors (asst trainer), Lane, Feebery, Affleck, Hammond, Mills, Smith, Watson, A Burgon, Banks (trainer). Standing: Jennings (coach), Stimpson, Clarke, Corkhill, Grice, Elliott, Walker, Haden, Lawrence, Henshall (sec/mgr). Seated: Taylor, Jones, Fenner, H Burgon, MacCartney, Riley, Rickards, Lewis, Caiels. Front: Rowley, McAnish

Division Two Final Table

		p	w	d	l	f	a	pts
1	Grimsby Town	42	27	5	10	103	59	59
2	Preston North End	42	23	6	13	71	52	52
3	Bolton Wanderers	42	21	9	12	79	55	51
4	Brentford	42	22	7	13	85	60	51
5	Bradford Park Ave.	42	23	3	16	86	67	49
6	Bradford City	42	20	6	16	73	67	46
7	West Ham United	42	17	11	14	78	70	45
8	Port Vale	42	19	7	16	60	55	45
9	Oldham Athletic	42	17	10	15	72	60	44
10	Plymouth Argyle	42	15	13	14	69	70	43
11	Blackpool	42	15	13	14	62	64	43
12	Bury	42	17	9	16	70	73	43
13	Burnley	42	18	6	18	60	72	42
14	Southampton	42	15	8	19	54	58	38
15	Hull City	42	13	12	17	52	68	38
16	Fulham	42	15	7	20	48	67	37
17	Nottingham Forest	42	13	9	20	73	74	35
18	NOTTS COUNTY	42	12	11	19	53	62	35
19	Swansea Town	42	10	15	17	51	60	35
20	Manchester United	42	14	6	22	59	85	34
21	Millwall	42	11	11	20	39	68	33
22	Lincoln City	42	9	8	25	44	75	26

1934/35

22nd in Division Two (Relegated)

#		Date	Opponent	Score	Scorers	Att	Bramham A	Clarke GW	Corkhill WG	Fallon WJ	Feebery A	Green RCG	Grice F	Haden S	Higgins A	Hoult A	Jones F	Julian W	King TP	Knox T	Lawrence E	Lewis H	MacCartney CW	McGrath James	Mills PC	Poskett TW	Rankin JP	Rickards T	Shaw F	Smith HR	Stabb GH	Steele E	Walker G
1	Aug	25	Swansea Town	1-2	McGrath	11759		6		3					11					1	4	10	9	7	2		8						5
2		27	Barnsley	1-1	Clarke	10338		6		3					11					1	4	10	9	7	2		8						5
3	Sep	1	BURNLEY	1-0	McGrath	15363		6		3					11					1	4	10	9	7	2		8						5
4		3	BARNSLEY	1-4	MacCartney	8662		6		3					11					1	4		9	7	2		10	8					5
5		8	Oldham Athletic	0-1		7350			4	3					11					1	6		9	7	2		10	8					5
6		15	BOLTON WANDERERS	0-2		13783			4	11	3						9			1	6			7	2		10	8					5
7		22	Southampton	1-1	Rickards	4850			4	11	3									1	6	8		7	2		10	9					5
8		29	NOTTM. FOREST	3-5	McGrath, Higgins, Lewis	15254			4	11	3				8					1	6	10		7	2			9					5
9	Oct	6	BRADFORD CITY	2-3	Lawrence(p), Rankin	13187			4		3				8					1	6	11		7			10	9		5			2
10		13	Sheffield United	0-3		15173			4		3			10	8		2				6	11	9	7		1							5
11		20	Brentford	1-4	Higgins	15313			7	11	3			10	8						6		9		2	1				4			5
12		27	FULHAM	1-1	Fallon	11643			4	11	3			10	8						6				2	1						9	7	5
13	Nov	3	Bradford Park Ave.	0-0		6581			4	11	3			10	8						6				2	1						9	7	5
14		10	PLYMOUTH ARGYLE	1-3	Stabb	10927			4	11	3			10	8						6				2	1						9	7	5
15		17	Norwich City	2-7	Lewis, Steele	11297		4			3		5	11	8						6	10			2	1						9	7	
16		24	NEWCASTLE UNITED	0-1		9616		4			3										6	10		11	2	1						9	7	5
17	Dec	1	West Ham United	0-4		18390		4			3			10	11						6	8			2	1						9	7	5
18		8	BLACKPOOL	3-2	Stabb 2, Steele	10067		4			3			10	11					1	6				2		8					9	7	5
19		15	Bury	0-1		8346		4			3			10	11					1	6				2		8					9	7	5
20		22	HULL CITY	1-1	Steele	5673		4		11	3			6						1		10			2		8					9	7	5
21		25	Manchester Utd.	1-2	Steele	32965		4		11	3			10						1	6				2		8					9	7	5
22		26	MANCHESTER UTD.	1-0	Stabb	24599		4		11	3			10						1	6				2		8					9	7	5
23		29	SWANSEA TOWN	4-0	Shaw 3, Grice	13221		4		11	3			10						1	6				2					8		9	7	5
24	Jan	5	Burnley	0-4		10409		4		11	3			10						1	6				2					8		9	7	5
25		19	OLDHAM ATHLETIC	2-1	Stabb, Shaw	10984		4		11	3									1	6				2					8	10	9	7	5
26		30	Bolton Wanderers	1-5	Steele	8220		4		11	3									1	6				2					8	10	9	7	5
27	Feb	2	SOUTHAMPTON	3-1	Shaw 3	9240		4			3			6						1			9		2					8	10		7	5
28		9	Nottm. Forest	3-2	Shaw, Bramham 2	19197	9	4			3			6						1					2					8	10	11	7	5
29		16	Bradford City	0-2		2611	9	4			3			6						1					2					8	10	11	7	5
30		23	SHEFFIELD UNITED	0-1		11724	9	4			3	11	6							1					2					8	10		7	5
31	Mar	2	BRENTFORD	0-1		10252					3	11	6							1	4				2		8				10	9	7	5
32		9	Fulham	0-7		8634					3	11	6							1	4				2		8				10	9	7	5
33		16	BRADFORD PARK AVE.	1-1	Steele	9199		4				11	6				2								3	1		8	10	5	9	7	
34		23	Plymouth Argyle	0-4		8691		4				11	6	10			2	1							3			8	9			7	5
35		30	NORWICH CITY	1-0	Bramham	7259	9	4		3		11	6	10				1							2				8			7	5
36	Apr	6	Newcastle United	1-1	Bramham	12394	9	4		3		11	6	10				1							2				8			7	5
37		13	WEST HAM UNITED	0-2		9721	9	4		3		11	6	10				1							2				8	5		7	
38		19	Port Vale	3-5	Rankin, Corkhill, Steele	9010	9		4	3		11	6					1							2		10		8	5		7	
39		20	Blackpool	1-3	Stabb	15434			4	3		11	6	10				1							2				8	5	9	7	
40		22	PORT VALE	3-2	Bramham 2, Shaw	6765	9		4	3		11	6					1							2		10		8	5		7	
41		27	BURY	1-2	Shaw	3448	9		4			11	6		7		3								2	1		8	10	5			
42	May	4	Hull City	1-5	Shaw	2721			4	3		11	6					1							2		10		8	5	9	7	
					Apps		9	8	32	14	39	13	24	19	10	1	1	2	2	32	27	11	8	11	40	10	23	9	20	9	24	30	34
					Goals		6	1	1	1			1		2						1	2	1	3			2	1	11		6	7	

F.A. Cup

		Date	Opponent	Score		Att	Bramham A	Clarke GW	Corkhill WG	Fallon WJ	Feebery A	Green RCG	Grice F	Haden S	Higgins A	Hoult A	Jones F	Julian W	King TP	Knox T	Lawrence E	Lewis H	MacCartney CW	McGrath James	Mills PC	Poskett TW	Rankin JP	Rickards T	Shaw F	Smith HR	Stabb GH	Steele E	Walker G
R3	Jan	12	Wolverhampton Wand.	0-4		26754			4	11	3									1	6				2		10		8		9	7	5

		P	W	D	L	F	A	Pts
1	Brentford	42	26	9	7	93	48	61
2	Bolton Wanderers	42	26	4	12	96	48	56
3	West Ham United	42	26	4	12	80	63	56
4	Blackpool	42	21	11	10	79	57	53
5	Manchester United	42	23	4	15	76	55	50
6	Newcastle United	42	22	4	16	89	68	48
7	Fulham	42	17	12	13	76	56	46
8	Plymouth Argyle	42	19	8	15	75	64	46
9	Nottingham Forest	42	17	8	17	76	70	42
10	Bury	42	19	4	19	62	73	42
11	Sheffield United	42	16	9	17	79	70	41
12	Burnley	42	16	9	17	63	73	41
13	Hull City	42	16	8	18	63	74	40
14	Norwich City	42	14	11	17	71	61	39
15	Bradford Park Ave.	42	11	16	15	55	63	38
16	Barnsley	42	13	12	17	60	83	38
17	Swansea Town	42	14	8	20	56	67	36
18	Port Vale	42	11	12	19	55	74	34
19	Southampton	42	11	12	19	46	75	34
20	Bradford City	42	12	8	22	50	68	32
21	Oldham Athletic	42	10	6	26	56	95	26
22	NOTTS COUNTY	42	9	7	26	46	97	25

Back: Lawrence, Feebery, Knox, Watson, Poskett, H Smith, Julian, B Jones. Centre: Fallon, Stimpson, Mills, Walker, Grice, M Jones, Corkhill, F Jones, Bramham. Front: McGrath, Rankin, Rickards, MacCartney, C Jones (manager), Lewis, Hoult, Haden, Clarke

1935/36

9th in Division Three (South)

							Blyth G	Bramham A	Chandler A	Clarke GW	Corkhill WG	Fallon WJ	Featherby L	Feebery A	Green RCG	Grice F	Haden S	Hoult A	Julian W	Knox T	Lawrence E	Meads T	Millington J	Mills PC	Notley W	Rankin JP	Rickards T	Shaw F	Steele E	Walker G
1	Aug	31	Bristol Rovers	0-0		15197	1		9	4		8	3	10						6	11	2					7	5
2	Sep	4	GILLINGHAM	3-3	Green, Corkhill, Chandler	9863	1		9	4		8	3	10		7				6	11	2						5
3		7	CLAPTON ORIENT	2-0	Rickards, Chandler	11966	1		9	4			3	10		7				6	11	2			8			5
4		11	Gillingham	0-0		5162	1		9	4			3	10	6						11	2			8		7	5
5		14	Southend United	0-0		11948	1		9	4			3	10						6	11	2			8		7	5
6		18	BOURNEMOUTH	1-3	Mills(p)	7735	1		9	4			3	10						6	11	2			8		7	5
7		21	NORTHAMPTON T	3-0	Bramham 2, Corkhill	8929	1	9		4			3	11	10	7				6		2			8			5
8		28	Crystal Palace	0-0		16153	1	9		4			3	11	6	7				10		2			8			5
9	Oct	5	READING	1-3	Mills(p)	10875	1	9		4			3	11		7				6		2			8	10		5
10		12	Cardiff City	2-3	Meads, Chandler	11458	1		9	4		11	3		6	7				10		2			8			5
11		19	QUEENS PARK RANGERS	3-0	Notley 2, Meads	7369	1			5	4	11	3		6	7				10		2	9		8			
12		26	Brighton & Hove Alb.	1-5	Notley	8158	1			5	4	11	3		6		7			10		2	9		8			
13	Nov	2	EXETER CITY	3-1	Shaw, Notley, Lawton(og)	7302				5	4	11	3	10	6			1				2	9			8	7	
14		9	Bristol City	1-1	Notley	12343				5	4	11	3	10	6			1				2	9			8	7	
15		16	COVENTRY CITY	2-1	Fallon, Green	17902				5	4	11	3	10	6			1				2	9			8	7	
16		23	Swindon Town	1-2	Notley	8233				5	4	11	3	10	6			1				2	9			8	7	
17	Dec	7	Torquay United	1-0	Rickards	3817				5	4	11	3		6			1				2	9	10	8		7	
18		18	MILLWALL	0-0		2325				5	4	11	3	10	6			1				2	9		8		7	
19		25	LUTON TOWN	0-3		12186				5		11	3		6			1	4			2	9	10	8		7	
20		26	Luton Town	0-1		18100			9		4	11	3	10			7	1		6		2			8			5
21		28	BRISTOL ROVERS	6-0	Green 2, Chandler 2, Rickards, McLean(og)	8669			9		4	11	3	10			7	1		6		2			8			5
22	Jan	4	Clapton Orient	2-0	Chandler, Rickards	9003			9		4	11	3	10			7	1		6		2			8			5
23		18	SOUTHEND UNITED	1-2	Rickards	6584					4	11	3	10	6			1				2	9		8		7	5
24		25	Northampton T	1-3	Shaw	6285			9		4	11	10	3		6		1				2			8	7		5
25	Feb	1	CRYSTAL PALACE	3-1	Green, Bramham, Mills(p)	8385		9			4	11			6			1				2			8	7		5
26		8	Reading	1-3	Fallon	7811		9			4	11	3	10	6			1				2			8	7		5
27		12	ALDERSHOT	1-2	Fallon	2817		9			4	11	3		6			1		10		2			8	7		5
28		15	CARDIFF CITY	2-0	Fallon, Shaw	4639				5	4	11	3		6	7		1				2	9		8	10		
29		22	Queens Park Rangers	2-2	Fallon, Steele	6497				5	4	11	3		6			1				2	9		8	10	7	
30		27	Newport County	2-1	Shaw, Corkhill	2818				5	4	11	3		6			1				2	9		8	10	7	
31		29	BRISTOL CITY	1-1	Mills(p)	3154				5	4	11	3	9	6			1				2			8	10	7	
32	Mar	7	Millwall	1-2	Shaw	8604				5	4	11	3		6			1				2	9		8	10	7	
33		14	BRIGHTON & HOVE ALB.	1-1	Rickards	5263		9		5	4	11			6				2	1		3			8	10	7	
34		21	Coventry City	1-5	Steele	17145				5	4	11	3	10						1	6	2			8	9	7	
35		28	SWINDON TOWN	0-0		4798				4	8	11	3							1	6	2			9	10	7	5
36	Apr	4	Aldershot	1-3	Shaw	3321				5	4	11	3							1	6	2	9		8	10	7	
37		10	Watford	2-1	Rickards, Bramham	10191	1	9			4	11	3								6	2			8	10	7	5
38		11	TORQUAY UNITED	1-0	Notley	4445	1				4	11	3								6	2	9		8	10	7	5
39		13	WATFORD	0-2		6343	1				4	11	3								6	2	9		8	10	7	5
40		18	Exeter City	0-0		3888	1					11	3							4	6	2	9		8	10	7	5
41		25	NEWPORT COUNTY	6-2	Notley 2, Walker, Shaw, Millington, Rickards	2180	1					11	3							4	6	7	2	9	8	10		5
42	May	2	Bournemouth	1-0	Rickards	4872	1						3	11						4	6	7	2	9	8	10		5

	Blyth G	Bramham A	Chandler A	Clarke GW	Corkhill WG	Fallon WJ	Featherby L	Feebery A	Green RCG	Grice F	Haden S	Hoult A	Julian W	Knox T	Lawrence E	Meads T	Millington J	Mills PC	Notley W	Rankin JP	Rickards T	Shaw F	Steele E	Walker G
Apps	18	9	10	18	38	32	3	41	23	24	5	7	1	24	10	18	8	42	20	2	33	27	24	25
Goals		4	6		3	5			5						2	1	4	9	9		9	7	2	1

Two own goals

F.A. Cup

R1	Nov	30	Grantham	2-0	Fallon, Green	8000				5	4	11		3	10	6				1			2	9		8		7		
R2	Dec	14	TORQUAY UNITED	3-0	Fallon, Rickards, Hunt(og)	13224				5	4	11		3	10	6				1			2	9		8		7		
R3	Jan	11	TRANMERE ROVERS	0-0		25153			9		4	11		3	10					1	6		2	7		8				5
rep		15	Tranmere Rovers	3-4	Chandler, Rickards, Steele	15109			9		4	11		3	10					1	6		2			8		7	5

Division Three (South) Cup

R1	Sep	25	WATFORD	2-1	Green, Chandler	3000	1		9		4		10	3	11	6							2			8		7	5
R2	Oct	23	Swindon Town	3-4	Bramham, Shaw, Fallon	1814		9		5		11		5		6			7	1	4	10	2			8			

		p	w	d	l	f	a	pts
1	Coventry City	42	24	9	9	102	45	57
2	Luton Town	42	22	12	8	81	45	56
3	Reading	42	26	2	14	87	62	54
4	Queen's Park Rgs.	42	22	9	11	84	53	53
5	Watford	42	20	9	13	80	54	49
6	Crystal Palace	42	22	5	15	96	74	49
7	Brighton & Hove A.	42	18	8	16	70	63	44
8	Bournemouth	42	16	11	15	60	56	43
9	NOTTS COUNTY	42	15	12	15	60	57	42
10	Torquay United	42	16	9	17	62	62	41
11	Aldershot	42	14	12	16	53	61	40
12	Millwall	42	14	12	16	58	71	40
13	Bristol City	42	15	10	17	48	59	40
14	Clapton Orient	42	16	6	20	55	61	38
15	Northampton Town	42	15	8	19	62	90	38
16	Gillingham	42	14	9	19	66	77	37
17	Bristol Rovers	42	14	9	19	69	95	37
18	Southend United	42	13	10	19	61	62	36
19	Swindon Town	42	14	8	20	64	73	36
20	Cardiff City	42	13	10	19	60	73	36
21	Newport County	42	11	9	22	60	111	31
22	Exeter City	42	8	11	23	59	93	27

Back: Feebery, Grice, Knox, Blyth, Mills, Chandler. Standing: Banks (ass. trainer), Walker, Clarke, Corkhill, Lawrence, Bramham, Featherby, Seddon (trainer). Seated: Meads, Gillon, Millington, Smith (sec/mgr), Barnes (chairman), Godfrey (treasurer), Rickards, Haden, Fallon. Front: Hoult, Green, Steele, Julian

1936/37

2nd in Division Three (South)

#	Date		Opponent	Score	Scorers	Att	Blyth G	Chalmers W	Cooper S	Corkhill WG	Fallon WJ	Feebery A	Ferguson C	Gallacher HK	Hatton C	Julian W	Kavanagh T	Mardon HJ	McLenahan H	Millington J	Mills PC	Moulson C	Rickards T	Shaw F	Smith, James	Vasey RH	Wyness G
1	Aug	29	EXETER CITY	3-1	Shaw, Ferguson 2	10216	1	8		4	11	3	7								2			10	9	6	5
2	Sep	2	Crystal Palace	2-1	Fallon, Smith	11740	1	8		4	11	3	7								2			10	9	6	5
3		5	Reading	1-4	Shaw	11189	1	8		4	11	3	7								2			10	9	6	5
4		7	CRYSTAL PALACE	0-1		7042	1			4	11		7			3	6				2		8	10	9		5
5		12	QUEENS PARK RANGERS	1-2	Mills(p)	5013	1			4	11	3					6	9		7	2		8	10			5
6		19	Bristol City	1-1	Mills(p)	10330	1	8		4	11	3						9		7	2		10			6	5
7		26	TORQUAY UNITED	2-0	Chalmers, Fallon	16021	1	8		4	11	3		9						7	2			10		6	5
8	Oct	1	WALSALL	3-3	Gallacher 2, Mills(p)	10215	1	8				3		9						11	2	5	7	10		6	4
9		3	Bournemouth	0-1		11974	1	8		4	11	3		9							2	5	7	10		6	
10		10	Clapton Orient	1-1	Fallon	10467	1	8		4	11	3		9		2				7		5		10		6	
11		17	NORTHAMPTON T	3-2	Gallacher 3(1p)	14557	1	8		4	11	3	10	9							2	5	7			6	
12		24	Bristol Rovers	3-2	Gallacher 2, Vasey	13187	1	8		4	11	3	10	9							2	5	7			6	
13		31	MILLWALL	1-1	Ferguson	14195	1	8		4	11	3	10	9							2	5	7			6	
14	Nov	7	Swindon Town	2-2	Mardon, Ferguson	10410	1			4	11	3	10	9				8			2	5	7			6	
15		14	ALDERSHOT	3-0	Gallacher(p), Rickards, Corkhill	13360	1	8		4	11	3	10	9							2	5	7			6	
16		21	Gillingham	0-3		12215	1	8		4	11	3	10	9							2	5	7			6	
17	Dec	5	Southend United	3-2	Chalmers, Rickards, Corkhill	6838	1	8		4	11	3	10				6	9			2	5	7				
18		12	WATFORD	2-1	Gallacher 2	8187	1	8		4	11	3	10	9			6				2	5	7				
19		19	Brighton & Hove Alb.	2-2	Ferguson, Gallacher	10989	1	8		4	11	3	10	9			6				2	5	7				
20		25	Luton Town	1-2	Ferguson	17569	1	8		4	11	3	10	9			6		5		2		7				
21		26	Exeter City	3-1	Fallon, Chalmers, Ferguson	11679	1	8		4	11	3	10				9		5		2		7			6	
22		28	LUTON TOWN	2-1	Chalmers, Mardon	16987	1	8		4	11	3		9			10	5			2		7			6	
23	Jan	2	READING	1-0	Mardon	15484	1	8		4	11	3		9			10	5			2		7				6
24		9	Queens Park Rangers	2-0	Chalmers, Mardon	14938	1	8		4	11	3		9			10	6			2	5	7				
25		16	NEWPORT COUNTY	3-1	Fallon, Gallacher 2	10914	1	8		4	11	3		9			10	6			2	5	7				
26		23	BRISTOL CITY	1-0	Rickards	9033	1	8		4	11	3		9			10				2	5	7			6	
27		30	Torquay United	2-2	Gallacher(p), Rickards	2458	1	8		4	11	3	10	9							2	5	7			6	
28	Feb	6	BOURNEMOUTH	4-3	Chalmers 3, Gallacher	17695	1	8		4	11	3	10	9							2	5	7			6	
29		13	CLAPTON ORIENT	0-0		14316	1	8		4	11	3	10	9					6		2	5	7				
30		20	Northampton T	1-1	Hatton	18435	1			4	11	3		9	10		8	6			2	5	7				
31		27	BRISTOL ROVERS	4-3	Millington, Gallacher 3	13648	1	8		4	7	3		9			10			11	2	5				6	
32	Mar	8	Millwall	0-0		8644	1	8		4	7	3		9			10			11	2	5				6	
33		13	SWINDON TOWN	3-2	Gallacher, Cooper 2	16531	1	8	10	4	11	3		9							2	5	7			6	
34		20	Aldershot	1-0	Fallon	5613	1	8	10	4	11	3		9	7			5			2	6					
35		26	CARDIFF CITY	4-0	Gallacher 2, Chalmers, Ferguson	17664	1	8		4	11	3	10	9	7			5			2	6					
36		27	GILLINGHAM	2-0	Gallacher 2(1p)	20821	1	8		4	11	3	10	9				5			2	6	7				
37		29	Cardiff City	2-0	Rickards, Gallacher	20245	1	8		4	11	3	10	9				5			2	6	7				
38	Apr	3	Newport County	0-2		12324	1	8		4	11		10	9				5			2	3	7			6	
39		10	SOUTHEND UNITED	2-1	Mardon, Mills	15295	1	8	10	4	11					2		9	5		3	6	7				
40		17	Watford	2-0	Rickards 2	10586	1	8	10	4	11				7	2		5			3	6	9				
41		24	BRIGHTON & HOVE ALB.	0-1		29516	1	8	10	4	11	3		9				5			2	6	7				
42	May	1	Walsall	1-2	Gallacher	5902	1	8	10	4	11	3		9				5			2	6	7				
						Apps	42	38	6	41	41	38	22	32	4	8	2	14	17	7	41	31	33	9	4	22	10
						Goals		9	2	2	6		8	25	1			5		1	4		7	2	1	1	

F.A. Cup

R1	Nov	28	Gateshead	0-2		11456	1			4	11	3	10	9				8			2	5	7			6	

Division Three (South) Cup

R2	Oct	21	READING	3-2	Mardon 2, Rickards	3212	1	8			11					2	4	9			3	5	7	10		6	
R3	Nov	11	Luton Town	4-2	Mardon 2, Ferguson 2	3000	1	8		4	11	3	10					9			2	5	7			6	
SF	Apr	26	WATFORD	1-1	Morgan (og)	1300	1	8		4			10	9		2			5	11	3		7			6	

SF replay held over to season 1937/38

		p	w	d	l	f	a	pts
1	Luton Town	42	27	4	11	103	53	58
2	NOTTS COUNTY	42	23	10	9	74	52	56
3	Brighton & Hove A.	42	24	5	13	74	43	53
4	Watford	42	19	11	12	85	60	49
5	Reading	42	19	11	12	76	60	49
6	Bournemouth	42	20	9	13	65	59	49
7	Northampton Town	42	20	6	16	85	68	46
8	Millwall	42	18	10	14	64	54	46
9	Queen's Park Rgs.	42	18	9	15	73	52	45
10	Southend United	42	17	11	14	78	67	45
11	Gillingham	42	18	8	16	52	66	44
12	Clapton Orient	42	14	15	13	52	52	43
13	Swindon Town	42	14	11	17	75	73	39
14	Crystal Palace	42	13	12	17	62	61	38
15	Bristol Rovers	42	16	4	22	71	80	36
16	Bristol City	42	15	6	21	58	70	36
17	Walsall	42	13	10	19	63	85	36
18	Cardiff City	42	14	7	21	54	87	35
19	Newport County	42	12	10	20	67	98	34
20	Torquay United	42	11	10	21	57	80	32
21	Exeter City	42	10	12	20	59	88	32
22	Aldershot	42	7	9	26	50	89	23

Back: Wyness, Kavanagh, Chalmers, Blyth, Shaw, Vasey, Millington. Standing: Ratcliffe (trainer), Julian, Mills, Feebery, Corkhill, Lowery, Walker, Rickards, Haden (asst. trainer). Seated: J Smith, P Smith (sec/mgr), Hobson and Walker (directors), Barnes (chairman), Towers and Phillip (directors), Fallon. Front: Ferguson, Taylor, Stevens, Flewitt, Mardon

1937/38

11th in Division Three (South)

						Beech A	Blyth G	Brannon MK	Burditt K	Chalmers W	Clayton S	Cooper S	Corkhill WG	Dean WR	Fallon WJ	Feebery A	Gallacher HK	Gallagher J	Halton R	Hatton C	Hindmarsh JS	Houghton R	Julian W	Mardon HJ	McLenahan H	Mills PC	Moulson C	Rickards T	Riley J	Roy JR	Vasey RH
1	Aug	28	SWINDON TOWN	3-0	Fallon, Corkhill, Chalmers	17313	6	1			8		10	4		11	3	9		7							5	2				
2	Sep	1	Exeter City	3-0	Gallacher, Corkhill, Angus(og)	8799	6	1			8		10	4		11	3	9		7							5	2				
3		4	Aldershot	1-0	Chalmers	7513	6	1			8			4		11	3	10		7					9			5	2				
4		8	EXETER CITY	0-0		14179	6	1			8			4		11	3	9		7	10							5	2				
5		11	MILLWALL	1-1	Mardon	15637	6	1				8	11	4			3				10				9	5			2		7		
6		18	Reading	2-0	Gallacher 2(1p)	14690	6	1			8		10	4		11	3	9										5	2		7		
7		22	BRISTOL CITY	2-0	Gallacher, Cooper	10937	6	1			8		10	4		11	3	9										5	2		7		
8		25	CRYSTAL PALACE	0-1		18164	6	1			8		10	4		11	3	9										5	2		7		
9	Oct	2	Cardiff City	2-2	Rickards, McLenahan	35468		1					10	4		11	3		6		8					9	5	2		7		
10		7	MANSFIELD TOWN	2-0	Fallon, Mardon	13632		1			8		10	4		11	3		6						9			5	2		7		
11		9	Newport County	0-3		11574	6	1			8		10	4		11	3							2	9	5					7		
12		16	BOURNEMOUTH	1-2	Mardon	15218		1						4		11	3	9		8					10	5	2			7		6
13		23	Brighton & Hove Alb.	1-0	Marriott(og)	9231		1			8			4						11	10				9	5	2	3		7		6
14		30	QUEENS PARK RANGERS	2-2	Chalmers, Hatton	11705		1			8			4		11					10				9	5	2	3		7		6
15	Nov	6	Southend United	1-2	Fallon	8674		1						4		11				7	10					5	2	3	9			6
16		13	CLAPTON ORIENT	1-0	Chalmers	11030	10	1			8			4		11		9	5	7	6						2	3				
17		20	Torquay United	3-0	Gallacher 2, Hatton	4286		1			8			4		11		9	5	7	6						2	3	10			
18	Dec	4	Bristol Rovers	1-1	O'Mahoney(og)	5572		1			8			4		11		9	5	7	6						2	3	10			
19		11	NORTHAMPTON T	5-0	*See below	9988		1					10	8		11		9	5							6	2	3	7			
20		18	Walsall	0-1		4483		1					10	8		11		9	5							6	2	3	7			
21		27	GILLINGHAM	1-0	Rickards	23337		1					10	8		11			5							6	2	3	7	9		
22	Jan	1	Swindon Town	0-1		9897		1					10	8		11			5							6	2	3	7	9		
23		15	ALDERSHOT	1-0	Chalmers	8125		1					10	8		11		9		6						5	2	3	7			
24		24	Millwall	0-5		12521	8	1						4		11		9		10	6					5	2	3	7			
25		29	READING	2-1	Hatton, Fallon	11046			1	9	8			4		11				10	6					5	2	3	7			
26	Feb	5	Crystal Palace	1-3	Fallon	16244		1		8	7					11			5	10	4					6	2	3		9		
27		12	CARDIFF CITY	2-0	Rickards, Fallon	13278		1		9	10	8		4		11					6					5	2	3	7			
28		19	NEWPORT COUNTY	1-1	Rickards	12843		1		8		7		4		11					10	6				5	2	3	9			
29		26	Bournemouth	1-1	Fallon	8599		1			8			4		11					10	6	7			5	2	3	9			
30	Mar	5	BRIGHTON & HOVE ALB.	0-3		14816		1			8			4		11	3				6	7				2	5	10	9			
31		12	Queens Park Rangers	1-2	Hatton	19078		1			8			4	9	11					10	6				5	2	3	7			
32		16	Gillingham	1-2	Chalmers	3949		1			7	8		4	9				6		10					5	2	3			11	
33		19	SOUTHEND UNITED	0-2		12878		1					8	4	9						10					5	2	3	7		11	6
34		26	Clapton Orient	0-2		7483		1											5		6						2	3		9	11	
35	Apr	2	TORQUAY UNITED	0-0		6470		1			9	10	8	11	4				5		6	2						3			7	
36		9	Mansfield Town	2-1	Hatton, Gallagher	11190		1					8	11	4		3		9		10	6				2	5				7	
37		15	Watford	0-2		14984		1				10	8	11	4		3		9		6					2	5				7	
38		16	BRISTOL ROVERS	1-1	Cooper	7215		1					8	10	4		3		9		6					2	5		7		11	
39		18	WATFORD	1-2	Gallagher	8789		1					8	10	4				9		6		2			3	5		7		11	
40		23	Northampton T	0-2		11175	6	1						10	4		3		9	8						2	5		7		11	
41		30	WALSALL	3-1	Hatton 2, Mills(p)	2828	6	1					8	11	4		3				10	7				2	5		9			
42	May	7	Bristol City	1-3	Riley(p)	13781		1			10			11	4		3		5			7				2	6	8	9			

Scorers in game 19: Chalmers 2, Richards, Gallacher, Fallon

	Apps	13	39	3	12	27	15	17	41	3	29	19	13	21	6	21	18	4	3	8	29	40	30	30	7	9	5
	Goals					8		2	2		8		7	2	7					3	1	1		5	1			

Three own goals

F.A. Cup

R3	Jan	8	Aldershot	3-1	Chalmers, Gallagher, Rickards	9000		1					10	8		4		11		9						6				5	2	3	7			
R4		22	Huddersfield Town	0-1		29480		1						8		4		11		9	10					6				5	2	3	7			

Division Three (South) Cup

1936/37 Semi-final replay

| Sep | 13 | Watford | 3-8 | Mardon, Halton, Rickards | 500 | | 1 | | | | | | | | | | | 3 | 7 | 10 | 4 | 11 | 2 | 9 | | | | 8 | | | | | |

Also played: D Roberts (5), S Haden (6)

1937/38 Competition

| R2 | Nov | 10 | WATFORD | 0-2 | | 1000 | 10 | | 1 | | 8 | | | 4 | | | | | 11 | | 6 | 7 | | | | 9 | 5 | 2 | 3 | | | |

	p	w	d	l	f	a	pts
1 Millwall	42	23	10	9	83	37	56
2 Bristol City	42	21	13	8	68	40	55
3 Queen's Park Rgs.	42	22	9	11	80	47	53
4 Watford	42	21	11	10	73	43	53
5 Brighton & Hove A.	42	21	9	12	64	44	51
6 Reading	42	20	11	11	71	63	51
7 Crystal Palace	42	18	12	12	67	47	48
8 Swindon Town	42	17	10	15	49	49	44
9 Northampton Town	42	17	9	16	51	57	43
10 Cardiff City	42	15	12	15	67	54	42
11 NOTTS COUNTY	42	16	9	17	50	50	41
12 Southend United	42	15	10	17	70	68	40
13 Bournemouth	42	14	12	16	56	57	40
14 Mansfield Town	42	15	9	18	62	67	39
15 Bristol Rovers	42	13	13	16	46	61	39
16 Newport County	42	11	16	15	43	52	38
17 Exeter City	42	13	12	17	57	70	38
18 Aldershot	42	15	5	22	39	59	35
19 Clapton Orient	42	13	7	22	42	61	33
20 Torquay United	42	9	12	21	38	73	30
21 Walsall	42	11	7	24	52	88	29
22 Gillingham	42	10	6	26	36	77	26

Back: Rickards, Feebery, McLenahan, Fallon, Cooper, Vasey, Cottam. Standing: Ratcliffe (trainer), Halton, Moulson, Corkhill, Brannon, Blyth, Mills, Chalmers, Roberts, Haden (ass. trainer). Steated: Mardon, H Gallacher, Miller (director), Barnes (chairman), Towers (director), Beech, Julian. Front: Hatton, Hindmarsh, Stevenson, R Houghton

1938/39

11th in Division Three (South)

#		Date	Opponent	Score	Scorers	Att	Blood JF	Burditt K	Clayton S	Cooper S	Coulston W	Dean WR	Dowall W	Feebery A	Flower T	Gallagher J	Gaughran BM	Hatton C	Hindmarsh JS	Houghton R	Martin DK	McLenahan H	Mills PC	Moulson C	Protheroe S	Read CW	Roy JR	Taylor GA	Taylor T	Towler BE	Watson JB	Wyllie J	Young A
1	Aug	27	Swindon Town	1-4	Gaughran	13370		6							1		9					5	2	3	11	10	7				8		4
2		31	CRYSTAL PALACE	0-1		10434		6				9			1			7				5	2	3		10	11				8		4
3	Sep	3	TORQUAY UNITED	5-1	Dean 2, Watson 2, Head(og)	7698				11		9		3	1			10	4			5	2			6	7				8		
4		7	Bristol City	1-2	Cooper	17038				11		9		3	1			10	4			5	2			6	7				8		
5		10	Clapton Orient	1-1	Hatton	8573								3	1		9	10	4	7		5	2			6	11				8		
6		17	NEWPORT COUNTY	2-0	Dean, Cooper	10834				10		9		3	1			7	4			5	2		11	6					8		
7		24	Northampton T	1-2	Cooper	13949				10		9		3	1			7	4			5	2			6				11	8		
8	Oct	1	READING	2-0	Watson, Towler	10550			8	10				3	1			7	4			5	2			6				11	9		
9		8	ALDERSHOT	1-1	Cooper	13334			8	10				3	1			7	4				2	5		6				11	9		
10		15	Bristol Rovers	0-0		7872			8	10				3	1			7	4				2	5		6				11	9		
11		22	IPSWICH TOWN	2-1	Cooper, Towler	9918			8	10				3	1			7	4				2	5						11	9	6	
12		29	Bournemouth	2-3	Hatton, Towler	7585		6		10				3	1			8	4				2	5			7			11	9		
13	Nov	5	WALSALL	0-0		8811				10		9		3	1				4	7			2	5		6				11	8		
14		12	Mansfield Town	0-2		9852		9	8	11				3	1			10	4	7				5		6							
15		19	QUEENS PARK RANGERS	0-0		13363		7	8	11				3	1			10	4		9		2	5		6							
16	Dec	3	EXETER CITY	3-1	Martin 2, Clayton	10129		10	8	11				3	1				4		9		2	5		6					7		
17		17	BRIGHTON & HOVE ALB.	4-3	Martin 2, Towler, Hatton	8073			8					3	1			10	4		9		2	5		6			7	11			
18		24	SWINDON TOWN	2-0	Martin 2	9998			8					3	1			10	4		9		2	5		6			7	11			
19		26	Watford	1-0	Taylor	2522			8					3	1			10	4		9		2	5		6			7	11			
20		27	WATFORD	0-3		21208			8					3	1			10	4		9		2	5		6			7	11			
21		31	Torquay United	2-0	Hatton 2	2859	3		8	11					1			10	4		9		2	5		6			7				
22	Jan	14	CLAPTON ORIENT	1-0	Martin	10811	3	10	8	11					1				4		9		2	5		6			7				
23		28	NORTHAMPTON T	1-0	Clayton	10924	3		8	11					1			10	4		9		2	5		6			7				
24	Feb	2	Newport County	1-2	Watson	7010	3			11					1			10	4		9		2	5		6			7		8		
25		4	Reading	1-3	Martin	7342	3			11					1			10	4		9		2	5		6			7		8		
26		11	Aldershot	3-0	Martin 3	5634				11				3	1			10	6		9		2	5		8			7				4
27		18	BRISTOL ROVERS	3-1	Cooper 2, Hatton	10229				11				3	1			10	6		9		2	5		8			7				4
28		25	Ipswich Town	2-0	Martin, Cooper	10161				11				3	1			10	6		9		2	5		8			7				4
29	Mar	4	BOURNEMOUTH	0-1		8539				11				3	1			10	6		9		2	5		8			7				4
30		11	Walsall	3-3	Martin 2, Hatton	6465				11				3	1			10	6		9		2	5		8			7				4
31		18	MANSFIELD TOWN	1-1	Cooper	11629				11				3	1			10	6		9		2	5		8			7				4
32		25	Queens Park Rangers	1-0	Read	9164	3			10					1			8	4		9		2	5		6			7	11			
33	Apr	1	SOUTHEND UNITED	4-1	Towler 2, Mills(p), Clayton	9467	3		8	10					1				4		9		2	5		6			7	11			
34		7	Port Vale	1-3	Mills(p)	9658	3			10					1			8	4		9		2	5		6			7	11			
35		8	Exeter City	0-1		5916			8					3	1			10	4		9		2	5		6			7	11			
36		10	PORT VALE	4-0	Towler, Martin 2, Read	10401				10				3	1			8	4		9		2	5		6			7	11			
37		15	CARDIFF CITY	1-1	Cooper	7640				10				3				8	4		9		2	5			1	7		11			6
38		17	Cardiff City	1-4	Towler	5070				10				3				8	4		9		2	5			1	7		11			6
39		22	Brighton & Hove Alb.	0-2		5508				10				3				8	4		9		2	5		6	1	7		11			
40		25	Southend United	0-1		2270		10		6				3				8	4		9		2	5			1	7		11			
41		29	Crystal Palace	1-5	Towler	6861								3		9		10	4				2	5			1	7		11	8		6
42	May	6	BRISTOL CITY	0-0		4623				6	7			3		9		10		8			2	5		4	1			11			
			Apps				8	8	16	33	1	6	6	27	36	2	2	37	39	4	26	8	41	36	2	36	6	6	25	22	17	1	11
			Goals						3	10		3					1	7			16		2			2			1	9	4		

One own goal

F.A. Cup

R3	Jan	7	BURNLEY	3-1	Cooper 2, Clayton	14500	3		8	11					1			10	4		9		2	5		6			7				
R4		21	WALSALL	0-0		34462	3		8	11					1			10	4		9		2	5		6			7				
rep		26	Walsall	0-4		9563	3		8	11					1			10	4		9		2	5		6			7				

Division Three (South) Cup

| R1 | Oct | 12 | Mansfield Town | 0-3 | | 1616 | | 9 | | | | | | 3 | 1 | | | 10 | 8 | 4 | 7 | | 2 | | | | | | | 11 | | 6 | |

W Dallman played at no. 5

		p	w	d	l	f	a	pts
1	Newport County	42	22	11	9	58	45	55
2	Crystal Palace	42	20	12	10	71	52	52
3	Brighton & Hove A.	42	19	11	12	68	49	49
4	Watford	42	17	12	13	62	51	46
5	Reading	42	16	14	12	69	59	46
6	Queen's Park Rgs.	42	15	14	13	68	49	44
7	Ipswich Town	42	16	12	14	62	52	44
8	Bristol City	42	16	12	14	61	63	44
9	Swindon Town	42	18	8	16	72	77	44
10	Aldershot	42	16	12	14	53	66	44
11	NOTTS COUNTY	42	17	9	16	59	54	43
12	Southend United	42	16	9	17	61	64	41
13	Cardiff City	42	15	11	16	61	65	41
14	Exeter City	42	13	14	15	65	82	40
15	Bournemouth	42	13	13	16	52	58	39
16	Mansfield Town	42	12	15	15	44	62	39
17	Northampton Town	42	15	8	19	51	58	38
18	Port Vale	42	14	9	19	52	58	37
19	Torquay United	42	14	9	19	54	70	37
20	Clapton Orient	42	11	13	18	53	55	35
21	Walsall	42	11	11	20	68	69	33
22	Bristol Rovers	42	10	13	19	55	61	33

Back: McLenahan, Moulson, Dean, Feebery, Hatton. Standing: Mellors (trainer), Roy, Mills, Flower, Blood, Taylor, O'Neill, Gallagher, England (trainer). Seated: Hindmarsh, Burditt, Houghton, Parkes (sec/mgr), Read, Watson, Protheroe. Front: Cooper, Wyllie, Young, Gaughran

1939/40

League Jubilee Fund (Friendly Game)

Aug	19	NOTTM. FOREST	1-1	Knox		6000	Wheldon E	Mills PC	Chester TH	Rayner F	Moulson C	Coulston W	Knox JP	Martin DK	Hatton C	Cooper S

Third Division (South)

1	Aug	26	BOURNEMOUTH	2-1	Hatton, Martin		10772	Flower T	Mills PC	Ringrose A	Rayner F	Moulson C	Coulston W	Knox JP	Martin DK	Hatton C	Cooper S
2	Sep	2	Cardiff City	4-2	Martin 2, Hatton, Mackenzie		17324	Flower T	Mills PC	Chester TH	Rayner F	Moulson C	Coulston W	Mackenzie J	Martin DK	Hatton C	Cooper S

Friendlies

1	Sep	23	Doncaster Rovers	2-4	Read, Bycroft (og)	3000	Flower T	Mills PC	McNaughton	Rayner F	Moulson C	Coulston W	Clayton S	Read CW	Hatton C	Cooper S
2		30	WOLVERHAMPTON W.	1-4	Rayner	5000	Flower T	Mills PC	Chester TH	Buckley FL	Moulson C	Weightman E	Rayner F	Read CW	Cooper S	Towler BE
3	Oct	7	Northampton Town	0-6		3000	Wheldon E	Mills PC	Chester TH	Nicholas JT	Barker JW	Hann R	Crooks SD	Lambert R	England	Duncan D
4		14	Nottm. Forest	1-2	Crooks	4000	Wakeman A	Mills PC	Wilcox GE	Nicholas JT	Barker JW	Hann R	Crooks SD	Hatton C	Houghton WE	Duncan D
5	Nov	4	BIRMINGHAM	1-0	Duncan		Flower T	Mills PC	Wilcox GE	Buckley FL	Barker JW	Hann R	Walsh W	Harrison R	Jones B	Duncan D
6	Dec	16	Hull City	5-4	Duncan 2, Mackenzie, Clayton, Nicholas (p)		Hall B	Nicholas JT	Wilcox GE	Buckley FL	Barker JW	Ward TV	Brookbanks E	Mackenzie J	Coleman E	Duncan D
7		25	COVENTRY CITY	1-1	Nicholas (p)		Hall B	Nicholas JT	Wilcox GE	Musson W	Barker JW	Ward TV	Crooks SD	Hall GW	Coleman E	Duncan D
8		26	Coventry City	2-8	Duncan, Mackenzie		Hall B	Nicholas JT	England E	Musson W	Barker JW	Ward TV	Hall GW	Mackenzie J	Coleman E	Duncan D
9		30	WEST BROMWICH ALB.	4-0	Clayton, Mackenzie, Duncan, og		Hall B	Nicholas JT	Wilcox GE	Ward T	Hann R	Read CW	Crooks SD	Clayton S	Hall GW	Duncan D

League: East Midlands Region

1	Oct	21	ROTHERHAM UNITED	2-0	Crooks, Harrison	2000	Hall B	Mills PC	Wilcox GE	Nicholas JT	Barker JW	Hann R	Crooks SD	Walsh W	Harrison R	Duncan D
2		28	Sheffield Wednesday	1-1	Duncan	3000	Hall B	Mills PC	Wilcox GE	Nicholas JT	Barker JW	Hann R	Walsh W	Crooks SD	Harrison R	Duncan D
3	Nov	11	Doncaster Rovers	1-2	Harrison	5479	Hall B	Mills PC	Wilcox GE	Nicholas JT	Barker JW	Hann R	Crooks SD	Walsh W	Harrison R	Duncan D
4		18	CHESTERFIELD	1-4	Glover	5000	Hall B	Mills PC	Wilcox GE	Nicholas JT	Barker JW	Hann R	Crooks SD	Hilliard G	Glover P	Duncan D
5		25	Barnsley	1-2	Duncan	1500	Hall B	Mills PC	Wilcox GE	Nicholas JT	Barker JW	Hann R	Crooks SD	Coleman E	Glover P	Duncan D
6	Dec	2	GRIMSBY TOWN	1-2	Crooks	7000	Hall B	Mills PC	Wilcox GE	Nicholas JT	Bailey L	Read CW	Crooks SD	Mackenzie J	Glover P	Duncan D
7		9	Sheffield United	1-7	Crooks	3000	Hall B	Mills PC	Wilcox GE	Nicholas JT	Bailey L	Read CW	Crooks SD	Mackenzie J	Harrison R	Duncan D
8	Jan	13	Mansfield Town	4-6	Towler 2, Buckley, Nicholas	2200	Hall B	Nicholas JT	Wilcox GE	Ward TV	Hann R	Ward TV	Crooks SD	Buckley FL	Mackenzie J	Towler BE
9	Mar	2	NOTTM. FOREST	4-3	Clayton, Crooks, Mackenzie, Towler	4000	Wilkinson N	Nicholas JT	Mason J	Corkhill WG	Barker JW	Ward TV	Clayton S	Mackenzie J	Towler BE
10		9	DONCASTER ROVERS	4-0	Towler 2, Duncan, Steele	3000	Wilkinson N	Nicholas JT	Beattie A	Corkhill WG	Barker JW	Ward TV	Clayton S	Steele FC	Towler BE	Duncan D
11		16	Chesterfield	1-3	Crooks	6000	Wilkinson N	Nicholas JT	Beattie A	Corkhill WG	Barker JW	Ward TV	Mackenzie J	Steele FC	Towler BE	Duncan D
12		22	MANSFIELD TOWN	2-2	Corkhill, Groves	4000	Wilkinson N	Nicholas JT	Beattie A	Corkhill WG	Barker JW	Ward TV	Crooks SD	Groves A	Towler BE	Duncan D
13		23	BARNSLEY	0-6		3000	Wilkinson N	Nicholas JT	Beattie A	Corkhill WG	Barker JW	Ward TV	Crooks SD	Clayton S	Brookbanks E	Duncan D
14		25	Rotherham United	2-3	Read, Towler	2000	Hall B	Nicholas JT	Beattie A	Corkhill WG	Baxter WA	Hague JK	Clayton S	Rayner F	Read CW	Towler BE
15		30	Grimsby Town	2-3	Clayton, Hatton	2500	Hall B	Griffiths J	Beattie A	Corkhill WG	Nicholas JT	Ward TV	Crooks SD	Clayton S	Mackenzie J	Hatton C	Duncan D
16	Apr	6	SHEFFIELD UNITED	3-0	Towler 2, Beattie	2114	Flower T	Mills PC	Mason J	Corkhill WG	Nicholas JT	Ward TV	Crooks SD	Groves A	Towler BE	Duncan D
17	May	4	Lincoln City	4-3	Mackenzie 2, Groves, Moss		Waite JH	Mills PC	Mason J	Waterall K	Corkhill WG	Munks JA	Moss G	Groves A	Towler BE	Duncan D
18		18	SHEFFIELD WEDNESDAY	1-4	Moss	1771	Bartram S	Mills PC	Mason J	Waterall K	Corkhill WG	Munks JA	Moss G	Mackenzie J	Mills A	Duncan D
19		25	Nottm. Forest	2-6	Duncan, PC Mills(p)		Bartram S	Mills PC	Mason J	Corkhill WG	Davies RG	Munks JA	Crooks SD	Mackenzie J	Moss G	Duncan D
20	Jun	1	LINCOLN CITY	3-0	Mackenzie 2, Crooks											

League Cup

PR	Apr	13	Mansfield Town	5-3	Hatton 2, Crooks, Duncan, O'Donnell	4500	Wakeman A	Nicholas JT	Mills PC	Corkhill WG	Hann R	Ward TV	Hatton C	O'Donnell F	Towler BE	Duncan D
R1/1		20	Arsenal	0-4		11521	Flower T	Lunn	Mills PC	Hann R	Nicholas JT	Ward TV	Massie A	O'Donnell F	Towler BE	Duncan D
R1/2		27	ARSENAL	1-5	PC Mills (p)	14755	Flower T	Nicholas JT	Mills PC	Corkhill WG	Hann R	Ward TV	Mackenzie J	O'Donnell F	Towler BE	Duncan D

1940/41

League South

#	Date	Opponent	Score	Scorers	Att	1	2	3	4	5	6	7	8	9	10	11
1	Aug 31	Stoke City	1-4	Crooks		Sidlow C	Nicholas JT	Beattie A	Massie A	Iverson RT	Keen E	Crooks SD	Edwards GR	Broome FH	Fenton M	Duncan D
2	Sep 7	STOKE CITY	3-2	Duncan, Fenton, McEwan	2000	Sidlow C	Sneddon T	Beattie A	Corkhill WG	Nicholas JT	Keen E	Crooks SD	Fenton M	Broome FH	McEwan F	Beattie R
3	28	Coventry City	1-1	Edwards	2000	Sidlow C	Smallwood E	Beattie A	Massie A	Nicholas JT	Iverson RT	Crooks SD	Smith JT	Broome FH	Edwards GR	Butler S
4	Oct 5	COVENTRY CITY	1-3	Crooks	2000	Sidlow C	Griffiths J	Beattie A	Massie A	Nicholas JT	Iverson RT	Crooks SD	Smith JT	Broome FH	Edwards GR	Duncan D
5	12	Walsall	2-3	Buckley, Crooks	3000	Sidlow C	Nicholas JT	Beattie A	Massie A	Lamb W	Iverson RT	Crooks SD	Buckley FL	Broome FH	Edwards GR	Duncan D
6	19	WALSALL	4-2	Broome 3, Nicholas (p)	1500	Sidlow C	Wilcox GE	Beattie A	Edwards GR	Nicholas JT	Massie A	Crooks SD	Smith JT	Broome FH	Duncan D	Butler S
7	26	West Bromwich Alb.	1-3	Edwards	2496	Sidlow C	Mills PC	Beattie A	Massie A	Nicholas JT	Buckley FL	Crooks SD	Smith JT	Broome FH	Edwards GR	Duncan D
8	Nov 2	West Bromwich Alb.	3-2	Broome, Buckley, Moss	2100	Mills PC	Findlay PA	Beattie A	Massie A	Nicholas JT	Buckley FL	Crooks SD	Cooper EJ	Broome FH	Moss G	Stein AW
9	9	Walsall	4-11	Broome 2, Crooks 2	400	Gilson H	Mills PC	Beattie A	Massie A	Nicholas JT	Buckley FL	Crooks SD	Cooper EJ	Broome FH	Moss G	Stein AW
10	16	WALSALL	2-1	Crooks 2	1000	Swinburne TA	Mills PC	Johnson JT	Beattie A	Nicholas JT	Buckley FL	Crooks SD	Cooper EJ	Broome FH	Gallacher P	Stein AW
11	30	BIRMINGHAM CITY	3-3	Broome, Duncan, Quinton (og)	600	Streten BR	Mills PC	Middleton L	Ellmer FB	Nicholas JT	Munks JA	Buckley FL	Cooper EJ	Broome FH	Crisp GH	Duncan D
12	Dec 7	Leicester City	0-6		1500	Streten BR	Mills PC	Middleton L	Ellmer FB	Nicholas JT	Buckley FL	Johnson JW	Cooper EJ	Broome FH	Gallacher P	Duncan D
13	21	Northampton Town	1-2	Vallance	4500	Streten BR	Beattie A	Johnson JT	Jackson H	Griffiths J	Buckley FL	Johnson JW	Cooper EJ	Broome FH	Vallance	Warburton G
14	25	Nottm. Forest	4-2	Broome,Johnson,Warburton,Shaw(og)	2265	Streten BR	Griffiths J	Beattie A	Jackson H	Nicholas JT	Buckley FL	Johnson JW	Warburton G	Broome FH	Vallance	Duncan D
15	28	LEICESTER CITY	4-2	Broome 2, Duncan 2	2000	Streten BR	Beattie A	Johnson JT	Jackson H	Nicholas JT	Buckley FL	Johnson JW	Vallance	Broome FH	Warburton G	Duncan D
16	Jan 11	West Bromwich Alb.	1-8	Hinsley	1403	Streten BR	Griffiths J	Johnson JT	Vallance	Nicholas JT	Buckley FL	Taylor GT	Cooper EJ	Broome FH	Hinsley C	Duncan D
17	25	Stoke City	2-2	Broome 2	300	Streten BR	Griffiths J	Elliott CS	Vallance	Nicholas JT	Boileau HA	Taylor GT	Crooks SD	Broome FH	Green T	Duncan D
18	Feb 1	STOKE CITY	2-1	Broome, Duncan	1000	Streten BR	Griffiths J	Elliott CS	Hinsley C	Nicholas JT	Boileau HA	Taylor GT	Crooks SD	Broome FH	Green T	Duncan D
19	Mar 15	NOTTM. FOREST	0-4		2000	Streten BR	Parr J	Johnson JT	Musson WU	Nicholas JT	Ellmer FB	Crooks SD	Hinsley C	Harrison R	Carter HS	Vause PG
20	Apr 12	Nottm. Forest	3-1	Newman 2, Lyman	2000	Streten BR	Parr J	Brook R	Musson WU	Nicholas JT	Johnson JT	Lyman CC	Buckley FL	Broome FH	Wright	Newman
21	14	Chesterfield	0-3		1300	Streten BR	Brook R	Johnson JT	Bingham	Padman	Ellmer FB	Wright	Berry	Clements	Moss G	Lyman CC

Game 16 also counted for Midland Cup

League Cup

Rd	Date	Opponent	Score	Scorers	Att	1	2	3	4	5	6	7	8	9	10	11
R1/1	Feb 15	WEST BROMWICH ALB.	4-0	Broome 2, Crooks, Hinsley	2700	Streten BR	Elliott CS	Johnson JT	Taylor GT	Nicholas JT	Boileau HA	Crooks SD	Davidson RT	Broome FH	Hinsley C	Duncan D
R1/2	22	West Bromwich Alb.	0-5		2581	Streten BR	Elliott CS	Johnson JT	Hinsley C	Nicholas JT	Boileau HA	Taylor GT	Green T	Broome FH	Davidson RT	Duncan D

1941/42

No League games played following bomb damage to Meadow Lane

1942/43

League North First Championship

#	Date	Opponent	Score	Scorers	Att	1	2	3	4	5	6	7	8	9	10	11
1	Aug 29	DERBY COUNTY	1-6	Steele	3000	Flower T	Challiner J	Benner R	Corkhill WG	Sharman F	Jones LJ	Barsby CF	Cairns WH	Steele FC	Moss G	Jessop W
2	Sep 5	Derby County	0-2		8000	Wilkinson N	Corkhill WG	Jones DO	Burgess R	Sharman F	Kirton J	Antonio GR	Steele FC	Cairns WH	Jones LJ	Jessop W
3	12	Mansfield Town	1-0	L Jones (p)	2000	Wilkinson N	Corkhill WG	Benner R	Burgess R	Sharman F	Kirton J	Antonio GR	Steele FC	Cairns WH	Jones LJ	Jessop W
4	19	MANSFIELD TOWN	3-1	Antonio, L Jones, Weaver		Wilkinson N	Corkhill WG	Jones DO	Kirton J	Sharman F	Weaver S	Coulston W	Antonio GR	Bowers J	Jones LJ	Burgess R
5	26	CHESTERFIELD	2-0	Hatton (p), Liddle	3500	Wilkinson N	Corkhill WG	Kirton J	Clarke GA	Sharman F	Burgess R	Coulston W	Steele FC	Bowers J	Hatton C	Liddle D
6	Oct 3	Chesterfield	1-6	L Jones		Parkin FW	Corkhill WG	Jones DO	Clarke GA	Sharman F	Burgess R	Booth LJ	Haines JWT	Bowers J	Jones LJ	Liddle D
7	10	Leicester City	3-1	Liddle 2, Booth		Wilkinson N	Corkhill WG	Jones DO	Clarke GA	Sharman F	Burgess R	Booth LJ	Antonio GR	Bowers J	Jones LJ	Liddle D
8	17	LEICESTER CITY	1-1	Bowers	4000	Wilkinson N	Corkhill WG	Jones DO	Clarke GA	Sharman F	Kirton J	Booth LJ	Clayton S	Bowers J	Jones LJ	Robinson P
9	24	LINCOLN CITY	3-6	Marsh 2, Collindridge		Wilkinson N	Corkhill WG	Jones DO	Clarke GA	Sharman F	Burgess R	Antonio GR	Haines JWT	Marsh JK	Kirton J	Collindridge C
10	31	Lincoln City	1-8	Bowers		Wilkinson N	Ellmer FB	Sharman F	Clarke GA	Fell J	Jones LJ	Brown E	Stillyards G	Bowers J	Bell T	Liddle D
11	Nov 7	Nottm. Forest	5-3	L Jones 2(1p), Bowers, Collindridge, Haines	5384	Wilkinson N	Benner R	Jones DO	Jones LJ	Sharman F	Kirton J	Booth LJ	Haines JWT	Bowers J	Liddle D	Collindridge C
12	14	NOTTM. FOREST	1-3	Antonio	4000	Wilkinson N	Benner R	Kirton J	Antonio GR	Sharman F	Liddle D	Booth LJ	Haines JWT	Bowers J	Moss G	Collindridge C
13	21	SHEFFIELD WEDNESDAY	2-2	Booth, Collindridge		Wilkinson N	Jones DO	Benner R	Clarke GA	Sharman F	Kirton J	Booth LJ	Antonio GR	Bowers J	Liddle D	Collindridge C
14	28	Sheffield Wednesday	1-3	Liddle	10000	Wilkinson N	Sharman F	Benner R	Clarke GA	Hughes S	Ellmer FB	Booth LJ	Jones LJ	Bowers J	Liddle D	Collindridge C
15	Dec 5	Northampton T	2-5	Brader, Collindridge	2000	Wilkinson N	Jones DO	Benner R	Clarke GA	Hughes S	Stancer LB	Coulston W	Antonio GR	Brader FW	Jones LJ	Collindridge C
16	12	NORTHAMPTON T	2-0	Brader, L Jones(p)		Wilkinson N	Corkhill WG	Jones DO	Clarke GA	Sharman F	Hughes S	Coulston W	Antonio GR	Brader FW	Jones LJ	Liddle D
17	19	LINCOLN CITY	4-2	Collindridge 3, Clarke		Wilkinson N	Corkhill WG	Jones DO	Liddle D	Hughes S	Kirton J	Clarke GA	Antonio GR	Brader FW	Jones LJ	Collindridge C
18	25	Lincoln City	1-8	GH Robinson		Parkin FW	Blood JF	Benner R	Clarke GA	Lilley K	Stancer LB	Brown M	Hodgkins JS	Tweed GE	Robinson GH	Liddle D

League North Second Championship

#	Date	Opponent	Score	Scorers	Att	1	2	3	4	5	6	7	8	9	10	11
19	Dec 26	DERBY COUNTY	2-3	Antonio, Bowers	15000	Hall B	Corkhill WG	Benner R	Hann R	Sharman F	Wright WA	Rickards CT	Antonio GR	Bowers J	Ramage PMF	Collindridge C
20	Jan 2	Derby County	2-1	Collindridge, Marsh	7000	Ramage PMF	Corkhill WG	Benner R	Burgess R	Sharman F	Hann R	Rickards CT	Antonio GR	Marsh JK	Jones LJ	Collindridge C
21	9	Lincoln City	2-0	Bowers, Collindridge			Corkhill WG	Benner R	Burgess R	Sharman F	Hann R	Rickards CT	Antonio GR	Bowers J	Jones LJ	Collindridge C
22	16	LINCOLN CITY	1-2	Bowers		Wilkinson N	Corkhill WG	Benner R	Burgess R	Sharman F	Jones LJ	Rickards CT	Antonio GR	Bowers J	Drury GB	Hinchcliffe T
23	23	SHEFFIELD UNITED	1-1	Marsh		Parkin FW	Corkhill WG	Marshall JG	Burgess R	Sharman F	Hughes S	Rickards CT	Antonio GR	Marsh JK	Ramage PMF	Grant EA
24	30	Sheffield United	2-3	Bowers, Jones		Wilkinson N	Corkhill WG	Marshall JG	Antonio GR	Hughes S	Ramage PMF	Clift BC	Jones LJ	Bowers J	Rawcliffe F	Maund JH
25	Feb 6	Mansfield Town	4-2	Rawcliffe 2, Jones(p), Rickards		Ashton P	Trim RF	Benner R	Hollis KB	Hughes S	Kirton J	Rickards CT	Jones LJ	Rickards CT	Rawcliffe F	Maund JH
26	13	MANSFIELD TOWN	2-0	Bowers, Maund		Wilkinson N	Benner R	Marshall JG	Hughes S	Leuty LH	Hughes S	Clift BC	Antonio GR	Bowers J	Jones LJ	Collindridge C
27	20	ROTHERHAM UNITED	4-0	Rickards 2, Antonio, Clift		Wilkinson N	Marshall JG	Benner R	Corkhill WG	Leuty LH	Hughes S	Clift BC	Antonio GR	Rickards CT	Rawcliffe F	Jones LJ
28	27	Rotherham United	2-2	Jones, Steele		Wilkinson N	Benner R	Marshall JG	Hann R	Leuty LH	Kirton J	Antonio GR	Jones LJ	Steele FC	Rawcliffe F	Davies W
29	Mar 6	Derby County	3-1	Antonio, Rickards, Towler	10540	Wilkinson N	Corkhill WG	Bacuzzi J	Barke JL	Leuty LH	Kirton J	Jones LJ	Jones LJ	Rickards CT	Towler BE	Collindridge C
30	13	DERBY COUNTY	2-2	Jones, Rickards	15100	Wilkinson N	Vincent NE	Corkhill WG	Barke JL	Leuty LH	Kirton J	Hughes S	Jones LJ	Rickards CT	Towler BE	Collindridge C
31	20	Sheffield United	1-4	Collindridge (p)		Wilkinson N	Vincent NE	Corkhill WG	Barke JL	Leuty LH	Kirton J	Hughes S	Jones LJ	Rickards CT	Towler BE	Collindridge C
32	27	SHEFFIELD UNITED	2-1	Rickards, Towler	12000	Wilkinson N	Bacuzzi J	Corkhill WG	Barke JL	Leuty LH	Kirton J	Davies W	Jones LJ	Rickards CT	Rawcliffe F	Towler BE
33	Apr 3	STOKE CITY	1-1	Rawcliffe		Wilkinson N	Corkhill WG	Benner R	Barke JL	Leuty LH	Kirton J	Davies W	Jones LJ	Bowers J	Rawcliffe F	Towler BE
34	10	Stoke City	1-1	Rickards	1000	Ashton P	Corkhill WG	Barke JL	Clarke GA	Leuty LH	Kirton J	Duns L	Jones LJ	Rickards CT	Rawcliffe F	Liddle D
35	17	Nottm. Forest	1-1	Duns	4443	Wilkinson N	Barke JL	Burgess R	Leuty LH	Kirton J	Duns L	Jones LJ	Rickards CT	Towler BE	Collindridge C	
36	24	NOTTM. FOREST	2-1	Jones, Rickards		Ashton P	Corkhill WG	Benner R	Rawcliffe F	Leuty LH	Barke JL	Duns L	Rickards CT	Lawton T	Jones LJ	Martin EJ
37	26	Coventry City	0-7		4384	Parkin FW	Corkhill WG	Benner R	Rigby NE	Hughes S	Barke JL	Brown GH	Rickards CT	Brader FW	Rawcliffe F	Parker A
38	May 1	COVENTRY CITY	2-1	Marsh, Towler(p)		Wilkinson N	Corkhill WG	Benner R	Burgess R	Leuty LH	Barke JL	Duns L	Rickards CT	Marsh JK	Jones LJ	Towler BE

Games 19 to 32 inclusive also counted for the League Cup
(Games 19 - 28 were a qualifying competition).

1943/44

League North First Championship

#	Date	Opponent	Score	Scorers	Att													
1	Aug 28	Lincoln City	5-4	Rawcliffe 2, Lager 2, Antonio		Wilkinson N	Corkhill WG	Challinor J	Burgess R	Smith L	Kirton J	Antonio GR	Jones LJ	Lager EW	Rawcliffe F	Towler BE
2	Sep 4	LINCOLN CITY	0-0		5000	Wilkinson N	Corkhill WG	Challinor J	Burgess R	Gray R	Kirton J	Antonio GR	Jones LJ	Lager EW	Rawcliffe F	Collindridge C
3	11	DERBY COUNTY	3-1	Drury 2, Anderson	5087	Wilkinson N	Jones DO	Challinor J	Corkhill WG	Gray R	Kirton J	Anderson J	Drury GB	Jones LJ	Rawcliffe F	Collindridge C
4	18	Derby County	2-4	Collindridge 2 (1p)	8000	Bloomfield W	Jones DO	Challinor J	Corkhill WG	Burgess R	Kirton J	Gray R	Jones LJ	Rawcliffe F	Collindridge C	Marshall JG
5	25	Chesterfield	0-3		7000	Wilkinson N	Marshall JG	Challinor J	Corkhill WG	Gray R	Kirton J	Ross J	Stancer LB	Brader FW	Jones LJ	Collins AD
6	Oct 2	CHESTERFIELD	1-0	Hatfield	4000	Donaldson HA	Corkhill WG	Marshall JG	Johnson J	Gray R	Keen E	Brunt GR	Hazel	Hatfield B	Jones LJ	Flint K
7	9	MANSFIELD TOWN	0-2			Donaldson HA	Corkhill WG	Challinor J	Keen E	Gray R	Kirton J	Brunt GR	Jones LJ	Hatfield B	Stancer LB	Collins AD
8	16	Mansfield Town	0-4		3500	Donaldson HA	Corkhill WG	Benner R	Russell D	Smith L	Gray R	Clarke GA	Jones LJ	Kirton J	Pettitt	Collindridge C
9	23	Leicester City	0-5			Donaldson HA	Corkhill WG	Marshall JG	Hann R	Sharman F	Gray R	Slack L	Jones LJ	Rawcliffe F	Iddon H	Towler BE
10	30	LEICESTER CITY	1-9	Antonio	5000	Donaldson HA	Drysdale J	Corkhill WG	Unwin S	Gray R	Towler BE	Houghton WE	Rawcliffe F	Martin DK	Antonio GR	Roberts D
11	Nov 6	NOTTM. FOREST	0-1		6000	Donaldson HA	Corkhill WG	Marshall JG	Nicholls H	Smith L	Gray R	Roberts D	Ball WE	Hatfield B	Jones LJ	Collindridge C
12	13	Nottm. Forest	4-0	Hunter 2, Walker, Collindridge(p)	5300	Streten BR	Corkhill WG	Bridges	Nicholls H	Smith L	Gray R	Hunter J	Antonio GR	Walker E	Jones LJ	Collindridge C
13	20	Sheffield Wednesday	0-1			Jepson A	Corkhill WG	Davidson DBL	Nicholls H	Gray R	Walters H	Hunter J	Antonio GR	Walker E	James J (2)	Murphy G
14	27	SHEFFIELD WEDNESDAY	0-0			Jepson A	Corkhill WG	Davidson DBL	Nicholls H	Gray R	Walters H	Hunter J	Hewitt	Wright J	Jones LJ	Collindridge C
15	Dec 4	NORTHAMPTON T	2-5	Wright 2		Hinton E	Skidmore W	Davidson DBL	Nicholls H	Melling F	Walters H	Lane H	Jones LJ	Wright J	Gardner	Towler BE
16	11	Northampton T	1-1	Wright		Clack FE	Pritchard R	Davidson DBL	Nicholls H	Godfrey L	Alderton JH	Lane H	Lane H	Walsh W	Murphy G	Summerfield A
17	18	Lincoln City	5-8	Ledger 3, Lane, Walsh	1629	Rickards CT	Rigby NE	Davidson DBL	Nicholls H	Gray R	Jones LJ	Ledger JK	Vincent NE	Walsh W	Lane H	Towler BE
18	25	LINCOLN CITY	2-5	Walsh, Martin		Wilkinson N	Benner R	Davidson DBL	Ashworth	Rigby NE	Fletcher	Ledger JK	Walsh W	Martin FA	Towler BE	Collindridge C

League North Second Championship

#	Date	Opponent	Score	Scorers	Att													
19	Dec 27	LEICESTER CITY	1-2	Edwards	10000	Oakley JC	Gutteridge R	Davidson DBL	Nicholls H	Godfrey L	Gray R	Ledger JK	Edwards G	Walsh W	Towler BE	Collindridge C
20	Jan 1	Leicester City	2-7	Knott, Towler		Jepson A	Gutteridge R	Marshall JG	Nicholls H	Godfrey L	Bye JH	Ledger JK	Lane H	Knott H	Walsh W	Towler BE
21	8	MANSFIELD TOWN	5-0	Dimond 2, Collindridge, Edwards, Ledger		Jepson A	Parr J	Davidson DBL	Nicholls H	Smith L	Gray R	Ledger JK	Edwards G	Dimond S	Jones LJ	Collindridge C
22	15	Mansfield Town	0-1		3500	Graham R	Nicholas J	Davidson DBL	Musson WU	Gray R	Towler BE	Ledger JK	Edwards G	Dimond S	Jones LJ	Rothwell E
23	22	Nottm. Forest	2-0	Dimond, Edwards	6803	Streten BR	Godfrey L	Davidson DBL	Nicholls H	Gray R	Musson WU	Ledger JK	Edwards G	Dimond S	Jones LJ	Smith J
24	29	NOTTM. FOREST	0-3		8000	Major L	Godfrey L	Gray R	Walters H	Rist FH	Musson WU	Ledger JK	Edwards G	Dimond S	Jones LJ	Rothwell E
25	Feb 5	DERBY COUNTY	0-2		7000	Jones J	Gutteridge R	Godfrey L	Nicholls H	Walters H	Walters H	Edwards G	Haycock F	Dimond S	Jones LJ	Collins AD
26	12	Derby County	3-7	Davis, Edwards, Flint	8000	Jones J	Godfrey L	Gutteridge R	Corkhill WG	Gray R	Gray R	Edwards G	Rawcliffe F	Davis RD	Towler BE	Flint K
27	19	Sheffield Wednesday	0-2		7000	Bradley G	Godfrey L	Gutteridge R	Walters H	Gray R	Towler BE	Ledger JK	Edwards G	Walsh W	Rawcliffe F	Collindridge C
28	26	SHEFFIELD WEDNESDAY	1-5	Davis	3000	Bradley G	Rigby NE	Hepworth R	Godfrey L	Gray R	Walters H	Ledger JK	Edwards G	Davis RD	Stancer LB	Towler BE
29	Mar 11	Walsall	1-2	Rickards		Whitehead J	Godfrey L	Davidson DBL	Rigby NE	Barke JL	Gray R	Edwards G	Stancer LB	Rickards CT	Ledger JK	Collindridge C
30	18	NORTHAMPTON T	1-4	Gray		Whitehead J	Becci A	Hepworth R	Rigby NE	Gray R	Davidson DBL	Ledger JK	Brown E	Walsh W	Stancer LB	Flint K
31	25	Northampton T	1-4	Gray		Thorpe WF	Davidson DBL	Hepworth R	Rigby NE	Marshall JG	Gray R	Ledger JK	Brown E	Walsh W	Stancer LB	Flint K
32	Apr 1	Doncaster Rovers	0-6			Kirkpatrick S	Marshall JG	Rigby NE	Southwell AA	Barke JL	Ledger JK	Higson S	Mordue J	Rollinson	Flint K
33	8	DONCASTER ROVERS	0-1			Thorpe WF	Davidson DBL	Marshall JG	Southwell AA	Barke JL	Stancer LB	DeLisle	Hogg F	Smith J	Openshaw	Ledger JK
34	10	Nottm. Forest	0-3			Thorpe WF	Davidson DBL	Kirkham R	Rigby NE	Greaves	Gregory H	Roberts D	Smith J	Flintson	Flint K
35	15	Mansfield Town	0-5		1000	Simpson C	Hepworth R	Everett HP	Unwin S	Southwell AA	Morley J	Smeeton J	Stancer LB	Walker E	Griffiths K	Flint K
36	22	MANSFIELD TOWN	3-2	Allen, Simpson, Wilson	1500	Thorpe WF	Everett HP	Kirkham R	Unwin S	Barton P	Morley J	Smith J	Simpson C	Allen W	Marsh JK	Wilson
37	29	COVENTRY CITY	1-4	Collindridge		Nugent S	Kirkpatrick S	Hepworth R	Unwin S	Barton P	Everett HP	Tyroll	Collindridge C	Potts	Morley J	Gascoigne D
38	May 6	Coventry City	2-8	Gascoigne 2	1775	Morgan	Everett HP	Moran A	Barton P	Barton P	Unwin S	Van Gelden J	Gascoigne D	Allen W	Renshaw	Drinkwater

Games 19 to 28 inclusive also counted for League Cup, 29 to 31 for the Midland Cup

1944/45

League North First Championship

1 Aug	26	Lincoln City	2-4	Knowles, Morrad	3000	Clack FE	Hepworth R	Benner R	Hogg F	Barton P	Chapman RJF	Van Gelden J	Carrick R	Morrad FG	O'Neill T	Knowles C
2 Sep	2	LINCOLN CITY	4-5	Morrad 2, Davie, Hepworth	3000	Clack FE	Hepworth R	Barton P	Hogg F	Wright WA	Stancer LB	Dixon W	Morrad FG	Davie J	O'Neill T	Flint K
3	9	SHEFFIELD WEDNESDAY	2-0	Davie 2	6000	Carter J	Hepworth R	Pomphrey EA	Hogg F	Wright WA	Long D	Edwards WJ	Morrad FG	Davie J	O'Neill T	Collindridge C
4	16	Sheffield Wednesday	1-6	Morrad	10000	Carter J	Hepworth R	Pomphrey EA	Hogg F	Wright WA	Long D	Flint K	Stancer LB	Morrad FG	O'Neill T	Carter
5	23	Nottm. Forest	1-2	Hepworth (p)	10000	Clack FE	Hepworth R	Pomphrey EA	Long D	Barton P	Everett HP	Edwards WJ	Hogg F	Davie J	White A	Morrad FG
6	30	NOTTM. FOREST	0-0		9000	Clack FE	Hepworth R	Pomphrey EA	Southwell AA	Barton P	Baker D	White A	Hogg F	Davie J	Morrad FG	Flint K
7 Oct	7	BARNSLEY	0-3		5000	Streten BR	Hepworth R	Pomphrey EA	Southwell AA	Southwell AA	Baker D	Piercy C	Morrad FG	Davie J	Stephenson R	Piercy C
8	14	Barnsley	2-6	Collindridge, Davie	5000	Streten BR	Hepworth R	Pomphrey EA	Hogg F	Southwell AA	Morrad FG	Piercy C	Wood CC	Davie J	O'Neill T	Collindridge C
9	21	Doncaster Rovers	1-3	Davie	4361	Streten BR	Hepworth R	Pomphrey EA	Southwell AA	Wright WA	Morrad FG	Edwards WJ	Sewell J	Davie J	Stephenson R	Piercy C
10	28	DONCASTER ROVERS	0-2		2000	Mowl WJ	Hepworth R	Pomphrey EA	Southwell AA	Moulson C	Morrad FG	Duggan	Sewell J	Davie J	Stephenson R	Towler BE
11 Nov	4	DERBY COUNTY	1-4	Sewell	9000	Mowl WJ	Hepworth R	Pomphrey EA	Southwell AA	Moulson C	Morrad FG	Gascoigne D	Sewell J	Davie J	Hogg F	Collindridge C
12	11	Derby County	3-6	Coen 2, Sewell	10000	Mowl WJ	Hepworth R	Pomphrey EA	Southwell AA	Sparrow	Hogg F	Coen L	Sewell J	Davie J	Parker A	Piercy C
13	18	Sheffield United	0-6		8000	Mowl WJ	Hepworth R	Kingwell	Southwell AA	Bicknell R	Sparrow	Coen L	Sewell J	Davie J	Parker A	Stephenson R
14	25	SHEFFIELD UNITED	1-0	Airlie	2000	Mowl WJ	Bacuzzi J	Hepworth R	Southwell AA	Rigby NE	Hogg F	Coen L	Sewell J	Airlie S	Strain N	Towler BE
15 Dec	2	ROTHERHAM UNITED	0-2		4000	Mowl WJ	Rigby NE	Hepworth R	Southwell AA	Moulson C	Hogg F	Coen L	Sewell J	Windle R	Flint K	Flint K
16	6	Rotherham United	1-2	Davie	8000	Mowl WJ	Bacuzzi J	Hepworth R	Southwell AA	Bicknell R	Hogg F	Sewell J	Strain N	Davie J	McMullen J	Piercy C
17	16	CHESTERFIELD	0-3		3000	Mowl WJ	Southwell AA	Brooks	Towler BE	Bicknell R	Hogg F	Davie J	Strain N	Morrad FG	McMullen J	Stancer LB
18	23	Chesterfield	0-8		7000	Bradshaw	Hepworth R	Skidmore W	Bicknell R	Southwell AA	Hogg F	Huntley	Strain N	Hughes A	Brooks	Towler BE

League North Second Championship

19 Dec	26	MANSFIELD TOWN	0-2			Oakley JC	Hepworth R	Marshall JG	Corkhill WG	Moulson C	Southwell AA	Sewell J	Hogg F	Brooks	Towler BE	Stephenson R
20	30	Mansfield Town	1-3	Towler	3000	Oakley JC	Southwell AA	Hepworth R	Pithie DS	Moulson C	Hogg F	Summers	Sewell J	Bicknell R	Towler BE	Mynard LD
21 Jan	6	Chesterfield	1-3	Collindridge	5000	Oakley JC	Hepworth R	Southwell AA	Taylor IL	Moulson C	Stancer LB	Connor	Sewell J	Coen L	Towler BE	Collindridge C
22	13	CHESTERFIELD	1-3	Lewis	4000	Stanowski	Hepworth R	Southwell AA	Towler BE	Moulson C	Hogg F	Sewell J	McPherson IB	Coen L	Lewis G	Pavlov M
23	20	Derby County	0-7		3500	Bradshaw	Griffiths J	Marshall JG	Southwell AA	Barke IL	Hogg F	Coen L	McPherson IB	Shell FH	Lewis G	Johnston TD
24	27	DERBY COUNTY	2-4	Collindridge, Lewis	6000	Mowl WJ	Griffiths J	Marshall JG	Allen RHA	Moulson C	Hogg F	Coen L	McPherson IB	Collindridge C	Lewis G	Bellis A
25 Feb	3	LEICESTER CITY	1-4	Southwell	5000	Mowl WJ	Hepworth R	Everett HP	Southwell AA	Everett HP	Moulson C	Coen L	McPherson IB	Shell FH	Strain N	Collindridge C
26	10	Leicester City	1-4	Wright	7500	Wiseman G	Hepworth R	Allen RHA	Taylor JL	Southwell AA	Moulson C	Coen L	Sewell J	Brooks	McPherson IB	Wright H
27	17	Nottm. Forest	4-1	Collindridge 2, McPherson, Towler	8000	Wiseman G	Hepworth R	Marshall JG	Towler BE	Morby JH	Everett HP	Coen L	McPherson IB	Southwell AA	Sewell J	Collindridge C
28	24	NOTTM. FOREST	1-2	Morrad	10000	Streten BR	Hepworth R	Ball E	Towler BE	Morby JH	Everett HP	Coen L	McPherson IB	Morrad FG	Lewis G	Collindridge C
29 Mar	3	Lincoln City	2-3	Sewell 2	2500	Hepworth R	Blood JF	Brooks	Towler BE	Morby JH	Everett HP	Sewell J	McPherson IB	Townrow RF	Lewis G	Gallago
30	10	Coventry City	0-4		3166	Wiseman G	Marshall JG	Blood JF	Marshall JG	Morby JH	Everett HP	Lamb HE	Lewis G	Hepworth R	Sewell J	Stephenson R
31	24	Coventry City	0-1		4339	Rollett E	Marshall JG	Allen RHA	Baker D	Morby JH	Stancer LB	Akers W	McPherson IB	Hepworth R	Coen L	Flint K
32	31	COVENTRY CITY	1-2	Flaherty	2000	Rollett E	Southwell AA	Allen RHA	Stancer LB	Morby JH	Baker D	Windle R	McPherson IB	Hepworth R	Flaherty E	Towler BE
33 Apr	2	Nottm. Forest	0-6		6920	Taylor J	Hepworth R	Everett HP	Unwin S	Peacock E	Stancer LB	Coen L	Hubbard J	Collindridge C	Flaherty E	Flint K
34	7	Port Vale	4-1	Strain 2, McPherson, Sewell	7000	Wiseman G	Bramley E	Everett HP	Southwell AA	Morby JH	Baker D	Windle R	McPherson IB	Strain N	Sewell J	Stephenson R
35	14	PORT VALE	2-1	Holmes, Strain	2000	Wiseman G	Bramley E	Allen RHA	Southwell AA	Morby JH	Baker D	Windle R	McPherson IB	Strain N	Sewell J	Holmes E
36	21	NOTTM. FOREST	1-3	Strain	4000	Andrews G	Southwell AA	Allen RHA	Foster J	Peacock E	Baker D	Windle R	Hubbard J	Strain N	Hubbard J	Holmes E
37	28	Nottm. Forest	5-2	McPherson 2, Sewell, Siddons, Toothill	3000	Wiseman G	Bramley E	Hutchinson J	Goodwin FN	Hubbard J	Siddons F	Siddons F	McPherson IB	Parker A	Sewell J	Toothill R
38 May	5	Grimsby Town	1-3	Parker	4000	Kirby N	Hutchinson J	Hepworth R	Hubbard J	Hoyle D	Probert	Wildgoose C	McPherson IB	Parker A	Sewell J	Toothill R
39	12	GRIMSBY TOWN	1-3	McPherson	2000	Wiseman G	Bramley E	Allen RHA	Southwell AA	Baker D	Hoyle D	Huntley	McPherson IB	Parker A	Sewell J	O'Neill T

Games 19 to 28 inclusive also counted for League Cup, 31, 32, 34 and 35 for the Midland Cup

1945/46

Third Division South (Northern Section)

#		Date	Opponent	Score	Scorers	Att.	1	2	3	4	5	6	7	8	9	10	11
1	Sep	8	Ipswich Town	0-1		10605	Wiseman G	Southwell AA	Taylor WB	Goodman	Peacock E	Hubbard J	McPherson IB	Pye J	Strain N	Hatton C	Beresford R
2		12	Southend United	3-7	Pye 2, Beresford	4227	Wiseman G	Southwell AA	Allen RHA	Ellmer FB	Parker A	Stancer LB	Beresford R	McPherson IB	Strain N	Pye J	Morrad FG
3		15	IPSWICH TOWN	1-1	McPherson	9142	Wiseman G	Southwell AA	Allen RHA	Hubbard J	Blagg EA	Stancer LB	McPherson IB	Pye J	Strain N	Sewell J	Beresford R
4		19	PORT VALE	3-1	Beresford 2, McPherson	5857	Wiseman G	Southwell AA	Allen RHA	Hubbard J	Ruecroft EJ	Tapping FH	Beresford R	McPherson IB	Woodcock E	Pye J	Meredith RD
5		22	NORWICH CITY	2-2	Pye (p), Sewell	10800	Wiseman G	Southwell AA	Allen RHA	Hubbard J	Harris K	Tapping FH	Beresford R	Pye J	Sewell J	McPherson IB	Toothill R
6		29	Norwich City	1-5	Pye	11692	Wiseman G	Corkhill WG	Allen RHA	Hubbard J	Southwell AA	Tapping FH	Beresford R	Sewell J	Tapping FH	Pye J	Alexander T
7	Oct	4	SOUTHEND UNITED	4-1	Pye 3, Beresford	4048	Wiseman G	Southwell AA	Allen RHA	Harris K	Peacock E	Hubbard J	Beresford R	McPherson IB	Tapping FH	Pye J	Strain N
8		6	Northampton T	2-1	Beresford, McPherson	7151	Wiseman G	Southwell AA	Allen RHA	Harris K	Corkhill WG	Hubbard J	Beresford R	McPherson IB	Hubbard J	Pye J	Strain N
9		13	NORTHAMPTON T	7-1	*see below	12576	Wiseman G	Southwell AA	Hutchinson J	Harris K	Sweet	Hubbard J	Beresford R	McPherson IB	Hubbard J	Pye J	Briggs R
10		20	MANSFIELD TOWN	1-0	Pye	17960	Wiseman G	Southwell AA	Hutchinson J	Harris K	Sweet	Hubbard J	Beresford R	McPherson IB	Hubbard J	Pye J	Alexander T
11		27	Mansfield Town	3-2	Beresford, Harris, Pye	8794	Wiseman G	Southwell AA	Robinson GF	Harris K	Corkhill WG	Hubbard J	Beresford R	McPherson IB	Airlie S	Pye J	Meredith RD
12	Nov	3	Queens Park Rangers	0-6		14527	Wiseman G	Southwell AA	Robinson GF	Harris K	Corkhill WG	Hubbard J	Beresford R	Hubbard J	Howarth G	McPherson IB	Meredith RD
13		10	QUEENS PARK RANGERS	0-1		22286	Flower T	Southwell AA	Ratcliffe PC	Harris K	Corkhill WG	Peacock E	Beresford R	McPherson IB	Howarth G	Pye J	Strain N
14	Dec	1	CLAPTON ORIENT	1-0	Meredith	13823	Kirby A	Southwell AA	Ratcliffe PC	Harris K	Corkhill WG	Read CW	Beresford R	Pye J	Parker A	McPherson IB	Meredith RD
15		8	Clapton Orient	3-3	McPherson 2, Pye		Thorne	Southwell AA	Ratcliffe PC	Harris K	Corkhill WG	Peacock E	McPherson IB	Pye J	Iceton OL	Sewell J	Parks A
16		22	Walsall	3-3	Parks, Pye, Sewell	3267	Kirby A	Southwell AA	Ratcliffe PC	Harris K	Corkhill WG	Goodwin FN	McPherson IB	Pye J	Sewell J	Parks A	Rhodes K
17		24	WALSALL	2-0	Pye 2	11871	Kirby A	Southwell AA	Ratcliffe PC	Harris K	Corkhill WG	Rossington K	Sewell J	McPherson IB	Sewell J	Pye J	Parks A
18		25	Watford	2-7	Hubbard, Meredith	3589	Kirby A	Southwell AA	Ratcliffe PC	Harris K	Corkhill WG	Peacock E	Beresford R	Pye J	Hubbard J	Parks A	Meredith RD
19		26	WATFORD	1-2	McPherson	17374	Kirby A	Robinson GF	Ratcliffe PC	Hubbard J	Corkhill WG	Peacock E	Girdham A	McPherson IB	Woodcock E	Pye J	Meredith RD
20		29	Port Vale	0-3		8000	Kirby A	Southwell AA	Allen RHA	Hubbard J	Corkhill WG	Peacock E	Beresford R	McPherson IB	Woollacott H	Pye J	Meredith RD

Scorers in game 9: Hubbard 2, McPherson 2, Beresford, Briggs, Pye

Third Division South Cup (Northern Section) Qualifying Competition

#		Date	Opponent	Score	Scorers	Att.	1	2	3	4	5	6	7	8	9	10	11
21	Jan	12	MANSFIELD TOWN	1-2	Pye	10796	Grant AF	Southwell AA	Allen RHA	Hubbard J	Corkhill WG	Peacock E	McPherson IB	Pye J	Ratcliffe PC	Moss G	Meredith RD
22		19	Mansfield Town	0-2		4430	Rollett E	Allen RHA	Ratcliffe PC	Corkhill WG	Southwell AA	Hoyle D	Beresford R	McPherson IB	Hubbard J	Jones A	Parks A
23		26	Port Vale	1-2	Cumberledge (og)	2632	Wilkinson N	Southwell AA	Ratcliffe PC	Corkhill WG	Brown AW	Sheen J	Hubbard J	Pye J	Dickson W	McPherson IB	Beresford R
24	Feb	2	PORT VALE	3-2	Beresford, Parks, Sheen	7000	Bland P	Ratcliffe PC	Allen RHA	Corkhill WG	Brown AW	Southwell AA	Beresford R	Pye J	Sheen J	Parks A	Meredith RD
25		9	Walsall	0-2		8088	Brown GR	Southwell AA	Ratcliffe PC	Southwell AA	Sheen J	Hubbard J	Beresford R	Pye J	McPherson IB	Parks A	Meredith RD
26		16	WALSALL	1-0	Hubbard	12109	Brown GR	Southwell AA	Ratcliffe PC	Corkhill WG	Brown AW	Hubbard J	Beresford R	Pye J	McPherson IB	Pye J	Hatton C
27		23	WATFORD	2-1	Beresford, O'Brien (og)	10921	Brown GR	Southwell AA	Ratcliffe PC	Baker D	Haines J	Hubbard J	Beresford R	Parks A	Hatton C	Pye J	Morrad FG
28	Mar	2	Watford	2-6	Beresford, Hatton	1500	Kirby A	Southwell AA	Allen RHA	Corkhill WG	Brown AW	Haines J	Beresford R	Parks A	Smith R	Hatton C	Morrad FG
29		9	Northampton T	1-2	Lovering	7755	Brown GR	Southwell AA	Ratcliffe PC	Allen RHA	Bagnall R	Sheen J	Beresford R	McPherson IB	Lovering W	Pye J	Morrad FG
30		16	NORTHAMPTON T	1-2	Pye	9925	Kirby A	Ratcliffe PC	Allen RHA	Corkhill WG	Southwell AA	Haines J	Beresford R	Pye J	Lovering W	Hatton C	Morrad FG
31		23	IPSWICH TOWN	1-0	Haines	9966	Brown GR	Southwell AA	Ratcliffe PC	Corkhill WG	Page D	Stewart R	Beresford R	Pye J	Haines J	McPherson IB	Parks A
32		30	Ipswich Town	2-1	Hatton, Rowley	10474	Brown GR	Southwell AA	Ratcliffe PC	Harris K	Clover G	Corkhill WG	Girdham A	Hatton C	Rowley W	Parks A	Morrad FG
33	Apr	6	Queens Park rangers	1-3	Ridyard (og)	13818	Brown GR	Southwell AA	Ratcliffe PC	Harris K	Bagnall R	Harris K	Girdham A	Parks A	Beresford R	Hubbard J	Howard
34		13	QUEENS PARK RANGERS	0-3		9000	Brown GR	Southwell AA	Ratcliffe PC	Corkhill WG	Bagnall R	Corkhill WG	Beresford R	McPherson IB	Haines J	Pye J	Morrad FG
35		19	NORWICH CITY	0-1		12000	Brown GR	Southwell AA	Robinson GF	Corkhill WG	Smith L	Hubbard J	Dean	Pye J	Barnard CH	Parks A	Toothill R
36		22	Norwich City	1-2	Pye	16000	Brown GR	Southwell AA	Robinson GF	Corkhill WG	Smith L	Baker D	Beresford R	Sail GH	Barnard CH	Pye J	Parks A

F.A. Cup

#		Date	Opponent	Score	Scorers	Att.	1	2	3	4	5	6	7	8	9	10	11
R1/1	Nov	17	BRADFORD CITY	2-2	McPherson, Hubbard	20000	Flower T	Southwell AA	Robinson GF	Harris K	Corkhill WG	Peacock E	Beresford R	Pye J	Hubbard J	McPherson IB	Stancer LB
R1/2		24	Bradford City	2-1	McPherson, Parker	11000	Kirby A	Southwell AA	Robinson GF	Harris K	Corkhill WG	Peacock E	Beresford R	McPherson IB	Hubbard J	Pye J	Parker A
R2/1	Dec	8	Northampton T	1-3	McPherson	10000	Kirby A	Southwell AA	Ratcliffe PC	Harris K	Corkhill WG	Peacock E	Beresford R	McPherson IB	Hubbard J	Pye J	Meredith RD
R2/2		15	NORTHAMPTON T	1-0	Martin	18000	Kirby A	Southwell AA	Ratcliffe PC	Harris K	Corkhill WG	Peacock E	Beresford R	Pye J	Martin DK	Hubbard J	Meredith RD

Ties played over two legs in season 1945/46

1946/47

12th in Division Three (South)

						Allen R	Bagnall R	Baxter WA	Beresford R	Brown C	Brown HT	Corkhill WG	Cumner HR	Dickson W	Fallon WJ	Flanagan DC	Freeman A	Gannon E	Houghton WE	Hubbard J	Jayes AG	Lockie AI	Lunn H	Morrad FG	Parks A	Robinson GF	Sewell J	Southwell AA	Toser E	Whittaker FJ	Wright BAW
1	Aug	31	BOURNEMOUTH	1-0	Brown C	26779				7	8	1	2	10		5		4		6					11	3			9	
2	Sep	7	Cardiff City	1-2	Lever(og)	24779				7	8	1	2	10		5		4		6					11	3			9	
3		11	BRISTOL CITY	0-3		17522				7	8	1	2	10				4		6		9			11	3		5		
4		14	NORWICH CITY	3-0	Sewell, Hubbard, Parks	18210		2			8	1	6	7				4		9	5				11	3	10			
5		21	Watford	2-2	Sewell, Hubbard	10100	3				8	1	2	7			11	4		9	5						10	6		
6		23	Port Vale	1-4	Cumner(p)	8574				9	8	1	2	7				4		6	5				11	3	10			
7		28	Northampton T	1-2	Beresford	11906		2		9	8	1	6	7				4			5				11	3	10			
8	Oct	3	PORT VALE	3-2	Brown C 2, Sewell	9542		2		9	8	1	6	7				4			5				11	3	10			
9		5	ALDERSHOT	2-0	Sewell 2	17298				7	8	1	2	11				4		6	5					3	10		9	
10		12	Brighton & Hove Alb.	2-3	Lunn, Sewell(p)	9419			6		8	1	2					4				9	5	7		11	3	10			
11		19	IPSWICH TOWN	1-2	Cumner	19886			6		8	1		11				4				9	5	7			3	10	2		
12		26	Leyton Orient	3-1	Jayes 2, Sewell	7613			6				1	11				4				9	5	7		8	3	10	2		
13	Nov	2	QUEENS PARK RANGERS	1-2	Sewell	26734			6					11				4				9	5	7		10	3	8	2		
14		9	Southend United	0-3		10100			6				1	11				4				9	5	7		10	3	8	2		
15		16	BRISTOL ROVERS	6-0	Jayes, Gannon, Lunn 2, Sewell 2	14390			6				1	8		11		4				9	5	7			3	10	2		
16		23	Mansfield Town	0-1		10899			6				1	4	8		11					9	5	7			3	10	2		
17	Dec	7	Crystal Palace	1-2	Jayes	12461			6				1		8		11	4				9	5	7			3	10	2		
18		21	Walsall	0-2		8801			6					1	8		11	4					5	7		10	3	9	2		
19		25	SWINDON TOWN	0-0		18439			6				1		8		11	4				9	5	7			3	10	2		
20		26	Swindon Town	2-4	Jayes, Brown C	17894					9	1					11	4		6		8	5	7			3		2		
21		28	Bournemouth	2-1	Brown C, Flanagan	13491					10	1		8		9		4		6		11	5	7			3		2		
22	Jan	4	CARDIFF CITY	1-1	Flanagan	28450						1		8		9		4		6		11	5	7			3	10	2		
23		18	Norwich City	2-2	Sewell, Lunn	16834	5						1	6	8			4	11	9				7			3	10	2		
24		23	TORQUAY UNITED	0-2		6295	5							6	8			4	11	9				7			3	10	2			1
25		25	WATFORD	4-1	Cumner, Sewell, Houghton, Jayes	9511							1	6	8			4	11			9	5	7			3	10	2		
26	Feb	1	NORTHAMPTON T	1-0	Sewell	13096							1	4	8	6			11			9	5	7			3	10	2		
27		8	Aldershot	1-1	Cumner	2974							1	4	8	6			11			9	5	7			3	10	2		
28	Mar	8	Queens Park Rangers	1-4	Sewell	9455			6				1		8		11	4				9	5	7				10	2		3	
29		22	Bristol Rovers	1-4	Cumner	11888			5					8	6			4	11			9		7			3	10	2			1
30		29	MANSFIELD TOWN	5-1	Fallon 2, Sewell 2, Houghton	12157			5				1	3	8	6	11	4	7			9						10	2			
31	Apr	4	EXETER CITY	0-0		15014			5				1	3	8	6	11	4	7			9						10	2			
32		5	Torquay United	2-1	Sewell 2	4064			5				1	3	8	6	11	4	7									10	2		9	
33		7	Exeter City	2-2	Sewell, Fallon	10796			5				1	3	8	6	11	4	7			10						9	2			
34		12	CRYSTAL PALACE	0-0		14890			5				1	3	8	6	11	4	7	9								10	2			
35		19	Reading	1-1	Parks	9446			5				1	3		6		4	7			10				11		8	2		9	
36		26	WALSALL	3-1	Whittaker, Dickson, Parks	10790			5				1	3		6		4	7			11				8		10	2		9	
37	May	3	Bristol City	1-1	Houghton	12210			5					3		6		4	11	9				7		8		10	2		1	
38		10	BRIGHTON & HOVE ALB.	2-0	Lunn, Whittaker(p)	12926			5				1	3		6		4	11					7		8		10	2		9	
39		17	Ipswich Town	2-1	Sewell 2	10301			5				1	3	8	6		4	11	9				7				10	2			
40		24	SOUTHEND UNITED	0-2		14041			5	9			1		8	6		4	11					7			3	10	2			
41		26	LEYTON ORIENT	1-2	Dickson	10785			5	9			1	4	8	6			7					11			3	10	2			
42		29	READING	1-0	Jayes	6142	5			6				3				7	4	11		9				8		10	2		1	
			Apps				1	6	25	9	13	36	29	35	15	15	2	2	38	18	13	26	23	24	1	17	29	37	32	2	10	2
			Goals						1		5			5	2	3	2		1	3	2	7		5		3		21			2	

Played in game 13: JA Dewick (1). In game 20: JK Marsh (10).

One own goal

F.A. Cup

R1	Nov	30	Leyton Orient	2-1	Jayes, Cumner	11800			6				1		8		11	4				9	5	7			3	10	2			
R2	Dec	14	SWINDON TOWN	2-1	Sewell, Fallon	18522			6				1		8		11	4				9	5	7			3	10	2			
R3	Jan	11	Luton Town	0-6		21820								10	1		8			4	11	6	9	5	7			3		2			

		p	w	d	l	f	a	pts
1	Cardiff City	42	30	6	6	93	30	66
2	Queen's Park Rgs.	42	23	11	8	74	40	57
3	Bristol City	42	20	11	11	94	56	51
4	Swindon Town	42	19	11	12	84	73	49
5	Walsall	42	17	12	13	74	59	46
6	Ipswich Town	42	16	14	12	61	53	46
7	Bournemouth	42	18	8	16	72	54	44
8	Southend United	42	17	10	15	71	60	44
9	Reading	42	16	11	15	83	74	43
10	Port Vale	42	17	9	16	68	63	43
11	Torquay United	42	15	12	15	52	61	42
12	NOTTS COUNTY	42	15	10	17	63	63	40
13	Northampton Town	42	15	10	17	72	75	40
14	Bristol Rovers	42	16	8	18	59	69	40
15	Exeter City	42	15	9	18	60	69	39
16	Watford	42	17	5	20	61	76	39
17	Brighton & Hove A.	42	13	12	17	54	72	38
18	Crystal Palace	42	13	11	18	49	62	37
19	Leyton Orient	42	12	8	22	54	75	32
20	Aldershot	42	10	12	20	48	78	32
21	Norwich City	42	10	8	24	64	100	28
22	Mansfield Town	42	9	10	23	48	96	28

Back: Cumner, Sewell, Allen, Lunn, Robinson, unknown, unknown, Bagnall, Adamson. Centre: C Jackson, unknown, Beresford, Hubbard, Southwell, Gannon, H Brown, Morrad, unknown, Cobley, unknown, C Brown. Front: Corkhill, Fisher (secretary), Hobson (director), Barnes (chairman), Cottee (treasurer), Stollery (manager), Whittaker, Linnell (director), Fallon, Parks

1947/48

6th in Division Three (South)

#	Date		Opponent	Score	Scorers	Att	Adamson H	Bagnall R	Baxter WA	Brown HT	Corkhill WG	Cumner HR	Dickson W	Evans FJ	Freeman A	Gannon E	Houghton WE	Howe HA	Jayes AG	Keeble FW	Lawton T	Lyman CC	Marsh JK	Molloy P	Orgill H	Parks A	Pimbley DW	Rigby NE	Sewell J	Southwell AA
1	Aug	23	Ipswich Town	0-2		14196			5	1				6	9		4	7	3	11		8							10	2
2		28	BOURNEMOUTH	1-2	Sewell	14065			5	1			11	6	9		4	7	3			8							10	2
3		30	BRISTOL CITY	3-1	Sewell, Houghton, Evans	18980			5	1	6	11			9		4	7	3							8			10	2
4	Sep	3	Bournemouth	0-2		16885			5			2	11	6	9		4	7							1	8			10	3
5		6	Reading	1-3	Sewell	11726			5	1	3	11	6	7			4					9				8			10	2
6		11	QUEENS PARK RANGERS	1-1	Lyman	19335			5	1	6	11				7	4		3			9				8			10	2
7		13	WALSALL	1-0	Cumner	20031			5	1	6	11	8			7	4		3			9							10	2
8		18	Queens Park Rangers	1-4	Keeble	15708			5	1	3	11	6			7	4			8		9							10	2
9		20	Leyton Orient	1-2	Sewell	11508			5	1	6					7	4		3	9		11				8			10	2
10		27	EXETER CITY	1-1	Lyman	20851			5	1	6	11		9		7	4		3			8							10	2
11	Oct	4	Newport County	1-3	Marsh	14015			5	1	6	11				7	4		3			9	8						10	2
12		11	PORT VALE	2-1	Cumner, Gannon	20172			5	1	6	11				7	4		3			8	9						10	2
13		18	Swindon Town	1-1	Marsh	18198			5	1	6	11				7	4		3			8	9						10	2
14		25	TORQUAY UNITED	0-0		23155			5	1	6	11				7	4		3			8	9						10	2
15	Nov	1	Crystal Palace	1-1	Marsh	16019			5	1	6	11				7	4		3	8			9						10	2
16		8	ALDERSHOT	0-2		20827			5	1	6	11				7	4		3	8			9						10	2
17		15	Northampton T	2-1	Lawton, Marsh	18272			5	1	6	11				4	7	3			9		10						8	2
18		22	BRISTOL ROVERS	4-2	Lawton 2, Sewell 2	31450			5	1	6	11				4	7	3			9		10						8	2
19	Dec	26	SWANSEA TOWN	5-1	Lawton 2, Freeman, Marsh, Sewell	42256	5			1	6	11				7	4	3			9		10						8	2
20		27	Swansea Town	1-1	Marsh	23573		6		1	5	11				7	4	3					9	1	10				8	2
21	Jan	3	Bristol City	0-1		35287		6	1		5	11		7			4	3			9		10						8	2
22		17	READING	5-1	Sewell 3, Marsh, Lawton	34866	5	6	1		4	11				7		3			9		10						8	2
23		31	Walsall	1-2	Lawton	20383		6	1		5					7	4	3			9		10			11			8	2
24	Feb	7	LEYTON ORIENT	1-4	Lawton	28875	5	6	1							7	4	3			9	11	10						8	2
25		14	Exeter City	1-0	Parks	16962		6	1		5					7	4	3				11	9			10			8	2
26		21	NEWPORT COUNTY	4-1	Sewell 2, Lawton, Lyman	17762		6	1		5					7	4	3			9	11				10			8	2
27		28	Port Vale	2-1	Lawton, Sewell	18147		6	1		5					7	4	3			9	11				10			8	2
28	Mar	6	SWINDON TOWN	2-1	Marsh 2	27767			1		5					7	4	3				11	9			10	6		8	2
29		13	Torquay United	2-2	Lyman, Marsh	8290		4	1		5					7		3				11	9			10	6		8	2
30		20	CRYSTAL PALACE	1-0	Lyman	30558		3	1		5					7	4	3			9	11	10				6		8	2
31		26	SOUTHEND UNITED	2-1	Lawton 2	35689			1		5					7	4	3			9	11	10				6		8	2
32		27	Aldershot	0-1		12750			1		5	7					4	3			9	11	10				6		8	2
33		29	Southend United	2-1	Cumner, Sheard(og)	17613		6	1		5	11					4	3			9		7				10		8	2
34	Apr	3	NORTHAMPTON T	3-2	Lawton 2, Lowery(og)	30903			1		5	11				7	4	3			9		10				6		8	2
35		7	Watford	3-1	Cumner, Sewell, Marsh	12532		6	1		5	11				7	4	3					9				10		8	2
36		10	Bristol Rovers	0-2		12451		6	1		5	11				7	4	3					9			8	10			2
37		15	IPSWICH TOWN	0-1		33505			1		5	11				7	4				9		10				6	3	8	2
38		17	NORWICH CITY	0-0		19183	6		1		5	11				7	4	3					9				10		8	2
39		22	BRIGHTON & HOVE ALB.	4-0	Pimbley, Sewell, Marsh, Cumner	19585		6	1		5	11					4	3			9		7				10		8	2
40		24	Brighton & Hove Alb.	3-1	Lawton 2, Cumner	19572			1		5	11				7	4	3			9		10				6		8	2
41		28	Norwich City	1-0	Lawton	37863			1		5	11				7	4	3			9		10				6		8	2
42	May	1	WATFORD	3-3	Lawton, Freeman, Sewell(p)	23174			1		6	11				7	4	3			9		10	5					8	2
			Apps				1	3	32	40	39	31	6	7	31	40	6	37	1	4	19	21	30	1	2	13	14	1	41	42
			Goals								6		1	2	1	1				1	18	5	12			1	1		17	

Two own goals

F.A. Cup

#	Date		Opponent	Score	Scorers	Att	Adamson H	Baxter WA	Brown HT	Corkhill WG	Cumner HR	Gannon E	Houghton WE	Howe HA	Lawton T	Lyman CC	Marsh JK	Sewell J	Southwell AA
R1	Nov	29	HORSHAM	9-1	Lawton 3, Sewell 3, Marsh 2, Freeman	24815		5	1	6	11	7	4	3	9		10	8	2
R2	Dec	13	STOCKTON	1-1	Sewell	30156		5	1	6	11	7	4	3	9		10	8	2
rep		20	Stockton	4-1	Lawton 3, Cumner	34261			1	5	11	7	4	3	9		10	8	2
R3	Jan	10	Birmingham City	2-0	Corkhill, Marsh	53000	6	1		4	11	7		3	9		10	8	2
R4		24	Swindon Town	0-1		27000		6	1	5	11	7	4	3	9		10	8	2

R2 after extra time. R2 replay at Middlesbrough

Played in R2 replay: J Hubbard (at no. 6)

	p	w	d	l	f	a	pts
1 Queen's Park Rgs.	42	26	9	7	74	37	61
2 Bournemouth	42	24	9	9	76	35	57
3 Walsall	42	21	9	12	70	40	51
4 Ipswich Town	42	23	3	16	67	61	49
5 Swansea Town	42	18	12	12	70	52	48
6 NOTTS COUNTY	42	19	8	15	68	59	46
7 Bristol City	42	18	7	17	77	65	43
8 Port Vale	42	16	11	15	63	54	43
9 Southend United	42	15	13	14	51	58	43
10 Reading	42	15	11	16	56	58	41
11 Exeter City	42	15	11	16	55	63	41
12 Newport County	42	14	13	15	61	73	41
13 Crystal Palace	42	13	13	16	49	49	39
14 Northampton Town	42	14	11	17	58	72	39
15 Watford	42	14	10	18	57	79	38
16 Swindon Town	42	10	16	16	41	46	36
17 Leyton Orient	42	13	10	19	51	73	36
18 Torquay United	42	11	13	18	63	62	35
19 Aldershot	42	10	15	17	45	67	35
20 Bristol Rovers	42	13	8	21	71	75	34
21 Norwich City	42	13	8	21	61	76	34
22 Brighton & Hove A.	42	11	12	19	43	73	34

Back: Ratcliffe (trainer), Gannon, Southwell, H Brown, Howe, Baxter, F Evans. Front: Freeman, Sewell, Lawton, Marsh, Parks, Corkhill

1948/49

11th in Division Three (South)

#	Date		Opponent	Score	Scorers	Att	Adamson H	Baxter WA	Brown AW	Brown HT	Chapman H	Corkhill WG	Evans FJ	Freeman A	Gannon E	Hold O	Houghton WE	Howe HA	Johnston TD	Lawton T	Marsh JK	McCavana WT	Mowl JW	Pimbley DW	Praski	Purvis B	Rigby NE	Russell RL	Sewell J	Smith RL	Southwell AA	Stone G
1	Aug	21	Torquay United	1-3	Sewell	10627				1		5		7	4			3	11	9	10						6	8		2	
2		26	WALSALL	2-0	Male(og), Johnston	35319				1		5		7	4			3	11	9	10						6	8		2	
3		28	BRISTOL ROVERS	4-1	Marsh, Sewell, Johnston, Lawton	33747		6		1		5		7	4				11	9	10					3		8		2	
4	Sep	2	Walsall	2-3	Sewell 2	14845		6		1		5		7	4				11	9	10					3		8		2	
5		4	Newport County	3-3	Sewell, Houghton, Marsh	16776		6		1		5			4		7	3	11	9	10							8		2	
6		9	IPSWICH TOWN	9-2	*See below	30985	6	5		1					4		7		11	9	10					3		8		2	
7		11	SWANSEA TOWN	1-1	Lawton	36471	6	5		1					4		7		11	9	10					3		8		2	
8		15	Ipswich Town	2-3	O'Mahoney(og), Lawton	21231	6	5		1		3			4		7		11	9	10							8		2	
9		18	Reading	4-1	Houghton, Evans 2, Johnston	23651	6	5		1			10		4		7	3	11	9								8		2	
10		23	SWINDON TOWN	1-2	Marsh	19527	6	5		1			9		4		7	3	11		10							8		2	
11		25	CRYSTAL PALACE	5-1	Johnston, Marsh 2, Sewell 2	24061	6	5		1					4		7	3	11	9		10						8		2	
12	Oct	2	Watford	1-1	Evans	22612	6	5		1			10		4		7	3	11	9								8		2	
13		9	Norwich City	0-3		29998	6			1					4		7	3	11	9	10							8		2	
14		16	EXETER CITY	9-0	Hold, Sewell 4, Lawton 4	36615	6		5	1					4	10	7	3	11	9								8		2	
15		23	Millwall	2-3	Sewell, Johnston	44627	6		5	1					4	10	7	3	11	9								8		2	
16		30	ALDERSHOT	2-0	Sewell, Johnston	35706	6		5	1				7	4			3	11	9								8		2	
17	Nov	6	Leyton Orient	1-3	Hold	16123	6		5	1			9	7	4	10		3	11									8		2	
18		13	PORT VALE	2-1	Johnston, Hold	29332									4	10	7	3	11	9		1						8		2	
19		20	Bristol City	1-3	Johnston	29663		6	5					7	4	10			11	9		1						8		2	
20	Dec	4	Brighton & Hove Alb.	2-3	Johnston, Hold	22994		4	5							10	7	3	11	9			1	6				8		2	
21		18	TORQUAY UNITED	5-0	Hold, Sewell 2, Johnston, Lawton	23007	6	5							4	10	7		11	9						3		8	1	2	
22		25	Northampton T	2-1	Johnston, Sewell	17724	6	5							4	10	7		11	9						3		8	1	2	
23		27	NORTHAMPTON T	2-0	Hold, Sewell	31171	6	5							4	10	7		11	9						3		8	1	2	
24	Jan	1	Bristol Rovers	2-3	Johnston, Hold	12617	6	5							4	9	7		11				10			3		8	1	2	
25		15	NEWPORT COUNTY	11-1	*See below	26843	6	5							4		7		11	9			10			3		8	1	2	
26		22	Swansea Town	1-3	Johnston	26493	6	5				4				10	7		11	9						3		8	1	2	
27	Feb	5	READING	1-0	Sewell	33165	6								4	10	7		11	9						3	5	8	1	2	
28		12	SOUTHEND UNITED	0-0		29188	6	5							4		7		11	9			10			3		8	1	2	
29		19	Crystal Palace	5-1	Johnston 3, Evans, Lawton	30925	6	5					10		4		7		11	9						3		8	1	2	
30		26	WATFORD	4-0	Johnston 3, Evans	31930	6	5					10		4		7		11	9						3		8	1	2	
31	Mar	5	NORWICH CITY	2-1	Lawton, Evans	34285	6	5					10		4		7		11	9						3		8	1	2	
32		12	Exeter City	1-3	Clark(og)	14374	6	5					10				7		11	9			4			3		8	1	2	
33		19	MILLWALL	1-3	Houghton	33818	6	5			4					10			11	9					7	3		8	1	2	
34		26	Aldershot	1-0	Johnston	9534	6	5			4		10				7		11	9						3		8	1	2	
35	Apr	2	LEYTON ORIENT	2-1	Houghton, Johnston	29740	6		5		4					10	7		11	9		2				3		8	1		
36		9	Port Vale	0-1		12198	6		5		4						7		11	9		2	10			3		8	1		
37		15	Bournemouth	1-2	Hold	24141	6	4	5		10			7		9			11			2				3		8	1		
38		16	BRISTOL CITY	2-1	Sewell 2	27149			5		4					9	7		11					6		3		8	1	2	
39		18	BOURNEMOUTH	2-3	Evans, Lawton	28161			5		4		10						11	9					7	3		8	1	2	
40		23	Swindon Town	0-3		17716	6				4					10		3	11	9					7			8	1	2	5
41		30	BRIGHTON & HOVE ALB.	1-1	Lawton	19829	6				4			7		10			11	9						3		8	1	2	5
42	May	7	Southend United	2-3	Sewell, Hold	12256	6				4			7		10	11		9							3		8	1	2	5
			Apps				33	27	13	17	10	7	10	10	29	19	31	15	41	36	11	3	8	3	21	5	2	42	22	39	3
			Goals									7				9	6		24	20	6							26			

*Scorers in game 6: Lawton 4, Sewell, Marsh, Houghton, Johnston, Bell(og). In game 25: Sewell 4, Johnston 2, Lawton 4, Houghton
Played in game 19: JS MacDonald (3). In game 38: J Jackson (10)

Four own goals

F.A. Cup

#	Date		Opponent	Score	Scorers	Att	Adamson H	Baxter WA	Brown HT	Gannon E	Hold O	Houghton WE	Howe HA	Johnston TD	Lawton T	Marsh JK	Purvis B	Sewell J	Southwell AA
R1	Nov	27	PORT VALE	2-1	Lawton 2	36514	6	5		4	10	7	3	11	9	1		8	2
R2	Dec	11	BARROW	3-2	Johnston 2, Lawton	36710	6	5	1	4	10	7	3	11	9			8	2
R3	Jan	8	Plymouth Argyle	1-0	Sewell	40000	6	5		4	10	7		11	9		3	8	2
R4		29	Liverpool	0-1		61003	6	5		4	10	7		11	9		3	8	2

R3 after extra time

		p	w	d	l	f	a	pts
1	Swansea Town	42	27	8	7	87	34	62
2	Reading	42	25	5	12	77	50	55
3	Bournemouth	42	22	8	12	69	48	52
4	Swindon Town	42	18	15	9	64	56	51
5	Bristol Rovers	42	19	10	13	61	51	48
6	Brighton & Hove A.	42	15	18	9	55	55	48
7	Ipswich Town	42	18	9	15	78	77	45
8	Millwall	42	17	11	14	63	64	45
9	Torquay United	42	17	11	14	65	70	45
10	Norwich City	42	16	12	14	67	49	44
11	NOTTS COUNTY	42	19	5	18	102	68	43
12	Exeter City	42	15	10	17	63	76	40
13	Port Vale	42	14	11	17	51	54	39
14	Walsall	42	15	8	19	56	64	38
15	Newport County	42	14	9	19	68	92	37
16	Bristol City	42	11	14	17	44	62	36
17	Watford	42	10	15	17	41	54	35
18	Southend United	42	9	16	17	41	46	34
19	Leyton Orient	42	11	12	19	58	80	34
20	Northampton Town	42	12	9	21	51	62	33
21	Aldershot	42	11	11	20	48	59	33
22	Crystal Palace	42	8	11	23	38	76	27

1949/50

Champions of Division Three (South) - Promoted

#	Date		Opponent	Score	Scorers	Att	Adamson H	Baxter WA	Boyes WE	Broome FH	Brunt GR	Chapman H	Corkhill WG	Crookes RE	Deans T	Evans FJ	Evans W	Freeman A	Johnston TD	Lawton T	Pimbley DW	Purvis B	Rigby NE	Robinson P	Sewell J	Simpson A	Smith RL	Southwell AA	Stone G
1	Aug	20	SOUTHEND UNITED	2-0	FJ Evans, Sewell	33507	6	5				4					7		10			11	9		3		8		1	2	
2		24	Norwich City	3-4	Lawton, W Evans, Sewell	32131	6	5				4					7		10			11	9		3		8		1	2	
3		27	Bristol Rovers	3-0	Lawton 2, Johnston	24816	6	5				4					7		10			11	9			3	8		1	2	
4	Sep	1	NORWICH CITY	5-0	FJ Evans 2, W Evans, Lawton, Johnston	35304	6	5				4					7		10			11	9			3	8		1	2	
5		3	BOURNEMOUTH	2-0	Lawton 2	34606	6	5				4					7		10			11	9			3	8		1	2	
6		8	EXETER CITY	3-3	Johnston 2, Lawton	32268	4		8					11			7		10			6	9			3			1	2	5
7		10	Crystal Palace	2-1	W Evans, Johnston	26847	6					4	5	8			7		10			11	9			3			1	2	
8		17	WATFORD	1-0	Sewell	34055	6	5				4					7		10			11	9			3	8		1	2	
9		24	Reading	1-0	W Evans	29134	6	5				4					7		10			11	9			3	8		1	2	
10	Oct	1	LEYTON ORIENT	7-1	Sewell 2, W Evans 2, Lawton 2, Johnston	36436	6	5				4					7		10			11	9			3	8		1	2	
11		8	Newport County	1-1	Sewell	21543	6	5				4				2	7		10			11	9			3	8	1			
12		15	BRISTOL CITY	4-1	Sewell 2, Southwell, Lawton	38055	6	5				4				2			10			11	9			3	8	1		7	
13		22	Brighton & Hove Alb.	3-2	Lawton 2(1p), Johnston	17411	6	5				4				3	7		10			11	9				8	1		2	
14		29	WALSALL	1-1	Lawton (p)	42789	6	5		7		4				3			10			11	9				8	1		2	
15	Nov	5	Millwall	3-1	Lawton, Sewell 2	19527	6	5		7		4				3			10			11	9				8	1		2	
16		12	SWINDON TOWN	3-0	Lawton 3 (2p)	37220	6	5		7		4				2			10			11	9			3	8	1			
17		19	Torquay United	0-0		13824	6	5		7		4				2			10			11	9			3	8	1			
18	Dec	3	Nottm. Forest	2-1	Lawton, Broome	37903	6	5		7		4				2			10			11	9			3	8	1			
19		17	Southend United	0-2		14628	6			7		4				2			10			11	9			3	8	5	1		
20		24	BRISTOL ROVERS	2-0	Broome, FJ Evans	32079	6	5		11		4				2	7		10				9			3	8	1			
21		26	IPSWICH TOWN	2-0	Sewell, Johnston	40419	6	5				4				2	7		10			11	9			3	8	1			
22		27	Ipswich Town	4-0	Sewell, Lawton 2, Johnston	22982	6	5				4				2	7		10			11	9			3	8	1			
23		31	Bournemouth	0-3		22651	6	5				4					7		10			11	9			3	8		1	2	
24	Jan	14	CRYSTAL PALACE	0-1		31381	6	5		7	9								10			11		4		3	8		1	2	
25		21	Watford	1-2	FJ Evans	17611	6				9	4					7		10			11				3	8	5	1	2	
26		28	ALDERSHOT	3-1	Broome, FJ Evans, Sewell	27076	6			7		4				2	9		10			11				3	8	5	1		
27	Feb	4	READING	4-0	Sewell, Broome, Lawton, Johnston	36245	6			7		4				2			10			11	9			3	8	5	1		
28		18	Leyton Orient	4-1	Sewell, Johnston 2, Broome	21633	6			7		4				2			10			11	9			3	8	5	1		
29		25	NEWPORT COUNTY	7-0	Sewell 3, Lawton 2(1p), Johnston, W Evans	28427	6			7		4				2			10			11	9			3	8	5	1		
30	Mar	4	Bristol City	0-4		32491	6			7		4				2			10			11	9			3	8	5	1		
31		11	BRIGHTON & HOVE ALB.	4-2	Tennant(og), Chapman, Lawton, Johnston	34283	6	5		7		8				2			10			11	9			3	4	1			
32		18	Walsall	3-3	Lawton, Johnston, Simpson	19589	6	5		7		8				2			10			11	9			3	4	1			
33		25	MILLWALL	2-0	Simpson 2	31061	6	5		7		4				2			10			11	9			3	8	1			
34	Apr	1	Swindon Town	1-1	Simpson	19876	6	5				4				2			10			11	9			3	7	8	1		
35		7	PORT VALE	3-1	Boyes, Lawton, Simpson	32097	6	5	11	7		4				2			10				9			3	8	1			
36		8	TORQUAY UNITED	1-1	Lawton	43456	6	5	11	7		4				2			10				9			3	8	1			
37		10	Port Vale	1-3	Lawton	15380	10	6			11					2	7						9		3		4	8	1	5	
38		15	Aldershot	0-2		9758	6	5				4				2			10			11	9			3	8	7	1		
39		22	NOTTM. FOREST	2-0	Sewell, Lawton	46000	6	5		7		4				2			10			11	9			3	8		1		
40		27	NORTHAMPTON T	2-0	Lawton 2	31928	6	5		7		4				2			10			11	9			3	8		1		
41		29	Northampton T	1-5	Broome	9971	6	5		7		4				2	9		10			11				3		8	1		
42	May	6	Exeter City	2-2	Broome, Crookes	10301	6	5		9	8		11	2			10	7							3	4		1		
					Apps		42	33	3	24	1	39	1	3	29	20	41	1	37	37	1	3	36	2	32	16	42	18	1		
					Goals				1	7		1			1		6	7		15	31					19	5		1		

One own goal

F.A. Cup

			Opponent	Score	Scorers	Att	Adamson H	Baxter WA	Boyes WE	Broome FH	Brunt GR	Chapman H	Corkhill WG	Crookes RE	Deans T	Evans FJ	Evans W	Freeman A	Johnston TD	Lawton T	Pimbley DW	Purvis B	Rigby NE	Robinson P	Sewell J	Simpson A	Smith RL	Southwell AA	Stone G
R1	Nov	26	TILBURY	4-0	Broome 2, Lawton, Sewell	28584	6	5		7		4				2			10			11	9			3	8	1			
R2	Dec	10	Rochdale	2-1	Johnston, Lawton	24231	6			7		4				2			10			11	9			3	8	5	1		
R3	Jan	7	BURNLEY	1-4	Johnston	44000	6	5				4							10	7		11	9			3	8		1	2	

		p	w	d	l	f	a	pts
1	NOTTS COUNTY	42	25	8	9	95	50	58
2	Northampton Town	42	20	11	11	72	50	51
3	Southend United	42	19	13	10	66	48	51
4	Nottingham Forest	42	20	9	13	67	39	49
5	Torquay United	42	19	10	13	66	63	48
6	Watford	42	16	13	13	45	35	45
7	Crystal Palace	42	15	14	13	55	54	44
8	Brighton & Hove A.	42	16	12	14	57	69	44
9	Bristol Rovers	42	19	5	18	51	51	43
10	Reading	42	17	8	17	70	64	42
11	Norwich City	42	16	10	16	65	63	42
12	Bournemouth	42	16	10	16	57	56	42
13	Port Vale	42	15	11	16	47	42	41
14	Swindon Town	42	15	11	16	59	62	41
15	Bristol City	42	15	10	17	60	61	40
16	Exeter City	42	14	11	17	63	75	39
17	Ipswich Town	42	12	11	19	57	86	35
18	Leyton Orient	42	12	11	19	53	85	35
19	Walsall	42	9	16	17	61	62	34
20	Aldershot	42	13	8	21	48	60	34
21	Newport County	42	13	8	21	67	98	34
22	Millwall	42	14	4	24	55	63	32

Back: Baxter, Deans, Southwell, R Smith, Houghton (manager), Rigby, Chapman, Adamson. Centre: Broome, Sewell, Lawton, W Evans, Johnston.
Front: F Evans, Simpson

1950/51

17th in Division Two

#	Date		Opponent	Score	Scorers	Att	Adamson H	Baxter WA	Bradley G	Broome FH	Brunt GR	Chapman H	Corkhill WG	Crookes RE	Deans T	Evans FJ	Evans W	Johnston TD	Lawton T	Leuty LH	Mann R	McPherson K	Paxton JW	Purvis B	Rigby NE	Robinson P	Roby D	Sewell J	Simpson A	Smith RL	Southwell AA
1	Aug	19	COVENTRY CITY	0-2		41088	6	5		7		4			2			10	11						3			8	9	1	
2		24	Queens Park Rangers	0-1		15962	6								2	9		10	11									8	5	1	
3		26	Cardiff City	0-2		36646	6			9		4		8	2	7		10	11				3						5	1	
4		31	QUEENS PARK RANGERS	3-3	W Evans, Crookes, Broome	33631	6			7		4		8	2			10	11	9			3						5	1	
5	Sep	2	BIRMINGHAM CITY	0-1		34648	6			7				8	3			10	11	9					4				5	1	2
6		4	Leicester City	1-1	Johnston	37169	6			7					3			10	11	9					4			8	5	1	2
7		9	Grimsby Town	4-1	Broome, Johnston, Sewell 2	21432	6		1	7			5	10	2			11		9					4			8			3
8		16	DONCASTER ROV.	1-2	Broome	39719	6		1	7					2			10	11	9					4			8	5		3
9		23	PRESTON NORTH END	1-3	Simpson	44277	6		1	7					2		11			9	5				4			8	10		3
10		30	Bury	0-0		21328			1	7					10	2			11	9	5	8		3	4			6			
11	Oct	7	Sheffield United	2-1	Sewell 2	37569			1	7			2	10					11	9	5		3		4			8	6		
12		14	LUTON TOWN	2-2	Johnston, Sewell	34054			1	7			2	10					11	9	5				4			8	6		3
13		21	Southampton	0-1		26105			1						11	2		7	10	9	5				4			8	6		3
14		28	BARNSLEY	2-1	Johnston, Lawton	39435			1	8			3	11	2			7	10	9	5				4				6		
15	Nov	4	Brentford	3-1	Johnston, Broome 2	26393			1	8			3	11	2			7	10	9	5				4				6		
16		11	BLACKBURN ROVERS	1-1	Broome(p)	35487			1	8			3		2			7	11	9	5				4			10	6		
17		18	Leeds United	1-0	Sewell	29728			1	9			3	11	2			7	10		5				4			8	6		
18		25	WEST HAM UNITED	4-1	Lawton 2, Sewell, W Evans	27073			1	10			3		2			7	11	9	5				4			8	6		
19	Dec	2	Swansea Town	1-2	Broome	22457			1	10			3		2			7	11	9	5				4			8	6		
20		9	HULL CITY	2-2	Leuty, Lawton	32708	6		1	10			3	11	2			7		9	5				4			8			
21		16	Coventry City	2-1	Lawton 2	25102			1				3	11	2			7	10	9	5				4			8	6		
22		23	CARDIFF CITY	1-2	Johnston	27634			1				3	11	2			7	10	9	5				4			8	6		
23		25	Chesterfield	0-0		20848			1				3	11	2			7	10	9	5				4			8	6		
24		26	CHESTERFIELD	1-0	Leuty (p)	35649			1				3	11	2			7	10	9	5				4			8	6		
25		30	Birmingham City	4-1	Sewell 2, Crookes 2	33770			1	7			3	11	2				10	9	5				4			8	6		
26	Jan	13	GRIMSBY TOWN	3-2	Johnston, Broome, Sewell	24849			1	9			3	11	2			7	10		5				4			8	6		
27		20	Doncaster Rov.	2-3	Sewell, Johnston	26045		5		9			3	11	2			7	10						4			8	6	1	
28	Feb	3	Preston North End	1-3	Johnston	35597				7			3	11	2				10	9	5				4			8	6	1	
29		17	BURY	4-2	Lawton 2, W Evans, Johnston	21008				7			3					10	11	9	5				4			8	6	1	2
30		24	SHEFFIELD UNITED	3-0	Sewell 2, Johnston	31290							3					10	11	9	5				4	7		8	6	1	2
31	Mar	3	Luton Town	1-1	Crookes	17398							3	7				10	11		5	9			4			8	6	1	2
32		10	SOUTHAMPTON	2-2	Sewell, Leuty	25712				7					3			10	11		5	9			4			8	6	1	2
33		17	Barnsley	0-2		12932	6							7	3			10	11		5	9			4					1	2
34		24	BRENTFORD	2-3	Broome, Johnston	24936				8				7	3			10	11	9	5				4			6		1	2
35		26	Manchester City	0-0		32047				7					11	3		8	10	9	5				4			6		1	2
36		31	Blackburn Rovers	0-0		17626				7					11	3		10	8	9	5				4			6		1	2
37	Apr	7	LEEDS UNITED	0-0		23466				7					11	3		10	8	9	5				4			6		1	2
38		14	West Ham United	2-4	Johnston 2	23226				7					3			10	11	9	5	6			4			8	1	1	2
39		21	SWANSEA TOWN	3-2	Broome, Crookes, Adamson	17787	8			9	7			11	3			10			5				4				6	1	2
40		28	Hull City	0-1		24190	8			9	7			11	2			10			5			3	4				6	1	
41		30	MANCHESTER CITY	0-0		13873	8		1		7			11	3			10			5	9			4				6		2
42	May	5	LEICESTER CITY	2-3	Crookes, Lawton	24092			1		7			10	3		8	11	9	5					4				6		2
			Apps				14	2	22	33	4	4	21	31	37	2	35	37	30	33	1	5	2	1	4	38	1	26	39	20	20
			Goals				1			10				6			3	14	9	3								14	1		

F.A. Cup

	Date		Opponent	Score	Scorers	Att	Adamson H	Baxter WA	Bradley G	Broome FH	Brunt GR	Chapman H	Corkhill WG	Crookes RE	Deans T	Evans FJ	Evans W	Johnston TD	Lawton T	Leuty LH	Mann R	McPherson K	Paxton JW	Purvis B	Rigby NE	Robinson P	Roby D	Sewell J	Simpson A	Smith RL	Southwell AA
R3	Jan	6	SOUTHAMPTON	3-4	Broome, Leuty(p), Simpson	29260			1	7			3	11	2				10	9	5				4			8	6		

		p	w	d	l	f	a	pts
1	Preston North End	42	26	5	11	91	49	57
2	Manchester City	42	19	14	9	89	61	52
3	Cardiff City	42	17	16	9	53	45	50
4	Birmingham City	42	20	9	13	64	53	49
5	Leeds United	42	20	8	14	63	55	48
6	Blackburn Rovers	42	19	8	15	65	66	46
7	Coventry City	42	19	7	16	75	59	45
8	Sheffield United	42	16	12	14	72	62	44
9	Brentford	42	18	8	16	75	74	44
10	Hull City	42	16	11	15	74	70	43
11	Doncaster Rovers	42	15	13	14	64	68	43
12	Southampton	42	15	13	14	66	73	43
13	West Ham United	42	16	10	16	68	69	42
14	Leicester City	42	15	11	16	68	58	41
15	Barnsley	42	15	10	17	74	68	40
16	Queen's Park Rgs.	42	15	10	17	71	82	40
17	NOTTS COUNTY	42	13	13	16	61	60	39
18	Swansea Town	42	16	4	22	54	77	36
19	Luton Town	42	9	14	19	57	70	32
20	Bury	42	12	8	22	60	86	32
21	Chesterfield	42	9	12	21	44	69	30
22	Grimsby Town	42	8	12	22	61	95	28

Back: Unknown, Purvis, Corkhill, Bradley, Linnell (director), Crookes, King, unknown. Standing: Potts (asst-trainer), Robinson, Simpson, Southwell, Baxter, R Smith, Chapman, Adamson, Rigby, unknown, Moore (trainer). Seated: Houghton (manager), F Evans, Broome, Sewell, Barnes (chairman), Lawton, W Evans, Johnston, W Fisher (secretary). Front: unknown, Jackson, Deans, Wylie.

1951/52

15th in Division Two

#		Date	Opponent	Score	Scorers	Att	Adamson H	Allen HA	Baxter WA	Bradley G	Broome FH	Brown RM	Brunt GR	Corkhill WG	Crookes RE	Deans T	Evans W	Jackson J	Johnston TD	Lawton T	Leuty LH	McCormack JC	McPherson I	McPherson K	Mitchell A	Robinson P	Simpson A	Smith RL	Southwell AA	Wylie RM
1	Aug	18	COVENTRY CITY	2-1	Crookes 2	34001					8				10	3			11	9	5		7			4	6	1	2	
2		25	Swansea Town	1-1	Lawton	17905					8				10	3			11	9	5		7			4	6	1	2	
3		30	BARNSLEY	4-0	Lawton(p), Broome 2, Johnston	15507					8				10	3			11	9	5		7			4	6	1	2	
4	Sep	1	BURY	2-1	Lawton 2	30915					8				10	3			11	9	5		7			4	6	1	2	
5		6	HULL CITY	4-0	Lawton, Broome, Johnston, McPherson	38203					8				10	3			11	9	5		7			4	6	1	2	
6		8	Luton Town	0-6		24511	6				8				10	3			11	9	5		7			4		1	2	
7		12	Barnsley	1-2	Crookes	16148								11		2	8	3	10				9			4	6	1		
8		15	NOTTM. FOREST	2-2	Broome, Crookes	44087			5		7				11	3	10		8	9						4	6	1	2	
9		20	Hull City	3-1	Lawton 2, Johnston	35499			5		7	11	8			3			10	9						4	6	1	2	
10		22	QUEENS PARK RANGERS	0-0		27734			5		8	11	6			3			10	9				7		4		1	2	
11		29	Blackburn Rovers	0-2		25560			6		8	11				3	7			9	5	10				4		1	2	
12	Oct	6	Brentford	0-1		28214					9	11	4		10	3			8		5		7			6			2	
13		13	DONCASTER ROV.	1-0	Crookes	23087					9		4		11	3		8			5		7			6		1	2	10
14		20	Everton	5-1	Jackson 4, Crookes	49604							4		11	3		8		9	5		7			6		1	2	10
15		27	SOUTHAMPTON	3-4	Jackson, Broome(p), Crookes	31540					9		4		11	3		8			5		7			6		1	2	10
16	Nov	3	Sheffield Wednesday	0-6		46530							4		11	3		8		9	5		7			6		1	2	10
17		10	LEEDS UNITED	1-2	Jackson	25307				1			4		11	3		8		9	5		7			6			2	10
18		17	Rotherham Utd.	0-2		20961				1					11	3	10	8		9	5		7			4	6		2	
19		24	CARDIFF CITY	1-1	Jackson	19452				1		7			11	3	10	8			5	9				4	6		2	
20	Dec	1	Birmingham City	0-2		26554					7		4		11	3		8	10	9	5						6	1	2	
21		8	LEICESTER CITY	2-3	Crookes 2	27065					8				10	3			11	9	5		7			4	6	1	2	
22		15	Coventry City	2-0	Broome, McCormack	20275		2			8				11	3				9	5	10	7			4	6	1		
23		22	SWANSEA TOWN	2-0	Broome, McCormack	22184	6				10				11	3				9	5	8	7			4		1	2	
24		25	SHEFFIELD UNITED	3-1	McCormack, Adamson, McPherson	30019	6				10				11	3				9	5	8	7			4		1	2	
25		26	Sheffield United	0-1		39383	6	2	5	1					10				11	9	3	8	7			4				
26		29	Bury	1-2	Broome	14942	6		5		10				11					8	3	9	7			4		1	2	
27	Jan	5	LUTON TOWN	5-4	* See below	22808	6				10				11	3				8	5	9	7			4		1	2	
28		19	Nottm. Forest	2-3	McCormack, Broome	40005	6			1	10				11	3				8	5	9	7			4			2	
29		26	Queens Park Rangers	4-1	Lawton 2, McCormack, Crookes	18891	6			1	7		4		11	3		10		9	5	8							2	
30	Feb	9	BLACKBURN ROVERS	0-1		26177	6	2		1	7		4		11	3		10		9	5	8								
31		16	BRENTFORD	5-2	* See below	22503	6			1	8				11	3			9		5		7			4			2	
32	Mar	1	Doncaster Rov.	5-1	Lawton 2, Crookes 2, McPherson	22467	6			1	8				10	3			11	9	5		7			4			2	
33		8	EVERTON	0-0		29380	6	2		1	8				10	3			11	9	5		7			4				
34		15	Southampton	0-4		20604	6			1	8				10	3				11	5	9	7			4			2	
35		22	SHEFFIELD WEDNESDAY	2-2	Crookes, Broome	33230			6	1	7				10	3				11	5	9	8			4			2	
36		29	Leeds United	0-1		12867			2	6	1	7			10	3				11	5		8	9		4				
37	Apr	5	ROTHERHAM UTD.	0-3		13161			2	6	1	7			10	3				11	5		8	9		4				
38		11	West Ham United	1-2	Crookes	22859			2		1				11	3	10	8			5	9	7			4	6			
39		12	Cardiff City	0-1		24178	8	2	5	1	7				11	3	10					9					6		4	
40		14	WEST HAM UNITED	1-0	Robinson	16306	8	2		1	10				11	3					5	9	7			6			4	
41		19	BIRMINGHAM CITY	5-0	Wylie 4, Adamson	24360	8	2		1					11	3					5	9	7			4	6			10
42		26	Leicester City	1-1	McPherson	21318	8	2		1	11					3					5	9	7			4	6			10
			Apps				17	11	10	19	32	7	11	1	38	40	7	11	20	29	38	17	34	2	1	38	17	23	32	7
			Goals				2				13				15			7	4	12		6	6			1				4

*Scorers in game 27: McCormack, McPherson, Crookes, Broome, Owen (og)
In game 31: Broome 2 (1p), Lawton, Johnston, McPherson

One own goal

F.A. Cup

		Date	Opponent	Score	Scorers	Att	Adamson H	Allen HA	Baxter WA	Bradley G	Broome FH	Brown RM	Brunt GR	Corkhill WG	Crookes RE	Deans T	Evans W	Jackson J	Johnston TD	Lawton T	Leuty LH	McCormack JC	McPherson I	McPherson K	Mitchell A	Robinson P	Simpson A	Smith RL	Southwell AA	Wylie RM
R3	Jan	12	STOCKTON	4-0	Broome 2, Lawton, McCormack	22805	6		5	1	10				11					8	3	9	7			4			2	
R4	Feb	2	PORTSMOUTH	1-3	Lawton	46500	6			1	7		4		11	3		10		9	5	8							2	

Jackson, Cruickshank, King, Adamson, R Smith, Bradley, Wade, unknown, unknown. Centre: K McPherson, Corkhill, unknown, Southwell, Robinson, Leuty, Simpson, Deans, V Smith, Baxter. Seated: Moore (trainer), I McPherson, Broome, Houghton (manager), Lawton, W Evans, Johnston, Potts (assistant trainer). Front: Brunt, Wylie, Guyler, unknown.

		p	w	d	l	f	a	pts
1	Sheffield Wed.	42	21	11	10	100	66	53
2	Cardiff City	42	20	11	11	72	54	51
3	Birmingham City	42	21	9	12	67	56	51
4	Nottingham Forest	42	18	13	11	77	62	49
5	Leicester City	42	19	9	14	78	64	47
6	Leeds United	42	18	11	13	59	57	47
7	Everton	42	17	10	15	64	58	44
8	Luton Town	42	16	12	14	77	78	44
9	Rotherham United	42	17	8	17	73	71	42
10	Brentford	42	15	12	15	54	55	42
11	Sheffield United	42	18	5	19	90	76	41
12	West Ham United	42	15	11	16	67	77	41
13	Southampton	42	15	11	16	61	73	41
14	Blackburn Rovers	42	17	6	19	54	63	40
15	NOTTS COUNTY	42	16	7	19	71	68	39
16	Doncaster Rovers	42	13	12	17	55	60	38
17	Bury	42	15	7	20	67	69	37
18	Hull City	42	13	11	18	60	70	37
19	Swansea Town	42	12	12	18	72	76	36
20	Barnsley	42	11	14	17	59	72	36
21	Coventry City	42	14	6	22	59	82	34
22	Queen's Park Rgs.	42	11	12	19	52	81	34

1952/53

19th in Division Two

							Adamson H	Allen HA	Baxter WA	Bradley G	Broome FH	Brunt GR	Crookes RE	Deans T	Edwards J	Evans W	Groome PB	Jackson J	Jarvis H	Johnston TD	Leuty LH	Linton JA	Lovell FW	McCormack JC	McPherson I	McPherson K	Robinson P	Simpson A	Smith RL	Southwell AA	Wade A	Wylie RM
1	Aug	23	Leicester City	0-3		29584	8	2		1			11	3							5			9	7			4	6				10
2		28	ROTHERHAM UTD.	2-1	Jackson, McCormack	23216	4	3		1			11	2				8			6	5		9	7								10
3		30	NOTTM. FOREST	3-2	McCormack 2, Crookes	39920	4			1			11	2				8			6	5		9	7							3	10
4	Sep	1	Rotherham Utd.	3-2	Broome, Crookes, McCormack	17043	4	3	5	1	7		11	2				8	6			9											10
5		6	SOUTHAMPTON	1-2	Wylie	25160	4	3					11	2				8			6	5		9	7					1			10
6		11	FULHAM	1-1	Jackson	18509	4			1	7		11	2			3	8			6	5		9									10
7		13	Bury	1-0	Wylie	12445	4			1			11	2				8			6	5		9	7							3	10
8		15	Fulham	0-6		14072	4		3	1			11	2				8			6	5		9	7								10
9		20	BIRMINGHAM CITY	2-0	Crookes, Wylie	24538	4			1			11	2				8			6	5		9	7							3	10
10		27	Luton Town	1-5	Johnston	13557	4			1			11	2				8			6	5		9	7							3	10
11	Oct	4	LEEDS UNITED	3-2	McCormack 3	22836	4			1	7		11	2				8			6	5		9								3	10
12		11	Everton	0-1		40626	4			1			11	2							6	5		9	7				8			3	10
13		18	BRENTFORD	4-0	Jackson 2, I McPherson, Harper(og)	26033	4						11	2				8			6	5		9	7					1		3	10
14	Nov	1	SWANSEA TOWN	3-4	McCormack, Johnston 2	21171	4						11	2				8			6	5		9	7					1		3	10
15		8	Huddersfield T	0-1		28205	4						11	2				8			6	5	1	9	7							3	10
16		15	SHEFFIELD UNITED	0-3		23889	4						11	2				8			6	5	1		7	9						3	10
17		22	Barnsley	2-1	McCormack, Johnston	11626	4					7	11	2						6	10	5	1	9								3	8
18		29	LINCOLN CITY	1-1	McCormack	18802	4			1			11	2	7					6	10	5		9								3	8
19	Dec	6	Hull City	0-6		18333	4							2	10					6	8	5	1	9	11							3	7
20		13	BLACKBURN ROVERS	5-0	K McPherson 4, Edwards	10222	4		5	1	7		11	2	10	8				6						9						3	
21		20	LEICESTER CITY	2-2	Evans, K McPherson	16168	4		5	1	7		11	2	10	8				6						9						3	
22		25	West Ham United	2-2	Broome(p), K McPherson	23614	4		5	1	7		11	3	10	8				6		2				9							
23		27	WEST HAM UNITED	1-1	Evans	24189	4		5	1	7		11	3	10	8				6		2				9							
24	Jan	1	Blackburn Rovers	2-3	Broome(p), K McPherson	27303	4		5	1	7		11	3	10	8				6		2				9							
25		3	Nottm. Forest	0-1		38002	4			1			11	3	10	8					5			7	9	6			2				
26		17	Southampton	1-1	Evans	16262	4				7		11	3	10	8				6	5	1			9				2				
27		24	BURY	2-1	Johnston 2	18750	4				7			3	11	8				6	5	1			9				2				10
28	Feb	7	Birmingham City	2-3	Evans, Jackson	24522		2	5				11	3	10	8		9			6		1	7			4						
29		19	LUTON TOWN	1-2	Broome(p)	8648	4			1	7			3	11	8				6	5				9				2				10
30		21	Leeds United	1-3	Edwards	22922	4						11	3	10	8				6	5	1		7	9				2				
31	Mar	5	EVERTON	2-2	K McPherson, Edwards	7529	4							3	11	8					5				9	6			2				10
32		7	Brentford	0-5		16147	4				7		11	3	10	8		6			5	1			9				2				
33		14	DONCASTER ROV.	4-3	K McPherson 2, Crookes 2	17906	4						11	3	10					6	5	1		7	9				2				8
34		21	Swansea Town	1-5	McCormack	20304	4						11	3	10					6	5	1		7	9				2				8
35		28	HUDDERSFIELD T	1-0	Wylie	15816	4			1			11	3	10					6	5			7	9				2				8
36	Apr	3	PLYMOUTH ARGYLE	0-4		18363	4			1	7		11	3	10		9			6	5								2				
37		4	Sheffield United	1-2	Crookes	33603				1		4	11	3	10					6	5			7	9				2				8
38		6	Plymouth Argyle	2-2	Adamson, Broome	18330	8			1	9	4	11	3		10				6	5								2				7
39		11	BARNSLEY	1-0	Adamson	13855	10			1	8	4	11	3						6	5								2				7
40		18	Lincoln City	0-3		14747				1		4	11	3		10		8		6	5				9				2				7
41		22	Doncaster Rov.	0-2		10063		2		1		4	8	3	11		9			6	5					7							10
42		25	HULL CITY	2-0	McCormack 2	11699				1		4	11	3			10			6	5		8	9					2				7
			Apps				37	6	8	28	16	7	38	42	21	13	1	21	5	37	38	11	1	25	16	19	4	2	3	28	3	32
			Goals				2				5		6		3	4		5		6				13	1	10							4

One own goal

F.A. Cup

R3	Jan	10	Leicester City	4-2	McPherson 2, Crookes, Broome(p)	30889	4				7		11	3		8				6	5	1			9				2				10
R4		31	Bolton Wanderers	1-1	McPherson	40048	4				7		11	3		8				6	5	1			9				2				10
rep	Feb	5	BOLTON WANDERERS	2-2	Jackson, McPherson	33669	4				7		11	3		8		10		6	5	1			9				2				
r2		9	Bolton Wanderers	0-1		23171	4				7		11	3		8				6	5	1			9				2				10

R4 replay after extra time. Replay 2 at Hillsborough

	p	w	d	l	f	a	pts
1 Sheffield United	42	25	10	7	97	55	60
2 Huddersfield Town	42	24	10	8	84	33	58
3 Luton Town	42	22	8	12	84	49	52
4 Plymouth Argyle	42	20	9	13	65	60	49
5 Leicester City	42	18	12	12	89	74	48
6 Birmingham City	42	19	10	13	71	66	48
7 Nottingham Forest	42	18	8	16	77	67	44
8 Fulham	42	17	10	15	81	71	44
9 Blackburn Rovers	42	18	8	16	68	65	44
10 Leeds United	42	14	15	13	71	63	43
11 Swansea Town	42	15	12	15	78	81	42
12 Rotherham United	42	16	9	17	75	74	41
13 Doncaster Rovers	42	12	16	14	58	64	40
14 West Ham United	42	13	13	16	58	60	39
15 Lincoln City	42	11	17	14	64	71	39
16 Everton	42	12	14	16	71	75	38
17 Brentford	42	13	11	18	59	76	37
18 Hull City	42	14	8	20	57	69	36
19 NOTTS COUNTY	42	14	8	20	60	88	36
20 Bury	42	13	9	20	53	81	35
21 Southampton	42	10	13	19	68	85	33
22 Barnsley	42	5	8	29	47	108	18

Back: Allen, Simpson, Southwell, K McPherson, Broome, Jackson, King. Standing: Brunt, Johnston, Bradley, Wade, R Smith, Cruickshank, Mann, Jarvis, McCormack, V Smith. Seated: Morley (director), Deans, Robinson, Evans, Leuty, Barnes (president), Baxter, Crookes, Wylie, Adamson. Front: Watts, Carver, Broadbent, Guyler, Groome.

1953/54

14th in Division Two

#		Date	Opponent	Score	Scorers	Att	Adamson H	Allen HA	Baxter WA	Bradley G	Broadbent AH	Brunt GR	Carver GF	Chatham RH	Coole W	Crookes RE	Cruickshank FJ	Deans T	Edwards J	Jarvis H	Johnston TD	Laird A	Leuty LH	Leverton R	Lovell FW	McCormack JC	Southwell AA	Taylor JE	Wade A	Wills GF	Wylie RM
1	Aug	19	Leeds United	0-6		18432	4			1						11		3	10		6		7	5		9	2				8
2		22	Bury	3-3	Johnston, McCormack, Lovell	12168	4			1		7				11		3			6		5		8	9	2				10
3		27	OLDHAM ATHLETIC	2-0	McCormack 2	15091	4			1		7				11		3			6		5		8	9	2				10
4		29	DONCASTER ROV.	1-5	Brunt	10117	4			1	8	7				11		3	10		6		5			9	2				
5	Sep	1	Oldham Athletic	3-1	Johnston 2, Carver	22083		4		1		7	8			11		3			6	10	5			9	2				
6		5	Blackburn Rovers	0-2		23244		4		1		7	8			11		3			6	10	5			9	2				
7		10	EVERTON	0-2		12515		4		1			8			11		3			6	10	5			9	2				7
8		12	DERBY COUNTY	0-1		23899		4	5	1			8			11		3			6	7			10	9	2				
9		19	Brentford	0-0		12770		4	5	1			8			11		3			6	10				9	2				7
10		23	Everton	2-3	Johnston, Wills	32005		4		1								3			6	10	9		8		2		5	11	7
11		26	BRISTOL ROVERS	1-5	Lovell	15318		4		1							3	11			6	10	5		8	9				2	7
12	Oct	3	Lincoln City	0-3		16448		4		1					7	11		3			6		5	9	10		2				8
13		10	Nottm. Forest	0-5		30559			5	1					7	11		3	10		6	4		9			2				8
14		17	LUTON TOWN	1-2	Leverton	12208		4		1					7	11		3			6	9	5	8			2				10
15		24	Plymouth Argyle	3-3	Johnston, Wylie, Crookes	16656	4			1					7	11		3			6	9	5	8			2				10
16		31	SWANSEA TOWN	3-0	Southwell, Johnston, Coole	12084	4			1					7	11		3			6	9	5	8			2				10
17	Nov	7	Rotherham Utd.	1-0	Wylie	12189	4			1					7	11		3			6	9	5	8			2				10
18		14	LEICESTER CITY	1-1	McCormack	27806	4			1					7	11		3			6		5	8		9	2				10
19		21	Stoke City	1-0	Crookes	17887	4			1					7	11		3			6	9	5	8			2				10
20		28	FULHAM	0-0		19336	4			1					7	11		3			6	9	5	8			2				10
21	Dec	5	West Ham United	2-1	Johnston, Crookes	16236	4			1					7	11		3			6	9	5	8			2				10
22		12	LEEDS UNITED	2-0	Johnston, Crookes	17552	4			1					7	11		3			6	9	5	8			2				10
23		19	BURY	0-0		12494	4			1					7	11		3			6	9	5	8			2				10
24		25	Birmingham City	0-3		30489	4			1					7	11		3			6	9	5	8			2				10
25		26	BIRMINGHAM CITY	2-1	McCormack, Leverton	20986	6			1			4			7		3				11	5	10		9	2				8
26	Jan	2	Doncaster Rov.	2-4	Johnston, McCormack	14233	6	4		1								3				11	5	10		9	2			7	8
27		16	BLACKBURN ROVERS	0-5		15044	4			1					7			3			6	11	5	10		9	2				8
28		23	Derby County	0-0		18302	4			1					6	7	11	3				9	5	10			2				8
29	Feb	6	BRENTFORD	2-0	Crookes 2	10507	4			1					6	7	11	3				9	5	10			2				8
30		13	Bristol Rovers	1-1	Chatham	20719	4			1					6	7	11	3				9	5	10			2				8
31		20	LINCOLN CITY	1-1	Johnston	21091	4	2		1					6	7	11	3				9	5				8				10
32		27	NOTTM. FOREST	1-1	Taylor	36988	4	2		1					6	7	11	3				9	5				8				10
33	Mar	6	Luton Town	1-2	Taylor	14623	4			1					6	7	11	3				9	5				2	8			10
34		13	PLYMOUTH ARGYLE	2-0	Johnston, Crookes	11157	4			1					6	7	11	3				9	5				2	8			10
35		20	Swansea Town	2-2	Coole, Taylor	15744	4			1					6	7	11	3					5	9			2	8			10
36		27	STOKE CITY	2-1	Crookes, Taylor	11877	4	3		1					6	7	11						5	9			2	8			10
37	Apr	3	Fulham	3-4	Johnston 2, Wylie	17796	4			1					6	7	11	3				9	5				2	8			10
38		10	ROTHERHAM UTD.	1-2	Wylie	11894	4			1					6	7	11	3				9	5				2	8			10
39		16	Hull City	2-0	Crookes, Taylor	24031	6			1					4	7	11	3				9	5				2	8		7	10
40		17	Leicester City	2-2	Johnston 2	32142	6			1					4	7	11	3				9	5				2	8			10
41		19	HULL CITY	1-1	Wylie	13022	6			1					4	7	11	3					5			9	2	8			10
42		24	WEST HAM UNITED	3-1	McCormack 2, Johnston	9971	4			1					7	11		3			6		5			9	2	8			10
					Apps		32	13	3	42	1	6	5	14	29	37	1	40	4	20	38	1	39	21	6	16	39	12	2	3	38
					Goals					1	1	1	2	9					16			2	2	8	1	5			1		5

F.A. Cup

			Opponent	Score	Scorer	Att	Adamson			Bradley					Coole			Deans			Johnston		Leuty	Leverton		McCormack	Southwell				Wylie
R3	Jan	9	Everton	1-2	Wylie	49737	4			1					7			3			6	11	5	10		9	2				8

		p	w	d	l	f	a	pts
1	Leicester City	42	23	10	9	97	60	56
2	Everton	42	20	16	6	92	58	56
3	Blackburn Rovers	42	23	9	10	86	50	55
4	Nottingham Forest	42	20	12	10	86	59	52
5	Rotherham United	42	21	7	14	80	67	49
6	Luton Town	42	18	12	12	64	59	48
7	Birmingham City	42	18	11	13	78	58	47
8	Fulham	42	17	10	15	98	85	44
9	Bristol Rovers	42	14	16	12	64	58	44
10	Leeds United	42	15	13	14	89	81	43
11	Stoke City	42	12	17	13	71	60	41
12	Doncaster Rovers	42	16	9	17	59	63	41
13	West Ham United	42	15	9	18	67	69	39
14	NOTTS COUNTY	42	13	13	16	54	74	39
15	Hull City	42	16	6	20	64	66	38
16	Lincoln City	42	14	9	19	65	83	37
17	Bury	42	11	14	17	54	72	36
18	Derby County	42	12	11	19	64	82	35
19	Plymouth Argyle	42	9	16	17	65	82	34
20	Swansea Town	42	13	8	21	58	82	34
21	Brentford	42	10	11	21	40	78	31
22	Oldham Athletic	42	8	9	25	40	89	25

Back: Moore (trainer), Adamson, Southwell, Leuty, Bradley, Wade, Jarvis, McCormack. Front: Jarvis, Leverton, Johnston, Poyser (manager), Deans, Wylie, Crookes

1954/55

7th in Division Two

						Adamson H	Bradley G	Broadbent AH	Carver GF	Chatham RH	Coole W	Crookes RE	Cruickshank FJ	Deans T	Jackson I	Jarvis H	Johnston TD	Leuty LH	Leverton R	Lister E	Loxley H	McCormack JC	Rawson K	Roby D	Southwell AA	Taylor JE	Wade A	Wills GF	Wylie RM
1	Aug	21	DERBY COUNTY	2-3	Coole, Wylie	29528	4	1			6	7	11		3				9	5						2	8			10
2		23	Port Vale	1-1	Taylor	26805	4	1			6	7	11		3				9	5						2	8			10
3		28	West Ham United	0-3		19638	4	1		8	5	7	11		3				6							2	9			10
4	Sep	2	PORT VALE	1-1	Chatham	17723	4	1			6	7	11		3					5			9			2	8			10
5		4	BLACKBURN ROVERS	3-1	Coole, Crookes, McCormack	14918	4	1			6	7	11		3					5			9			2	8			10
6		9	PLYMOUTH ARGYLE	2-0	Chatham, McCormack	14497	4	1			6	7	11		3					5			9			2	8			10
7		11	Fulham	1-3	Johnston	26619	4	1				7			3				6	5			9			2	8		11	10
8		15	Plymouth Argyle	3-1	Taylor, Wills, Broadbent	17173	4	1	11						3				6	5			9			2	8		7	10
9		18	SWANSEA TOWN	2-1	Taylor 2	17928	4	1	11						3				6	5			9			2	8		7	10
10		25	Nottm. Forest	1-0	McCormack	30348	4	1	11		6				3					5			9			2	8		7	10
11	Oct	2	Liverpool	1-3	Wills	37643	4	1	11		6				3					5			9			2	8		7	10
12		9	STOKE CITY	1-0	Leverton	22266	4	1	11		6				3					5	9						2	8		7	10
13		16	Middlesbrough	0-2		20585	4	1	11	8	6				3					5	9						2			7	10
14		23	LINCOLN CITY	2-1	Wylie, McCormack	19474	4	1	11		6				3					10	5			9			2			7	8
15		30	Hull City	2-5	Johnston, Broadbent	22995	4	1	11						3			6	10	5			9			2			7	8
16	Nov	6	LUTON TOWN	3-3	Johnston, Wylie, Broadbent	10395	4	1	11						3			6	10				9			2		5	7	8
17		13	Rotherham Utd.	0-2		11740	4	1	9				11		3			6	10	5						2			7	10
18		20	LEEDS UNITED	1-2	Broadbent	14519	4	1	11	8					3			6	9	5						2			7	10
19		27	Bury	2-1	Wylie, Broadbent	12495	4	1	11						3				6		10		9	5		2			7	8
20	Dec	4	BIRMINGHAM CITY	3-2	Johnston 2, Broadbent	13477	4	1	11						3				6		10		9	5		2			7	8
21		11	Ipswich Town	1-0	Wylie	12442	4	1	11						3				6	5	10		9			2			7	8
22		18	Derby County	1-1	Wylie	15857	4	1	11						3				6	5	10		9			2			7	8
23		25	BRISTOL ROVERS	2-0	Wylie, Broadbent	19647	4	1	11						3	9			6	5	10					2			7	8
24		27	Bristol Rovers	4-1	Broadbent, Leverton, Jackson 2	28885	4	1	11						3	9			6	5	10					2			7	8
25	Jan	1	WEST HAM UNITED	5-1	Jackson 4, Broadbent(p)	20290	4	1	11						3	9			6	5	10					2			7	8
26		15	Blackburn Rovers	5-4	Jackson 2, Wills 2, Wylie	18664	4	1	11						3	9			6	5	10					2			7	8
27	Feb	5	Swansea Town	0-3		21527	4	1	11						3	9			6	5	10					2			7	8
28		12	NOTTM. FOREST	4-1	Wills 2, Jackson, Broadbent	31104	4	1	11						3	9			6	5	10					2			7	8
29	Mar	3	LIVERPOOL	0-3		11026	4	1	11						3	9			6	5	10					2			7	8
30		5	MIDDLESBROUGH	1-3	Jackson	22354	4	1	11						3	9			6	5	10					2			7	8
31		16	Lincoln City	2-1	Wills, Leverton	8082	4	1							3	9			6	5	10				7	2			11	8
32		19	HULL CITY	3-1	Wylie, Jackson, Roby	15103	4	1							3	9			6	5	10				7	2			11	8
33		26	Luton Town	1-3	Wills	16917	4	1			6				3	9				5	10				7	2			11	8
34		28	Stoke City	0-3		8173		1			6			2	3	9				5	10				7	4			11	8
35	Apr	2	ROTHERHAM UTD.	3-2	Crookes, Wills, Broadbent	15812	4	1	10		6		11		3	9				5						2			7	8
36		8	Doncaster Rov.	2-4	Wylie, Graham(og)	12223	4	1	10		6		11		3	9				5						2			7	8
37		9	Leeds United	0-2		24564	4	1	10		6		11	2	3	9				5									7	8
38		11	DONCASTER ROV.	4-0	Jackson 3, Cruickshank	13144	4	1			6			2	3	9				5		11						8	7	10
39		16	BURY	2-1	Jackson, Redman(og)	12545	4	1	11		6			2	3	9				5								8	7	10
40		23	Birmingham City	1-1	Wills	28018	4	1	11		6			2	3	9				5								8	7	10
41		27	FULHAM	0-0		8236	4	1	11		6			2	3	9				5								8	7	10
42		30	IPSWICH TOWN	2-1	Jackson 2	10812	4	1	11						3	9				5				6		2	8		7	10
					Apps	41	42	30	3	20	7	10	6	42	20	4	25	38	18	1	1	15	2	4	37	17	1	36	42
					Goals			11		2	2	2	1		17		5		3			4		1		4		10	10

Two own goals

F.A. Cup

R3	Jan	8	Middlesbrough	4-1	Wylie 2, Broadbent, Wills	30503	4	1	11						3	9			6	5	10					2			7	8
R4		29	Sheffield Wednesday	1-1	Conwell (og)	53138	4	1	11						3	9			6	5	10					2			7	8
rep	Feb	3	SHEFFIELD WEDNESDAY	1-0	Jackson	36506	4	1	11						3	9			6	5	10					2			7	8
R5		19	CHELSEA	1-0	Broadbent	41457	4	1	11						3	9			6	5	10					2			7	8
R6	Mar	12	YORK CITY	0-1		47310	4	1	11						3	9			6	5	10					2			7	8

R4 replay after extra time

		p	w	d	l	f	a	pts
1	Birmingham City	42	22	10	10	92	47	54
2	Luton Town	42	23	8	11	88	53	54
3	Rotherham United	42	25	4	13	94	64	54
4	Leeds United	42	23	7	12	70	53	53
5	Stoke City	42	21	10	11	69	46	52
6	Blackburn Rovers	42	22	6	14	114	79	50
7	NOTTS COUNTY	42	21	6	15	74	71	48
8	West Ham United	42	18	10	14	74	70	46
9	Bristol Rovers	42	19	7	16	75	70	45
10	Swansea Town	42	17	9	16	86	83	43
11	Liverpool	42	16	10	16	92	96	42
12	Middlesbrough	42	18	6	18	73	82	42
13	Bury	42	15	11	16	77	72	41
14	Fulham	42	14	11	17	76	79	39
15	Nottingham Forest	42	16	7	19	58	62	39
16	Lincoln City	42	13	10	19	68	79	36
17	Port Vale	42	12	11	19	48	71	35
18	Doncaster Rovers	42	14	7	21	58	95	35
19	Hull City	42	12	10	20	44	69	34
20	Plymouth Argyle	42	12	7	23	57	82	31
21	Ipswich Town	42	11	6	25	57	92	28
22	Derby County	42	7	9	26	53	82	23

Back: Wills, Johnston, Southwell, Bradley, Leuty, Adamson, Wade. Centre: Poyser (manager), Taylor, McCormack, Deans, Wylie, Crookes, Moore (trainer). Front: Cruickshank.

1955/56

20th in Division Two

#		Date	Opponent	Score	Scorers	Att	Abthorpe J	Adamson H	Bradley G	Bulch RS	Carver GF	Chatham RH	Coole W	Crookes RE	Cruickshank FJ	Deans T	Groome PB	Jackson J	Johnston TD	Leuty LH	Leverton R	Linton JA	Lister E	Loxley H	McCormack JC	McGrath, John	Roby D	Russell PW	Smith GH	Southwell AA	Taylor JE	Wade A	Wills GF	Wylie RM
1	Aug	20	Middlesbrough	0-3		20291		4	1					11	3				9								6	8			2		7	10
2		25	BARNSLEY	2-2	Jackson 2	15517		4	1					11	3			9		5							6	8			2		7	10
3		27	BRISTOL CITY	3-2	Cruickshank(p), Wills, Roby	14596		4	1			5		11	3				9								6	8			2		7	10
4		31	Barnsley	1-3	Wylie	16636		4	1			5		11	3				9								6	8			2		7	10
5	Sep	3	West Ham United	1-6	Abthorpe	16710	9	4				5		11	3							1					6	7			2	8		10
6		7	Fulham	1-1	Johnston	16455		4				5	7		3				9			1	11				6	8			2			10
7		10	Port Vale	0-0		14733				4		5	7		3				9			1	11				6	8			2			10
8		15	FULHAM	3-4	Johnston 2, McGrath	9563				4		5			3				9		7	1	11			6	8			2			10
9		17	Rotherham Utd.	1-1	Johnston	10479		6		4		5	7		3				9			1	11					8			2			10
10		24	SWANSEA TOWN	1-5	Cruickshank	16679		6		4		5			3				9	7	1							8			2		11	10
11	Oct	1	Nottm. Forest	2-0	Crookes 2	26373		4				5		11	2	3			6		9	1						10					7	8
12		8	SHEFFIELD WEDNESDAY	1-1	Roby	23356		4				5		11	2	3			6		9	1						10					7	8
13		15	Doncaster Rov.	1-1	Abthorpe	10170	9	4				5		11	2	3			6			1						10					7	8
14		22	BLACKBURN ROVERS	1-2	Wills	13926	9	4				5		11	2	3			6			1						10					7	8
15		29	Stoke City	2-0	Crookes 2	15737	9					5		11	2	3			6			1			4			10					7	8
16	Nov	5	PLYMOUTH ARGYLE	3-0	Wills, Crookes, Abthorpe	12466	9					5		11	2	3			6			1			4			10					7	8
17		12	Liverpool	1-2	Jackson	32654					8	5		11	2		3	9	6			1			4			10					7	
18		19	LEICESTER CITY	1-1	McGrath	25622					8	5		11	2		3	9	6			1			4			10					7	
19		26	Lincoln City	0-2		12815						5		11	2		3	9	6						4			10	1				7	8
20	Dec	3	BRISTOL ROVERS	5-2	Wylie 3, Roby, Taylor	15255						5		11	2		3	9	6						4			7	1		10			8
21		10	Hull City	0-2		12842						5		11	2		3	9	6						4			7	1		10			8
22		17	MIDDLESBROUGH	5-0	Roby 2, Jackson, Crookes, Taylor	9693						5		11	2		3	9	6							4		7	1		10			8
23		24	Bristol City	3-1	Taylor 2, Roby	24075						5		11	2		3	9	6							4		7	1		10			8
24		26	Leeds United	0-1		24869						5		11	2		3	9	6							4		7	1		10			8
25		27	LEEDS UNITED	2-1	Cruickshank(p), Jackson	23910						5			2		3	9	6							4		7	1		10		11	8
26		31	WEST HAM UNITED	0-1		18708						5			2		3	9	6							4		7	1		10		11	8
27	Jan	14	Port Vale	1-3	Bulch	17370				9		5			2		3		6							4		7	1		10		11	8
28		21	ROTHERHAM UTD.	1-2	Taylor(p)	12616						5			2		3		6					9		4		7	1		10		11	8
29	Feb	4	Swansea Town	1-5	Coole	13114						5	7		2		3	9	6							4			1		10		11	8
30		11	NOTTM. FOREST	1-3	Jackson	17509						5	7		2		3	9	6							4			1	2	10		11	8
31		18	Leicester City	0-4		25977		4	1	9		5	7		3											6				2	10		11	8
32		25	DONCASTER ROV.	3-2	Wills, Chatham, McCormack	13762		4	1			6				3					10				9			7		2		5	11	8
33	Mar	3	Blackburn Rovers	0-2		18697		4	1			6				3					10				9			7		2		5	11	8
34		10	HULL CITY	0-2		12707		4	1			6		11		3									9			7		2		5	10	8
35		17	Plymouth Argyle	1-1	Wills	19946			1			6				3	10	11						4	9				5	2			7	8
36		24	LIVERPOOL	2-1	McCormack 2(1p)	13915			1			6				3	10							4	9		7	5		2			11	8
37		30	Bury	0-4		11708			1			6				3	10		9					4			7	5		2			11	8
38		31	Sheffield Wednesday	0-1		31330			1			6				3	9							4			7	5		2	10		11	8
39	Apr	2	BURY	2-1	Loxley, Wylie	13742			1			6				3	10							4	9		7	5		2			11	8
40		7	LINCOLN CITY	2-2	McCormack, Jackson	14234			1			6				3	10							4	9		7	5		2			11	8
41		14	Bristol Rovers	0-2		15455			1			6				3	10							4	9		7	5		2			11	8
42		21	STOKE CITY	1-3	Jackson	10918			1			4				3	10							6	9		7	5		2			11	8
			Apps				5	16	16	6	2	40	6	20	31	9	21	24	28	2	6	14	4	13	9	20	38	8	12	23	14	3	32	40
			Goals				3			1			1	1	6	3		8	4					1	4	2	6				5		5	5

F.A. Cup

R3	Jan	7	FULHAM	0-1		21500						5		11	2		3	9	6							4	7	1		10			8

Back: Sheridan, Cruickshank, Abthorpe, Leuty, Broome (coach), Wade, Kirkham, Parry, Groome. Standing: Potts (trainer), Southwell, Birch, McGrath, Bradley, Adamson, Linton, Johnston, Lister, Poyser (manager). Seated: Noon, Wills, Taylor, Jackson, Deans, Wylie, Crookes, Leverton. Front: Roby, Bircumshaw, Hill.

		p	w	d	l	f	a	pts
1	Sheffield Wed.	42	21	13	8	101	62	55
2	Leeds United	42	23	6	13	80	60	52
3	Liverpool	42	21	6	15	85	63	48
4	Blackburn Rovers	42	21	6	15	84	65	48
5	Leicester City	42	21	6	15	94	78	48
6	Bristol Rovers	42	21	6	15	84	70	48
7	Nottingham Forest	42	19	9	14	68	63	47
8	Lincoln City	42	18	10	14	79	65	46
9	Fulham	42	20	6	16	89	79	46
10	Swansea Town	42	20	6	16	83	81	46
11	Bristol City	42	19	7	16	80	64	45
12	Port Vale	42	16	13	13	60	58	45
13	Stoke City	42	20	4	18	71	62	44
14	Middlesbrough	42	16	8	18	76	78	40
15	Bury	42	16	8	18	86	90	40
16	West Ham United	42	14	11	17	74	69	39
17	Doncaster Rovers	42	12	11	19	69	96	35
18	Barnsley	42	11	12	19	47	84	34
19	Rotherham United	42	12	9	21	56	75	33
20	NOTTS COUNTY	42	11	9	22	55	82	31
21	Plymouth Argyle	42	10	8	24	54	87	28
22	Hull City	42	10	6	26	53	97	26

1956/57

20th in Division Two

#	Date		Opponent	Score	Scorers	Att	Bircumshaw PB	Bradley G	Bulch RS	Carver GF	Chatham RH	Cruickshank FJ	Groome PB	Jackson J	Johnston TD	Kirkham R	Lane JG	Linton JA	Lister E	Loxley H	Maddison F	McGrath, John	Roby D	Russell PW	Smith GH	Southwell AA	Taylor JE	Tucker K	Wills GF	Wylie RM
1	Aug	18	BURY	2-2	Taylor, Jackson	14857	1			6	2	3		10			9			4				5			8		11	7
2		23	LIVERPOOL	1-1	Wills	14671	1			6	2	3		10			9			4				5			8		11	7
3		25	Grimsby Town	1-2	Wills	18462	1			6	2	3		10			9			4			7	5					11	8
4		29	Liverpool	3-3	Wylie, Lane, Jackson	41095	1			6	2	3		10			9			4			7	5					11	8
5	Sep	1	DONCASTER ROV.	1-2	Lane	14412				6	2	3		10			9			4			7	5	1				11	8
6		8	Stoke City	0-6		18556	1			6	2	3		10			9			4			7	5					11	8
7		13	LEYTON ORIENT	1-3	Lane	10447	1		10	4	2	3	6				9						7	5					11	8
8		15	MIDDLESBROUGH	2-1	Russell, Jackson	10190	1		10	6	2		9				7			4	3			5					11	8
9		22	Leicester City	3-6	Jackson, Wills, Bradley	28806	1		10	6	2	3	9				7			4				5					11	8
10		29	BRISTOL ROVERS	0-2		12720			10	6	2	3	9				7			4				5	1				11	8
11	Oct	6	BRISTOL CITY	1-1	Lane	12005			10	5			6				7			4	3		8	9	1	2			11	
12		13	Sheffield United	1-5	Wills	21737			10	5			9				7			4	3		8	6	1	2			11	
13		20	NOTTM. FOREST	1-2	Lane	31585			10	6							9			4	3		7	5	1	2			11	8
14		27	Port Vale	2-1	Lane, Wills	13137			10	6							9			4	3		7	5	1	2			11	8
15	Nov	3	ROTHERHAM UTD.	1-5	Lane	12870			10	6							9			4	3		7	5	1	2			11	8
16		10	Lincoln City	0-1		11615			10								9			6	3	4	7	5	1	2			11	8
17		17	SWANSEA TOWN	1-4	Wills	10248			10									11		6	3	4	7	5	1	2			9	8
18		24	Fulham	1-5	McGrath	15360			6	3						1		11				4	7	5		2	10		9	8
19	Dec	1	BARNSLEY	3-2	Wills 3	11133			6		3			10	11	1						4	7	5		2			9	8
20		8	West Ham United	1-2	Wills	14875			6		3			10	11	1						4	7	5		2			9	8
21		15	Bury	1-2	Jackson	8364					3			10	11	1	7				6	4		5		2			9	8
22		22	GRIMSBY TOWN	0-1		4869			6		3			10	11	1	7					4		5		2			9	8
23		24	HUDDERSFIELD T	1-2	Wills	9165			8		3	2	10			11	1			6		4		5					9	7
24		26	Huddersfield T	0-3		7483			4		3	2	9			11	1			6			7	5					10	8
25		29	Doncaster Rov.	2-4	Loxley, Wills	11911			10	4	3					2	7	1	11	6				5					9	8
26	Jan	12	STOKE CITY	5-0	Jackson 2, Wylie 2, McGrath	13886		4	6		3			9				1				8	7	5		2			11	10
27		19	Middlesbrough	0-0		23085	11	4	6		3			9				1				8	7	5		2				10
28	Feb	2	LEICESTER CITY	0-0		42489		4	6		3			9				1				8	7	5		2			11	10
29		9	Bristol Rovers	0-3		17081		4	6		3			9				1				8	7	5		2			11	10
30		20	Bristol City	0-3		19288		4	6		3			9				1					7	5		2	8		11	10
31		23	SHEFFIELD UNITED	2-2	Russell 2	5712	11	4	6		3							1				8	7	5		2			9	10
32	Mar	9	PORT VALE	3-1	Jackson 2, Russell	17234		4	6	2	3			9				1				8	10	5				11	7	
33		16	Rotherham Utd.	0-0		9482		4	6	2	3			9				1					8	5				11	7	10
34		23	LINCOLN CITY	3-0	Wylie, Wills, Tucker	17375		4	6	2	3							1					8	7	5			11	9	10
35		30	Swansea Town	1-2	Wills	13826		4	6	2	3							1					8	7	5			11	9	10
36	Apr	6	FULHAM	0-0		17121		4	6	2	3							1					8	7	5			11	9	10
37		13	Barnsley	1-1	Tucker	7652		4	6	2	3							1						7	5			8	11	9	10
38		19	Blackburn Rovers	1-1	Wills	24367		4	6	2	3							1						7	5			8	11	9	10
39		20	WEST HAM UNITED	4-1	Wills 2, Russell, Tucker	17803		4	6	2	3							1						7	5			8	11	9	10
40		23	BLACKBURN ROVERS	2-0	Taylor 2	27613		4		2	3							1		6				7	5			8	11	9	10
41		27	Leyton Orient	2-2	Wills 2	12424		4		2	3							1		6				7	5			8	11	9	10
42	May	1	Nottm. Forest	4-2	Taylor 2, Roby, Wylie	32046		4	6	2	3							1						7	5			8	11	9	10
			Apps				2	8	17	33	28	34	11	25	4	1	21	25	3	22	8	17	33	42	9	18	10	11	41	39
			Goals					1						9			7			1			2	5			5		19	5

Game 9: Bradley injured (43 mins), Wills went in goal

F.A. Cup

R3	Jan	5	RHYL	1-3	Bircumshaw	16231	11			10	3						7	1		6		4		5		2			9	8

		p	w	d	l	f	a	pts
1	Leicester City	42	25	11	6	109	67	61
2	Nottingham Forest	42	22	10	10	94	55	54
3	Liverpool	42	21	11	10	82	54	53
4	Blackburn Rovers	42	21	10	11	83	75	52
5	Stoke City	42	20	8	14	83	58	48
6	Middlesbrough	42	19	10	13	84	60	48
7	Sheffield United	42	19	8	15	87	76	46
8	West Ham United	42	19	8	15	59	63	46
9	Bristol Rovers	42	18	9	15	81	67	45
10	Swansea Town	42	19	7	16	90	90	45
11	Fulham	42	19	4	19	84	76	42
12	Huddersfield Town	42	18	6	18	68	74	42
13	Bristol City	42	16	9	17	74	79	41
14	Doncaster Rovers	42	15	10	17	77	77	40
15	Leyton Orient	42	15	10	17	66	84	40
16	Grimsby Town	42	17	5	20	61	62	39
17	Rotherham United	42	13	11	18	74	75	37
18	Lincoln City	42	14	6	22	54	80	34
19	Barnsley	42	12	10	20	59	89	34
20	NOTTS COUNTY	42	9	12	21	58	86	30
21	Bury	42	8	9	25	60	96	25
22	Port Vale	42	8	6	28	57	101	22

Back: Southwell, Jackson, Lane, Russell, Loxley, Maddison, Noon. Centre: Broome (coach), McGrath, Johnston, Smith, Cruickshank, Linton, Groome, Bulch, Potts (trainer). Seated: Sheridan, Taylor, Bircumshaw, Wills, Poyser (manager), Lister, Roby, Wylie, Gissing

1957/58

21st in Division Two (Relegated)

#		Date		Opponent	Score	Scorers	Att	Asher T	Bradley G	Bulch RS	Carver GF	Chatham RH	Cruickshank FJ	Gissing JW	Groome PB	Jackson J	Lane JG	Linton JA	Loxley H	Maddison F	McGrath John	Newsham S	Noon H	Parry C	Pritchard RT	Rawson K	Robledo E	Roby D	Russell PW	Sheridan J	Tucker K	Wills GF	Wylie RM
1	Aug	24		Sheffield United	0-1		20920			4			3		2			1	6			9						7	5		11	8	10
2		29		FULHAM	1-5	Tucker	18238			4			3		2			1	6			9						7	5		11	8	10
3		31		BLACKBURN ROVERS	1-1	Wills	17927			4			3		2	9		1			6	8							5		11	7	10
4	Sep	4		Fulham	0-1		14607				6		3		2	9		1			4	8						7	5			11	10
5		7		Ipswich Town	1-2	Jackson	17018			4			3		2	10	9	1			6	8						7	5			11	
6		12		SWANSEA TOWN	2-4	Wills 2	11397	10			6		3		2		9	1			4	8							5		11	7	
7		14		HUDDERSFIELD T	1-1	McGrath	15584	10			6		2					1		3	8	9							5	4	11	7	
8		19		Swansea Town	3-1	Asher, Carver, Tucker	19353	10			6		2					1		3	8	9							5	4	11	7	
9		21		LINCOLN CITY	1-0	Newsham	18059	10					2					1		3	6	8						7	5	4	11	9	
10		28		Bristol Rovers	2-5	Roby, Russell	20415				6		3		2			1			8	10				4		7	5		11	9	
11	Oct	5		DERBY COUNTY	1-0	Newsham	23966		1		6		2							3		10				8		7	5	4	11	9	
12		12		Grimsby Town	0-2		14328	8			6		2					1		3		10						7	5	4	11	9	
13		19		STOKE CITY	1-2	Newsham	13125	10			6		2					1		3	8	9						7	5	4		11	
14		26		Bristol City	1-3	Carver	18394				6		2	7			8	1	5	3		10							9	4		11	
15	Nov	2		CARDIFF CITY	5-2	Wills 2, Newsham 2, Lane	14911	10			6		2	7			9	1				8			3	5				4		11	
16		9		Liverpool	0-4		39735	10			6		2	7			9	1				8			3				5	4		11	
17		16		MIDDLESBROUGH	2-0	Lane, Asher	13800	10			6		2	7			9	1			4	8			3				5			11	
18		23		Leyton Orient	2-2	Wills, Asher	12361	10	1		6		2	7			9				4	8			3	5						11	
19		30		CHARLTON ATHLETIC	2-1	Lane, Asher	14961	10	1		6	2	3	7			9				4	8				5						11	
20	Dec	7		Doncaster Rov.	0-4		8674	10	1			2	3								4	8	6			5		7			11	9	
21		14		ROTHERHAM UTD.	1-0	Newsham	10857	10	1			2	3				9		6			8		7		5				4		11	
22		21		SHEFFIELD UNITED	1-0	Lane	12070	10	1			2	3				9		6			8		7		5				4		11	
23		25		BARNSLEY	2-3	Loxley, Wills	11343	10	1			2	3				9		6			8		7		5				4		11	
24		26		Barnsley	1-1	Sheridan	20307	10	1			2	3			9			6		4			7						5	8	11	
25		28		Blackburn Rovers	0-3		24605		1				3			9			6		4			7		2	10		5	8		11	
26	Jan	11		IPSWICH TOWN	0-3		13612		1			2	3			8	9		6		4						10	5			11	7	
27		18		Huddersfield T	0-3		9173	10	1			2	3				9		6		4	8		7		5						11	
28	Feb	1		Lincoln City	2-2	Wills, Lane	8573	10			6	2				8	9	1	4					3				7	5			11	
29		15		Derby County	1-2	Lane	21304	10			6	2				8	9	1	4					3				7	5			11	
30		22		LEYTON ORIENT	0-1		11494	10			6	2					9	1				8		3				7	5	4		11	
31	Mar	1		Stoke City	1-0	Lane	16452				6	2				8	9	1	4			10		3				7	5			11	
32		8		BRISTOL CITY	0-1		10042				6	2				8	9	1	4			10		3	5			7				11	
33		15		Cardiff City	0-2		11116				6	2				8	9	1	4			10		3	5			7				11	
34		22		LIVERPOOL	0-2		13040				6	2						1	4			10		3				7	5		11	9	8
35		29		Middlesbrough	1-3	Lane	14879				6	2					10	1	4					3	5			7			11	9	8
36	Apr	4		West Ham United	1-3	Wills	29866				6	2	3				10	1	4						5			7			11	9	8
37		5		GRIMSBY TOWN	2-0	Lane, Wylie	11555		1		6	2					10		4					3	5			7			11	9	8
38		8		WEST HAM UNITED	1-0	Wills(p)	18317		1		6	2		11			10		4					3	5			7				9	8
39		12		Charlton Athletic	1-4	Lane	21612		1		6	2		7			10		4					3	5			11				9	8
40		19		DONCASTER ROV.	0-5		16102		1		6	2					10		4					3	5			7			11	9	8
41		23		BRISTOL ROVERS	0-0		13467				6	2		7				1	4			9		3	5				8		11		10
42		26		Rotherham Utd.	3-1	Newsham 2, Lane	7222					2		7			8	1	6			9		3	5				4		11		10
						Apps		20	15	4	28	23	28	10	7	11	26	27	24	7	17	31	1	6	18	19	2	25	24	17	17	42	13
						Goals		4			2					1	11		1		1	8						1	1	1	2	10	1

F.A. Cup

				Opponent	Score	Scorers	Att																										
R3	Jan	4		TRANMERE ROVERS	2-0	Tucker(p), Jackson	13394		1			2	3			8	9		6		4							10	5		11	7	
R4		25		BRISTOL CITY	1-2	Pritchard	18395		1		6	2					9		4			8			3			10	5		11	7	

	p	w	d	l	f	a	pts
1 West Ham United	42	23	11	8	101	54	57
2 Blackburn Rovers	42	22	12	8	93	57	56
3 Charlton Athletic	42	24	7	11	107	69	55
4 Liverpool	42	22	10	10	79	54	54
5 Fulham	42	20	12	10	97	59	52
6 Sheffield United	42	21	10	11	75	50	52
7 Middlesbrough	42	19	7	16	83	74	45
8 Ipswich Town	42	16	12	14	68	69	44
9 Huddersfield Town	42	14	16	12	63	66	44
10 Bristol Rovers	42	17	8	17	85	80	42
11 Stoke City	42	18	6	18	75	73	42
12 Leyton Orient	42	18	5	19	77	79	41
13 Grimsby Town	42	17	6	19	86	83	40
14 Barnsley	42	14	12	16	70	74	40
15 Cardiff City	42	14	9	19	63	77	37
16 Derby County	42	14	8	20	60	81	36
17 Bristol City	42	13	9	20	63	88	35
18 Rotherham United	42	14	5	23	65	101	33
19 Swansea Town	42	11	9	22	72	99	31
20 Lincoln City	42	11	9	22	55	82	31
21 NOTTS COUNTY	42	12	6	24	44	80	30
22 Doncaster Rovers	42	8	11	23	56	88	27

1958/59

23rd in Division Three (Relegated)

#		Date	Opponent	Score	Scorers	Att	Asher T	Bircumshaw PB	Brown K	Butler JH	Carver GF	Chatham RH	Cruickshank FJ	Forrest JR	Gissing JW	Hateley A	Horobin R	Kilford JD	Lane JG	Langford JW	Linton JA	Loxley H	Newsham S	Newton J	Noon H	Parry C	Roby D	Russell ET	Russell PW	Sheridan J	Stone M	Twigg RL	Withers A	Wylie RM
1	Aug	23	ACCRINGTON STANLEY	1-1	Newsham	14872					6	2	3					9		11	1	4	10			7		5					8
2		27	Wrexham	2-3	Wylie, Parry	15541					6		3				2			11	1	4	10		9	7		5					8
3		30	Halifax Town	1-1	Newsham	9789							3				2			11	1	4	10		9	7	6	5					8
4	Sep	4	WREXHAM	2-0	Roby, Newsham	11906	10						3				2			11	1		9			7	6	5	4				8
5		6	NEWPORT COUNTY	1-1	Roby	12249							3		7		2			11	1		9			10	6	5	4				8
6		11	HULL CITY	1-1	Parry	8584					6		3				2			11	1		9		7	10		5	4				8
7		13	Chesterfield	0-1		12774	8				6		3				2			11	1		9		7	10		5	4				
8		15	Hull City	0-5		8521					6		3				2	9	11	1			10			7	4	5	8				
9		20	BURY	1-1	Roby	10077							3				2	9	11	1		10			7	6	5	4				8
10		25	SOUTHAMPTON	1-2	Roby	6171							3				2	9	11	1		8			7	6	5	4				10
11		27	MANSFIELD TOWN	3-4	Roby 2, Newsham(p)	16510							3				2	9	11	1		8			7	6	5	4				10
12	Oct	1	Southampton	0-3		16548					6		3				2	9	11	1	4				7	10	5					8
13		4	Swindon Town	1-3	Wylie	13478					6		3				2		11	1	4				7	9	5	8				10
14		9	BRENTFORD	0-0		4381					6		3				2		11	1	4	9			7		5	8				10
15		11	Rochdale	2-1	Newsham 2(1p)	5306		11			6		3		7		2			1	4	9			10		5	8				
16		18	DONCASTER ROV.	2-2	Newsham 2	9341		11			6		3		7		2			1	4	9			10		5					8
17		25	Plymouth Argyle	0-3		25750					6		3		7		2		11	1		9			10		5	4				8
18	Nov	1	TRANMERE ROVERS	1-1	Roby	9107							3		7		2	9		1		10		6	11		5	4				8
19		8	Stockport County	1-1	Hateley	10181	8						3		7	9	2			1				6	10		5	4				11
20		22	Norwich City	3-3	Carver, Newsham, Sheridan	13637		11		5	10		3				8	2		1	6	9			7			4				
21		29	BOURNEMOUTH	4-3	Horobin 2, Newsham, Loxley	7463		11		5	10		3				8	2		1	6	9			7			4				
22	Dec	13	SOUTHEND UNITED	1-4	Lane	7121				5		2	3				8		9	11	1	6	10		7			4				
23		20	Accrington Stanley	0-3		5299		11			6		3				8	2		1	9	10			7		5	4				
24		26	BRADFORD CITY	1-3	Loxley	8376	10				6		3				11	2		1	9				8	7		5				8
25		27	Bradford City	1-4	Roby	16230	8						3				10	2		1	6			4	7	11	5	9				
26	Jan	3	HALIFAX TOWN	4-4	Horobin 2, Loxley, Brown	8909	10		9		6		3				8	2		1	4				7		5				11	
27		10	READING	3-1	Cruickshank, Horobin, Withers	10156	10		9		6		3				8	2		1					7		5	4			11	
28		31	CHESTERFIELD	3-1	Brown 2, Newsham	14871			9		6		3				8	2		1	5	10			7			4			11	
29	Feb	7	Bury	1-0	Forrest	6555			9	2	6		3	10			8			1	5				7			4			11	
30		14	Mansfield Town	0-3		13376			9	2			3	10			8			1	5		6		7			4			11	
31		21	SWINDON TOWN	1-0	Forrest	10575			9	2			3	10			8			1	5		6		7			4			11	
32		23	Colchester Utd.	1-4	Horobin	4404				2			3	10			8			1	5	9	6		7			4			11	
33		28	ROCHDALE	1-1	Roby	6394				2	6		3	10			8			1	5	9			7			4			11	
34	Mar	7	Doncaster Rov.	1-2	Carver	4663				2	6		3	10		9	8			1	4				7	5					11	
35		14	PLYMOUTH ARGYLE	1-2	Withers	7369				2	6		3	10			8		9		5				7			4		1	11	
36		16	Newport County	1-3	Horobin	5869				2	6		3	10			8		9		5				7			4		1	11	
37		21	Tranmere Rovers	3-0	Roby 2, Brown	9493		9	2	6		3	10			8				1	5				7			4			11	
38		27	Queens Park Rangers	1-2	Roby	12044				2	6		3		7	9	11			1	5	10			8			4				
39		28	STOCKPORT COUNTY	0-2		9761				2	6		3	10	11	9	8			1	5				7			4				
40		30	QUEENS PARK RANGERS	0-1		6956		11	9	2	6		3	10			8				4				7	5		1				
41	Apr	4	Reading	1-3	Roby	8285	10				6		3	9			11				4		2		7	5	8	1				
42		11	NORWICH CITY	1-3	Horobin	13289					6		3	10			8				4	9	2		7	5		1			11	
43		18	Bournemouth	0-0		8130					6		3	10			8				4	9	2		7	5		1			11	
44		21	Brentford	0-4		11738	8				6		3	10			7				4	9	2			5		1			11	
45		25	COLCHESTER UTD.	0-1		4733	8				6		3	10			7				4		2			5		1			11	
46		29	Southend United	2-5	Withers, Anderson(og)	5774	8				6		3	9			7					10	2			5	4	1			11	
			Apps				11	6	8	15	33	2	46	17	8	4	27	26	10	16	37	33	28	1	11	6	43	9	32	34	7	2	17	16
			Gls						4		2			1	2		1	8	1			3	11			2	13			1			3	2

AN Bates played at 9 in game 45

One own goal

F.A. Cup

		Date	Opponent	Score	Scorer	Att																												
R1	Nov	15	BARROW	1-2	Bircumshaw	11030		11			6		3				2	7		1		9		4	10		5	8					

		p	w	d	l	f	a	pts
1	Plymouth Argyle	46	23	16	7	89	59	62
2	Hull City	46	26	9	11	90	55	61
3	Brentford	46	21	15	10	76	49	57
4	Norwich City	46	22	13	11	89	62	57
5	Colchester United	46	21	10	15	71	67	52
6	Reading	46	21	8	17	78	63	50
7	Tranmere Rovers	46	21	8	17	82	67	50
8	Southend United	46	21	8	17	85	80	50
9	Halifax Town	46	21	8	17	80	77	50
10	Bury	46	17	14	15	69	58	48
11	Bradford City	46	18	11	17	84	76	47
12	Bournemouth	46	17	12	17	69	69	46
13	Queen's Park Rgs.	46	19	8	19	74	77	46
14	Southampton	46	17	11	18	88	80	45
15	Swindon Town	46	16	13	17	59	57	45
16	Chesterfield	46	17	10	19	67	64	44
17	Newport County	46	17	9	20	69	68	43
18	Wrexham	46	14	14	18	63	77	42
19	Accrington Stanley	46	15	12	19	71	87	42
20	Mansfield Town	46	14	13	19	73	98	41
21	Stockport County	46	13	10	23	65	78	36
22	Doncaster Rovers	46	14	5	27	50	90	33
23	NOTTS COUNTY	46	8	13	25	55	96	29
24	Rochdale	46	8	12	26	37	79	28

Back: Kilford, Blenkinsop, Butler, Twigg, Linton, Stone, Noon, Sheridan, Loxley. Standing: Dixon (masseur), Harvey, Hateley, Rawson, Cruickshank, Chatham, P Russell, ET Russell, Kirkham, Wheeler (trainer). Seated: Ramirez, Wylie, Roby, Carver, Lane, Newsham, Asher, Hill. Front: Felice, Newton, Parry.

1959/60

2nd in Division Four (Promoted)

#	Date		Opponent	Score	Scorers	Att	Beeby O	Bircumshaw PB	Butler JH	Carver GF	Cruickshank FJ	Edwards RT	Forrest JR	Gibson APS	Gissing JW	Hateley A	Horobin R	Joyce C	Loxley H	Newsham S	Newton J	Noon H	Rawson K	Roby D	Sheridan J	Smith GH	Withers A
1	Aug	22	CHESTER	2-1	Roby, Horobin	9652			2	6	3		9				10	8						5	7	4	1	11
2		26	Crewe Alexandra	1-2	Roby	10283			2	6	3		9				10	8				4	5	7		1	11
3		29	Crystal Palace	1-1	Newsham	16466		11	2	6	3							7		10		4	5	8		1	9
4	Sep	3	CREWE ALEXANDRA	4-1	Newsham 2, Horobin 2	9861			2	6	3		10				8			9			5	7	4	1	11
5		5	BRADFORD PARK AVE.	0-1		12139			2	6	3		10		7					9			5	8	4	1	11
6		7	Gateshead	0-0		6618			2	6			10	4			8			9		3	5	7		1	11
7		12	Stockport County	1-3	Forrest	7662			2	6			10				8			9		3	5	7	4	1	11
8		17	GATESHEAD	4-0	Forrest 3, Withers	8793			2	6			10				8			9		3	5	7	4	1	11
9		19	EXETER CITY	3-0	Roby, Horobin, Forrest	11982			2	6			10				8			9		3	5	7	4	1	11
10		21	Hartlepool Utd.	4-2	Newsham 2, Roby, Forrest	3926			2	6			10				8			9		3	5	7	4	1	11
11		26	Watford	2-4	Forrest, Carver	10131			2	6			10	4			8		5	9		3		7		1	11
12	Oct	1	HARTLEPOOL UTD.	4-0	Newsham 2(1p), Horobin, Withers	10732	3		2	6			10				8		5	9		4		7		1	11
13		3	OLDHAM ATHLETIC	3-1	Roby, Horobin, Carver	14015	3		2	6			10				8		5	9		4		7		1	11
14		6	Carlisle Utd.	0-2		9004	3		2	6			10				8		5	9		4		7		1	11
15		10	WORKINGTON	2-0	Newsham 2(1p)	13280	3		2	6			10				8		5	9		4		7		1	11
16		15	CARLISLE UTD.	2-1	Newsham 2	12232	3		2	6			10				8		5	9		4		7		1	11
17		17	Doncaster Rov.	4-0	Newsham 3, Forrest	4705	3		2	6			10				8		5	9		4		7		1	11
18		24	NORTHAMPTON T	2-1	Newsham, Withers	14867	3		2	6			10				8		5	9		4		7		1	11
19		31	Torquay United	1-3	Newsham	8272	3		2	6			10				8		5	9		4		7		1	11
20	Nov	7	MILLWALL	2-1	Newsham, Withers	16018	3	11	2	6			10				8		5	9		4				1	7
21		21	GILLINGHAM	3-1	Horobin, Forrest, Bircumshaw	13856	3	11	2	6			10				8		5	9		4				1	7
22		28	Barrow	3-4	Newsham 2(1p), Forrest	5507	3	11	2				4				8		5	9				10	6	1	7
23	Dec	12	Darlington	2-5	Newsham(p), Forrest	3977	3	11	2	6			10				8		5	9					4	1	7
24		19	Chester	1-2	Forrest	4209	3	11	2				10					8	5	9		4		7	6	1	
25		26	ROCHDALE	2-1	Bircumshaw 2	14582		11	2			3	10					8	5	9		4		7	6	1	
26		28	Rochdale	4-1	Bircumshaw 2, Forrest, Roby	4044		11	2				10	4				8	5	9		3		7	6	1	
27	Jan	2	CRYSTAL PALACE	7-1	Joyce 3, Bircumshaw 2, Forrest, Roby	15804		11	2				10	4				8	5	9		3		7	6	1	
28		9	Southport	2-1	Bircumshaw, Joyce	4161		11	2				10	4				8	5	9		3		7	6	1	
29		16	Bradford Park Ave.	1-1	Newsham	8114		11	2				10	4				8	5	9		3		7	6	1	
30		23	STOCKPORT COUNTY	3-0	Joyce 2, Bircumshaw	13113		11	2				10	4				8	5	9		3		7	6	1	
31		30	ALDERSHOT	5-3	Bircumshaw, Newsham, Roby, Joyce	12879		11	2				10	4				8	5	9		3		7	6	1	
32	Feb	6	Exeter City	3-3	Bircumshaw 2, Joyce	9479		11	2				10	4				8	5	9		3		7	6	1	
33		13	WATFORD	2-1	Forrest, Bircumshaw	18423		11	2	6			10	4				8	5	9		3		7		1	
34		27	Workington	1-0	Newsham	4983		11	2	6			10	4				8	5	9		3		7		1	
35	Mar	5	DONCASTER ROV.	3-4	Bircumshaw 2, Joyce	16469		11	2	6			10	4				8	5	9		3		7		1	
36		12	Northampton T	2-4	Bircumshaw 2	8902		11	2				10	4				8	5	9		3		7	6	1	
37		19	TORQUAY UNITED	1-1	Hateley	15041		11	2	6					9	8			5			3		7	4	1	10
38		26	Millwall	1-1	Withers	12189	7		2	6			10		9	8			5			3			4	1	11
39	Apr	2	SOUTHPORT	4-1	Hateley 2, Forrest, Withers	12320			2	6			10		9	8			5			3		7	4	1	11
40		9	Gillingham	1-0	Forrest	7655		11	2	6			10		9	8			5			3		7	4	1	
41		16	BARROW	1-2	Hateley	15634		11	2	6			10		9	8			5			3		7	4	1	
42		18	WALSALL	2-1	Roby, Hateley	22788			2	6			10		9	8		5				3		7	4	1	11
43		19	Walsall	2-2	Withers, Forrest	14752			2				10	6	9	8		5				3		7	4	1	11
44		23	Aldershot	1-1	Hateley	6502			2				10	6	9	8		5			4	3		7		1	11
45		30	DARLINGTON	5-4	Roby 2, Forrest, Joyce, Withers	13386			2				10	6	9	8		5			4	3		7		1	11
46	May	3	Oldham Athletic	3-0	Hateley 2, McGill(og)	3628			2				10	6	9	8		5			4	3		7		1	11
					Apps		13	22	46	31	5	1	44	17	1	10	25	22	36	34	3	41	10	42	26	46	31
					Goals			18		2			19			8	7	10		23				11			8

One own goal

F.A. Cup

R	Date		Opponent	Score	Scorers	Att	Beeby O	Bircumshaw PB	Butler JH	Carver GF	Cruickshank FJ	Edwards RT	Forrest JR	Gibson APS	Gissing JW	Hateley A	Horobin R	Joyce C	Loxley H	Newsham S	Newton J	Noon H	Rawson K	Roby D	Sheridan J	Smith GH	Withers A
R1	Nov	14	Hastings United	2-1	Bircumshaw 2	5757	3	11	2	6			10				8		5	9		4				1	7
R2	Dec	5	BATH CITY	0-1		25889	3		2	6			10				8		5	9				7	4	1	11

		p	w	d	l	f	a	pts
1	Walsall	46	28	9	9	102	60	65
2	NOTTS COUNTY	46	26	8	12	107	69	60
3	Torquay United	46	26	8	12	84	58	60
4	Watford	46	24	9	13	92	67	57
5	Millwall	46	18	17	11	84	61	53
6	Northampton Town	46	22	9	15	85	63	53
7	Gillingham	46	21	10	15	74	69	52
8	Crystal Palace	46	19	12	15	84	64	50
9	Exeter City	46	19	11	16	80	70	49
10	Stockport County	46	19	11	16	58	54	49
11	Bradford Park Ave.	46	17	15	14	70	68	49
12	Rochdale	46	18	10	18	65	60	46
13	Aldershot	46	18	9	19	77	74	45
14	Crewe Alexandra	46	18	9	19	79	88	45
15	Darlington	46	17	9	20	63	73	43
16	Workington	46	14	14	18	68	60	42
17	Doncaster Rovers	46	16	10	20	69	76	42
18	Barrow	46	15	11	20	77	87	41
19	Carlisle United	46	15	11	20	51	66	41
20	Chester	46	14	12	20	59	77	40
21	Southport	46	10	14	22	48	92	34
22	Gateshead	46	12	9	25	58	86	33
23	Oldham Athletic	46	8	12	26	41	83	28
24	Hartlepools United	46	10	7	29	59	109	27

Back: Carver, E Russell, Hateley, J Butler, Forrest, Newton, Roby. Standing: P Bircumshaw, Beeby, Cruickshank, McDowall, Sheridan, Stone, Newsham, Noon, Gibson Seated: Withers, Hill (manager), 4 directors, P Russell. Front: Joyce, Loxley, Horobin

1960/61

5th in Division Three

#		Date	Opponent	Score	Scorers	Att	Bircumshaw A	Bircumshaw PB	Butler JH	Carver GF	Edwards RT	Forrest JR	Gibson APS	Gissing JW	Hampton IK	Hateley A	Horobin R	Joyce C	Loxley H	Newton J	Noon H	Rawson K	Roby D	Sheridan J	Simcoe KE	Smith GH	Withers A
1	Aug	20	Watford	2-2	Joyce, Forrest	16218			2	6		10				9		8	5		3		7	4		1	11
2		25	QUEENS PARK RANGERS	2-1	Withers, Horobin	15174			2	6						9	10	8	5		3		7	4		1	11
3		27	BOURNEMOUTH	3-2	Hateley 2, Joyce	12115			2	6						9	10	8	5		3		7	4		1	11
4		29	Queens Park Rangers	0-2		8365		11	2	6		5				9		8			3		7	4	10	1	
5	Sep	3	Bradford City	2-2	PB Bircumshaw, Hateley	9689		11	2	6						9		8	5		3		7	4		1	10
6		8	READING	4-2	PB Bircumshaw 2, Joyce, Hateley	14309		11	2	6						9		8	5		3		7	4		1	10
7		10	BARNSLEY	5-1	Hateley 3, PB Bircumshaw, Sheridan	13936		11	2	6						9		8	5		3		7	4		1	10
8		14	Reading	0-2		6327		11	2				6			9		8	5		3		7	4		1	10
9		17	Newport County	2-2	Hateley, Joyce	7799		11	2			10	6			9		8			3	5		4		1	7
10		20	Bristol City	1-2	Roby	14839			2			10	6			9		8	5		3		7	4		1	11
11		24	COLCHESTER UTD.	4-2	Hateley 2, Roby, Joyce	14134			2	6		10				9		8	5		3		7	4		1	11
12		29	BRISTOL CITY	3-0	Hateley, Roby, Forrest	14230			2	6		10				9		8	5		3		7	4		1	11
13	Oct	1	Grimsby Town	1-1	Hateley	12448			2	6		10				9		8	5		3		7	4		1	11
14		3	Hull City	1-3	PB Bircumshaw	12199		11	2	6		10				9		8	5		3		7	4		1	
15		8	SWINDON TOWN	1-0	PB Bircumshaw	11483		11	2	6		10				9		8	5		3		7	4		1	
16		15	Torquay United	2-2	Joyce, Hateley	8010			2	6		10				9		8	5		3		7	4		1	11
17		22	PORT VALE	2-2	Hateley, PB Bircumshaw	10725		11	2	6		10				9	7	8	5		3			4		1	
18		29	Southend United	1-3	Forrest	5296		11	2	6		10				9	7	8	5		3			4		1	
19	Nov	12	Bury	0-7		8884			2	6		10				9	8				3	5	7	4		1	11
20		19	WALSALL	3-1	Joyce, Hateley, PB Bircumshaw	12574		11	2	6		10				9		8			3	5	7	4		1	
21	Dec	10	Tranmere Rovers	3-2	Horobin, Forrest, Hateley	5668			2	6		10				9	8		5		3		7	4		1	11
22		17	WATFORD	3-1	Forrest 2, Hateley	10262			2	6		10				9	8		5		3		7	4		1	11
23		26	Coventry City	2-2	Horobin, Forrest	18793			2	6		10				9	8		5		3		7	4		1	11
24		27	COVENTRY CITY	3-0	Carver, Roby(p), Austin(og)	26759			2	6		10	5			9	8				3		7	4		1	11
25		31	Bournemouth	3-1	Horobin 3	7974			2	6		10	5			9	8				3		7	4		1	11
26	Jan	14	BRADFORD CITY	2-1	Hateley, Horobin	12421			2	6		10	5			9	8				3		7	4		1	11
27		21	Barnsley	2-5	Horobin, Forrest	5522			2	6		10	5			9	8				3		7	4		1	11
28		28	CHESTERFIELD	1-0	Forrest	7555			2	6		10	5			9	8				3		7	4		1	11
29	Feb	4	NEWPORT COUNTY	6-0	Withers 3, Horobin 2, Hateley	10673			2	6		10	5			9	8				3		7	4		1	11
30		11	Colchester Utd.	2-1	Hateley, Withers	4634			2	6		10	5			9	8		4		3		7			1	11
31		18	GRIMSBY TOWN	0-1		22292			2	6		10	5			9	8		4		3		7			1	11
32		25	Halifax Town	1-0	Hateley	4242			2	6		10	4			9	8		5		3		7			1	11
33	Mar	4	TORQUAY UNITED	0-1		14181			2	6			4			9	8	10	5		3		7			1	11
34		8	Shrewsbury Town	0-4		8330		11	2	6			4			9	8		5		3		7			1	10
35		11	Port Vale	3-1	PB Bircumshaw 3	10931		11	2	6			4			9	8		5		3		7			1	10
36		18	SOUTHEND UNITED	1-2	Hateley	10530		11	2	6			4			9	8		5		3		7			1	10
37		23	HALIFAX TOWN	1-1	Hateley	8346		11		6	2		5			9	8				3		7	4		1	10
38		25	Chesterfield	1-3	Gissing	6154		11			2		5	7	6	9	8				3			4		1	10
39	Apr	1	BURY	0-3		10489				6	2	10	5	7		9	8				3			4		1	11
40		3	Brentford	0-3		5416	3	11		6	2	10	5	7			8							4	9	1	
41		4	BRENTFORD	0-0		3933	3	11		6	2	10				9	8		5	4			7			1	
42		8	Walsall	1-2	Christie(og)	14508				6	2	10				9	8	11	5		3		7	4		1	
43		15	SHREWSBURY TOWN	2-1	Hateley, Forrest	7271				6	2	10				9	8	11	5		3		7	4		1	
44		22	Swindon Town	0-1		8904				6	2	10				9	8	11	5		3		7	4		1	
45		27	HULL CITY	2-1	Horobin, Hateley	4941		11		6	2					9	8	10	5		3		7	4		1	
46		29	TRANMERE ROVERS	4-1	Hateley 2, Withers, Joyce	7076				6	2					9	8	10	5		3		7	4		1	11
					Apps		2	19	36	42	10	31	21	3	1	45	31	25	32	1	44	3	40	38	2	46	34
					Goals					1		10	1			27	11	8					4	1			6

Two own goals

F.A. Cup

R1	Nov	5	Aldershot	0-2		7498			2	6		10				9	11	8	5		3		7	4		1	

F.L. Cup

R1	Oct	20	BRIGHTON & HOVE ALB.	1-3	Noon	10449			2	6		10				9		8	5		3		7	4		1	11

		p	w	d	l	f	a	pts
1	Bury	46	30	8	8	108	45	68
2	Walsall	46	28	6	12	98	60	62
3	Queen's Park Rgs.	46	25	10	11	93	60	60
4	Watford	46	20	12	14	85	72	52
5	NOTTS COUNTY	46	21	9	16	82	77	51
6	Grimsby Town	46	20	10	16	77	69	50
7	Port Vale	46	17	15	14	96	79	49
8	Barnsley	46	21	7	18	83	80	49
9	Halifax Town	46	16	17	13	71	78	49
10	Shrewsbury Town	46	15	16	15	83	75	46
11	Hull City	46	17	12	17	73	73	46
12	Torquay United	46	14	17	15	75	83	45
13	Newport County	46	17	11	18	81	90	45
14	Bristol City	46	17	10	19	70	68	44
15	Coventry City	46	16	12	18	80	83	44
16	Swindon Town	46	14	15	17	62	55	43
17	Brentford	46	13	17	16	56	70	43
18	Reading	46	14	12	20	72	83	40
19	Bournemouth	46	15	10	21	58	76	40
20	Southend United	46	14	11	21	60	76	39
21	Tranmere Rovers	46	15	8	23	79	115	38
22	Bradford City	46	11	14	21	65	87	36
23	Colchester United	46	11	11	24	68	101	33
24	Chesterfield	46	10	12	24	67	87	32

Back: Noon, Simcoe, Horobin, Edwards, Dixon (physio), Newsham, Gibson, Roby, Withers. Centre: Beeby, Joyce, Smith, Rawson, Forrest, McDowall, Hateley, Loxley. Front: Hill (manager), Butler, Newton, Sheridan, Gissing, Carver, Bircumshaw, Wheeler (trainer).

1961/62

13th in Division Three

League

							Astle J	Bircumshaw A	Bircumshaw PB	Butler JH	Butler PL	Carver GF	Edwards RT	Flower AJ	Forrest JR	Fry KF	Gibson APS	Hampton IK	Hateley A	Horobin R	Jones B	Joyce C	Loxley H	Moore B	Newsham S	Noon H	Sheridan J	Smith GH	Withers A	Woodford R
1	Aug	19	BRISTOL CITY	1-0	Horobin(p)	10203						6	2		10				9	8		7	5			3	4		1	11
2		23	Crystal Palace	1-4	Withers	28567						6	2		10				9	8		7	5			3	4		1	11
3		26	Bradford Park Ave.	2-3	Hateley, Forrest	11476						6	2		10				9	8		7	5			3	4		1	11
4		31	CRYSTAL PALACE	0-0		11633						6	2		10				9	8		7	5			3	4		1	11
5	Sep	2	GRIMSBY TOWN	2-0	Forrest, Welbourne(og)	9289						6	2		10				9	8		7	5			3	4		1	11
6		7	PETERBOROUGH UTD.	2-2	Hateley, Loxley	19466			11			6	2		10	4			9	8			5			3			1	7
7		9	Coventry City	2-2	Horobin, PB Bircumshaw	13366			11			6	2		10				9	8						3	4		1	7
8		16	BRENTFORD	3-1	Edwards, Hateley, Newsham	7979				2		6	7						9	8			5		10	3	4		1	11
9		21	PORT VALE	2-3	Hateley 2	8676				2		6			10				9	8		7	5			3	4		1	11
10		23	Reading	2-4	Horobin, Withers	11169	7			2		6	10							8			5		9	3	4		1	11
11		25	Port Vale	0-1		11707				2	1	6	7		10							8	5		9	3	4			11
12		30	NEWPORT COUNTY	8-1	*See below	6356			9	2	1				8		6			7			5		10	3	4			11
13	Oct	4	Bournemouth	1-2	Forrest	15610			9	2	1				8		6			7			5		10	3	4			11
14		7	PORTSMOUTH	2-1	PB Bircumshaw 2	9889			9			6	2							7		8	5		10	3	4		1	11
15		12	BOURNEMOUTH	3-2	Hateley 3	11859			9			6	2						10	7		8	5			3	4		1	11
16		14	Barnsley	0-2		7100			9			6	2						10	7		8	5			3	4		1	11
17		28	Watford	1-3	PB Bircumshaw	10086			11			6	2						9	8		10	5			3	4		1	7
18	Nov	11	Torquay United	3-3	Horobin 2, Hateley	3773			11			6	2		10				9	8			5			3	4		1	7
19		18	LINCOLN CITY	1-0	Forrest	9215			11			6	2		10				9	8			5			3	4		1	7
20	Dec	2	QUEENS PARK RANGERS	0-0		7980				2		6			10				9	8			5	7		3	4		1	11
21		16	Bristol City	0-6		12805				2		6			10				9	8			5	7		3	4		1	11
22		23	BRADFORD PARK AVE.	4-2	Hateley 3, Horobin	6868	8	3				6	2					5	9	10			7				4		1	11
23		26	SHREWSBURY TOWN	3-2	Horobin(p), Moore, Walters(og)	10197	8	3				6	2					5	9	10			7				4		1	11
24	Jan	13	Grimsby Town	1-2	Sheridan	5998	8	3			1	6	2					5	9	10			7				4			11
25		20	COVENTRY CITY	2-0	Hateley 2	8827		3			1	6	2		8			5	9	10			7				4			11
26		27	Northampton T	2-1	Withers, Hateley	11813		3			1	6	2		8			5	9	10			7				4			11
27	Feb	2	Brentford	1-0	Hateley	9227		3			1	6	2		8			5	9	10			7				4			11
28		10	READING	2-2	Horobin, Spiers(og)	9312	8	3			1	6	2					5	9	10			7				4			11
29		17	Newport County	0-2		2597		3		2	1	6			8			5	9	10			7				4			11
30		24	Portsmouth	0-0		14442		3	8	2	1					7		5	9	10						6	4			11
31	Mar	3	BARNSLEY	0-2		7379		3	8	2	1	6				7		5	9	10							4			11
32		10	Hull City	1-2	Moore	3911						6	2	11	10		5	3	9			8		7			4	1		
33		17	WATFORD	1-0	PB Bircumshaw	6987		3	11			6	2			7	5		9	8		10					4	1		
34		23	Swindon Town	0-1		7427		3	11			6	2			7	5		9			10					4	1	8	
35		28	Shrewsbury Town	0-3		3880		3				6	2	10	7	5		9	8	11							4	1		
36		31	TORQUAY UNITED	2-0	Jones, PB Bircumshaw	4975		3	11			6	2		8	7	5		10		9						4	1		
37	Apr	3	HULL CITY	3-0	Hateley 2, PB Bircumshaw (p)	3688		3	11			6	2			7	5		10	8	9						4	1		
38		6	Lincoln City	2-2	Jones, Hateley	6111		3	11			6	2			7	5		10	8	9						4	1		
39		9	Halifax Town	2-1	Sheridan, Fry	3293	8	3	11			6	2			7	5		10		9						4	1		
40		12	SWINDON TOWN	0-1		5369		3	9				2			7	5		10	8					6		4	1		11
41		14	NORTHAMPTON T	1-4	PB Bircumshaw	5974		3	9				2			7	5		10	8					6		4	1		11
42		20	Southend United	2-3	Horobin, Forrest	8339		3	11		1	6	2		10	7	5		9	8							4			
43		21	Queens Park Rangers	0-2		10043		3	11		1	6	5		10	7		2	9	8							4			
44		23	SOUTHEND UNITED	2-0	Horobin(p), Forrest	5158		3			1	6	2		10	7	5		9	8				11						4
45		28	HALIFAX TOWN	0-0		4822	8				1	6	2	10		7	5	3	9					11						4
46		30	Peterborough Utd.	0-2		7873			3	11	2								8		10	5	9		6		1	7		4

*Scorers in game 12: PB Bircumshaw 3, Withers 2, Newsham, Horobin, Herrity (og).

	Apps	7	23	23	12	15	40	37	2	25	15	27	3	40	40	5	15	21	14	6	25	42	31	35	3
	Goals			11			1	6	1					19	11	2		1	2	2		2		5		

Four own goals

F.A. Cup

R1	Nov	4	YEOVIL TOWN	4-2	Withers 2, Hateley, PB Bircumshaw	11375			11			6	2		10				9	8			5			3	4		1	7
R2		15	Margate	1-1	Loxley	7864			11		2	6			10				9	8			5			3	4		1	7
rep		30	MARGATE	3-1	PB Bircumshaw 2, Hateley	12302			11		2	6			10				9	8			5			3	4		1	7
R3	Jan	6	MANCHESTER CITY	0-1		25015	8	3				6	2					5	9	10			7				4		1	11

F.L. Cup

R1	Sep	14	DERBY COUNTY	2-2	Horobin 2	14654					2	6	7		10	5			9	8						3	4		1	11
rep		27	Derby County	2-3	PB Bircumshaw, Forrest	12494			10	2		6			8				9	7		5				3	4		1	11

R1 replay after extra time

Back: PB Bircumshaw, Astle, JH Butler, Edwards, A Bircumshaw. Standing: Carver, Gibson, Smith, Loxley, P Butler, Sheridan, Moore. Seated: Wheeler (trainer), Joyce, Horobin, Forrest, Hateley, Hill (manager). Front: Nixon, Withers

		p	w	d	l	f	a	pts
1	Portsmouth	46	27	11	8	87	47	65
2	Grimsby Town	46	28	6	12	80	56	62
3	Bournemouth	46	21	17	8	69	45	59
4	Queen's Park Rgs.	46	24	11	11	111	73	59
5	Peterborough Utd.	46	26	6	14	107	82	58
6	Bristol City	46	23	8	15	94	72	54
7	Reading	46	22	9	15	77	66	53
8	Northampton Town	46	20	11	15	85	57	51
9	Swindon Town	46	17	15	14	78	71	49
10	Hull City	46	20	8	18	67	54	48
11	Bradford Park Ave.	46	20	7	19	80	78	47
12	Port Vale	46	17	13	16	65	58	47
13	NOTTS COUNTY	46	17	9	20	67	74	43
14	Coventry City	46	16	11	19	64	71	43
15	Crystal Palace	46	14	14	18	83	80	42
16	Southend United	46	13	16	17	57	69	42
17	Watford	46	14	13	19	63	74	41
18	Halifax Town	46	15	10	21	62	84	40
19	Shrewsbury Town	46	13	12	21	73	84	38
20	Barnsley	46	13	12	21	71	95	38
21	Torquay United	46	15	6	25	76	100	36
22	Lincoln City	46	9	17	20	57	87	35
23	Brentford	46	13	8	25	53	93	34
24	Newport County	46	7	8	31	46	102	22

1962/63

7th in Division Three

#	Date		Opponent	Score	Scorers	Att	Agnew DY	Astle J	Bircumshaw A	Brown R	Butler PL	Carver GF	Daykin B	Edwards RT	Flower AJ	Fry KF	Gibson APS	Hampton IK	Hateley A	Jones B	Loxley H	Moore B	Sheridan J	Smith GH	Tait RJ	Withers A
1	Aug	18	Coventry City	0-2		22832	3			8	1	6		2		7	5		10	9			4		11	
2		23	WATFORD	1-3	Brown	6113	3			8	1		6	2	10	7	5		9				4			11
3		25	BOURNEMOUTH	2-0	Hateley, Moore	6749	3	10		8	1		6	2			5		9			7	4		11	
4		28	Watford	0-4		11423	3	10		8	1		6	2		7	5		9		4				11	
5	Sep	1	BARNSLEY	2-0	Brown, Hateley(p)	6347		10	3	8						5	2		9	7	6		4	1	11	
6		6	READING	1-0	Hateley	5798		10	3	8						5	2		9	7	6		4	1	11	
7		8	Colchester Utd.	2-2	Jones, Astle	5399		10	3	8						7	5	2		9	6		4	1	11	
8		12	Reading	1-1	Astle	5780		10	3	8						7	5	2		9	6		4	1	11	
9		15	SOUTHEND UNITED	2-1	Brown, Astle	7128		10	3	8						7	5	2		9	6		4	1	11	
10		20	BRISTOL CITY	3-2	Loxley, Fry, Jones	5993		10	3	8						7	5	2		9	6		4	1	11	
11		22	Millwall	2-0	Jones 2	15953		10	3	8			6			7	5	2		9			4	1	11	
12		29	SHREWSBURY TOWN	1-5	Jones	10363		10		8			3			7	5	2		9	6		4	1	11	
13	Oct	1	Port Vale	1-1	Jones	9245		10		8			3			7	5	2		9	6		4	1	11	
14		6	Queens Park Rangers	1-0	Jones	15594		10					3			7	5	2		9	6		4	1	11	
15		11	PORT VALE	1-0	Tait	14320		10		8			2			7	5	3		9	6		4	1	11	
16		13	HULL CITY	1-1	Fry	9595		10					8			3	7	5	2		9	6		4	1	11
17		20	Crystal Palace	1-1	Carver	13700		10			7		8			3		5	2		9	6		4	1	11
18		27	WREXHAM	3-2	Jones 2, Astle	8496		10					8			3	7	5	2		9	6		4	1	11
19	Nov	10	BRISTOL ROVERS	1-3	Hateley(p)	5950		10		8						3		5	2	9	7	6		4	1	11
20		17	Brighton & Hove Alb.	3-1	Edwards 2, Bircumshaw	6187		11	3					6		10		5	2		9	4	7	8	1		
21	Dec	1	Swindon Town	1-3	Jones	11977		11	3					6		10		5	2		9	4	7	8	1		
22		8	PETERBOROUGH UTD.	2-0	Hateley, Edwards	5640		8	3							10	7	5	2	9		6		4	1	11	
23		15	COVENTRY CITY	1-1	Astle	6793		8	3							10	7	5	2	9		6		4	1	11	
24		22	Bournemouth	1-3	Edwards	9629		8	3							10	7	5	2	9		6		4	1	11	
25		26	NORTHAMPTON T	2-1	Astle, Hateley	6614		8	3							10	7	5	2	9		6		4	1		11
26	Jan	12	Barnsley	1-3	Hateley	7719		8	3				4			10	7	5	2	9		6			1		11
27	Feb	23	QUEENS PARK RANGERS	3-2	Hateley 3 (2p)	8268		8	3				6			10	7	5	2	9	11			4	1		
28	Mar	9	CRYSTAL PALACE	0-2		5536		8	3				6			10	7	5	2	9	11			4	1		
29		12	Carlisle Utd.	2-4	Hateley 2 (1p)	6732		8	3	10		6						5	2	9	7			4	1	11	
30		16	Wrexham	1-5	Jones	8059		8	3			6					11	5	2	9		10		4	1		
31		21	CARLISLE UTD.	1-0	Astle	3455		8	3							10	11	5	2	9		6	7	4	1		
32		23	HALIFAX TOWN	5-0	Hateley 3, Astle, Edwards	5076		8	3							10	11	5	2	9		6	7	4	1		
33		30	Bristol Rovers	1-1	Astle	5970		8	3							10	11	5	2	9		6	7	4	1		
34	Apr	2	Northampton T	2-2	Astle, Hateley	14606		8	3							2	11	5		9		6	7	4	1	10	
35		6	BRIGHTON & HOVE ALB.	0-1		7001		8	3							2	11	5		9		6	7	4	1	10	
36		12	BRADFORD PARK AVE.	3-2	Astle, Loxley, Tait	6382		8	3	10						2	7	5		9		6		4	1	11	
37		16	Bradford Park Ave.	0-5		8258		8	3	10						2	7	5		9		6		4	1	11	
38		20	SWINDON TOWN	2-0	Hateley 2	5609		8	3							2	11	5		9		6	7	4	1	10	
39		24	Shrewsbury Town	2-2	Astle, Hateley	4381		8	3							2	11	5		9		6	7	4	1	10	
40		27	Peterborough Utd.	0-0		10287		8	3							2	11	5		9		6	7	4	1	10	
41		30	Bristol City	1-1	Waterhouse (og)	12197		8	3							2	11	5		9		6	7	4	1	10	
42	May	4	MILLWALL	3-3	Tait 2, Hateley	6457		8	3							2	11	5		9		6	7	4	1	10	
43		7	Halifax Town	1-2	Tait	1781		8	3							2	11	7	5	9		6		4	1	10	
44		13	Southend United	2-1	Astle, Flower	8210		8	3							2	11	7	5	9		6		4	1	10	
45		17	COLCHESTER UTD.	6-0	Astle 2, Hateley 2(1p), Flower, Tait	4103		9	3							2	11	7	5	8		6		4	1	10	
46		20	Hull City	1-1	Astle	4145		8	3							2	11	7	5	9		6		4	1	10	
				Apps			4	44	34	18	4	13	3	38	18	26	46	29	32	22	38	13	44	42	34	4
				Goals				16	1	3		1		5	2	2			22	11	2	1			6	

One own goal

F.A. Cup

| R1 | Nov | 3 | PETERBOROUGH UTD. | 0-3 | | 24473 | | 10 | | 8 | | | 3 | | | 7 | 5 | 2 | | 9 | 6 | | 4 | 1 | 11 | |

F.L. Cup

R2	Sep	26	Southend United	3-2	Astle, Brown, Fry	5500		10	3	8				6		7	5	2		9			4	1	11	
R3	Oct	17	SWINDON TOWN	5-0	Astle 2, Jones, Loxley, Sheridan	7012		10					8			3	7	5	2	9	6		4	1	11	
R4	Nov	14	Birmingham City	2-3	Moore, Sheridan	13187			3				6		10			5	2	9	4	7	8	1		11

		p	w	d	l	f	a	pts
1	Northampton Town	46	26	10	10	109	60	62
2	Swindon Town	46	22	14	10	87	56	58
3	Port Vale	46	23	8	15	72	58	54
4	Coventry City	46	18	17	11	83	69	53
5	Bournemouth	46	18	16	12	63	46	52
6	Peterborough Utd.	46	20	11	15	93	75	51
7	NOTTS COUNTY	46	19	13	14	73	74	51
8	Southend United	46	19	12	15	75	77	50
9	Wrexham	46	20	9	17	84	83	49
10	Hull City	46	19	10	17	74	69	48
11	Crystal Palace	46	17	13	16	68	58	47
12	Colchester United	46	18	11	17	73	93	47
13	Queen's Park Rgs.	46	17	11	18	85	76	45
14	Bristol City	46	16	13	17	100	92	45
15	Shrewsbury Town	46	16	12	18	83	81	44
16	Millwall	46	15	13	18	82	87	43
17	Watford	46	17	8	21	82	85	42
18	Barnsley	46	15	11	20	63	74	41
19	Bristol Rovers	46	15	11	20	70	88	41
20	Reading	46	16	8	22	74	78	40
21	Bradford Park Ave.	46	14	12	20	79	97	40
22	Brighton & Hove A.	46	12	12	22	58	84	36
23	Carlisle United	46	13	9	24	61	89	35
24	Halifax Town	46	9	12	25	64	106	30

Back: Wheeeler (trainer), Astle, Butler, Loxley, Sheridan, Smith, Daykin, Coleman (manager). Centre: Ford (assistant trainer), Agnew, Bircumshaw, Carver, Fry, Brown, Flower, Hateley. Front: Gibson, Edwards, Withers, Jones, Tait.

1963/64

24th in Division Three (Relegated)

#		Date	Opponent		Score	Scorers	Att	Agnew DY	Astle J	Barber MJ	Bates B	Bircumshaw A	Bly TG	Butler PL	Carver GF	Edwards RT	Flower AJ	Froggatt J	Fry KF	Gibson APS	Hampton IK	Holder DJ	Jones B	Lowe E	Loxley H	Povey VR	Robinson LJ	Sheridan J	Smith GH	Tait RJ	Woodfield T	Woolley R
1	Aug	24	Brentford		1-4	Bly	13320		8	11		3	9			2				5					6	7			4	1	10	
2		29	COVENTRY CITY		0-3		18669		8	11		3	9			2				5					6	7			4	1	10	
3		31	SHREWSBURY TOWN		0-1		7788		8	11		3	9			2				5					6	7			4	1	10	
4	Sep	7	Bristol City		0-2		9440		8			3	9	6	4					5	2		11			7				1	10	
5		10	Coventry City		0-2		27796		10			3	9	1	6	4	11			5	2		8			7						
6		14	PORT VALE		2-0	Bly, Tait	7309		8			3	9	1	6	4	11		7	5	2										10	
7		16	Mansfield Town		0-4		16560		8	11		3	9	1		4			7	5	2								6		10	
8		21	Peterborough Utd.		1-5	Astle	11791		8	11		3	9	1	6	4			7	5	2										10	
9		28	Crewe Alexandra		1-0	Barber	5284		10	11		3	9	1		4			7	5	2		8		6							
10	Oct	3	MANSFIELD TOWN		1-0	Jones	14014		10	11		3	9	1		4			7	5	2		8		6							
11		5	CRYSTAL PALACE		1-1	Bly	7207		10	11		3	9	1		4			7	5	2		8		6							
12		9	Reading		2-3	Edwards, Astle	8403		10	11		3	9	1		4			7	5	2				6	8						
13		12	WATFORD		1-2	Astle	6887		10	11		3	9	1		4			7	5	2				6	8						
14		17	READING		0-1		5271		8	11		3	9	1		4			7	5	2				6						10	
15		19	Queens Park Rangers		2-3	Edwards, Astle	7175		8	11		3		1		4			7	5	2		9		6						10	
16		24	WALSALL		0-1		6548		8	11		3		1		4	10		7		2	5	9		6							
17		26	WREXHAM		3-0	Edwards, Tait, Barber	4724		8	11		3		1		4			7		2	5	9		6						10	
18		29	Walsall		1-2	Astle	10598		8	11		3		1		4			7		2	5	9		6						10	
19	Nov	2	Bournemouth		1-1	Astle	9762		8	11		3		1		4			7		2	5	9		6						10	
20		23	MILLWALL		2-0	Tait, Snowden(og)	5205		8			3		1		4	11		7		2	5	9		6						10	
21		30	Colchester Utd.		0-4		4377	3	8	9		2		1		4	11		7			5			6						10	
22	Dec	14	BRENTFORD		2-0	Fry, Barber	3744	3	9	11		2				4			7	5					6			8	1			
23		21	Shrewsbury Town		2-5	Astle, Tait	3738	3	8	11		2	9			4			7	5					6				1		10	
24		26	Oldham Athletic		0-2		15869	3	8	11		2	9	1	10	4			7	5				6								
25		28	OLDHAM ATHLETIC		4-2	Astle 3, Fry	7976	3	8	11		2	9		10	4			7	5				6					1			
26	Jan	11	BRISTOL CITY		1-1	Edwards	5824	3	8	11		2	9		10	4			7	5				6					1			
27		18	Port Vale		1-0	Astle	7337	3	8	11		2	9		10	4				5				6		7			1			
28		25	HULL CITY		0-1		9065	3	8	11		2	9		10	4				5				6		7			1			
29	Feb	1	PETERBOROUGH UTD.		0-0		7206	3	9	11		2			10	4				5				6		7		8	1			
30		8	CREWE ALEXANDRA		0-0		5380	3	9	11		2			6	4				5						7		8	1		10	
31		15	Crystal Palace		0-2		15867	3	9	11		2			6	4				5						7		8	1		10	
32		22	Watford		0-2		11370	3	8	11						4				5	2				6	7		9	1		10	
33		29	SOUTHEND UNITED		1-1	Flower	3610	3	8						10	4	11			5	2				6	7		9	1			
34	Mar	3	Barnsley		1-2	Bly	3709	3					8		10	4	11			5	2				6	7		9	1			
35		7	Wrexham		0-4		4947	3	8						10	4				5	2				6	7		9	1	11		
36		14	BOURNEMOUTH		1-3	Fry(p)	2640	3					9		10	4	11		7	5	2				6			8	1			
37		20	Southend United		1-3	Edwards	7575	3								4	11		7	5	2		9	6				8	1		10	
38		26	LUTON TOWN		1-1	Jones	4406	3					9		6		11		7	5	2		8					4	1		10	
39		28	BARNSLEY		1-1	Flower	3607	3					9		6		11		7	5	2		8					4	1		10	
40		30	Luton Town		0-2		8387	3	8						6		10	11	7	5	2		9					4	1			
41	Apr	4	Millwall		1-6	Fry	5418	3	8				9		6	2	11		7	5								4	1			10
42		9	Bristol Rovers		3-4	Fry 2(1p), Woolley	3883		8			2			6		11		7	5							3		1		10	4	9
43		11	COLCHESTER UTD.		3-1	Flower 2, Woolley	3913		8			2		1			11		7			5		6			3				10	4	9
44		18	Bristol Rovers		0-4		7102		8		11	2			1			10	7			5		6			3				4	9	
45		22	Hull City		1-4	Flower	5106	3	8			2	9	1			11	10	7	5				6							4		
46		25	QUEENS PARK RANGERS		2-2	Flower, Tait	2862	3	8				9	1	6		11		7	5	2										10	4	
				Apps				23	41	28	1	35	27	22	22	39	17	2	32	38	27	8	15	8	25	16	3	18	24	26	5	4
				Goals					11	3			4			5	6		6				2							5		2

One own goal

F.A. Cup

		Date	Opponent		Score	Scorers	Att																										
R1	Nov	16	FRICKLEY COLLIERY		2-1	Astle, Tait	5896		8			3		1		4	11		7				2	5	9	6					10		
R2	Dec	7	Doncaster Rovers		1-1	Bly	8810	3	8	11		2	9			4			7	5					6				1		10		
rep		10	DONCASTER ROVERS		1-2	Tait	10607	3	8	11		2	9			4			7	5					6				1		10		

F.L. Cup

		Date	Opponent		Score	Scorers	Att																										
R2	Sep	25	BLACKBURN ROVERS		2-1	Jones, Astle	7030		10	11		3	9	1		4			7	5	2		8		6								
R3	Nov	5	BRADFORD PARK AVE.		3-2	Astle, Fry(p), Edwards	4002		8	11		3		1		4			7		2	5	9		6						10		
R4		13	PORTSMOUTH		3-2	Tait 2, Fry(p)	6132		8			3		1		4	11		7		2	5	9		6						10		
R5	Dec	17	MANCHESTER CITY		0-1		7330	3	8	11		2	9			4			7	5					6				1		10		

		p	w	d	l	f	a	pts
1	Coventry City	46	22	16	8	98	61	60
2	Crystal Palace	46	23	14	9	73	51	60
3	Watford	46	23	12	11	79	59	58
4	Bournemouth	46	24	8	14	79	58	56
5	Bristol City	46	20	15	11	84	64	55
6	Reading	46	21	10	15	79	62	52
7	Mansfield Town	46	20	11	15	76	62	51
8	Hull City	46	16	17	13	73	68	49
9	Oldham Athletic	46	20	8	18	73	70	48
10	Peterborough Utd.	46	18	11	17	75	70	47
11	Shrewsbury Town	46	18	11	17	73	80	47
12	Bristol Rovers	46	19	8	19	91	79	46
13	Port Vale	46	16	14	16	53	49	46
14	Southend United	46	15	15	16	77	78	45
15	Queen's Park Rgs.	46	18	9	19	76	78	45
16	Brentford	46	15	14	17	87	80	44
17	Colchester United	46	12	19	15	70	68	43
18	Luton Town	46	16	10	20	64	80	42
19	Walsall	46	13	14	19	59	76	40
20	Barnsley	46	12	15	19	68	94	39
21	Millwall	46	14	10	22	53	67	38
22	Crewe Alexandra	46	11	12	23	50	77	34
23	Wrexham	46	13	6	27	75	107	32
24	NOTTS COUNTY	46	9	9	28	45	92	27

1964/65

13th in Division Four

League

#	Date		Opponent	Result	Scorers	Att	Agnew DY	Astle J	Barber MJ	Bates B	Bircumshaw A	Bly TG	Carver GF	Coates DP	Docherty B	Edwards RT	Fawell D	Flower AJ	Froggatt J	Gibson APS	Hampton IK	Hannah G	Kavanagh E	Lowe E	Pace DJ	Povey VR	Rayner J	Robinson LJ	Sheridan J	Smith GH	Tait B	Woolley R
1	Aug	22	Wrexham	0-4		7911	3	8	11			9	6			2				5		10	7						4	1		
2		27	TRANMERE ROVERS	2-4	Astle, Flower(p)	7694	3	9							10			11		5	2	8	7	6					4	1		
3		29	SOUTHPORT	0-0		4916	3	9							10	5		11		6	2	8	7						4	1		
4		31	Tranmere Rovers	0-4		11715		8			3				10	5		11		6	2		7						4	1	9	
5	Sep	5	Bradford Park Ave.	2-2	Kavanagh, Gibson(p)	7064		9	11		3				10	5			8	6	2		7						4	1		
6		10	DARLINGTON	4-2	Sheridan, Docherty, Rayner, Astle	8460		9	11		3				10	5				6	2		7				8		4	1		
7		12	ALDERSHOT	0-0		7659		9	11		3				10	5				6	2		7				8		4	1		
8		14	Darlington	1-5	Gibson	5125		9			3				10	5		11		6			7				8	2	4	1		
9		18	Doncaster Rov.	0-0		11362	3	9						2	10	5		11		6			7				8		4	1		
10		26	CHESTERFIELD	5-1	Raynor 3, Kavanagh, Astle	7482	3	9						2	10	5		11		6			7				8		4	1		
11		28	Newport County	1-3	Astle	5802	3	9				8		2	10	5		11					7				6		4	1		
12	Oct	3	YORK CITY	3-1	Sheridan, Rayner, Povey	6490	3							2			6	10	5			8	7			11	9		4	1		
13		8	NEWPORT COUNTY	1-0	Povey	6137	3							2			6	10	5			8	7			11	9		4	1		
14		10	Brighton & Hove Alb.	0-6		14195	3							2			6		5		10	8	7			11	9		4	1		
15		17	OXFORD UNITED	0-0		4971	3		11					2			6	10	5			8					7		4	1	9	
16		22	CREWE ALEXANDRA	2-0	Docherty, Rayner	3970	3							2			6	10	5		11	8					7	9	4	1		
17		24	Barrow	0-2		2149	3							2			8	10	5		11	6					7	9	4	1		
18		29	STOCKPORT COUNTY	2-0	Hannah, Rayner	4312								3			6			9	11	5	2	10	7			8		4	1		
19		31	HARTLEPOOL UTD.	1-0	Edwards	4924	3							2			6	10	9		11	5					7		8	4	1		
20	Nov	7	Rochdale	1-1	Sheridan	4804	3							2			6	10	9		11	5					7		8	4	1		
21		21	Bradford City	2-0	Edwards, Flower	3127	3							2			6	10	9		11	5					7		8	4	1		
22		28	CHESTER	1-1	Rayner	5878	3							2			6	10	9		11	5					7		8	4	1		
23	Dec	12	WREXHAM	1-3	Rayner	4706	3							2			6	11	10			5				7	9		8	4	1		
24		19	Southport	0-0		1800	3							2			6	10			11	5				9	7		8	4	1	8	
25		26	Lincoln City	0-1		4969	3							2			6				11	5	10			9	7	8		4	1		
26		28	LINCOLN CITY	2-1	Pace 2	4472	3							2			6				11	5	10			9	7	8		4	1		
27	Jan	2	BRADFORD PARK AVE.	3-3	Rayner 2, Pace	6205	3							2			6				11	5	10			9	7	8		4	1		
28		16	Aldershot	2-1	Flower, Pace	3910	3							2			6				11	5	10			9	7	8		4	1		
29		23	DONCASTER ROV.	5-2	Pace 3, Walton 2(2og)	8045	3							2			6				11	5	10			9	7	8		4	1		
30	Feb	6	Chesterfield	0-0		7014	3							2			6				11	5	10			9	7	8		4	1		
31		13	York City	1-2	Flower	6188	3							2			6				11	5	10			9	7	8		4	1		
32		20	BRIGHTON & HOVE ALB.	1-2	Coates	5002	3							6		2					11	5	10	7		9		8		4	1		
33		24	Torquay United	1-2	Pace	3905	3							6		2					11	5	10	7		9		8		4	1		
34		27	Oxford United	0-4		7837	3						4	6	10	2	8	11				5		7		9					1		
35	Mar	6	BARROW	4-1	Pace, Povey, Kavanagh, Gibson(p)	4294	3						4	6		2						5	10	7		9	11	8			1		
36		10	Crewe Alexandra	1-2	Kavanagh	4094	3						4	6		2						5	10	7		9	11	8			1		
37		13	Hartlepool Utd.	2-2	Gibson(p), Pace	5031	3							6	8	2		11		5			10			9			4	1		7
38		20	ROCHDALE	0-0		3219	3							6	8	2		11		5			10			9			4	1		7
39		27	Millwall	1-4	Pace	6324	3								10	5		11		6	2					9	7	8	4	1		
40	Apr	3	BRADFORD CITY	1-0	Pace	3707					3				8	10	5	11		6	2					9	7		4	1		
41		10	Chester	1-4	Flower	5684					3				8	10	5	11		6	2					9	7		4	1		
42		17	TORQUAY UNITED	0-0		5046			11		3				6		8			10	5	2				9			4	1		7
43		19	Halifax Town	1-1	Bates	1913			11	3					6		8			10	5	2				9			4	1		7
44		20	HALIFAX TOWN	4-0	Edwards 2, Rayner, Flower	4080			11	3					6	8	7			5	2					9	10		4	1		
45		23	Stockport County	1-0	Rayner	5880			11	3					6	8	7			5	2					9	10		4	1		
46		29	MILLWALL	1-2	Edwards	10729			11	3					6	8	7			5	2					9	10		4	1		
			Apps				33	11	5	5	35	2	6	34	25	37	1	35	2	40	15	22	25	1	24	19	32	1	43	46	3	4
			Goals					4		1			1	2	5			6		4		1	4		12	3	13		3			

Two own goals

F.A. Cup

R1	Nov	14	CHELMSFORD CITY	2-0	Rayner, Kavanagh	9870	3							2			6	10	9		11	5				7		8	4	1		
R2	Dec	5	Brentford	0-4		9400	3							2			6	10	9		11	5				7		8	4	1		

F.L. Cup

R1	Sep	2	NEWPORT COUNTY	3-2	Astle 2, Froggatt	2881		9	11		3				10	5			8	6	2		7						4	1		
R2		23	Torquay United	2-1	Astle 2	4734	3	9			2				10	5		11		6			7				8		4	1		
R3	Oct	26	Chelsea	0-4		6596					3				8	10	5		11	6	2		7			9			4	1		

Back: Gibson, Sheridan, Astle, Edwards, Coates, Woolley, Flower, Lee, Hampton, Shrewsbury. Centre: Coleman (scout), Agnew, Hannah, Bircumshaw, Butler, Smith, Froggatt, Woodfield, L Robinson, Bly, Wheeler (trainer). Front: B Tait, Kavanagh, Docherty, Ward, J Robinson, Lowe (player/manager), Barber, Carver, Stead, Povey.

Division Four final table

		p	w	d	l	f	a	pts
1	Brighton & Hove A.	46	26	11	9	102	57	63
2	Millwall	46	23	16	7	78	45	62
3	York City	46	28	6	12	91	56	62
4	Oxford United	46	23	15	8	87	44	61
5	Tranmere Rovers	46	27	6	13	99	56	60
6	Rochdale	46	22	14	10	74	53	58
7	Bradford Park Ave.	46	20	17	9	86	62	57
8	Chester	46	25	6	15	119	81	56
9	Doncaster Rovers	46	20	11	15	84	72	51
10	Crewe Alexandra	46	18	13	15	90	81	49
11	Torquay United	46	21	7	18	70	70	49
12	Chesterfield	46	20	8	18	58	70	48
13	NOTTS COUNTY	46	15	14	17	61	73	44
14	Wrexham	46	17	9	20	84	92	43
15	Hartlepools United	46	15	13	18	61	85	43
16	Newport County	46	17	8	21	85	81	42
17	Darlington	46	18	6	22	84	87	42
18	Aldershot	46	15	7	24	64	84	37
19	Bradford City	46	12	8	26	70	88	32
20	Southport	46	8	16	22	58	89	32
21	Barrow	46	12	6	28	59	105	30
22	Lincoln City	46	11	6	29	58	99	28
23	Halifax Town	46	11	6	29	54	103	28
24	Stockport County	46	10	7	29	44	87	27

1965/66

8th in Division Four

#		Date	Opponent	Result	Scorers	Att
1	Aug	21	DARLINGTON	0-0		7388
2		23	Stockport County	3-1	Bates 2, Shiels	11670
3		28	Lincoln City	2-1	Pace 2	6613
4	Sep	4	SOUTHPORT	1-2	Pace	5903
5		11	CHESTER	3-3	Bates 2, Shiels	4916
6		16	STOCKPORT COUNTY	1-1	Beresford	6623
7		18	Halifax Town	1-0	Moulden	2523
8		25	PORT VALE	3-1	Bates 2, Shiels	6086
9	Oct	1	Crewe Alexandra	0-1		3760
10		7	COLCHESTER UTD.	1-0	Hampton	5681
11		9	Bradford Park Ave.	0-4		4501
12		16	ALDERSHOT	2-0	Beresford 2	5407
13		25	Newport County	2-1	Kirkup, Rowland(og)	3985
14		30	TORQUAY UNITED	1-1	Bates	7174
15	Nov	6	Chesterfield	0-0		8575
16		20	Luton Town	1-5	Shiels	6486
17		22	Colchester Utd.	1-4	Still	2768
18		27	BARROW	0-2		3442
19	Dec	11	DONCASTER ROV.	1-2	Still	5049
20		27	Tranmere Rovers	3-0	Still 2, Shiels	10592
21	Jan	1	BRADFORD PARK AVE.	2-0	Still, Bates	6277
22		8	Rochdale	2-0	Sheridan, Flower	2677
23		15	NEWPORT COUNTY	1-1	Bates	4605
24		29	Darlington	0-1		7712
25	Feb	5	LINCOLN CITY	2-1	Still, Beresford	5122
26		12	Barnsley	1-1	Gibson(p)	2516
27		19	Southport	0-1		5297
28		26	Chester	1-1	Benskin	8704
29	Mar	5	BARNSLEY	0-1		5894
30		9	Aldershot	0-0		3593
31		12	HALIFAX TOWN	1-1	Carver	3961
32		19	Port Vale	1-0	Flower	5619
33		26	CREWE ALEXANDRA	0-1		3265
34	Apr	2	CHESTERFIELD	2-0	Still 2	1927
35		8	Wrexham	3-1	Beresford, Kirkup, Thompson	7262
36		9	Hartlepool Utd.	0-2		4001
37		11	WREXHAM	3-1	Still, Beresford, Shiels	4667
38		16	LUTON TOWN	1-1	Edwards	4740
39		23	Barrow	1-2	Agnew	4151
40		27	Bradford City	4-0	Beresford 2, Still, Flower	2370
41		30	HARTLEPOOL UTD.	1-0	Kirkup	4448
42	May	6	Doncaster Rov.	3-0	Gibson, Beresford 2	16389
43		9	Torquay United	0-2		8928
44		13	TRANMERE ROVERS	1-2	King(og)	4642
45		18	BRADFORD CITY	2-1	Still, Beresford	3130
46		21	ROCHDALE	3-3	Still 2, Bates	3488

Two own goals

F.A. Cup

R1	Nov	13	Southend United	1-3	Sheridan	5375

F.L. Cup

R1	Sep	1	CHESTERFIELD	0-0		6076
rep		8	Chesterfield	1-2	Bates	2188

Final Table

		p	w	d	l	f	a	pts
1	Doncaster Rovers	46	24	11	11	85	54	59
2	Darlington	46	25	9	12	72	53	59
3	Torquay United	46	24	10	12	72	49	58
4	Colchester United	46	23	10	13	70	47	56
5	Tranmere Rovers	46	24	8	14	93	66	56
6	Luton Town	46	24	8	14	90	70	56
7	Chester	46	20	12	14	79	70	52
8	NOTTS COUNTY	46	19	12	15	61	53	50
9	Newport County	46	18	12	16	75	75	48
10	Southport	46	18	12	16	68	69	48
11	Bradford Park Ave.	46	21	5	20	102	92	47
12	Barrow	46	16	15	15	72	76	47
13	Stockport County	46	18	6	22	71	70	42
14	Crewe Alexandra	46	16	9	21	61	63	41
15	Halifax Town	46	15	11	20	67	75	41
16	Barnsley	46	15	10	21	74	78	40
17	Aldershot	46	15	10	21	75	84	40
18	Hartlepools United	46	16	8	22	63	75	40
19	Port Vale	46	15	9	22	48	59	39
20	Chesterfield	46	13	13	20	62	78	39
21	Rochdale	46	16	5	25	71	87	37
22	Lincoln City	46	13	11	22	57	82	37
23	Bradford City	46	12	13	21	63	94	37
24	Wrexham	46	13	9	24	72	104	35

Back: Coates, Hampton, Bates, Moulden, Shiels, Woolley, Gibson, Hannah, Carver, Pace. Centre: Bircumshaw, Flower, Barber, Smith, Sheridan, Butler, Kirkup, Still, Edwards. Front: Wheeler (trainer), Agnew, Stead, Northridge, Rogers, Beresford, Ward, Coleman (manager).

1966/67

20th in Division Four

#	Date		Opponent	Score	Scorers	Att	Agnew DY	Bates B	Beresford J	Bowers J	Cargill J	Chalmers L	Clarke D	Coates DP	Crispin T	Edwards RT	Flower AJ	Garner W	Gibson APS	Hampton IK	Harkin T	Marshall S	Needham DW	Rose MJ	Shrewsbury P	Smith GH	Smith, Jack	Still RG	Thompson T	Thorne T	Upton F	Watson DV	Wileman R
1	Aug	20	Bradford Park Ave.	1-4	Bates	6283		7	10	11		2				6			5	3		8					1		9	4			
2		27	PORT VALE	0-0		5648		7	10			2	11			6	8		5	3							1		9	4			
3	Sep	3	Crewe Alexandra	1-4	Edwards	3098		7	10			2	11			6			5	3							1		9	4	8		
4		7	WREXHAM	2-2	Thompson, Marshall	3878	3					2	11			4	7	9	6			10	5				1			8			
5		10	BARROW	2-2	Marshall 2	4029	3	7			1		11			4		9	6	2		10	5							8			
6		16	York City	1-4	Baker(og)	4909		7			1	2	11			6			5	3		8						10	9	4			
7		19	Southport	1-2	Marshall	6249		7				2	11			6			5	3		8					1	10	9	4			
8		24	LINCOLN CITY	2-1	Marshall 2	5167		7				2	11			4			5	3	9	8					1	10			6		
9		26	Wrexham	2-3	Marshall. Gibson(p)	6554		7				2	11			4			5	3	9	8					1	10			6		
10	Oct	1	Chesterfield	1-1	Harkin	5341						2	11			4	7		5	3	9	8					1	10			6		
11		8	ALDERSHOT	3-0	Beresford 2, Harkin	4911			10	7		2	11			4			5	3	9						1	8			6		
12		15	Luton Town	5-2	Upton 2, Harkin 2, Gibson(p)	5743			10	7		2	11			4			5	3	9						1	8			6		
13		19	SOUTHPORT	0-1		6491			10	7		2	11			4			5	3	9						1	8			6		
14		22	BARNSLEY	0-3		6373			10	7		2	11			4			5	3	9						1	8			6		
15		29	Newport County	0-1		3670		7	12			2	11			4			5		9	8					1	10	3		6		
16	Nov	1	CREWE ALEXANDRA	1-1	Harkin	2919			10				11			4	7		5	2	9	12					1	8	3		6		
17		5	BRENTFORD	3-2	Harkin 2, J Smith	3883			10				11			4	7		5	2	9						1	8	3		6		
18		12	Halifax Town	2-5	J Smith 2	2461			10				11			4	7		5	2	9						1	8	3		6		
19		19	HARTLEPOOL UTD.	0-0		3922		7				2	11			6			5		10						1	8	9	3	4		
20	Dec	3	BRADFORD CITY	1-3	J Smith	3913						2	11			4	7		5		9	8					1	10	3		6		
21		17	BRADFORD PARK AVE.	2-1	Bates 2	3051		7				2	11	4		8	12		5		9						1	10	3		6		
22		27	ROCHDALE	2-0	J Smith 2	4810		7				2	11	4		8	12		5		9						1	10	3		6		
23		31	Port Vale	0-0		5359		7				2		4		8	11		5		9				12		1	10	3		6		
24	Jan	14	Barrow	1-0	Edwards	7243		7				2		4		8	11		5		9						1	10	3		6		
25		21	YORK CITY	2-0	Edwards, Harkin	4718		7			1	2		4		8	11		5		9							10	3		6		
26		27	Rochdale	1-1	J Smith	2358		7			1	2		4		8	11		5		9							10	3		6		
27	Feb	4	Lincoln City	1-2	Harkin	5122		7			1	2		4		8	11		5		9							10	3		6		
28		11	CHESTERFIELD	0-2		5791			10		1	2	11	4		8			5		9				7			12	3		6		
29		18	Southend United	0-1		8476	10	6			1	2		4		8	11		5	12	9								7	3				
30		25	Aldershot	1-4	Chalmers	3855	7	6			1	2	12	4		8			5		10	11								3		9		
31	Mar	4	LUTON TOWN	1-2	Harkin	3909	7	11			1			4					6	2	10		5					8	3		9		
32		10	SOUTHEND UNITED	1-0	Bates	3858	7	11			1			4					5	2		8	6					10	3		9		
33		18	Barnsley	0-0		5278	7							4					6	2	10	8	5	1				11	3		9		
34		24	Chester	2-1	J Smith, Gibson(p)	4292	7							4					10		6	2	8	5	1			9	3				11
35		25	EXETER CITY	0-1		4258	7							4				10	6	2		8	5	1				9	3		12		11
36		28	CHESTER	3-0	Bates, Marshall 2	3398	7	11				2		6					4		10	8	5	1							9	3	
37	Apr	1	Brentford	0-1		6283	7	11				2		6					4			8	5	1				10	3		9		
38		8	HALIFAX TOWN	2-1	Still 2	3024	7	11						6					4	2		8	5	1				10	3		9		
39		10	Stockport County	0-2		8856	7	11						6					4	2		8	5	1				10	3		9		
40		15	Hartlepool Utd.	1-2	Bates	4674	11	6			2			4					5				7	1				9	10	3		8		
41		22	NEWPORT COUNTY	2-1	Marshall 2	3455	7					2		4	3		11		6			8	5	1				10			9		
42		26	STOCKPORT COUNTY	2-2	Marshall, Bates	4536	7					2		4	3		11		6			8	5		1				10		9		
43		29	Bradford City	1-3	Upton	3856	7					2		4	3		11		6	12		8	5		1				10		9		
44	May	6	TRANMERE ROVERS	0-0		4209	7					2		4	3		11		6			8	5	1				12	10		9		
45		13	Exeter City	0-1		3417	7					2			3		11		5				8	4	1			10	6		9		
46		17	Tranmere Rovers	0-3		6817	7					2	11		3				5					4	1			10	6		9	8	

	Apps	2	35	21	5	10	35	24	24	6	30	22	2	46	24	28	25	17	12	2	24	32	12	37	2	34	4	2
	Goals		7	2			1				3			3		10	12					8	2	1			3		

One own goal

F.A. Cup

R1	Nov	26	Oldham Athletic	1-3	Marshall	12200						2	11			4	7		5		9	8					1	10		3		6		

F.L. Cup

R1	Aug	24	MANSFIELD TOWN	1-1	Beresford	7002		7	10			2	11			6	8		5	3							1		9	4			
rep		29	Mansfield Town	0-3		6081		7	10			2	11			6	8		5	3		12					1		9	4			

		p	w	d	l	f	a	pts
1	Stockport County	46	26	12	8	69	42	64
2	Southport	46	23	13	10	69	42	59
3	Barrow	46	24	11	11	76	54	59
4	Tranmere Rovers	46	22	14	10	66	43	58
5	Crewe Alexandra	46	21	12	13	70	55	54
6	Southend United	46	22	9	15	70	49	53
7	Wrexham	46	16	20	10	76	62	52
8	Hartlepools United	46	22	7	17	66	64	51
9	Brentford	46	18	13	15	58	56	49
10	Aldershot	46	18	12	16	72	57	48
11	Bradford City	46	19	10	17	74	62	48
12	Halifax Town	46	15	14	17	59	68	44
13	Port Vale	46	14	15	17	55	58	43
14	Exeter City	46	14	15	17	50	60	43
15	Chesterfield	46	17	8	21	60	63	42
16	Barnsley	46	13	15	18	60	64	41
17	Luton Town	46	16	9	21	59	73	41
18	Newport County	46	12	16	18	56	63	40
19	Chester	46	15	10	21	54	78	40
20	NOTTS COUNTY	46	13	11	22	53	72	37
21	Rochdale	46	13	11	22	53	75	37
22	York City	46	12	11	23	65	79	35
23	Bradford Park Ave.	46	11	13	22	52	79	35
24	Lincoln City	46	9	13	24	58	82	31

1967/68

17th in Division Four

						Ball GH	Bates B	Bradd LJ	Cartwright M	Chalmers L	Crispin T	Elliott JW	Farmer RJ	Gadsby MD	Gibson APS	Marshall S	McGovern P	Murphy, F. John	Murphy, James B	Needham DW	Oakes DR	Pring KD	Rose MJ	Rushton B	Smith KW	Smith, Jack	Thompson T	Watson CR	Watson DV	Weaver E	Yeomans K
1	Aug	19	CHESTER	1-2	Marshall	6599		11		2					3	8					6		1	4	10	9				5	7
2		26	Chesterfield	0-4		5932	7			2		11			3	8					6		1	10		9	4		5		
3	Sep	2	EXETER CITY	1-0	J Smith	3741				2		11			5	8					4		1		10	9	3			6	7
4		6	Port Vale	0-0		4338	7			2		11			5	8					4		1	12	10	9	3			6	
5		9	Darlington	2-2	Marshall, KW Smith	4642	7			2		11			5	8				9	4		1		10		3			6	
6		16	ALDERSHOT	0-1		4451				2		11			5	8					6	4	1		9		3			10	7
7		23	Workington	1-5	Marshall	2109	12					3	11		5	8					4		1		10		6			9	7	2
8		25	Port Vale	1-4	KW Smith	4021				2		11			5	8					4		1		10		3			9	7
9		30	LINCOLN CITY	0-0		6238				2		11			3	10					5	8	1		6		4			9	7
10	Oct	4	CREWE ALEXANDRA	1-0	DV Watson	5550	12	9		2					3	7					5	8	1		6		4			10	11
11		7	BRADFORD PARK AVE.	0-0		7355	12	9		2				4	3	7					5	8	1		6					10	11
12		14	Brentford	1-2	Elliott	7443	8	9		2			4		3	12					5	7	1		6					10	
13		21	ROCHDALE	2-0	Bradd, Elliott	5832		9		2		10	4		3			11			5	7	1		6					8	
14		25	Crewe Alexandra	0-4		6308		9		2		10	4		3			11			5	7	1		6	12				8	
15		28	York City	2-4	Bates 2	4982	7	9		2			4		3			11			5		1		6	10				8	12
16	Nov	4	NEWPORT COUNTY	3-1	Weaver, Bradd, Collins(og)	4472	3	8	9	2		11	4		5								1		6	10					7
17		10	Hartlepool Utd.	1-3	Weaver	4141	2	8	9		3	11	4		5								1		6	10				12	7
18		15	Exeter City	3-3	Gibson, Weaver, Farmer	4009	2						8		11	10					5		1		6	9	4				3	7
19		18	SWANSEA TOWN	3-2	Weaver, J Smith, Thompson	5180	2						10	8	11	12					5		1		6	9	4				3	7
20		25	Barnsley	1-3	Marshall	8361	2					3	11	8		10	12				5		1		6	9	4				7	
21	Dec	2	WREXHAM	1-1	Elliott	4878	2		12				11	8		3	10				5		1		6	9	4				7	
22		16	Chester	3-1	Bradd 2, Farmer(p)	3576	2		9				11	4	1			6			5				3	8				10	7	
23		23	CHESTERFIELD	1-0	FJ Murphy	9990	2		9				11	4	1	12		6			5				3	8				10	7	
24		26	Bradford City	1-5	Farmer	11013	2	7	9				11	4	1	12		6			5				3	8				10		
25		30	BRADFORD CITY	1-0	Bates	7404	2	10	9				11	4	1	6					5	7			3	8						
26	Jan	13	DARLINGTON	0-0		4426	2	8	9				11	4	1	6			12		5	7			3	10						
27		20	Aldershot	0-0		4354	2	7	9						1	6			8	10	5	4	11		3							
28	Feb	3	WORKINGTON	2-1	Bradd 2	5259	2		9				11	4	1	6	8				5	7			3	10						
29		10	Lincoln City	3-1	Farmer, KW Smith (p), Marshall	6554	2		9				11	4	1	6					5	7			3	10						
30		17	HALIFAX TOWN	1-3	KW Smith (p)	5880	2		9				11	4	1	6	8		12		5	7			3	10						
31		24	Swansea Town	0-2		5803	2						11	4	1	6		12		10	5	8	7		3	9						
32	Mar	2	BRENTFORD	2-1	JB Murphy, Farmer	4486	2						11	4	1	6			10	8	5				3	9						
33		8	Doncaster Rov.	1-3	Pring	9765	2		8	12			11	4		6			9	5		7	1		3	10						
34		16	Rochdale	0-0		1895	7		9	2			12	4		6					10	5		11	1	3	8						
35		23	YORK CITY	1-1	Bradd	4174	8		9	2			11	4				12		6	10	5		7	1	3							
36		30	Newport County	0-1		2023	8		9	2			11	4						6	10	5		7	1	3							
37	Apr	6	HARTLEPOOL UTD.	0-3		4976	8		9	2			11	4		12				6	10	5		7	1	3							
38		12	Luton Town	0-2		16631	4	7		2			11			5	12		10	6		8			1	3	9						
39		13	Bradford Park Ave.	4-1	JB Murphy,FJ Murphy,Bates,Burgin(og)	2165	4	7		2	5		11						10	6		8			1	3	9						
40		15	LUTON TOWN	2-2	Bates, JB Murphy(p)	7920	3	7		2			11			5			10	8		4			1	6	9						
41		20	BARNSLEY	1-4	Elliott	8674	3	7		2			11			5	12		10	8		4			1	6	9						
42		22	Southend United	1-0	Bradd	9673	3		9	2			11	10			7			8		4			1	6	5						
43		27	Wrexham	0-2		3933	3		9	2			11	10			7			8		4	12		1	6	5						
44	May	1	DONCASTER ROV.	0-2		4070			9	2			11			5			8	10		4	7			3	6		1				
45		4	SOUTHEND UNITED	4-3	Bradd 2, Elliott, J Smith	3848			9	2			11	4		5			8			6	7	1		3	10						
46		10	Halifax Town	1-0	Pring	1802			9	2			11	4		5					10	12	6	7	1	3	8						
			Apps				28	19	28	15	16	2	40	30	11	39	24	3	18	16	31	25	17	34	3	45	33	13	1	21	17	1
			Goals					5	10				5	5		1	5		2	3				2		4	3	1		1	4	

Game 10: Rose injured (32 mins), Gibson went in goal

Two own goals

F.A. Cup

| R1 | Dec | 9 | Runcorn | 0-1 | | 6246 | 2 | | 10 | | | | 11 | 8 | | 3 | | | 12 | | | 5 | | 1 | | 6 | 9 | 4 | | | 7 | |

F.L. Cup

| R1 | Aug | 23 | ROTHERHAM UTD. | 0-1 | | 4492 | 7 | | | 2 | | | | | 3 | 8 | | | | 12 | 4 | | 1 | 11 | 10 | 9 | 6 | | 5 | | | |

Back: Ball, KW Smith, Rose, J Smith, Needham, Gibson. Front: Oakes, Pring, Bates, Bradd, JB Murphy, Elliott

		p	w	d	l	f	a	pts
1	Luton Town	46	27	12	7	87	44	66
2	Barnsley	46	24	13	9	68	46	61
3	Hartlepools United	46	25	10	11	60	46	60
4	Crewe Alexandra	46	20	18	8	74	49	58
5	Bradford City	46	23	11	12	72	51	57
6	Southend United	46	20	14	12	77	58	54
7	Chesterfield	46	21	11	14	71	50	53
8	Wrexham	46	20	13	13	72	53	53
9	Aldershot	46	18	17	11	70	55	53
10	Doncaster Rovers	46	18	15	13	66	56	51
11	Halifax Town	46	15	16	15	52	49	46
12	Newport County	46	16	13	17	58	63	45
13	Lincoln City	46	17	9	20	71	68	43
14	Brentford	46	18	7	21	61	64	43
15	Swansea Town	46	16	10	20	63	77	42
16	Darlington	46	12	17	17	47	53	41
17	NOTTS COUNTY	46	15	11	20	53	79	41
18	Port Vale	46	12	15	19	61	72	39
19	Rochdale	46	12	14	20	51	72	38
20	Exeter City	46	11	16	19	45	65	38
21	York City	46	11	14	21	65	68	36
22	Chester	46	9	14	23	57	78	32
23	Workington	46	10	11	25	54	87	31
24	Bradford Park Ave.	46	4	15	27	30	82	23

1968/69

19th in Division Four

#	Date		Opponent	Score	Scorers	Att	Ball GH	Barker RJ	Bates B	Bradd LJ	Butlin BD	Cartwright M	Elliott IW	Farmer RJ	Gibson APS	Masson DS	Murphy, F.John	Murphy, James B.	Needham DW	Oakes DR	Pring KD	Rose MJ	Smith GWC	Smith KW	Smith, Jack	Stubbs BH	Wilson A	Worthington PR
1	Aug	10	Lincoln City	0-5		8177	3		8	9		2	11		6					10	5	12	7	1		4			
2		17	SOUTHEND UNITED	2-2	Bradd 2	5227	2		8	9			11		6					10	5	12	7	1		3	4		
3		24	Bradford Park Ave.	1-1	JB Murphy	2395	2		8	9			11		6					10	5	12	7	1		3	4		
4		28	HALIFAX TOWN	1-2	Bradd	4980	2		8	9					6					10	5			1		3	4		7	
5		31	ALDERSHOT	0-2		5311	2		7	9					6		10		8	5	12	11		1	3	4			
6	Sep	7	NEWPORT COUNTY	3-1	KW Smith, Bradd, JB Murphy	3579	2		11	9				8					10	5	6	7		1	3	4			
7		14	Darlington	2-3	JB Murphy, Masson	6291	2		11	9				7		10			8	5	12			1	6	4			3
8		17	Grimsby Town	0-2		2361	2		8							10			9	5	7	11			6	4			3
9		21	SWANSEA TOWN	0-3		4167	2		11	9					4	5	10		7			12		1	6		8		3
10		28	Wrexham	2-3	Bradd, Masson	4522	2		11	9					6	5	10		8		4	7	1						3
11	Oct	5	Chesterfield	2-0	Bradd, JB Murphy	5611	2		11	9					4	6	10		8	5		7	1						3
12		8	Halifax Town	1-3	Bradd	3630	2		11	9					4	6	10		8	5	12	7	1						3
13		12	PORT VALE	0-0		4127	2		11	9					4	6	10		8	5		7	1						3
14		19	Exeter City	0-0		4123	2		11	9					4	6	10			5	7		1			8			3
15		26	BRENTFORD	0-2		4173	2		11	9					4	6	10			5	7		1			8			3
16	Nov	4	Peterborough Utd.	0-1		4552	2		8	9			11	4	6					5	10	7	1		3				
17		9	CHESTER	3-2	Bates, Bradd, Masson	3089	2		8	9			11	4	6	10				5		7	1		3				
18		23	YORK CITY	0-0		3295			7	9			11	4	6	10			8	5			1		3				2
19		30	Rochdale	0-0		2673			7	9			11	4	6	10			8	5			1		3	12			2
20	Dec	7	Bradford City	1-1	Needham	4280				7			11	4	6	10			8	5			1		3	9			2
21		14	Port Vale	2-0	J Smith, Elliott	4169				7			11	4	6	10			8	5			1		3	9			2
22		21	EXETER CITY	3-1	Bradd 2, Masson	4605		8	7	9			11	4	6	10				5			1	3					2
23		26	CHESTERFIELD	2-1	Masson(p), Barker	9801		8	7	9			11	4	6	10				5			1		3				2
24	Jan	4	Scunthorpe Utd.	1-2	Barker	3410	12	8	7	9			11	4	6	10				5			1		3				2
25		11	BRADFORD CITY	0-2		4776	2	8	7	9			11	4	6	10				5			1						3
26		18	Chester	1-3	Masson	5033	2	8	7	9			11	4	6	10				5			1		12				3
27		25	PETERBOROUGH UTD.	2-1	Masson, Butlin	5740		8	7		9			4	6	10				5		11	1		3				2
28	Feb	1	DONCASTER ROV.	1-1	Needham	6587		8	7		9		12	4	3	10				5	6	11	1						2
29		22	Colchester Utd.	1-1	Butlin	6612		8	7		9			4		10				5	3	11	1			6			2
30	Mar	1	LINCOLN CITY	0-0		5870		8	4	7	9			6		10				5	3	11	1						2
31		5	SCUNTHORPE UTD.	1-0	Butlin	3311		8	4	7	9			6		10				5	3	11	1						2
32		7	Southend United	0-4		11185		8	11	7	9			4	3	10				5	6	12	1						2
33		11	Doncaster Rov.	0-0		10255	2	8	7		9			4		10				5	6		1						3
34		15	BRADFORD PARK AVE.	5-0	Butlin 2, Barker 2, Brown(og)	3629	2	8	7		9			11	4	10				5	6		1						3
35		22	Aldershot	0-0		5352	2	8	7		9			11	4	10				5	6		1						3
36		26	Brentford	0-0		3361	2	8	7		9			11	4	10				5	6		1						3
37		29	Newport County	0-0		1769	2	8	7	12	9			11	4	10				5	6		1						3
38	Apr	5	WREXHAM	5-0	Masson 2, Butlin, Elliott, Barker	5325	2	8		7	9			11	4	10				5	6		1						3
39		7	GRIMSBY TOWN	2-1	Butlin, Masson	6307	2	8		7	9			11	4	10				5	6		1						3
40		8	Workington	1-1	Masson	1707	2	8	7		9					4	10			5	6	11	1						3
41		12	Swansea Town	0-3		1984	2	8			9			11	4	10				5	6	7	1						3
42		16	WORKINGTON	0-0		4305	2	8		7	9			12	4	10				5	6	11	1						3
43		19	DARLINGTON	0-0		4444	2	8	7	10	9			4						5	6	11	1						3
44		23	York City	0-2		3095	2	8	7		9			4		10				5	6	11	1						3
45		28	ROCHDALE	1-1	Butlin	3678	2	8	7		9			4		10				5	6	11	1						3
46	May	2	COLCHESTER UTD.	2-0	Masson 2	3576	2	8	7		9			4		10				5	6	11	1		12				3
			Apps				34	25	42	31	20	1	24	39	27	38	1	17	44	31	27	36	10	20	13	2	1	38
			Goals					5	1	10	8		2			13		4	2						1	1			

One own goal

F.A. Cup

| R1 | Nov | 16 | Doncaster Rov. | 0-1 | | 8318 | | | 8 | 9 | | | 11 | 4 | 6 | 10 | | | | 5 | | 7 | 1 | | 3 | | | | 2 |

F.L. Cup

| R1 | Aug | 14 | Grimsby Town | 0-0 | | 4627 | 2 | | 8 | 9 | | | 11 | | 6 | | | | | 10 | 5 | 12 | 7 | 1 | | 3 | 4 | | |
| rep | | 21 | GRIMSBY TOWN | 0-1 | | 6082 | 2 | | 8 | 9 | | | 11 | | 6 | | | | | 10 | 5 | | 7 | 1 | | 3 | 4 | | |

	p	w	d	l	f	a	pts
1 Doncaster Rovers	46	21	17	8	65	38	59
2 Halifax Town	46	20	17	9	53	37	57
3 Rochdale	46	18	20	8	68	35	56
4 Bradford City	46	18	20	8	65	46	56
5 Darlington	46	17	18	11	62	45	52
6 Colchester United	46	20	12	14	57	53	52
7 Southend United	46	19	13	14	78	61	51
8 Lincoln City	46	17	17	12	54	52	51
9 Wrexham	46	18	14	14	61	52	50
10 Swansea Town	46	19	11	16	58	54	49
11 Brentford	46	18	12	16	64	65	48
12 Workington	46	15	17	14	40	43	47
13 Port Vale	46	16	14	16	46	46	46
14 Chester	46	16	13	17	76	66	45
15 Aldershot	46	19	7	20	66	66	45
16 Scunthorpe United	46	18	8	20	61	60	44
17 Exeter City	46	16	11	19	66	65	43
18 Peterborough Utd.	46	13	16	17	60	57	42
19 NOTTS COUNTY	46	12	18	16	48	57	42
20 Chesterfield	46	13	15	18	43	50	41
21 York City	46	14	11	21	53	75	39
22 Newport County	46	11	14	21	49	74	36
23 Grimsby Town	46	9	15	22	47	69	33
24 Bradford Park Ave.	46	5	10	31	32	106	20

Back: Bradd, J Smith, Rose, Needham, Gadsby, Stubbs, D Smith. Standing: Wheeler (trainer), Imlach (coach), Ball, Farmer, Pring, Hallam, Cartwright, Jackson (assistant trainer), Gray (manager). Seated: Elliott, FJ Murphy, Saunders, JB Murphy, Gibson, Oakes, KW Smith, Bates. Front: Walsh, Rowe.

1969/70

7th in Division Four

#		Date	Opponent	Result	Scorers	Att	Ball GH	Barker RJ	Billington B	Bradd LJ	Butlin BD	Buxton IR	Crickmore C	Gould G	Hobson J	Holder S	Jones M	Masson DS	McDerment WS	McMorran J	Needham DW	Nixon JC	Oakes DR	Rose MJ	Ryan J	Smith KW	Stubbs BH	Watling BJ	Worthington PR
1	Aug	9	OLDHAM ATHLETIC	0-0		6584	8			9				11		4	10	3		5			1	7	6				2
2		16	Brentford	0-1		6364	2			9					11	4	10		8	5		6	1	7					3
3		23	COLCHESTER UTD.	1-1	Hobson	4901	2			9	12				11		4		8	5		6	1	7					3
4		27	Crewe Alexandra	1-1	Masson	2963	2	8		9					11			10	4	5		6	1	7					3
5		30	Peterborough Utd.	0-1		5986	2	8		9					11			10	4	5		6	1	7					3
6	Sep	6	GRIMSBY TOWN	2-1	Masson, Butlin	4991	2	8			9				11			10	4	5		6	1	7	3	12			
7		13	Chester	1-0	Barker	3645	2	8			9				11			10	7	5		6	1		3	4			
8		17	LINCOLN CITY	2-0	Butlin 2	6479	2	8			9				11			10		5		6	1	7	3	4			
9		20	EXETER CITY	4-0	Masson, Butlin, Barker, Hobson	6358	2	8			9	12			11			10		5		6	1	7	3	4			
10		27	Aldershot	0-2		5139	2	8			9				11			10	12	5		6	1	7	3	4			
11		30	Northampton T	1-3	Needham	6609	2	8			9				11			10		5		6	1	7	3	4			
12	Oct	4	YORK CITY	0-2		5883	2	8			9				11			10	4	5		6	1	7	3				
13		8	BRENTFORD	1-0	Hobson	4664	2	10		9		8			11			4		5		6	1	7	12				3
14		11	Chesterfield	0-5		10170		10		9		8			11			4		5		6	1	7	2				3
15		18	NEWPORT COUNTY	4-1	Buxton, Barker 2, Butlin	4394	2	10		7	9	8			11			4		5		12	1			6			3
16		25	Bradford Park Ave.	3-1	Smith, Bradd, Masson(p)	3219	2	10		9					11			4		5		6	1	7	8				3
17	Nov	1	SWANSEA TOWN	0-1		5604	2	10		9		8			11			4		5		6	1	7	12				3
18		8	Wrexham	0-2		8805	2	8	11	9					7			4				6	1		10	5			3
19		22	Workington	2-0	Barker, Masson	1916	2	8		9					11			10				4	1	7		6			3
20		29	SCUNTHORPE UTD.	3-1	Masson 2, Smith	3497	2	8		9					11			10		5		4	1	7	3	6			
21	Dec	13	CHESTER	3-0	Masson 2, Barker	4231	2	9	12	10					11			8		5		4	1	7	3	6			
22		26	Colchester Utd.	1-2	Ryan	4759	2	8		9					11			10		5		4	1	7	3	6			12
23		27	PETERBOROUGH UTD.	2-2	Barker, Masson(p)	6924	2	10	6	9					11			8		5			1	7	3	4			12
24	Jan	3	Grimsby Town	1-2	Barker	3791	2	8			9				11			10		5			1	7	3	6			
25		10	Exeter City	1-1	Barker	3872	2	9	10						11		4	8		5	7				3	6	1		
26		17	ALDERSHOT	3-0	Bradd, Masson 2	4854	2	9		8					11			10		5	7	4				6	1		3
27		24	Southend United	5-2	Needham, Stubbs, Barker 2, Bradd	5263	2	10		8					11			8		5	7	4				6	1		3
28		31	York City	2-1	Nixon 2	3897	2	10		9					11		12	8		5	7	4				6	1		3
29	Feb	7	CHESTERFIELD	1-1	Hobson	15346	2	9		8					11					5	7	4			10	6	1		3
30		14	Oldham Athletic	0-5		3943	2	9	10	8					11					5	7	4			12	6	1		3
31		21	WREXHAM	3-2	Barker, Masson, Nixon	6742	2	9							11			8		5	7	4	1		10	6			3
32		28	Newport County	0-1		1339	2	9							11			8		5	7	4	1		10	6	12		3
33	Mar	2	Hartlepool Utd.	0-4		1797	2	9	12	8					11					5	7	4	1		10	6			3
34		11	DARLINGTON	4-1	Masson 2, Hobson, Bradd	3742	2	9	12	8					11			10		5		4			7	6	1		3
35		14	Scunthorpe Utd.	3-2	Masson 2, Barker	3960	2	9		8		11			7			10		5		4				6	1		3
36		18	SOUTHEND UNITED	2-0	Masson, Barker	5828	2	9		8		11			7			10		5		4				6	1		3
37		21	HARTLEPOOL UTD.	1-0	Bradd	5313	2	10		9		11			7			8		5		4				6	1		3
38		28	Darlington	2-1	Hobson, Masson(p)	1768	2	9		8		11			7			10		5		4				6	1		3
39		30	BRADFORD PARK AVE.	5-2	Masson 2(1p), Crickmore, Bradd 2	8897	2	9		8		11			7			10		5		4				6	1		3
40		31	Swansea Town	1-1	Barker	13983	2	9		8		11			7			10		5		4				6	1		3
41	Apr	4	CREWE ALEXANDRA	0-1		7014	2	9		8		11			7			10		5		4			12	6	1		3
42		8	PORT VALE	1-2	Barker	5070	2	9		8		11			7			10		5		4				6	1		3
43		15	Lincoln City	4-2	Barker 2, Bradd, Masson	5518	2	9		8		11			7			10		5		4				6	1		3
44		18	Port Vale	1-1	Masson	8042	2	10		9		11			7			8		5		4				6	1		3
45		21	WORKINGTON	0-3		3155	2	9		8		11			7			10		5		4				6	1		3
46		24	NORTHAMPTON T	2-0	Barker, Stubbs	2456		9		8		11		7	12	4		10		5		2			3	6	1		

| | Apps | 43 | 44 | 7 | 35 | 10 | 5 | 12 | 1 | 45 | 1 | 6 | 43 | 3 | 6 | 45 | 9 | 43 | 27 | 24 | 24 | 36 | 20 | 34 |
| | Goals | | 19 | | 8 | 5 | 1 | 1 | | 6 | | | 23 | | | 2 | 3 | | | 1 | 2 | 2 | | | |

F.A. Cup

| R1 | Nov | 15 | ROTHERHAM UTD. | 0-3 | | 8769 | 2 | 8 | | 9 | | 12 | | | 11 | | | 10 | | | | 6 | 1 | 7 | 4 | 5 | | | 3 |

F.L. Cup

| R1 | Aug | 13 | Mansfield Town | 1-3 | Barker | 6727 | | 8 | | | 9 | | | | 11 | | 4 | 10 | 3 | | 5 | | | 1 | 7 | 6 | | | 2 |

		p	w	d	l	f	a	pts
1	Chesterfield	46	27	10	9	77	32	64
2	Wrexham	46	26	9	11	84	49	61
3	Swansea Town	46	21	18	7	66	45	60
4	Port Vale	46	20	19	7	61	33	59
5	Brentford	46	20	16	10	58	39	56
6	Aldershot	46	20	13	13	78	65	53
7	NOTTS COUNTY	46	22	8	16	73	62	52
8	Lincoln City	46	17	16	13	66	52	50
9	Peterborough Utd.	46	17	14	15	77	69	48
10	Colchester United	46	17	14	15	64	63	48
11	Chester	46	21	6	19	58	66	48
12	Scunthorpe United	46	18	10	18	67	65	46
13	York City	46	16	14	16	55	62	46
14	Northampton Town	46	16	12	18	64	55	44
15	Crewe Alexandra	46	16	12	18	51	51	44
16	Grimsby Town	46	14	15	17	54	58	43
17	Southend United	46	15	10	21	59	85	40
18	Exeter City	46	14	11	21	57	59	39
19	Oldham Athletic	46	13	13	20	60	65	39
20	Workington	46	12	14	20	46	64	38
21	Newport County	46	13	11	22	53	74	37
22	Darlington	46	13	10	23	53	73	36
23	Hartlepool	46	10	10	26	42	82	30
24	Bradford Park Ave.	46	6	11	29	41	96	23

Back: Redmile, K Smith, Worthington, Bradd, Ryan, Gould. Standing: Butlin, Needham, Stubbs, Rose, Watling, Jones, McMorran, Oakes. Seated: Wheeler (trainer), Terry, Hobson, Barker, Masson, Ball, McDerment, Jackson (assistant trainer). Front: McGlinchey, Holder, Lamb

1970/71

Champions of Division Four - Promoted

#	Date		Opponent	Score	Scorers	Att	Ball GH	Barker RJ	Bradd LJ	Brindley JC	Brown RE	Cozens JW	Crickmore C	Hateley A	Hobson J	Jones M	Masson DS	Needham DW	Nixon JC	Oakes DR	Stubbs BH	Watling BJ	Worthington PR
1	Aug	15	York City	0-0		4476		8	9	2			11		7		10	5		4	6	1	3
2		22	BARROW	3-1	Crickmore, Barker 2	5826		9	8	2			11			6	10	5	7	4		1	3
3		29	Aldershot	1-0	Nixon	8689		9	8	2			11		12		10	5	7	4	6	1	3
4	Sep	2	CREWE ALEXANDRA	5-1	Barker 2, Crickmore, Needham, Nixon	6463		9	8	2			11		12	6	10	5	7	4		1	3
5		5	SOUTHEND UNITED	2-1	Bradd, Masson	9025			8	2		9	11		12	6	10	5	7	4		1	3
6		12	Colchester Utd.	3-2	Stubbs, Barker, Bradd	4285		9	8	2			11				10	5	7	4	6	1	3
7		19	BRENTFORD	0-0		10281		9	8	2			11				10	5	7	4	6	1	3
8		23	NEWPORT COUNTY	2-0	Barker, Nixon	8445		9	8	2			11				10	5	7	4	6	1	3
9		26	Exeter City	1-0	Barker	6093		9	8	2			11				10	5	7	4	6	1	3
10		30	Hartlepool Utd.	1-2	Bradd	2772		9	8	2			11			12	10	5	7	4	6	1	3
11	Oct	3	WORKINGTON	2-2	Bradd, Masson	7474		9	8	2			11			12	10	5	7	4	6	1	3
12		10	Grimsby Town	1-2	Nixon	5482		9	8	2			11				10	5	7	4	6	1	3
13		17	YORK CITY	2-1	Barker 2	7690		9	8	2	1		11				10	5	7	4	6		3
14		21	DARLINGTON	3-0	Crickmore(p), Nixon, Masson	6285		9	8	2	1		11			4		10	5	7		6		3
15		24	OLDHAM ATHLETIC	2-0	Needham, Crickmore	10028		9	8	2	1		11			4	10	5	7		6		3
16		31	Scunthorpe Utd.	1-0	Masson	5801		9	8	2			11			4	10	5	7	12	6	1	3
17	Nov	7	NORTHAMPTON T	1-0	Nixon	21012		9		2			11	8		4	10	5	7		6	1	3
18		11	LINCOLN CITY	0-0		10276		9	12	2			11	8		4	10	5	7		6	1	3
19		14	Southport	1-2	Hateley 2	3392		8		2			11	9		4	10	5	7		6	1	3
20		28	Peterborough Utd.	1-1	Hateley	7116		8	10	2			11	9		4		5	7	12	6	1	3
21	Dec	5	BOURNEMOUTH	2-1	Crickmore(p), Hateley	11711	2	8	10				11	9		4		5	7		6	1	3
22		19	Barrow	2-1	Hateley, Bradd	2672	2	8	10				11	9		4		5	7		6	1	3
23		26	CAMBRIDGE UNITED	4-1	Jones, Needham 2, Bradd	15722	2	9	8			10	11			4		5	7	12	6	1	3
24	Jan	9	HARTLEPOOL UTD.	3-0	Barker 2, Hateley	11540	2	8					11	9		4	10	5	7		6	1	3
25		16	Darlington	3-2	Hateley, Albeson (2 og)	5096	2	8					11	9		4	10	5	7	12	6	1	3
26		23	Chester	1-2	Edwards (og)	5835		8		2			11	9		4	10	5	7	12	6	1	3
27		30	PETERBOROUGH UTD.	6-0	Masson, Bradd, Hateley 3, Needham	9440		12	8	2			11	9		4	10	5	7		6	1	3
28	Feb	6	Bournemouth	1-1	Hateley	15431			8	2			11	9		4	10	5	7		6	1	3
29		13	CHESTER	2-1	Bradd, Nixon	10545			8	2			11	9		4	10	5	7		6	1	3
30		20	Lincoln City	1-0	Masson	10849		12	8	2			11	9		4	10	5	7		6	1	3
31		22	Stockport County	0-1		2926			8	2			11	9		4	10	5	7		6	1	3
32		27	SCUNTHORPE UTD.	3-0	Masson, Bradd, Crickmore	10750		12	8	2			11	9		4	10	5	7		6	1	3
33	Mar	6	Oldham Athletic	3-1	Bradd, Hateley 2	17953		12	8	2			11	9		4	10	5	7		6	1	3
34		9	Newport County	1-2	Masson	2129			8	2			11	9		4	10	5	7		6	1	3
35		13	SOUTHPORT	3-1	Masson, Barker, Hateley	11182		12	8	2			11	9		4	10	5	7		6	1	3
36		17	STOCKPORT COUNTY	5-1	Masson, Nixon, Crickmore 2, Stubbs	10704			8	2			11	9		4	10	5	7		6	1	3
37		20	Northampton T	1-1	Hateley	11923			8	2			11	9		4	10		7	6	5	1	3
38		26	Southend United	0-1		7010			8	2			11	9		4	10	5	7		6	1	3
39	Apr	3	ALDERSHOT	3-0	Crickmore, Masson, Hateley	8747		12	8	2			11	9		4	10	5	7		6	1	3
40		8	Workington	1-0	Barker	2986		8		2			11	9		4	10	5	7		6	1	3
41		10	Cambridge United	1-2	Hateley	6935		8		2			11	9		4	10	5	7		6	1	3
42		12	COLCHESTER UTD.	4-0	Hateley 3, Masson	14084		8		2			11	9		4	10	5	7	6		1	3
43		17	GRIMSBY TOWN	1-0	Masson	12182		8		2			11	9		4	10	5	7		6	1	3
44		24	Brentford	2-2	Crickmore, Hateley	9299		8	12	2			11	9		4	10	5	7		6	1	3
45		28	Crewe Alexandra	2-1	Bradd, Masson	4222			8	2			11	9		4	10	5	7		6	1	3
46	May	1	EXETER CITY	1-1	Hateley	18002		12	8	2			11	9			10	5	7	4	6	1	3
					Apps		5	37	37	41	3	2	46	29	4	37	42	45	45	21	42	43	46
					Goals			13	11				10	22		1	14	5	8		2		

Three own goals

F.A. Cup

R1	Nov	21	PORT VALE	1-0	Crickmore(p)	15965		8	10	2			11	9		4		5	7		6	1	3
R2	Dec	12	Bury	1-1	Nixon	6968	2	8	10				11	9		4		5	7	12	6	1	3
rep		21	BURY	3-0	Hateley, Crickmore, Needham	15508	2	8	10				11	9		4		5	7	12	6	1	3
R3	Jan	2	Leicester City	0-2		33770	2	8	10				11	9		4		5	7		6	1	3

F.L. Cup

R1	Aug	19	Aston Villa	0-4		17843	12	9	8	2			11		7		10	5		4	6	1	3

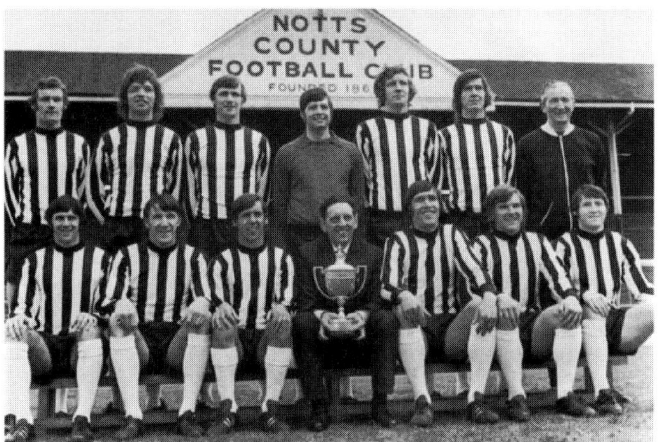

		p	w	d	l	f	a	pts
1	NOTTS COUNTY	46	30	9	7	89	36	69
2	Bournemouth	46	24	12	10	81	46	60
3	Oldham Athletic	46	24	11	11	88	63	59
4	York City	46	23	10	13	78	54	56
5	Chester	46	24	7	15	69	55	55
6	Colchester United	46	21	12	13	70	54	54
7	Northampton Town	46	19	13	14	63	59	51
8	Southport	46	21	6	19	63	57	48
9	Exeter City	46	17	14	15	67	68	48
10	Workington	46	18	12	16	48	49	48
11	Stockport County	46	16	14	16	49	65	46
12	Darlington	46	17	11	18	58	57	45
13	Aldershot	46	14	17	15	66	71	45
14	Brentford	46	18	8	20	66	62	44
15	Crewe Alexandra	46	18	8	20	75	76	44
16	Peterborough Utd.	46	18	7	21	70	71	43
17	Scunthorpe United	46	15	13	18	56	61	43
18	Southend United	46	14	15	17	53	66	43
19	Grimsby Town	46	18	7	21	57	71	43
20	Cambridge United	46	15	13	18	51	66	43
21	Lincoln City	46	13	13	20	70	71	39
22	Newport County	46	10	8	28	55	85	28
23	Hartlepool	46	8	12	26	34	74	28
24	Barrow	46	7	8	31	51	90	22

Back: Jones, Needham, Bradd, Watling, Stubbs, Worthington, Wheeler (physio). Front: Nixon, Barker, Masson, Sirrel (manager), Hateley, Brindley, Crickmore

1971/72

4th in Division Three

#	Date		Opponent	Score	Scorers	Att	Ball GH	Barker RJ	Bolton IR	Bradd LJ	Brindley JC	Brown RE	Carlin W	Carter SC	Cooper T	Cozens JW	Crickmore C	Hateley A	Hulme J	Jones M	Mansley A	Masson DS	Needham DW	Nixon JC	Richardson J	Stubbs BH	Watling BJ	Worthington PR
1	Aug	14	ROCHDALE	4-0	Mansley, Masson, Stubbs, Hateley	10879		12		8	2	1						9		4	11	10	5	7		6		3
2		21	Chesterfield	2-1	Bradd, Hateley	12276		12		8	2	1		5				9		4	11	10		7		6		3
3		28	BOLTON WANDERERS	1-2	Hateley	15658	2	12		8		1						9		4	11	10	5	7		6		3
4		30	Port Vale	3-0	Masson, Bradd, Hateley	5298				8	2	1						9		4	11	10	5	7		6		3
5	Sep	4	Walsall	2-1	Hateley 2	6780		12		8	2	1						9		4	11	10	5	7		6		3
6		11	SHREWSBURY TOWN	1-0	Mansley	13328		12		8	2	1	4					9		6	11	10	5	7				3
7		18	Brighton & Hove Alb.	1-1	Needham	13443		12		8	2	1	4					9		6	11	10	5	7				3
8		25	BRISTOL ROVERS	2-3	Masson(p), Roberts(og)	13101				8	2	1	4					9		12	11	10	5	7		6		3
9		29	BOURNEMOUTH	1-1	Masson(p)	13342				8	2	1	4					9		12	11	10	5	7		6		3
10	Oct	2	Swansea City	1-1	Masson	9703				8	2	1	11		12			9		4		10	5	7		6		3
11		9	PLYMOUTH ARGYLE	1-0	Bradd	11828				8	2	1	4			9					12	11	10	5	7		6		3
12		16	Rochdale	1-1	Bradd	4848				8	2	1	4			9					12	11	10	5	7		6		3
13		20	Blackburn Rovers	2-0	Bradd 2	6935				8	2	1	4			11		9				10	5	7		6		3
14		23	OLDHAM ATHLETIC	2-0	Needham 2	14419				8	2	1	4			11		9		12		10	5	7		6		3
15		30	York City	2-0	Nixon, Hateley	8302				8	2	1	4			11		9		12		10	5	7		6		3
16	Nov	6	MANSFIELD TOWN	2-0	Bradd, Needham	16905				8	2	1	4			11		9				10	5	7		6		3
17		13	Aston Villa	0-1		37462				8	2	1	4			11		9		12		10	5	7		6		3
18		27	Bradford City	3-2	Bradd, Cooper(og), Cozens	6826				8	2	1	4			11		9		12		10	5	7		6		3
19	Dec	4	BARNSLEY	3-0	Cozens 2, Bradd	12639				8	2	1	4			11		9		12		10	5	7		6		3
20		18	WALSALL	3-0	Bradd 2, Hateley	11775				8	2	1	4			11		9				10	5	7		6		3
21		27	Wrexham	1-1	Cozens	12680				8	2	1	4			11		9		12		10	5	7		6		3
22	Jan	1	BRIGHTON & HOVE ALB.	1-0	Bradd	16401				8	2	1	4			11		9		12		10	5	7		6		3
23		8	Bolton Wanderers	2-1	Cozens, Carlin	8380				8	2	1	4			11		9		5		10		7		6		3
24		22	Bournemouth	0-2		21154				8	2	1	4		12	11		9		5		10		7		6		3
25		29	BLACKBURN ROVERS	1-0	Bradd	12375				8	2	1	4			11		9		6		10		7		5		3
26	Feb	12	Oldham Athletic	1-0	Hateley	8621				8	2	1	4	7		11		9		6		10		12		5		3
27		19	YORK CITY	2-2	Hateley, Bradd	12351				8	2	1	4	7		11		9		6		10		12		5		3
28		26	Mansfield Town	1-1	Bradd	16784				8	2	1	4	7		11		9		5		10		7		6		3
29	Mar	4	ASTON VILLA	0-3		34208				8	2	1	4						11	9		5	10		7		6		3
30		11	Plymouth Argyle	1-1	Bradd	12157				9	2		8	11					5	4		10		7		6	1	3
31		14	Rotherham Utd.	2-2	Masson, Cozens	10359				9	2		8			11			6	4		10		7		5	1	3
32		18	CHESTERFIELD	1-4	Stubbs	14701			12	10	2		8			11		9	6	4				7		5	1	3
33		22	ROTHERHAM UTD.	1-1	Worthington	11522				9	2	1	8	11		12			6	4		10		7		5		3
34		25	Shrewsbury Town	1-1	Bradd	5211				9	2	1	8	11					6	4		10		7		5		3
35	Apr	1	WREXHAM	1-0	May(og)	12060	2			9		1	10	11		12			6	4		10		7		5		3
36		3	SWANSEA CITY	5-0	Bradd, Masson, Cozens 2, Nixon	14019				9		1		11		8			6	4		10	5	7		2		3
37		4	Bristol Rovers	2-0	Carter, Cozens	11998				9		1		11		8			6	4		10	5	7	12	2		3
38		8	Torquay United	1-1	Masson(p)	6478				9		1		11	6	8				4		10	5	7	12	2		3
39		12	HALIFAX TOWN	3-1	Cozens 2, Carter	14979				9	2	1		11		8				4		10	5	7		6		3
40		15	BRADFORD CITY	2-0	Bradd, Cozens	16315				9	2	1		11		8				4		10	5	7		6		3
41		18	Halifax Town	1-3	Bradd	3943				9	2	1		11	12	8				4		10	5	7		6		3
42		22	Barnsley	1-2	Masson	6264				9	2	1		11		8				4		10	5	7		6		3
43		26	PORT VALE	2-1	Masson(p), Carter	9033				9	2	1		11	12	8				4		10	5	7		6		3
44		29	TRANMERE ROVERS	1-0	Cozens	9885				9	2	1		11	12	8				4		10	5	7		6		3
45	May	3	TORQUAY UNITED	2-1	Bradd, Masson	8921				9	2	1		11		8				4		10	5	7		6		3
46		8	Tranmere Rovers	1-2	Needham	4212				9	2	1	4	11	12	8				6		10	5	7				3
			Apps				2	6	1	46	41	43	31	18	8	33	1	28	8	44	11	45	32	46	2	43	3	46
			Goals							21			1	3		13		10			2	11	5	2		2		1

Three own goals

F.A. Cup

	Date		Opponent	Score	Scorers	Att	Bradd LJ	Brindley JC	Brown RE	Carlin W	Cozens JW	Hateley A	Hulme J	Masson DS	Needham DW	Nixon JC	Stubbs BH	Worthington PR
R1	Nov	20	NEWPORT COUNTY	6-0	Hateley, Cozens, Bradd, Nixon, Stubbs, Carlin	11976	8	2	1	4	11	9		10	5	7	6	3
R2	Dec	11	South Shields	3-1	Masson, Cozens, Bradd	8144	8	2	1	4	11	9		10	5	7	6	3
R3	Jan	15	Watford	4-1	Cozens 2, Nixon, Masson	13488	8	2	1	4	11	9	5	10		7	6	3
R4	Feb	5	Derby County	0-6		39450	8	2	1	4	11	9	6	10		7	5	3

F.L. Cup

	Date		Opponent	Score	Scorers	Att	Barker RJ	Bradd LJ	Brindley JC	Brown RE	Carlin W	Hateley A	Jones M	Mansley A	Masson DS	Needham DW	Nixon JC	Richardson J	Stubbs BH	Worthington PR
R1	Aug	17	Leyton Orient	1-1	Nixon	8263		8	2	1	5	9	6	11	10		7		4	3
rep		25	LEYTON ORIENT	3-1	Hateley, Nixon, Bradd	3607	12	8		1		9	4	11	10	5	7	2	6	3
R2	Sep	8	GILLINGHAM	1-2	Bradd	12650	12	8	2	1		9	4	11	10	5	7		6	3

		p	w	d	l	f	a	pts
1	Aston Villa	46	32	6	8	85	32	70
2	Brighton & Hove A.	46	27	11	8	82	47	65
3	Bournemouth	46	23	16	7	73	37	62
4	NOTTS COUNTY	46	25	12	9	74	44	62
5	Rotherham United	46	20	15	11	69	52	55
6	Bristol Rovers	46	21	12	13	75	56	54
7	Bolton Wanderers	46	17	16	13	51	41	50
8	Plymouth Argyle	46	20	10	16	74	64	50
9	Walsall	46	15	18	13	62	57	48
10	Blackburn Rovers	46	19	9	18	54	57	47
11	Oldham Athletic	46	17	11	18	59	63	45
12	Shrewsbury Town	46	17	10	19	73	65	44
13	Chesterfield	46	18	8	20	57	57	44
14	Swansea City	46	17	10	19	46	59	44
15	Port Vale	46	13	15	18	43	59	41
16	Wrexham	46	16	8	22	59	63	40
17	Halifax Town	46	13	12	21	48	61	38
18	Rochdale	46	12	13	21	57	83	37
19	York City	46	12	12	22	57	66	36
20	Tranmere Rovers	46	10	16	20	50	71	36
21	Mansfield Town	46	8	20	18	41	63	36
22	Barnsley	46	9	18	19	32	64	36
23	Torquay United	46	10	12	24	41	69	32
24	Bradford City	46	11	10	25	45	77	32

1972/73

2nd in Division Three - Promoted

#		Date	Opponent	Score	Scorers	Att	Bradd LJ	Brindley JC	Brown RE	Carlin W	Carter SC	Cooper T	Cozens JW	Dyer P	Jones M	Mann AF	Masson DS	McManus CE	Needham DW	Nixon JC	Randall K	Scanlon I	Stubbs BH	Vinter M	Worthington PR
1	Aug	12	Shrewsbury Town	0-0		3775		2	1			8	9		4	10			5	7		11	6	12	3
2		19	BOLTON WANDERERS	1-0	Masson	11129	10	2	1						4	11	8		5	7	9		6		3
3		26	York City	1-1	Masson(p)	4318	8	2	1						4	11	10		5	7	9		6		3
4		28	Tranmere Rovers	2-0	Randall 2	3651	10	2	1				12		4	11	8		5	7	9		6		3
5	Sep	2	WALSALL	1-1	Nixon	9554	8	2	1						4	11	10		5	7	9	12	6		3
6		9	Southend United	1-2	Bradd	6035	10	2	1			12			4	3	8		5	7	9		6		
7		16	ROCHDALE	2-2	Needham, Nixon	7991	10	2	1				11		4	3	8		5	7	9		6		
8		19	Charlton Athletic	1-6	Bradd	6156	9	2	1				11	4		6	3	10	5	7	8				
9		23	Watford	0-1		8363	9		1				11	4		6	12	10	5	7	8		2		3
10		27	SWANSEA CITY	2-0	Nixon, Masson	6118	9	2	1				11				10	4	5	7	8		6		3
11		30	BRENTFORD	1-0	Randall	8152	9	2	1				11			12	10	4	5	7	8		6		3
12	Oct	7	Halifax Town	1-0	Masson(p)	3233	10	2	1				11	7		8	4		5		9		6		3
13		14	BOURNEMOUTH	0-2		11914	9	2	1				11	7		10	4		5	12	8		6		3
14		21	Wrexham			5404	9	2	1	4	11		8			10			5		7		6		3
15		25	ROTHERHAM UTD.	2-0	Needham, Bradd	6199	9	2	1	4						11	10		5	7	8		6		3
16		28	PORT VALE	1-1	Randall	8544	8	2	1	4	12					11	10		5	7	9		6		3
17	Nov	4	Swansea City	0-3		3508	9	2	1	4						11	10		5	7	8		6		3
18		7	Bristol Rovers			6695	9	2	1		8			11		4		10	1	5	12	7		6		3
19		11	CHARLTON ATHLETIC	3-1	Randall 2 (1p), Needham	7069	9	2	1	4						11	10		5	7	8		6		3
20		25	OLDHAM ATHLETIC	2-4	Randall(p), Bradd	7329	9	2	1	4	11						10		5	7	8	12	6		3
21	Dec	2	Grimsby Town	1-3	Randall(p)	9149	8	2	1	4	11				12		10		5	7	9		6		3
22		16	CHESTERFIELD	2-0	Nixon, Randall(p)	6891	9	2	1	4	11						12	10	5	7	8		6		3
23		23	Scunthorpe Utd.	0-1		3983	9	2	1		11					12	10	4	5	7	8		6		3
24		26	WATFORD	1-0	Franks(og)	9282	9	2	1		11						10	4	5	7	8		6		3
25		30	Bolton Wanderers	2-2	Stubbs, Bradd	17800	8	2	1		11						10	4	5	7	9		6		3
26	Jan	6	YORK CITY	1-0	Masson	6202	9	2	1		11						10	4	5	7	8		6		3
27		23	Walsall	3-1	Randall, Stubbs, Carlin	4395	9	2	1	6	11						10	4		7	8		5		3
28		27	SOUTHEND UNITED	2-0	Bradd, Nixon	7903	9	2	1	12	11						10	4	5	7	8		6		3
29		30	Rotherham Utd.	4-1	Nixon 2, Randall, Masson	6572	9	2	1	12	11						10	4	5	7	8		6		3
30	Feb	3	BRISTOL ROVERS	2-0	Randall, Nixon	11938	9	2	1		11						10	4	5	7	8		6		3
31		10	Rochdale	1-4	Nixon	3092	9	2	1	12	11						10	4	5	7	8		6		3
32		17	SHREWSBURY TOWN	1-0	Nixon	8903	9	2	1	10					12		11	4	5	7	8		6		3
33		24	Chesterfield	2-0	Masson 2	8755	9	2	1	10	11							4	5	7	8		6		3
34	Mar	3	HALIFAX TOWN	3-0	Stubbs, Nixon, Bradd	9820	9		1	10	11				12		6	4	5	7	8		2		3
35		7	Blackburn Rovers	0-2		13626	9		1	10					12		6	4	5	7	8	11	2		3
36		10	Bournemouth	1-1	Nixon	14830	9	2	1	10							11	4	5	7	8		6		3
37		17	WREXHAM	1-0	Bradd	10068	9	2	1	11					12		6	4	5	7	10			8	3
38		21	PLYMOUTH ARGYLE	2-0	Vinter, Randall	12889	9	2	1	10					12		6	4	5	7	11			8	3
39		24	Port Vale	1-1	Randall(p)	8920	8	2	1	11					12		6	4	5	7	9			10	3
40		31	Oldham Athletic	1-1	Needham	12570	9	2	1	10							11	4	5	7	8		6		3
41	Apr	7	GRIMSBY TOWN	4-0	Randall 2, Nixon, Mann	16208	9	2	1	11	12						10	4	5	7	8		6		3
42		14	Plymouth Argyle	4-1	Nixon 2, Carter, Randall	11997		2	1	11	8						10	4	5	7	9		6		3
43		20	Brentford	1-1	Needham	11658		2	1	10	7						11	4	5	9	8		6		3
44		21	BLACKBURN ROVERS	0-0		22712	9	2		10							11	4	1	5	7	8		6		3
45		23	SCUNTHORPE UTD.	2-0	Bradd, Nixon	15697	9	2		10							11	4	1	5	7	8		6		3
46		28	TRANMERE ROVERS	4-1	Nixon, Randall(2p), Needham	23613	8	2		10							11	4	1	5	7	9		6		3
			Apps				43	43	42	28	27	1	9	6	13	42	44	4	45	44	45	4	42	4	43
			Goals				9			1	1					1	8		6	17	19		3	1	

One own goal

F.A. Cup

		Date	Opponent	Score	Scorers	Att	Bradd	Brindley	Brown	Carlin	Carter	Cooper	Cozens	Dyer	Jones	Mann	Masson	McManus	Needham	Nixon	Randall	Scanlon	Stubbs	Vinter	Worthington
R1	Nov	18	Altrincham	1-0	Randall(p)	4211	9	2	1	4							11	10	5	7	8		6		3
R2	Dec	9	LANCASTER CITY	2-1	Randall(p), Bradd	6613	9	2	1	4					6		11	10	5	7	8				3
R3	Jan	13	SUNDERLAND	1-1	Bradd	15142	8	2	1		11						10	4	5	7	9		6		3
rep		15	Sunderland	0-2		30033	9	2	1		11						10	4	5	7	8		6		3

F.L. Cup

		Date	Opponent	Score	Scorers	Att																			
R1	Aug	16	YORK CITY	3-1	Randall, Nixon, Mann	8078	10	2	1			8			4	11			5	7	9		6		3
R2	Sep	6	SOUTHPORT	3-2	Needham, Mann, Cozens	7004	10	2	1				11		4	3	8		5	7	9		6		
R3	Oct	3	Southampton	3-1	Cozens 2, Bradd	11095	9	2	1	12	11		7				10	4	5		8		6		3
R4		31	STOKE CITY	3-1	Randall(p), Bradd, Stubbs	20297	9	2	1	4							11	10	5	7	8		6		3
R5	Nov	22	Chelsea	1-3	Osgood(og)	22580	9	2	1	4							11	10	5	7	8		6		3

Watney Cup

		Date	Opponent	Score		Att																			
R1	Jul	29	SHEFFIELD UNITED	0-3		14405	9	2	1			8			4	3	10		5	7		11	6		

		p	w	d	l	f	a	pts
1	Bolton Wanderers	46	25	11	10	73	39	61
2	NOTTS COUNTY	46	23	11	12	67	47	57
3	Blackburn Rovers	46	20	15	11	57	47	55
4	Oldham Athletic	46	19	16	11	72	54	54
5	Bristol Rovers	46	20	13	13	77	56	53
6	Port Vale	46	21	11	14	56	69	53
7	Bournemouth	46	17	16	13	66	44	50
8	Plymouth Argyle	46	20	10	16	74	66	50
9	Grimsby Town	46	20	8	18	67	61	48
10	Tranmere Rovers	46	15	16	15	56	52	46
11	Charlton Athletic	46	17	11	18	69	67	45
12	Wrexham	46	14	17	15	55	54	45
13	Rochdale	46	14	17	15	48	54	45
14	Southend United	46	17	10	19	61	54	44
15	Shrewsbury Town	46	15	14	17	46	54	44
16	Chesterfield	46	17	9	20	57	61	43
17	Walsall	46	18	7	21	56	66	43
18	York City	46	13	15	18	42	46	41
19	Watford	46	12	17	17	43	48	41
20	Halifax Town	46	13	15	18	43	53	41
21	Rotherham United	46	17	7	22	51	65	41
22	Brentford	46	15	7	24	51	69	37
23	Swansea City	46	14	9	23	51	73	37
24	Scunthorpe United	46	10	10	26	33	72	30

Back: Stubbs, Brown, Bradd, Vinter, McManus, Dyer. Standing: Fenton (youth coach), Scanlon, Jones, Bolton, Cozens, Worthington, Needham, Cooper, Potrac, unknown, Wheeler (trainer). Seated: Nixon, Brindley, Masson, Sirrel (manager), Hopcroft (director), Dunnett (chairman), Levin (director), Carlin, Mann, Carter. Front: Newell, Richards

1973/74

10th in Division Two

	Date	Opponent	Score	Scorers	Att	Bolton IR	Bradd LJ	Brindley JC	Brown RE	Carlin W	Carter SC	Cliff E	Collier G	Dyer P	Mann AF	Masson DS	McManus CE	McVay DR	Needham DW	Nixon JC	O'Brien R	Probert EW	Randall K	Scanlon I	Stubbs BH	Vinter M	Worthington PR
1	Aug 25	Crystal Palace	4-1	Stubbs, Vinter, Randall 2	20841		2	1		7					11	4		6				10	9		5	12	3
2	Sep 1	SUNDERLAND	1-4	Carter	15322		9	2	1	8	11				12	4			5	7			10		6		3
3	8	Carlisle Utd.	0-3		6109		8	2			11					4	1		5	7		10	9		6		3
4	11	LUTON TOWN	1-1	Bradd	8509		9	2							11	4	1		5	7		10	8		6		3
5	15	SWINDON TOWN	2-0	Randall, Bradd	9264		9	2							11	4	1		5	7		10	8		6		3
6	19	Oxford United	1-2	Bradd	6995		9	2							11	4	1		5	7		10	8		6		3
7	22	Portsmouth	2-1	Mann, Bradd	14443		9	2							11	4	1		5	7		10	8		6	12	3
8	29	ASTON VILLA	2-0	Probert, Bradd	15872		9	2							11	4	1		5	7		10	8		6	12	3
9	Oct 2	OXFORD UNITED	0-0		9927		9	2							11	4	1		5	7		10	8		6		3
10	6	Blackpool	1-0	Mann	11072		9	2							11	4	1		5	7		10	8		6	12	3
11	13	FULHAM	2-1	Masson(2p)	11981		9	2					12		11	4	1		5	7		10	8		6		3
12	20	PRESTON NORTH END	2-1	Stubbs, Mann	12479		9	2							11	4	1		5	7		10	8		6		3
13	27	Sheffield Wednesday	0-0		14252		9	2							11	4	1		5	7		10	8		6		3
14	Nov 3	MILLWALL	3-3	Nixon, Dorney(og), Needham	12243		8	2							11	4	1		5	7		10	9		6		3
15	10	West Bromwich Alb.	1-2	Randall	15564		9	2							11	4	1		5	7		10	8		6		3
16	17	Bolton Wanderers	3-1	Stubbs, Randall 2	12139		9	2							11	4	1		5	7		10	8		6		3
17	24	MIDDLESBROUGH	2-2	Bradd, Masson	16314		9	2							11	4	1		5	7		10	8		6	12	3
18	Dec 1	Bristol City	2-2	Masson(p), Mann	10436		8	2							11	4	1	6	5	7		10	9			12	3
19	8	ORIENT	2-4	Bradd, Masson(p)	11264		9	2							11	4	1	6	5	7		10	8				3
20	15	HULL CITY	3-2	Stubbs, Nixon, Masson(p)	8574		9	2	1						11	4		12	5	7		10	8		6		3
21	22	Aston Villa	1-1	Randall(p)	20825		9	2	1						11	4		6	5	7		10	8				3
22	26	NOTTM. FOREST	0-1		32310		9	2	1				12		11	4		6	5	7		10	8				3
23	29	CARLISLE UTD.	0-3		10209		9	2	1				12		11	4		6	5	7		10	8				3
24	Jan 1	Sunderland	2-1	Masson 2	22581			2	1		7	3			11	4		6	5	9		10	8				
25	20	CRYSTAL PALACE	1-3	Randall	14748		9	2	1		11				10			6	5	7		4	8				3
26	26	Cardiff City	0-1		8432	4	9	2			11			7	10		1	6	5				8				3
27	Feb 2	Hull City	0-1		6384	12	9	2			7	3			11	4	1	6	5			10	8				
28	5	Luton Town	1-1	Probert	4908	5	9	2			11	3			6	8	1	4		12		10	7				
29	9	PORTSMOUTH	4-0	Randall 2, Masson(p), Roberts(og)	8665		9	2			11				6	8	1	4	5			10	7	3			
30	16	Fulham	0-2		7515	12	8	2			7				3	10	1	4	5			11	9	6			
31	19	Swindon Town	4-1	Masson, Randall 2, Bradd	3482		9	2			11				3	8	1	4	5			10	7	6			
32	23	BLACKPOOL	0-3		11092		9	2			11				3	8	1	4	5	12		10	7	6			
33	Mar 3	Nottm. Forest	0-0		29962		9	2				3			11	8	1	4	5			10	7	6			
34	9	SHEFFIELD WEDNESDAY	1-5	Mann	9378		9	2				3			11	8	1	4	5			10	7	6			
35	16	Preston North End	2-0	Stubbs, Bradd	8907	4	9	2			12				11	8	1	5			3	10	7	6			
36	23	WEST BROMWICH ALB.	1-0	Stubbs	9672	4	9	2							11	10	1	8	5	12	3		7	6			
37	30	Millwall	0-0		5906	4	9	2							11	10	1	8	5	12	3		7	6			
38	Apr 6	Middlesbrough	0-4		27823	3	7	2							10	8	1	4	5	12	11		9	6			
39	13	BOLTON WANDERERS	0-0		8349	6	9	2							11	8	1	10	5	12	3		7	4			
40	15	CARDIFF CITY	1-1	Randall	6975	4		2					12		10	8	1		5		3	7	9	11	6		
41	20	Orient	1-1	Masson	11711	6	10	2							11	4	1	8	9		3		7	12	5		
42	27	BRISTOL CITY	2-1	Rodgers(og), Bradd	6991	6	11	2							4	1	8	9		3	10	7			5		

	Apps	12	39	42	8	1	14	5	3	1	40	40	34	25	39	31	8	35	42	2	32	6	25
	Goals		10				1				5	11			1	2		2	13		6	1	

Three own goals

F.A. Cup

| R3 | Jan 5 | West Bromwich Albion | 0-4 | | 13022 | | 2 | 1 | | | 7 | | | | 11 | 4 | | 6 | 5 | 9 | | 10 | 8 | | | 12 | 3 |

F.L. Cup

| R1 | Aug 28 | DONCASTER ROV. | 3-4 | Randall 2, Stubbs | 7735 | | 2 | 1 | | | 7 | | | | 11 | 4 | | 6 | | 8 | | 10 | 9 | | 5 | 12 | 3 |

		p	w	d	l	f	a	pts
1	Middlesbrough	42	27	11	4	77	30	65
2	Luton Town	42	19	12	11	64	51	50
3	Carlisle United	42	20	9	13	61	48	49
4	Orient	42	15	18	9	55	42	48
5	Blackpool	42	17	13	12	57	40	47
6	Sunderland	42	19	9	14	58	44	47
7	Nottingham Forest	42	15	15	12	57	43	45
8	West Bromwich Alb.	42	14	16	12	48	45	44
9	Hull City	42	13	17	12	46	47	43
10	NOTTS COUNTY	42	15	13	14	55	60	43
11	Bolton Wanderers	42	15	12	15	44	40	42
12	Millwall	42	14	14	14	51	51	42
13	Fulham	42	16	10	16	39	43	42
14	Aston Villa	42	13	15	14	48	45	41
15	Portsmouth	42	14	12	16	45	62	40
16	Bristol City	42	14	10	18	47	54	38
17	Cardiff City	42	10	16	16	49	62	36
18	Oxford United	42	10	16	16	35	46	36
19	Sheffield Wed.	42	12	11	19	51	63	35
20	Crystal Palace	42	11	12	19	43	56	34
21	Preston North End	42	9	14	19	40	62	31
22	Swindon Town	42	7	11	24	36	72	25

Back: Cliff, Randall, Needham, McManus, Brown, Worthington, Stubbs, Bradd. Front: Nixon, Brindley, Mann, Carter, Masson, Carlin, Probert

1974/75

14th in Division Two

#	Date		Opponent	Result	Scorers	Att	Benjamin T	Bolton IR	Bradd LJ	Brindley JC	Brown RE	Carter SC	Mann AF	Masson DS	McManus CE	McVay DR	Needham DW	Nixon JC	O'Brien R	Probert EW	Randall K	Richards P	Scanlon I	Stubbs BH	Vinter M
1	Aug	17	Bristol Rovers	0-0		14319			10	2		12	11	4	1		5		7	3	8	9		6	
2		20	FULHAM	1-1	Bradd	9468			10	2			11	4	1		5		7	3	8	9		6	
3		24	OLDHAM ATHLETIC	1-0	Needham	9353			10	2			11	4	1		5		8	3	7	9		12	6	
4		28	Fulham	0-3		9373			9	2			10	4	1		5		12	3	8	7		11	6	
5		31	York City	2-2	Bradd 2	6558			9	2			10	4	1		5			3	8	7		11	6	
6	Sep	7	SOUTHAMPTON	3-2	Randall, Stubbs, Masson(p)	8923			9	2			10	4	1		5			3	8	7		11	6	
7		14	Norwich City	0-3		17362	12		9	2	1		10	4			5			3	8	7		11	6	
8		21	WEST BROMWICH ALB.	0-0		10004			9	2	1		10	4			5			3	8	7		11	6	
9		24	ORIENT	1-1	Scanlon	7883			9	2	1		10	4			5			3	8	7		11	6	
10		28	Bolton Wanderers	1-1	Scanlon	10347			9	2	1		10	4			5			3	8	7		11	6	
11	Oct	5	PORTSMOUTH	1-1	Stubbs	8573			9	2	1	12	10	4			5			3	8	7		11	6	
12		12	Manchester Utd.	0-1		46565			9	2	1	7	10	4			5			3	8			11	6	
13		15	Oldham Athletic	0-1		9240			9	2	1	7	10	4			5			3	8			11	6	
14		19	OXFORD UNITED	4-1	Scanlon 2, Bradd, Carter	8116			9	2	1	7	10	4			5			3	8			11	6	12
15		26	Bristol City	0-3		10343			9	2	1	7	10	4			5			3	8			11	6	
16	Nov	2	HULL CITY	5-0	O'Brien, Randall(p), Scanlon, Probert, Vinter	9032				2	1	7		8		4	5		3	10	9		11	6	12
17		9	Aston Villa	1-0	Needham	22182		8		2	1	7	10	4			5		3		9		11	6	12
18		16	SHEFFIELD WEDNESDAY	3-3	Scanlon 3(1p)	14170		8		2	1	7	10	4			5		3		9		11	6	12
19		23	Sunderland	0-3		25677		8		2	1	7	10	4			5				9	3	11	6	12
20		30	MILLWALL	2-1	Bolton, Randall	9248		8		2	1	7	12	4			5			10	9	3	11	6	
21	Dec	7	Blackpool	1-3	Vinter	4922		8		2	1	7	11	4			5		3	10	9			6	12
22		14	BRISTOL ROVERS	3-2	Aitkin(og), Randall, Stubbs	7628		4		2	1	7	11				5			8	9	3		6	10
23		21	Cardiff City	0-0		6646		4	12	2		7	11		1		5			8	9	3		6	10
24		26	NORWICH CITY	1-1	Mann	13977		4	10	2		7	11		1		5			8	9	3		6	
25		28	Nottm. Forest	2-0	Bradd, Carter	25013		4	9	2		7	11		1		5			10	8	3		6	12
26	Jan	11	BLACKPOOL	0-0		10601		6	9	2		7	11		1		5			10	8	3		4	
27		18	Millwall	0-3		4963		4	10	2		7	11		1		5		3	8	9			6	12
28	Feb	1	ASTON VILLA	1-3	Scanlon	16651		4	9	2		7	10		1		5		3	8			11	6	
29		8	Hull City	0-1		6700		4	9	2					1	10	5		3	8	7		11	6	
30		15	SUNDERLAND	0-0		15855		4		2					1	10	5		3	8	9		11	6	7
31		22	Sheffield Wednesday	1-0	Vinter	14900		6		2		12			1	10	5		3	8	7		11	6	9
32	Mar	1	YORK CITY	2-1	Bradd, Needham	8835		4	12	2		7			1	10	5		3	8			11	6	9
33		8	Orient	1-0	Scanlon	4352		4	12	2		7			1	10	5		3	8			11	6	9
34		15	BOLTON WANDERERS	1-1	Vinter	8196		4	12	2		7			1	10	5		3	8			11	6	9
35		22	Southampton	2-3	Scanlon 2	12973		4	12	2		7			1	10	5		3	8			11	6	9
36		25	NOTTM. FOREST	2-2	Scanlon, Richardson(og)	20303		4	12	2		7			1	10	5		3	8			11	6	9
37		29	CARDIFF CITY	0-2		8105		4	12	2		7			1	10	5		3	8			11	6	9
38	Apr	2	West Bromwich Alb.	1-4	McVay	7812	6		12	2		7	10		1	4	5		3	8			11		9
39		5	BRISTOL CITY	1-2	Probert	7227	6		10	2	1	7					8	5	3	4	9		11		
40		12	Portsmouth	1-1	Scanlon	10966		4		2		7			1	8	5		3	10	9		11	6	
41		19	MANCHESTER UTD.	2-2	Probert, Randall	17320		4		2		7			1	8	5		3	10	9		11	6	
42		26	Oxford United	2-1	Randall 2	6316		4		2		7			1	10	5		3	8	9			6	11

	Apps	2	25	30	42	17	31	28	21	25	15	42	4	35	39	30	7	32	40	20
	Goals		1	6			2	1	1			1	3		1	3	7		14	3	4

Two own goals

F.A. Cup

R3	Jan	3	PORTSMOUTH	3-1	Randall 2, Needham	14723		4	10	2		7	11		1		5			8	9	3		6	
R4		24	Queens Park Rangers	0-3		23428		4	10	2		7	11		1		5		3	8	9			6	

F.L. Cup

R2	Sep	10	Southampton	0-1		10649			12	9	2	1		10	4			5		3	8	7		11	6	

Back: McVay, Brindley, Randall, McManus, Brown, Needham, Stubbs, Wheeler (trainer). Front: O'Brien, Nixon, Probert, Scanlon, Sirrel (manager), Masson, Bradd, Bolton, Mann

		p	w	d	l	f	a	pts
1	Manchester United	42	26	9	7	66	30	61
2	Aston Villa	42	25	8	9	79	32	58
3	Norwich City	42	20	13	9	58	37	53
4	Sunderland	42	19	13	10	65	35	51
5	Bristol City	42	21	8	13	47	33	50
6	West Bromwich Alb.	42	18	9	15	54	42	45
7	Blackpool	42	14	17	11	38	33	45
8	Hull City	42	15	14	13	40	53	44
9	Fulham	42	13	16	13	44	39	42
10	Bolton Wanderers	42	15	12	15	45	41	42
11	Oxford United	42	15	12	15	41	51	42
12	Orient	42	11	20	11	28	39	42
13	Southampton	42	15	11	16	53	54	41
14	NOTTS COUNTY	42	12	16	14	49	59	40
15	York City	42	14	10	18	51	55	38
16	Nottingham Forest	42	12	14	16	43	55	38
17	Portsmouth	42	12	13	17	44	54	37
18	Oldham Athletic	42	10	15	17	40	48	35
19	Bristol Rovers	42	12	11	19	42	64	35
20	Millwall	42	10	12	20	44	56	32
21	Cardiff City	42	9	14	19	36	62	32
22	Sheffield Wed.	42	5	11	26	29	64	21

1975/76

5th in Division Two

							Benjamin T	Birchenall AJ	Bolton IR	Bradd LJ	Brindley JC	Carter SC	King J	Lane F	Mann AF	McManus CE	McVay DR	Needham DW	O'Brien R	Probert EW	Randall K	Richards LG	Richards P	Scanlon I	Sims J	Smith DF	Stubbs BH	Vinter M
1	Aug	16	Charlton Athletic	2-1	Bradd, Probert	9618			4	9	2	7				1	8	5		10	12			3	11		6	
2		19	Orient	1-1	Probert	5223			4	9		7		3		1	10	5		8				2	11		6	
3		23	SOUTHAMPTON	0-0		9439			4	9		7				1	10	5	3	8	12			2	11		6	
4		30	Nottm. Forest	1-0	Bradd	19757			4	9		7				1	10	5	3	8				2	11		6	
5	Sep	6	CARLISLE UTD.	1-0	Probert	8005			4	9		7				1	10	5	3	8				2	11		6	
6		13	York City	2-1	Scanlon(p), McVay	6129			4	9		7				1	10	5	3	8				2	11		6	12
7		20	LUTON TOWN	1-0	Scanlon	11173			4	9		7				1	10	5	3	8				2	11		6	
8		23	Hull City	2-0	Bradd 2	8068			4	9		7				1	10	5	3	8				2	11		6	
9		27	Sunderland	0-4		27565			4	9		7				1	10	5	3	8				2	11		6	12
10	Oct	4	BRISTOL CITY	1-1	Needham	10802			4	9		7				1	10	5	3	8				2	11		6	12
11		11	OXFORD UNITED	0-1		11742			4	9	2	7				1	8	5	10					3	11		6	12
12		18	Bolton Wanderers	1-2	Bolton	16659			4	9					10	1	8	5	3		7			2	11		6	
13		25	PORTSMOUTH	2-0	Scanlon(p), Probert	9594			4	9						1	8	5	3	10	7			2	11		6	12
14	Nov	1	West Bromwich Alb.	0-0		12610			4	9	12	7			10	1		5	3	8				2	11		6	
15		4	PLYMOUTH ARGYLE	1-0	Scanlon	9239			12	9		7			10	1	8	5	3	4				2	11		6	
16		8	BRISTOL ROVERS	1-1	Bradd	10930				9		7			10	1	8	5	3	4				2	11		6	
17		15	Chelsea	0-2		18229				9	12	7			10	1	8	5	3	4				2	11		6	
18		22	BOLTON WANDERERS	1-1	Bradd	12964			4	9	2	7			10	1	12	5	3	8					11		6	
19		29	Blackpool	0-1		5747			4	9	2	7			10	1	6	5	3	8					11			12
20	Dec	6	BLACKBURN ROVERS	3-0	Bolton, Bradd, Scanlon	10252			4	9	2				10	1		5	3	8					11		6	7
21		13	Southampton	1-2	Vinter	12571			4	9	2				10	1	12	5	3	8					11		6	7
22		20	CHARLTON ATHLETIC	2-0	O'Brien, Sims	10017			4	9	2				10	1		5	3						11	7	6	
23		26	Fulham	2-3	Vinter, Scanlon	11887			7	9	2				10	1		5	3	4					11	8	6	12
24		27	OLDHAM ATHLETIC	5-1	Bradd 2, Scanlon 2, Sims	14706			7	9					10	1	4	5	3					2	11	8	6	
25	Jan	10	YORK CITY	4-0	Sims 2, Bradd, Vinter	10136				9			12	8	10	1		5	3	4				2		7	6	11
26		17	Carlisle Utd.	2-1	Bradd, Vinter	7654			12	9				8	10	1		5	3	4				2	11		6	7
27	Feb	7	Plymouth Argyle	3-1	Probert, Scanlon, Vinter	11576				9				7	10	1		5	3	4				2	11	8	6	12
28		14	Bristol Rovers	0-0		7946			4	9					10	1	6	5	3	8				2	11	7		12
29		21	CHELSEA	3-2	Scanlon, Sims, Bradd	14528				9			12		10	1		5	3	4				2	11	8	6	7
30		24	HULL CITY	1-2	Bolton	15293			12	9		7			10	1		5	3	4				2	11		6	8
31		28	Portsmouth	3-1	Bradd 2, Scanlon	9126			7	9	2				10	1		5	3	4					11	8	6	12
32	Mar	6	WEST BROMWICH ALB.	0-2		20032			4	8	2				10	1		5	3	9					11	7	6	12
33		13	Oxford United	1-2	Sims	5737		8		9	2			1	10			5	3	4					11	7	6	
34		20	BLACKPOOL	1-2	Mann	10427		8		12	2			1	10		4	5	3						11	7	6	9
35		27	Blackburn Rovers	1-2	Mann	8472		8		9			12		10	1	4	5	3					2		7	6	11
36	Apr	3	SUNDERLAND	0-0		14811		8		9			11		10	1		5	3					2		7	4	6
37		10	Luton Town	1-1	Sims	8277		8		9			11		10	1		5	3					2	12	7	4	6
38		13	NOTTM. FOREST	0-0		29279	12			9			7		10	1		5	3					2	11	8	4	6
39		17	FULHAM	4-0	Bradd, O'Brien, Scanlon, Benjamin	8819	12			9					10	1	8	5	3					2	11	7	4	6
40		19	Oldham Athletic	2-2	Bradd, Mann	7346	12			9					10	1	7	5	3					2	11	8	4	6
41		24	Bristol City	2-1	O'Brien, Benjamin	24614	12			9					10	1	8	5	3					2	11	7	4	6
42		27	ORIENT	2-0	Needham, Sims	8515	11			9					10	1	7	5	3			12		2		8	4	6
					Apps		5	5	27	42	14	24	3	2	31	40	27	42	40	30	4	1	32	38	19	7	40	20
					Goals		2		3	16					3		1	2	3	5					12	8			5

F.A. Cup

| R3 | Jan | 3 | LEEDS UNITED | 0-1 | | 31192 | | | 4 | 9 | | 12 | | | 10 | 1 | | 5 | 3 | | | | | 2 | 11 | 8 | | 6 | 7 |

F.L. Cup

R2	Sep	9	SUNDERLAND	2-1	Stubbs, Bradd	10384			4	9		7				1	10	5	3	8				2	11		6	12
R3	Oct	8	Leeds United	1-0	Scanlon	19122			4	9	2	7				1	8	5	10					3	11		6	
R4	Nov	11	Everton	2-2	Scanlon(p), Stubbs	19169				9	12	7			10	1	8	5	3	4				2	11		6	
rep		25	EVERTON	2-0	Bradd 2	23404			6	9	2	7			10	1	8	5	3	4					11			
R5	Dec	3	Newcastle United	0-1		31223			8	9	2				10	1	7	5	3	4		12			11		6	

		p	w	d	l	f	a	pts
1	Sunderland	42	24	8	10	67	36	56
2	Bristol City	42	19	15	8	59	35	53
3	West Bromwich Alb.	42	20	13	9	50	33	53
4	Bolton Wanderers	42	20	12	10	64	38	52
5	NOTTS COUNTY	42	19	11	12	60	41	49
6	Southampton	42	21	7	14	66	50	49
7	Luton Town	42	19	10	13	61	51	48
8	Nottingham Forest	42	17	12	13	55	40	46
9	Charlton Athletic	42	15	12	15	61	72	42
10	Blackpool	42	14	14	14	40	49	42
11	Chelsea	42	12	16	14	53	54	40
12	Fulham	42	13	14	15	45	47	40
13	Orient	42	13	14	15	37	39	40
14	Hull City	42	14	11	17	45	49	39
15	Blackburn Rovers	42	12	14	16	45	50	38
16	Plymouth Argyle	42	13	12	17	48	54	38
17	Oldham Athletic	42	13	12	17	57	68	38
18	Bristol Rovers	42	11	16	15	38	50	38
19	Carlisle United	42	12	13	17	45	59	37
20	Oxford United	42	11	11	20	39	59	33
21	York City	42	10	8	24	39	71	28
22	Portsmouth	42	9	7	26	32	61	25

Back: Probert, P Richards, Bradd, Randall, Benjamin, Mann. Standing: Wheeler (trainer), McVay, Needham, McManus, Regan, Lane, Stubbs, Bolton, O'Brien, Fenton (coach). Seated: Brindley, Carter, Scanlon, Sirrel (manager), Dunnett (chairman), McCool, Kane, Smith. Front: Weightman, L Richards, Towle

1976/77

8th in Division Two

#		Date	Opponent	Score	Scorers	Att	Benjamin T	Bolton IR	Bradd LJ	Busby MG	Carter SC	Hooks P	Mair G	Mann AF	McManus CE	McVay DR	Needham DW	O'Brien R	Probert EW	Richards LG	Richards P	Ross I	Scanlon I	Sims J	Smith DF	Stubbs BH	Vinter M
1	Aug	21	MILLWALL	1-2	Bradd	8469			9					12	1	7	5	3	4		2		11		10	6	8
2		25	Chelsea	1-1	Probert	17426	12		9					6	1	10	5	3	4		2		11		8		7
3		28	Plymouth Argyle	2-1	Sims, Vinter	14539	12							11	1	10	5	3	4		2			9	8	6	7
4	Sep	4	BOLTON WANDERERS	0-1		9347	12				11			9	1	10	5	3	4		2				8	6	7
5		11	Cardiff City	3-2	Needham, Vinter 2	11960					12			10	1		5	3	4		2		11	9	8	6	7
6		18	BLACKPOOL	2-0	Scanlon, Mann	9598					12			10	1		5	3	4		2		11	9	8	6	7
7		25	Bristol Rovers	1-5	Needham	6251		12			7			3	1		5		4		2		11	10	8	6	9
8	Oct	2	OLDHAM ATHLETIC	1-0	Scanlon(p)	9123								10	1	12	5	3	4		2		11	9	8	6	7
9		9	Blackburn Rovers	1-6	Probert	7993		12						3	1	10	5		4		2		11	9	8	6	7
10		16	ORIENT	0-1		8192		3						6	1		5		10		2	4	11	12	9		8
11		23	Hereford United	4-1	Sims 2, Needham, Busby	7462				9				3	1		5		10		2	4	11	7		6	8
12		30	CARLISLE UTD.	2-1	Ross, Probert	8327				9	12			3	1		5		10		2	4	11	7		6	8
13	Nov	6	Sheffield United	0-1		18355				9	12			3	1		5		10		2	4	11	7		6	8
14		13	WOLVERHAMPTON W.	1-1	Bradd	14234			9	8	12			10	1		5	3	4		2		11			6	7
15		20	Fulham	5-1	Vinter 2, Carter, Busby, Howe(og)	12191			9	10	7		12	6	1		5	3	4		2		11				8
16		27	LUTON TOWN	0-4		10009			9	10	7			3	1		5		4		2		11	12		6	8
17	Dec	4	Southampton	1-2	Vinter	14153			9	10	7			6	1	3			4		2		11			5	8
18		27	HULL CITY	1-1	Needham	10634			9	10	7			6	1		5	3	4		2		11			12	8
19	Jan	3	Carlisle Utd.	2-0	Vinter, Mann	8295			9	4	7			10	1		5	3			2				11	6	8
20		22	Millwall	5-2	Bradd 2, Vinter 3	10240			9	4	7			10	1		5	3			2				11	6	8
21		29	Charlton Athletic	1-1	Needham	8863			9	4	7			10	1		5	3			2				11	6	8
22	Feb	5	PLYMOUTH ARGYLE	2-0	Needham, Mann	9079			9	4	7			10	1		5	3			2				11	6	8
23		12	Bolton Wanderers	0-4		22355			9	4	7			10	1		5	3			2		12	11		6	8
24		15	CHELSEA	2-1	Stubbs, Carter(p)	11902			9	4	7			10	1		5	3			2				11	6	8
25		19	CARDIFF CITY	1-0	Bradd	9401			9	4	7			10	1		5	3			2		12		11	6	8
26		26	Blackpool	1-1	Vinter	10275			9	4	7			6	1		5	3			2		11		10	6	8
27	Mar	2	BURNLEY	5-1	Carter 2(2p), Thompson(og), Vinter, Bradd	8492			9	4	7		12	6	1		5	3			2		11		10		8
28		5	BRISTOL ROVERS	2-1	Busby, Carter	10058			9	4	7			11	1		5	3			2		12		10	6	8
29		8	Nottm. Forest	2-1	Anderson(og), Carter(p)	31004	6		9	10	7			4	1		5	3			2		12		11		8
30		12	Oldham Athletic	1-1	Bradd	9771			9	4	7		8	6	1		5	3			2		11	12	10		
31		19	BLACKBURN ROVERS	0-0		9343			9	4	7		8	10	1		5	3			2		11			6	
32		26	Orient	0-1		4635	12		9	4	7			10	1	8	5	3			2		11			6	
33		28	SHEFFIELD UNITED	2-1	Carter 2(1p)	9275			9	4	7			10	1		5	3			2		11	8		6	
34	Apr	1	HEREFORD UNITED	3-2	Bradd 2, Scanlon	8080			9	4	7			10	1		5	3			2		11	8	12	6	
35		8	Hull City	1-0	Daniel(og)	7225			9	4	7			10	1		5	3			2		8	11	6		12
36		9	NOTTM. FOREST	1-1	Bradd	32518	2		9	4	7			11	1		5	3						10	8	6	12
37		11	Wolverhampton Wand.	2-2	Bradd, Mann	25549			9	4	7			10	1		5	3			2		12		11	6	8
38		16	FULHAM	0-0		14847			9	4	7			11	1		5	3			2		12		11	6	8
39		23	Luton Town	2-4	Bradd, Mann	9585			9	4	7			10	1		5	3			2		12		11	6	8
40		30	SOUTHAMPTON	3-1	Carter(p), Richards P, Scanlon	11021		3	9	4	7			10	1		5				2		11	8		6	12
41	May	7	Burnley	1-3	Scanlon	11699		6	9	4	7			10	1		5	3			2		11	8			12
42		14	CHARLTON ATHLETIC	0-1		7845	6			4	7	11	9		1		5	3		10	2			8	12		
					Apps		7	5	30	32	36	1	5	41	42	8	41	33	18	1	41	4	31	20	29	33	36
					Goals				12	3	9			5			6		3		1	1	5	3		1	12

Four own goals

F.A. Cup

R3	Jan	8	ARSENAL	0-1		17328			9	4	7			10	1		5	3			2				11	6	8

F.L. Cup

R2	Sep	1	Scunthorpe United	2-0	McVay, Vinter	6208	9				12				1	7	5	3	4		2		11		10	6	8
R3		22	Derby County	1-1	O'Brien	24881					12			10	1		5	3	4		2		11	9	7	6	8
rep	Oct	4	DERBY COUNTY	1-2	Scanlon(p)	16276					12			6	1	10	5	3	4		2		11	9	7		8

Anglo-Scottish Cup

QR	Aug	7	NOTTM. FOREST	0-0		4258			9		7			10	1	8	5	3	4		2		11	12		6	
QR		10	Bristol City	0-2		3372	12		9		7			10	1	8	5	3	4		2		11			6	
QR		14	West Bromwich Alb.	1-3	Sims	6396	12								1	10	5	3	4		2		11	7	8	6	9

League tables for 1976/77 onwards will be found on page 197

Back: P Richards, Scanlon, McManus, Bradd, Benjamin. Standing: Wheeler (trainer), L Richards, Vinter, McVay, Sprigg, Lane, Probert, Bolton, O'Brien, Addison (coach). Seated: Smith, Towle, Needham, Fenton (manager), Carter, Stubbs, Mann. Front: Mair, Mitchell, Hooks

1977/78

15th in Division Two

						Benjamin T	Birchenall AJ	Bradd LJ	Busby MG	Carter SC	Chapman RD	Hooks P	Hunt D	Ladd I	Mann AF	McManus CE	McVay DR	O'Brien R	Richards LG	Richards P	Scanlon I	Sims J	Smith DF	Stubbs BH	Vinter M	Wood GT
1	Aug	20	BLACKBURN ROVERS	1-1	Bradd	8237	6		9	4	7	5	12			1		3		2	11		10		8	
2		23	Bristol Rovers	2-2	Carter, Busby	5167	6		9	4	7	5				1		3	12	2	11		10		8	
3		27	Tottenham Hotspur	1-2	Vinter	25839	6			4	7	5				1		3	11	2		9	10	12	8	
4	Sep	3	SOUTHAMPTON	2-3	Sims, Bradd	9088	6		12		7	4				1		3	11	2		9	10	5	8	
5		10	CARDIFF CITY	1-1	O'Brien	7330		11	9	4	7	5				12	1	3		2		8	10	6		
6		17	Fulham	1-5	Bradd	6064			9	4	7	5				12	1	3	11	2			10	6	8	
7		24	BLACKPOOL	1-1	Stubbs	7200	2	9	12		4	5				10	1	3	8		7			6	11	
8	Oct	1	Luton Town	0-2		7593	2	7	9				8	10	5	11	1	3		4		12		6		
9		4	Sheffield United	1-4	Hooks	12495	2	10			7	4	8			6	1	3	11			9		5		
10		8	ORIENT	1-1	Bradd	7482			9		7	5	12			11	1	3		2			4	6	8	
11		15	Oldham Athletic	1-2	Vinter	8717		8	9		10	5				11	1	3		2	12		4	6	7	
12		22	CHARLTON ATHLETIC	2-0	Carter, Vinter	8273	6				7	5				10	1	3		2		9	8	4	11	
13		29	Mansfield Town	3-1	O'Brien, Mann, Vinter	11237	6	8	12		7	5				10	1	3		2		9		4	11	
14	Nov	5	BRIGHTON & HOVE ALB.	1-0	Vinter	9549		6			7	4	12			10	1	8	3	2		9		5	11	
15		12	Burnley	1-3	Carter(p)	9734		10			7	6	12			11	1	4	3	2		8		5	9	
16		19	SUNDERLAND	2-2	Bradd, Mann	12247		6	9		7	4	12			11	1	10	3	2				5	8	
17		26	Millwall	0-0		5654		6	9			4	7			10	1	8	3	2			12	5	11	
18	Dec	3	STOKE CITY	2-0	Vinter, Hooks	9309		10			7	4	8			11	1	6	3	2				5	9	
19		10	Crystal Palace	0-2		14691		6			7	4	11			10	1	8	3	2			12	5	9	
20		17	BURNLEY	3-0	Hooks, Thompson(og), Vinter	7639		6			7	4	10			11	1	8	3	2				5	9	
21		26	Bolton Wanderers	0-2		24559		6	8			4	11			10	1	2	3	7			12	5	9	
22		27	HULL CITY	2-1	O'Brien 2	9486		6	8			4	11			10	1	2	3				12	7	5	9	
23		31	BRISTOL ROVERS	3-2	Bradd 2, Hooks	8471		6	8			4	11			10	1	2	3				12	7	5	9	
24	Jan	2	Blackburn Rovers	0-1		14394		6	8			4	11			10	1	2	3				7		5	9	
25		14	TOTTENHAM HOTSPUR	3-3	Bradd 2, Vinter	15709			9		7	4				10	1	6	3	2			8		5	11	
26		21	Southampton	1-3	Vinter	20174			9			4	12			10	1	6	3	2			8		5	11	
27	Feb	25	LUTON TOWN	2-0	Bradd, Mann	8558		8	9		7	4				10	1	6	3	2					5	11	
28	Mar	4	Orient	0-0		5828		6	9		7	4				10	1	8	3	2					5	11	
29		7	Blackpool	2-2	O'Brien, Carter	6783		6	9		7	4				11	1	10	3	2			12		5	8	
30		11	OLDHAM ATHLETIC	3-2	Vinter 2, Carter(p)	8916		6	9		7	4				11	1	10	3	2			12		5	8	
31		17	Charlton Athletic	0-0		5856	5	10	9		7	4	6				1	8	3	2			12			11	
32		21	MANSFIELD TOWN	1-0	Vinter	10587		6	9		7	4	8				1	10	3	2					5	11	
33		25	Hull City	1-1	Vinter	5392		6	9		7	4	10				1	8	3	2			12		5	11	
34		27	BOLTON WANDERERS	1-1	Vinter	15718		6	9		7	4	8				1	10	3	2			12	5		11	
35	Apr	1	Brighton & Hove Alb.	1-2	Vinter	20315	4	6	9		7	5	10				1	8	3	2			12			11	
36		4	FULHAM	1-1	Vinter	7378	5		9		7	4	6				1	10	3	2			8			11	
37		8	MILLWALL	1-1	Vinter	7509	5	6	9		7	4	12	8		10	1		3	2						11	
38		15	Sunderland	1-3	Sims	14673	5		9		7	4		10		6	1			2			8			11	3
39		22	CRYSTAL PALACE	2-0	Vinter, Bradd	7710			9		7	4	6			10	1	8	3	2					5	11	
40		25	SHEFFIELD UNITED	1-2	Vinter	8234			9		7	4	12	6		10	1	8	3	2					5	11	
41		29	Stoke City	1-1	Bradd	13890	12		9		7	4	6			10	1	8	3	2					5	11	
42	May	3	Cardiff City	1-2	O'Brien	9506	10		9		7	4	6				1	8	3	2					5	11	
					Apps		16	28	34	5	36	42	19	12	1	31	42	27	41	7	36	4	22	14	35	39	1
					Goals				12	1	5		4			3			6				2		1	19	

One own goal

F.A. Cup

R3	Jan	6	Charlton Athletic	2-0	Vinter 2	9228		6	8		11	4	12			10	1	2	3				7	5	9	
R4		31	Brighton & Hove Alb.	2-1	Vinter 2	23590		6	9		7	4	12			10	1	8	3	2					5	11	
R5	Feb	18	Millwall	1-2	Chapman	12176		6	9		7	4	12			10	1	8	3	2					5	11	

F.L. Cup

| R2 | Aug | 30 | Birmingham City | 2-0 | Carter(p), Sims | 14993 | 6 | | | 4 | 7 | 5 | | | | 1 | | 3 | 11 | 2 | | 9 | 10 | | 8 | |
| R3 | Oct | 25 | Nottm. Forest | 0-4 | | 26931 | 6 | | | | 7 | 4 | | | | 10 | 1 | | 3 | | 2 | 12 | 9 | 8 | 5 | 11 | |

Anglo-Scottish Cup

PR	Aug	6	HULL CITY	1-0	Vinter	4020	6			4	7	5					1		3		2	11	10	8		9	
PR		9	Oldham Athletic	0-0		3243	6			4	7	5					1		3	12	2	11	10	8		9	
PR		12	Sheffield United	5-4	Chapman, Sims 2, Scanlon, Hooks	8000	6			4	7	5	12				1		3		2	11	10			9	
PO	Sep	6	SHEFFIELD UNITED	3-0	Smith, Stubbs, O'Brien	5279			9	4	7	5	12				1		3		2	11	8	10	6		
QF1		13	Motherwell	1-1	Bradd	4734	6		9	4	12		10			11	1		3		2			7	5		
QF2		27	MOTHERWELL	1-0	Vinter	5396	2	7	9			5				10	1		3	4		11	8		6	12	
SF1	Oct	18	ST. MIRREN	1-0	Mann	5384		6	9		7	4				10	1		3		2			8	5	11	
SF2	Nov	1	St. Mirren	0-2		4345	8			12	7	4				10	1	6	3		2		9		5	11	

A play off with Sheffield United was required.
SF2 game after extra time.

EW Probert played in third PR game (at 8) and in QF1 (8)

1978/79

6th in Division Two

#		Date	Opponent	Score	Scorers	Att	Benjamin T	Blockley JP	Carter SC	Green R	Hooks P	Hunt D	Mair G	Mann AF	Masson DS	McCulloch I	McManus CE	McVay DR	O'Brien R	Richards P	Stubbs BH	Vinter M	Wood GT
1	Aug	19	West Ham United	2-5	McCulloch 2	25387	4	5	7		9			10		8	1	12	3	2	6	11	
2		22	MILLWALL	1-1	Vinter	7060	4	5	7	12				10		9	1	8	3	2	6	11	
3		26	BLACKBURN ROVERS	2-1	Blockley, Vinter	7774	4	5			9			8			7	1		3	2	6	11	10
4	Sep	2	Burnley	1-2	McCulloch	9787	4	5		9	12	8		10			7	1		3	2	6	11	
5		9	Leicester City	1-0	Vinter	14485	4	5		9				10		8	7	1		3	2	6	11	
6		16	ORIENT	1-0	Masson	8190	4	5		9				10		8	7	1		3	2	6	11	
7		22	Charlton Athletic	1-1	Vinter	8643	4	5		9				10	12	8	7	1		3	2	6	11	
8		30	NEWCASTLE UNITED	1-2	Hooks	11813	4			9	12	10		6		8	7	1		3	2	5	11	
9	Oct	7	Cardiff City	3-2	Hooks 2, McCulloch	7952	4	5			9	12		10		8	7	1		3	2	6	11	
10		14	BRISTOL ROVERS	2-1	Vinter, O'Brien(p)	8646	4				9	10		6		8	7	1		3	2	5	11	
11		21	Luton Town	0-6		8561	4				9	10		6		8	7	1	12	3	2	5	11	
12		28	CAMBRIDGE UNITED	1-1	McCulloch	8437	4				12	9		10		6	8	7	1	2	3		5	11	
13	Nov	4	Wrexham	1-3	O'Brien	10891	4				10	9	6			11	8	7	1	2	3		5	
14		11	WEST HAM UNITED	1-0	O'Brien(p)	11002	4				9	10		6		8	7	1		3	2	5	11	
15		18	Blackburn Rovers	4-3	Hooks, Vinter, Masson, Hunt	7833	4				9	10		6	8		7	1	12	3	2	5	11	
16		21	BURNLEY	1-1	Masson	8520	4				9	10		6	8		7	1		3	2	5	11	
17		25	BRIGHTON & HOVE ALB.	1-0	Hooks	8851	4				9	10		6	8		7	1		3	2	5	11	
18	Dec	2	Fulham	1-1	Hooks	7591	4				9	10		6	8		7	1		3	2	5	11	
19		9	CRYSTAL PALACE	0-0		11011	4				9	10		6	8		7	1		3	2	5	11	
20		16	Preston North End	1-1	Vinter	10730	4				9	10		6	8		7	1		3	2	5	11	
21		23	SUNDERLAND	1-1	O'Brien(p)	11281	4	6			9			10	8		7	1		3	2	5	11	
22		26	Oldham Athletic	3-3	Hooks, Vinter, Blockley	8262	4	12			9	10		6	8		7	1		3	2	5	11	
23		30	Stoke City	0-2		21393	4	12			9	10		6	8		7	1		3	2	5	11	
24	Jan	20	Orient	0-3		4803	4				9	10		6	8		7	1	12	3	2	5	11	
25	Feb	3	CHARLTON ATHLETIC	1-1	Mann	7958		4			9	10		6	8		7	1		3	2	5	11	
26		24	Bristol Rovers	2-2	Hooks, Vinter	6887		4			9	10		6	8		7	1		3	2	5	11	
27	Mar	3	LUTON TOWN	3-1	Mann, Hunt, Hooks	7624		4			9	10		6	8		7	1		3	2	5	11	
28		10	Cambridge United	1-0	Mann	5157		4			9	10		6	8		7	1	12	3	2	5	11	
29		13	SHEFFIELD UNITED	4-1	Vinter 3, McCulloch	10372		4			9	10		6	8		7	1		3	2	5	11	
30		24	Millwall	1-0	O'Brien	5679		4			9	10		6	8		7	1	12	3	2	5	11	
31		27	CARDIFF CITY	1-0	McCulloch	8211	12	4			9	10		6	8		7	1		3	2	5	11	
32		31	Brighton & Hove Alb.	0-0		21382		4			9	10		6	8		7	1		3	2	5	11	
33	Apr	7	FULHAM	1-1	Blockley	9465	12	4			9	10		6	8		7	1		3	2	5	11	
34		10	Sheffield United	1-5	McCulloch	15186		4			9	10		6	8		7	1		3	2	5	11	
35		13	Sunderland	0-3		34027		4		12	9	10		6	8		7	1		3	2	5	11	
36		14	OLDHAM ATHLETIC	0-0		7023	12	4			9	10		6	8		7	1		3	2	5	11	
37		18	Newcastle United	2-1	Hooks, O'Brien(p)	12017		4			9	10		6	8		7	1	12	3	2	5	11	
38		21	PRESTON NORTH END	0-0		7009		4			9	10	8	6			7	1		3	2	5	11	
39		24	LEICESTER CITY	0-1		8702		4			9	10	6	12	8		7	1		3	2	5	11	
40		28	Crystal Palace	0-2		23454		4			9	10		6	8		7	1	12	3	2	5	11	
41	May	1	WREXHAM	1-1	Mair	4374		4			9	10	6	12	8		7	1			2	5	11	3
42		5	STOKE CITY	0-1		21571		4			9			6	10	8	7	1		3	2	5	11	
					Apps		27	29	2	9	38	37	4	40	37	42	42	11	41	40	42	41	2	
					Goals			3			10	2	1	3	3	8			6			12		

F.A. Cup

R3	Jan	9	READING	4-2	Vinter, Hooks, Mann, Masson	8265		4			9	10		6	8		7	1		3	2	5	11	
R4		27	Arsenal	0-2		39173		4			9	10		6	8		7	1		3	2	5	11	

F.L. Cup

R1/1	Aug	12	Scunthorpe Utd.	1-0	Hooks	2389	4	5	7		8			10				1		3	2	6	9	11
R1/2		15	SCUNTHORPE UTD.	3-0	Carter 2, Hooks	5064	4	5	7		9			10		8		1		3	2	6	11	12
R2		30	Crewe Alexandra	0-2		3178	4	5			9	12		10	8		7	1		3	2	6	11	

Anglo-Scottish Cup

PR	Jul	31	Mansfield Town	0-1		5354		5	12	9		4		10			7	1	8	3	2	6	11	
PR	Aug	5	NORWICH CITY	2-1	Blockley, Carter	4209	4	5	12		9	8		10			7	1		3	2	6	11	
PR		8	Leyton Orient	3-2	Vinter, Benjamin, Carter(p)	2511	4	5	7	12	9					8		1		3	2	6	11	10

Back: Chapman, Hunt, McVay, Mann, Richards, Benjamin. Centre: Wheeler (trainer), Stubbs, Green, King, McManus, Blockley, Sims, Murphy (coach). Front: Carter, Hooks, McCulloch, Sirrel (manager), Vinter, O'Brien, Smith

1979/80

17th in Division Two

#	Date		Opponent	Score	Scorers	Att	Avramovic R	Beavon MS	Benjamin T	Blockley JP	Christie T	Doherty J	Hooks P	Hunt D	Kilcline B	Leonard MC	Mair G	Manns P	Masson DS	McCulloch I	O'Brien R	Richards P	Shelton G	Stubbs BH	Wood GT
1	Aug	18	CARDIFF CITY	4-1	McCulloch, Mair, Richards, Masson	7157	1			4	11		9	10			6		8	7	3	2		5	
2		21	Shrewsbury Town	1-1	Christie	7369	1			6	9		10	4			11		8	7	3	2		5	
3		25	Burnley	1-0	Mair	7005	1		12	6	9		10	4			11		8	7	3	2		5	
4	Sep	1	QUEENS PARK RANGERS	1-0	Masson	8745	1			6	9		10	4			11		8	7	3	2		5	
5		8	Leicester City	0-1		16595	1			6	9		10	4			11		8	7	3	2		5	
6		15	LUTON TOWN	0-0		9582			12	6	9		10	4		1	11		8	7	3	2		5	
7		22	SWANSEA CITY	0-0		8319				6	9		10	4		1	11		8	7	3	2		5	
8		29	Wrexham	0-1		9173			12	6	9		10	4		1	11		8	7	3	2		5	
9	Oct	6	Bristol Rovers	3-2	Blockley, McCulloch, Christie	5422				10	4	9			6	5	1	11	12	8	7	3	2			
10		9	SHREWSBURY TOWN	5-2	Mair, O'Brien 2(2p), McCulloch, Benjamin	7361			10	6	9			12	4		1	11		8	7	3	2		5	
11		13	OLDHAM ATHLETIC	1-1	Masson	8540			10	4	9			12	6		1	11		8	7	3	2		5	
12		20	Fulham	3-1	Hooks, McCulloch 2	6280	1		10	6			9	4			11		8	7	3	2		5	
13		27	WEST HAM UNITED	0-1		12256	1		10	6	12		9	4			11		8	7	3	2		5	
14	Nov	3	Cardiff City	2-3	Blockley, Hunt	8316			10	6	12		9	4	1		11		8	7	3	2		5	
15		10	PRESTON NORTH END	2-1	Mair, Christie	8602	1		10	6	12		9	4			11		8	7	3	2		5	
16		17	Sunderland	1-3	Masson	21896	1		10	6	12		9	4			11		8	7	3	2		5	
17		24	CHELSEA	2-3	Hooks, O'Brien	12646	1		10		12		9	4	6		11		8	7	3	2		5	
18	Dec	1	Watford	1-2	O'Brien	12170	1			4	6	12	9	10			11		8	7	3	2		5	
19		8	BIRMINGHAM CITY	1-1	O'Brien(p)	11383	1	10		6	12		9	4			11		8	7	3	2		5	
20		15	Orient	0-1		4115	1	10	5	6	12		9	4			11		8	7	3	2			
21		22	NEWCASTLE UNITED	2-2	O'Brien 2(2p)	11224	1	10		6	12		9	4			11		8	7	3	2		5	
22		26	Charlton Athletic	0-0		6894	1	10		6	12		9	4			11		8	7	3			5	
23		29	BURNLEY	2-3	Hunt, Christie	7596	1	10	2	6	12		9	4			11		8	7	3			5	
24	Jan	1	CAMBRIDGE UNITED	0-0		7722	1	10	2	6	9			4			11		8	7	3			5	
25		12	Queens Park Rangers	3-1	Christie, Hooks, Hunt	9613			2	6	9	7	10	4	5	1	11		8		3				12
26		19	LEICESTER CITY	0-1		14849			2	6	9	7	10	4	12	1	11		8		3			5	
27	Feb	2	Luton Town	1-2	Donaghy(og)	9007	1		2	6	9	12	10	4			11		8	7	3			5	
28		9	Swansea City	1-0	Hooks	13213	1		2	6	7	10	9	4			11		8		3			5	
29		23	Oldham Athletic	0-1		7241	1		2	6	11	7	9	4	12		10		8		3			5	
30		26	WREXHAM	1-1	O'Brien(p)	6684	1		2	6	9			4			11	10	8	7	3			5	
31	Mar	1	FULHAM	1-1	Hunt	6968	1		2	6	9			4			11	10	8	7	3			5	
32		11	West Ham United	2-1	Christie, Stubbs	24894	1		4		9			10	6		11		8	7	3	2		5	
33		15	BRISTOL ROVERS	0-0		5693	1		6		9		12	4	3		10		8	11		2	7	5	
34		22	Preston North End	0-2		7407	1		10		9			12	6		11		8	7	3	2	4	5	
35		29	SUNDERLAND	0-1		10817	1				9			12	10	6	11		8	7	3	2	4	5	
36	Apr	2	Newcastle United	2-2	Christie, Benjamin	22005	1		10		9			12	6		11		8	7	3	2	4	5	
37		5	CHARLTON ATHLETIC	0-0		6254	1		10		9			12	6		11		8	7	3	2	4	5	
38		8	Cambridge United	3-2	McCulloch, Christie, O'Brien	5546	1		10		9				6		11		8	7	3	2	4	5	
39		12	WATFORD	1-2	Hooks	7279	1		8		9		12	10	6		11			7	3	2	4	5	
40		19	Chelsea	0-1		24002	1		10		9			8	6		11			7	3	2	4	5	
41		26	ORIENT	1-1	O'Brien(p)	5505	1		10		9			4	6		11		8	7	3	2		5	
42	May	3	Birmingham City	3-3	Mair, Christie, Kilcline	33863	1		4		9			12	10	6	11		8	7	3	2		5	
					Apps		33	6	34	30	41	5	34	38	16	9	42	3	40	38	41	32	8	39	1
					Goals				2	2	9		5	4	1		5			4	6	10	1	1	

One own goal

F.A. Cup

R3	Jan	5	WOLVERHAMPTON W.	1-3	Hunt	15668			2	6	9		10	4	5	1	11		8	7	3				

F.L. Cup

R2/1	Aug	28	TORQUAY UNITED	0-0		5865	1		12	6			10	4			11	9	8	7	3	2		5	
R2/2	Sep	5	Torquay United	1-0	Hooks	4531	1			6	9		10	4	5		11		8	7	3	2			
R3		25	Grimsby Town	1-3	O'Brien(p)	11881				6	9		10	4			11		8	7	3	2		5	

Played in game 3: C King (at no. 1)

Anglo-Scottish Cup

PR	Aug	4	Mansfield Town	1-0	Christie	3587	1		8	6	9	12	11	4						10	7	3	2	5	
PR		7	SHEFFIELD UNITED	0-1		4340	1		8	6	9			4				12	11	10	7	3	2	5	
PR		11	CAMBRIDGE UNITED	1-3	Hooks	2553	1		8	6	9		11	4					12	10	7	3	2	5	

1980/81

Second in Division Two: Promoted

						Avramovic R	Beavon DG	Benjamin T	Christie T	Doherty J	Goodwin M	Harkouk R	Hooks P	Hunt D	Kelly EP	Kilcline B	Leonard MC	Mair G	Manns P	Masson DS	McCulloch I	McParland II	O'Brien R	Richards P	Wood GT
1	Aug	16	BOLTON WANDERERS	2-1	Christie, Hooks	7459	1		2	9					11	10	4	5			8	7		3	6	
2		20	Newcastle United	1-1	Masson	17272	1		2	9					11	10	4	5			8	7		3	6	12
3		23	SHEFFIELD WEDNESDAY	2-0	Christie, McCulloch	10246	1		2	9					11	10	4	5	12		8	7		3	6	
4		30	West Ham United	0-4		21769	1		2	9					11	10	4	5	12		8	7		3	6	
5	Sep	6	QUEENS PARK RANGERS	2-1	Christie, Hunt	7097	1		2	9					12	10	4	5		11	8	7		3	6	
6		13	Swansea City	1-1	Kilcline	10921	1		2	9					12	10	4	5		11	8	7		3	6	
7		20	Bristol City	1-0	Masson	8253	1		2					9	11	10	4	5			8	7		3	6	12
8		27	CARDIFF CITY	4-2	Kelly, McCulloch, O'Brien(p), Hooks	7229	1		2	9				8	11	10	4	5				7		3	6	
9	Oct	4	Luton Town	1-0	Hunt	8786	1		2	9					11	10	4	5			8	7		3	6	
10		7	GRIMSBY TOWN	0-0		7800	1		2	9					11	10	4	5			8	7		3	6	
11		11	BRISTOL ROVERS	3-1	Harkouk, Hooks, Christie	7292	1		2	9				12	11	10	4	5			8	7		3	6	
12		18	Orient	2-0	Gray(og), McCulloch	5829	1		2	9				12	11	10	4	5			8	7		3	6	
13		21	Oldham Athletic	1-0	McCulloch	5876	1		2	9				4	11	10		5			8	7		3	6	
14		25	BLACKBURN ROVERS	2-0	McCulloch 2	13500	1		2	9				4	11	10		5			8	7		3	6	
15	Nov	1	Wrexham	1-1	Hooks	6221	1		2	9				4	11	10	12	5			8	7		3	6	
16		8	DERBY COUNTY	0-0		16560	1		2	9				8	11	10	4	5				7		3	6	
17		11	NEWCASTLE UNITED	0-0		8093	1		2	9				8	11	10	4	5				7		3	6	12
18		22	Shrewsbury Town	1-1	Christie	5352	1		2	9				8	11	10	4	5				7	12	3	6	
19		25	Bolton Wanderers	0-3		7344	1		2	9				12	11	10	4	5			8	7		3	6	
20		29	CHELSEA	1-1	Harkouk	14419	1		2	9				12	11	10	4	5			8	7		3	6	
21	Dec	6	Watford	0-2		11180	1		2	9				11	12	10	4	5			8	7		3	6	
22		13	OLDHAM ATHLETIC	0-2		6565	1		2		4		9		10			5			7	8		3	6	11
23		19	Bristol Rovers	1-1	McCulloch	3552			2		12		7		10		4	5	1		8	9		3	6	11
24		27	Preston North End	2-2	Harkouk, Manns	6551		11	2	9	4		10			6		5	1	7	8		12			3
25	Jan	10	SHREWSBURY TOWN	0-0		7139		6	2	9			10	11		4		5	1	7	8		12			3
26		17	WEST HAM UNITED	1-1	Hooks	13745	1		2	9				11		10	4	5			8	7		3	6	
27		31	Sheffield Wednesday	2-1	Christie, McCulloch	22685	1		2	9				12	11	10	4	5			8	7		3	6	
28	Feb	7	SWANSEA CITY	2-1	Masson, McCulloch	8628			2	9					11	10	4	5	1		8	7		3	6	
29		14	Queens Park Rangers	1-1	McCulloch	11457	1		2	9					11	10	4	5			8	7		3	6	
30		20	Cardiff City	1-0	Christie	4958	1		2	9				12	11	10	4	5			8	7		3	6	
31		28	BRISTOL CITY	2-1	O'Brien(p), Christie	7609	1		2	9				12	11	10	4	5			8	7		3	6	
32	Mar	7	LUTON TOWN	0-1		8075	1		2	9				12	11	10	4	5			8	7		3	6	
33		14	Grimsby Town	1-2	Christie	12184	1	11	2	9	4					10		5			8	7		3	6	
34		21	ORIENT	1-0	O'Brien	6846	1		2	9	4				11	10		5			8	7		3	6	
35		28	Blackburn Rovers	0-0		14391	1		2	9	4				11	10		5			8	7		3	6	
36	Apr	5	WREXHAM	1-1	Hunt	10959	1		2	9	4				11	10		5			8	7		3	6	
37		11	Derby County	2-2	Goodwin, Christie	17922	1	11	2	9	4					10		5			8	7		3	6	
38		18	PRESTON NORTH END	0-0		8485	1		11	2	9	4	12			10		5			8	7		3	6	
39		20	Cambridge United	2-1	Christie 2	5507	1		2	9					11	10		5			8	7		3	6	
40		25	WATFORD	1-2	Goodwin	10345	1		2	9	4	12	11			10		5			8	7		3	6	
41	May	2	Chelsea	2-0	Christie, Harkouk	13324	1		2	9	4		8		11	10		5				7		3	6	
42		5	CAMBRIDGE UNITED	2-0	Christie, McCulloch	12489	1		2	9	4		8		11	10		5				7		3	6	
					Apps		38	5	42	39	3	10	25	36	42	27	42	4	4	36	39	2	40	40	7	
					Goals					14		2	4	5	3	1	1			1	3	11		3		

One own goal

F.A. Cup

R3	Jan	3	BLACKBURN ROVERS	2-1	Manns, Christie	7885		6	2	9			10	11		4		5	1	7	8					3
R4		24	PETERBOROUGH UTD.	0-1		11714	1		2	9					12	11	10	4	5			8	7		3	6	

F.L. Cup

R1/1	Aug	8	Grimsby Town	0-1		7402	1		2	9					11	10	4	5		12	8	7		3	6	
R1/2		12	GRIMSBY TOWN	3-0	Christie, Kelly, Mair	4718	1		2	9					11	10	4	5		12	8	7		3	6	
R2/1		26	Newport County	1-1	Hunt	6708	1		2	9					11	10	4	5		12	8	7		3	6	
R2/2	Sep	2	NEWPORT COUNTY	2-0	O'Brien(p), Christie	4714	1		2	9						10	4	5		11	8	7		3	6	
R3		23	QUEENS PARK RANGERS	4-1	O'Brien(p), Christie, Kelly, Hooks	6644	1		2	9				11	10	4	5			8	7		3	6		
R4	Oct	29	Manchester City	1-5	Christie	26363	1		2	9				4	11	10					8	7		3	6	12

Anglo-Scottish Cup

Q	Aug	2	ORIENT	2-2	Hunt, Harkouk	2450	1			9			11	12	8	4	6				10	7		3	2	
Q		4	Fulham	1-0	O'Brien(p)	1500	1		2					9	10	4	5		11		8	7		3	6	
Q		6	Bristol City	1-1	Hooks	1678	1		2					7	10	4	5		11		8	9			6	3
QF1	Sep	16	MORTON	2-0	Christie, Hunt	3558	1		2	9				11	10	4	5				8	7		3	6	
QF2		30	Morton	1-1	O'Brien	3500	1		2	9				4	11	10		5			8	7		3	6	12
SF1	Nov	4	Kilmarnock	2-1	Robertson(og), Harkouk	2900	1		2				9	11	10	4	5			12	8	7			6	3
SF2		18	KILMARNOCK	5-2	*See below	4314	1		2	9			7	11	10	4	5			12	8			3	6	
F1	Mar	24	Chesterfield	0-1		10190	1		2	9	4			11		10		5			8	7		3	6	
F2		31	CHESTERFIELD	1-1	Masson	12951	1		2	9	4		12	11	10			5			8	7		3	6	

Scorers in SF2: O'Brien(p), Harkouk, Kilcline, Christie, Hooks   Played in first game: BH Stubbs (5)
Second leg of final after extra time. Chesterfield won 2-1 on aggregate score

1981/82

15th in Division One

#	Date		Opponent	Score	Scorers	Att	Avramovic R	Benjamin T	Chiedozie J	Christie T	Goodwin M	Harkouk R	Hooks P	Hunt D	Kilcline B	Lahtinen A	Mair G	Masson DS	McCulloch I	McParland II	O'Brien R	Richards P	Worthington N
1	Aug	29	Aston Villa	1-0	McCulloch	30097	1	2	7	9	12	4	11	10	5				8			3	6
2	Sep	1	MANCHESTER CITY	1-1	Christie	14493	1	2	7	9	12	4	11	10	5				8			3	6
3		5	COVENTRY CITY	2-1	Christie, Hunt	10891	1	2	7	9	4		11	10	5				8			3	6
4		12	Swansea City	2-3	O'Brien(p), McCulloch	14738	1	2	7	9	4		11	10	5	12			8			3	6
5		19	IPSWICH TOWN	1-4	Osman(og)	12540	1	2	7	9			11	4	5	12		8	10			3	6
6		22	Everton	1-3	McCulloch	22186	1	2		9	4		11	10	5			12	8	7		3	6
7		26	Wolverhampton Wand.	2-3	Berry(og), Goodwin	11594	1	2		9	4		11	10	5				8	7		6	3
8	Oct	3	ARSENAL	2-1	Hunt, Kilcline	10785	1	2		9	4		11	10	5			12	8	7		6	3
9		10	SUNDERLAND	2-0	Christie 2	10668	1	2		9	4		11	10	5	6			8	7	3		
10		17	Southampton	1-3	Mair	18900	1	2	4	9				10	5	6	11	8	7		3		
11		24	WEST HAM UNITED	1-1	Masson	12456	1		7		2		10	4		5	11	8	9		3	6	
12		31	Manchester Utd.	1-2	McCulloch	45928	1	2		12	7		10	4		5	11	8	9		3	6	
13	Nov	7	Leeds United	0-1		19552	1	2	7	9			10	4	5	12		8	11		3	6	
14		21	Brighton & Hove Alb.	2-2	McCulloch, Mair	13851	1	2	7		8		10	4	5		11		9		3	6	
15		24	EVERTON	2-2	Hooks, McCulloch	7749	1	2	7		8		10	4	5		11		9		3	6	
16		28	TOTTENHAM HOTSPUR	2-2	O'Brien, Kilcline	15550	1	2	7		8		10	4	5		11		9		3	6	
17	Dec	5	Birmingham City	1-2	McCulloch	11914	1	2	7		8		10	4	5		11		9		3	6	
18	Jan	16	ASTON VILLA	1-0	Christie	9590	1	2	9	12	4		10	5			11	8		7	3	6	
19		23	Nottm. Forest	2-0	Hooks, Christie	26158	1	2		9	4		10		5		11	8		7	3	6	
20		26	LIVERPOOL	0-4		14399	1	2		9	4		10		5		11	8	12	7	3	6	
21		30	Ipswich Town	3-1	Mair, Kilcline, Hooks	21614	1	2	7	12	4		10		5		11	8	9		3	6	
22	Feb	6	SWANSEA CITY	0-1		10062	1	2	7	12	4		10		5		11	8	9		3	6	
23		13	Arsenal	0-1		18229	1	2	7	12	4		10		5		11	8	9		3	6	
24		16	Coventry City	5-1	Goodwin, Harkouk, Mair, Christie, Chiedozie	10237	1	2	7	12	4	8	10		5		11		9		3	6	
25		20	WOLVERHAMPTON W.	4-0	McCulloch 2, Mair 2	10168	1	2	7	12	4	8	10		5		11		9		3	6	
26		27	Sunderland	1-1	McCulloch	12910	1	2	7	12	4	8	10		5		11		9		3	6	
27	Mar	6	SOUTHAMPTON	1-1	Mair	12465	1	2	7		4	8	10		5		11		9		3	6	
28		13	West Ham United	0-1		22145	1	2	7	12	4	8	10		5		11		9		3	6	
29		20	MANCHESTER UTD.	1-3	Harkouk	17048	1	2		10		8			5		11	4	9	7	3	6	
30		24	West Bromwich Alb.	4-2	McCulloch 3, Mair	12637	1	2		10	4	8		12	5		11		9	7	3	6	
31		27	LEEDS UNITED	2-1	Harkouk, Hunt	13307	1	2		10	4	8		12	5		11		9	7	3	6	
32	Apr	2	Liverpool	0-1		30126	1	2	10		4	8		12	5		11		9	7	3	6	
33		10	Middlesbrough	0-3		10402	1	2	7	12	4	8	10	5			11		9		3	6	
34		12	NOTTM. FOREST	1-2	Christie	19304	1	2	7	10	4	8		5			11		9	12	3	6	
35		17	BRIGHTON & HOVE ALB.	4-1	Christie 3, Goodwin	7616	1	2	7	10	4	8		5			11		9	12	3	6	
36		24	Tottenham Hotspur	1-3	McCulloch	38017	1	2	7	10	4			8	5		11		9	12	3	6	
37		26	STOKE CITY	3-1	McCulloch, Harkouk(p), Mair	8650	1	2	7	10	4	8		12	5		11		9		3	6	
38	May	1	BIRMINGHAM CITY	1-4	McCulloch	10704	1	2	7	10	4	8			5		11		9		3	6	
39		5	Manchester City	0-1		24443	1	2	7	10	4			8	5		11		9	12	3	6	
40		8	Stoke City	2-2	Christie(p), Richards	11011	1	2	7	10	4	12		8	5		11		9		3	6	
41		11	MIDDLESBROUGH	0-1		6707	1	2	7	12	4	10		8	5		11		9		3	6	
42		15	WEST BROMWICH ALB.	1-2	Chiedozie	8726	1	2	7	10	4			8	5	3	11		9	12		6	

	Apps	42	41	32	35	38	18	28	30	36	8	34	16	40	12	39	40	2
	Goals			2	12	3	4	3	3	3		9	1	16		2	1	

Two own goals

F.A. Cup

| R3 | Jan | 5 | ASTON VILLA | 0-6 | | 12321 | | 2 | 7 | 12 | 10 | | 9 | 4 | | | 5 | 11 | 8 | | 3 | 6 | |

Played at no. 1: MC Leonard

F.L. Cup

| R2/1 | Oct | 7 | Lincoln City | 1-1 | Hooks | 4943 | 1 | 2 | | 9 | 4 | | 11 | 10 | 5 | 6 | | 8 | 7 | | 3 | | |
| R2/2 | | 27 | LINCOLN CITY | 2-3 | Mair, Masson | 6292 | 1 | | 7 | | 12 | 2 | | 10 | 4 | | 5 | 11 | 8 | 9 | | 3 | 6 |

F.L. Group Cup

PR	Aug	15	Lincoln City	1-1	Mair	2959	1	2		9	4		8	10			11		7		3	6	5
PR		19	Peterborough Utd.	1-3	Manns	2463	1	2			4		8	10			11		7		3	6	5
PR		22	Norwich City	0-3		4038	1	2			4		9	10			11		8	7	3	6	5

P Manns played in each game, in position 12, 9 and 12 respectively

1982/83

15th in Division One

#	Date		Opponent	Score	Scorers	Att.	Avramovic R	Benjamin T	Chiedozie J	Christie T	Clarke DA	Fashanu J	Goodwin M	Harkouk R	Hooks P	Hunt D	Kilcline B	Lahtinen A	Leonard MC	Mair G	McCulloch I	McParland IJ	O'Brien R	Richards P	Worthington N
1	Aug	28	SWANSEA CITY	0-0		8048	1	2	10	9			8			4	5	12		11		7		6	3
2	Sep	1	Sunderland	1-1	Christie	18997	1	2	7	9			8			4	5	10		11		12		6	3
3		4	Luton Town	3-5	Kilcline, Chiedozie, Goodwin	9071	1	2	7	9			10	8		4	5			11		12		6	3
4		7	MANCHESTER CITY	1-0	Goodwin	9369	1	2	7	9			10	8		4	5			11				6	3
5		11	EVERTON	1-0	Harkouk(p)	9188	1	2	7	9			10	8		4	5			11				6	3
6		18	Arsenal	0-2		20556	1	2	7	9			10	8		4	5	12		11				6	3
7		25	IPSWICH TOWN	0-6		8475	1	2	7	9			10	8		4	5				11			6	3
8	Oct	2	Southampton	0-1		16230	1	2	7				10	8	12	4	5				9	11		6	3
9		9	ASTON VILLA	4-1	Mortimer(og), Christie, Mair, McCulloch	8977	1	2	7	8	10		12			4	5			11	9			6	3
10		16	Coventry City	0-1		8314	1	2	7	8	10					4	5	12		11	9			6	3
11		23	Tottenham Hotspur	2-4	Christie, Chiedozie	26183	1		7	8	10		12			4	5	2		11	9			6	3
12		30	WATFORD	3-2	Kilcline, McCulloch, Hooks	9158	1		7	8	10		2		12	4				11	9			6	3
13	Nov	6	Norwich City	2-1	Mair, Christie	12591	1		7	8	10		2		4		5			11	9			6	3
14		13	BIRMINGHAM CITY	0-0		9118	1		7	8	10		2		4		5	12		11	9			6	3
15		20	LIVERPOOL	1-2	Christie	16897	1		7	8			10		4		5	12		11	9			6	3
16		27	Brighton & Hove Alb.	2-0	McCulloch 2	9971	1	2	7	8					10	4	5			11	9			6	3
17	Dec	4	NOTTM. FOREST	3-2	McCulloch, Hooks, Christie	23552	1	2	7	8					10	4	5			11	9			6	3
18		11	Manchester Utd.	0-4		33618	1	2	7	8			12		10	4	5			11	9			6	3
19		18	WEST HAM UNITED	1-2	Worthington	8441	1	2	7	9	12	8			10	4	5			11				6	3
20		27	West Bromwich Alb.	2-2	Fashanu, Goodwin	17756	1	2	7	12		8	10			4	5			11	9			6	3
21		28	STOKE CITY	4-0	Mair, McCulloch 2, Goodwin	11591	1	2	7			8	10		12	4	5			11	9			6	3
22	Jan	1	Liverpool	1-5	Fashanu	33663	1	2	7			8	10		12	4	5			11	9			6	3
23		3	SUNDERLAND	0-1		9317	1	2	7			8	10		12	4	5			11	9			6	3
24		15	Swansea City	0-2		8999	1	2		12		8	10			4	5			11	9	7		6	3
25		22	ARSENAL	1-0	Fashanu	9718	1	2	7	12	12	8	10			4	5			11	9			6	3
26	Feb	5	Everton	0-3		14546	1	2	7			8	10			4	5			11	9			6	3
27		15	SOUTHAMPTON	1-2	McCulloch	5846	1	2	7		3	8	10		12	4	5			11	9			6	3
28		19	Manchester City	1-0	Fashanu	21199			7			8	2		11	4		5	1		9	12	10	6	3
29		26	COVENTRY CITY	5-1	Fashanu 2, Lahtinen, McCulloch, Hooks	8676			7			8	2		11	4		5	1		9	12	10	6	3
30	Mar	5	TOTTENHAM HOTSPUR	3-0	Hunt, Chiedozie 2	11841			7			8	2		11	4	5		1		9	12	10	6	3
31		8	Aston Villa	0-2		17452			7	12		8	2		11	4	5				9		10	6	3
32		12	Watford	3-5	Christie, Worthington, Fashanu	16273	1	4	7	10	11	8	2				5		1		9	12		6	3
33		19	NORWICH CITY	2-2	Worthington, Christie(p)	8059		2	7	10	11	8		12		4	5		1		9			6	3
34		26	Birmingham City	0-3		11744	1	2		10	12		8	7		4	5				9		11	6	3
35	Apr	2	Stoke City	0-1		16316	1	2		10	3		12	7		4	5	8			9			6	11
36		4	WEST BROMWICH ALB.	2-1	McCulloch, Christie(p)	8696	1	2	7	8	3		4				5	10			9			6	11
37		9	Ipswich Town	0-0		15945	1	2	7	8			4			3	5	10			9	12		6	11
38		16	LUTON TOWN	1-1	Chiedozie	8897	1	2	7	8			4	12		3	5	10			9			6	11
39		23	Nottm. Forest	1-2	Lahtinen	25554	1	2	7	8			4	12		3	5	10			9			6	11
40		30	BRIGHTON & HOVE ALB.	1-0	Kilcline	7326	1	2	7	8	12		4			3	5	10			9			6	11
41	May	7	West Ham United	0-2		17534	1	2	7	8	12		4			3	5	10			9			6	11
42		14	MANCHESTER UTD.	3-2	Harkouk 2, McParland	14395	1	6	9	10				7		2	3	8				11		4	5
			Apps				36	34	39	33	16	15	34	14	17	37	40	17	6	25	34	11	5	42	41
			Goals						5	9		7	4	3	3	1	3	2		3	10	1			3

One own goal

F.A. Cup

R3	Jan	8	Leicester City	3-2	Fashanu 2, McCulloch	18384	1	2	7			8	10			4	5			11	9			6	3
R4		29	Middlesbrough	0-2		17114	1	2	7	12		8	10			4	5			11	9			6	3

The Milk Cup

R2/1	Oct	6	Aston Villa	2-1	Chiedozie, Clarke	16312	1	2	7	9	12		8			4	5			11	10			6	3
R2/2		26	ASTON VILLA	1-0	Hunt	6921	1		7	8	10		2		12	4	5			11	9			6	3
R3	Nov	9	CHELSEA	2-0	Christie(p), Hooks	8852	1		7	8	10		2		4		5	12		11	9			6	3
R4	Dec	7	WEST HAM UNITED	3-3	McCulloch, Christie, Hunt	7525	1	2	7	8					10	4	5			11	9			6	3
rep		21	West Ham United	0-3		12906	1	2	7	8	11	9	10			4	5			12				6	3

Back: Richards, Christie, Leonard, Avramovic, Hunt, Benjamin, O'Brien. Centre: Wheeler (trainer), Hooks, Worthington, Lahtinen, Kilcline, Harkouk, Wood, Walker (youth coach), Wilkinson (manager). Front: McCulloch, Manns, Mair, Sirrel (general manager), McParland, Chiedozie, Goodwin

1983/84

21st in Division One - Relegated

#		Date	Opponent	Score	Scorers	Att	Armstrong KC	Benjamin T	Chiedozie J	Christie T	Clarke DA	Davis DJ	Fashanu J	Goodwin M	Harkouk R	Hodson S	Hunt D	Jones MR	Kilcline B	Lahtinen A	Leonard MC	Mair G	McCulloch I	McDonagh JM	McParland IJ	O'Neill M	Richards P	Roeder G	Worthington N
1	Aug	27	Leicester City	4-0	O'Neill, Christie 3	15583			7	9			8	4	10	6			5	2				1		12	11		3
2		30	BIRMINGHAM CITY	2-1	Harkouk 2	11031			7	9			8	4	10	6			5	2				12	1		11		3
3	Sep	3	IPSWICH TOWN	0-2		9023			7	12			8	4	10	6			5	2				9	1		11		3
4		6	Coventry City	1-2	Fashanu	11016			7				8	4	10	6			5	2				9	1		11		3
5		10	Watford	1-3	Harkouk	12896			7	12			8	4	10	6			5	2				9	1		11		3
6		17	ARSENAL	0-4		10217	2		7	12			8	4	10	6			5						1		11		3
7		24	West Ham United	0-3		20613	2	12	8						10	6			5			11		9	1	7	4		3
8	Oct	1	EVERTON	0-1		7949	2		7	8				4	10	6			5			12		9	1		11		3
9		16	Nottm. Forest	1-3	Christie(p)	26657	2		7	9			8	4	10	6			5						1		11	12		3
10		22	STOKE CITY	1-1	Kilcline	7684	2			9			8	4	10	6			5			11			1		12	7		3
11		29	Tottenham Hotspur	0-1		29198	2	8	9					4		6			5			11		1	12	10	7		3
12	Nov	5	West Bromwich Alb.	0-2		10760	2	8	9					4					5			11		1	12	10	7	6	3
13		12	NORWICH CITY	1-1	Fashanu	7882		11	9				8	2	10	5								1		7	4	6	3
14		19	Southampton	2-0	Christie, Fashanu	15009		11	9				8	2	10	5								1		7	4	6	3
15		26	ASTON VILLA	5-2	Christie 2(1p), Chiedozie 2, Harkouk	8960		11	9				8	2	10	5								1		7	4	6	3
16	Dec	3	Queens Park Rangers	0-1		10217		11	9				8	2	10	5								1		7	4		3
17		10	SUNDERLAND	6-1	*See below	7123	6	11	9				8	2		5								1	10	7	4		3
18		17	Liverpool	0-5		22436	6	11	9				8	2		5								12	1	10	7	4	3
19		26	LUTON TOWN	0-3		9789		11	9				8	2	12	5			6						10	1	7	4		3
20		27	Manchester Utd.	3-3	Christie(p), Fashanu 2	41544		11	9	12			8	2	10	5			6					1		7	4		3
21		31	Ipswich Town	0-1		14170		11	9	12			8	2	10	5			6					1		7	4		3
22	Jan	2	WEST HAM UNITED	2-2	Christie, O'Neill	8667		11	9	8				2	10	5			6					1		7	4		3
23		14	LEICESTER CITY	2-5	Chiedozie, Harkouk	10707		11	9					2	10	5			6					8	1	12	7	4	3
24		21	Arsenal	1-1	Chiedozie	20110	2	11	9	3					12	5			6		1			8		7	4		10
25	Feb	4	Everton	1-4	McParland(p)	13191	2	11		3			7		10	5		12	6		1			8		9	4		
26		11	WATFORD	3-5	Harkouk, Christie 2(1p)	8070	2	11	9	3					10	5			6					8	1	7	4		
27		21	TOTTENHAM HOTSPUR	0-0		7943	2	11	9	3					12	10			5		6		1	8		7	4		
28		25	Stoke City	0-1		11725	2	11	9	3					12	10			5					8		7	4		
29	Mar	3	WEST BROMWICH ALB.	1-1	Christie(p)	7373		11	9	3					10				6		5	2	1	8		12	7	4	
30		13	Norwich City	1-0	O'Neill	12116		11	9	3								2	6		5		1	10	8		7	4	
31		17	COVENTRY CITY	2-1	O'Neill, Christie(p)	6564	5	11	9	3								2	6				1	10	8		7	4	
32		24	Birmingham City	0-0		9040	5	11	9	3				6				2					1	10	8		7	4	
33		31	NOTTM. FOREST	0-0		18357	5	11	9	3								2	6				1	10	8		7	4	
34	Apr	7	Wolverhampton Wand.	1-0	Hunt	7481	5	11	9	3								2	6				1	10	8	12	7	4	
35		14	MANCHESTER UTD.	1-0	Christie	13911	5			3							12	2	6				1	10	8	11	7	4	
36		21	Luton Town	2-3	Christie, Chiedozie	8181	5	11	8	3							12	2	6				1	10		9	7	4	
37		28	Aston Villa	1-3	Chiedozie	13052	5	11		3							9	2	6				1	10		8	7	4	
38	May	1	WOLVERHAMPTON W.	4-0	Chiedozie, Christie 2, Hunt	5378	5	11	9	3							12	2	6				1	10		8	7	4	
39		5	QUEENS PARK RANGERS	0-3		7309	5	11	9								3	2	6				1	10		8	7	4	
40		7	Sunderland	0-0		14517	5	11	9		3			6	10	2							1	12		8	7	4	
41		12	LIVERPOOL	0-0		18745	5	11	9	3				6	10	2	5						1			8	7	4	
42		17	SOUTHAMPTON	1-3	Christie	6035		11	9	3				6		2	5	12					1	10		8	7	4	

*Scorers in game 17: Christie, Worthington, McParland, Chiedozie 2, Richards

Apps	10	15	40	39	20	1	17	29	32	13	39	2	24	6	18	17	22	24	21	38	34	4	24
Goals			9	19			5		6		2		1						2	4	1		1

F.A. Cup

Rd	Date	Opponent	Score	Scorers	Att																							
R3	Jan	8	BRISTOL CITY	2-2	Christie 2(1p)	11042			11	9	8			2	10		5		6					12	1		7	4		3
rep		10	Bristol City	2-0	Kilcline, McCulloch	16107			11	9				2	10	5			6					8	1		7	4		3
R4	Feb	1	Huddersfield Town	2-1	Kilcline, Harkouk	13634	2		11	9	3				10		5		6		1			8		12	7	4		
R5		18	MIDDLESBROUGH	1-0	Chiedozie	17487	2		11	9	3				10		6		5		1			8			7	4		
R6	Mar	10	EVERTON	1-2	Chiedozie	19534			11	8	3				12				6		5	2	1	9		10	7	4		

The Milk Cup

Rd	Date	Opponent	Score	Scorers	Att																							
R2/1	Oct	3	Aldershot	4-2	Kilcline, Christie 2, Fashanu	4458	2		7	8			9	4	10	6			5						1		11			3
R2/2		25	ALDERSHOT	4-1	Hunt 2, Christie 2	3439	2	8	9					4		6			5		11			1	12	10	7			3
R3	Nov	8	Birmingham City	2-2	Harkouk, Chiedozie	10484		8	9	12				2	4				5					1	11	10	7	6		3
rep		22	BIRMINGHAM CITY	0-0		8268			11	9			8	2	10	5								1		7	4	6		3
r2		29	Birmingham City	0-0		9678			11	9			8	2	10	5								1		7	4	6		3
r3	Dec	5	BIRMINGHAM CITY	1-3	O'Neill	7361	6		11	9			8	2	10	5								1	12	7	4			3

R3 replay and replay 2 after extra time

Back: Chiedozie, Benjamin, Leonard, Fashanu, McDonagh, Lahtinen, Goodwin. Centre: Short (trainer), Christie, Harkouk, Kilcline, O'Brien, Mair, Walker (coach). Front: Worthington, McCulloch, Lloyd (manager), Sirrel (general manager), Clarke, Richards

1984/85

20th in Division Two - Relegated

#		Date	Opponent	Score	Scorers	Att	Beaver D	Benjamin T	Burke SJ	Burns K	Clarke DA	Davis DI	Daws A	Downing K	Fashanu J	Goodwin M	Harkouk R	Hodson S	Hunt D	Jones MR	Lahtinen A	Leonard MC	McDonagh JM	McParland II	O'Neill M	Richards P	Robinson MJ	Sims SF	Waitt M	Watson DV	Yates D	Young AF
1	Aug	25	LEEDS UNITED	1-2	Harkouk	12497					3			9	8		10	2	6	4	5	1		11	7							
2		28	Brighton & Hove Alb.	1-2	Fashanu	13773					3			9	8	12	10	2	6	4	5	1		11	7							
3	Sep	1	Charlton Athletic	0-3		4656					3			9	8	12	10	2	6	4	5	1		11	7							
4		4	BARNSLEY	0-2		4703					3			9	8		10	2	6	4	5	1		11	7							
5		8	MIDDLESBROUGH	3-2	Goodwin, Harkouk, Hunt	4911					3			11	8	12	10	2	6			1		7	4		5					9
6		15	Sheffield United	0-3		12628					3				8	9	10	2	6			1		11	7	4	5					
7		22	BLACKBURN ROVERS	0-3		5246		3			11				8	9	10	2	6			1		7	4		5					
8		29	Shrewsbury Town	2-4	Harkouk 2	3504	11	3							8	9	10	2	6			1		7	4		5	12				
9	Oct	6	Wolverhampton Wand.	3-2	Harkouk, O'Neill, Pender(og)	7676								3	8	11	10		6		2	1		7	4		5	12				9
10		14	CARDIFF CITY	0-2		5893									8	11	10	2	6		3	1		7	4		5					9
11		20	BIRMINGHAM CITY	1-3	Goodwin	5788								10	8	4		2	6		3	1		11	7		5					9
12		27	Oldham Athletic	2-3	Harkouk, Sims	3273		3	11						8		10	2	4			1		7	9	6	5					12
13	Nov	3	GRIMSBY TOWN	1-1	Fashanu	5750		3	11						8	6	10	2	5			1		7	9	4						12
14		10	Portsmouth	1-3	Goodwin	12287		3	11						8	6	10	2	5			1		7	9	4						
15		17	HUDDERSFIELD T	0-2		6051		3	11						12	6	10	2				1	7	9	4		5					8
16		24	Carlisle Utd.	0-1		3165		2	12						8	6	10		11		3	1		7	4				5			9
17	Dec	1	OXFORD UNITED	2-0	Hunt, Young	6282		2			3				9	8		10				1	12	7	4		6		5			11
18		8	Manchester City	0-2		20109		2			3				4	10		11				1	12	7	8		6		5			9
19		16	FULHAM	2-1	Harkouk(p), Young	4917		2			3				8	9		11				1	12	7	4		6		5			10
20		26	Wimbledon	2-3	Harkouk 2	2992		2			3				8	9		11				1		7	4		6	10	5			12
21		29	Barnsley	0-0		7447		2			3				8	9		11				1		7	4		6	10	5			
22	Jan	1	CRYSTAL PALACE	0-0		5725		2			3			10	8	9		11				1		7	4		6		5			
23		12	SHEFFIELD UNITED	0-0		8119					3				8	4						1	11	7	2		6	10	5			9
24		19	Leeds United	0-5		11364					3					4		8			1		11	7	2		6	10	5			9
25		26	CHARLTON ATHLETIC	0-0		3409					3				8	10		11		2		1		7	4		6	12	5			9
26	Feb	2	SHREWSBURY TOWN	1-3	Hunt	4421		5			3				8	10		11		2	1			7	4		6	9				12
27		9	Middlesbrough	1-0	Waitt	3364		5			3				8	7		11		2	1				4	12	6	9				10
28		23	Grimsby Town	0-2		4967		8		4	3					7	10		11	2	1						9	6	12	5		
29	Mar	2	OLDHAM ATHLETIC	0-0		4202		11		4	3				8	7	10				1			2	9		6	12	5			
30		9	Birmingham City	1-2	Sims	9071		11			3		4		8	7	10				1			2	9		6	12	5			
31		17	Cardiff City	4-1	Daws, Harkouk, Young 2	3631						3	8			6	7	10				1		2	11	4			5			9
32		23	WOLVERHAMPTON W.	4-1	Fashanu, Harkouk 2, Young	5561						3	11		8	6	7	10				1		2		4			5			9
33		30	Blackburn Rovers	0-1		7132		11			3				8	4	7	10				1		2	12	6			5			9
34	Apr	2	PORTSMOUTH	1-3	Harkouk	5631		10				3	9		8	4	7					1		2	11	6	12	5			
35		6	WIMBLEDON	2-3	Fashanu, Harkouk	4800							12		8	4	7		11			1		3	9	6	10	5	2			
36		8	Crystal Palace	0-1		4744							11	3	8	4	7		10			1		2	9	6	12		5			
37		14	BRIGHTON & HOVE ALB.	1-2	Richards	4671							11	3		4			10			1		7	2	12	6		5	8		9
38		20	Huddersfield T	2-1	Fashanu, Young(p)	4117		2							8	7			10			1		11		3	12	6	5	4		9
39		27	CARLISLE UTD.	3-0	Fashanu, Goodwin(p), Watson	4051							3		8	7	11		10			1				2	9	6		5	4		
40	May	4	Oxford United	1-1	Fashanu	9944							3		8	7			10	6	1		11		2	9			5	4		
41		6	MANCHESTER CITY	3-2	Fashanu, Harkouk, Young	17812							3	8	7		11	10				1		12	2		6		5	4		9
42		11	Fulham	0-1		4891							3	8	7		11	10		5	1				2	12	6			4	9	
			Apps				1	21	5	2	22	4	7	12	32	38	35	14	37	4	14	31	11	20	26	35	14	34	13	25	8	24
			Goals										1		8	4	15		3						1	1		2	1	1		7

One own goal

F.A. Cup

		Date	Opponent	Score	Scorers	Att																											
R3	Jan	5	GRIMSBY TOWN	2-2	McParland 2	6202					3				8	4		11				1	12	7	2		6	10	5			9
rep		8	Grimsby Town	2-4	Harkouk, Wilkinson(og)	6743					3				8	6					2	1	11	7	4		5	10				9

The Milk Cup

		Date	Opponent	Score	Scorers	Att																											
R2/1	Sep	25	Charlton Athletic	1-0	Goodwin	4012	11	3							8	9	10	2	6			1		7	4		5					
R2/2	Oct	9	CHARLTON ATHLETIC	2-0	O'Neill, Harkouk(p)	3453									8	11	10	2	6		3	1		7	4		5					9
R3		30	BOLTON WANDERERS	6-1	Harkouk 3, Sims, Richards, Young	4547		3	11						12	10	2	6				1		8	7	4	5					9
R4	Nov	21	Norwich City	0-3		14540		2	11						8	6	10				3	1		7	4				5			9

Back: Beaver, Clarke, Dalton, McDonagh, Hunt, Richards. Centre: Walker (coach), Jones, Lahtinen, Leonard, O'Neill, Harkouk, Short (trainer).
Front: Benjamin, Downing, Fashanu, Lloyd (manager), Hodson, McParland, Goodwin

1985/86

8th in Division Three

						Barnes PL	Benjamin T	Clarke DA	Davies JG	Davis DJ	Daws A	Downing K	Edge D	Fairclough W	Goodwin M	Harbottle M	Harkouk R	Hesford I	Hunt D	Kevan DJ	Leonard MC	McParland IJ	Mimms R	Richards P	Robinson MJ	Sims SF	Smalley P	Waitt M	Yates D	Young AF
1	Aug	17	CARDIFF CITY	1-4	Young	3856		4	3				11		8		10			1	7	2		5				6	9
2		24	Blackpool	3-1	Young 2, Harkouk	4011		4	3						8		10			1	7	2		5	12			6	9
3		26	DONCASTER ROV.	1-1	McParland	3922		4	3				11				10	8		1	7	2		5	12			6	9
4		31	Plymouth Argyle	1-0	Harkouk	5105		4	3						8		10		11	1	7	2		5				6	9
5	Sep	7	GILLINGHAM	1-1	Young	3624		4	3						8				11	1	7	2		5		10		6	9
6		14	Bournemouth	0-0		4235		4	3						8				11	1	7	2		5		10		6	9
7		17	YORK CITY	3-1	Goodwin, Young, McParland	3708		4	3						8	12			11	1	7	2		5		10		6	9
8		22	Darlington	3-2	Harbottle, McParland, Waitt	3786		4	3					2	8	10			11	1	7			12	5		9	6	
9		28	BURY	2-2	Young, Waitt	4528		4	3						8				11	1	7	2		12	5		10	6	9
10	Oct	1	Bristol Rovers	1-1	McParland	3549		4	3						8				11	1	7	2		5		10		6	9
11		5	Derby County	0-2		14406		4	3						8				11	1	7	2		12	5		10	6	9
12		12	BRISTOL CITY	4-0	Hunt 3, McParland	4332		4	3		12				8				11	1	7	2		5		10		6	9
13		19	CHESTERFIELD	2-1	Waitt, Goodwin(p)	5776		4	3						8				11	1	7	2		12	5		10	6	9
14		22	Wigan Athletic	1-3	Robinson	3374		4	3						8	12			11	1	7	2		10	5			6	9
15		27	LINCOLN CITY	3-2	Harkouk 2, McParland	6120		4	3						8		10		11	1	7	2		5				6	9
16	Nov	2	Walsall	0-0		4967		4	3						8		10		11	1	7	2		5				6	9
17		6	Reading	1-3	Harkouk(p)	6986		4	3						8		10		11	1	7	2		12	5			6	9
18		9	BOLTON WANDERERS	1-0	Yates	4497		4	3						8				11	1	7	2		10	5			6	9
19		23	Newport County	2-1	McParland, Goodwin	1946		4	3						8		10		11	1	7			12	5	2	9	6	
20		30	SWANSEA CITY	3-0	Hunt, Goodwin(p), McParland	3912		4	3						8			1	11		7			10	5	2	9	6	
21	Dec	14	Rotherham Utd.	0-1		3820		4	3						8			1	11		7			12	5	2	10	6	9
22		22	BLACKPOOL	1-2	Hunt	5926		4	3		5				8		12	1	11		7				2	10	6		9
23		26	WOLVERHAMPTON W.	4-0	Harkouk, McParland, Waitt, Goodwin	5264		4	3					12	8		10	1	11		7				5	2	9	6	
24		28	Doncaster Rov.	1-2	Edge	3673		4	3		6			10	8	12		1	11		7				5	2	9		
25	Jan	11	PLYMOUTH ARGYLE	2-0	Hunt, McParland	4953		4	3		6			10	2	8			11	1	7			12	5		9		
26		18	Cardiff City	3-1	Waitt, Mullen(og), McParland	2410		4			3			10	8			1	11		7				5	2	9	6	
27		21	Brentford	1-1	Hunt	4002		4			5		3	10	8			1	11		7					2	9	6	
28	Feb	1	Gillingham	0-4		4368		4	3		5				2			10	1	11	12	7					8	9	6	
29		4	WIGAN ATHLETIC	1-1	Yates	3369	12	4	3		5			10	2			7	1	11							8	9	6	
30		8	Chesterfield	2-2	Edge, Waitt	3623			3					10	2	8		7	1	11					5	4	9	6	
31	Mar	1	Bury	4-2	Waitt, Hunt, Harkouk, Barnes	2379	12		3		6					8	10		11	1	7				5	4	9	2	
32		4	BRISTOL ROVERS	0-0		3183	12		3		6			10		8			11	1	7				5	4	9	2	
33		8	DERBY COUNTY	0-3		13086		4	3		6			12		8		10	11	1	7				5		9	2	
34		15	Bristol City	0-3		5701	7	4								8		10						12	1	3	5	2	9	6	
35		22	Lincoln City	2-0	Waitt 2	3468	9	4			3					8		10		11					7	1		5	2	12	6	
36		29	BRENTFORD	0-4		3857	11	4	12	1	3					8		10						7			5	2	9	6	
37		31	Wolverhampton Wand.	2-2	Waitt, Goodwin	3774		4	11	1	3				12	8		10						7			5	2	9	6	
38	Apr	5	READING	0-0		3711		4	11	1	3					8								7			5	2	9	6	
39		8	WALSALL	3-1	Waitt 2, Barnes	2490	10	4	11	1	3					8								7			5	2	9	6	
40		12	Bolton Wanderers	0-1		4688	10	4	11	1	3					8								7		5		2	9	6	
41		15	BOURNEMOUTH	3-1	Davis, McParland, Waitt	2423	10	4	11	1	3					8								7			5	2	9	6	
42		19	NEWPORT COUNTY	1-2	Waitt	3279	10	4	11	1	3					8								7			5	2	9	6	
43		22	York City	2-2	Barnes, McParland (p)	3211	10	4	11		3					8								7			5	2	9	6	
44		26	Swansea City	0-0		3869	10	4	11	1	3					8								7		12	5	2	9	6	
45	May	3	ROTHERHAM UTD.	1-0	McParland	3123	10	2	11	1	3					8							4	7			5		9	6	
46		6	DARLINGTON	5-0	Yates 2, McParland, Clarke, Barnes	2345	10	2	11	1	3					8							4	7			5		9	6	

Played in game 43: RT Dalton (1). In game 46: C Jackson (12).
Game 24: Hesford sent off, Hunt went in goal.

	Apps	14	43	42	10	22	1	3	10	5	43	4	20	10	34	3	23	44	2	20	12	41	26	37	44	19
	Goals	4		1		1			2		6	1	7		8			15		1				14	4	6

One own goal

F.A. Cup

R1	Nov	17	SCARBOROUGH	6-1	Hunt, Harkouk 3, Young, McParland	5621		4	3						8		10		11	1	7	2		5				6	9
R2	Dec	7	WREXHAM	2-2	Waitt 2	4569		4	3						8				11	1	7			5	2	10	6	9
R3		10	Wrexham	3-0	Clarke, Waitt, McParland	2645		4	3						8				11	1	7			5	2	10	6	9
R4	Jan	13	Stoke City	2-0	Waitt, McParland	12219		4	3		6			10		8			11	1	7			12	5		9	2	
R5		25	TOTTENHAM HOTSPUR	1-1	McParland	17546		4			3			10	2	8	12		11	1	7				5	9	6	
rep		29	Tottenham Hotspur	0-5		17393		4			3			10			8		11	1	7				5	2	9	6	

The Milk Cup

R1/1	Aug	20	DONCASTER ROVERS	1-0	Clarke	2425		4	11		3					8		10			1	7	2		5	12			6	9
R1/2	Sep	3	Doncaster Rovers	1-2	Goodwin	2679		4	3						8		10		11	1	7	2		5		12		6	9
R2/1		24	Fulham	1-1	Goodwin	2324		4	3						8	12			11	1	7	2		10	5		9	6	
R2/2	Oct	8	FULHAM	2-4	Young, McParland	3054		4	11							12			8		1	7	2					10	6	9

R1 won an away goals. R2/2 after extra time

Freight Rover Trophy

R1	Jan	16	DONCASTER ROVERS	1-0	McParland	1642		4	3		6			10		8				1	11			7			14	5	12	9	2	
R1	Mar	11	Mansfield Town	0-1		3447		4			3					8		10		11	1	7					5	6	9	2	
po		20	MANSFIELD TOWN	0-1		2409		4			3				12	8		10		11		7	1				5	2	9	6	

Play off with Mansfield needed to decide group winner

1985/86. Back: Richards, Clarke, Hunt, Dalton, Benjamin, Davis, Goodwin. Centre: Walker (coach), Downing, Smalley, Young, Waitt, Robinson, Yates, Short (physio). Front: McDonagh, Daws, Harkouk, Sirrel (manager), Sims, McParland, Leonard.

1986/87. Back: Davis, Benjamin, Leonard, Hunt, Barnes. Centre: Jones (physio), Sims, Waitt, Yates, Bate (chief coach). Front: Smalley, Clarke, Edge, Sirrel (manager), Kevan, Harbottle, McParland

1986/87

7th in Division Three

#	Month	Date	Opponent	Score	Scorers	Att	Benjamin T	Campbell DA	Clarke DA	Crichton P	Davis DJ	Downing K	Fairclough W	Goodwin M	Hunt D	Jackson C	Kevan DJ	Leonard MC	McParland JJ	Sims SF	Smalley P	Thompson DS	Waitt M	Yates D	Young RA
1	Aug	23	WIGAN ATHLETIC	2-0	Waitt, McParland(p)	3533	4				3			8	10			1	11	5	2	7	9	6	12
2		31	Swindon Town	2-1	McParland, Goodwin	7350	4				3			8	10			1	11	5	2	7	9	6	
3	Sep	6	BOURNEMOUTH	1-1	Waitt	3619	4		12		3			8	10			1	11	5	2	7	9	6	
4		13	Darlington	1-2	Yates	1814	4		3				12	8	10			1	11	5	2	7	9	6	
5		16	Port Vale	1-1	Waitt	3725	4		11		3			8	10			1		5	2	7	9	6	12
6		20	FULHAM	2-3	McParland, Thompson	4452	4		11		3			8	10			1	7	5	2	12	9	6	
7		27	Chesterfield	2-1	McParland, Clarke	3249	2		11		3			8	10			1	7	5	12	4		6	9
8		30	BRISTOL ROVERS	3-0	Clarke, Yates, Sims(p)	3409	2		11		3			8	10			1	7	5	12	4		6	9
9	Oct	4	Bolton Wanderers	1-1	Hartford(og)	4248	2		11		3			8			10	1	7	5	12	4		6	9
10		11	ROTHERHAM UTD.	5-0	Sims 2(2p), McParland 2, Thompson	4132			11		3		12	8			10	1	7	5	2	4		6	9
11		18	Blackpool	1-3	Young	5325	6		11		3		12	8			10	1	7		2	4		5	9
12		21	MIDDLESBROUGH	1-0	McParland	4405	6		11	1	3			8			10		7		2	4		5	9
13		25	DONCASTER ROV.	3-1	Young, McParland 2	4179	6		11	1	3			8			10		7		2	4		5	9
14	Nov	1	Newport County	1-1	Young	1980	6		11	1	3			8			10		7		2	4	12	5	9
15		4	Brentford	0-1		3057	6		11	1	3			8			10		7		2	4	12	5	9
16		8	WALSALL	2-1	McParland, Clarke	5267	6		11	1	3			8			10		7		2	4	12	5	9
17		22	Gillingham	1-3	Waitt	5514	6		11		3				8		10	1	7		2	4	12	5	9
18		29	BRISTOL CITY	2-0	Goodwin, McParland	3987	6		11		3			8			10	1	7		2	4	9	5	
19	Dec	13	YORK CITY	5-1	Yates 2, Thompson 2, Clarke	3614	6		11		3			8			10	1	7		2	4	9	5	12
20		21	Carlisle Utd.	2-0	Yates, Waitt	2811	6				3			8	11		10	1	7		2	4	9	5	
21		26	MANSFIELD TOWN	0-0		8820	6				3			8	11		10	1	7		2	4	9	5	12
22		27	Bury	2-0	Clarke, McParland	3232	6		11		3			8			10	1	7		2	4	9	5	12
23	Jan	3	GILLINGHAM	3-1	Waitt 3	5832			11		3			8	6		10	1	7		2	4	9	5	12
24		24	Bournemouth	0-3		6022	6		11		3			8			10	1	7		2	4	9	5	
25		31	DARLINGTON	2-2	Yates 2	4196	2				3	11		8			10	1	7		6	4	9	5	12
26	Feb	7	PORT VALE	4-1	McParland 3(1p), Waitt	5277					3	11		8	6		10	1	7		2	4	9	5	12
27		14	Fulham	1-3	McParland	3054		11			3			8	6		10	1	7		2	4	9	5	
28		17	Chester City	2-1	Thompson, Goodwin	2792		11			3			8	6		10	1	7		2	4	9	5	
29		21	CHESTERFIELD	2-1	McParland 2(1p)	5020		11			3			8	6		10	1	7		2	4	9	5	12
30		28	Bristol Rovers	0-0		2978		11			3			8		6	10	1	7		2	4	9	5	12
31	Mar	3	NEWPORT COUNTY	5-2	Goodwin, Waitt, McParland 2, Kevan	3814		11			3			8		6	10	1	7		2	4	9	5	12
32		7	Doncaster Rov.	2-1	Waitt 2	2564		11			3		6	8			10	1	7		2	4	9	5	
33		14	BLACKPOOL	3-2	Campbell, Yates, Young	5920		11			3			8	6		10	1	7		2	4	9	5	12
34		17	Middlesbrough	0-2		9845		11			3			8	6		10	1	7		2	4	9	5	12
35		21	Rotherham Utd.	1-1	McParland	3787		11			3			8	6		10	1	7		2	4	9	5	
36		24	Wigan Athletic	0-1		3171		11			3			8	6		10	1	7		2	4	9	5	12
37		28	BOLTON WANDERERS	0-0		4776		11			3			8	6		10	1	7		2	4	9	5	12
38	Apr	4	Walsall	1-1	Downing	5206		10			3	11	12	8	6			1	7		2	4		5	9
39		11	BRENTFORD	1-1	Yates	4358		10			3	11		8	6			1	7		2	4		5	9
40		18	CHESTER CITY	1-1	Thompson	4528		10			3	11		8	6		12	1	7		2	4		5	9
41		21	Mansfield Town	2-1	Hunt, Thompson	6094		10			3	11	12	8	6			1	7		2	4		5	9
42		26	CARLISLE UTD.	2-1	McParland, Campbell	4808		10			3	11		8	6	12		1	7		2	4		5	9
43		28	SWINDON TOWN	2-3	Hunt, McParland	6354					3	11	10	8	6	5	12	1	7		2	4			9
44	May	2	Bristol City	1-3	McParland	9189	6	10	12		3			8	5		4	1	7		2	11			9
45		4	BURY	1-2	Clarke	4457		10	11		3			6	8	5		1	7		2	4	9		12
46		9	York City	1-1	Young	3760			11		3		6	8	5		10	1	7		2	4	9		12

Game 11: Leonard injured (28 mins), Davis went in goal

	Benjamin T	Campbell DA	Clarke DA	Crichton P	Davis DJ	Downing K	Fairclough W	Goodwin M	Hunt D	Jackson C	Kevan DJ	Leonard MC	McParland JJ	Sims SF	Smalley P	Thompson DS	Waitt M	Yates D	Young RA
Apps	24	18	23	5	45	8	9	45	30	4	33	41	45	10	46	46	32	42	35
Goals		2	6			1		4	2		1		24	3		7	12	9	5

One own goal

F.A. Cup

Rd	Month	Date	Opponent	Score	Scorers	Att	Benjamin T	Campbell DA	Clarke DA	Crichton P	Davis DJ	Downing K	Fairclough W	Goodwin M	Hunt D	Jackson C	Kevan DJ	Leonard MC	McParland JJ	Sims SF	Smalley P	Thompson DS	Waitt M	Yates D	Young RA
R1	Nov	15	CARLISLE UNITED	1-1	Davis	4626	6		11		3			8			10	1	7		2	4	12	5	9
rep		18	Carlisle United	3-0	Young, McParland 2	3742	6		11		3			8			10	1	7		2	4	12	5	9
R2	Dec	7	MIDDLESBROUGH	0-1		7415	6		11		3			8	14		10	1	7		2	4	9	5	12

Littlewoods Challenge Cup

Rd	Month	Date	Opponent	Score	Scorers	Att	Benjamin T	Campbell DA	Clarke DA	Crichton P	Davis DJ	Downing K	Fairclough W	Goodwin M	Hunt D	Jackson C	Kevan DJ	Leonard MC	McParland JJ	Sims SF	Smalley P	Thompson DS	Waitt M	Yates D	Young RA
R1/1	Aug	26	PORT VALE	1-3	McParland	2127	4				3			8	10			1	11	5	2	7	9	6	12
R1/2	Sep	3	Port Vale	1-4	Waitt	3436	2			10	3			8	6			1	11	5		7	9	4	12

Freight Rover Trophy

Rd	Month	Date	Opponent	Score	Scorers	Att	Benjamin T	Campbell DA	Clarke DA	Crichton P	Davis DJ	Downing K	Fairclough W	Goodwin M	Hunt D	Jackson C	Kevan DJ	Leonard MC	McParland JJ	Sims SF	Smalley P	Thompson DS	Waitt M	Yates D	Young RA
PR	Nov	24	GILLINGHAM	0-5		1668	12		11		3			8	6		10	1	7		2	4	9	5	14
PR	Jan	5	Northampton Town	0-3		3578			11		3			8	6		10	1			2	4	9	5	7

Played in game 2: PL Barnes (at no. 12)

1987/88

4th in Division Three

		Opponent	Score	Scorers	Att	Barnes PL	Belford D	Birtles G	Davis DJ	Fairclough W	Gray AM	Hart P	Kevan DJ	Leonard MC	Lund G	McParland IJ	McStay W	Mills G	Pike G	Smalley P	Thompson DS	Thorpe A	Withe C	Yates D
1	Aug 15	WIGAN ATHLETIC	4-4	Pike 2(1p), Birtles 2	6344			9	3		6		4	1	8	7		11	10	2	12			5
2	22	York City	5-3	McParland 2, Thompson, McKenzie(og), Pike	2939		1	9	3		6		4		12	8		7	10	2	11			5
3	29	GRIMSBY TOWN	0-0		5322			6	3		12		4	1	9	8		7	10	2	11			5
4	Sep 1	Fulham	0-0		4767			9	3	11	6		4	1	12	8		7	10	2				5
5	5	SOUTHEND UNITED	6-2	McParland 2, Lund, Pike 3(2p)	4166			9	3	14			4	1	12	8		7	10	2	11			5
6	12	Northampton T	1-0	Lund	6023	12		9	3	14			4	1	11	8		7	10	2				5
7	15	ALDERSHOT	2-1	Lund, Pike	4835			9	3	12			4	1	11	8		7	10	2				5
8	19	BRISTOL CITY	0-1		5705			9		3			4	1	11	8		7	10	2	12			5
9	26	Chesterfield	0-2		3466			9		3			4	1	12	8		7	10	2	11			5
10	29	BRISTOL ROVERS	1-1	Birtles	4334			9		3			4	1		8		7	10	2	11			5
11	Oct 3	Chester City	2-1	Mills, Pike	3375			9		14			6	1	12	8		7	10	2	11		3	5
12	11	MANSFIELD TOWN	1-1	Mills	8573			9	4	11			6	1		8		7	10	2			3	5
13	17	Doncaster Rov.	1-0	Lund	2645			9	4	11			6	1		8		7	10	2			3	5
14	20	BURY	3-0	Lund 2, Birtles	4044			9	4	11			6	1	8	12		7	10	2			3	5
15	24	Gillingham	1-3	Withe	5551			9	4	11			6	1		8		7	10	2			3	5
16	31	SUNDERLAND	2-1	Birtles 2	8854			9		14			6	4	1	12	8		7	10	2	11		3	5
17	Nov 3	Rotherham Utd.	1-1	Green(og)	4157			9	4	11			6	1		8		7	10	2			3	5
18	7	BRENTFORD	3-0	Withe, McParland 2	5634			9	4	11			6	1		8		7	10	2		12	3	5
19	21	WALSALL	3-1	McParland 2, Lund	7211			6	12				4	1	9	8		7	10	2			11	3	5
20	28	Brighton & Hove Alb.	1-1	Yates	8733			9	12	4		6		1	14	8		7	10	2			11	3	5
21	Dec 12	Port Vale	3-1	Pike, McParland 2	3358			9	4			6		1		8		7	10	2			11	3	5
22	19	PRESTON NORTH END	4-2	McParland 2, Pike 2	5734			6		12			4	1	9	8		7	10	2			11	3	5
23	26	CHESTERFIELD	2-0	Lund, Mills	8677			6					4	1	9	8		7	10	2			11	3	5
24	28	Blackpool	1-1	Lund	4627			6					4	1	9	8		7	10	2			11	3	5
25	Jan 1	Grimsby Town	0-0		5297					12		6	4	1	9	8		7	10	2			11	3	5
26	2	NORTHAMPTON T	3-1	Lund, Thorpe 2	8153	14		6		12			4	1	9	8		7	10	2			11	3	5
27	9	YORK CITY	3-0	Mills, Thorpe, Lund	5924			6					4	1	9	8		7	10	2			11	3	5
28	16	Bristol City	1-2	Lund	9558	14		6		12			4	1	9	8		7	10	2			11	3	5
29	30	FULHAM	5-1	McParland 3(1p), Yates, Lund	6110			6	3	12			4	1	9	8		7	10	2	11			5
30	Feb 5	Southend United	2-1	Pike, McParland(p)	3905			6					4	1	9	8		7	10	2			11	3	5
31	13	BLACKPOOL	2-3	McParland(p), Thorpe	5803			6					4	1	9	8		7	10	2			11	3	5
32	20	Wigan Athletic	1-2	McParland	5182				3			6		1	9	8		7	10	2			11	4	5
33	23	Aldershot	2-0	McParland 2	2880							6		1	9	8	4	7	10	2			11	3	5
34	27	CHESTER CITY	1-0	Lund	5869			9		14		6		1	12	8	4	7	10	2			11	3	5
35	Mar 2	Bristol Rovers	1-1	Twentyman(og)	4075			6		12				1	9	8	4	7	10	2			11	3	5
36	5	DONCASTER ROV.	2-0	Lund 2	5816			6					4	1	9	8		7	10	2			11	3	5
37	12	Mansfield Town	1-1	Pike(p)	8002	12		6	3	14			4	1	9	8		7	10	2				11	5
38	19	Sunderland	1-1	Barnes	24071	12		6					4	1	9	8	11	7	10	2				3	5
39	26	GILLINGHAM	0-1		6478	14		6	3	12			4	1		9	8	7	10	2				11	5
40	Apr 2	Brentford	0-1		4388	12		9				6	4	1		11	8	7	10	2				3	5
41	4	BRIGHTON & HOVE ALB.	1-2	Barnes	7422	11		6		12			4	1	9	8	14	7	10	2				3	5
42	9	Bury	1-0	Birtles	2527	11		9		12		6		1		8	4	7	10	2				3	5
43	23	ROTHERHAM UTD.	4-0	Lund 3, Mills	7021	8		6						1	9			7	12	2			11	3	5
44	30	Walsall	1-2	Lund	11913	8		6		12			4	1	9	14		7	10	2			11	3	5
45	May 2	PORT VALE	1-2	Thorpe	7702			6		12			4	1	9	8	14	7		2			11	3	5
46	7	Preston North End	2-1	McParland, Pike	5822			6		4				1	9	8	2	7	10	12			11	3	5

	Apps	11	1	43	20	29	4	23	32	45	40	43	9	46	46	46	9	23	35	46
	Goals	2		7							20	21		5	14		1	5	2	2

Three own goals

Play Offs

		Opponent	Score	Scorers	Att																			
SF1	May 15	WALSALL	1-3	Yates	11522	12		6		4				1	9	8	2	7	10				11	3	5
SF2	18	Walsall	1-1	Yates	8901	8		9		4		6		1	12	14	2	7	10				11	3	5

F.A. Cup

		Opponent	Score	Scorers	Att																			
R1	Nov 15	CHESTERFIELD	3-3	Kevan, McParland, Birtles	4850			9				6	4	1		8		7	10	2			11	3	5
rep	17	Chesterfield	1-0	Pike(p)	4482			6					4	1	9	8		7	10	2			11	3	5
R2	Dec 5	Port Vale	0-2		5039	12				4		6		1	9	8		7	10	2			11	3	5

Littlewoods Challenge Cup

		Opponent	Score	Scorers	Att																			
R1/1	Aug 18	Wolverhampton Wand.	0-3		5980			9	3		6		4	1	8	7		11	10	2	12			5
R1/2	25	WOLVERHAMPTON W.	1-2	Gray	2730			6	3		9		4	1		8		7	10	2	11			5

Played in R1/1: C Jackson (14)

Sherpa Van Trophy

		Opponent	Score	Scorers	Att																			
PR	Oct 13	NORTHAMPTON T	1-0	Withe	2351			9	4	11			6	1		8		7	10	2			3	5
PR	Nov 24	Brentford	2-3	Birtles, McParland	2005			6		4				1	9	8		7	10	2			11	3	5
R1	Jan 20	CARDIFF CITY	2-0	Barnes, McParland	2704	8		6	3	14			4	1	9	12		7		2			11	10	5
QF	Feb 9	Colchester Utd.	3-2	McParland, Thorpe, Lund	1564			6					4	1	9	8		7	10	2			11	3	5
SFS	Mar 9	Brighton & Hove Alb.	5-1	Thorpe, McParland 2, Barnes 2	8499	12		6					4	1	9	8		7	10	2			11	3	5
FS1	Apr 12	WOLVERHAMPTON W.	1-1	McParland	10041			9		3		6	4	1	12	8	14	7	10	2			11		5
FS2	19	Wolverhampton Wand.	0-3		18413			9		3		6		1	12	8	4	7	10	2			11		5

174

1988/89

9th in Division Three

#	Date		Opponent	Score	Scorers	Att	Barnes PL	Birtles G	Cherry S	Davison AJ	Draper M	Fairclough W	Johnson T	Kevan DJ	Law N	Leonard MC	Lund G	McParland JJ	McStay W	Mills G	Norton D	O'Riordan D	Palmer C	Pike G	Rimmer S	Thorpe A	Turner P	Withe C	Yates D
1	Aug	27	BRISTOL CITY	0-0		6285		9						6	1	12	8		7	2	4		10		11		3	5
2	Sep	3	Blackpool	1-0	Mills	4669		9						6	1	12	8		7	2	4		10		11		3	5
3		10	NORTHAMPTON T	0-1		6340		9						6	1		8	12	7	2	4		10		11		3	5
4		17	Wolverhampton Wand.	0-0		10870		9			11			6	1		8	12	7	2	4		10				3	5
5		20	Huddersfield T	1-3	Yates	5655		9						6	1	12	8		7	2	4		10		11		3	5
6		24	PRESTON NORTH END	0-0		5045							14	12	6	1	9	8	10	7	2	4				11		3	5
7	Oct	1	Mansfield Town	1-1	McParland	5908		9				12		4	6	1		8	2	7				10		11		3	5
8		4	CHESTERFIELD	4-0	Thorpe, McStay, Yates, Pike(p)	4520		9						4	6	1	8		2	7				10		11		3	5
9		9	CHESTER CITY	2-2	Birtles 2	5771		9						4	6	1		8	2	7				10		11		3	5
10		15	Bristol Rovers	0-2		4183	8							4	6	1	12		2	7				10		11		3	5
11		22	READING	3-3	Thorpe, Law, Mills(p)	5170		9				2		4	6	1	12	8		7				14		11		3	5
12		29	FULHAM	0-1		5214	12	9							6	1	8			7	2	4		10		11		3	5
13	Nov	5	Bury	1-1	Lund	2692	14	9							6	1	8		12	7	2	4		10		11		3	5
14		8	Brentford	1-2	O'Riordan	4013		9							6	1	8		2	7		4		10		11		3	5
15		12	SOUTHEND UNITED	1-1	Mills	5037	6						10			1	9		2	7		4			8	11		3	5
16		26	GILLINGHAM	1-2	Rimmer	4611	6							4	12	1	9			7		2		10	8	11		3	5
17	Dec	3	Aldershot	3-2	Kevan, Lund, Rimmer	2191					8			4	5	1	9	12	7			6			10	11		3	2
18		18	Wigan Athletic	1-0	McParland	3016		6				11			5	1	9	8	12	7		4		10				3	2
19		26	SHEFFIELD UNITED	1-4	Pike	11590						11			5	1	9	8	2	7		4		10	12	14		3	6
20		31	BOLTON WANDERERS	2-0	Lund, Law	5097	6					11			5	1	9	8	2	7		4		10				3	
21	Jan	2	Port Vale	0-1		7084	6					11			5	1	9	8	2	7		4		10		12		3	
22		7	Swansea City	0-2		5808	6					11			12	1	9	8	2	7		4		10		14		3	5
23		14	BLACKPOOL	1-1	Lund	4748						11			6	1	9	8	2	7		4		10		12		3	5
24		21	Northampton T	3-1	McParland 2(1p), Draper	3704					12	2		6		1	9	8		7		4		10		11		3	5
25		29	WOLVERHAMPTON W.	1-1	O'Riordan	9058					10			6	2	1	9	8		7		4		12		11		3	5
26	Feb	4	MANSFIELD TOWN	2-1	Pike, Coleman(og)	5924	12				10		14		2	1	9	8		7		4		6		11		3	5
27		11	Chesterfield	0-3		4943	12				10	14			2	1	9	8		7		4				11		3	5
28		18	Chester City	0-1		3165	8		1		11				6		9			7		4	2	10				3	5
29		25	BRISTOL ROVERS	1-0	Barnes	5176	8		1		11				6		9	12	2	7		5	4	10				3	
30		28	CARDIFF CITY	2-0	Kevan, Withe	4266	8		1					11	6		9		2	7		5	4	10		12		3	
31	Mar	4	Reading	3-1	Barnes 3	4153	8		1					11	6		9			12		4	2	10		14	7	3	5
32		11	BURY	3-0	Lund, Barnes, McParland	5727	8		1					11	6		9	12	2			4		10			7	3	5
33		14	Fulham	1-2	McParland(p)	3402	8		1				14	11	6		9	12	2			4		10			7	3	5
34		18	Bristol City	4-0	Barnes 2, O'Riordan, Draper	6407	8		1		11	14			6		9		2			4		10		12	7	3	5
35		25	PORT VALE	1-4	Yates	7328	8	12	1		11				6		9		2			4		10		14	7	3	5
36		27	Sheffield United	1-1	Yates	13039	8		1		12	10			6		9		2			4				11	7	3	5
37	Apr	1	WIGAN ATHLETIC	1-0	Thorpe	4929	8		1		10	14			6		9		2			4		12		11	7	3	5
38		4	SWANSEA CITY	1-0	Lund	3940			1		12	8			6		9		2			4		10		11	7	3	5
39		8	Bolton Wanderers	3-3	Turner, Thorpe, Crombie(og)	4521			1		12			8	6		9		2			4		10		11	7	3	5
40		15	Preston North End	0-3		6735			1	8	3	12		6		9		2			5	4	10		11	7			
41		18	Cardiff City	1-0	Yates	3073			1			8	10	4	6		9							12	2	11	7	3	5
42		22	HUDDERSFIELD T	3-0	Draper, Johnson 2	5499			1		8	10	11		6		9					4	2				7	3	5
43		28	Southend United	1-1	Johnson	3931			1		8	10	11		6		9				12						7	3	5
44	May	1	BRENTFORD	3-0	Lund, Bates(og), Yates	4989			1		8		11	14	6		9		10			4	2			12	7	3	5
45		6	ALDERSHOT	4-1	Lund, Turner, Johnson, Law(p)	4261			1		8	12	11		6		9		10			4	2				7	3	5
46		13	Gillingham	1-2	Law(p)	2871			1		8	14	11		6		9		10			4	2			12	7	3	5

	Barnes PL	Birtles G	Cherry S	Davison AJ	Draper M	Fairclough W	Johnson T	Kevan DJ	Law N	Leonard MC	Lund G	McParland JJ	McStay W	Mills G	Norton D	O'Riordan D	Palmer C	Pike G	Rimmer S	Thorpe A	Turner P	Withe C	Yates D
Apps	15	20	18	1	20	20	10	18	44	27	42	23	33	29	8	43	11	36	4	36	16	45	41
Goals	7	2			3		4	2	4		8	6	1	3		3		3	2	4	2	1	6

Three own goals

F.A. Cup

Round	Date		Opponent	Score	Scorers	Att	Barnes PL	Birtles G	Cherry S	Davison AJ	Draper M	Fairclough W	Johnson T	Kevan DJ	Law N	Leonard MC	Lund G	McParland JJ	McStay W	Mills G	Norton D	O'Riordan D	Palmer C	Pike G	Rimmer S	Thorpe A	Turner P	Withe C	Yates D
R1	Nov	19	Darlington	2-1	Thorpe, Pike	2110		6						4		1	9			7		2		10	8	11		3	5
R2	Dec	10	Hartlepool Utd.	0-1		3182		6				11			5	1	9	12		7		4		10	8			3	2

Littlewoods Challenge Cup

Round	Date		Opponent	Score	Scorers	Att	Barnes PL	Birtles G	Cherry S	Davison AJ	Draper M	Fairclough W	Johnson T	Kevan DJ	Law N	Leonard MC	Lund G	McParland JJ	McStay W	Mills G	Norton D	O'Riordan D	Palmer C	Pike G	Rimmer S	Thorpe A	Turner P	Withe C	Yates D
R1/1	Aug	30	MANSFIELD TOWN	5-0	McParland 3, Pike, Mills	4428		9						6	1	12	8		7	2	4		10		11		3	5
R1/2	Sep	6	Mansfield Town	0-1		2695		9			11			6	1	12	8	14	7	2	4		10				3	5
R2/1		27	TOTTENHAM HOTSPUR	1-1	Birtles	9279		9					12	4	6	1		8	2	7				10		11		3	5
R2/1	Oct	11	Tottenham Hotspur	1-2	Thorpe	14953		9						4	6	1		8	2	7				10		11		3	5

Sherpa Van Trophy

Round	Date		Opponent	Score	Scorers	Att	Barnes PL	Birtles G	Cherry S	Davison AJ	Draper M	Fairclough W	Johnson T	Kevan DJ	Law N	Leonard MC	Lund G	McParland JJ	McStay W	Mills G	Norton D	O'Riordan D	Palmer C	Pike G	Rimmer S	Thorpe A	Turner P	Withe C	Yates D
PR	Nov	29	Mansfield Town	1-1	Yates	2477	14				7	12		4	6	1	9		2					10		8	11	3	5
PR	Dec	6	CHESTERFIELD	1-1	Yates	2005	14				8	7	11	4	5	1	9	12				6				10		3	2
R1	Jan	17	Brentford	0-2		3194					12	11		10	6	1	9		2	7		4				8	14	3	5

1989/90

3rd in Division Three - Promoted after Play Off

						Barnes PL	Bartlett K	Chapman G	Cherry S	Chiedozie J	Draper M	Fairclough W	Fleming G	Johnson T	Kevan DJ	Law N	Lund G	McStay W	Norris S	Norton D	O'Riordan D	Palmer C	Platnauer N	Robinson PJ	Short, Craig	Stant P	Thomas D	Turner P	Yates D
1	Aug	19	Leyton Orient	1-0	Stant	5364			1		7	4					9				8	2	3	6		10		11	5
2		26	BLACKPOOL	0-1		4852	14		1		7			12			9				8	2	3	6	4	10		11	5
3	Sep	2	Bristol Rovers	2-3	Yates, Johnson	4753			1		12	7		11			9	14			8	2	3	6	4	10			5
4		9	READING	0-0		4697			1		7			11	9							2	3	6	4	10		8	5
5		15	Chester City	3-3	Chapman, Short, Draper	2394			11	1	7			12			9	14			2		3	6	4	10		8	5
6		23	ROTHERHAM UTD.	2-0	Chapman 2	5891			11	1	7			10			9					2	3	6	4			8	5
7		26	BOLTON WANDERERS	2-1	Johnson, Lund	5392			11	1	7			10			9					2	3	6	4			8	5
8		30	Swansea City	0-0		3075			11	1	7			10			9					2	3	6	4	12		8	5
9	Oct	7	Walsall	2-2	Johnson, Draper	4592			11	1	7			10			9					2	3	6	4			8	5
10		14	TRANMERE ROVERS	1-0	Chapman	6332	12		11	1	7			10			9					2	3	6	4			8	5
11		17	Bristol City	0-2		8331	10		11	1	7						9	14				2	3	6	4	12		8	5
12		21	PRESTON NORTH END	2-1	Palmer, Johnson	5276			11	1	7			10			9					2	3	6	4			8	5
13		28	Northampton T	0-0		3734			11	1	7	5					9				10	2	3	6	4	12		8	
14		31	BRENTFORD	3-1	Turner, Lund 2	4586			11	1	7			10			9				14	2	3	6	4	12		8	5
15	Nov	4	Mansfield Town	3-1	Robinson, Johnson 2	6016	11			1	7			10			9					2	3	6	4	12		8	5
16		11	WIGAN ATHLETIC	1-1	Lund	5443	11			1	7			10			9					2	3	6	4	12		8	5
17		25	Huddersfield T	2-1	Turner, Yates	5416				1	7						9				11	2	3	6	4	10		8	5
18	Dec	2	FULHAM	2-0	Johnson, Robinson	5133				1	12			7			9	14			11	2	3	6	4	10		8	5
19		16	Cardiff City	3-1	Stant 2, Turner	3610				1	7				12		9				11	2	3	6	4	10		8	5
20		26	SHREWSBURY TOWN	4-0	Stant 2, Yates, Turner	7819				1	7	12		11			9					2	3	6	4	10		8	5
21		30	BIRMINGHAM CITY	3-2	Palmer, Johnson, Lund	7786				1	7	12		11			9					2	3	6	4	10		8	5
22	Jan	1	Crewe Alexandra	0-1		4786				1	7	8		12	14		9				11	2	3	6	4	10			5
23		6	BURY	0-4		6059	14			1	7	12		11			9					2	3	6	4	10		8	5
24		13	Blackpool	0-0		3146	10			1	7			11			9					2	3	6	4			8	5
25		20	LEYTON ORIENT	1-0	Palmer	5344	10			1	7			11			9					2	3	6	4			8	5
26	Feb	3	Rotherham Utd.	2-1	Barnes, Yates	7218	10			1	7						9					2	3	6	4			8	5
27		10	CHESTER CITY	0-0		5184	10			1	12	2		7			9			14	11		3	6	4			8	5
28		17	Fulham	2-5	Yates, Johnson	4625	10			1	7			12		14	9			2	11		3	6	4			8	5
29		24	HUDDERSFIELD T	1-0	Lund	7632	10	12		1	7			11			9					2	3	6	4			8	5
30	Mar	3	Bury	2-3	Johnson, Draper(p)	3007	10	14		1	12			7			9				11	2	3	6	4			8	5
31		6	SWANSEA CITY	2-1	Lund, Palmer	4859				10	1	12	7		11		3	9			14	2		6	4			8	5
32		10	Bolton Wanderers	0-3		8420			10	1		7	2		12		4	9			11	14		3	6				8	5
33		17	WALSALL	2-0	Bartlett, Johnson	5207		10	12	1		7	2		11			9			14			3	6	4			8	5
34		19	Tranmere Rovers	0-2		9718		10		1			3		12			9				7	11	2		6	4			8	5
35		24	BRISTOL CITY	0-0		9598		9		1					7							2	11		3	6	4		10	8	5
36		31	Preston North End	4-2	Norton, Yates, Bartlett 2	5810		9	12	1					11						2	7		3	6	4		14	10	8	5
37	Apr	7	Brentford	1-0	Bartlett	5105		9	7	1					11							2		3	6	4		12	10	8	5
38		10	NORTHAMPTON T	3-2	Johnson(p), Thomas, Stant	5396		9		1					11							2		3	6	4	7	10	8	5
39		14	CREWE ALEXANDRA	2-0	Johnson, Bartlett	6403		9		1					11							2		3	6	4	7	10	8	5
40		17	Shrewsbury Town	2-2	Johnson, Bartlett	3536		9		1					11				7			2		12	3	6	4		10	8	5
41		21	CARDIFF CITY	2-1	Short, Bartlett	5532		9	12	1					11				10			7		2	3	6	4			8	5
42		24	Birmingham City	2-1	Lund, Palmer	10533		9		1		12			11				10			7		2	3	6	4			8	5
43		26	BRISTOL ROVERS	3-1	Turner, Johnson 2(1p)	10151		9		1					11				10					2	3	6	4		7	8	5
44		28	Wigan Athletic	1-1	A Johnson (og)	2433		9	12	1					11				10		14			2	3	6	4		7	8	5
45	May	3	Reading	1-1	Bartlett	3132		9		1					11				10					2	3	6	4		7	8	5
46		5	MANSFIELD TOWN	4-2	Lund, Turner, Johnson 2(1p)	6906		9		1					11				10					2	3	6	4		7	8	5
				Apps		13	14	19	46	1	34	8	3	40	3	3	40	3	1	15	17	37	44	46	44	22	10	44	45
				Goals		1	8	4			3			18			9			1		5		2	2	6	1	6	6

One own goal

Play offs

SF1	May	13	Bolton Wanderers	1-1	Lund	15108		9		1					11				10			12		2	3	6	4		7	8	5
SF2		16	BOLTON WANDERERS	2-0	Johnson, Bartlett	15197		8		1					10				9			2		4	3	6			7	11	5
F		27	Tranmere Rovers	2-0	Johnson, Short	29252		9		1					11				10					2	3	6	4		7	8	5

Final at Wembley Stadium

F.A. Cup

R1	Nov	18	Doncaster Rovers	0-1		3817				1		7			10			9			11		2	3	6	4	12		8	5

Littlewoods Challenge Cup

R1/1	Aug	22	Shrewsbury Town	0-3		2848				1		7	4		14			9	12			8	2	3	6		10		11	5
R1/2		29	SHREWSBURY TOWN	3-1	Robinson, Short, Stant	2559				1		7	12		8			9					2	3	6	4	10		11	5

Leyland-DAF Cup

PR	Nov	28	Fulham	1-0	Palmer	1317				1		7	14		12			9				11	2	3	6	4	10		8	5
PR	Dec	12	PETERBOROUGH UTD.	2-2	Draper, Lund	1616	14			1		7	6		11			9					12	2	3		4	10		8	5
R1	Jan	23	Bristol City	1-0	Barnes	4902	10			1		7						9				11	2	3	6	4			8	5
QF	Feb	21	Hereford United	1-1	Barnes	3409	10			1			7		11				14			12	2	3	6	4	9		8	5
SFS	Mar	14	Maidstone United	1-0	Turner	2114	10			1				2			4	9			7	11		3	6				8	5
FS1		28	Bristol Rovers	0-1		6480		9		1					11							2	7		3	6	4	12		8	5
FS2	Apr	2	BRISTOL ROVERS	0-0		10857	9			1					11				12			2	7		3	6	4	14		8	5

QF won 4-3 on penalties after extra time. SFS after extra time.

176

1988/89. Back: Machin, Fairclough, Atkin, Leonard, Davison, Norton, Draper, Johnson. Centre: Barnwell (manager), Walker (youth coach), Law, Yates, Smalley, Lund, Jackson, Kevan, Hart (player coach), Newman (assistant manager). Front: Withe, McParland, McStay, Birtles, Pike, O'Riordan, Mills, Thorpe

1990/91, the season promotion to Division One was won in the play-offs. Back: Finch, Browne, Cox, O'Riordan, Walker, Telford, Thompson, Aldridge, Wells. Centre: Mick Jones, Stant, Palmer, Yates, Cherry, Blackwell, Craig Short, Lund, Platnauer, Wilson. Front: Robinson, Norton, Johnson, Turner, Derek Pavis, Neil Warnock, Draper, Bartlett, Thomas, Chapman.

1990/91

4th in Division Two - Promoted after Play Off

#	Date		Opponent	Score	Scorers	Att	Bartlett K	Brook G	Chapman G	Cherry S	Davis SM	Draper M	Harding P	Johnson T	Lund G	Nelson G	Norton D	O'Riordan D	Palmer C	Paris A	Platnauer N	Regis D	Robinson PJ	Short, Chris	Short, Craig	Thomas D	Turner P	Yates D
1	Aug	25	Hull City	2-1	Palmer, Lund	7385	9			1		8		11	10		12		2		3	6			4	7		5
2	Sep	1	OXFORD UNITED	3-1	Johnson, Lund, Melville(og)	6398	9			1		8		11	10		2		4		3	6				7		5
3		8	Middlesbrough	0-1		17301	9	12		1		8		11	10		2		4		3	6				7		5
4		15	PORTSMOUTH	2-1	Draper, Thomas	6433	9		12	1		8		11	10				2		3	6			4	7		5
5		18	BARNSLEY	2-3	Robinson, Lund	7187	9			1		8		11	10				2		3	6			4	7		5
6		22	Watford	3-1	Platnauer, Dublin(og), Bartlett	7973	9			1		8		11	10				2		3	6			4	7	12	5
7		29	BRISTOL ROVERS	3-2	Yates, Thomas, Robinson	6562	9			1		8		11	10				2		3	14	6		4	7	12	5
8	Oct	1	Port Vale	1-0	Johnson(p)	7723	9			1		8		11	10				2		3	6			4	7	12	5
9		6	Leicester City	1-2	Johnson	13597	9			1		12		11	10				2		3	14	6		4	7	8	5
10		13	WOLVERHAMPTON W.	1-1	Thomas	12835	9			1		12		11	10				2		3	14	6		4	7	8	5
11		20	MILLWALL	0-1		7605	9			1		12		11	10				2		3	14	6		4	7	8	5
12		23	Plymouth Argyle	0-0		6651	9			1		11	3		10				2			6			4	7	8	5
13		27	Oldham Athletic	1-2	Regis	12940	9			1		8	12	11	10				2		3	14	6		4	7		5
14		30	CHARLTON ATHLETIC	2-2	Balmer(og), Bartlett	5086	9			1		8		11	10				2		3	14	6	12	4	7		5
15	Nov	3	WEST HAM UNITED	0-1		10950	9			1		11	3	12					6	2		10			4	7	8	5
16		10	WEST BROMWICH ALB.	4-3	Bartlett 2, Regis, Draper(p)	8162	9			1		11	3			14			6	2		10	12		4	7	8	5
17		17	Ipswich Town	0-0		10573	9			1		11	3						6	2		10			4	7	8	5
18		24	SWINDON TOWN	0-0		6091	9			1		11	3		12				6	2		10			4	7	8	5
19	Dec	1	Sheffield Wednesday	2-2	Draper(p), Bartlett	23474	9			1		11	3						6	2		10			4	7	8	5
20		15	HULL CITY	2-1	Regis, Bartlett	5537	9			1		11	3						6	2		10			4	7	8	5
21		22	BRISTOL CITY	3-2	Regis 2, Draper	6586	9			1		11	3	12					6	2		10			4	7	8	5
22		26	Blackburn Rovers	1-0	Bartlett	8648	9			1		11	3						6	2		10			4	7	8	5
23		29	Newcastle United	2-0	Bartlett, Draper(p)	17536	9			1		11	3	8			2		6			10	4	12		7		5
24	Jan	1	BRIGHTON & HOVE ALB.	2-1	Bartlett, Chivers (og)	8238	9			1		11	3						6			10		2	4	7	8	5
25		12	Oxford United	3-3	Robinson, Turner, Yates	5358				1		11		9					6	2		10	3	12	4	7	8	5
26		19	MIDDLESBROUGH	3-2	Draper, Regis, Johnson	9323				1		11		9					6	2		10	3	12	4	7	8	5
27		22	Charlton Athletic	1-3	Regis	4516	9			1		11	3	12						2		10	6		4	7	8	5
28	Feb	2	Portsmouth	1-2	Johnson	12680	9			1		11	3	12					6	2	14	10			4	7	8	5
29		23	West Bromwich Alb.	2-2	Bartlett 2	11068	9			1		11	3	12	10				6	2	7	14			4		8	5
30	Mar	2	SHEFFIELD WEDNESDAY	0-2		15546	9			1		11	3	12					6	2		10			4	7	8	5
31		12	PORT VALE	1-1	Johnson	6305	9			1		11	3	12	10				6	2		14			4	7	8	5
32		16	Bristol Rovers	1-1	Johnson	4878	9			1		11	3	10					6		12			2	4	7	8	5
33		19	Wolverhampton Wand.	2-0	Johnson, Bartlett	12375	9			1				11					6		3	10		2	4	7	8	5
34		23	LEICESTER CITY	0-2		11532	9			1		14		11					6	12	3	10		2	4	7	8	5
35		30	BLACKBURN ROVERS	4-1	Bartlett, Johnson 3	6831	9			1		10	12	11					6		3	14		2	4	7	8	5
36	Apr	1	Bristol City	2-3	Johnson, O'Riordan	13466	9			1		10		11					6		3			2	4	7	8	5
37		6	NEWCASTLE UNITED	3-0	Regis 2, Chris Short	7806	9		12	1		10	3						6	5			11	2	4	7	8	
38		9	Barnsley	0-1		9801	9			1	14	10	3	12					6	5			11	2	4	7	8	
39		13	Brighton & Hove Alb.	0-0		9864	9			1		10		11					6	5	3		12	2	4	7	8	
40		16	WATFORD	1-0	Paris	6168			12	1		10		11					6	2	3		9		4	7	8	5
41		20	Millwall	2-1	Yates, Regis	10162			12	1		10		11					6	2	3		9		4	7	8	5
42		23	Swindon Town	2-1	Yates, Johnson	8287	14		12	1		10		11					6	2	3		9		4	7	8	5
43		27	PLYMOUTH ARGYLE	4-0	Draper, Regis 3(1p)	7370	14		12	1		10		11					6	2	3		9		4	7	8	5
44	May	4	OLDHAM ATHLETIC	2-0	Regis, Johnson	12311	14			1		10	12	11					6	2	3		9		4	7	8	5
45		7	IPSWICH TOWN	3-1	Johnson 2(1p), Regis	6902				1		10	12	11					6	2	3		9	5	4	7	8	
46		11	West Ham United	2-1	Draper 2	26551				1	12	10	7	11					6	2	3		9	5		4	8	
						Apps	40	1	6	46	2	45	24	37	16	2	4	31	40	15	13	37	19	15	43	44	38	41
						Goals	13					9		16	3			1	1	1	1	15	3	1		3	1	4

Four own goals

Play offs

			Opponent	Score	Scorers	Att																						
SF1	May	19	Middlesbrough	1-1	Turner	22343				1		10	7	11					6	2	3		9		5	4	12	8	
SF2		22	MIDDLESBROUGH	1-0	Harding	18249	14			1		10	7	11					6	2	3		9		5	4	12	8	
F	Jun	2	Brighton & Hove Alb.	3-1	Johnson 2, Regis	59940	12			1		10	14	11					6	2	3		9			4	7	8	5

Final at Wembley Stadium

F.A. Cup

			Opponent	Score	Scorers	Att																						
R3	Jan	5	Hull City	5-2	*See below	6655	9			1		11	3		10				6					12	2	4	7	8	5
R4		26	OLDHAM ATHLETIC	2-0	Turner, Craig Short	14002	9			1		11	3		10				6	2						4	7	8	5
R5	Feb	16	MANCHESTER CITY	1-0	Lund	18979	9			1		11	3		10				6	2	7			12	4		8	5	
R6	Mar	10	Tottenham Hotspur	1-2	O'Riordan	29686	9			1		11	3	12	10				6	2						4	7	8	5

*Scorers in R3: Buckley(og), Turner, O'Riordan, Bartlett, Lund

Rumbelows League Cup

			Opponent	Score	Scorers	Att																						
R1/1	Aug	29	Exeter City	1-1	Bartlett	3858	9			1		8		11	10		12		2		3	6			4	7		5
R1/2	Sep	4	EXETER CITY	1-0	Johnson	4204	9			1		8		11	10		2		12	4	3	6				7		5
R2/1		25	OLDHAM ATHLETIC	1-0	Johnson	7089	9			1		8		11	10				2		3	6			4	7	12	5
R2/2	Oct	10	Oldham Athletic	2-5	Johnson(p), Robinson	10757	9			1		14		11	10				2		3	12	6		4	7	8	5

R2 second leg after extra time

Zenith Data Systems Cup

			Opponent	Score	Scorers	Att																						
R1	Nov	20	PORT VALE	1-0	Regis	2320	9		14	1		11	3	12					6	2		10			4	7	8	5
R2	Dec	11	SUNDERLAND	2-2	Bartlett, Draper (p)	3003	9			1		11	3	14					6	2		10	12		4	7	8	5

R2 lost 1-3 on penalties after extra time

1991/92

21st in Division One - Relegated

#		Date	Opponent	Score	Scorers	Att	Agana T	Bartlett K	Cherry S	Devlin P	Draper M	Dryden R	Farina F	Harding P	Johnson M	Johnson T	Lund G	Matthews R	McClelland J	O'Riordan D	Palmer C	Paris A	Regis D	Rideout P	Short, Chris	Short, Craig	Slawson S	Thomas D	Turner P	Wells M	Williams A	Wilson K	Yates D
1	Aug	17	Manchester Utd.	0-2		46276		12	1		10					11				6	2	3	9		14	4		7	8				5
2		20	SOUTHAMPTON	1-0	Yates	7613			1		10			6		11					2	3	9			4		7	8				5
3		24	NOTTM. FOREST	0-4		21044		12	1		10			6		11					2	3	9		14	4		7	8				5
4		28	Chelsea	2-2	T Johnson, Bartlett	15847		10	1		12	8		6		11					2	3	9		14	4		7					5
5		31	West Ham United	2-0	Bartlett 2	20093		10	1		6	8				11					2	3	9			4		7	12				5
6	Sep	3	SHEFFIELD WEDNESDAY	2-1	T Johnson 2(1p)	12297		10	1		6	9			12	11					2	3				4		7	8				5
7		7	LIVERPOOL	1-2	T Johnson	16051		10	1		6	9				11					2	3	12			4		7	8				5
8		14	Coventry City	0-1		10624		10	1		6	9				11					2	3	12		14	4		7	8				5
9		17	Sheffield United	3-1	Bartlett 2, Rideout	19375		10	1		6	8				11						3		9	2	4		7					5
10		21	NORWICH CITY	2-2	Rideout, Bowen(og)	9488		10	1		6	8				11					12	3		9	2	4		7	14				5
11		28	Luton Town	1-1	T Johnson(p)	7629		10	1		12			6		11					8	3		9	2	4		7	14				5
12	Oct	6	MANCHESTER CITY	1-3	Thomas	11878		10	1		8			6		11					2	3	12	9		4		7	14				5
13		19	LEEDS UNITED	2-4	Lund, T Johnson	12970		10	1		6	14				11	9				2	3	12			4		7	8				5
14		26	Arsenal	0-2		30011		12	1		6	10		14	4	11	9				2	3						7	8				5
15	Nov	2	OLDHAM ATHLETIC	2-0	Rideout, T Johnson	6634		10	1		6	5		8		11	12				2	3		9		4		7	14				
16		16	Aston Villa	0-1		23020	10		1		6	8				11					2	3		9		4		7					5
17		23	Everton	0-1		24230	10		1		6	8				11					2	3		9	14	4		7	12				5
18		30	QUEENS PARK RANGERS	0-1		7891	10		1		6	3		8		11					2	14		9	5	4		7	12				
19	Dec	7	Tottenham Hotspur	1-2	Craig Short	23364	10		1		12			6		11					2	3		9	5	4		7	8				
20		20	Southampton	1-1	Slawson	8658	10		1							9					2	3			6	4	12	7	8				5
21		26	CHELSEA	2-0	Yates, T Johnson	11867	10		1							9					2	3			6	4		7	8				5
22		28	WEST HAM UNITED	3-0	Turner, Harding, Agana	11128	10		1							9					2	3			12	6	4	14	7	8				5
23	Jan	1	Crystal Palace	0-1		14202	10		1							9					2	3			12	6	4	14	7	8				5
24		11	Nottm. Forest	1-1	Dryden	30168	10	12	1			5				9					2	3				6	4	14	7	8				
25		18	MANCHESTER UTD.	1-1	T Johnson(p)	21055		10	1		6					9					2	3				5	4		7	8				
26	Feb	1	Leeds United	0-3		27323		10	1		6	5				11	9				2	3					4	12	7	8	14			
27		8	ARSENAL	0-1		11221	12	10	1		6					11					2	3				5	4		7	8		14		
28		22	Queens Park Rangers	1-1	Bartlett	8495		10	1			3				11					2					5	4	9	7			8		
29		25	WIMBLEDON	1-1	Craig Short	6198	12	10	1			3				11					2					5	4	9	7			8		
30	Mar	7	Wimbledon	0-2		3796	12		1		6	3			8	11	14		4		2					5		9	10		7			
31		10	ASTON VILLA	0-0		8391			1		6	3			8	11	14		4		2					5		12		8	7			
32		14	Oldham Athletic	3-4	Draper, Williams, Lund	12125		10	1		6	3			14		9		5		2					4	12		8		7			11
33		17	EVERTON	0-0		7480		10	1		6	3					9		11		2					5	4		8		7			12
34		21	Sheffield Wednesday	0-1		23910		10	1		6	3			14		9		11		2					8	4	12	7					5
35		28	CRYSTAL PALACE	2-3	Craig Short, Wilson	7675			1		6	3	14				9		11		2					4	12		8			7	10	5
36		31	Liverpool	0-4		25457			1		6	3	14				9				2				12	4			8			7	10	5
37	Apr	7	TOTTENHAM HOTSPUR	0-2		9205			1		6	3	11	8			9				2				5	4	14	12			7	10	
38		11	COVENTRY CITY	1-0	Sansom(og)	6655		10	1	9	6	3		8	5			14			2					4		12			7	11	
39		18	Norwich City	1-0	Matthews	12100		10	1		6	3		8	5			14			2					12	4	9			7	11	
40		20	SHEFFIELD UNITED	1-3	Bartlett	12605		10	1		6	3		8	5			12			2					4		9			7	11	
41		25	Manchester City	0-2		23426	9		10	1		6	3		8	5			4	12		2									7	11	
42	May	2	LUTON TOWN	2-1	Matthews 2	11380	9			1	12	6			8						2					5	4		3			7	11	

Played in game 36: PJ Robinson (11). In game 41: PR Cox (14).

	Apps	13	29	42	2	35	29	3	29	5	31	13	5	6	1	41	27	9	11	27	38	13	36	29	1	15	8	25
	Goals	1	7			1	1		1		9	2	3						3		3	1	1		1	1	2

Two own goals

F.A. Cup

Round	Date		Opponent	Score	Scorers	Att																											
R3	Jan	5	WIGAN ATHLETIC	2-0	T Johnson, Turner	5913	10		1					9		11	12				2	3		7	6	4	14		8				5
R4	Feb	4	BLACKBURN ROVERS	2-1	Lund, Draper	12173		10	1		6	5				11	9				2	3				4	12	7	8				
R5		15	Norwich City	0-3		14511	11	10	1		6	14		9		12					2	3			5	4		7	8				

Rumbelows League Cup

Round	Date		Opponent	Score	Scorers	Att																											
R2/1	Sep	24	Port Vale	1-2	T Johnson	4722		10	1			8		6		11						3	9		2	4		7	12				5
R2/2	Oct	9	PORT VALE	3-2	Bartlett 2, T Johnson(p)	4419		10	1		6	12				11					2	3	14	9		4		7	8				5

Lost on away goals rule a.e.t.

Zenith Data Systems Cup

Round	Date		Opponent	Score	Scorers	Att																											
R2	Oct	22	Sheffield United	3-3	Draper, Bartlett, Slawson	3291		10	1		6	7		8	4	11					2	3	9				12			14			5
QF	Nov	26	SHEFFIELD WEDNESDAY	1-0	Harding	4118	10		1			3		8		11				6	2			9	5	4		7	12				
SF	Jan	8	LEICESTER CITY	1-2	Chris Short	11559	10		1		12			9		11					2	3		7	6	4	14		8				5

SF after extra time

1992/93

17th in Division One of the Football League

#		Date	Opponent	Score	Scorers	Att	Agana T	Bartlett K	Catlin R	Cherry S	Cox PR	Devlin P	Dijkstra M	Draper M	Dryden R	Johnson M	Lund G	Matthews R	Murphy S	O'Riordan D	Palmer C	Reeves D	Robinson D	Short, Chris	Short, Craig	Slawson S	Smith D	Smith M	Thomas D	Turner P	Turner R	Walker R	Williams A	Wilson K
1	Aug	16	Birmingham City	0-1		10614	9			1				7		5		10		6	2			4			11		3				8	12
2		22	LEICESTER CITY	1-1	D Smith(p)	10502	9			1			3	7		5				6	2				4	10	11			14			8	12
3		25	WATFORD	1-2	Slawson	6276	9			1			3	7		5				6	2					10	11			4			8	12
4		29	Peterborough Utd.	3-1	D Smith, Wilson, Williams	6720			1				3	7		4				6	2		5			10	11			12			8	9
5	Sep	5	BARNSLEY	1-3	Craig Short	6205			1				5	7					12	6	2		3	4		10	11		14	8				9
6		12	Watford	3-1	Draper, Lund, Slawson	7077				1			5	7		9		4	6	2			3			12	11			8				10
7		19	Millwall	0-6		6689				1			2	7		9		4	6			5				12	11			3	8				10
8		26	LUTON TOWN	0-0		5992				1		12		7		4	9			6	5				2		10	11			3	8				
9		29	Tranmere Rovers	1-3	Murphy	5410				1		10		7		4	9		5	6					2			11			3	8				
10	Oct	3	Bristol Rovers	3-3	Bartlett, D Smith, O'Riordan	5015		10		1		14		7		5	9		12	6					2			11	4		3	8				
11		10	GRIMSBY TOWN	1-0	Lund	6442		10		1		11		7		5	9			6	2								4	3	8				
12		17	Swindon Town	1-5	Thomas	7912		10		1		11		7		5	9		14	6	2					12			4	3	8				
13		24	OXFORD UNITED	1-1	Turner P	5228	10			1		11		7		5	9			6	4		2						3	12		8			
14		31	Sunderland	2-2	Chris Short, Slawson	15501	10			1				7		5	9				4		2		12				3	8		6		11
15	Nov	3	DERBY COUNTY	0-2		14268	10			1		12		7		5	9				4		2			11			3	8		6		
16		7	West Ham United	0-2		12345		12		1		7			10	5	9				4		2			11			3	8		6		
17		14	WOLVERHAMPTON W.	2-2	Bartlett 2	8494		12		1		7				5	9			6	4		2			11			3	8			10	14
18		21	Southend United	1-3	Bartlett	2651		10		1		11			7		9		14	6	4		2			12			3		5	8			
19		28	Bristol City	0-1		9086	9	10		1			3	8		6				14	2					12	11		4		5				7
20	Dec	5	NEWCASTLE UNITED	0-2		14841	9	10		1			3	7						14	2		6			12	11		4		5				8
21		12	CAMBRIDGE UNITED	1-0	R Turner	5037	9	10		1			3	7			12			6			2				11		4		5		14		8
22		19	Portsmouth	0-0		8943	9	10		1			3	7							2						11	12	4		5		6		8
23		28	BRENTFORD	1-1	Agana	6892	9	10		1			3	7						6			2				11		4		5				8
24	Jan	9	MILLWALL	1-2	Thomas	6148	9	10		1								12	14	6			2				11	3	4		5		7		8
25		16	Luton Town	0-0		6729	9			1		8		7	3	6		12			5						11		4				2		10
26		23	Leicester City	1-1	Draper	15716	9			1	5	7		8	3	6		12					2				11		4						10
27		26	TRANMERE ROVERS	5-1	*See below	5642	9			1	5	7		8		3	10			6			2				11		4						12
28		30	Charlton Athletic	1-2	Draper	8337	9			1	5	7		8		3	10			6			2				11		4				14		12
29	Feb	6	BIRMINGHAM CITY	3-1	D Smith(p), Matthews, Bartlett	8550	9	12		1	5	7		8		3		10		6			2				11					4			
30		21	PETERBOROUGH UTD.	1-0	D Smith(p)	7468	9	12		1	5	10		8		3		7		6			2				11					4			
31		27	Grimsby Town	3-3	Devlin, Draper, Lund	5871	9			1	5	10		8		3	7			6			2				11		4			12			
32	Mar	6	BRISTOL ROVERS	3-0	Draper 2, Devlin	6455	9	12		1	5	10		8		3	7			6			2				11		4						
33		9	Wolverhampton Wand.	0-3		11482		9		1	5	10		8		3	7			6			2				11		4					14	12
34		13	WEST HAM UNITED	1-0	Walker	10272				1	5	12		8		3	7			6			2				11		4			6	10	9	
35		16	Barnsley	0-0		6372				1	5	10		8		3	7								11				4			6	2	9	
36		20	Newcastle United	0-4		29871				1	5	10		8		3	7						2				12	11	4			6	14	9	
37		23	SOUTHEND UNITED	4-0	Lund, Cox, Draper 2	6109				1	5	10		8		3	7						2				12	11	4		14	6		9	
38	Apr	3	BRISTOL CITY	0-0		6634	12			1	5	10		8		3	7				14						11		4			6		9	
39		6	Cambridge United	0-3		4583	12			1	5	10		8		3	7			14	9		2				11		4			6			
40		10	CHARLTON ATHLETIC	2-0	Thomas, Draper	6202	7			1	5	10		8		3				2	9						12	11	4			6			14
41		12	Brentford	2-2	Devlin, Walker	8045	7			1	5	10		8		3					9						14	11	4			6			2
42		17	PORTSMOUTH	0-1		11014	7			1	5	10		8		3	12				9		2				11		4			6			14
43		24	SWINDON TOWN	1-1	Reeves	8382	12			1	5	10		8		3	7			9							11			2		6			4
44	May	1	Oxford United	1-1	Walker	6171	12			1	5	10		8		3	7			9							11			2		6			4
45		5	Derby County	0-2		13326	12			1	5	10		8		3	7			9					14		11			2		6			4
46		8	SUNDERLAND	3-1	Reeves, D Smith, Draper	14417	12			1	5	10		8		3	7			9							11		6	2					4
			Apps				29	16	2	44	21	32	11	44	2	37	28	8	8	17	31	9	1	31	3	20	37	5	37	20	8	12	22	32
			Goals				2	5			1	3		11			4	2	1	1				2		1	1	3	8		3	1	3	1	1

*Scorers in game 27: Matthews, D Smith 2(1p), Agana, Draper
Played in game 1: P Harding (14). In game 41, M Wells (12)

F.A. Cup

		Date	Opponent	Score		Att	Agana T	Bartlett K	Catlin R	Cherry S	Cox PR	Devlin P	Dijkstra M	Draper M	Dryden R	Johnson M	Lund G	Matthews R	Murphy S	O'Riordan D	Palmer C	Reeves D	Robinson D	Short, Chris	Short, Craig	Slawson S	Smith D	Smith M	Thomas D	Turner P	Turner R	Walker R	Williams A	Wilson K
R3	Jan	12	SUNDERLAND	0-2		8522	9			1				3			12	10		6			2			14	11		4		5		7	8

Coca Cola Cup

		Date	Opponent	Score	Scorers	Att																												
R2/1	Sep	22	WOLVERHAMPTON W.	3-2	Lund 2, Robinson	4197				1				7		4	9			6		5	2				10	11		3	8			
R2/2	Oct	7	Wolverhampton Wand.	1-0	O'Riordan	11146		10		1		11		7		5	9		12	6	2				4					3	8			
R3		27	CAMBRIDGE UNITED	2-3	Draper, Agana	3742	10			1		11		7			9			4			2					3	6			5	8	12

Anglo-Italian Cup

		Date	Opponent	Score	Scorers	Att																												
PR	Sep	2	Derby County	2-4	Craig Short, O'Riordan	6767		1					7		5			6			2	4	10	11		3	8		14			9	
PR		15	BARNSLEY	1-1	Palmer	2115				1			3	7		4	9		5	6	2						14	11		12	8			10

Played in first PR game: T Gallagher (no. 12)

1993/94

7th in Division One

							Agana T	Cherry S	Cox PR	Devlin P	Dijkstra M	Draper M	Foster CJ	Gallagher T	Johnson M	King P	Legg A	Lund G	Matthews R	McSwegan G	Murphy S	Palmer C	Reeves D	Reid P	Sherlock P	Short, Chris	Simpson M	Slawson S	Thomas D	Turner P	Walker R	Williams A	Wilson K
1	Aug	14	MIDDLESBROUGH	2-3	Draper(p), Lund	9392	1	5	7		8			3			11	12		9			10							4	6	14	2
2		21	Peterborough Utd.	1-1	Draper	6890		5	7		8			3			11	9					12							4	6	10	2
3		28	SUNDERLAND	1-0	Draper	9166		1	7		8			3			11	9								4	5	10			6		2
4	Sep	4	Tranmere Rovers	1-3	Simpson	6317		1	7		8			3			11	9					12			4	5	10			6		2
5		11	WEST BROMWICH ALB.	1-0	Draper	9870		1	7		8			3			11	9		12						4		10		5	6		2
6		18	Watford	1-3	Draper	6959		1	7	4	8			3				10		9			12			14		11		5	6		2
7		25	DERBY COUNTY	4-1	McSwegan 3, P Turner	11000	12	1		7	6	8					11	10		9				2						3	4	5	
8	Oct	2	Leicester City	2-3	Draper(p), McSwegan	16319		1	5	7		8					11	10		9				2						3	4	6	
9		9	BRISTOL CITY	2-0	McSwegan(p), Draper	6418		1		7		8		2			11	10		9	6									3	4	5	
10		16	Luton Town	0-1		6366		1	12	7		8		2	3		11	10		9	6					4					5		14
11		20	Millwall	0-2		5887	9	1	5	7				2	3		11	10		12										4	6		8
12		23	PORTSMOUTH	1-1	Walker	6683	12	1	5	7				2		3	11	10		9										8	4	6	
13		30	Nottingham Forest	0-1		26721	9	1		7		8		2	11	3		10		12										6	4	5	
14	Nov	2	Wolverhampton Wan.	0-3		15989	11	1	12	7		8		2	4	3		10		9										14	6	5	
15		6	CRYSTAL PALACE	3-2	McSwegan 2(1p), Lund	6904	11	1		6		8		2	4	3		10		9							12			14	5		
16		13	Charlton Athletic	1-5	Agana	7226	11	1		7		8		2	5	3		10	12											6	4		
17		20	STOKE CITY	2-0	Robinson, P Turner	9815	11	1		7		8		2	5	3		9												6			10
18		28	OXFORD UNITED	2-1	Devlin, Agana	5302	11	1		7		8		2	3			9												6	5		10
19	Dec	5	Crystal Palace	2-1	Devlin 2	13704	11	1		7		8		2	3			9			4									6	5		10
20		11	MILLWALL	1-3	Lund	6516	11	1		7		8		2	3			9		12	4									6	5		10
21		18	Middlesbrough	0-3		7869	11	1	2	7		8			3			9		12	4									6	5		10
22		27	Grimsby Town	2-2	Lund, Devlin	7781	11	1	2	7	5	8			3			9		10										4	6		
23	Jan	1	Bolton Wanderers	2-4	P Turner, Lund	11041		1	2	7	4	8			5			9	12	10							11			6			2
24		3	SOUTHEND UNITED	2-1	Draper, Dijkstra	6503		1	4	7	3	8			5			9	11	10										6			2
25		11	BIRMINGHAM CITY	2-1	Devlin, McSwegan	7212		1		7	3	8	5		4		10	9	11	12			2					6					
26		15	LUTON TOWN	1-2	Agana	6589	11	1		7	3	8	5		4		10	9		12										6			
27		22	Bristol City	2-0	Legg, Agana	7458	11	1		7		8	5				10	9												6			
28	Feb	5	Portsmouth	0-0		9359	11	1		7	6	8	5					9			2		10	3						4			
29		12	NOTTM. FOREST	2-1	McSwegan, Palmer	17911		1		7	14	8	5		6		12	9		11	2		10	3						4			
30		19	Birmingham City	3-2	McSwegan, Wilson, Legg	12913		1	12		3	8	5		6		11	9		10	2		7							4			14
31		22	PETERBOROUGH	2-1	McSwegan 2	6106		1	12		3	8	5				7	9		10	2			6						4			11
32	Mar	1	BARNSLEY	3-1	Draper 2, Lund	6297		1	2	7	3	8	5				11	9		10			6				12			4			
33		5	Sunderland	0-2		16269		1	2	7	3	8	5				11	9	12	10			6										4
34		12	WATFORD	1-0	Lund	6379		1	6	7		8		2			3	9		10				11						4	5		2
35		16	West Bromwich Alb.	1-1		14594		1	6	7		8			5		3	9	12	10				11						4			2
36		26	LEICESTER CITY	4-1	McSwegan, Matthews, Lund 2	11907		1				8			5		11	9	7	10	3	6								4			2
37		30	Southend United	0-1		3758		1			12	8			5		11	9	7	10	3	6								4			2
38	Apr	2	GRIMSBY TOWN	2-1	Matthews, Draper	7205		1		12		8			5		11	9	7	10	3	6								4			2
39		4	Barnsley	3-0	Devlin, Lund, McSwegan	6827		1		7		8			5		11	9		10	3	6								4			2
40		9	BOLTON WANDERERS	2-1	Murphy, Devlin	7270		1		7		8			5		11	9		10	3	6								4			2
41		12	TRANMERE ROVERS	0-0		6318		1		7		8			5		11	9	12	10	3	6								4			2
42		16	WOLVERHAMPTON W.	0-2		13438		1		7	5	8					11	9	10	12	3	6								4			2
43		20	Derby County	1-1	Draper	18602		1	6	7	5	8					11	9		12	3	6								4			
44		23	Stoke City	0-0		16453	10	1		7	5	8			12			9		11	3	6								4			2
45		30	CHARLTON ATHLETIC	3-3	Draper(p), Lund, McSwegan	7019	11	1		7		8			5			9		10	3	6								4			2
46	May	8	Oxford United	1-2	Draper	8487	7	1			4	8			5		11	9	12	10	3	6											2
			Apps				20	45	19	41	18	44	9	13	34	6	30	46	12	37	11	22	4	5	7	6	6	4	7	40	21	2	29
			Goals				4			7	1	14			2		11	2	15	1	1							1		3	1		1

R Catlin played in game 2, at 1
S Goater played in game 16 at 9
D Robinson played in games 17 and 18 at 4, scoring once
JP Gannon played in games 26 and 27, at 2. D Yates played in 46, at 14

F.A. Cup

R3	Jan	8	SUTTON UNITED	3-2	Draper, Agana, Devlin	6805	11	1	4	7	3	8			5		12	9	14	10										6			2
R4		29	WEST HAM UNITED	1-1	Lund	14952	11	1	14	7	6	8					10	9		12	5	2		3						4			
rep	Feb	9	West Ham United	0-1		23273		1		7	6	8			5		10	9	12	11	2			3						4			

R4 replay after extra time

Coca Cola Cup

1/1	Aug	17	HULL CITY	2-0	Lund, Cox	3003			5	7		8			3		11	10		9		14								12	6	4	2
1/2		24	Hull City	1-3	Draper	2222		1	5	7		8			3		11			9						12	14			10	6	4	2
2/1	Sep	22	Newcastle United	1-4	Srnicek(og)	25887		1		14	12	8			3			10		9			2	7				4	5	6			11
2/2	Oct	5	NEWCASTLE UTD.	1-7	McSwegan	6068	10	1	5	7	6	8					11	14		9			2					12	3	4			

Round 1 won on away goals   Played in R1/1: R Catlin (1)

Anglo-Italian Cup

PR	Aug	31	DERBY COUNTY	3-2	Legg 2, Lund	3276		1		7		8			3		11	9					4	5	10					6			2
PR	Sep	15	Nottingham Forest	1-1	Lund	7347		1		7	2	8			3		11	14		9						12	10		5	6			4
IR	Oct	12	ASCOLI	4-2	Legg, Lund 2, Draper	3756		1	12	7		8		2			11	10		9		6							3	4	5		
IR	Nov	9	PISA	3-2	Agana, Devlin, Lund	3253	11	1		7	9	8		2	5	3		10	14								12			4	6		
IR		16	Brescia	1-3	Draper	2000		1		7	8			2	5	3		10	9										11	4			
IR	Dec	22	Ascona	1-0	McSwegan	1000	11	1	2	7	4	8			5		9	10												6	3		12
SF1	Jan	26	Southend United	0-1		3706	10	1		7	6	8	5		2		11	9			4			3						6			
SF2	Feb	16	SOUTHEND UNITED	1-0	Devlin	5485		1		7	3	8	5		6		10	9		11	2			12						4			2
F	Mar	20	Brescia	0-1		17185	12	1		7	3	8			5		11	9		10	6									4			2

SF2 won 4-3 on penalties a.e.t. Final at Wembley Stadium

1994/95

24th in Division One (Relegated): Anglo-Italian Cup Winners

						Agana T	Butler PJF	Cherry S	Daniel R	Devlin P	Emenalo M	Gallagher T	Galloway M	Hogg GJ	Jemson NB	Johnson M	Legg A	Lund G	Marsden C	Matthews R	McSwegan G	Mills G	Murphy S	Nicol S	Reece PJ	Russell KJ	Sherlock P	Short, Chris	Simpson M	Turner P	Walker R	White DW	Williams JN	Yates D
1	Aug	13	Portsmouth	1-2	Sherlock	10487	7		1							3	8	9			10		5				12		11	4			
2		21	WOLVERHAMPTON W.	1-1	Simpson	8569	7		1		3						8	9		12	10		5						11	4			6
3		27	Sheffield United	3-1	Lund, McSwegan 2	15301	7		1		11	3					8	9			10		5						12	4			6
4		30	OLDHAM ATHLETIC	1-3	McSwegan	6604	7		1		11	3					8	9		12	10		5			2				4			6
5	Sep	3	SWINDON TOWN	0-1		6537	12		1		7	3					8	9		11	10		5							4			6
6		10	Bristol City	1-2	Jemson	6670			1			4	2			7	5	8	12		9	10									3			6
7		13	Barnsley	1-1	Lund	3928			1		9		2			7	5	8	12			10									4	3		6
8		17	STOKE CITY	0-2		8282			1		9	3	2			7	5	8	12			10									11	4			6
9		24	CHARLTON ATHLETIC	3-3	Agana,Lund,Sturgess(og)	5726	11		1		7					10	5	8	9			12		3			2				4			6
10	Oct	1	Reading	0-2		7465	11		1		7					10	3	8	9		12			2	6						4			5
11		8	PORT VALE	2-2	Williams, Agana	6903	11		1		7						3		9		12			2	6						4	8	10	5
12		15	Watford	1-3	Williams	7008	11	8	1		7						12	3	9					2	6				4			14	10	5
13		23	DERBY COUNTY	0-0		6390	11	8			7						12	6	9					2		1					4	3	10	5
14		29	Burnley	1-2	Davis (og)	12876	11	8		6	7		2					9			10					1					4	3	12	5
15	Nov	1	Southend United	0-1		4302	11	8		3	7		2					9				9	10			1		14			4	6	12	5
16		5	SUNDERLAND	3-2	Devlin 2, Legg	8890	11	8		3	7		2				6	10			9					1		12			4			5
17		19	Bolton Wanderers	0-2		11698	11	8		3	7						6			12	10	9		2	5	1					4			
18		26	WEST BROMWICH ALB.	2-0	Turner, Lund	10088	11	8	1	3	7	10					6		9					2							4			5
19	Dec	3	Derby County	0-0		14278	11	8	1		7						6	3	9					10	2	12					4			5
20		6	TRANMERE ROVERS	1-0	Devlin	4703	11	8	1		7						6	3		9	4			10	2	12								5
21		10	Wolverhampton Wan.	0-1		25786	11	8	1		7					14	6	3	9	10				2	12					4				5
22		17	PORTSMOUTH	0-1		6383	11	8	1		7					12	6	3	9	10				2	14					4				5
23		26	MILLWALL	0-1		6758	11	8	1		7						6	3						10	2					4		9		5
24		28	Middlesbrough	1-2	McSwegan	21558	11	8	1							12	6	3		7	14	10	2	5						4		9		
25		31	LUTON TOWN	0-1		6249		8	1		7					14	6	3		10	12	11	2	5						4		9		
26	Jan	14	BURNLEY	3-0	Devlin, White, McSwegan	8698	12	8	1		7						6	3		11	10		2	5						4		9		
27		21	Sunderland	2-1	Lund, Matthews	14334		8			7						6	3	9		11			2	5	10					4		12		
28		28	Grimsby Town	1-2	White	5161		8			7						6	3	9		11			2	5	10					4		12		
29	Feb	4	Tranmere Rovers	2-3	Legg, Devlin (p)	6105	9				7				6		11	3		8			2	5	10					12	4		14		
30		7	BOLTON WANDERERS	1-1	Matthews	7374	9				7				6		11	3			12			2	5	10					8	4				
31		11	SOUTHEND UNITED	2-2	Legg, Matthews	6768	9				7				6		11	3	14	8			2	5	10					12	4				
32		18	West Bromwich Alb.	2-3	Devlin 2	13748					7				6		11	3	12	8	9		2	5	10					14	4				
33		25	READING	1-0	Agana	7184	12				7				6		14	11		8			2	5		9					10	4				
34	Mar	4	Charlton Athletic	0-1		13863	11				7				6		14						2	5	10	9		8			4		12		
35		11	SHEFFIELD UNITED	2-1	Simpson, White	11102	12				7				6			11					2	5	10	9				14	4		8		
36		14	Oldham Athletic	1-1	Devlin	5465	12				7				6			11					2	5	10	9		14			4		8		
37		21	BRISTOL CITY	1-1	White	5692	9		1		7				6		14	11					2		10	4		3		12			8		
38		25	Stoke City	1-2	White	10170			1		7	9			6			11					14	5	10		12	2			4		8		
39	Apr	1	BARNSLEY	1-3	Devlin	6834			1		7				6		14	11		9	3			10		2					4		8		
40		8	Luton Town	0-2		6428			1			12		14			11						3	5	10	9				2	7	4	8		
41		15	MIDDLESBROUGH	1-1	White	9377	12							11	6								3	5	10	1	9			2	7	4	8		
42		19	Millwall	0-0		5471						14		11	6		12						3	5	10	1	9			2	7	4	8		
43		22	GRIMSBY TOWN	0-2		5286		4				12		11	6		14						3	5	10	1	9			2	7		8		
44		29	WATFORD	1-0	White	5083		4				9		11	6						14		3	5	10	1		12		2	7		8		
45	May	3	Swindon Town	0-3		8262		4				9		11	6						12		3	5	10	1				2	7		8		
46		7	Port Vale	1-1	McSwegan	9452								11	6						9		3	5	10	1				2	7	4	8		
			Apps				31	20	25	5	40	7	7	7	17	11	31	34	23	7	18	22	34	35	19	11	11	5	13	19	38	7	20	5	21
			Goals				3				9					1		3	5		3	6							1		2	1		7	2	

CR Hoyle played in games 1,2 and 40 at 2, 2 and 6 respectively
PR Cox played in games 4-6 at 2, 6 and 2
M Kuhl played in games 6 and 7 at 11
JB Kearton played in games 27 -36 at 1 (10 games). M Forsyth played at 3 in games 33 to 36, 38 and at 5 in games 37 and 39 (7 appearances).
S Slawson played in game 39 (at 12). ID Ridgway in game 45 (14).

Two own goals

F.A. Cup

R3	Jan	8	MANCHESTER CITY	2-2	White, Matthews	12376		8	1		7					6	3			11	10	2	5							4		9		
rep		18	Manchester City	2-5	McSwegan, Matthews	14261		8	1		7					6	3	12		11	10	2	5							4		9		

Coca Cola Cup

2/1	Sep	20	Bristol City	1-0	Devlin	2546	14		1		7					12	5	8	9			10		3			2		11	4				6
2/2		27	BRISTOL CITY	3-0	Lund 2, Jemson	2721	11		1		7					10	3	8	9		12			2	6					4				5
R3	Oct	26	TOTTENHAM HOTSPUR	3-0	McSwegan 2, Agana	16952	11	8			7					6	9			14	10	2	12		1					4	3			5
R4	Nov	30	Norwich C	0-1		14030	11	8	1		7					6	3	9			10	2								4				5

Anglo-Italian Cup

PR	Aug	24	Ascoli	1-1	Devlin	1300	10		1		7	3						9		12			6				8			11	4			5
PR	Sep	6	LECCE	1-0	Turner	2495	9				7	3	2			5	8			11	10				1					12	4				6
PR	Oct	5	Atalanta	1-1	Agana	2300	11		1			3				10		12	9	7		2	6							4	8			5
PR	Nov	15	VENEZIA	3-3	Devlin, Marsden, Murphy	2861	11	8		3	7	2				6				10	9		12		1					4				5
SF1	Jan	24	STOKE CITY	0-0		5135		8			7					6	3	9		12			2	5	10					4		11		
SF2		31	Stoke City	0-0		10741	9	8			14			6		12	3						2	5	10						7	4	11		
F	Mar	19	Ascoli	2-1	Agana, White	11704	9		1		7	12	14			6	11						3	5		13			2	10	4	8		

SF2 after extra time. County won 3-2 on penalties
Final played at Wembley Stadium
Played in first PR game; CR Hoyle (2), PR Cox (14). Played in SF1 amd SF2; JB Kearton (1). Played in SF1; S Slawson (14)

1995/96

4th in Division Two

#		Date	Opponent	Score	Scorers	Att	Agana T	Arkins V	Ashcroft L	Baraclough IR	Battersby A	Derry SP	Devlin P	Finnan SJ	Gallagher T	Galloway M	Hogg GI	Hunt JM	Jemson NB	Jones G	Legg A	Marsden C	Martindale G	McSwegan G	Mills G	Murphy S	Nicol S	Richardson IG	Rogers PA	Short, Chris	Simpson M	Strodder GI	Turner P	Walker R	Ward D	White DW	Wilder CJ
1	Aug	12	Wrexham	1-1	Turner	4338	10						7			6					11	8			12	2						5	4	3	1	9
2		19	WYCOMBE WANDERERS	2-0	Legg, White	5552	10						7			6					11	8			12	2						5	4	3	1	9
3		26	Peterborough United	1-0	White	5618	12						7		8			10			11				2		6				14	5	4	3	1	9
4		29	BRADFORD CITY	0-2		6168							7		8			10			11				12	2	6					5	4	3	1	9
5	Sep	2	Brighton & Hove Albion	0-1		5267	10						7						12		11	8			2		6					5	4	3	1	9
6		9	BOURNEMOUTH	2-0	White 2 (1p)	4875	12						7		2						11				8		6				10	5	4	3	1	9
7		12	STOCKPORT COUNTY	1-0	Devlin	4588	14						7		2	12					11				8		6				10	5	4	3	1	9
8		16	Shrewsbury Town	1-0	White	2892	14	12					7		2	8					11				6						10	5	4	3	1	9
9		23	BRISTOL CITY	2-2	Legg, White	5251	14	10							2	8					11				6		4				12	7	5		3	1	9
10		30	Crewe Alexandra	2-2	Agana, White	4260	11	10							2	8					12				6		4				14	7	5		3	1	9
11	Oct	7	Carlisle United	0-0		6058	11	12					7		2	8					4				6							10	5		3	1	9
12		14	ROTHERHAM UNITED	2-1	Devlin, Gallagher	5480		10	3				7		2						11				6		4					8	5			1	9
13		21	Bristol Rovers	3-0	Nicol, Arkins, Legg	6062		10	3				7		2						11				12	6	4					8	5			1	9
14		28	SWINDON TOWN	1-3	Legg	8725		10	3				7		2						11				6		4					8	5			1	9
15	Nov	1	BRENTFORD	4-0	Devlin, Arkins 2, Murphy	3958	13	10					7		2	12					11				14	6	4					8	5			1	9
16		4	Burnley	4-3	Arkins, Devlin 2(1p), Baraclough	10511	12	10	3					9	7						11				2	6	4					8	5			1	
17		18	CHESTERFIELD	4-1	Gallagher, Strodder, Nicol, Arkins	6747		10	3					9	7						11				2	6	4					8	5			1	
18		25	Swansea City	0-0		2327		10	3					9	7						11				2	6						8	5	4		1	
19	Dec	9	Bristol City	2-0	Strodder, White	5617	14	10	3					9	7						11				2	6						8	5	4		1	12
20		16	CREWE ALEXANDRA	0-1		5869		10	3					9	7						11				2	6						8	5	4		1	12
21		23	BLACKPOOL	1-1	Arkins	5522		10	3				7				6				11				2	8					12	5	4		1	9
22	Jan	13	Wycombe Wanderers	1-1	Rogers	4908			3	10			8		2		6				11				4			7				5			1	9
23		20	WREXHAM	2-1	Arkins	5014		12	3	10			9		14						11				4		6	8				5			1	7	2
24	Feb	3	PETERBOROUGH UTD.	1-0	Battersby	5067		9	5	10	8						4				11				3		6	7		12					1		2
25		10	Walsall	0-0		4378	11	9		3	10		7		2		6								5		8								1		4
26		17	Stockport County	0-2		6179	11	10	3				9		7										4		8					6	5			1	2
27		24	SHREWSBURY TOWN	1-1	Rogers	4559			10	3	12		9		7						11				4		8					6	5			1	2
28		27	Bournemouth	2-0	Devlin, Hunt	3191	11		3	10	9				7		6								4		8						5			1	2
29	Mar	2	HULL CITY	1-0	Battersby	4528	11		3	10					7				9						4		8				12	5			1	2
30		6	WALSALL	2-1	Battersby, Jones	4050	11	12	3	10			7				6		9						4		8						5			1	
31		9	Blackpool	0-1		7187	11		3	10					12		6		9				7		4		8						5			1	
32		12	YORK CITY	2-2	Jones, Battersby	3462	11		3	10	2		7		8		6		9				12		4								5			1	
33		16	OXFORD UNITED	1-1	Martindale	5140	11		3	10	2		7				6		9				12		4		8						5			1	
34		19	Bradford City	0-1		3622	11	2	3	10			7		12		6		9				7		4		8						5			1	
35		23	York City	3-1	Martindale 2, Jones	3126			3		2		7				11		9				10		4		6	8					5			1	
36		26	Hull City	0-0		2589			3		2		7			4	6		9				10				11	8					5			1	
37		30	CARLISLE UNITED	3-1	Jones 2, Martindale	4515			11	3	12	2	7			4			9				10				6	8					5			1	
38	Apr	2	Rotherham United	0-2		3232			11	3		2	7						9				10		4		6	8					5			1	
39		6	Swindon Town	0-1		12311			11	3	14	2	7		12		6		9				10		4			8	7	5			1				
40		9	BRISTOL ROVERS	4-2	* See below	4661	12		11	3	14		7						9				10		4		6	8				5			1		2
41		13	Brentford	0-0		4588	11			3	12		7						9				10		4		6	8				5			1		2
42		16	Oxford United	1-1	Murphy	6934	11	12	3	14	2		7						9				10		4		6	8				5			1		
43		20	BURNLEY	1-1	Battersby	5697	11		14	3	12	2	7						9				10		4		6	8				5			1		
44		23	BRIGHTON & HOVE ALB	2-1	Battersby 2	3501	11			3	10	2	7			5	8		9				12		4		6		14				1				
45		27	SWANSEA CITY	4-0	Murphy, Agana, Martindale, Finnan	5051	11			3	10	2	7						12				9		4		6	8				5			1		
46	May	4	Chesterfield	0-1		6708	11		14	12	3	10	2	7						13			9		4		6	8							1		
			Apps				29	23	6	35	21	12	26	17	22	9	10	10	3	18	25	3	16	3	13	39	13	15	21	2	23	43	12	11	46	20	9
			Goals				2	7		2	7		6	2	2			1		5	4		6			3	2		2			3	1			8	

Scorers in game 40: Strodder, Martindale, Baraclough, Finnan
Played in games 30 (at 2) and 31 (at 2, substituted): CR Hoyle

Play Offs

		Date	Opponent	Score	Scorers	Att																													
SF1	May	12	Crewe Alexandra	2-2	Finnan, Martindale	4931	11			3	10	2	7							9			12		4		6	8				5			1		
SF2		15	CREWE ALEXANDRA	1-0	Martindale	9640	11			3	10	2	7										9		4		6	8				5			1		
F		26	Bradford City	0-2		39972	11			3	10	2	7						12				9		4		6	8				5			1		

Final at Wembley Stadium

F.A. Cup

		Date	Opponent	Score	Scorers	Att																													
R1	Nov	12	York City	1-0	Legg	4228		10	3					9	7						11				2	6	4					8	5			1	
R2	Dec	2	Telford United	2-0	Gallagher, Legg	2831		10	3					9	7						11				2	6						8	5	4		1	12
R3	Jan	6	MIDDLESBROUGH	1-2	Rogers	12621	13	10	3				9		2		6				11					8		7			12	5	4		1	14

Coca Cola Cup

		Date	Opponent	Score	Scorers	Att																													
R1/1	Aug	15	LINCOLN CITY	2-0	White 2	3494	10						7			6					11	8			12	2						5	4	3	1	9
R1/2		22	Lincoln City	2-0	White 2	2636										6		10			11				2		8					7	5	4	3	1	9
R2/1	Sep	20	Leeds United	0-0		12384	10	12					7						6		11				5					2	8		4	3	1	9
R2/2	Oct	3	LEEDS UNITED	2-3	White 2 (1p)	12477	11	10						7	8				12		4				6					2		5		3	1	9

Auto Windscreens Shield

		Date	Opponent	Score	Scorers	Att																													
R1	Oct	17	Chesterfield	1-2	White	2150	11	10						14	4	7		13			12				5			2	8				3	1	9		
R1	Nov	7	STOCKPORT COUNTY	1-0	Devlin	2015	11	10					9		7	6		13			3		2		4			12	8	5				1	14		
R2		27	Doncaster Rovers	3-1	Murphy, Agana, Devlin	1714	10						9		7	8	4				3		2		6							5			1	12	
QF	Jan	9	York City	0-1		2075	14	11			10		9			12	6				3				2	4			8		7	5			1		

Played in R1: MI Redmile (at 6)

1996/97

Bottom of Division Two: Relegated

#		Date	Opponent	Score	Scorers	Att	Agana T	Arkins V	Baraclough IR	Battersby A	Cunnington SG	Derry SP	Dudley CB	Farrell SP	Finnan SJ	Gallagher T	Galloway M	Hendon IM	Hogg GI	Hunt JM	Jones G	Kennedy PHJ	Martindale G	Mendez G	Murphy S	Nogan LM	Pollitt MF	Redmile MJ	Regis D	Richardson IG	Ridgway JD	Robinson PJ	Rogers PA	Simpson M	Strodder GJ	Walker R	Ward D	White DW	Wilder CJ	Wilkes T
1	Aug	17	PRESTON NORTH END	2-1	Jones, Martindale	6879		<u>10</u>	3	13		2							6		12	11	9									<u>8</u>			7	5		1		4	
2		24	Stockport County	0-0		5271		<u>10</u>	3	12									6			11	9	4							7	8			5			1		2	
3		31	YORK CITY	0-1		4600		<u>10</u>	3	12									<u>6</u>			11	13	9	4							7	8			5			1		2	
4	Sep	7	Plymouth Argyle	0-0		8109	11		3			4							6			10	7	12	5								8						1		2	9
5		10	WATFORD	2-3	Martindale (p), Robinson	3660	10		3	13		4							6			<u>11</u>	7	12	5								8						1		2	9
6		14	MILLWALL	1-2	Baraclough	4473	11		<u>9</u>	3	12	4							6			10	7		5								8						1		2	
7		21	Bournemouth	1-0	Jones	3678	11	9	3			4							6			<u>10</u>	7	12	5								8					13	1		2	
8		28	WREXHAM	0-0		4216	11	<u>9</u>	3	13		4							6			<u>10</u>	7	12	5								8						1		2	
9	Oct	1	Gillingham	0-1		5583	12		3	<u>10</u>		<u>4</u>							6			13	7	11	5							9	8						1		2	
10		5	Wycombe Wanderers	0-1		4606	13	9	3			<u>4</u>							6				7	12	5							10	8						1		2	11
11		8	Peterborough United	3-1	Agana, Heald(og), Martindale	5456	11	<u>9</u>	3			4							6			12	7	10	5								8						1		2	
12		12	BRISTOL ROVERS	1-1	Agana	4558	11	<u>9</u>			12	4							6			13	7	10	5								8			3			1		2	
13		15	CHESTERFIELD	0-0		4265	<u>10</u>	12				4		9					6			13	11	<u>8</u>	5								7			3			1		2	
14		19	Burnley	0-1		9368				12		4		9					6				7	13	5								8			<u>3</u>			1		11	
15		26	Bristol City	0-4		9540	12		3	<u>9</u>		4			7				6	8		10	11		5															1		2	
16		29	WALSALL	2-0	Strodder, Agana	3127	11					8		10					6				7	9	4											5	3		1		2	
17	Nov	2	SHREWSBURY TOWN	1-2	Derry	4363	<u>11</u>					8		9	13				6			12	7	<u>10</u>	5											4	3	1			2	
18		9	Luton Town	0-2		6134	11					6		9					4			10	7										8				5	3	1			2	
19		23	Blackpool	0-1		3598	13	9				2			11				4	12		10	<u>7</u>								6		8				5	3	1				
20		30	BRISTOL CITY	2-0	Arkins, Robinson	4693	12	9	3			6			11				4			10	<u>7</u>										8				5		1			2	
21	Dec	3	Brentford	0-2		3675		9	3	12		6			7				4			<u>10</u>	11										8				5		1			2	
22		14	ROTHERHAM UNITED	0-0		3954	11	9	3			6			7				4			<u>10</u>	12										8				5		1			2	
23		20	Crewe Alexandra	0-3		3125	10	12	3			<u>6</u>			7				4				11	9				5						8					1			2	
24		26	Watford	0-0		9065	11		3					9	7				4				10					5		6	12	8						1			2	
25	Jan	11	Wrexham	3-3	Farrell, Martindale 2 (1p)	3272	12		3			6		10	7	8			13			<u>11</u>	9		4												5		1			2	
26		18	GILLINGHAM	1-1	Martindale (p)	5008	<u>11</u>		3	13		6		<u>10</u>	7				12				9		4									8			5		1			2	
27		25	Walsall	1-3	Battersby	3261	11		3	9		6		12	<u>7</u>				10						4									8			5	13	1			2	
28	Feb	1	LUTON TOWN	1-2	Richardson	4866			3	9		7			13				<u>6</u>			<u>8</u>	12		4					<u>10</u>	14	11			5			1		2	
29		4	BOURNEMOUTH	0-2		2757			3	10		2			13	14			6			<u>9</u>	12		4					11		8			5			1		7	
30		8	Shrewsbury Town	1-2	Regis	2692	<u>10</u>		3	12					13	7			6						4	9		11	8							5		1			2	
31		15	BLACKPOOL	1-1	Butler (og)	5281			3	<u>9</u>			12	13		7			6								10	4				11			<u>8</u>	5		1			2	
32		22	Bury	0-2		3430			3	13			12		9				<u>7</u>								10	1	4				11	8			5					2	
33		25	Millwall	0-1		5907			12	13			7		<u>9</u>	8		2	6								10	1	4				11				5					<u>3</u>	
34	Mar	1	BRENTFORD	1-1	Strodder	4323							7		12	8		2	6								<u>10</u>	1	4	<u>9</u>		11			13	5					<u>3</u>	
35		8	CREWE ALEXANDRA	0-1		4047			3				7			8		2	6				13				<u>10</u>	1	4	<u>9</u>	11	12				5						
36		15	Rotherham United	2-2	Regis, Redmile	2605			3		12	7	13					2	6								<u>10</u>	1	4	<u>9</u>	11								8	5		
37		22	STOCKPORT COUNTY	1-2	Baraclough	4238			3				12		11			2	6	8					1	4	9			<u>7</u>											10	5	
38		25	BURY	0-1		3036			3	13			12		7			2	<u>6</u>						14		1	4	10	<u>11</u>		8									<u>9</u>	5	
39		29	Preston North End	0-3		9472			3				10						<u>6</u>				12	<u>11</u>			4	13	14	7	8						5	2	1			<u>9</u>	
40		31	PETERBOROUGH UTD.	0-0		3848			3		8	6	10											<u>11</u>			4	13		7	12						5	2	1			<u>9</u>	
41	Apr	5	York City	2-1	Dudley, Redmile	3115				8	6	10	12		3												4	13		7	<u>11</u>				5	2	1			<u>9</u>	
42		12	WYCOMBE WANDERERS	1-2	Derry	4290			3	8	6	10			<u>7</u>				4				12				4			<u>9</u>		13	11			5	2	1	14			
43		15	PLYMOUTH ARGYLE	2-1	Heathcote (og), Jones	2423			3	<u>8</u>	<u>9</u>				7				2			13	11				4					12				5	6	1	<u>10</u>			
44		20	Bristol Rovers	0-1		6309			3	8	<u>9</u>	14			7				2			11	<u>10</u>				4						12			5	<u>6</u>	1	13			
45		26	BURNLEY	1-1	Dudley	4591			<u>3</u>		8	11	13					2			7	10	<u>9</u>				4			12						5	14	1				
46	May	3	Chesterfield	0-1		5736			3		<u>8</u>	11	<u>10</u>		7			2	6		9	12				1	<u>4</u>		13						5						

Played in one game: WJ Diuk (46, at 14), C Ludlam (14, at 2, subbed), PR Mitchell (45, at 6)

	Apps	23	15	38	18	8	39	10	14	23	1		5	12	35	9	27	22	28	3	16	6	8	23	10	19	6	37	1	1	28	16	38	9	37	3
	Goals	3	1	2	1		2	2	1						3		6					2	2	1		2			2								

One own goal

F.A. Cup

			Opponent	Score	Scorers	Att																																	
R1	Nov	17	Newcastle Town	2-0	Kennedy, Robinson	3918		13				6			10	7			4	12	<u>9</u>	11			5					8							<u>3</u>	1		2	
R2	Dec	7	ROCHDALE	3-1	Jones, Arkins, Agana	3584	13	<u>9</u>	3	12		6			7				4		10	<u>11</u>									8		5					1		2	
R3	Jan	14	ASTON VILLA	0-0		13315	<u>11</u>		3	12		<u>6</u>		<u>10</u>	7		14					9			4						8		5	13	1			2			
rep		22	Aston Villa	0-3		25006	<u>11</u>		3			<u>6</u>		10	7		13					9			4						8		5	12	1			2			

R1 played at Stoke City

Coca Cola Cup

| R1/1 | Aug | 20 | BURY | 1-1 | Jones | 2141 | | <u>10</u> | 3 | | | 2 | | | | | | | 6 | | | 11 | | 9 | | | | | | | 7 | 8 | | | 5 | | | 1 | | 4 | |
| R1/2 | Sep | 3 | Bury | 0-1 | | 2571 | | 12 | 3 | 10 | | 2 | | | | | | | | | | 11 | 9 | | 6 | | | | | | | <u>7</u> | 8 | | | 5 | | | 1 | | 4 | |

Auto Windscreens Shield

| R1 | Dec | 9 | Scarborough | 1-0 | Martindale (p) | 952 | | | 3 | | | | | <u>7</u> | 12 | | | | 8 | | | 9 | | | 1 | 4 | | | 11 | 13 | 6 | | | | 5 | | | <u>2</u> | | 10 | |
| R2 | Jan | 28 | Scunthorpe United | 1-1 | Hunt | 1076 | | | | | | <u>9</u> | | | 2 | 7 | | 5 | 6 | | | 14 | 10 | | | 1 | | | <u>8</u> | 12 | | 4 | | | 3 | | | | | 13 | |

R2 a.e.t.. Lost 2-4 on penalties. Played at 11 (substituted) in R2: AR Roddie

1997/98

Champions of Division Three: Promoted

#	Date		Opponent	Score	Scorers	Att	Baraclough IR	Cunnington SG	Derry SP	Diuk WJ	Dudley CB	Dyer AC	Farrell SP	Finnan SJ	Hendon IM	Hogg GJ	Hughes AJ	Jackson JJ	Jones G	Kiwomya AD	Lormor A	Martindale G	Mitchell PR	Otto R	Pearce DA	Pollitt MF	Poric A	Redmile MI	Richardson IG	Robinson PJ	Robson M	Strodder GI	Ward D	White DW
1	Aug	9	ROCHDALE	2-1	Robson (p), Redmile	4173	12		6		9			7	2				10						3			4	13	8	11	5	1	14
2		16	Hull City	3-0	Redmile, White, Jones	7412	13	11	6					7	2				10						3			4	12	8		5	1	9
3		23	LINCOLN CITY	1-2	White	5707	11				12			7	2	5			10			13			3			4	6	8			1	9
4		30	Cardiff City	1-1	Finnan	6191	11		12					7	2	5			10			13			3			4	6	8			1	9
5	Sep	2	Hartlepool United	1-1	Baraclough (p)	2010	11		6					7	2	5			10						3			4	12	8			1	9
6		7	SCUNTHORPE UNITED	2-1	Redmile, Derry	5009	6		7	12					2				10		9		11		3			4		8		5	1	
7		13	MANSFIELD TOWN	1-0	Martindale	6706	6		7		14					13	2		10		9		11	3				4		8		5	1	12
8		20	Shrewsbury Town	2-1	Jones, Finnan	2532	6	8	7		13					12	2		10		9		11	3				4	14			5	1	
9		27	Scarborough	2-1	Baraclough (p), Farrell	2751	6		7		9			12	11	2			10						3			4	8	13		5	1	
10	Oct	4	DARLINGTON	1-1	Dudley	4428	6		7		9			12	11	2			13	10					3			4	8			5	1	
11		11	MACCLESFIELD T	1-1	Richardson	4871	6		7		9			12	13	2			14	10			11	3				4	8			5	1	
12		18	Swansea City	2-1	Jones, Jackson	3668	3		7					9	11			13	10			12					4	6		8	5	1	
13		21	Rotherham United	1-1	Farrell	3161	4		6					9	7	2		12	10			13			3					8	11	5	1	
14		25	CAMBRIDGE UNITED	1-0	Jones	4279	4		7					9	11	2			10			12			3					8	6	5	1	
15	Nov	1	Barnet	2-1	Baraclough, Derry	2530	6		8					9	7	2			10			12			3				4	13	11	5	1	
16		4	CHESTER CITY	1-2	Strodder	3104	6		8					9	7	2			10			12			3				4	13	11	5	1	
17		8	EXETER CITY	1-1	Strodder	5107	6		8		10			9	7	2				13					3			12	4		11	5	1	
18		18	Colchester United	0-2		2635	11		8						7	2		6		10	9			13	3			4	12			5	1	
19		22	Leyton Orient	1-1	Farrell	4321	6		8					9	7	2		12		10								4	3	13	11	5	1	
20		29	PETERBOROUGH UTD.	2-2	Jones, Robson	8006	6		8		13			9	7	2			10									4	3	12	11	5	1	
21	Dec	3	Brighton & Hove Albion	1-0	Farrell	1239	3		8		13			9	7	2			10			12						4		6	11	5	1	
22		13	DONCASTER ROVERS	5-2	*see below	4024	6		8					9	7	2			10	14		13			3			4		12	11	5	1	
23		20	Torquay United	2-0	Farrell 2	2536	6		8					9	7	2			10	13		12			3			4		14	11	5	1	
24		26	Scunthorpe United	2-1	Jones 2	4781	6		8					9	7	2			10			13			3			4		12	11	5	1	
25		28	HARTLEPOOL UNITED	2-0	Farrell 2	6073	6		8					9	7	2			10						3			4		12	11	5	1	
26	Jan	10	Rochdale	2-1	Jones, Robinson	2387	6		8					9	7	2			10			12			3			4	5		11		1	
27		17	CARDIFF CITY	3-1	Robinson, Jones 2	6214	6		8					9	7	2			10			12			3			4	5		11		1	
28		20	HULL CITY	1-0	Richardson	4017	6		8					9	7				10						3			4	5	11	2	1		
29		24	Lincoln City	5-3	Farrell 2,Baraclough,Strodder,Jones	6059	6		11					9	7				10			12			3			2	4	8		5	1	
30		31	Mansfield Town	2-0	Jones 2	6786	6							9	7	2	12		10						3			11	4	8		5	1	
31	Feb	7	SHREWSBURY TOWN	1-1	Jones	5790	6							9	7	2	12		10						3			11	4	8		5	1	
32		14	Darlington	2-0	Jones, Finnan	2781	6	12						9	7	2			10						3			11	4	8		5	1	
33		21	SCARBOROUGH	1-0	Farrell	5645	6	12						9	7	2				14			10	13	3			11	4	8		5	1	
34		24	SWANSEA CITY	2-1	Jones 2	4484	3	6						9	7	2			10			13	12					11	4	8		5	1	
35		28	Macclesfield Town	0-2		5112	6				13			9	7		5					2	3			1		11	4	8	12			
36	Mar	3	Exeter City	5-2	Robson, Farrell 2, Jones 2	2966	6				13	3		9	7	2	5		10	12				1				4	8	11				
37		7	BARNET	2-0	Jones, Hughes	6081	6					3		9	7	2	5		10	13								4	8	11	12			
38		14	Chester City	1-0	Jones	2753	6					3		9	7	2	5	14	10	13								4	8	11	12			
39		21	COLCHESTER UNITED	0-0		6284		12				6	9	7	2		4	14	10			13			3					8	11	5	1	
40		28	LEYTON ORIENT	1-0	Robson	8389						6	9	7	2		4	13	10						3		12			8	11	5	1	
41	Apr	3	Peterborough United	0-1		6498						6	9	7	2		11	12	10						3			13	4	8		5	1	
42		11	BRIGHTON & HOVE ALB	2-2	Hughes, Jones	5344					13	6		7			11	9	10						3	2		4		8	12	5	1	
43		13	Doncaster Rovers	2-1	Strodder, Finnan	2485		13			12	2		7			6	9	10						3			4		8	11	5	1	
44		18	TORQUAY UNITED	3-0	Pearce, Jones 2	5183	13				12			2	7		6	9	10				14		3			4		8	11	5	1	
45		25	Cambridge United	2-2	Jones 2	4009				13		6	9	7			8	14	10						3	2		4		12	11	5	1	
46	May	2	ROTHERHAM UNITED	5-2	Jones 2, Pearce, Farrell, Robinson	12431						2	9				6	12	10						3	7		4		8	11	5	1	

Scorers in game 22: Baraclough 2 (1p), Utley (og), Finnan, Farrell

	Apps	38	9	28	1	17	10	35	44	38	4	15	15	44	2	7	22	1	4	38	2	4	34	30	40	28	39	44	6
	Goals	6		2		1		15	5			2	1	28			1			2			3	2	3	4	4		2

One own goal

F.A. Cup

	Date		Opponent	Score	Scorers	Att																											
R1	Nov	16	COLWYN BAY	2-0	Hogg, Richardson	3074			14		10			9	7	13	2		12						3			4	6	8	11	5	1	
R2	Dec	6	Preston North End	2-2	Finnan, Derry	7583	3		8		14			7	2				13	9		10						12		4		6	11	5	1	
rep		16	PRESTON NORTH END	1-2	Farrell	3052	6		8		13			9	7	2			10			14			3				4		12	11	5	1	

Coca Cola Cup

	Date		Opponent	Score	Scorers	Att																											
R1/1	Aug	12	Darlington	1-1	White	2189	12		6					7	2				10						3			4		8	11	5	1	9
R1/2		26	DARLINGTON	2-1	Baraclough (p), Hendon	1925	11			12				7	2	6			10			13			3			4	8			5	1	9
R2/1	Sep	16	TRANMERE ROVERS	0-2		1779	6	13	14		12			7	2				10				11		3			4		8		5	1	9
R2/2		23	Tranmere Rovers	1-0	Dudley	3287	3	6	8		10			9	7	2	12		13					11				4	5				1	

R1/2 a.e.t.   Played at 14 in R2/2: SD Stevens

Auto Windscreens Shield

	Date		Opponent	Score		Att																											
R1	Jan	27	Burnley	0-2		2442	6	8		14						10		11	9	2		3			4		5	7				1		

Played at 12: T Henshaw. At 13, D Randall.

1998/99

16th in Division Two

					Beadle PCWJ	Billy CA	Bolland PG	Creaney GT	Dudley CB	Dyer AC	Fairclough CH	Farrell SP	Finnan SJ	Garcia A	Grant KT	Hendon IM	Holmes R	Hughes AJ	Jackson JJ	Jones G	Liburd RJ	Matthews LJ	Murray S	Owers G	Pearce DA	Quayle M	Rapley KJ	Redmile MJ	Richardson IG	Robson M	Stallard M	Strodder GJ	Tierney F	Torpey SDJ	Ward D	Warren MW
1	Aug	8	Oldham Athletic	3-1	Richardson, Farrell 2	5709		14				5	9			2		8			10	12		11	7	3			4	6					13	1
2		15	BOURNEMOUTH	1-2	Hendon (p)	5269	7				3	5	9			2		8			10	12		11	6				4		14				13	1
3		22	Northampton Town	1-1	Torpey	6141				12	13	5				2		8			10	3		11	7				4	6					9	1
4		29	MANCHESTER CITY	1-1	Hendon (p)	10316						5	12	13		2		8	9		3			11	7				4	6					10	1
5		31	Macclesfield Town	1-0	Hendon	3148	13					5	12	6		2		8			10	3		11	7				4						9	1
6	Sep	5	WIGAN ATHLETIC	0-1		4445	12					5		6		2		8			10	3		11	7				4						9	
7		8	Blackpool	0-1		3849	6				2	5	9					8		13	10	3		11	7		12		4							1
8		12	FULHAM	1-0	Murray	5805	8					5		6		2			12	13	10	3		11	7		9						4			1
9		18	Walsall	2-3	Jones, Hughes	3991					14	5		6		2		8	13	10	3		11	7		9		12					4			1
10		26	MILLWALL	3-1	Murray, Hendon (p), Jones	5016					12	5		6	13	2		8		10	3	9		11	7								4			1
11	Oct	3	Wycombe Wanderers	1-1	Strodder	4164					3	5		6	14	2		8			10	12	9	11	7						13		4			1
12		10	LINCOLN CITY	2-3	Hendon (p), Hughes	6458						5	13	6	7	2		8			10	3	9	11	12								4			1
13		17	Burnley	1-1	Pearce	10559			12					6	7			8			10	3	9			11		5					4			1
14		20	Chesterfield	0-3		4506							9	6	7	2		8			10	3	14	13	12	11		5					4			1
15		24	BRISTOL ROVERS	1-1	Garcia	4822						5	9	6	8	2			12		13	3		7	11				4							1
16		31	STOKE CITY	1-0	Farrell	8546						5	9	6	8	2					12			11	7	3			4							1
17	Nov	7	York City	1-1	Fairclough	3391						5	9	6	8	2		12			13			11	7	3			4							1
18		21	COLCHESTER UNITED	1-3	Murray	4598						5			13	2		8	14	10	12			11	7	3			4	6						1
19		28	Wrexham	0-1		2811								8		2		5			10			11	7	3			4	6						1
20	Dec	12	PRESTON NORTH END	2-3	Kidd (og), Richardson	5096						5			8	2					13	10		11	7	3			4	6				12	14		1
21		19	Gillingham	0-4		6072						3			12	2			10			8		11	7			13	4	6			5				1
22		26	NORTHAMPTON T	3-1	Grant, Tierney, Richardson	6131									9	2		8	13	10	12			11	7	3			4	6				5			1
23		28	Reading	0-1		13026									9	2		8	13	10	12			11	7	3			4	6			14	5			1
24	Jan	9	OLDHAM ATHLETIC	0-1		4669					14				13	9	2	8	11	10	12			7	3				4	6				5			1
25		16	Bournemouth	0-2		5968		8			14					9	2			12	10	5		11	7	3			4	6		13					1
26		30	READING	1-1	Owers	5192		8		13	3				9	2					10	5		11	7	12			4					14		1	6
27	Feb	13	BLACKPOOL	0-1		4778		7		12	3			8	9	2					10	5		11					4					13		1	6
28		16	Wigan Athletic	0-3		2971		10			9				8	2					14	5		11	7	12			4	6				13		1	3
29		20	Fulham	1-2	Owers	11909	10		9		11					2		13			12	5			7	3			4	6						1	8
30		23	Luton Town	1-0	Rapley	4851	10	8								2						4			7	3	9							11		1	5
31		27	WALSALL	2-1	Creaney, Hendon (p)	6172		8	14		10				13	2						4			7	3	9	12	6					11		1	5
32	Mar	6	Millwall	3-1	Richardson 2, Beadle	6042	10		13		12				2							4			7	3	9	8	6					11		1	5
33		13	YORK CITY	4-2	Richardson 2, Tierney, Beadle	5400	10		7		2							12				4				3	9	8	6		13			11		1	5
34		16	Manchester City	1-2	Stallard	26502	10		7		2				13			12				4				3	14	8	6		9			11		1	5
35		20	Stoke City	3-2	Beadle, Liburd, Stallard	9565	10		7		5					2						4				3		12	8	6		9			11		1	
36		27	Bristol Rovers	1-1	Creaney	5899	10		7		2	8										4			13	12	3	14	5		9			11			1	6
37	Apr	3	BURNLEY	0-0		6625			8	10		13		12				2	14						7	3		4	5		9			11		1	6
38		5	Lincoln City	1-0	Tierney	5745		2	7			4							12						13	3		10	5	8	9			11		1	6
39		10	CHESTERFIELD	2-0	Powers, Stallard	5121	10	2	8		13				12			14							11	7	3	4	5		9					1	6
40		13	WREXHAM	1-1	Garcia	3294	10	2	8		12				13			14							11	7	3	4	5	6	9					1	
41		16	Colchester United	1-2	Stallard	4215	10				12							14	4						11	2	3	13	5	8	9		7			1	6
42		24	LUTON TOWN	1-2	Redmile	5583	10			7								4		12					11	2	3	14	5	8	9	13				1	6
43		27	WYCOMBE WANDERERS	1-0	Creaney (p)	4271	10			7	8							12		4					11	2	3		5		9					1	6
44	May	1	Preston North End	1-1	Rapley	11862	10	14	7		8							12		4					11	2	3	13	5		9					1	6
45		4	MACCLESFIELD TOWN	1-1	Hughes	3747		6	7		8					2	4			11						3		10	5		9			12	1		
46		8	GILLINGHAM	0-1		7815	13	7	14		8								4						11	2	3		10	5	9			12			6

Played in one game in goal: PR Gibson (46), AL Goram (6), B Parkin (12)
DJ Foley played at 9 in games 20 (subbed) and 21 (subbed)
P Devlin played in 5 games; 15, 16, 17 at 10 and 18, 19 at 9

Apps	14	6	13	16	4	29	16	11	13	19	6	32	8	30	10	28	35	5	35	39	33	5	16	41	23	2	14	11	20	6	43	18
Goals	3		3			1	3		2	1	6		3		2	1			3	3	1		2	1	7		4	1	3	1		

One own goal

F.A. Cup

R1	Nov	15	Hendon	0-0		1627						5	9			2		8			10	12		11	7	3			4	6					1	
rep	Dec	1	HENDON	3-0	Owers, Jones 2	2230			13						8	2		9	5	10	14			11	7	3	12		4	6						1	
R2		5	WIGAN ATHLETIC	1-1	Jones	3591					5				8	2			10	9				11	7	3	12		4	6						1	
rep		15	Wigan Athletic	0-0		3292					5				13	2		10		8				11	7	3			4	6		9		12		1	
R3	Jan	2	Sheffield United	1-1	Jones	12264									9	2		8	13	10	14			11	7	3			4	6				5		1	
rep		23	SHEFFIELD UNITED	3-4	(aet) Jones 2, Murray	7489							9			2		8		10	5			11	7	3			4	6				14	12	1	

R2 reply won 4-2 on penalties a.e.t. Played at 12 in R3: J Pennant

Worthington Cup

| R1/1 | Aug | 11 | MANCHESTER CITY | 0-2 | | 5795 | 7 | | | | 14 | 5 | 9 | | | 2 | | | | | 10 | 13 | | 11 | 8 | 3 | | | 4 | | | | 6 | | 12 | 1 | |
| R1/2 | | 19 | Manchester City | 1-7 | Torpey | 10063 | 7 | | 12 | 14 | 5 | | | | | 2 | | | 10 | 3 | | | | 8 | 6 | | | | 4 | | 11 | | | | 9 | 1 | |

Played at 13 in R2/2: T Henshaw

Auto Windscreens Shield

| R1 | Dec | 22 | HULL CITY | 0-1 | | 1109 | | | | | | | | | 8 | | | 2 | 3 | 10 | | | | | 6 | 12 | | | | | | 5 | 7 | | 1 | |

Played at 4: T Henshaw; at 9, DJ Foley; at 11, D Rabat; at 13, J Samuels; at 14, J Pennant

1999/2000

8th in Division Two

#		Date	Opponent	Score	Scorers	Att	Allsopp D	Angell BAM	Beadle PCWI	Blackmore CG	Bolland PG	Brough M	Cross D	Darby DA	Dyer AC	Farrell SP	Fenton NL	Ford R	Gibson PR	Heffernan P	Holmes R	Howell D	Hughes AJ	Liburd RJ	Lindley JE	Murray S	Owers G	Pearce DA	Ramage CD	Rapley KJ	Redmile MI	Richardson IG	Robson M	Stallard M	Tierney F	Ward D	Warren MW	Webster A
1	Aug	7	LUTON TOWN	0-0		6141			10	3	13			14						2		4			4		11			7		5	8	12	9		1	6	
2		14	Colchester United	3-0	Hughes, Stallard, Blackmore	3986				3				10	12					2		4					11			8	14	5	7	13	9		1	6	
3		21	SCUNTHORPE UNITED	3-0	Ramage, Stallard 2	5506			13	3				10						2		4	12				11			8	14	5	7		9		1	6	
4		28	Cambridge United	1-1	Stallard	4329			12	3				10						2		4					11	13		8	14	5	7		9		1	6	
5	Sep	3	Wrexham	3-2	Darby 2, Stallard	5030			14	3	12			10						2		4					11	13		8		5	7		9		1	6	
6		11	BLACKPOOL	2-1	Ramage, Stallard	5512			13	3	14			10						2		4					11	12		8		5	7		9		1	6	
7		18	Cardiff City	1-2	Stallard	6568			14	3				10						2		4		12			11	13		8		5	7		9		1	6	
8		25	BRISTOL ROVERS	0-2		6197			14	3				10						2		4					11	12		8	13	5	7		9		1	6	
9	Oct	2	Oldham Athletic	2-1	Darby, Ramage	5143				5				10						2		4					11	3		8	12	13	7		9		1	6	
10		9	Bury	3-1	Stallard, Blackmore, Owers	3620				7	10				13		6			2		4				12	11	3	8		5			9		1		
11		16	WYCOMBE WANDERERS	2-1	Fenton, Richardson	5710			13		10				9		12	6		2		4					11	3	8		5	7			1			
12		19	CHESTERFIELD	1-0	Ramage	4749					10				9	7		6		2		4	3				11			8	13	5			12	1			
13		23	Bristol Rovers	1-0	Rapley	8188					10				9	12		4		2		7	14				11	3		8	13	5					1	6	
14		26	BRENTFORD	0-1		5075									10	3		4		2		7				12	11			8	13	5			9		1	6	
15	Nov	3	Stoke City	1-0	Dyer	11619					10				9			4		2		7	12				11	3		8	14	5	6				1	13	
16		6	GILLINGHAM	1-1	Allsopp	6023	9			3	11				12			4		2								13	7	8	10	5	6				1		
17		12	Preston North End	0-2		14226				3					11			4		2		10	13				7		8	14	5	6		9	12		1		
18		23	OXFORD UNITED	0-1		4020	9			3				10				4		2			11				7		8		5	6		13		1	12		
19		27	BRISTOL CITY	4-4	* See below	5374	9							10	13			4		2		11					7	3	8		5			14	12	1	6		
20	Dec	4	Luton Town	2-2	Richardson, Owers	5583												4		2		11					7	3	8	13	5	10		9	12	1	6		
21		11	BOURNEMOUTH	5-1	Angell 3, Richardson, Stallard	4199		10		3	8				13					2		12		11	7						5	4		9		1	6		
22		18	Millwall	0-1		7917		10		3	8									2			13	11	7						12	5	4		9		1	6		
23		26	WIGAN ATHLETIC	0-2		8176		10		3	8									2		13		11	7					12		5	4		9		1	6		
24		28	Reading	0-0		7703		10		3	14				13			4		2		12			7				8		5	11		9		1	6		
25	Jan	3	BURNLEY	2-0	Angell 2	8229		10			11					4		2					3		12	7			8		5	6		9		1		
26		8	Bournemouth	1-1	Owers	4344		10			11							2				12	3			7			8	13	5	4		9		1	6		
27		15	COLCHESTER UNITED	1-2	Rapley	4931					11							2				14	3		13	7			8	10	5	4		9	12	1	6		
28		22	Scunthorpe United	0-1		4035												2				8	4			7	3			10		5		9	11	1	6		12
29	Feb	5	Brentford	2-0	Tierney, Rapley	5106							13		9			2				8	4			7	3	12	10		5			11	1	6		
30		12	WREXHAM	2-1	Dyer, Hughes	5474				2			13		9							8	4			7	3	12	10		5			11	1	6		
31		15	CAMBRIDGE UNITED	2-3	Owers, Hughes (p)	4053							12		9			2				8	4			7	3		10		5		13	11	1	6		
32		19	Bristol City	2-2	Liburd, Hughes (p)	10029							14		9			2				8	4			7	3	13	10	12	5			11	1	6		
33		26	CARDIFF CITY	2-1	Hughes (p), Dyer	5334							10	12	13			14				11	2			7	3		8		5	4		9		1	6		
34	Mar	4	Blackpool	1-2	Stallard	4277		2		10				6	13								12			4			7	3	8			5		9	11	1		
35		7	Gillingham	1-0	Richardson	6915					10	11			3	12		2					4			7						13		6	9		1		
36		11	STOKE CITY	0-0		9677						13	11		3	12		2				10	4			7			8		5	6		9		1			
37		18	Oxford United	3-2	Dyer, Hughes 2 (1p)	4544						14	11		12	3	13			2		10	4			7			8		5			9		1	6		
38		21	PRESTON NORTH END	1-0	Redmile	6401							11		9	3	13			2		10	4			7			8	12	5					1	6		
39		25	Wigan Athletic	0-2		6094							11		9	3	12			2		10	4			7			8	13	5	6				1			
40	Apr	1	MILLWALL	1-1	Darby	7032							10	3	12			2				11	4			7			8	13	5	6		9		1			
41		8	Burnley	1-2	Stallard	13022						11	10	3	13							4	2			7			8	12	5	6		9		1			
42		15	READING	1-2	Darby	4791						12	11	10	3							4	2			7			8	13	5			9		1	6		
43		21	Wycombe Wanderers	0-2		4369						4	11		9	3			1			12				7			8	10	5			13			6		
44		24	OLDHAM ATHLETIC	0-1		3728						4	11			3					13	12				6			7	8	10	5		9		1			
45		29	Chesterfield	1-2	Bolland	2455					5	8	11	14		3					13	2				4			7		10			9	12	1	6		
46	May	6	BURY	2-2	Dyer, Stallard	4017						2	8	11	9	3			13				4			7				10	5			14	12	1	6		

Scorers in game 19: Holland (og), Stallard, Dyer, Warren

Apps	3	6	8	21	25	11	1	28	30	9	13	1	1	2	41	1	35	31	1	9	45	20	40	29	41	33	2	36	13	45	33	1
Goals	1	5		2	1			5	6		1						7	1			4		4	3	1	4		13	1		1	

One own goal

F.A. Cup

| R1 | Oct | 30 | BOURNEMOUTH | 1-1 | Rapley | 3674 | | | | 11 | | | | 6 | | | | | | 2 | | 10 | | | | | | | 5 | 8 | 7 | | 4 | | 9 | 12 | 1 | 3 | |
| rep | Nov | 9 | Bournemouth | 2-4 | Redmile, Tierney | 4026 | | | | 3 | | | | 10 | | | | | | 2 | | 11 | 4 | | 9 | 7 | | | 8 | 12 | 5 | 6 | | | 13 | 1 | | | |

Worthington Cup

R1/1	Aug	10	Bury	0-1		1893			10	3				13						2		7		11	12		8			5	6		9		1	4		
R1/2		24	BURY	2-0	Blackmore, Ramage (p)	2494			13	3	14			10						2		11			7	12	8			5	6		9		1	4		
R2/1	Sep	14	Huddersfield Town	1-2	Ramage	6900			14	3	13			10						2		11		12			7	2	8		5	6		9		1	4		
R2/2		21	HUDDERSFIELD TOWN	2-2	Blackmore, Darby	4104			12	3	13			10					1	2		11					7		8		5	6		9	14		4		

Auto Windscreens Shield

| R1 | Dec | 7 | BLACKPOOL | 0-1 | | 1167 | | | | 13 | 14 | | | 12 | 10 | | | | | | | 11 | | | | | 7 | 3 | 8 | 5 | 6 | | 9 | 2 | 1 | 4 | | |

2000/01

8th in Division Two

							Allsopp D	Bolland PG	Brough M	Calderwood C	Dyer AC	Farrell SP	Fenton NL	Gibson PR	Hamilton IR	Holmes R	Hughes AJ	Ireland C	Jacobsen A	Jorgensen H	Joseph D	Liburd RJ	McCann GS	McDermott A	Moreau F	Murray S	Newton AL	Nicholson KJ	Owers G	Pearce DA	Ramage CD	Rapley KJ	Redmile MI	Richardson IG	Stallard M	Thomas GR	Ward D	Warren MW
1	Aug	12	Luton Town	1-0	Stallard	7059					10				12	4					11	3		2					7		8		5			9		1	6
2		19	MILLWALL	3-4	Ramage 2, Stallard	6046					4				12						11	3		2					7		8		5			9		1	6
3		26	Stoke City	1-0	Stallard	13041					4				10		12				11	3		2					7		8	13			5	9		1	6
4		28	CAMBRIDGE UNITED	0-1		5020					12						13				11	3	10	2					7		8	14	5		4	9		1	6
5	Sep	2	Oldham Athletic	1-0	Owers	4424					4				10		12				11	3		2					7		8	13			5	9		1	6
6		9	BRISTOL ROVERS	1-1	Stallard	5511					2	12			10		4				11	3							7		8	13	14	5	9			1	6
7		12	SWANSEA CITY	0-1		3395						13			11			2				3		12					7		8	14	5	4	9			1	6
8		16	Northampton Town	0-1		5703								1	11			2			13	3		12					7		8		5	4	9				6
9		23	BRENTFORD	2-2	Joseph, Hughes	4164		8							10		13				11	3		2					7			14	5	4	9			1	6
10		30	Walsall	1-5	Stallard	5211		8			10	4			11		6		13		12	3		2					7				5			9			6
11	Oct	6	Wycombe Wanderers	1-3	Stallard	5080		8			2	13	5		10		4		14		11								7	3	12					9			6
12		14	WIGAN ATHLETIC	2-2	Farrell, Hughes	4567					4	10	5	1	11		12				13			2					7	3	8					9			6
13		17	BURY	1-0	Stallard	3461						10	5	1	11		12	4						2					7	3	8					9			6
14		21	Peterborough United	0-1		5889						10	5	1	11		2	3						13					7						4	9			6
15		24	Bournemouth	1-0	Stallard	3556						5	1	11		10	3		12					2					7						4	9			6
16		28	SWINDON TOWN	3-2	Farrell, Ramage, Joseph (p)	4502						9	5	1	10	12		4			11			2		13			7	3	8	14								6
17	Nov	4	Bristol City	0-4		10250						9	5	1	10			6			11			2		12			7	3	8			4					
18		25	Oxford United	3-2	Allsopp 2 (1p), Newton	4765	9	8				10	5	1	11			6			13			2					7	3				4					
19	Dec	2	Colchester United	0-2		3280	10	8					5	1	11			12			6			2					13	7	3				4	9			
20		16	READING	3-2	Allsopp 2, Stallard (p)	5106	10					5			11		8	6					2				12		7	3				4	9		1	
21		23	WREXHAM	1-0	Liburd	6206	10		12			5					8				6	13	2			11	14		7	3				4	9		1	
22		26	Rotherham United	0-0		7673	10		11			5						6					2						8	7	3				4	9		1	
23		30	Millwall	3-2	Hughes 2, Owers	11495	10		11						2	4	6				12	3					13	8	7					5	9		1	
24	Jan	1	STOKE CITY	2-2	Liburd, Richardson	9125	10		11			5			2	8		6			12	3							7					4	9		1	13
25		13	Cambridge United	2-2	Stallard, Allsopp (p)	4029	10		11			5				13	8	6			12	3		2					7					4	9		1	
26		20	ROTHERHAM UNITED	4-1	* see below	7010	10					5					2	12	6							11	8		7					4	9		1	
27	Feb	3	OLDHAM ATHLETIC	1-0	Allsopp	5212	10		13				14	5		11		4	3	6				2					8		7	12			9		1	
28		10	Bristol Rovers	0-0		6914	10		11				5		7		4			6				2		12			8			3			9		1	
29		13	LUTON TOWN	1-3	Stallard	4333	10		11				5		13		7			6			12	4		2	14	8				3			9		1	
30		17	NORTHAMPTON T	2-0	Stallard, Fenton	6320	12		11				10	5		7			4	6			13	2		8						3			9		1	
31		20	Swansea City	1-0	Brough	4058	10		11				5					7	4	6	13		12	2		8						3			9		1	
32		24	Brentford	1-3	Allsopp	4366	10		11				13	5				4	6				7	2		8	12					3			9		1	
33	Mar	3	WALSALL	2-0	Farrell, Allsopp	6077	10		12			11					13	2	6				5			8					7	3			9	4	1	
34		6	Wigan Athletic	1-1	Fenton	5021	10		13				5					2			12	6				11	8				7	3			9	4	1	
35		17	Bury	1-1	Allsopp	3487	10			4		12	5					2				6					11				7	3			9	8	1	
36		23	PETERBOROUGH UTD.	3-3	Allsopp (p), Nicholson, Stallard	6510	10			5		13					4	2				6			12		11				7	3			9	8	1	
37		27	Port Vale	0-1		4602	10			4		14	5				8	2		12		6					11				13	7	3			9		1	
38		31	Reading	1-2	Owers	11624	10			5		12			11		4	6	2							14					13	7	3			9	8	1	
39	Apr	10	Wrexham	1-1	Thomas	2741	10		11	5		9					13	6	2		12								3	7				4		8	1	
40		14	BOURNEMOUTH	0-2		5186	10					5					6	3		2	13	12			11		14		7					4	9	8	1	
41		16	Swindon Town	2-1	Joseph, Stallard	7117	12					5						4	6		10	8		2			13	11	7	3					9		1	
42		21	BRISTOL CITY	2-1	Nicholson, Allsopp	5369	10		12			5					2	6	13								13	8	4	7	3				9	4	1	
43		26	WYCOMBE WANDERERS	0-2		3574	14		11			5					2	6		10			13			8	4	7	3				12	9		1	
44		28	Port Vale	3-2	Allsopp 2 (1p), Owers	5236	10	8				5					6							12			2	11	7	3					9	1	
45	May	3	COLCHESTER UNITED	2-2	Stallard, Jacobsen	2860	10	8									6					5					2	11	7	3				4	9		1	
46		5	OXFORD UNITED	2-1	Joseph, Stallard	5513	10						7			5	6		11			2					8	3					4	9		1	

Scorers in game 26: Jacobsen, Liburd, Hughes, Stallard
C Cramb played in games 7 (at 10, subbed), 8 (at 10) and 9 (at 12)
P Heffernan played at 12 in game 14
JE Lindley played in goal in games 10 and 11

Apps	29	7	16	5	9	19	30	9	25	5	30	16	29	5	27	31	2	25	5	11	20	11	40	27	15	7	8	25	42	8	35	16
Goals	13		1			3	2				5		2		4	3					1	2	4		3			1	17	1		

F.A. Cup

R1	Dec	8	Gravesend & Northfleet	2-1	Stallard, Hughes	2376		13				5			11		10	6					12	2		8			7	3				4	9		1	
R2		12	Wigan Athletic	1-1	Stallard	3886	10					5			11		8	6						2					7	3				4	9		1	
rep		19	WIGAN ATHLETIC	2-1	(aet) Liburd 2	3349	10		13			5					8	6						2		11			7	3				4	9		1	
R3	Jan	6	Wimbledon	2-2	Hughes, Stallard	4391	10		11			5			13	12	8	6				3					2		7					4	9		1	
rep		27	WIMBLEDON	0-1	(aet)	9084	10		12			14	5		11		8	6				3					13	2	7					4	9		1	

Worthington Cup

R1/1	Aug	22	Hull City	0-0		2675					4				7						11	3	10	2					8		12		5			9		1	6
R1/2	Sep	5	HULL CITY	2-0	Stallard 2 (1p)	1907					4	14			10		13				11	3		2					7		8	12		5	9			1	6
R2/1		19	WATFORD	1-3	Stallard (p)	2346								1	10						11			2					7	3	8	12	5	4	9				6
R2/2		26	Watford	2-0	McDermott, Hughes	7677		8			10	5			13		6				14	11		2					7	3				4	9		1	

R2 lost on away goals rule   JE Lindley played at 12 in R2/2

LDV Vans Trophy

R1	Jan	9	Port Vale	0-3		1919		10						1	11	2					5	9							7										4

Also played: B Gellert (3), M Dunn (6, subbed), R Ford (8), P Heffernan (12)

2001/02

19th in Division Two

#	Date		Opponent	Score	Scorers	Att	Allsopp D	Baraclough IR	Bolland PG	Brough M	Cas M	Caskey DM	Chilvers LC	Fenton NL	Garden SR	Grayson SN	Hackworth A	Hamilton IR	Heffernan P	Holmes R	Ireland C	Jorgensen H	Liburd RJ	McNamara NA	Mildenhall SJ	Nicholson KJ	Owers G	Quinn SJ	Richardson IG	Richardson LN	Riley PA	Stallard M	Stone DJC	Warren MW	Whitley J	Wilkie L
1	Aug	11	Port Vale	2-4	Cas, Allsopp	6076	10	3			7	8		5						6		13			1	11	2					9		12		4
2		18	CAMBRIDGE UNITED	2-1	Ireland, Stallard	5744	10	3			11	8		5						6	2		1			7						9		12		4
3		25	Northampton Town	2-0	Baraclough, Stallard	4648	10	3			11	8		2					12	6	4		1			7						9		5		
4		27	CHESTERFIELD	1-1	Owers	6236	10	3			11	8		2						6	4		1	12	7							9		5		
5	Sep	8	WREXHAM	2-2	Allsopp 2 (1p)	4776	10	3			11	8		2		5	13			6			1	12	7							9		4		
6		15	BRENTFORD	0-0		5043	10	3			11	8		5			12	7					1	6	2		13					9		4		
7		18	Tranmere Rovers	2-4	Caskey, Cas	7343	10	3			11	8		5			13	7					1	6	2		12					9		4		
8		22	Colchester United	1-0	Allsopp	3796	10	3			11	8		2		5	13	4			12		1		7		6		9							
9		25	PETERBOROUGH UTD.	1-0	Stallard	5633	10	3			11	8		2		5	12	4					1		7		6		9							
10		29	Oldham Athletic	1-4	Stallard	6864	10	3			11	8		2		5	12	4					1		7		6		9							
11	Oct	6	WYCOMBE WANDERERS	0-1		4483	10	3			11	8		2		5	14	4				12	1	13	7		6		9							
12		13	Stoke City	0-1		13220	10	3		4	11	8				2	13						1	12	7		6		9					5		
13		20	READING	3-4	Allsopp 2 (1p), Grayson	5604	10	3		4	11	8				2	9	12			7		1		13		6		14					5		
14		23	BRIGHTON & HOVE ALB	2-2	Fenton, I Richardson	5092	10	3		4	11			2		5	9	12			8		1		7		6		13							
15		27	Bournemouth	2-4	Hackworth, Allsopp	3209	10			4	11	14		2		5	8	13			3		1		7		6		9					12		
16	Nov	3	QUEEN'S PARK RANGERS	0-2		6231	10		4	12	11	8	3	6		5	9						1	13	7								14	2		
17		9	Huddersfield Town	2-2	Baraclough, Caskey	10168	10	11	4	13	7	8	3	5			14						1	12			6						9	2		
18		20	Blackpool	0-0		4118	10	11	4		7	8	3	5			12						1				6	2					9			
19		24	CARDIFF CITY	0-0		6313	10	11	4	12	7	8	3	5			9						1				6	2								
20	Dec	1	Bristol City	2-3	Quinn, Chilvers	9411	10	3			4	8	6				9		13	5			1		7	11		2					12			
21		11	Wigan Athletic	1-1	Heffernan	3827	10	3	8	4		12		5			9						1	11		7	6			13			2			
22		15	BURY	1-2	Quinn	4395	10	3	4	13	14	8		5	1		9							11			7	6		12			2			
23		21	SWINDON TOWN	3-1	Quinn, Caskey, Cas	4197	10	3	4	12	11	8		2	1		13		14	5						7	9	6								
24		26	Wrexham	1-2	Allsopp	3707	10	11	4					2	1		9		12	3	5				13	7	8	6		14						
25		29	Chesterfield	1-2	Fenton	5139			4		11	8		2	1		9			5			12		7	10	6		3							
26	Jan	12	Cambridge United	2-0	Caskey. Heffernan	3747			7	4	11	8		5			13		10	6			1	12	2				3	9						
27		19	PORT VALE	1-3	Fenton	6006	10		8	4	11	8	3	2						5			1		7		6	12	9							
28		22	Swindon Town	0-1		3821	10		7	4	11	8	3	5			12				13		1				6	2		9						
29		26	Wycombe Wanderers	0-3		5574	10		7	4		8	2	5			13				11	1			12		6		3	9						
30		29	NORTHAMPTON T	0-3		4182			4	13		8	3	5	1		9		10		12			11	14		7		6	2						
31	Feb	2	OLDHAM ATHLETIC	0-2		4555	10	3			7	8	4	1		12	9			11							6	2						5		
32		9	Reading	1-2	Liburd	13564	10	3			7	8		4	1		13			6	11				12			2		9				5		
33		16	STOKE CITY	0-0		7501	10	3	4		7	8			1		9			6	11				12			2		13				5		
34		19	WIGAN ATHLETIC	1-3	I Richardson	3358	10	3	4		7	8		12	1				14	6	11						13	2		9				5		
35		23	Brentford	1-2	Caskey	5367	10	3				8		4	1		9			6				12	11	7		2					5		
36		26	COLCHESTER UNITED	1-1	Allsopp	3140	10	3			11	8		5	1		9		6	4				12	7			2								
37	Mar	2	TRANMERE ROVERS	3-0	Allsopp 3	4562	10	3		4	7	8		6	1		14		9	5	12	11	13					2								
38		5	Peterborough United	1-0	Allsopp	4415	10			4	7	8		6	1		12		9	5	11				3			2								
39		9	Bury	4-0	Allsopp 2, Heffernan, Cas	5435	10			4	7	8		5	1		9		6		11	14			3			2					12			
40		16	BRISTOL CITY	2-0	Cas, Heffernan	7521	10			4	7	8		5	1		12		9	6	11				3			2								
41		23	Brighton & Hove Albion	2-2	Allsopp, Cas	6538	10	12		4	7	8		5	1		13		9	6					3			2					2		11	
42		30	BOURNEMOUTH	2-0	Allsopp 2	9014	10	14		12	7	8		5	1		13		9	6	11				3			2						4		
43	Apr	1	Queen's Park Rangers	2-3	Heffernan, Baraclough	10966	10	3				8		6	1		13		9	5	7				11			2						12	4	
44		6	BLACKPOOL	1-0	Allsopp (p)	7783	10	12	13		11			6	1		9			5	4				3	7		2						8		
45		13	Cardiff City	1-2	Liburd	17105	10		13		11			6	1		9		12	5	4				3	7		2						8		
46		20	HUDDERSFIELD T	2-1	Allsopp, Nicholson	15618	10		12		7	8		5	1		9			6	11				3			2			13			4		
					Apps		43	33	19	21	40	42	9	42	21	10	33	9	23	27	2	25	4	26	24	30	6	24	21	6	26	6	17	6	2		
					Goals		19	3			6	5	1	3			1	1		6				1		2			1	3	2		4				

Game 25: Mildenhall went in goal after Garden was dismissed

F.A. Cup

R	Date		Opponent	Score	Scorers	Att																												
R1	Nov	17	Cambridge United	1-1	Allsopp	3061	10	11	4	12	7	8	3	5		14						13	1				6	2		9							
rep		27	CAMBRIDGE UNITED	2-0	Allsopp, Owers	2661	10	11		4	7	8	3	5		9				12			1		2		6					13					
R2	Dec	8	Wycombe Wanderers	0-3		4725	10	3	7	4		8		5		9		11	13				1	12			6					2					

Worthington Cup

R	Date		Opponent	Score	Scorers	Att																												
R1	Aug	21	Mansfield Town	4-3	Allsopp 3, Mildenhall	4553	10	3			11	8		2				12		6	13	14	1	4	7							9		5		
R2	Sep	11	MANCHESTER CITY	2-4	Allsopp (p), Stallard	5972	10	3	13		11	8		2		5	14	12					1	6	7							9		4		

R2 after extra time

LDV Vans Trophy

R	Date		Opponent	Score	Scorers	Att																												
R1	Oct	16	YORK CITY	2-0	Allsopp, Hackworth (p)	1128	9	3		7	8	4		1	2	10	12	13			14			11			6						5			
R2		30	Bury	3-2	Caskey, Allsopp 2	1197	9	3	12		8	4		2		6	10	11					1	7									13	5		
QF	Dec	4	OLDHAM ATHLETIC	0-1		1047	12	3		7		14		2	1		10		13	8	4			11		9		6			5					

R2 a.e.t, won on sudden death

2002/03

15th in Division Two

#	Date		Opponent	Score	Scorers	Att	Allsopp D	Ashton JJ	Baraclough IR	Bolland PG	Brough M	Cas M	Caskey DM	Deeney S	Fenton NL	Francis WD	Garden SR	Hackworth A	Harrad SN	Heffernan P	Holmes R	Ireland C	Jupp DA	Liburd RJ	McCarthy P	Mildenhall SJ	Nicholson KJ	Ramsden SP	Richardson IG	Riley PA	Stallard M	Stone DJC	Whitley J
1	Aug	10	WYCOMBE WANDERERS	1-1	Cas	6012	10		11	4		7	8		5	1						6		3							9	2	
2		13	Crewe Alexandra	3-0	Allsopp 2, Stallard	6141	10		11	4	13	7	8		5	1					12	6		14							9	2	
3		17	Stockport County	0-0		5047	10		11	4		7	8		5	1						6		3							9	2	
4		24	WIGAN ATHLETIC	0-2		6302	10		11	4		7	8		5	1				13		6		14					3	12	9	2	
5		26	Barnsley	0-0		10431	10		11	4		7	8		5	1						6		13					3	12	9	2	
6		31	BRENTFORD	2-2	Stallard, Heffernan	5551	10		11	4			8		5	1				7		6							3	12 13	9	2	
7	Sep	7	OLDHAM ATHLETIC	1-3	Heffernan	5435	10		11				4	8	5	1				7		6		14					3	13 12	9	2	
8		14	Luton Town	2-2	Bolland, Allsopp	6456	10		11	4	13		8		5	1				9		6		2					3	7	12		
9		17	Port Vale	2-3	Bolland, Allsopp	3505	10			4	11		8		5	1				12		6		2					3	7 13	9		
10		21	CARDIFF CITY	0-1		6118	10			4	14	7	8		5	1	12			13				11					3	2 6	9		
11		28	Cheltenham Town	4-1	Stallard 2, Allsopp 2	4565	10	4	11			4	7	12	8	5	1				14		13		11					3	6	9	2	
12	Oct	5	PETERBOROUGH UTD.	2-2	Stallard, Cas	6548	10			4	7	12	8		5	1				14		13		11					3	6	9	2	
13		12	Huddersfield Town	0-3		9984	10			13	7	4	8		5	1				12				11					3	14 6	9	2	
14		19	NORTHAMPTON T	2-1	Stallard, Heffernan	6009	10			4	7	12			5	1				11									3	2 6	9		8
15		26	Chesterfield	0-0		4539	10			4	7		12		5	1				11									3	2 6	9		8
16		29	SWINDON TOWN	1-1	Bolland	4797	10			4	7	14	13		5	1				11									3	2 6	9	12	8
17	Nov	9	MANSFIELD TOWN	2-2	Liburd, Caskey	10302	14	5		4	7	11	12			1				10				13					3	2	9	6	8
18		23	COLCHESTER UNITED	2-3	Allsopp, Brough	4626	10	6	11		7	13	4		5	1				9			2						3		12		8
19		30	Blackpool	1-1	Baraclough	5843	10	4	11			8			5	12				7			2			1				6	3	9	
20	Dec	3	Bristol City	2-3	Stallard 2	10690	10	4	11				14		5	13				12			2			1			7	6	3	9	8
21		14	QUEEN'S PARK RANGERS	3-0	Liburd, Fenton, Allsopp	5343	10		11				4		2							6	7	3	1					5	9		8
22		21	Tranmere Rovers	2-2	Stallard 2 (1p)	8275			11			7	4		2		10	13				6		3	1	12				5	9		8
23		26	BARNSLEY	3-2	Stallard (p), Richardson, Baraclough	7413			11			7	12				10	13				6		3					1	2 5	9		8
24		28	Plymouth Argyle	0-1		11901			11			7	13	4			9	12				6		10	1	3	2			5			14	8
25	Jan	1	Wigan Athletic	1-3	Stallard	6009	10		11			7	14	4								6	12	3	1	13	2			5	9		8
26		18	Brentford	1-1	Fenton	5112	10		11			4			5					12		6	7		1	3	2				9		8
27		21	STOCKPORT COUNTY	3-2	Stallard, Heffernan, Caskey	4392	10		11			4			2					13		6	7		1	3	12	5			9		
28		25	PLYMOUTH ARGYLE	0-2		6329	10		11				4		2					8		6		12	1	3	7	5			9		
29	Feb	1	Wycombe Wanderers	1-3	Stallard	5690			11				4		2				14	10	3	6	12	8	1	13	7	5			9		
30		4	CREWE ALEXANDRA	2-2	Caskey (p), Allsopp	3875	13		11	12			4		5				14	10	2	6		8	1	3	7				9		
31		8	Mansfield Town	2-3	Stallard 2	8134	10		11	4	12		8		2					13		6		3	1		7	5			9		
32		15	BRISTOL CITY	2-0	Stallard (p), Heffernan	5754			11	4	7		8		2	12				10		6		3	1		13	5			9		
33		22	Oldham Athletic	1-1	Heffernan	5657			11	4	7		8		2	13		12		10		6		3	1		14	5			9		
34	Mar	1	LUTON TOWN	2-1	Heffernan 2	6778			11	4			8			7				10		6		2	1	3	13	5	12		9		
35		4	PORT VALE	1-0	Stallard	6302			11	4	7		8							10		6		2	1	3	12	5			9	13	
36		8	Cardiff City	2-0	Stallard 2 (1p)	11389				4	8				2					10		6		11	1	3	7	5			9		
37		15	CHESTERFIELD	1-1	Stallard	6801				4	8		13		2	12				10		6		11	1	3	7	5			9		
38		18	Northampton Town	0-2		5254		12		4	11		8		2			13		10		6		3	1		7	5			9		
39		22	Swindon Town	0-5		4246				4	11		8		2		5	7		12		10	13	6	1		3				9		14
40		29	HUDDERSFIELD T	3-2	Heffernan, Stallard 2 (2p)	5872			11	8	13				1	5	12			10		6		7	2		3			4	9		
41	Apr	5	BLACKPOOL	3-1	Heffernan, Ireland, Fenton	5551	13		11	8					1	5	12	14		10		6		7	2		3			4	9		
42		12	Colchester United	1-1	Stallard	3435	12		11	8					1	5				10		6		7	2		3			4	9		
43		19	TRANMERE ROVERS	0-1		5715	10		11			4	13	1	5			7				6		8	2		3	12			9		
44		21	Queen's Park Rangers	0-2		13585	10		11			7	8	1	5			12				6		2			3		4		9		
45		26	Peterborough United	0-1		5381	13		11			7	8	1	5			10				6		2			3	12	4		9		
46	May	3	CHELTENHAM TOWN	1-0	Allsopp	9710	4		11			7	8	1	5	12		10				6					3	2			9		
					Apps		33	4	34	29	31	18	39	7	40	10	18	9	5	36	4	37	8	32	6	21	37	32	34	3	45	15	12
					Goals		10		2	3	1	2	3		3					10		1		2						1	24		

F.A. Cup

R1	Nov	16	Southport	2-4	Allsopp 2	3519	10		14			7	11	4		5	1			13		6	12						3		9	2	8

Worthington Cup

R1	Sep	10	Oldham Athletic	2-3	Stallard, Heffernan	4205	10		11			4	8		2		1	12		13		6	3						7	5	9		

LDV Vans Trophy

R1	Oct	22	WIGAN ATHLETIC	2-3	Richardson, Bolland	1020	14			13	4	7			5					10	12			11		1	3		6		9	2	8

2003/04

23rd in Division Two: Relegated

#	Date		Opponent	Score	Scorers	Attendance
1	Aug	9	Bristol City	0-5		12050
2		16	WREXHAM	0-1		4768
3		23	Swindon Town	0-4		5758
4		25	PETERBOROUGH UTD.	0-1		5177
5		30	Barnsley	1-1	Heffernan	9087
6	Sep	6	LUTON TOWN	1-1	Barras	7505
7		13	Chesterfield	1-0	Bolland	4367
8		16	RUSHDEN & D'MNDS	1-3	Stallard	4250
9		20	TRANMERE ROVERS	2-2	Stallard, Platt	4215
10		27	Blackpool	1-2	Stallard (p)	6206
11	Oct	1	Sheffield Wednesday	1-2	Stallard	20354
12		4	COLCHESTER UNITED	3-0	Heffernan 2, Riley	4187
13		11	BOURNEMOUTH	0-1		4419
14		18	Stockport County	2-2	Caskey, Platt	4727
15		21	Grimsby Town	0-2		4274
16		25	BRENTFORD	2-0	Platt, Caskey	4145
17	Nov	1	HARTLEPOOL UNITED	1-0	Baldry	5011
18		15	Port Vale	0-1		4900
19		22	BRIGHTON & HOVE ALB	1-2	Heffernan (p)	5051
20		29	Oldham Athletic	1-0	Heffernan	5190
21	Dec	13	WYCOMBE WANDERERS	1-1	Heffernan	5014
22		20	Plymouth Argyle	0-3		9923
23		26	QUEEN'S PARK RANGERS	3-3	Heffernan 3 (1p)	7702
24		28	Luton Town	0-2		7181
25	Jan	6	Peterborough United	2-5	Riley 2	3855
26		10	BRISTOL CITY	1-2	Butler (og)	6403
27		17	Wrexham	1-0	Parkinson	4212
28		24	SWINDON TOWN	1-2	Heffernan (p)	6663
29		31	BARNSLEY	1-1	Parkinson	7355
30	Feb	7	Queen's Park Rangers	2-3	Parkinson, Richardson	14412
31		14	Bournemouth	0-1		6332
32		21	STOCKPORT COUNTY	4-1	Heffernan 4 (1p)	5618
33		28	Brentford	3-2	Richardson, Heffernan, Scully	4478
34	Mar	2	GRIMSBY TOWN	3-1	* see below	6011
35		6	PLYMOUTH ARGYLE	0-0		8057
36		13	Wycombe Wanderers	1-1	Heffernan	5125
37		16	Rushden & Diamonds	1-2	Scully	4030
38		20	CHESTERFIELD	1-1	Fenton	7808
39		27	Tranmere Rovers	0-4		7308
40	Apr	3	BLACKPOOL	4-1	Scully, Heffernan 2, Scoffham	5100
41		10	Colchester United	1-4	Richardson	3782
42		12	SHEFFIELD WEDNESDAY	0-0		9601
43		17	Hartlepool United	0-4		5629
44		24	PORT VALE	1-2	Heffernan	5834
45	May	1	Brighton & Hove Albion	0-1		6618
46		8	OLDHAM ATHLETIC	1-1	Barras	6715

Scorers in game 34: Antoine-Curier, Heffernan, Scoffham
CK Rhodes played at 13 in game 25
PM Arphexad played in 3 games 36 to 38 in goal
WD Francis played at 12 in games 1, 18 and 26
JA Bewers played at 12 in games 40, 45 and 46
KJ Wilson played in game 43 at 12 and games 45 and 46 at 3

F.A. Cup

	Date		Opponent	Score	Scorers	Attendance
R1	Nov	9	SHILDON	7-2	* See below	4016
R2	Dec	6	Gravesend & Northfleet	2-1	Fenton, Platt	2998
R3	Jan	3	Middlesbrough	0-2		15061

Scorers in R1: Fenton, Platt 2, Nicholson, Richardson, Barras, Heffernan

Carling Cup

	Date		Opponent	Score	Scorers	Attendance
R1	Aug	12	Preston North End	0-0		5016
R2	Sep	23	IPSWICH TOWN	2-1	Baldry, Stallard (p)	4059
R3	Oct	29	Chelsea	2-4	Barras, Stallard	35997

R1 won 7-6 on penalties a.e.t.

LDV Vans Trophy

	Date		Opponent	Score		Attendance
R1	Oct	15	BARNSLEY	0-0		1220

Lost 2-4 on penalties a.e.t.

2004/05

19th in Football League Two

#		Date	Opponent	Score	Scorers	Att	Baudet J	Bolland PG	Deeney S	Edwards M	Elliot R	Friars EC	Gill MJ	Gordon KG	Harrad SN	Henderson W	Hurst G	Kuduzovic F	McFaul S	Mildenhall SJ	Oakes ST	O'Grady CJ	Palmer CL	Pead CG	Pipe DR	Richardson IG	Robinson MLStC	Scoffham S	Scully ADT	Sofiane Y	Stallard M	Ullathorne R	Whitlow MW	Williams M	Wilson KJ	Zadkovich RA
1	Aug	7	CHESTER CITY	1-1	Baudet (p)	6432	4	8		2			7	9	12		10			1					11	5					3	6			
2		10	Kidderminster Harriers	0-0		2927	4	8		6			7	9		1	10	14							11	5			12			3		13	2	
3		14	Bristol Rovers	1-2	Hurst	8225	4	8		6			7	9		1	10								2	5			11			3		13	12	
4		21	YEOVIL TOWN	1-2	Gordon	5024	4	8		6			7	9		1	10								2	5			11			3		12	13	
5		28	Lincoln City	2-1	Scully 2	5173	4	8	12	6			7		13	1	10								2	5			11			3		9	14	
6		30	OXFORD UNITED	0-1		5288	4	8	1	6			7				10	14							2	5			11			3	12	9	13	
7	Sep	4	CHELTENHAM TOWN	0-0		4302	4	8	1	13			7	10	14			12								5			11			3	6	9	2	
8		11	Northampton Town	0-0		5471	4	8		5			7	13		1	10							6	2		14		11	9		3	12			
9		18	SOUTHEND UNITED	1-2	Hurst	4487	4	8		4			12			1	14							7	2	5	10		11	9		3	6	13		
10		25	Rochdale	3-0	Hurst 3	2370	4	8					7			1	9				14			12	10	5			11	13		3	6		2	
11	Oct	2	LEYTON ORIENT	1-2	Baudet (p)	5141	4	8					7	13		1	9				10			6	11				14	12		3	5		2	
12		10	Macclesfield Town	2-1	Hurst 2	2456	4	8						9		1	10				7	12	11	6								3	5		2	
13		16	Mansfield Town	1-3	Gordon	7682	4	8	1				7	14			10				11	9	6		2				12			3	5		13	
14		19	DARLINGTON	1-1	Hurst	3620	4	8	1		12		9				10				7	13	6						11			3	5		2	
15		23	BOSTON UNITED	2-1	Gordon, Palmer	5434	4	8	1				13	9			10				7	14	6		12				11			3	5		2	
16		30	Rushden & Diamonds	1-5	Pipe	3504		8	1		13	2		9			10	12			7		6		14				11			3	5		4	
17	Nov	6	SHREWSBURY TOWN	3-0	Bolland, Hurst, Palmer	5745	5	8	1				12	9			10		6		7		11		2								3	4			
18		20	Bury	0-1		2938	4	8	1				13	9			10	12	6				3		7	5			11						2	
19		27	CAMBRIDGE UNITED	2-1	Williams, Palmer	5080	4	8	1				14	9					6		11	13	3		7								12	5	10	2	
20	Dec	7	Grimsby Town	2-3	Oates, Gordon	4030	4						7	9		1	14		6		8	13	11		2				12					5	10	3	
21		11	WYCOMBE WANDERERS	0-1		6529							13	7		1	10	12	6		8	4	3		2				11					5	9		
22		18	Swansea City	0-4		6609	5	8	1				7	9	10		13				12	3			2				11			14		6	4		
23		28	Scunthorpe United	0-0		6399	4	8	1				7	9	10						11		6									3	5		2	
24	Jan	1	Cheltenham Town	2-0	Hurst, Palmer	3375	4	8	1				7	9			10				11		6									3	5		2	
25		3	ROCHDALE	0-0		5258	4	8	1					9			10		7			11	6						12			3	5	13	2	
26		15	Southend United	0-0		5304	4		1				7	9			10	12	8		6		2						11				5		3	
27		22	SCUNTHORPE UNITED	2-0	Hurst, Gordon	6429	5	13	1				7	9			10		6		8		12		2				11			3		14	4	
28		25	MACCLESFIELD TOWN	0-5		3586	5	13	1				7	9			10		6		8		2						11			3		12	4	
29		29	Leyton Orient	0-2		3440	5	7	1					9	12		10		6		13		2						11			3			4	
30	Feb	5	MANSFIELD TOWN	0-1		10005	5	8	1				7	9			12		6		13	14	2						11		10	3			4	
31		12	Darlington	2-1	Pipe, Wilson	4213		8	1				7				10		6		11		2								9	3	5	12	4	
32		15	NORTHAMPTON T	0-0		4645	12	8	1				7	13			10		6		11		2								9	3	5		4	
33		19	RUSHDEN & D'MNDS	1-1	Baudet (p)	4556	4	8	1				7	9	14		10	12	11		6		2						13			3	5		2	
34		26	Wycombe Wanderers	2-1	Wilson, Oates	4199	5	8	1				7		12		10		6		11		2							9	3			4		
35	Mar	5	SWANSEA CITY	1-0	Stallard	4644	5	8	1			12	7		13		10	6			11		2						9	3						
36		12	KIDDERMINSTER HARRIERS	1-3	Stallard	4358		8	1		12	5	7		13		10	6			11		2							9	3			14	4	
37		16	Boston United	0-4		2229		8	1				7		13		10	6			11		2						12	9	3	5			4	
38		19	Chester City	2-3	Hurst, Zadkovich	2324		8			1	5	7		13		10	6			11		2							9	3				4	12
39		26	BRISTOL ROVERS	1-2	Hurst	4258	5	8			1		7				10	2	6									13	12	9	3			4	11	
40		29	Yeovil Town	3-1	Oakes, Hurst, Stallard	7221	5	2	1				7				10		6		11								12	9	3			4	8	
41	Apr	2	LINCOLN CITY	1-0	Baudet (p)	7103	5	2	1				7				10		6		11		12						14	13	9	3			4	8	
42		9	Oxford United	1-2	Baudet	4436	5	8	1				7		12		10	13			3		2							9				6	4	11
43		16	GRIMSBY TOWN	2-2	Oakes 2	5478	5	8	1				7				10	4	6		3		2						12	13	9					11
44		23	Shrewsbury Town	1-1	Harrad	4202	5		1					4	7		8				6		11						10	12	9			3		
45		30	BURY	0-1		6424	5		1					4	7		8				6		11		2				10		9			12	3	13
46	May	7	Cambridge United	0-0		4723	5		1				12	7			14	13			6		3		2				10	11	9				4	8

Match 36: Elliot took over in goal after Deeney dismissed

	Apps	Goals
Baudet J	39	5
Bolland PG	40	1
Deeney S	32	
Edwards M	9	
Elliot R	4	
Friars EC	9	
Gill MJ	43	5
Gordon KG	27	5
Harrad SN	16	1
Henderson W	11	
Hurst G	41	14
Kuduzovic F	3	
McFaul S	24	
Mildenhall SJ	1	
Oakes ST	31	5
O'Grady CJ	9	4
Palmer CL	25	2
Pead CG	5	
Pipe DR	41	2
Richardson IG	10	3
Robinson MLStC	2	
Scoffham S	7	
Scully ADT	31	2
Sofiane Y	4	
Stallard M	16	3
Ullathorne R	36	
Whitlow MW	24	1
Williams M	18	2
Wilson KJ	41	1
Zadkovich RA	8	

F.A. Cup

R	Date	Opponent	Score	Scorers	Att																										
R1	Nov 13	WOKING	2-0	Baudet (p), Gordon	4700	5	8	1				13	9			10		6		7		11		2				12			3		4	
R2	Dec 4	Swindon Town	1-1	Oakes	5768	4		1				7	9					6		8	12	11		2				13					5	10	3
rep	15	SWINDON TOWN	2-0	Gordon 2	3770		8	1				7	9	10		13	12					3		2				11			5		6	4	
R3	Jan 8	MIDDLESBROUGH	1-2	Scully	13671		8	1				7	9	14		10				13		6		2				11			3	5	12	4	

Carling Cup

| R1 | Aug 25 | Bradford City | 2-1 | Ullathorne, Richardson | 3517 | 4 | 8 | 1 | 6 | | | 7 | | | | 10 | | | | | | | | 2 | 5 | | | 11 | | | 3 | | 9 | 12 | |
| R2 | Sep 21 | West Ham United | 2-3 | Wilson, Richardson | 11111 | | 8 | 1 | 4 | | | 7 | | | | 9 | | | | | | | | 10 | 5 | | | 11 | | | 3 | 6 | 13 | 2 | |

R1 a.e.t.

LDV Vans Trophy

| R1 | Sep 28 | WREXHAM | 2-3 | Sofiane, Hurst | 1359 | 5 | | | | 4 | 7 | 13 | | 1 | 9 | | | | | 10 | 6 | 8 | | | | | 12 | 11 | | | 3 | | 2 | | |

FA Cup action: Scully gives Notts a 2nd minute lead against Middlesbrough...

....the perfect start for acting manager Ian Richardson

2005/06

21st in Football League Two

#		Date	Opponent	Score	Scorers	Att	Baudet J	Berry TM	Chillingworth DT	Crooks LR	Dadi E	De Bolla GM	Doyle NLR	Edwards M	Friars EC	Frost S	Gill MJ	Gordon KG	Hurst G	Long SW	Marshall SA	Martin DA	McGoldrick DJ	McMahon LJ	Needham LP	O'Callaghan BP	Palmer CL	Pilkington KW	Pipe DR	Scoffham S	Sheridan J	Sissoko N	Tann AJ	Ullathorne R	White AD	Williams M	Wilson KJ	Zadkovich RA
1	Aug	6	Torquay United	0-0		3754	6							4				10			3		8			2	11	1	7	9	12			13	14		5	
2		9	WREXHAM	1-0	Long	4382	6							4			13		12	14			8			2	11	1	7	9				3	10		5	
3		13	LINCOLN CITY	2-1	Scoffham, Baudet	6153	6							4				12		13			8			2	11	1	7	9				3	10		5	
4		20	Stockport County	1-1	Wiliams (og)	3922	6							4				14	10		11	12	8			2		1	7	9				3	13		5	
5		27	BRISTOL ROVERS	2-0	Hurst 2	4405	6							4				8		10	12			14			2	11	1	7	9				3	13		5	
6		29	Mansfield Town	3-2	Hurst 2, Edwards	6444	6							4					10	8		14	7			2	11	1		9	12			3	13		5	
7	Sep	2	Darlington	1-1	White	5273	6							4				8	12	10						11		1	7	9	13			3	14		5	
8		10	CHESTER CITY	1-0	Hurst	5404	6							4				8		10						2	11	1	7	9	12			3	13		5	
9		17	Shrewsbury Town	0-2		4011	6							4				8	9	10		11				2	12	1	7		14			3	13		5	
10		24	RUSHDEN & D'MNDS	0-0		5142		14						4				8	9	10	12		13	6			2		1	7		11			3			5	
11		27	Grimsby Town	0-4		5577		9						4				8			13		12	10	6		2		1	7		11			3			5	
12	Oct	1	Macclesfield Town	1892				10						4				8	9	12	13		6				2		1	7	14	11			3			5	
13		7	BOSTON UNITED	1-2	Edwards	6632	6	8						4				12		13				10			2		1	7	9	11			3	14		5	
14		15	Rochdale	0-3		3348	6	8						4					9	11		3	10				2		1	7	14	13						5	12
15		22	CARLISLE UNITED	0-0		5347	6							4	5			13		10	7			12	8				1		9	11			3			2	
16		29	Bury	3-2	Hurst 3	2671	6							4	5			13		10	11			8			12		1	7	9				3	14		2	
17	Nov	12	CHELTENHAM TOWN	2-3	Baudet (p), Edwards	4903	6							4				13		10	11			8					1	7			5	3	9	12	2	
18		19	Boston United	2-1	Hurst, White	2921	6							4						10				11		8			1	7			5	3	9		2	
19		26	TORQUAY UNITED	2-2	Edwards, De Bolla	4442	6				12			4						10	13			11		8			1	7			5	3	9		2	
20	Dec	6	Peterborough United	0-2		2833	6				12			4						10	13			8	11	2			1	7		14	3		9		5	
21		10	Wrexham	1-1	Sheridan	4726	6							9	4	5				10				8	11				1	7		13			3	12		2	
22		17	STOCKPORT COUNTY	2-0	Baudet, Friars	4261	6							9	4	5	12				8				11				1	7		10			3	13		2	
23		26	Oxford United	0-3		5626	6							9	4	5								8	11	7	12		1			14	10		3	13		2	
24		31	Leyton Orient	0-1		3715	6							10	4						8			12	11	2	5		1	7				3	9				
25	Jan	2	BARNET	1-0	Martin	5249	6							4							3		8	11	2	5		1	7	12	10				9			
26		7	DARLINGTON	3-2	Scoffham, Martin, Baudet (p)	4244	6							4							3		8	11	2	5		1	7	13	10				9		12	
27		14	Wycombe Wanderers	0-2		5185	6			2		12		4									8	11	9	5	1	7		10		13			3				
28		21	SHREWSBURY TOWN	2-1	Pipe, Wilson	5438	6			2	9	10		4							3			11		8			1	7		12		13			5		
29		24	NORTHAMPTON T	2-2	Pipe, Crooks	4884	6			2	9	10		4							3			11		8			1	7		12					5		
30		28	Chester City	2-0	Baudet (p), Dadi (p)	2599	6			2	9	10		4							3			11	13	8	1	7	12							5		
31	Feb	4	GRIMSBY TOWN	0-1		6456	6			2	9	10		4							12		3		11		8	1	7	13							5		
32		11	Rushden & Diamonds	0-1		3113	6			2	10	13		4									3		12	14	8		1	7	9	11						5		
33		14	WYCOMBE WANDERERS	1-2	O'Callaghan	3710	6		9	3	10	13		4										8	11	2		1	7			12					5		
34		18	PETERBOROUGH UTD.	1-2	Dadi (p)	6012	6		9	3	10	14		12										8	11	2	13	1	7			4					5		
35		25	Lincoln City	1-2	Edwards	5262			10		14		6	4									12	8		2	11	1	7	9		13			3		5		
36	Mar	4	MANSFIELD TOWN	2-2	Palmer, Chillingworth	9779	6		13	2	9		8	4									12				11	1	7		10				3		5		
37		11	Bristol Rovers	2-1	Chillingworth, Scoffham	6280	6		10	5			8	4							12					2	11	1	7	14	13				3	9			
38		18	OXFORD UNITED	0-0		5265	6		10	5			8	4								14				2	11	1	7	9	13				3	12			
39		25	Northampton Town	0-2		6077	6		10	5	12		8	4												2	11	1	7	9	14				3	13			
40	Apr	1	LEYTON ORIENT	1-1	Edwards	5007	6		10	5			8	4								13			11		11	1	2	9	7				3	14			
41		8	Barnet	1-2	Scoffham	2841	6		10	5			8	4					13								11		7	1	2	9				3	12			
42		15	MACCLESFIELD TOWN	1-1	Edwards	4393	6		13	5			8	4							1	3		12	11	2	10		7	9									
43		17	Carlisle United	1-2	Scoffham	10735	6			2			8	4			14			13		3			11	12	10	1	7	9					5				
44		22	ROCHDALE	1-1	Martin	4413	6		13	2			5	4			12					3		8	11	10		1	7	9									
45		29	Cheltenham Town	0-2		4518	6		12	2			8	4			13					3			11		10	1	7	9					5				
46	May	6	BURY	2-2	Martin, Baudet (p)	9817	6		13		10		8	4			12					2		14	11		5	1	7	9					3				
				Apps			42	5	13	18	11	14	12	46	5	4	14	6	18	19	1	22	6	29	22	33	29	45	43	30	27	3	5	33	26	1	34	1
				Goals			6		2	1	2	1		7	1				9	1		4				1	1		2	5	1				2		1	

One own goal

F.A. Cup

| R1 | Nov | 5 | Bristol City | 2-0 | Baudet, Tann | 4221 | 5 | | | | | | | 4 | | | 8 | | 10 | 11 | | | 6 | | | 12 | | 1 | 7 | 9 | | 2 | 3 | 13 | | | |
| R2 | Dec | 3 | Torquay United | 1-2 | McMahon (p) | 2407 | 5 | | | | 9 | | | 6 | | | | 13 | 10 | 12 | | | 8 | | | 2 | 14 | 1 | 7 | | 11 | | | 3 | | | 4 | | |

Carling Cup

| R1 | Aug | 23 | Watford | 1-3 | Palmer | 7011 | 5 | | | | | | | 6 | | | 8 | | 10 | | 3 | | | 2 | 11 | 1 | 7 | 13 | | | | | 12 | 9 | | 4 | | |

LDV Vans Trophy

| R1 | Oct | 18 | Northampton Town | 2-5 | Long, McMahon (p) | 2041 | 5 | 8 | | | | | 6 | | | | | | 7 | 1 | | 13 | 11 | | 12 | | | | | | | | | 3 | 9 | 10 | 4 | | |

C Chilaka played at 2

LAST DAY ADVENTURES 2005/06 - NOTTS 2 BURY 2

There was a mathematical chance of County being relegated to the Conference on the last day of the season.

You could cut the atmosphere with a knife. 0-2 down, but in the 84th minute Martin scores for Notts.

Pressure, what pressure? Baudet slots home an 87 minute penalty.....

...with understandable relief all round!

2006/07

#	Date		Opponent	Score	Scorers	Att	Byron M	Curtis TD	Deeney S	Dudfield LG	Edwards M	Gleeson DE	Hunt SJ	Lee JB	Martin DA	McCann HA	McMahon D	Mendes AJHA	Needham LP	N'Toya T	Parkinson AJ	Pilkington KW	Pipe DR	Ross I	Sheridan J	Silk GL	Smith JA	Somner MJ	Walker J	Weston M	White A
1	Aug	5	Lincoln City	1-1	Hughes (og)	6046	14			10	4			9		3		12			13	11	1	2	8		7	6			5
2		8	SHREWSBURY TOWN	1-1	Edwards	4386	14			10	4					3		9			12	11	1	2	8	13	7	6			5
3		12	WYCOMBE WANDERERS	1-0	Mendes	4053				10	4	7	14		8	3		9			12	11	1	2	13			6			5
4		19	Rochdale	1-0	White	2321					4	7	14	9	13	3		10			12	11	1	2	8			6			5
5		26	PETERBOROUGH UTD.	0-0		6353					4	7		9	8	3		10			12	11	1	2				6			5
6	Sep	2	Milton Keynes Dons	2-3	Lee, Martin	6323					12	4	7	13	9	8	3				10	11	1	2	14			6			5
7		9	ACCRINGTON STANLEY	3-2	Edwards, Martin 2	4677					4	7	5	9	6	3		10	14	12	11		1	2	8		13				5
8		12	Chester City	0-0		1818				10	4	7		9	8	3		12				11	1	2	13			6			5
9		16	Barnet	3-2	White, Parkinson, Lee	2317				10	4	7	14	9	8	3		12				11	1	2	13			6			5
10		23	SWINDON TOWN	1-1	White	6079					14	4	7	9	8	3		10			13	11	1	2	12			6			5
11		26	STOCKPORT COUNTY	1-0	Mendes	4021					12	4	7	14	9		3	10			13	11	1	2	8			6			5
12		30	Torquay United	1-0	Dudfield	2815					14	4	7	8	9		3	10			12	11	1	2	13			6			5
13	Oct	7	Mansfield Town	2-2	Edwards, Dudfield	6182					10	4		13		14	3	9			12	11	1	2	8	7		6			5
14		14	BRISTOL ROVERS	1-2	Mendes	5797					13	4	7	6	9	14	3	12		10		11	1	2	8						5
15		21	Grimsby Town	2-0	Mendes, Lee	4029					14	4	7	13	9	12	3	10				11	1	2	8			6			5
16		28	BURY	0-1		4770					4	7	13	9	10	3		11	14			1	2	8	12			6			5
17	Nov	4	Boston United	3-3	Lee 2, White	2539					12	4		7	9	13	3	10			11		1		8	2		6			5
18		18	WREXHAM	2-1	Parkinson, Lee	4416					14	4	7		9		3	12	10		11		1	2	8				13	6		5
19		25	Walsall	1-2	Ross	5402					12	4	13		9		3	14	10		11		1	2	8	6	7					5
20	Dec	5	HARTLEPOOL UNITED	0-1		3546					14	4	7		9		3	10	13		11		1	2	8			12	6			5
21		9	MACCLESFIELD TOWN	1-2	Martin	4036		1		12	4			9	14	3	10	13			11			2	8		6	7			5
22		16	Darlington	1-0	White	3253		1		10	4				14	3	12	9	13	11					8		2	7	6		5
23		22	HEREFORD UNITED	0-1		4106		1		10	4				13	3	9	11	14	12				2	8		6	7			5
24		26	Stockport County	0-2		5823				13	4			9	12	3		10			11		1	2			7	8	6			5
25		30	Swindon Town	1-1	Dudfield	6805				10	12		4	9	14	3		13			11		1	2	8			7	6			5
26	Jan	1	CHESTER CITY	1-2	Lee	4019				10			4	9	13	3		14			11		1	2	8		12	7	6			5
27		13	Accrington Stanley	2-1	Dudfield, Lee	1702				10	4			3	9	7		12			11		1	2	14		13	8	6			5
28		20	TORQUAY UNITED	5-2	Mendes, Smith, Parkinson, Lee 2	4311				10	4			3	9	11		13	7		12		1				2	8	6			5
29		27	Hereford United	2-3	Lee 2	3280				10	4	2			9	7		13			11	1				12	3	8	6			5
30		30	BARNET	1-1	Dudfield (p)	3010				10	4			5	9	7	3	12			11	1					2	8	6			
31	Feb	3	LINCOLN CITY	3-1	Smith, Lee, Dudfield	7019				10	4			5	9		3				11		1		7		2	8	6			13
32		10	Wycombe Wanderers	0-0		4836				10	4			5	9		3	13			11		1		7		2	8	6			12
33		17	ROCHDALE	1-2	Lee	4493				10	4			5	9	13	3				14		1		7		2	8	6			12
34		20	Shrewsbury Town	0-2		3369				10	4			7	9		3	12			11		1			6	2	8	13			5
35		24	MK DONS	2-2	Smith (p), Hunt	4031			1		4		7	9			3			10	12	11		6	2			13	8			5
36	Mar	3	Peterborough United	0-2		5014			1	10	4			5		12	3		9		13	11		7			2	8	6			
37		10	MANSFIELD TOWN	0-0		10034			1	10	4			7			3				9	13	11		6	2		12	8		13	5
38		17	Bristol Rovers	0-2		4642			1	10	4			7			3				9	11			6	12		2	8		13	5
39		24	Bury	1-0	N'Toya	2310				10	4			5	9	13	3			11		12	1	2	8			7	6			
40		31	GRIMSBY TOWN	2-0	Newey (og), Smith	4724				10	4			5	9		3			11		12	1	2	7		13	8	6	14		
41	Apr	7	BOSTON UNITED	2-0	Lee, Somner	4170				10	4			5	9		3					11	1	2	7		6	8	12	13	14	
42		9	Wrexham	1-0	Spender (og)	4557				10	4			5	13		3				14	11	1		7		2	8	6	9	12	
43		14	WALSALL	1-2	Dudfield	7080				10	4			5	9		3					13	1	2	12		7	8	6	11	14	
44		20	Hartlepool United	1-1	Parkinson	6174	14			10	4			5	9	12	3					11	1	2	8			6	13	7	
45		28	DARLINGTON	0-1		5264	5			10	4				9	12	3					11	1	2	14		7	8	6	13		
46	May	5	Macclesfield Town	1-1	Parkinson	4114	6			10	4			5	9	13	3					11	1	2			7	8	12	14		
			Apps				3	2	7	41	45	17	32	38	29	43	7	37	1	21	45	39	39	36	3	30	27	38	8	4	35
			Goals							7	3		1	15	4			5		1	5				1		4	1			5

Three own goals

F.A. Cup

	Date		Opponent	Score	Scorers	Att																									
R1	Nov	11	Leyton Orient	1-2	Dudfield	3011				12	3	13		10		5		11		14	9	1	6	8		2		7			4

Carling Cup

	Date		Opponent	Score	Scorers	Att																									
R1	Aug	22	Crystal Palace	2-1	Dudfield, Martin	4481	8	1		11	3	14	5		6			12	13	10					7	9	2				4
R2	Sep	20	Middlesbrough	1-0	N'Toya	11148	8	1		11	3	13	4			5		12	14	10					6	9	2		7		
R3	Oct	24	SOUTHAMPTON	2-0	Edwards, Lee	6731		1			3	13	5	10	14			11		12	9		6	8		2		7			4
R4	Nov	7	WYCOMBE WANDERERS	0-1		7395		1		12	3				10	13	5		11		14	9		6	8		2		7			4

Johnstone's Paint Trophy

	Date		Opponent	Score	Scorers	Att																									
R1	Oct	17	BARNET	0-1		1291			1	11			14	3		8				6	5	10				9	12	2		7		4

Played at 13: S Akers

Home to Southampton in the League Cup. Mike Edwards celebrates after his 13th minute goal.....

.. and Jason Lee added a second before half-time to give Notts a 2-0 win over the Championship side.

The July 2006 team group. From left, back: Austin McCann, Mike Edwards, Alan White, Steve Hunt, Dan Martin, Junior Mendes, Matt Somner. Middle: Mike Whitlow (coaching staff), Stef Frost, Bobby Wilson, Tom Hannigan, Saul Deeney, Kevin Pilkington, Jason Lee, Lawrie Dudfield, Dan Gleeson, John Haselden (physio). Front: Andy Parkinson, Jake Sheridan, Tcham N'Toya, Tom Curtis, John Gannon (assistant-manager), Steve Thompson (manager), David Pipe, Liam Needham, Ian Ross, Gary Silk.

Jason Lee, Player's Player of the Year, and Mike Edwards, Player of the Year, 2006/07

FOOTBALL LEAGUE TABLES 1976/77 to 2006/07

1976/77 Division 2

		p	w	d	l	f	a	pts
1	Wolverhampton Wan.	42	22	13	7	84	45	57
2	Chelsea	42	21	13	8	73	53	55
3	Nottingham Forest	42	21	10	11	77	43	52
4	Bolton Wanderers	42	20	11	11	75	54	51
5	Blackpool	42	17	17	8	58	42	51
6	Luton Town	42	21	6	15	67	48	48
7	Charlton Athletic	42	16	16	10	71	58	48
8	NOTTS COUNTY	42	19	10	13	65	60	48
9	Southampton	42	17	10	15	72	67	44
10	Millwall	42	15	13	14	57	53	43
11	Sheffield United	42	14	12	16	54	63	40
12	Blackburn Rovers	42	15	9	18	42	54	39
13	Oldham Athletic	42	14	10	18	52	64	38
14	Hull City	42	10	17	15	45	53	37
15	Bristol Rovers	42	12	13	17	53	68	37
16	Burnley	42	11	14	17	46	64	36
17	Fulham	42	11	13	18	54	61	35
18	Cardiff City	42	12	10	20	56	67	34
19	Orient	42	9	16	17	37	55	34
20	Carlisle United	42	11	12	19	49	75	34
21	Plymouth Argyle	42	8	16	18	46	65	32
22	Hereford United	42	8	15	19	57	78	31

1977/78 Division 2

		p	w	d	l	f	a	pts
1	Bolton Wanderers	42	24	10	8	63	33	58
2	Southampton	42	22	13	7	70	39	57
3	Tottenham Hotspur	42	20	16	6	83	49	56
4	Brighton & Hove A.	42	22	12	8	63	38	56
5	Blackburn Rovers	42	16	13	13	56	60	45
6	Sunderland	42	14	16	12	67	59	44
7	Stoke City	42	16	10	16	53	49	42
8	Oldham Athletic	42	13	16	13	54	58	42
9	Crystal Palace	42	13	15	14	50	47	41
10	Fulham	42	14	13	15	49	49	41
11	Burnley	42	15	10	17	56	64	40
12	Sheffield United	42	16	8	18	62	73	40
13	Luton Town	42	14	10	18	54	52	38
14	Orient	42	10	18	14	43	49	38
15	NOTTS COUNTY	42	11	16	15	54	62	38
16	Millwall	42	12	14	16	49	57	38
17	Charlton Athletic	42	13	12	17	55	68	38
18	Bristol Rovers	42	13	12	17	61	77	38
19	Cardiff City	42	13	12	17	51	71	38
20	Blackpool	42	12	13	17	59	60	37
21	Mansfield Town	42	10	11	21	49	69	31
22	Hull City	42	8	12	22	34	52	28

1978/79 Division 2

		p	w	d	l	f	a	pts
1	Crystal Palace	42	19	19	4	51	24	57
2	Brighton & Hove A.	42	23	10	9	72	39	56
3	Stoke City	42	20	16	6	58	31	56
4	Sunderland	42	22	11	9	70	44	55
5	West Ham United	42	18	14	10	70	39	50
6	NOTTS COUNTY	42	14	16	12	48	60	44
7	Preston North End	42	12	18	12	59	57	42
8	Newcastle United	42	17	8	17	51	55	42
9	Cardiff City	42	16	10	16	56	70	42
10	Fulham	42	13	15	14	50	47	41
11	Orient	42	15	10	17	51	51	40
12	Cambridge United	42	12	16	14	44	52	40
13	Burnley	42	14	12	16	51	62	40
14	Oldham Athletic	42	13	13	16	52	61	39
15	Wrexham	42	12	14	16	45	42	38
16	Bristol Rovers	42	14	10	18	48	60	38
17	Leicester City	42	10	17	15	43	52	37
18	Luton Town	42	13	10	19	60	57	36
19	Charlton Athletic	42	11	13	18	60	69	35
20	Sheffield United	42	11	12	19	52	69	34
21	Millwall	42	11	10	21	42	61	32
22	Blackburn Rovers	42	10	10	22	41	72	30

1979/80 Division 2

		p	w	d	l	f	a	pts
1	Leicester City	42	21	13	8	58	38	55
2	Sunderland	42	21	12	9	69	42	54
3	Birmingham City	42	21	11	10	58	38	53
4	Chelsea	42	23	7	12	66	52	53
5	Queen's Park Rgs.	42	18	13	11	75	53	49
6	Luton Town	42	16	17	9	66	45	49
7	West Ham United	42	20	7	15	54	43	47
8	Cambridge United	42	14	16	12	61	53	44
9	Newcastle United	42	15	14	13	53	49	44
10	Preston North End	42	12	19	11	56	52	43
11	Oldham Athletic	42	16	11	15	49	53	43
12	Swansea City	42	17	9	16	48	53	43
13	Shrewsbury Town	42	18	5	19	60	53	41
14	Orient	42	12	17	13	48	54	41
15	Cardiff City	42	16	8	18	41	48	40
16	Wrexham	42	16	6	20	40	49	38
17	NOTTS COUNTY	42	11	15	16	51	52	37
18	Watford	42	12	13	17	39	46	37
19	Bristol Rovers	42	11	13	18	50	64	35
20	Fulham	42	11	7	24	42	74	29
21	Burnley	42	6	15	21	39	73	27
22	Charlton Athletic	42	6	10	26	39	78	22

1980/81 Division 2

		p	w	d	l	f	a	pts
1	West Ham United	42	28	10	4	79	29	66
2	NOTTS COUNTY	42	18	17	7	49	38	53
3	Swansea City	42	18	14	10	64	44	50
4	Blackburn Rovers	42	16	18	8	42	29	50
5	Luton Town	42	18	12	12	61	46	48
6	Derby County	42	15	15	12	57	52	45
7	Grimsby Town	42	15	15	12	44	42	45
8	Queen's Park Rgs.	42	15	13	14	56	46	43
9	Watford	42	16	11	15	50	45	43
10	Sheffield Wed.	42	17	8	17	53	51	42
11	Newcastle United	42	14	14	14	30	45	42
12	Chelsea	42	14	12	16	46	41	40
13	Cambridge United	42	17	6	19	53	65	40
14	Shrewsbury Town	42	11	17	14	46	47	39
15	Oldham Athletic	42	12	15	15	39	48	39
16	Wrexham	42	12	14	16	43	45	38
17	Orient	42	13	12	17	52	56	38
18	Bolton Wanderers	42	14	10	18	61	66	38
19	Cardiff City	42	12	12	18	44	60	36
20	Preston North End	42	11	14	17	41	62	36
21	Bristol City	42	7	16	19	29	51	30
22	Bristol Rovers	42	5	13	24	34	65	23

1981/82 Division 1

		p	w	d	l	f	a	pts
1	Liverpool	42	26	9	7	80	32	87
2	Ipswich Town	42	26	5	11	75	53	83
3	Manchester United	42	22	12	8	59	29	78
4	Tottenham Hotspur	42	20	11	11	67	48	71
5	Arsenal	42	20	11	11	48	37	71
6	Swansea City	42	21	6	15	58	51	69
7	Southampton	42	19	9	14	72	67	66
8	Everton	42	17	13	12	56	50	64
9	West Ham United	42	14	16	12	66	57	58
10	Manchester City	42	15	13	14	49	50	58
11	Aston Villa	42	15	12	15	55	53	57
12	Nottingham Forest	42	15	12	15	42	48	57
13	Brighton & Hove A.	42	13	13	16	43	52	52
14	Coventry City	42	13	11	18	56	62	50
15	NOTTS COUNTY	42	13	8	21	61	69	47
16	Birmingham City	42	10	14	18	53	61	44
17	West Bromwich Alb.	42	11	11	20	46	57	44
18	Stoke City	42	12	8	22	44	63	44
19	Sunderland	42	11	11	20	38	58	44
20	Leeds United	42	10	12	20	39	61	42
21	Wolverhampton Wan.	42	10	10	22	32	63	40
22	Middlesbrough	42	8	15	19	34	52	39

1982/83 Division 1

		p	w	d	l	f	a	pts
1	Liverpool	42	24	10	8	87	37	82
2	Watford	42	22	5	15	74	57	71
3	Manchester United	42	19	13	10	56	38	70
4	Tottenham Hotspur	42	20	9	13	65	50	69
5	Nottingham Forest	42	20	9	13	62	50	69
6	Aston Villa	42	21	5	16	62	50	68
7	Everton	42	18	10	14	66	48	64
8	West Ham United	42	20	4	18	68	62	64
9	Ipswich Town	42	15	13	14	64	50	58
10	Arsenal	42	16	10	16	58	56	58
11	West Bromwich Alb.	42	15	12	15	51	49	57
12	Southampton	42	15	12	15	54	58	57
13	Stoke City	42	16	9	17	53	64	57
14	Norwich City	42	14	12	16	52	58	54
15	NOTTS COUNTY	42	15	7	20	55	71	52
16	Sunderland	42	12	14	16	48	61	50
17	Birmingham City	42	12	14	16	40	55	50
18	Luton Town	42	12	13	17	65	84	49
19	Coventry City	42	13	9	20	48	59	48
20	Manchester City	42	13	8	21	47	70	47
21	Swansea City	42	10	11	21	51	69	41
22	Brighton & Hove A.	42	9	13	20	38	68	40

1983/84 Division 1

		p	w	d	l	f	a	pts
1	Liverpool	42	22	14	6	73	32	80
2	Southampton	42	22	11	9	66	38	77
3	Nottingham Forest	42	22	8	12	76	45	74
4	Manchester United	42	20	14	8	71	41	74
5	Queen's Park Rgs.	42	22	7	13	67	37	73
6	Arsenal	42	18	9	15	74	60	63
7	Everton	42	16	14	12	44	42	62
8	Tottenham Hotspur	42	17	10	15	64	65	61
9	West Ham United	42	17	9	16	60	55	60
10	Aston Villa	42	17	9	16	59	61	60
11	Watford	42	16	9	17	68	77	57
12	Ipswich Town	42	15	8	19	55	57	53
13	Sunderland	42	13	13	16	42	53	52
14	Norwich City	42	12	15	15	48	49	51
15	Leicester City	42	13	12	17	65	68	51
16	Luton Town	42	14	9	19	53	66	51
17	West Bromwich Alb.	42	14	9	19	48	62	51
18	Stoke City	42	13	11	18	44	63	50
19	Coventry City	42	13	11	18	57	77	50
20	Birmingham City	42	12	12	18	39	50	48
21	NOTTS COUNTY	42	10	11	21	50	72	41
22	Wolverhampton Wan.	42	6	11	25	27	80	29

1984/85 Division 2

		p	w	d	l	f	a	pts
1	Oxford United	42	25	9	8	84	36	84
2	Birmingham City	42	25	7	10	59	33	82
3	Manchester City	42	21	11	10	66	40	74
4	Portsmouth	42	20	14	8	69	50	74
5	Blackburn Rovers	42	21	10	11	66	41	73
6	Brighton & Hove A.	42	20	12	10	54	34	72
7	Leeds United	42	19	12	11	66	43	69
8	Shrewsbury Town	42	18	11	13	66	53	65
9	Fulham	42	19	8	15	68	64	65
10	Grimsby Town	42	18	8	16	72	64	62
11	Barnsley	42	14	16	12	42	42	58
12	Wimbledon	42	16	10	16	71	75	58
13	Huddersfield Town	42	15	10	17	52	64	55
14	Oldham Athletic	42	15	8	19	49	67	53
15	Crystal Palace	42	12	12	18	46	65	48
16	Carlisle United	42	13	8	21	50	67	47
17	Charlton Athletic	42	11	12	19	51	63	45
18	Sheffield United	42	10	14	18	54	66	44
19	Middlesbrough	42	10	10	22	41	57	40
20	NOTTS COUNTY	42	10	7	25	45	73	37
21	Cardiff City	42	9	8	25	47	79	35
22	Wolverhampton Wan.	42	8	9	25	37	79	33

1985/86 Division 3

		p	w	d	l	f	a	pts
1	Reading	46	29	7	10	67	51	94
2	Plymouth Argyle	46	26	9	11	88	53	87
3	Derby County	46	23	15	8	80	41	84
4	Wigan Athletic	46	23	14	9	82	48	83
5	Gillingham	46	22	13	11	81	54	79
6	Walsall	46	22	9	15	90	64	75
7	York City	46	20	11	15	77	58	71
8	NOTTS COUNTY	46	19	14	13	71	60	71
9	Bristol City	46	18	14	14	69	60	68
10	Brentford	46	18	12	16	58	61	66
11	Doncaster Rovers	46	16	16	14	45	52	64
12	Blackpool	46	17	12	17	66	55	63
13	Darlington	46	15	13	18	61	78	58
14	Rotherham United	46	15	12	19	61	59	57
15	Bournemouth	46	15	9	22	65	72	54
16	Bristol Rovers	46	14	12	20	51	75	54
17	Chesterfield	46	13	14	19	61	64	53
18	Bolton Wanderers	46	15	8	23	54	68	53
19	Newport County	46	11	18	17	52	65	51
20	Bury	46	12	13	21	63	67	49
21	Lincoln City	46	10	16	20	55	77	46
22	Cardiff City	46	12	9	25	53	83	45
23	Wolverhampton Wan.	46	11	10	25	57	98	43
24	Swansea City	46	11	10	25	43	87	43

1986/87 Division 3

		p	w	d	l	f	a	pts
1	Bournemouth	46	29	10	7	76	40	97
2	Middlesbrough	46	28	10	8	67	30	94
3	Swindon Town	46	25	12	9	77	47	87
4	Wigan Athletic	46	25	10	11	83	60	85
5	Gillingham	46	23	9	14	65	48	78
6	Bristol City	46	21	14	11	63	36	77
7	NOTTS COUNTY	46	21	13	12	77	56	76
8	Walsall	46	22	9	15	80	67	75
9	Blackpool	46	16	16	14	74	59	64
10	Mansfield Town	46	15	16	15	52	55	61
11	Brentford	46	15	15	16	64	66	60
12	Port Vale	46	15	12	19	76	70	57
13	Doncaster Rovers	46	14	15	17	56	62	57
14	Rotherham United	46	15	12	19	48	57	57
15	Chester City	46	13	17	16	61	59	56
16	Bury	46	14	13	19	54	60	55
17	Chesterfield	46	13	15	18	56	69	54
18	Fulham	46	12	17	17	59	77	53
19	Bristol Rovers	46	13	12	21	49	75	51
20	York City	46	12	13	21	55	79	49
21	Bolton Wanderers	46	10	15	21	46	58	45
22	Carlisle United	46	10	8	28	39	78	38
23	Darlington	46	7	16	23	45	77	37
24	Newport County	46	8	13	25	49	86	37

1987/88 Division 3

		p	w	d	l	f	a	pts
1	Sunderland	46	27	12	7	92	48	93
2	Brighton & Hove A.	46	23	15	8	69	47	84
3	Walsall	46	23	13	10	68	50	82
4	NOTTS COUNTY	46	23	12	11	82	49	81
5	Bristol City	46	21	12	13	77	62	75
6	Northampton Town	46	18	19	9	70	51	73
7	Wigan Athletic	46	20	12	14	70	61	72
8	Bristol Rovers	46	18	12	16	68	56	66
9	Fulham	46	19	9	18	69	60	66
10	Blackpool	46	17	14	15	71	62	65
11	Port Vale	46	18	11	17	58	56	65
12	Brentford	46	16	14	16	53	59	62
13	Gillingham	46	14	17	15	77	61	59
14	Bury	46	15	14	17	58	57	59
15	Chester City	46	14	16	16	51	62	58
16	Preston North End	46	15	13	18	48	59	58
17	Southend United	46	14	13	19	65	83	55
18	Chesterfield	46	15	10	21	41	70	55
19	Mansfield Town	46	14	12	20	48	59	54
20	Aldershot	46	15	8	23	64	74	53
21	Rotherham United	46	12	16	18	50	66	52
22	Grimsby Town	46	12	14	20	48	58	50
23	York City	46	8	9	29	48	91	33
24	Doncaster Rovers	46	8	9	29	40	84	33

1988/89 Division 3

1	Wolverhampton Wan.	46	26	14	6	96	49	92
2	Sheffield United	46	25	9	12	93	54	84
3	Port Vale	46	24	12	10	78	48	84
4	Fulham	46	22	9	15	69	67	75
5	Bristol Rovers	46	19	17	10	67	51	74
6	Preston North End	46	19	15	12	79	60	72
7	Brentford	46	18	14	14	66	61	68
8	Chester City	46	19	11	16	64	61	68
9	NOTTS COUNTY	46	18	13	15	64	54	67
10	Bolton Wanderers	46	16	16	14	58	54	64
11	Bristol City	46	18	9	19	53	55	63
12	Swansea City	46	15	16	15	51	53	61
13	Bury	46	16	13	17	55	67	61
14	Huddersfield Town	46	17	9	20	63	73	60
15	Mansfield Town	46	14	17	15	48	52	59
16	Cardiff City	46	14	15	17	44	56	57
17	Wigan Athletic	46	14	14	18	55	53	56
18	Reading	46	15	11	20	68	72	56
19	Blackpool	46	14	13	19	56	59	55
20	Northampton Town	46	16	6	24	66	76	54
21	Southend United	46	13	15	18	56	75	54
22	Chesterfield	46	14	7	25	51	86	49
23	Gillingham	46	12	4	30	47	81	40
24	Aldershot	46	8	13	25	48	78	37

1989/90 Division 3

1	Bristol Rovers	46	26	15	5	71	35	93
2	Bristol City	46	27	10	9	76	40	91
3	NOTTS COUNTY	46	25	12	9	73	53	87
4	Tranmere Rovers	46	23	11	12	86	49	80
5	Bury	46	21	11	14	70	49	74
6	Bolton Wanderers	46	18	15	13	59	48	69
7	Birmingham City	46	18	12	16	60	59	66
8	Huddersfield Town	46	17	14	15	61	62	65
9	Rotherham United	46	17	13	16	71	62	64
10	Reading	46	15	19	12	57	53	64
11	Shrewsbury Town	46	16	15	15	59	54	63
12	Crewe Alexandra	46	15	17	14	56	53	62
13	Brentford	46	18	7	21	66	66	61
14	Leyton Orient	46	16	10	20	52	56	58
15	Mansfield Town	46	16	7	23	50	65	55
16	Chester City	46	13	15	18	43	55	54
17	Swansea City	46	14	12	20	45	63	54
18	Wigan Athletic	46	13	14	19	48	64	53
19	Preston North End	46	14	10	22	65	79	52
20	Fulham	46	12	15	19	55	66	51
21	Cardiff City	46	12	14	20	51	70	50
22	Northampton Town	46	11	14	21	51	68	47
23	Blackpool	46	10	16	20	49	73	46
24	Walsall	46	9	14	23	40	72	41

1990/91 Division 2

1	Oldham Athletic	46	25	13	8	83	53	88
2	West Ham United	46	24	15	7	60	34	87
3	Sheffield Wed.	46	22	16	8	80	51	82
4	NOTTS COUNTY	46	23	11	12	76	55	80
5	Millwall	46	20	13	13	70	51	73
6	Brighton & Hove A.	46	21	7	18	63	69	70
7	Middlesbrough	46	20	9	17	66	47	69
8	Barnsley	46	19	12	15	63	48	69
9	Bristol City	46	20	7	19	68	71	67
10	Oxford United	46	14	19	13	69	66	61
11	Newcastle United	46	14	17	15	49	56	59
12	Wolverhampton Wan.	46	13	19	14	63	63	58
13	Bristol Rovers	46	15	13	18	56	59	58
14	Ipswich Town	46	13	18	15	60	68	57
15	Port Vale	46	15	12	19	56	64	57
16	Charlton Athletic	46	13	17	16	57	61	56
17	Portsmouth	46	14	11	21	58	70	53
18	Plymouth Argyle	46	12	17	17	54	68	53
19	Blackburn Rovers	46	14	10	22	51	66	52
20	Watford	46	12	15	19	45	59	51
21	Swindon Town	46	12	14	20	65	73	50
22	Leicester City	46	14	8	24	60	83	50
23	West Bromwich Alb.	46	10	18	18	52	61	48
24	Hull City	46	10	15	21	57	85	45

1991/92 Division 1

1	Leeds United	42	22	16	4	74	37	82
2	Manchester United	42	21	15	6	63	33	78
3	Sheffield Wed.	42	21	12	9	62	49	75
4	Arsenal	42	19	15	8	81	46	72
5	Manchester City	42	20	10	12	61	48	70
6	Liverpool	42	16	16	10	47	40	64
7	Aston Villa	42	17	9	16	48	44	60
8	Nottingham Forest	42	16	11	15	60	58	59
9	Sheffield United	42	16	9	17	65	63	57
10	Crystal Palace	42	14	15	13	53	61	57
11	Queen's Park Rgs.	42	12	18	12	48	47	54
12	Everton	42	13	14	15	52	51	53
13	Wimbledon	42	13	14	15	53	53	53
14	Chelsea	42	13	14	15	50	60	53
15	Tottenham Hotspur	42	15	7	20	58	63	52
16	Southampton	42	14	10	18	39	55	52
17	Oldham Athletic	42	14	9	19	63	67	51
18	Norwich City	42	11	12	19	47	63	45
19	Coventry City	42	11	11	20	35	44	44
20	Luton Town	42	10	12	20	38	71	42
21	NOTTS COUNTY	42	10	10	22	40	62	40
22	West Ham United	42	9	11	22	37	59	38

1992/93 Football League Division 1

1	Newcastle United	46	29	9	8	92	38	96
2	West Ham United	46	26	10	10	81	41	88
3	Portsmouth	46	26	10	10	80	46	88
4	Tranmere Rovers	46	23	10	13	72	56	79
5	Swindon Town	46	21	13	12	74	59	76
6	Leicester City	46	22	10	14	71	64	76
7	Millwall	46	18	16	12	65	53	70
8	Derby County	46	19	9	18	68	57	66
9	Grimsby Town	46	19	7	20	58	57	64
10	Peterborough Utd.	46	16	14	16	55	63	62
11	Wolverhampton Wan.	46	16	13	17	57	56	61
12	Charlton Athletic	46	16	13	17	49	46	61
13	Barnsley	46	17	9	20	56	60	60
14	Oxford United	46	14	14	18	53	56	56
15	Bristol City	46	14	14	18	49	67	56
16	Watford	46	14	13	19	57	71	55
17	NOTTS COUNTY	46	12	16	18	55	70	52
18	Southend United	46	13	13	20	54	64	52
19	Birmingham City	46	13	12	21	50	72	51
20	Luton Town	46	10	21	15	48	62	51
21	Sunderland	46	13	11	22	50	64	50
22	Brentford	46	13	10	23	52	71	49
23	Cambridge United	46	11	16	19	48	69	49
24	Bristol Rovers	46	10	11	25	55	87	41

1993/94 Division 1

1	Crystal Palace	46	27	9	10	73	46	90
2	Nottingham Forest	46	23	14	9	74	49	83
3	Millwall	46	19	17	10	58	49	74
4	Leicester City	46	19	16	11	72	59	73
5	Tranmere Rovers	46	21	9	16	69	53	72
6	Derby County	46	20	11	15	73	68	71
7	NOTTS COUNTY	46	20	8	18	65	69	68
8	Wolverhampton Wan.	46	17	17	12	60	47	68
9	Middlesbrough	46	18	13	15	66	54	67
10	Stoke City	46	18	13	15	57	59	67
11	Charlton Athletic	46	19	8	19	61	58	65
12	Sunderland	46	19	8	19	54	57	65
13	Bristol City	46	16	16	14	47	50	64
14	Bolton Wanderers	46	15	14	17	63	64	59
15	Southend United	46	17	8	21	63	67	59
16	Grimsby Town	46	13	20	13	52	47	59
17	Portsmouth	46	15	13	18	52	58	58
18	Barnsley	46	16	7	23	55	67	55
19	Watford	46	15	9	22	66	80	54
20	Luton Town	46	14	11	21	56	60	53
21	West Bromwich Alb.	46	13	12	21	60	69	51
22	Birmingham City	46	13	12	21	52	69	51
23	Oxford United	46	13	10	23	54	75	49
24	Peterborough Utd.	46	8	13	25	48	76	37

1994/95 Division 1

1	Middlesbrough	46	23	13	10	67	40	82
2	Reading	46	23	10	13	58	44	79
3	Bolton Wanderers	46	21	14	11	67	45	77
4	Wolverhampton Wan.	46	21	13	12	77	61	76
5	Tranmere Rovers	46	22	10	14	67	58	76
6	Barnsley	46	20	12	14	63	52	72
7	Watford	46	19	13	14	52	46	70
8	Sheffield United	46	17	17	12	74	55	68
9	Derby County	46	18	12	16	66	51	66
10	Grimsby Town	46	17	14	15	62	56	65
11	Stoke City	46	16	15	15	50	53	63
12	Millwall	46	16	14	16	60	60	62
13	Southend United	46	18	8	20	54	73	62
14	Oldham Athletic	46	16	13	17	60	60	61
15	Charlton Athletic	46	16	11	19	58	66	59
16	Luton Town	46	15	13	18	61	64	58
17	Port Vale	46	15	13	18	58	64	58
18	Portsmouth	46	15	13	18	53	63	58
19	West Bromwich Alb.	46	16	10	20	51	57	58
20	Sunderland	46	12	18	16	41	45	54
21	Swindon Town	46	12	12	22	54	73	48
22	Burnley	46	11	13	22	49	74	46
23	Bristol City	46	11	12	23	42	63	45
24	NOTTS COUNTY	46	9	13	24	45	66	40

1995/96 Division 2

1	Swindon Town	46	25	17	4	71	34	92
2	Oxford United	46	24	11	11	76	39	83
3	Blackpool	46	23	13	10	67	40	82
4	NOTTS COUNTY	46	21	15	10	63	39	78
5	Crewe Alexandra	46	22	7	17	77	60	73
6	Bradford City	46	22	7	17	71	69	73
7	Chesterfield	46	20	12	14	56	51	72
8	Wrexham	46	18	16	12	76	55	70
9	Stockport County	46	19	13	14	61	47	70
10	Bristol Rovers	46	20	10	16	57	60	70
11	Walsall	46	19	12	15	60	45	69
12	Wycombe Wanderers	46	15	15	16	63	59	60
13	Bristol City	46	15	15	16	55	60	60
14	Bournemouth	46	16	10	20	51	70	58
15	Brentford	46	15	13	18	43	49	58
16	Rotherham United	46	14	14	18	54	62	56
17	Burnley	46	14	13	19	56	68	55
18	Shrewsbury Town	46	13	14	19	58	70	53
19	Peterborough Utd.	46	13	13	20	59	66	52
20	York City	46	13	13	20	58	73	52
21	Carlisle United	46	12	13	21	57	72	49
22	Swansea City	46	11	14	21	43	79	47
23	Brighton & Hove A.	46	10	10	26	46	69	40
24	Hull City	46	5	16	25	36	78	31

1996/97 Division 2

1	Bury	46	24	12	10	62	38	84
2	Stockport County	46	23	13	10	59	41	82
3	Luton Town	46	21	15	10	71	45	78
4	Brentford	46	20	14	12	56	43	74
5	Bristol City	46	21	10	15	69	51	73
6	Crewe Alexandra	46	22	7	17	56	47	73
7	Blackpool	46	18	15	13	60	47	69
8	Wrexham	46	17	18	11	54	50	69
9	Burnley	46	19	11	16	71	55	68
10	Chesterfield	46	18	14	14	42	39	68
11	Gillingham	46	19	10	17	60	59	67
12	Walsall	46	19	10	17	54	53	67
13	Watford	46	16	19	11	45	38	67
14	Millwall	46	16	13	17	50	55	61
15	Preston North End	46	18	7	21	49	55	61
16	Bournemouth	46	15	15	16	43	45	60
17	Bristol Rovers	46	15	11	20	47	50	56
18	Wycombe Wanderers	46	15	10	21	51	56	55
19	Plymouth Argyle	46	12	18	16	47	58	54
20	York City	46	13	13	20	47	68	52
21	Peterborough Utd.	46	11	14	21	55	73	47
22	Shrewsbury Town	46	11	13	22	49	74	46
23	Rotherham United	46	7	14	25	39	70	35
24	NOTTS COUNTY	46	7	14	25	33	59	35

1997/1998 Division 3

1	NOTTS COUNTY	46	29	12	5	82	43	99
2	Macclesfield Town	46	23	13	10	63	44	82
3	Lincoln City	46	20	15	11	60	51	75
4	Colchester United	46	21	11	14	72	60	74
5	Torquay United	46	21	11	14	68	59	74
6	Scarborough	46	19	15	12	67	58	72
7	Barnet	46	19	13	14	61	51	70
8	Scunthorpe United	46	19	12	15	56	52	69
9	Rotherham United	46	16	19	11	67	61	67
10	Peterborough Utd.	46	18	13	15	63	51	67
11	Leyton Orient	46	19	12	15	62	47	66
12	Mansfield Town	46	16	17	13	64	55	65
13	Shrewsbury Town	46	16	13	17	61	62	61
14	Chester City	46	17	10	19	60	61	61
15	Exeter City	46	15	15	16	68	63	60
16	Cambridge United	46	14	18	14	63	57	60
17	Hartlepool United	46	12	23	11	61	53	59
18	Rochdale	46	17	7	22	56	55	58
19	Darlington	46	14	12	20	56	72	54
20	Swansea City	46	13	11	22	49	62	50
21	Cardiff City	46	9	23	14	48	52	50
22	Hull City	46	11	8	27	56	83	41
23	Brighton & Hove A.	46	6	17	23	38	66	35
24	Doncaster Rovers	46	4	8	34	30	113	20

1998/1999 Division 2

1	Fulham	46	31	8	7	79	32	101
2	Walsall	46	26	9	11	63	47	87
3	Manchester City	46	22	16	8	69	33	82
4	Gillingham	46	22	14	10	75	44	80
5	Preston North End	46	22	13	11	78	50	79
6	Wigan Athletic	46	22	10	14	75	48	76
7	Bournemouth	46	21	13	12	63	41	76
8	Stoke City	46	21	6	19	59	63	69
9	Chesterfield	46	17	13	16	46	44	64
10	Millwall	46	17	11	18	52	59	62
11	Reading	46	16	13	17	54	63	61
12	Luton Town	46	16	10	20	51	60	58
13	Bristol Rovers	46	13	17	16	65	56	56
14	Blackpool	46	14	14	18	44	54	56
15	Burnley	46	13	16	17	54	73	55
16	NOTTS COUNTY	46	14	12	20	52	61	54
17	Wrexham	46	13	14	19	43	62	53
18	Colchester United	46	12	16	18	52	70	52
19	Wycombe Wanderers	46	13	12	21	52	58	51
20	Oldham Athletic	46	14	9	23	48	66	51
21	York City	46	13	11	22	56	80	50
22	Northampton Town	46	10	18	18	43	57	48
23	Lincoln City	46	13	7	26	42	74	46
24	Macclesfield Town	46	11	10	25	43	63	43

1999/2000 Division 2

1	Preston North End	46	28	11	7	74	37	95
2	Burnley	46	25	13	8	69	47	88
3	Gillingham	46	25	10	11	79	48	85
4	Wigan Athletic	46	22	17	7	72	38	83
5	Millwall	46	23	13	10	76	50	82
6	Stoke City	46	23	13	10	68	42	82
7	Bristol Rovers	46	23	11	12	69	45	80
8	NOTTS COUNTY	46	18	11	17	61	55	65
9	Bristol City	46	15	19	12	59	57	64
10	Reading	46	16	14	16	57	63	62
11	Wrexham	46	17	11	18	52	61	62
12	Wycombe Wanderers	46	16	13	17	56	53	61
13	Luton Town	46	17	10	19	61	65	61
14	Oldham Athletic	46	16	12	18	50	55	60
15	Bury	46	13	18	15	61	64	57
16	Bournemouth	46	16	9	21	59	62	57
17	Brentford	46	13	13	20	47	61	52
18	Colchester United	46	14	10	22	59	82	52
19	Cambridge United	46	12	12	22	64	65	48
20	Oxford United	46	12	9	25	43	73	45
21	Cardiff City	46	9	17	20	45	67	44
22	Blackpool	46	8	17	21	49	77	41
23	Scunthorpe United	46	9	12	25	40	74	39
24	Chesterfield	46	7	15	24	34	63	36

2000/2001 Division 2

1	Millwall	46	28	9	9	89	38	93
2	Rotherham United	46	27	10	9	79	55	91
3	Reading	46	25	11	10	86	52	86
4	Walsall	46	23	12	11	79	50	81
5	Stoke City	46	21	14	11	74	49	77
6	Wigan Athletic	46	19	18	9	53	42	75
7	Bournemouth	46	20	13	13	79	55	73
8	NOTTS COUNTY	46	19	12	15	62	66	69
9	Bristol City	46	18	14	14	70	56	68
10	Wrexham	46	17	12	17	65	71	63
11	Port Vale	46	16	14	16	55	49	62
12	Peterborough Utd.	46	15	14	17	61	66	59
13	Wycombe Wanderers	46	15	14	17	46	53	59
14	Brentford	46	14	17	15	56	70	59
15	Oldham Athletic	46	15	13	18	53	65	58
16	Bury	46	16	10	20	45	59	58
17	Colchester United	46	15	12	19	55	59	57
18	Northampton Town	46	15	12	19	46	59	57
19	Cambridge United	46	14	11	21	61	77	53
20	Swindon Town	46	13	13	20	47	65	52
21	Bristol Rovers	46	12	15	19	53	57	51
22	Luton Town	46	9	13	24	52	80	40
23	Swansea City	46	8	13	25	47	73	37
24	Oxford United	46	7	6	33	53	100	27

2001/2002 Division 2

1	Brighton & Hove A.	46	25	15	6	66	42	90
2	Reading	46	23	15	8	70	43	84
3	Brentford	46	24	11	11	77	43	83
4	Cardiff City	46	23	14	9	75	50	83
5	Stoke City	46	23	11	12	67	40	80
6	Huddersfield Town	46	21	15	10	65	47	78
7	Bristol City	46	21	10	15	68	53	73
8	Queen's Park Rgs.	46	19	14	13	60	49	71
9	Oldham Athletic	46	18	16	12	77	65	70
10	Wigan Athletic	46	16	16	14	66	51	64
11	Wycombe Wanderers	46	17	13	16	58	64	64
12	Tranmere Rovers	46	16	15	15	63	60	63
13	Swindon Town	46	15	14	17	46	56	59
14	Port Vale	46	16	10	20	51	62	58
15	Colchester United	46	15	12	19	65	76	57
16	Blackpool	46	14	14	18	66	69	56
17	Peterborough Utd.	46	15	10	21	64	59	55
18	Chesterfield	46	13	13	20	53	65	52
19	NOTTS COUNTY	46	13	11	22	59	71	50
20	Northampton Town	46	14	7	25	54	79	49
21	Bournemouth	46	10	14	22	56	71	44
22	Bury	46	11	11	24	43	75	44
23	Wrexham	46	11	10	25	56	89	43
24	Cambridge United	46	7	13	26	47	93	34

2002/2003 Division 2

1	Wigan Athletic	46	29	13	4	68	25	100
2	Crewe Alexandra	46	25	11	10	76	40	86
3	Bristol City	46	24	11	11	79	48	83
4	Queen's Park Rgs.	46	24	11	11	69	45	83
5	Oldham Athletic	46	22	16	8	68	38	82
6	Cardiff City	46	23	12	11	68	43	81
7	Tranmere Rovers	46	23	11	12	66	57	80
8	Plymouth Argyle	46	17	14	15	63	52	65
9	Luton Town	46	17	14	15	67	62	65
10	Swindon Town	46	16	12	18	59	63	60
11	Peterborough Utd.	46	14	16	16	51	54	58
12	Colchester United	46	14	16	16	52	56	58
13	Blackpool	46	15	13	18	56	64	58
14	Stockport County	46	15	10	21	65	70	55
15	NOTTS COUNTY	46	13	16	17	62	70	55
16	Brentford	46	14	12	20	47	56	54
17	Port Vale	46	14	11	21	54	70	53
18	Wycombe Wanderers	46	13	13	20	59	66	52
19	Barnsley	46	13	13	20	51	64	52
20	Chesterfield	46	14	8	24	43	73	50
21	Cheltenham Town	46	10	18	18	53	68	48
22	Huddersfield Town	46	11	12	23	39	61	45
23	Mansfield Town	46	12	8	26	66	97	44
24	Northampton Town	46	10	9	27	40	79	39

2003/2004 Division 2

1	Plymouth Argyle	46	26	12	8	85	41	90
2	Queen's Park Rgs.	46	22	17	7	80	45	83
3	Bristol City	46	23	13	10	58	37	82
4	Brighton & Hove A.	46	22	11	13	64	43	77
5	Swindon Town	46	20	13	13	76	58	73
6	Hartlepool United	46	20	13	13	76	61	73
7	Port Vale	46	21	10	15	73	63	73
8	Tranmere Rovers	46	17	16	13	59	56	67
9	Bournemouth	46	17	15	14	56	51	66
10	Luton Town	46	17	15	14	69	66	66
11	Colchester United	46	17	13	16	52	56	64
12	Barnsley	46	15	17	14	54	58	62
13	Wrexham	46	17	9	20	50	60	60
14	Blackpool	46	16	11	19	58	65	59
15	Oldham Athletic	46	12	21	13	66	60	57
16	Sheffield Wed.	46	13	14	19	48	64	53
17	Brentford	46	14	11	21	52	69	53
18	Peterborough Utd.	46	12	16	18	58	58	52
19	Stockport County	46	11	19	16	62	70	52
20	Chesterfield	46	12	15	19	49	71	51
21	Grimsby Town	46	13	11	22	55	81	50
22	Rushden & Diamonds	46	13	9	24	60	74	48
23	NOTTS COUNTY	46	10	12	24	50	78	42
24	Wycombe Wanderers	46	6	19	21	50	75	37

2004/2005 Football League Two

1	Yeovil Town	46	25	8	13	90	65	83
2	Scunthorpe United	46	22	14	10	69	42	80
3	Swansea City	46	24	8	14	62	43	80
4	Southend United	46	22	12	12	65	46	78
5	Macclesfield Town	46	22	9	15	60	49	75
6	Lincoln City	46	20	12	14	64	47	72
7	Northampton Town	46	20	12	14	62	51	72
8	Darlington	46	20	12	14	57	49	72
9	Rochdale	46	16	18	12	54	48	66
10	Wycombe Wanderers	46	16	15	15	57	49	63
11	Leyton Orient	46	16	15	15	65	67	63
12	Bristol Rovers	46	13	21	12	60	57	60
13	Mansfield Town	46	15	15	16	56	56	60
14	Cheltenham Town	46	16	12	18	51	54	60
15	Oxford United	46	16	11	19	50	63	59
16	Boston United	46	14	16	16	62	58	58
17	Bury	46	14	16	16	54	54	58
18	Grimsby Town	46	14	16	16	51	52	58
19	NOTTS COUNTY	46	13	13	20	46	62	52
20	Chester City	46	12	16	18	43	69	52
21	Shrewsbury Town	46	11	16	19	48	53	49
22	Rushden & Diamonds	46	10	14	22	42	63	44
23	Kidderminster H.	46	10	8	28	39	85	38
24	Cambridge United	46	8	16	22	39	62	30

2005/2006 Football League Two

1	Carlisle United	46	25	11	10	84	42	86
2	Northampton Town	46	22	17	7	63	37	83
3	Leyton Orient	46	22	15	9	67	51	81
4	Grimsby Town	46	22	12	12	64	44	78
5	Cheltenham Town	46	19	15	12	65	53	72
6	Wycombe Wanderers	46	18	17	11	72	56	71
7	Lincoln City	46	15	21	10	65	53	66
8	Darlington	46	16	15	15	58	52	63
9	Peterborough Utd.	46	17	11	18	57	49	62
10	Shrewsbury Town	46	16	13	17	55	55	61
11	Boston United	46	15	16	15	50	60	61
12	Bristol Rovers	46	17	9	20	59	67	60
13	Wrexham	46	15	14	17	61	54	59
14	Rochdale	46	14	14	18	66	69	56
15	Chester City	46	14	12	20	53	59	54
16	Mansfield Town	46	13	15	18	59	66	54
17	Macclesfield Town	46	12	18	16	60	71	54
18	Barnet	46	12	18	16	44	57	54
19	Bury	46	12	17	17	45	57	52
20	Torquay United	46	13	13	20	53	66	52
21	NOTTS COUNTY	46	12	16	18	48	63	52
22	Stockport County	46	11	19	16	57	78	52
23	Oxford United	46	11	16	19	43	57	49
24	Rushden & Diamonds	46	11	12	23	44	76	45

2006/2007 Football League Two

1	Walsall	46	25	14	7	66	34	89
2	Hartlepool United	46	26	10	10	65	40	88
3	Swindon Town	46	25	10	11	58	38	85
4	Milton Keynes Dons	46	25	9	12	76	58	84
5	Lincoln City	46	21	11	14	70	59	74
6	Bristol Rovers	46	20	12	14	49	42	72
7	Shrewsbury Town	46	18	17	11	68	46	71
8	Stockport County	46	21	8	17	65	54	71
9	Rochdale	46	18	12	16	70	50	66
10	Peterborough Utd.	46	18	11	17	70	61	65
11	Darlington	46	17	14	15	52	56	65
12	Wycombe Wanderers	46	16	14	16	52	47	62
13	NOTTS COUNTY	46	16	14	16	55	53	62
14	Barnet	46	16	11	19	55	70	59
15	Grimsby Town	46	17	8	21	57	73	59
16	Hereford United	46	14	13	19	45	53	55
17	Mansfield Town	46	14	12	20	58	63	54
18	Chester City	46	13	14	19	40	48	53
19	Wrexham	46	13	12	21	43	65	51
20	Accrington Stanley	46	13	11	22	70	81	50
21	Bury	46	13	11	22	46	61	50
22	Macclesfield Town	46	12	12	22	55	77	48
23	Boston United	46	12	10	24	51	80	36
24	Torquay United	46	7	14	25	36	63	35

The Division Three (South) Championship squad of 1949/50. Back: Simpson, Houghton (manager), Southwell, Smith, Fisher (secretary), Chapman, Adamson, Moore (trainer), Rigby. Centre: FJ Evans, Broome, Sewell, Barnes (chairman), Lawton, W Evans, Johnston. Front: Baxter, Deans

FOOTBALL LEAGUE SEASONS 1888/89 TO 2006/07

	Div.	Pos.	Home: p	w	d	l	f	a	Away: p	w	d	l	f	a	Pts		Average attendances: Overall	Home	Away
1888/89	1	11	11	4	2	5	25	32	11	1	0	10	15	41	12		3881	3909	3850
1889/90	1	10	11	4	3	4	20	19	11	2	2	7	23	32	17		3619	3364	3900
1890/91	1	3	11	9	1	1	33	11	11	2	3	6	19	24	26		6398	7300	5579
1891/92	1	8	13	9	3	1	41	12	13	2	1	10	14	39	26		5088	5308	4850
1892/93	1	14	15	8	3	4	34	15	15	2	1	12	19	46	24	R	6417	6933	5900
1893/94	2	3	14	12	1	1	55	14	14	6	2	6	15	17	39		3478	3121	3862
1894/95	2	2	15	12	2	1	50	15	15	5	3	7	25	30	39		4855	4633	5111
1895/96	2	10	15	8	1	6	41	22	15	4	1	10	16	32	26		3328	3133	3536
1896/97	2	1	15	12	1	2	60	18	15	7	3	5	32	25	42	P	5224	4867	5607
1897/98	1	13	15	4	6	5	23	23	15	4	2	9	13	23	24		8283	8600	7967
1898/99	1	5	17	9	6	2	33	20	17	3	7	7	14	31	37		9806	10676	8935
1899/1900	1	15	17	5	7	5	29	22	17	4	4	9	17	38	29		8527	8941	8112
1900/01	1	3	17	13	2	2	39	18	17	5	2	10	15	28	40		10003	9441	10566
1901/02	1	13	17	12	2	3	44	19	17	2	2	13	7	38	32		9384	9118	9650
1902/03	1	15	17	8	5	4	25	16	17	4	2	11	16	33	31		9641	9235	10046
1903/04	1	13	17	9	3	5	27	26	17	3	2	12	10	35	29		10441	10235	10647
1904/05	1	18	17	1	7	9	16	33	17	4	1	12	20	36	18		9529	8059	11000
1905/06	1	16	19	8	9	2	34	21	19	3	3	13	21	50	34		10553	10026	11079
1906/07	1	18	19	6	9	4	31	18	19	2	6	11	15	32	31		11737	10526	12947
1907/08	1	18	19	9	3	7	24	19	19	4	5	10	15	32	34		12237	10526	13947
1908/09	1	15	19	9	4	6	31	23	19	5	4	10	20	25	36		13250	10237	16263
1909/10	1	9	19	10	5	4	41	26	19	5	5	9	26	33	40		11289	9947	12632
1910/11	1	11	19	9	6	4	21	16	19	5	4	10	16	29	38		12763	12684	12842
1911/12	1	16	19	9	4	6	26	20	19	5	3	11	20	43	35		12283	10947	13618
1912/13	1	19	19	6	4	9	19	20	19	1	5	13	9	36	23	R	12936	12053	13820
1913/14	2	1	19	16	2	1	55	13	19	7	5	7	22	23	53	P	12211	11789	12632
1914/15	1	16	19	8	7	4	28	18	19	1	6	12	13	39	31		10187	9053	11322
1919/20	1	21	21	9	8	4	39	25	21	3	4	14	17	49	36	R	18095	16476	19713
1920/21	2	6	21	12	5	4	36	17	21	6	6	9	19	23	47		16810	15286	18333
1921/22	2	13	21	10	7	4	34	18	21	2	8	11	13	33	39		12881	11810	13952
1922/23	2	1	21	16	1	4	29	15	21	7	6	8	17	19	53	P	14024	13143	14905
1923/24	1	10	21	9	7	5	21	15	21	5	7	9	23	34	42		16530	15333	17727
1924/25	1	9	21	11	6	4	29	12	21	5	7	9	13	19	45		15933	13000	18867
1925/26	1	22	21	11	4	6	37	26	21	2	3	16	17	48	33	R	16404	14908	17899
1926/27	2	16	21	11	4	6	45	24	21	4	1	16	25	72	35		11170	9825	12514
1927/28	2	15	21	10	4	7	47	26	21	3	8	10	21	48	38		11808	11065	12551
1928/29	2	5	21	13	4	4	51	24	21	6	5	10	27	41	47		14454	15090	13819
1929/30	2	22	21	8	7	6	33	26	21	1	8	12	21	44	33	R	11788	11333	12243
1930/31	3S	1	21	16	4	1	58	13	21	8	7	6	39	33	59	P	10721	12257	9185
1931/32	2	16	21	10	4	7	43	30	21	3	8	10	32	45	38		11920	11965	11874
1932/33	2	15	21	10	4	7	41	31	21	5	6	10	26	47	40		11587	11015	12158
1933/34	2	18	21	9	7	5	32	22	21	3	4	14	21	40	35		11913	12037	11789
1934/35	2	22	21	8	3	10	29	33	21	1	4	16	17	64	25	R	11197	10980	11413
1935/36	3S	9	21	10	5	6	40	25	21	5	7	9	20	32	42		8208	7320	9095
1936/37	3S	2	21	15	3	3	44	23	21	8	7	6	30	29	56		12725	14129	11321
1937/38	3S	11	21	10	6	5	29	17	21	6	3	12	21	33	41		11872	12354	11390
1938/39	3S	11	21	12	6	3	36	16	21	5	3	13	23	38	43		9126	10410	7842
1946/47	3S	12	21	11	4	6	35	19	21	4	6	11	28	44	40		13260	15376	11143
1947/48	3S	6	21	12	4	5	44	27	21	7	4	10	24	32	46		21546	25380	17712
1948/49	3S	11	21	15	3	3	68	19	21	4	2	15	34	49	43		25266	30002	20530
1949/50	3S	1	21	17	3	1	60	12	21	8	5	8	35	38	58	P	28064	35176	20953
1950/51	2	17	21	7	7	7	37	34	21	6	6	9	24	26	39		28000	30115	25884
1951/52	2	15	21	11	5	5	45	27	21	5	2	14	26	41	39		26341	26525	26156
1952/53	2	19	21	11	5	5	41	31	21	3	3	15	19	57	36		20441	19391	21491
1953/54	2	14	21	8	6	7	26	29	21	5	7	9	28	45	39		18090	16237	19943
1954/55	2	7	21	14	3	4	46	27	21	7	3	11	28	44	48		18481	16895	20066
1955/56	2	20	21	8	5	8	39	37	21	3	4	14	16	45	31		17075	15401	18748
1956/57	2	20	21	7	6	8	34	32	21	2	6	13	24	54	30		16644	15638	17650
1957/58	2	21	21	9	3	9	24	31	21	3	3	15	20	49	30	R	16066	14470	17663
1958/59	3	23	23	5	9	9	33	39	23	3	4	16	22	57	29	R	10056	9529	10582
1959/60	4	2	23	19	1	3	66	27	23	7	7	9	41	42	60	P	10718	13820	7616
1960/61	3	5	23	16	3	4	52	24	23	5	6	12	30	53	51		10577	11974	9180

FOOTBALL LEAGUE SEASONS - CONTINUED

	Div.	Pos.	Home: p	w	d	l	f	a	Away: p	w	d	l	f	a	Pts		Average attendances: Overall	Home	Away
1961/62	3	13	23	14	5	4	44	23	23	3	4	16	23	51	43		8972	8352	9592
1962/63	3	7	23	15	3	5	46	29	23	4	10	9	27	45	51		8214	6860	9568
1963/64	3	24	23	7	8	8	29	26	23	2	1	20	16	66	27	R	8015	6423	9606
1964/65	4	13	23	12	7	4	43	23	23	3	7	13	18	50	44		5874	5756	5991
1965/66	4	8	23	9	8	6	32	25	23	10	4	9	29	28	50		5533	4949	6117
1966/67	4	20	23	10	7	6	31	25	23	3	4	16	22	47	37		4790	4354	5226
1967/68	4	17	23	10	7	6	27	27	23	5	4	14	26	52	41		5671	5641	5702
1968/69	4	19	23	10	8	5	33	22	23	2	10	11	15	35	42		4705	4778	4632
1969/70	4	7	23	14	4	5	44	21	23	8	4	11	29	41	52		5428	5779	5076
1970/71	4	1	23	19	4	0	59	12	23	11	5	7	30	24	69	P	8713	10757	6668
1971/72	3	4	23	16	3	4	42	19	23	9	9	5	32	25	62		12190	13941	10440
1972/73	3	2	23	17	4	2	40	12	23	6	7	10	27	35	57	P	9231	10701	7760
1973/74	2	10	21	8	6	7	30	35	21	7	7	7	25	25	43		12391	11911	12871
1974/75	2	14	21	7	11	3	34	26	21	5	5	11	15	33	40		12071	10927	13216
1975/76	2	5	21	11	6	4	33	13	21	8	5	8	27	28	49		12036	12414	11658
1976/77	2	8	21	11	5	5	29	20	21	8	5	8	36	40	48		11896	10943	12849
1977/78	2	15	21	10	9	2	36	22	21	1	7	13	18	40	38		10552	9268	11836
1978/79	2	6	21	8	10	3	23	15	21	6	6	9	25	45	44		11071	9281	12862
1979/80	2	17	21	4	11	6	24	22	21	7	4	10	27	30	37		10648	8818	12477
1980/81	2	2	21	10	8	3	26	15	21	8	9	4	23	23	53	P	10046	9551	10540
1981/82	1	15	21	8	5	8	32	33	21	5	3	13	29	36	47		15966	11613	20319
1982/83	1	15	21	12	4	5	37	25	21	3	3	15	18	46	52		14002	10266	17739
1983/84	1	21	21	6	7	8	31	36	21	4	4	13	19	36	41	R	12815	9463	16167
1984/85	2	20	21	6	5	10	25	32	21	4	2	15	20	41	37	R	6790	6211	7368
1985/86	3	8	23	12	6	5	42	26	23	7	8	8	29	34	71		4405	4404	4407
1986/87	3	7	23	14	6	3	52	24	23	7	7	9	25	32	76		4555	4729	4381
1987/88	3	4	23	14	4	5	53	24	23	9	8	6	29	25	81		6152	6336	5968
1988/89	3	9	23	11	7	5	37	22	23	7	6	10	27	32	67		5360	5675	5045
1989/90	3	3	23	17	4	2	40	18	23	8	8	7	33	35	87	P	5657	6151	5163
1990/91	2	4	23	14	4	5	45	28	23	9	7	7	31	27	80	P	9795	8164	11426
1991/92	1	21	21	7	5	9	24	29	21	3	5	13	16	33	40	R	15258	10987	19530
1992/93	1*	17	23	10	7	6	33	21	23	2	9	12	22	49	52		8738	8151	9325
1993/94	1*	7	23	16	3	4	43	26	23	4	5	14	22	43	68		9674	8314	11034
1994/95	1*	24	23	7	8	8	26	28	23	2	5	16	19	38	40	R	8811	7195	10427
1995/96	2*	4	23	14	6	3	42	21	23	7	9	7	21	18	78		5215	5130	5300
1996/97	2*	24	23	4	9	10	20	25	23	3	5	15	13	34	35	R	4794	4239	5348
1997/98	3*	1	23	14	7	2	41	20	23	15	5	3	41	23	99	P	4760	5711	3809
1998/99	2*	16	23	8	6	9	29	27	23	6	6	11	23	34	54		6349	5616	7082
1999/2000	2*	8	23	9	6	8	32	27	23	9	5	9	29	28	65		6075	5667	6483
2000/01	2*	8	23	10	6	7	37	33	23	9	6	8	25	33	69		5689	5203	6175
2001/02	2*	19	23	8	7	8	28	29	23	5	4	14	31	42	50		6414	5956	6872
2002/03	2*	15	23	10	7	6	37	32	23	3	9	11	25	38	55		6583	6154	7012
2003/04	2*	23	23	6	9	8	32	27	23	4	3	16	18	51	42	R	6444	5940	6948
2004/05	L2*	19	23	6	7	10	21	27	23	7	6	10	25	35	52		4941	5384	4498
2005/06	L2*	21	23	7	11	5	30	26	23	5	5	13	18	37	52		4980	5467	4492
2006/07	L2*	13	23	8	6	9	29	25	23	8	8	7	26	28	62		4567	4974	4160

indicates renumbered divisions

NOTTS' LEAGUE RECORD AGAINST OTHER CLUBS

		Home:					Away:					Totals:		%
	p	w	d	l	f	a	w	d	l	f	a	f	a	won
Accrington	10	4	1	0	22	4	2	0	3	14	11	36	15	60.00
Accrington Stanley	4	1	1	0	4	3	1	0	1	2	4	6	7	50.00
Aldershot	36	12	2	4	35	14	8	5	5	18	17	53	31	55.56
Arsenal	44	14	2	6	48	36	6	5	11	19	30	67	66	45.45
Aston Villa	66	13	8	12	52	49	3	7	23	29	83	81	132	24.24
Barnet	6	2	1	0	4	1	2	0	1	6	5	10	6	66.67
Barnsley	62	15	4	12	63	49	3	15	13	29	47	92	96	29.03
Barrow	10	2	1	2	10	8	2	0	3	7	9	17	17	40.00
Birmingham City	52	13	8	5	48	26	5	6	15	25	44	73	70	34.62
Blackburn Rovers	86	19	15	9	80	49	12	7	24	54	91	134	140	36.05
Blackpool	56	13	6	9	45	35	6	9	13	30	42	75	77	33.93
Bolton Wanderers	74	14	13	10	48	44	9	7	21	39	75	87	119	31.08
Boston United	6	2	0	1	5	3	1	1	1	5	8	10	11	50.00
Bournemouth	52	13	2	11	44	38	6	7	13	23	37	67	75	36.54
Bradford City	46	11	7	5	35	23	10	3	10	36	41	71	64	45.65
Bradford Park Avenue	38	8	5	6	37	29	5	7	7	32	39	69	68	34.21
Brentford	60	15	9	6	49	27	5	10	15	27	50	76	77	33.33
Brighton & Hove Albion	46	11	5	7	38	29	7	7	9	31	38	69	67	39.13
Bristol City	94	25	12	10	80	46	9	9	29	50	92	130	138	36.17
Bristol Rovers	80	23	9	8	88	50	8	18	14	47	62	135	112	38.75
Burnley	50	16	7	2	64	19	3	7	15	18	41	82	60	38.00
Burton Swifts	8	4	0	0	22	4	2	2	0	8	3	30	7	75.00
Burton Wanderers	6	2	0	1	8	4	2	0	1	6	2	14	6	66.67
Bury	96	24	12	12	75	57	13	11	24	48	77	123	134	38.54
Cambridge United	20	6	2	2	15	8	4	4	2	14	13	29	21	50.00
Cardiff City	56	15	6	7	48	31	10	5	13	40	41	88	72	44.64
Carlisle United	18	7	1	1	14	7	3	1	5	9	13	23	20	55.56
Charlton Athletic	30	7	7	1	29	16	1	5	9	13	34	42	50	26.67
Chelsea	32	9	4	3	30	15	3	4	9	22	34	52	49	37.50
Cheltenham Town	6	1	1	1	3	3	2	0	1	6	3	9	6	50.00
Chester City	32	6	7	3	26	19	7	3	6	23	23	49	42	40.63
Chesterfield	48	15	7	2	41	18	6	7	11	19	33	60	51	43.75
Colchester United	30	7	4	4	31	16	4	3	8	18	31	49	47	36.67
Coventry City	30	10	3	2	28	14	5	3	7	22	26	50	40	50.00
Crewe Alexandra	30	8	3	4	37	11	5	2	8	18	26	55	37	43.33
Crystal Palace	42	7	6	8	30	26	6	5	10	24	32	54	58	30.95
Darlington	28	7	6	1	31	15	6	2	6	24	29	55	44	46.43
Darwen	8	4	0	0	15	2	1	0	3	5	8	20	10	62.50
Derby County	54	10	9	8	39	35	4	9	14	25	48	64	83	25.93
Doncaster Rovers	36	8	3	7	38	36	6	3	9	29	32	67	68	38.89
Everton	66	9	11	13	37	44	7	2	24	31	82	68	126	24.24
Exeter City	32	8	6	2	36	13	5	8	3	28	22	64	35	40.63
Fulham	58	13	10	6	53	28	4	3	22	33	80	86	108	29.31
Gainsborough Trinity	2	1	0	0	2	0	0	0	1	2	3	4	3	50.00
Gateshead	12	6	0	0	18	2	1	2	3	3	9	21	11	58.33
Gillingham	24	5	4	3	18	13	3	1	8	11	22	29	35	33.33
Glossop	4	0	2	0	2	2	1	1	0	1	0	3	2	25.00
Grimsby Town	62	18	4	9	55	32	4	9	18	35	57	90	89	35.48
Halifax Town	22	5	4	2	25	13	5	2	4	13	16	38	29	45.45
Hartlepool United	20	7	1	2	13	4	1	3	6	11	23	24	27	40.00
Hereford United	4	1	0	1	3	3	1	0	1	6	4	9	7	50.00
Huddersfield Town	24	8	2	2	21	11	2	3	7	8	21	29	32	41.67
Hull City	58	17	8	4	58	23	8	7	14	27	48	85	71	43.10
Ipswich Town	22	5	0	6	20	23	5	2	4	15	10	35	33	45.45
Kidderminster Harriers	2	0	0	1	1	3	0	1	0	0	0	1	3	0.00
Leeds City	2	1	0	0	4	0	1	0	0	4	2	8	2	100.00
Leeds United	32	8	3	5	25	20	1	3	12	7	40	32	60	28.13
Leicester City	42	5	8	8	35	30	6	4	11	29	39	64	69	26.19
Leyton Orient	60	17	6	7	51	26	8	9	13	34	39	85	65	41.67
Lincoln City	54	17	7	3	50	21	13	6	8	40	38	90	59	55.56
Liverpool	60	12	7	11	46	41	2	5	23	17	69	63	110	23.33
Loughborough	4	2	0	0	5	1	2	0	0	4	1	9	2	100.00
Luton Town	62	8	11	12	37	47	4	7	20	29	70	66	117	19.35
Macclesfield Town	10	0	3	2	4	10	2	2	1	4	4	8	14	20.00
Manchester City	58	14	8	7	44	26	3	4	22	18	63	62	89	29.31
Manchester United	48	10	5	9	33	33	4	9	11	27	41	60	74	29.17
Mansfield Town	32	8	6	2	27	15	6	4	6	23	27	50	42	43.75
Middlesbrough	54	15	7	5	50	34	4	2	21	23	64	73	98	35.19
Middlesbrough Ironopolis	2	1	0	0	3	0	0	1	0	0	0	3	0	50.00
Millwall	54	7	9	11	39	41	8	6	13	32	51	71	92	27.78
Milton Keynes Dons	6	0	2	1	5	6	0	0	3	4	8	9	14	0.00

LEAGUE RECORDS CONTINUED

		Home:						Away:					Totals:		%
	p	w	d	l	f	a	w	d	l	f	a	f	a	won
Newcastle United	60	12	7	11	37	39	5	8	17	34	75	71	114	28.33
Newport County	40	16	3	1	76	17	4	5	11	21	35	97	52	50.00
Northampton Town	46	17	3	3	45	23	6	7	10	24	35	69	58	50.00
Northwich Victoria	2	1	0	0	6	1	1	0	0	1	0	7	1	100.00
Norwich City	22	5	4	2	23	12	4	3	4	17	25	40	37	40.91
Nottingham Forest	86	14	15	14	66	64	14	8	21	41	56	107	120	32.56
Oldham Athletic	74	21	8	8	54	35	10	9	18	46	69	100	104	41.89
Oxford United	26	5	5	3	15	9	3	4	6	18	26	33	35	30.77
Peterborough United	34	7	8	2	27	16	4	3	10	13	25	40	41	32.35
Plymouth Argyle	36	13	1	4	32	14	7	6	5	26	26	58	40	55.56
Port Vale	82	22	9	10	91	50	13	10	18	50	65	141	115	42.68
Portsmouth	20	4	2	4	15	12	2	4	4	10	19	25	31	30.00
Preston North End	76	16	11	11	57	51	6	7	25	30	82	87	133	28.95
Queen's Park Rgrs	42	7	8	6	29	26	5	3	13	26	39	55	65	28.57
Reading	50	14	7	4	46	25	5	5	15	30	52	76	77	38.00
Rochdale	26	5	7	1	21	12	6	5	2	18	13	39	25	42.31
Rotherham Town	6	2	1	0	8	4	2	0	1	4	2	12	6	66.67
Rotherham United	40	14	2	4	40	20	5	9	6	21	24	61	44	47.50
Rushden & Diamonds	6	0	2	1	2	4	0	0	3	2	8	4	12	0.00
Scarborough	2	1	0	0	1	0	1	0	0	2	1	3	1	100.00
Scunthorpe United	14	7	0	0	16	2	3	1	3	7	7	23	9	71.43
Sheffield United	68	14	5	15	55	55	7	4	23	33	70	88	125	30.88
Sheffield Wednesday	58	13	8	8	42	33	5	8	16	21	49	63	82	31.03
Shrewsbury Town	32	8	4	4	27	20	2	7	7	16	31	43	51	31.25
Southampton	42	6	6	9	33	31	2	4	15	20	50	53	81	19.05
Southend United	52	14	6	6	48	32	6	3	17	28	48	76	80	38.46
Southport	10	2	1	2	8	5	2	1	2	5	4	13	9	40.00
Stockport County	30	11	2	2	32	12	3	6	6	11	17	43	29	46.67
Stoke City	74	16	11	10	59	40	11	10	16	31	51	90	91	36.49
Sunderland	74	20	12	5	69	36	6	10	21	35	85	104	121	35.14
Swansea City	68	18	5	11	63	42	5	11	18	28	63	91	105	33.82
Swindon Town	48	12	6	6	35	21	5	4	15	24	51	59	72	35.42
Thames	2	1	0	0	4	0	0	1	0	0	0	4	0	50.00
Torquay United	36	9	7	2	32	12	7	7	4	28	22	60	34	44.44
Tottenham Hotspur	34	7	6	4	27	16	3	2	12	18	36	45	52	29.41
Tranmere Rovers	28	7	4	3	25	13	4	1	9	20	32	45	45	39.29
Walsall	50	19	4	2	59	20	3	7	15	34	49	93	69	44.00
Watford	48	13	1	10	39	35	7	4	13	31	45	70	80	41.67
West Bromwich Albion	60	17	7	6	54	29	4	9	17	41	74	95	103	35.00
West Ham United	52	12	8	6	42	23	6	3	17	27	59	69	82	34.62
Wigan Athletic	20	2	4	4	12	16	1	3	6	7	17	19	33	15.00
Wolverhampton Wan.	66	15	11	7	71	40	5	8	20	32	67	103	107	30.30
Workington	10	2	2	1	6	6	3	1	1	6	6	12	12	50.00
Wrexham	46	13	8	2	38	20	4	6	13	25	46	63	66	36.96
Wycombe Wanderers	22	4	2	5	10	11	1	4	6	7	18	17	29	22.73
Yeovil Town	2	0	0	1	1	2	1	0	0	3	1	4	3	50.00
York City	32	10	4	2	34	15	6	6	4	27	26	61	41	50.00
Totals:	4434	1099	570	548	3911	2505	529	532	1156	2432	4028	6343	6533	

Of which:	p	w	d	l	f	a	w	d	l	f	a	tot. f	tot. a	pts
Top tier (old Div. 1)	1068	242	147	145	894	648	99	106	329	509	1064	1403	1712	983
Second tier (old Div. 2, Div. 1*)	1516	374	190	194	1380	899	175	188	395	844	1426	2224	2325	1550
Third tier (old Div. 3, Div. 2*)	920	227	118	115	767	507	116	125	219	505	768	1272	1275	1150
Last tier (old Div. 4, Lge 2*)	552	138	77	61	456	280	84	69	123	320	442	776	722	660
Division 3 (South)	378	118	38	33	414	171	55	44	90	254	328	668	499	428

Present day club names are used throughout; South Shields included with Gateshead and Wimbledon with Milton Keynes Dons.

PLAYER LIST: ONE LEAGUE GAME OR MORE

Name		D.o.B.	Place of Birth	Died	First Season	Last Season	Ints	Previous Club	Next Club	Appearances					Goals				
										Leg	FAC	FLC	Oth	PO	Leg	FAC	FLC	Oth	PO
Abrahams J	James	1867	New Mills		1891				Stockton	4	0	0	0	0	1	0	0	0	0
Abthorpe J	John	19/01/1933	Mansfield		1955			Wolves		5	0	0	0	0	3	0	0	0	0
Adamson H	Harry	27/06/1924	Kelty	1997	1947	1955		Jeanfield Swifts	Gainsborough Trin.	233	17	0	0	0	5	0	0	0	0
Agana PAO	Tony	02/10/1963	Bromley		1991	1996		Sheffield Utd.	Hereford Utd.	145	9	9	16	3	15	2	2	4	0
Agnew DY	David	04/08/1939	Kilwinning		1962	1966		Scunthorpe Utd.	Ilkeston T	85	4	2	0	0	1	0	0	0	0
Allan J	John	1872	Glasgow		1894	1897		Derby County	Heanor T	79	5	0	3	5	27	2	0	0	0
Allen H	Herbert	01/04/1899	Shifnal		1923			Wellington St.George	Stourbridge	1	0	0	0	0	0	0	0	0	0
Allen HA	Anthony 'Tanner'	27/10/1924	Beeston		1951	1953		Nottm. Forest	Corby T	30	0	0	0	0	0	0	0	0	0
Allen RHA	Robert	05/12/1916	Shepton Mallet		1946				Bristol City	1	0	0	0	0	0	0	0	0	0
Allin T	Thomas		Boston	1931	1888				Accrington	6	0	0	0	0	2	0	0	0	0
Allsebrook R	Dick	25/09/1892	Newstead	1961	1912	1919		Newstead	Ebbw Vale	97	3	0	0	0	2	0	0	0	0
Allsopp D	Danny	10/08/1978	Melbourne, Australia		1999			Man. City (loan)		108	8	3	4	0	43	4	4	3	0
					2000	2002		Man. City	Hull City										
Allsopp E	Elijah	13/07/1872	Milford	1953	1893	1896		Bury		59	3	0	1	1	20	2	0	1	0
Anderson J	John				1904			Port Glasgow Ath.	Port Glasgow Ath.	9	0	0	0	0	0	0	0	0	0
Andrews H	Harold	13/08/1903	Lincoln	1988	1927	1931		Lincoln City	Barnsley	134	6	0	0	0	55	3	0	0	0
Angell BAM	Brett	20/08/1968	Marlborough		1999			Stockport Co. (loan)		6	0	0	0	0	5	0	0	0	0
Antoine-Curier M	Mickael	05/03/1983	Orsay, France		2003			Sheffield Wed.	Grimsby Town	4	0	0	0	0	1	0	0	0	0
Arkins VT	Vinny	18/09/1970	Dublin		1995	1996		Shelbourne	Portadown	38	5	4	4	0	8	1	0	0	0
Armstrong KC	Ken	31/01/1959	Bridgnorth		1983			Southampton (loan)		10	0	0	0	0	0	0	0	0	0
Arnott W	Wattie	12/05/1861	Pollokshields	1931	1894		s	Queen's Park		1	1	0	0	0	0	0	0	0	0
Arphexad PM	Pegguy	18/05/1973	Les Abymes, Guadeloupe		2003			Coventry City (loan)		3	0	0	0	0	0	0	0	0	0
Ashcroft L	Lee	07/09/1972	Preston		1995			West Brom (loan)		6	0	0	0	0	0	0	0	0	0
Asher T	Tommy	21/12/1936	Dunscroft		1957	1958		Wath Ath.	Peterborough Utd.	31	0	0	0	0	4	0	0	0	0
Ashton JJ	Jon	04/10/1982	Nuneaton		2002			Leicester City (loan)		4	0	0	0	0	0	0	0	0	0
Ashurst W	Bill	04/05/1894	Willington	1947	1920	1926	e	Lincoln City	West Bromwich A.	200	22	0	0	0	0	0	0	0	0
Astle J	Jeff	13/05/1942	Eastwood	2002	1961	1964	e	Holy Trin.YC Kimberley	West Bromwich A.	103	5	8	0	0	31	1	9	0	0
Astley JE	Joseph	1899	Cradley Heath	1967	1928			Manchester Utd.	Nantwich T	4	0	0	0	0	0	0	0	0	0
Avramovic R	Raddy	29/11/1949	Rijeka, Croatia		1979	1982	yu	NK Rijeka	Inter Montreal	149	3	15	15	0	0	0	0	0	0
Bagnall R	Reg	22/11/1926	Brinsworth		1946	1947		Rotherham United	Ransome&Marles	9	1	0	0	0	0	0	0	0	0
Bagshaw JJ	Jimmy	25/12/1885	Derby	1966	1919	1920	e	Derby County	Watford	24	0	0	0	0	0	0	0	0	0
Bailey LF					1888					1	0	0	0	0	1	0	0	0	0
Bakewell GH	George	1864	Derby		1891				Derby County	5	1	0	0	0	1	0	0	0	0
Baldry SJ	Simon	12/02/1976	Huddersfield		2003			Huddersfield T	Boston U (trials)	35	3	2	1	0	1	0	1	0	0
Ball GH	Geoff	02/11/1944	Nottingham		1967	1971		Nottm. Forest	Ilkeston T	112	5	3	0	0	0	0	0	0	0
Ball WH	William	1876	West Derby	1929	1899	1900		Everton	Blackburn Rovers	65	5	0	0	0	2	0	0	0	0
Baraclough IR	Ian	04/12/1970	Leicester		1995	1997		Mansfield Town	QPR	212	15	12	6	3	15	0	1	0	0
					2001	2003		QPR	Scunthorpe Utd.										
Barber MJ	Mike	24/08/1941	Kensington		1963	1964		QPR		33	2	4	0	0	3	0	0	0	0
Barker RJ	Richie	23/11/1939	Loughborough		1968	1971		Derby County	Peterborough Utd.	112	5	4	0	0	37	0	1	0	0
Barley HF	Harry	1905	Grimsby	1958	1933			New Brighton	Scunthorpe Utd.	11	0	0	0	0	1	0	0	0	0
Barnes PL	Paul	16/11/1967	Leicester		1985	1989			Stoke City	53	1	0	11	2	14	0	0	5	0
Barras A	Tony	29/03/1971	Billingham		2003			Walsall	Macclesfield T	40	2	3	1	0	2	1	1	0	0
Barry LJ	Len	27/10/1901	Sneinton	1970	1920	1927	e	RAF Cranwell	Leicester City	146	7	0	0	0	10	1	0	0	0
Bartlett KF	Kevin	12/10/1962	Portsmouth		1989	1992		West Bromwich A.	Cambridge Utd.	99	6	7	3	5	33	1	3	2	1
Bassett EJ	Ted	01/01/1889	Deptford	1970	1913	1914		Dartford	Watford	44	1	0	0	0	5	0	0	0	0
Bates AN	Tony	06/04/1938	Blidworth		1958			Blidworth Coll.	Sutton T	1	0	0	0	0	0	0	0	0	0
Bates BF	Brian	04/12/1944	Beeston		1963	1968		Loughboro' College	Mansfield Town	128	2	7	0	0	24	0	1	0	0
Battersby A	Tony	30/08/1975	Doncaster		1995	1996		Sheffield Utd.	Bury	39	2	1	1	3	8	0	0	0	0
Baudet J	Julien	13/01/1979	Grenoble, France		2004	2005		Rotherham Utd.	Crewe Alexandra	81	4	2	2	0	11	2	0	0	0
Baxter WA	Bill	06/09/1917	Nottingham	1992	1946	1953		Nottm. Forest	Grantham	140	13	0	0	0	0	0	0	0	0
Beadle PCWJ	Peter	13/05/1972	Lambeth		1998	1999		Port Vale	Bristol City	22	0	4	0	0	3	0	0	0	0
Beaver D	David	04/04/1966	Kirkby-in-Ashfield		1984			App.		1	0	1	0	0	0	0	0	0	0
Beavon DG	David	08/12/1961	Nottingham		1980			Nottm. Schools	Lincoln City	5	1	0	0	0	0	0	0	0	0
Beavon MS	Stuart	30/11/1958	Wolverhampton		1979			Tottenham H (loan)		6	0	0	0	0	0	0	0	0	0
Beeby O	Oliver	02/10/1934	Whetstone, Leics		1959			Leicester City	Oxford United	13	2	0	0	0	0	0	0	0	0
Beech A	Albert	24/09/1912	Fenton	1985	1937			Huddersfield T	Northwich Vic.	13	0	0	1	0	0	0	0	0	0
Belford D	Dale	11/07/1967	Burton-on-Trent		1987			Sutton Coldfield T	VS Rugby	1	0	0	0	0	0	0	0	0	0
Bell E	Ernest				1891					5	1	0	0	0	0	0	0	0	0
Bemment FC	Fred	12/10/1884	Lowestoft	1957	1907			Norwich City	Chesterfield Town	9	0	0	0	0	0	0	0	0	0
Benjamin TL	Tristan	01/04/1957	St Kitts		1974	1986			Chesterfield	311	17	30	28	0	4	0	1	0	0
Benskin DW	Denis	28/05/1947	Ruddington		1965				Lockheed Leam.	4	0	0	0	0	1	0	0	0	0
Beresford JW	John	25/01/1946	Sheffield	2003	1965	1966		Chesterfield	Matlock T	50	1	2	0	0	13	0	1	0	0
Beresford RJ	Reg	29/06/1925	Lower Pilsley		1945	1946		Hardwick Col.	S Normanton	9	4	0	0	0	1	0	0	0	0
Berry TM	Tyrone	20/02/1987	Brixton		2005			Crystal Palace (loan)		5	0	0	1	0	0	0	0	0	0
Bettison FH	Harry	1891	Hucknall Torkard		1910			Netherfield Rgs	Grantham T	1	0	0	0	0	0	0	0	0	0
Bewers JA	Jon	10/09/1982	Wellingborough		2003			Aston Villa	Walsall	3	0	0	0	0	0	0	0	0	0
Billington BK	Brian	28/04/1951	Leicester		1969			Leicester City	Enderby T	7	0	0	0	0	0	0	0	0	0
Billy CA	Chris	02/12/1973	Huddersfield		1998			Plymouth Argyle	Bury	6	0	2	0	0	0	0	0	0	0
Birchenall AJ	Alan	22/08/1945	East Ham		1975			Leicester City (loan)		33	3	0	2	0	0	0	0	0	0
					1977			Leicester City	Memphis Rogues										
Bircumshaw A	Tony	08/02/1945	Mansfield		1960	1965		Mansfield St Johns	Hartlepool Utd.	148	6	11	0	0	1	0	0	0	0
Bircumshaw PB	Peter	29/08/1938	Mansfield						Bradford City	72	6	1	0	0	40	7	1	0	0
Bird WS	Walter	1891	Hugglescote	1965	1912	1914		Coalville Swifts	Grimsby Town	10	0	0	0	0	2	0	0	0	0
Birtles G	Garry	27/07/1956	Nottingham		1987	1988	e	Nottm. Forest	Grimsby Town	63	4	6	7	2	9	1	1	1	0
Bisby CC	Charlie	10/09/1904	Mexborough	1977	1926	1931		Denaby U	Coventry City	206	9	0	0	0	1	0	0	0	0
Blackmore CG	Clayton	23/09/1964	Neath		1999		w	Barnsley	Leigh RMI	21	1	4	1	0	2	0	2	0	0
Blockley JP	Jeff	12/09/1949	Leicester		1978	1979	e	Leicester City	Enderby T	59	3	6	6	0	5	0	0	1	0
Blood JF	Jack	02/10/1914	Nottingham	1992	1938			Johnson&Barnes	Exeter City	8	3	0	0	0	0	0	0	0	0

204

Name		D.o.B.	Place of Birth	Died	First Season	Last Season	Ints	Previous Club	Next Club	Appearances Leg	FAC	FLC	Oth	PO	Goals Leg	FAC	FLC	Oth	PO
Bly TG	Terry	22/10/1935	Fincham		1963	1964		Coventry City	Grantham	29	2	2	0	0	4	1	0	0	0
Blyth G	George	18/10/1906	Motherwell	1984	1935	1937		Hibernian	Grantham	99	3	0	4	0	0	0	0	0	0
Boertien P	Paul	21/01/1979	Haltwhistle		2003			Derby County (loan)		5	0	0	0	0	0	0	0	0	0
Bolland PG	Paul	23/12/1979	Bradford		1998	2004		Bradford City	Grimsby Town	172	8	9	5	0	6	0	0	1	0
Bolton IR	Ian	13/07/1953	Leicester		1971	1976		Birmingham City	Watford	70	3	5	0	0	4	0	0	0	0
Boreham RW	Reg	27/05/1896	High Wycombe	1976	1920			Wycombe Wan.	Arsenal	3	0	0	0	0	0	0	0	0	0
Boucher TC	Tom		1873	West Bromwich		1896	1898		Stourbridge	Bedminster	79	4	0	0	4	32	1	0	0	1
Bowers JA	Johnny	14/11/1939	Leicester		1966			Derby County		5	0	0	0	0	0	0	0	0	0
Boyes WE	Wally	05/01/1913	Killamarsh	1960	1949		e	Everton	Scunthorpe Utd.	3	0	0	0	0	1	0	0	0	0
Bradd LJ	Les	05/11/1947	Buxton		1967	1977		Rotherham Utd.	Stockport Co.	395	22	17	8	0	125	4	7	1	0
Bradley G	Gordon	20/05/1925	Scunthorpe	2006	1950	1957		Leicester City	Cambridge City	192	11	0	0	0	1	0	0	0	0
Bradley H	Herbert	1887	Padiham		1910			Bury	Preston NE	3	0	0	0	0	0	0	0	0	0
Brailsford JR	James	1877	Lincoln	1946	1897			Lincoln City	Lincoln City	1	0	0	0	0	0	0	0	0	0
Bramham A	Arnold	16/01/1912	West Melton	1989	1934	1935		Silverwood Coll.	Rotherham Utd.	18	0	0	1	0	10	0	0	1	0
Bramley C	Charlie	01/01/1870	Nottingham	1916	1891	1897		Notts Rangers	Retired	126	13	0	9	3	8	0	0	0	0
Brannan MH	Mike		1911	Wath-on-Dearne		1937			Barnsley	Grantham	3	0	0	2	0	0	0	0	0	0
Brealey H	Harry		1874	Nottingham		1894	1895			Hucknall St Johns	8	0	0	1	0	3	0	0	0	0
Brearley J	John		1875	West Derby	1944	1896	1897		Liverpool S End	Kettering T	9	0	0	0	1	0	0	0	0	1
					1900			Millwall Ath.	Middlesbrough										
Brindley JC	Bill	29/01/1947	Nottingham	2007	1970	1975		Nottm. Forest	Gillingham	223	12	14	1	0	0	0	0	0	0
Broadbent AH	Albert	20/08/1934	Dudley		1953	1954		Dudley T	Sheffield Wed.	31	5	0	0	0	11	2	0	0	0
Brodie GW	George	17/12/1898	Castle Douglas		1922			Wigan Borough	Castle Douglas	1	0	0	0	0	0	0	0	0	0
Brook G	Gary	09/05/1964	Dewsbury		1990			Blackpool (loan)		1	0	0	0	0	0	0	0	0	0
Broome FH	Frank	11/06/1915	Berkhamsted	1994	1949	1952	e	Derby County	Brentford	105	9	0	0	0	35	6	0	0	0
Brough M	Michael	01/08/1981	Nottingham		1999	2003			Stafford Rgs	89	9	1	4	0	2	0	0	0	0
Broughton M	Matt	08/10/1880	Grantham	1957	1904			Grantham	Watford	2	0	0	0	0	1	0	0	0	0
Brown AW	Alan	26/08/1914	Corbridge	1996	1948			Burnley	Sheff. Wed. (coach)	13	2	0	0	0	0	0	0	0	0
Brown C	Cyril	25/05/1918	Ashington	1990	1946			Sunderland	Boston U	13	1	0	0	0	5	0	0	0	0
Brown DC	Davie	26/11/1887	Broughty Ferry		1921			Stoke	Kilmarnock	14	0	0	0	0	7	0	0	0	0
Brown GH	George					1886	1888		Nottm Forest	Nottm Forest	19	5	0	0	0	1	0	0	0	0
Brown HT	Harry	09/04/1924	Kingsbury	1982	1946	1948		QPR	Derby County	93	9	0	0	0	0	0	0	0	0
Brown JA	John	20/03/1866	Nottingham	1955	1884	1888		Nottm High School		1	3	0	0	0	0	1	0	0	0
Brown K	Keith	01/01/1942	Hucknall		1958			West Ham Utd.	Rotherham Utd.	8	0	0	0	0	4	0	0	0	0
Brown R	Ralph	26/02/1944	Ilkeston		1962			Aston Villa	Nuneaton Boro	18	0	1	0	0	3	0	1	0	0
Brown REE	Roy	05/10/1945	Shoreham		1970	1974		Reading	Mansfield Town	113	9	10	1	0	0	0	0	0	0
Brown RM	Ray	11/02/1928	Carlisle		1951			Queen's Park		7	0	0	0	0	0	0	0	0	0
Brown W	Billy			Nottingham		1894			Nottm. Forest (loan)		1	0	0	1	0	0	0	0	0	0
Bruce D	Dan	20/10/1870	Bonhill	1931	1892	1895	s	Glasgow Rangers	Small Heath	89	9	0	9	2	47	3	0	1	1
Brunt GR	Geoff	24/11/1926	Nottingham	2000	1949	1953			Heanor T	29	1	0	0	0	1	0	0	0	0
Bulch RS	Bobby	01/01/1933	Washington		1955	1957		Washington	Darlington	27	0	0	0	0	1	0	0	0	0
Bull W	Walter	19/12/1874	Nottingham	1952	1894	1903		St. Andrews, Nottm.	Tottenham H	282	18	0	3	3	53	5	0	0	0
Burditt FCK	Ken	12/11/1906	Ibstock	1977	1937	1938		Millwall	Colchester Utd.	20	0	0	1	0	0	0	0	0	0
Burgon FA	Archie	28/03/1912	Nottingham	1994	1932	1933		Newark T	Grantham T	26	1	0	0	0	7	0	0	0	0
Burke J	Jimmy		1870	Scotland		1892	1893		Third Lanark	Grantham Rovers	15	2	0	1	1	4	1	0	0	0
Burke SJ	Steve	29/09/1960	Nottingham		1984			QPR (loan)		5	0	2	0	0	0	0	0	0	0
Burns JA	Henry	20/06/1865	Liverpool	1957	1891			West Bromwich A.	South Weald	1	0	0	0	0	0	0	0	0	0
Burns K	Kenny	23/09/1953	Glasgow		1984		s	Derby County (loan)		2	0	0	0	0	0	0	0	0	0
Burrows W	William					1893				Notts Olympic	1	0	0	1	0	0	0	0	0	0
Busby MG	Martyn	24/03/1953	High Wycombe		1976	1977		QPR	QPR	37	1	1	5	0	4	0	0	0	0
Butler JH	John	10/03/1937	Birmingham		1958	1961		Bestwood Coll.	Chester	109	3	3	0	0	0	0	0	0	0
Butler PJF	Peter	27/08/1966	Halifax		1994			West Ham Utd.	West Bromwich A.	20	2	2	3	0	0	0	0	0	0
Butler PL	Peter	03/10/1942	Nottingham		1961	1965		Bestwood YC	Bradford City	44	3	3	0	0	0	0	0	0	0
Butlin BD	Barry	09/11/1949	Rosliston		1968	1969		Derby County (loan)		30	0	1	0	0	13	0	0	0	0
Buxton IR	Ian	17/04/1938	Cromford		1969			Luton Town	Port Vale	5	1	0	0	0	1	0	0	0	0
Byron M	Michael	16/08/1987	Liverpool		2006			Hull City (loan)		3	0	0	0	0	0	0	0	0	0
Calderhead D	David	19/06/1864	Hurlford	1938	1889	1899	s	Q of South Wan.	Lincoln City (mngr)	278	25	0	8	7	12	0	0	0	0
Calderwood C	Colin	20/01/1965	Stranraer		2000		s	Nottm. Forest (loan)	Retired	5	0	0	0	0	0	0	0	0	0
Cale F	Fred		1875	Hucknall Torkard	1950	1895			Hucknall St Johns	Redhill U (Nottm)	1	0	0	0	0	0	0	0	0	0
Calladine CF	Charlie		1888	Wessington		1907			Notts Olympic		3	0	0	0	0	0	0	0	0	0
Campbell DA	David	02/06/1965	Eglinton		1986		n	Nottm. Forest (loan)		18	0	0	0	0	2	0	0	0	0
Cantrell J	Jimmy	07/05/1882	Sheepbridge	1960	1907	1912		Aston Villa	Tottenham H	131	5	0	0	0	64	1	0	0	0
Cargill JG	Jim	22/09/1945	Alyth		1966				Nottm. Forest	10	0	0	0	0	0	0	0	0	0
Carlin W	Willie	06/10/1940	Liverpool		1971	1973		Leicester City	Cardiff City	60	6	3	0	0	2	1	0	0	0
Carter AB	Alfred		1877	Basford	1951	1896	1898		Newstead Byron	Kettering T	20	1	0	0	0	5	0	0	0	0
Carter SC	Steve	23/04/1953	Great Yarmouth		1971	1978		Manchester City	Derby County	188	10	13	12	0	21	0	3	2	0
Cartwright M	Mick	09/10/1946	Birmingham		1967	1968		Coventry City	Rochdale	16	0	1	0	0	0	0	0	0	0
Carver GF	Gerry	27/06/1935	Worcester		1953	1965		Boldmere St Michaels		280	12	5	0	0	10	0	0	0	0
Cas M	Marcel	30/04/1972	Breda, Holland		2001	2002		RBC Roosendaal	Sheffield Utd.	58	3	3	3	0	8	0	0	0	0
Cashmore A	Arthur	30/10/1893	Birmingham	1969	1921			Cardiff City	Darlaston	14	4	0	0	0	6	0	0	0	0
Caskey DM	Darren	21/08/1974	Basildon		2001	2003		Reading	Bristol City	114	7	5	4	0	10	0	0	1	0
Catlin R	Bob	22/06/1965	Wembley		1992	1993		Marconi (Aust.)		3	0	1	1	0	0	0	0	0	0
Chadburn JL	John	12/02/1873	Mansfield	1923	1894	1896		Lincoln City	Wolves	50	2	0	6	1	15	0	0	1	0
Chalmers J	Jimmy	03/12/1877	Old Luce		1899			Preston NE	Beith	25	3	0	0	0	2	1	0	0	0
Chalmers LA	Len	04/09/1936	Geddington		1966	1967		Leicester City	Dunstable T (mngr)	51	1	2	0	0	1	0	0	0	0
Chalmers TK	Tommy		1882	Beith		1905	1908		Beith	Ilkeston U	18	1	0	0	0	1	0	0	0	0
Chalmers W	Willie	25/07/1904	Bellshill		1936	1937		Bury	Aldershot	65	1	0	4	0	17	1	0	0	0
Chandler ACH	Arthur	27/11/1895	Paddington	1984	1935			Leicester City	Leicester C (staff)	10	2	0	1	0	6	1	0	1	0
Chapman GA	Gary	01/05/1964	Bradford		1989	1990		Bradford City	Exeter City	25	0	0	3	0	4	0	0	0	0
Chapman HG	Herbert	19/01/1878	Kiveton Park	1934	1903			Sheffield Utd.	Northampton Town	7	0	0	0	0	1	0	0	0	0
Chapman H	Harry	04/03/1921	Liverpool	1990	1948	1950		Aston Villa	Gorleston	53	3	0	0	0	1	0	0	0	0
Chapman RD	Bob 'Sammy'	18/08/1946	Aldridge		1977			Nottm. Forest	Shrewsbury Town	42	3	2	7	0	0	1	0	1	0
Charlesworth G	George		1893	Bolsover	1964	1919			Sutton Junction	Sutton T	30	0	0	0	0	4	0	0	0	0

Name		D.o.B.	Place of Birth	Died	First Season	Last Season	Ints	Previous Club	Next Club	Appearances					Goals				
										Leg	FAC	FLC	Oth	PO	Leg	FAC	FLC	Oth	PO
Chatham RH	Ray	20/07/1924	Wolverhampton	1999	1953	1958		Wolves	Margate	127	3	0	0	0	4	0	0	0	0
Cherry SR	Steve	05/08/1960	Nottingham		1988	1994		Plymouth Argyle	Watford	266	14	17	25	6	0	0	0	0	0
Chiedozie JO	John	18/04/1960	Owerri, Nigeria		1981	1983	ng	Leyton Orient	Tottenham H	112	8	11	0	0	16	2	2	0	0
					1989			Non contract											
Childs H	Harry	07/11/1908	Acomb	1977	1928			West Stanley	Halifax Town	1	0	0	0	0	0	0	0	0	0
Chillingworth DT	Dan	13/09/1981	Cambridge		2005			Cambridge Utd (loan)		13	0	0	0	0	2	0	0	0	0
Chilvers LC	Liam	06/11/1981	Chelmsford		2001			Arsenal (loan)	Colchester Utd.	9	2	0	0	0	1	0	0	0	0
Chipperfield JJ	Jimmy	04/03/1894	Bethnal Green	1966	1921			Tottenham H	Northfleet	18	6	0	0	0	2	3	0	0	0
Christie TJ	Trevor	28/02/1959	Cresswell, Northumb'nd		1979	1983		Leicester City	Nottm. Forest	187	10	21	10	0	63	3	10	3	0
Clamp AF	Arthur	01/05/1884	Sneinton	1918	1906	1914			Sneinton	275	14	0	0	0	3	0	0	0	0
Clare WE	Edwin	1883	Basford	1944	1903	1904		Mansfield W'dhouse	Brighton & Hove A.	6	0	0	0	0	0	0	0	0	0
Clarke DA	David	25/09/1946	Long Eaton		1966			Nottm. Forest		24	1	2	0	0	0	0	0	0	0
Clarke DA	David	03/12/1964	Nottingham		1982	1986			Lincoln City	123	13	10	3	0	7	1	2	0	0
Clarke WG	William				1933	1935		West Bromwich A.	Dudley T	37	2	0	1	0	1	0	0	0	0
Clayton S	Stan	21/11/1912	Castleford	2002	1937	1938		Upton Colliery		31	5	0	0	0	3	1	0	0	0
Clements JE	John	1867	East Markham		1888	1889		St Saviors	Newton Heath	14	4	0	0	0	0	0	0	0	0
Cliff E	Eddie	30/09/1951	Liverpool		1973			Burnley	Chicago Sting	5	0	0	0	0	0	0	0	0	0
Clinch TH	Tom	1876	Bolton		1904			Reading		6	0	0	0	0	0	0	0	0	0
Coates DP	David	11/04/1935	Newcastle		1964	1966		Mansfield Town	Notts youth coach	66	2	3	0	0	1	0	0	0	0
Cock DJ	Donald	08/07/1896	Hayle	1974	1922	1924		Fulham	Arsenal	85	7	0	0	0	32	2	0	0	0
Coglin S	Steve	14/10/1903	Willenhall		1931			Grimsby Town	Worcester City	13	1	0	0	0	3	0	0	0	0
Coles FG	Gordon	1875	Nottingham	1947	1894	1895		Nottm Post Office	Nottm. Forest	1	0	0	2	0	0	0	0	0	0
Collier GH	Geoff	25/07/1950	Blackpool		1973			Macclesfield T	Macclesfield T	3	0	0	0	0	0	0	0	0	0
Connell A	Archie	22/04/1900	Darvel		1927			Queen of the South		4	0	0	0	0	1	0	0	0	0
Connor JH	Jack	1875	Staincross		1895			Newark	Newark	17	2	0	0	0	0	0	0	0	0
Cook J	Jack	27/07/1887	Sunderland	1952	1919	1923		Middlesbrough	Northampton Town	98	19	0	0	0	13	5	0	0	0
Cooke RJ	James	1893	Ilkeston		1919			Mansfield Mechanics	Ilkeston U	12	0	0	0	0	0	0	0	0	0
Cooke T	Thomas				1888			Notts Rangers (loan)		1	0	0	0	0	0	0	0	0	0
Cookson AE	Alfred	1873	Nottingham	1910	1896				Newark	3	0	0	0	0	0	0	0	0	0
Coole W	Billy	27/01/1925	Manchester	2001	1953	1955		Mansfield Town	Barrow	42	1	0	0	0	5	0	0	0	0
Cooper E	Edward	1891	Walsall		1920			Newcastle United	Stafford Rgs	4	0	0	0	0	0	0	0	0	0
Cooper J	Joe	1899	Newbold	1959	1922	1923		Chesterfield	Grimsby Town	31	2	0	0	0	4	0	0	0	0
Cooper S	Sedley	17/08/1911	Garforth	1981	1936	1938		Huddersfield T		56	3	0	0	0	14	2	0	0	0
Cooper T	Terry	11/03/1950	Croesyceiliog		1971	1972		Newport County	Lincoln City	9	0	1	1	0	0	0	0	0	0
Cope HW	Horace	24/05/1899	Treeton	1961	1920	1926		Treeton U	Arsenal	125	5	0	0	0	6	0	0	0	0
Corkhill WG	Bill	23/04/1910	Belfast	1978	1931	1938		Liverpool	Cardiff City	264	20	0	4	0	9	2	0	0	0
					1945	1951		Cardiff C	Scunthorpe U(trainer)										
Cornwell RL	Ralph	07/09/1901	Nottingham	1988	1923	1925		Sneinton Inst.	Norwich City	42	4	0	0	0	0	0	0	0	0
Coulston W	Walter	31/01/1912	Wombwell	1990	1938			Barnsley		1	0	0	0	0	0	0	0	0	0
Cox PR	Paul	06/01/1972	Nottingham		1991	1994			Kettering T	44	2	3	3	0	1	0	1	0	0
Cozens JW	John	14/05/1946	Hammersmith		1970	1972		Hillingdon Boro	Peterborough Utd.	44	4	3	0	0	13	4	3	0	0
Cramb C	Colin	23/06/1974	Lanark		2000			Crewe Alex. (loan)		3	0	0	0	0	0	0	0	0	0
Crank J	Joseph	1876	Leigh	1946	1896			Fairfield	Glossop NE	1	0	0	0	0	0	0	0	0	0
Crapper J	Joe	03/03/1899	Wortley	1989	1921			Swallownest	Huddersfield T	2	0	0	0	0	0	0	0	0	0
Craythorne R	Ben	21/01/1882	Aston	1953	1904	1913		Walsall	Darlington	282	14	0	0	0	12	0	0	0	0
Creaney GT	Gerry	13/04/1970	Coatbridge		1998			St Mirren	Queen of the South	16	0	0	0	0	3	0	0	0	0
Cresswell F	Frank	05/09/1908	South Shields	1979	1933			Chester	Chester	16	0	0	0	0	4	0	0	0	0
Crichton PA	Paul	03/10/1968	Pontefract		1986			Nottm. Forest (loan)		5	0	0	0	0	0	0	0	0	0
Crickmore CA	Charlie	11/02/1942	Hull		1969	1971		Norwich City	Retired	59	4	1	0	0	11	2	0	0	0
Crispin T	Tim	07/06/1948	Leicester		1966	1967			Lincoln City	8	0	0	0	0	0	0	0	0	0
Crone R	Bob	1870	Belfast	1943	1896	1897	i	Millwall Ath.	Bedminster	32	3	0	0	4	0	0	0	0	0
Crookes RE	Bobby	29/02/1924	Retford		1949	1955		Retford T	Worksop T	177	8	0	0	0	45	1	0	0	0
Crooks LR	Lee	14/01/1978	Wakefield		2005			Manchester C (loan)		18	0	0	0	0	1	0	0	0	0
Cross DB	David	07/09/1982	Bromley		1999					1	0	0	0	0	0	0	0	0	0
Cruickshank FJ	Frank	20/11/1931	Polmont		1953	1959		Nuneaton Boro	Cheltenham T	151	4	0	0	0	5	0	0	0	0
Cumner RH	Horace	31/03/1918	Cwmaman	1999	1946	1947	w	Arsenal	Watford	66	8	0	0	0	11	2	0	0	0
Cunnington SG	Shaun	04/01/1966	Bourne		1996	1997		West Bromwich A.	Kidderminster H	17	0	2	1	0	0	0	0	0	0
Currie JB	Blair	14/02/1896	Galston		1919			Glenleven Rovers		8	0	0	0	0	1	0	0	0	0
Cursham HA	Harry	27/11/1859	Wilford	1941	1877	1890	e	Repton School		9	43	0	0	0	2	49	0	0	0
Curtis TD	Tommy	01/03/1973	Exeter		2006			Chester City		2	0	2	0	0	0	0	0	0	0
Dadi E	Eugene	20/08/1973	Abidjan, Ivory Coast		2005			Nottm. Forest (loan)		11	0	0	0	0	2	0	0	0	0
Daft HB	Harry	05/04/1866	Radcliffe-on-Trent	1945	1885	1892	e	Trent College	Nottm. Forest	137	33	0	5	1	58	19	0	3	0
					1893	1894		Nottm. Forest	Newark										
Dainty HC	Herbert	02/06/1879	Geddington	1957	1903			Northampton T	Southampton	20	1	0	0	0	0	0	0	0	0
Dale GH	George	02/05/1883	Nottingham	1957	1914			Newark	Chelsea	18	1	0	0	0	5	0	0	0	0
Dalton RT	Tim	14/10/1965	Waterford		1985			Coventry City	Bradford City	1	0	0	0	0	0	0	0	0	0
Daly J	Joe	28/12/1897	Lancaster	1941	1920	1926		Cliftonville	Northampton Town	139	15	0	0	0	12	0	0	0	0
Daniel RC	Ray	10/12/1964	Luton		1994			Portsmouth (loan)		5	0	0	1	0	0	0	0	0	0
Darby DA	Duane	17/10/1973	Warley		1999			Hull City	Rushden & Diamonds	28	0	4	0	0	5	0	1	0	0
Davies JG	John	18/11/1959	Llandyssil		1985			Hull City (loan)		10	0	0	0	0	0	0	0	0	0
Davies W	Willie	16/02/1900	Troedyrhiwfuwch	1953	1927	1929	w	Cardiff City	Tottenham H	71	2	0	0	0	9	0	0	0	0
Davis AG	Arthur	1898	Birmingham	1955	1923	1927		QPR	Crystal Palace	140	6	0	0	0	51	3	0	0	0
Davis DJ	Darren	05/02/1967	Sutton-in-Ashfield		1983	1987			Lincoln City	92	6	6	7	0	1	0	0	0	0
Davis SM	Steve	30/10/1968	Hexham		1990			Southampton (loan)		2	0	0	0	0	0	0	0	0	0
Davison AJ	Aidan	11/05/1968	Sedgefield		1988		n	Billingham Synth.	Bury	1	0	0	0	0	0	0	0	0	0
Daws A	Tony	10/09/1966	Sheffield		1984	1985		Manchester Utd.	Sheffield Utd.	8	0	0	0	0	1	0	0	0	0
Daykin RB	Brian	04/08/1937	Long Eaton		1962			Derby County	Corinthians (Sydney)	3	0	0	0	0	0	0	0	0	0
Dean JT	Jerry	13/02/1881	Hadley		1904	1911		Wellington T	Shelley FC (Canada)	254	14	0	0	0	49	3	0	0	0
Dean WR	Bill 'Dixie'	22/01/1907	Birkenhead	1980	1937	1938	e	Everton	Sligo Rovers	9	0	0	0	0	3	0	0	0	0
Deans TS	Tommy	07/01/1922	Shieldhill	2000	1949	1955		Clyde	Boston U	239	14	0	0	0	0	0	0	0	0
Death WG	Billy	13/11/1899	Rotherham	1984	1920	1922		Rotherham T	Mansfield Town	21	2	0	0	0	4	0	0	0	0
De Bolla GMJ	Mark	01/01/1983	Camberwell		2005			Chesterfield		14	1	0	0	0	1	0	0	0	0

Name		D.o.B.	Place of Birth	Died	First Season	Last Season	Ints	Previous Club	Next Club	Appearances Leg	FAC	FLC	Oth	PO	Goals Leg	FAC	FLC	Oth	PO
Deeney S	Saul	12/03/1983	Derry		2002 2006	2004		Foyle Harps Burton Albion	Burton Albion	49	4	6	1	0	0	0	0	0	0
Deighton AD	Alex	1877	Gateshead		1897			Rock Ferry	Rock Ferry	10	1	0	0	0	1	0	0	0	0
Derry SP	Shaun	06/12/1977	Nottingham		1995	1997			Sheffield Utd.	79	7	5	0	3	4	1	0	0	0
Devey W	Will	12/04/1865	Perry Barr	1948	1896	1897		Burton Wanderers	Walsall	14	0	0	0	0	3	0	0	0	0
Devlin PJ	Paul	14/04/1972	Birmingham		1991	1998	s	Stafford Rangers	Birmingham City	146	8	12	19	0	25	1	1	6	0
Dewick JA	John	28/11/1919	Rotherham	1997	1946					1	0	0	0	0	0	0	0	0	0
Dickson W	Bill	15/04/1923	Lurgan		1946	1947	n	Glenavon	Chelsea	21	0	0	0	0	2	0	0	0	0
Dijkstra M	Meindert	28/02/1967	Eindhoven, Holland		1992	1993		Willem II (Holland)		29	3	2	8	0	1	0	0	0	0
Dinsdale N	Norman	20/06/1898	Hunslet	1970	1920	1927		Anston Ath.	Coventry City	267	27	0	0	0	11	0	0	0	0
Diuk WJ	Wayne	26/05/1980	Nottingham		1996	1997			Kettering T	2	0	1	1	0	0	0	0	0	0
Dixon H	Harry	1870	Kettering		1893			Kettering T	Kettering T	3	0	0	0	0	0	0	0	0	0
Dobson CF	Charley	09/09/1862	Basford	1939	1881	1888	e	Stonyhurst Col.		1	34	0	0	0	0	6	0	0	0
Docherty B	Benny	11/08/1941	Bellshill		1964			Cambuslang Rgs		25	2	3	0	0	2	0	0	0	0
Docherty E	Edward	1871	Glasgow		1892			Partick Thistle	Duntocher Harps	6	0	0	0	0	1	0	0	0	0
Dodd GF	George	07/05/1885	Whitchurch	1960	1907	1910		Workington	Chelsea	91	1	0	0	0	20	0	0	0	0
Doherty JC	Jim	31/01/1957	Douglas		1979	1980		Cumnock Juniors	Motherwell	8	0	0	1	0	0	0	0	0	0
Dolphin A	Alf	1890	Redditch	1940	1920			Oldham Athletic	Darlington	24	0	0	0	0	3	0	0	0	0
Donaldson J	Joe		Scotland		1898			Holytown Thistle		3	0	0	0	0	0	0	0	0	0
Donnelly S	Sam	1874	Annbank		1893	1894		Annbank	Blackpool	32	6	0	9	1	7	2	0	0	0
Dowall W	Bill		Thornliebank		1938			Ballymena		6	0	0	0	0	0	0	0	0	0
Downing KG	Keith	23/07/1965	Oldbury		1984	1986		Mile Oak Rovers	Wolves	23	0	0	0	0	1	0	0	0	0
Dowsey J	Jack	01/05/1905	Willington	1942	1928	1931		Sunderland	Northampton Town	98	5	0	0	0	4	0	0	0	0
Doyle NLR	Nathan	12/01/1987	Derby		2005			Derby County (loan)		12	0	0	0	0	0	0	0	0	0
Draper MA	Mark	11/11/1970	Long Eaton		1988	1993		Sandiacre T	Leicester City	222	10	15	20	3	41	2	2	5	0
Dryden RA	Richard	14/06/1969	Stroud		1991	1992		Exeter City	Birmingham City	31	3	2	2	0	1	0	0	0	0
Dudfield LG	Lawrie	07/05/1980	Southwark		2006			Boston United		41	1	3	1	0	7	1	1	0	0
Dudley CB	Craig	12/09/1979	Ollerton		1996	1998			Oldham Athletic	31	3	3	0	0	3	0	1	0	0
Dyer AC	Alex	14/11/1965	Forest Gate		1997	2000		Huddersfield T	Kingstonian	78	6	5	1	0	6	0	0	0	0
Dyer PD	Paul	24/01/1953	Leicester		1972	1973			Colchester Utd.	7	0	0	0	0	0	0	0	0	0
Earle HT	Harry	23/11/1868	East Grinstead	1951	1904			Clapton		23	1	0	0	0	2	0	0	0	0
Edge DJ	Declan	18/09/1965	Malacca, Malaysia		1985		nz	Gisbourne C (NZ)	Gisbourne C (NZ)	10	3	0	2	0	2	0	0	0	0
Edwards JW	Jack	23/02/1924	Salford	1978	1952	1953		Southampton	King's Lynn	25	0	0	0	0	3	0	0	0	0
Edwards M	Mike	25/04/1980	Hessle		2004	2006		Grimsby Town		100	3	7	1	0	10	0	1	0	0
Edwards RT	Dick	20/11/1942	Kirkby-in-Ashfield		1959	1966		E Kirkby Welfare	Mansfield Town	221	10	14	0	0	20	0	1	0	0
Elleman AR	Allan	03/11/1862	Birmingham	1939	1891		i	West Bromwich A.	Grimsby Town	6	0	0	0	0	2	0	0	0	0
Elliot R	Rob	30/04/1986	Chatham		2004			Charlton Ath. (loan)		4	0	0	0	0	0	0	0	0	0
Elliott JW	John	23/12/1946	Warkworth		1967	1968		Ashington	King's Lynn	64	2	2	0	0	7	0	0	0	0
Elliott S	Sid	14/01/1908	Sunderland	1986	1931	1933		Bristol City	Bradford City	51	2	0	0	0	16	0	0	0	0
Emberton FP	Teddy	23/06/1884	Thryston	1957	1904	1914		Stafford Rangers		365	17	0	0	0	2	1	0	0	0
Emenalo M	Michael	14/07/1965	Aba, Nigeria		1994		ng	RWD Molenbaek (Bel)	San Jose Earthquakes	7	0	0	4	0	0	0	0	0	0
Emmitt HW	Herbert	06/08/1857	Nottingham	1901	1881	1888			Nottm Forest	4	31	0	0	0	0	4	0	0	0
Evans FJ	Fred	20/05/1923	Petersfield		1947	1950		Portsmouth	Crystal Palace	39	0	0	0	0	14	0	0	0	0
Evans WE	Billy	05/09/1921	Birmingham	1960	1949	1952		Aston Villa	Gillingham	96	7	0	0	0	14	0	0	0	0
Fairclough CH	Chris	12/04/1964	Nottingham		1998			Bolton Wanderers	York City	16	1	2	0	0	1	0	0	0	0
Fairclough WR	Wayne	27/04/1968	Nottingham		1985	1989			Mansfield Town	71	3	3	11	2	0	0	0	0	0
Fallon WJ	Bill	14/01/1912	Larne	1989	1933 1946	1938	r	Dolphin (Dublin) Sheffield Wed.	Sheffield Wed. Exeter City	135	10	0	3	0	23	3	0	1	0
Farina F	Frank	05/09/1964	Darwin, Australia		1991		au	Bari - Italy (loan)		3	0	0	0	0	0	0	0	0	0
Farmer RJ	Ron	06/03/1936	Guernsey		1967	1968		Coventry City	Grantham	69	2	0	0	0	5	0	0	0	0
Farrell SP	Sean	28/02/1969	Watford		1996	2000		Peterborough Utd.	Burton Albion	88	7	3	1	0	22	1	0	0	0
Fashanu JS	Justin	19/02/1961	Hackney	1998	1982	1984		Nottm. Forest	Brighton & Hove A.	64	2	7	0	0	20	2	1	0	0
Fawell DS	Derek	22/03/1944	Hartlepool		1964			Spennymoor U	Lincoln City	1	0	0	0	0	0	0	0	0	0
Featherby WL	Len	28/07/1905	King's Lynn	1972	1935			Plymouth Argyle	Carlisle Utd.	3	0	0	1	0	0	0	0	0	0
Feebery A	Alf	10/09/1909	Hucknall	1989	1929	1938		Hucknall Congs	Bristol Rovers	221	7	0	4	0	1	0	0	0	0
Feeney WT	Tom	26/08/1910	Grangetown	1973	1932			Newcastle United	Lincoln City	17	0	0	0	0	2	0	0	0	0
Fenner T	Tom	12/05/1904	Warrington		1927	1933		Wigan Borough	Bradford City	158	5	0	0	0	69	1	0	0	0
Fenton NL	Nick	23/11/1979	Preston		1999	2003		Manchester C (loan)		168	12	7	5	0	10	2	0	0	0
Fenwick RW	Bob	29/09/1894	Walker	1973	1922	1924		Lincoln City	Lincoln City	6	0	0	0	0	0	0	0	0	0
Ferguson A	Sandy	1867	Glasgow	1894	1889	1890		Rangers	Newark	22	5	0	0	0	0	0	0	0	0
Ferguson C	Charlie	22/11/1910	Dunfermline	1995	1936			Middlesbrough	Luton Town	22	1	0	2	0	8	0	0	2	0
Ferguson JS	Jim	30/08/1896	Longriggend	1952	1927	1931		Brentford		158	6	0	0	0	0	0	0	0	0
Ferrier D	David				1894				Dundee	2	0	0	0	0	0	0	0	0	0
Finnan SJ	Steve	20/04/1976	Limerick		1995	1998	r	Birmingham C (loan)		97	7	4	1	3	7	1	0	0	1
Fisher F	Fred	1910	Hucknall		1929			Newark T	Torquay United	3	0	0	0	0	1	0	0	0	0
Flanagan DC	Daniel	24/11/1924	Dublin		1946			Dundalk	Shelbourne	2	0	0	0	0	2	0	0	0	0
Fleming GJ	Gary	17/02/1967	Derry		1989		n	Manchester C (loan)		3	0	0	1	0	0	0	0	0	0
Fletcher F	Fred	1877	Ripley		1894	1895		Derby County	Worcester Rovers	9	0	0	2	1	3	0	0	0	1
Fletcher HH	Harry	13/06/1873	Birmingham	1923	1897	1899		Grimsby Town	Grimsby Town	60	2	0	0	0	17	1	0	0	0
Flint WA	Billy	21/03/1890	Underwood	1955	1908	1925		Eastwood Rgs		376	32	0	0	0	40	1	0	0	0
Flower AJ	Tony	02/01/1915	Carlton, Notts		1961	1966			Halifax Town	129	5	6	0	0	17	0	0	0	0
Flower T	Tom	1915	Liverpool	1962	1938	1945		Liverpool		36	4	0	1	0	0	0	0	0	0
Foley DJ	Dominic	07/07/1976	Cork		1998		r	Wolves (loan)		2	0	0	1	0	0	0	0	0	0
Ford R	Ryan	03/09/1978	Worksop		1999	2000		Manchester Utd.	Ilkeston T	1	0	0	1	0	0	0	0	0	0
Forrest JR	Bobby	13/05/1931	Rossington	2005	1958	1961		Leeds United	Weymouth	117	6	3	0	0	37	0	1	0	0
Forsyth ME	Mike	20/03/1966	Liverpool		1994			Derby County	Wycombe Wan.	7	0	0	0	0	0	0	0	0	0
Foster CJ	Colin	16/07/1964	Chislehurst		1993			West Ham U (loan)		9	0	0	2	0	0	0	0	0	0
Foster JH	Jack	24/01/1889	Wombwell	1972	1919			Worksop T	Luton Town	32	3	0	0	0	1	0	0	0	0
Fountain RE	Richard	1882	Leeds		1905			Scarborough	Accrington Stanley	1	0	0	0	0	0	0	0	0	0
Francis WD	Willis	26/07/1985	Nottingham		2002	2003		Trainee	Grantham T	13	0	0	0	0	0	0	0	0	0
Fraser J	Jack	10/11/1876	Dumbarton	1952	1897	1898	s	Motherwell	Newcastle United	41	2	0	0	0	5	0	0	0	0
Freeman A	Tony	29/08/1928	Melton Mowbray	2004	1946	1949		Melton T	Boston U	44	6	0	0	0	2	1	0	0	0

Name		D.o.B.	Place of Birth	Died	First Season	Last Season	Ints	Previous Club	Next Club	Appearances Leg	FAC	FLC	Oth	PO	Goals Leg	FAC	FLC	Oth	PO
Friars EC	Emmet	14/09/1985	Derry		2004	2005		Foyle Harps		14	0	0	1	0	1	0	0	0	0
Froggatt F	Frank	21/03/1898	Sheffield	1944	1927	1930		Sheffield Wed.	Chesterfield	115	3	0	0	0	1	0	0	0	0
Froggatt JL	John	13/12/1945	Stanton Hill		1963	1964		E Kirkby Colliery	Ilkeston T	4	0	1	0	0	0	0	1	0	0
Frost S	Stef	03/07/1989	Eastwood		2005					4	0	0	0	0	0	0	0	0	0
Fry KF	Keith	11/04/1941	Cardiff		1961	1963		Newport County	Merthyr Tydfil	73	4	6	0	0	9	0	3	0	0
Gadsby MD	Mick	01/08/1947	Oswestry		1967			Ashbourne	York City	11	0	0	0	0	0	0	0	0	0
Galbraith					1888			Dundee		1	0	0	0	0	0	0	0	0	0
Gallacher HK	Hughie	02/02/1903	Bellshill	1957	1936	1937	s	Derby County	Grimsby Town	45	1	0	1	0	32	0	0	0	0
Gallagher J	Jimmy	02/09/1911	Bury	1972	1937	1938		Lancaster T	Exeter City	23	2	0	1	0	2	1	0	0	0
Gallagher TD	Tommy	25/08/1974	Nottingham		1992	1996				43	3	1	12	0	2	1	0	1	0
Galloway MA	Mick	13/10/1974	Nottingham		1994	1996			Gillingham	21	2	2	4	0	0	0	0	0	0
Gannon E	Eddie	03/01/1921	Dublin	1989	1946	1948	r	Shelbourne	Sheffield Wed.	107	11	0	0	0	2	0	0	0	0
Gannon JP	Jim	07/09/1968	Southwark		1993			Stockport Co. (loan)		2	0	0	0	0	0	0	0	0	0
Garcia A	Tony	18/03/1972	Pierre Patte, France		1998			Sheffield Wed.	Valenciennes	19	5	0	1	0	2	0	0	0	0
Garden SR	Stuart	10/02/1972	Dundee		2001	2003		Forfar Ath.	Ross County	52	1	1	2	0	0	0	0	0	0
Garner WD	Bill	14/12/1947	Leicester		1966			Bedford T	Loughborough U	2	0	0	0	0	0	0	0	0	0
Garratt FH	Fred	01/10/1888	Stanton Hill	1967	1909	1911		Stanton Hill Vic.	Stockport Co.	8	0	0	0	0	0	0	0	0	0
Gaughran BM	Benny	29/09/1915	Dublin	1977	1938			Sunderland	Dundalk	2	0	0	1	0	1	0	0	0	0
Gee E	Ellis	15/06/1877	Grassmoor	1948	1900	1906		Everton	Reading	214	14	0	0	0	21	2	0	0	0
Gibbon H	Harry	19/04/1906	Hetton-le-Hole	1972	1927			Sunderland	Seaham Harbour	3	0	0	0	0	0	0	0	0	0
Gibson APS	Alex	28/11/1939	Kirkconnel	2003	1959	1968		Auchinleck Talbot	Boston Utd.	347	10	16	0	0	10	0	0	0	0
Gibson PR	Paul	01/11/1976	Sheffield		1998	2000		Manchester Utd.	Northwich Vic.	11	0	2	1	0	0	0	0	0	0
Gibson T	Tommy	23/10/1888	Maxwelltown		1919	1922		Nottm. Forest	Southend Utd.	63	6	0	0	0	5	1	0	0	0
Gibson W	Will		1869	Cambuslang	1911	1896	1897		Sunderland	Bristol City	41	3	0	0	4	0	0	0	0	0
Gill MJ	Matthew	08/11/1980	Cambridge		2004	2005		Peterborough Utd.		57	5	3	1	0	0	0	0	0	0
Gissing JWD	John	24/11/1938	Stapleford		1957	1960			Chesterfield	22	0	0	0	0	1	0	0	0	0
Gleeson DE	Dan	17/02/1985	Cambridge		2006			Cambridge Utd.		17	1	3	1	0	0	0	0	0	0
Glen A	Alex	11/12/1878	Kilsyth		1903			Grimsby Town	Tottenham H	20	1	0	0	0	3	0	0	0	0
Goater LS	Shaun	25/02/1970	Hamilton, Bermuda		1993		bm	Rotherham U (loan)		1	0	0	0	0	0	0	0	0	0
Gooch PG	Percy	01/09/1882	Lowestoft	1956	1907			Birmingham	Norwich City	3	0	0	0	0	1	0	0	0	0
Goodwin MA	Mark	23/02/1960	Sheffield		1980	1986		Leicester City	Walsall	237	15	20	10	0	23	0	3	0	0
Goram AL	Andy	13/04/1964	Bury		1998		s	Rangers	Sheffield Utd.	1	0	0	0	0	0	0	0	0	0
Gordon KG	Gavin	24/06/1979	Manchester		2004	2005		Cardiff City		33	5	0	1	0	5	3	0	0	0
Goss W	William		1879	Nottingham		1899			Heanor T	Portsmouth	16	3	0	0	0	1	1	0	0	0
Goucher GH	George	18/05/1902	Shirebrook	1987	1926			Shirebrook	Nottm. Forest	1	0	0	0	0	0	0	0	0	0
Gould G	Geoff	07/01/1945	Blackburn		1969			Bradford		1	0	0	0	0	0	0	0	0	0
Grant KT	Kim	25/09/1972	Sekondi-Takaradi, Ghana		1998		gh	Millwall (loan)		6	0	0	0	0	1	0	0	0	0
Gray AM	Andy	30/11/1955	Glasgow		1987		s	Aston Villa (loan)		4	0	2	0	0	0	0	1	0	0
Grayson SN	Simon	16/12/1969	Ripon		2001			Blackburn R (loan)		10	0	1	2	0	1	0	0	0	0
Greatorex L	Laurie		1901	Unstone	1960	1924			Dronfield	Southend Utd.	4	0	0	0	0	0	0	0	0	0
Green AW	Arthur	12/05/1881	Aberystwyth	1966	1902	1906	w	Walsall	Nottm. Forest	134	8	0	0	0	56	3	0	0	0
Green R	Rick	23/11/1952	Scunthorpe		1978			Chesterfield	Scunthorpe Utd.	9	0	0	2	0	0	0	0	0	0
Green RCG	Ronnie	12/03/1912	Frampton Cotterell	1979	1934	1935		Arsenal	Charlton Ath.	36	4	0	1	0	5	1	0	1	0
Grice F	Frank	13/11/1908	Derby	1988	1931	1935		Linfield	Tottenham H	102	5	0	2	0	4	1	0	0	0
Grice R	Reuben		1886	Ruddington	1967	1910	1911		Grove Celtic	Rotherham County	4	0	0	0	0	0	0	0	0	0
Griffiths A	Arthur	16/03/1879	Aston		1903	1911		Bristol Rovers	Retired	163	8	0	0	0	1	0	0	0	0
Groome PB	Pat	16/03/1934	Nottingham		1952	1957		Bonsall	Skegness T	40	1	0	0	0	0	0	0	0	0
Gunn W	Billy	04/12/1858	Nottingham	1921	1882	1892	e	Nottm Forest		3	25	0	0	0	1	13	0	0	0
Guttridge FH	Frank	12/04/1866	Nottingham	1918	1888			Heanor T	Nottm Forest	18	1	0	0	0	0	0	0	0	0
					1894			Nottm. Forest	Nelson										
Hackworth A	Tony	19/05/1980	Durham		2001	2003		Leeds United	Scarborough	54	3	3	4	0	1	0	0	1	0
Haden S	Sam	17/01/1902	Royston, West Yorks	1974	1927	1937		Arsenal	Peterborough Utd.	289	11	0	1	0	36	2	0	0	0
Hadley A	Arthur	05/05/1876	Reading		1898	1901		Reading	Leicester Fosse	76	6	0	0	0	22	0	0	0	0
Haig P	Paul			Nottingham		1913			Eastwood Rgs	Mansfield Town	1	0	0	0	0	0	0	0	0	0
Hall GW	Willie	12/03/1912	Newark	1967	1930	1932	e	Ransome & Marles	Tottenham H	34	1	0	0	0	7	1	0	0	0
Hall WH	William					1894					2	0	0	0	0	0	0	0	0	0
Halton RL	Reg	11/07/1916	Leek	1988	1937			Manchester Utd.	Bury	6	1	0	2	0	7	0	0	1	0
Hamilton IR	Ian	14/12/1967	Stevenage		2000	2001		Sheffield Utd.	Lincoln City	34	4	5	3	0	0	0	0	0	0
Hamilton W	Billy	24/10/1904	Musselburgh	1984	1930			Accrington Stanley	Alloa Ath.	2	0	0	0	0	0	0	0	0	0
Hammond L	Len	12/09/1901	Rugby	1983	1933			Northampton Town	Rugby T	26	1	0	0	0	0	0	0	0	0
Hampson T	Tommy	02/05/1898	Bury		1929			Cardiff City	Nottm Coop Dairy	1	0	0	0	0	0	0	0	0	0
Hampton IK	Ivan	15/10/1942	Kimberley		1960	1966		Rotherham Utd.	Halifax Town	141	3	12	0	0	1	0	0	0	0
Handley G	George	01/10/1868	Burton-on-the-Wolds		1895			Loughborough T	Coalville T	1	0	0	0	0	0	0	0	0	0
Hannah G	George	11/12/1928	Liverpool	1990	1964	1965		Manchester City	Bradford City	25	0	1	0	0	1	0	0	0	0
Hannigan R	Richard					1898			Greenock Morton	Woolwich Arsenal	15	1	0	0	0	2	0	0	0	0
Harbottle MS	Mark	26/09/1968	Nottingham		1985			Nottm Forest	Scarborough	4	0	0	0	0	1	0	0	0	0
Harding PJ	Paul	06/03/1964	Mitcham		1990	1992			Birmingham City	54	6	1	5	3	1	0	0	1	1
Harker E	Ted		1862	Plumtree		1884	1888				2	12	0	0	0	0	2	0	0	0
Harkin JT	Terry	14/09/1941	Derry		1966		n	Cardiff City	Southport	28	1	0	0	0	10	0	0	0	0
Harkouk RP	Rachid	19/05/1956	Chelsea		1980	1985	al	QPR	Retired	144	11	13	7	0	39	5	5	3	0
Harper RRG	Rowland		1881	Lichfield	1949	1907	1908		Aston Villa	Mansfield Invicta	10	0	0	0	0	1	0	0	0	0
Harper T	Theo 'Fay'		1866	Brierley Hill		1892	1894		Mansfield Town	Mansfield Town	46	6	0	4	1	0	0	0	0	0
Harrad SN	Shaun	11/12/1984	Nottingham		2002	2004		Nottm Forest		29	3	0	0	0	1	0	0	0	0
Harris GT	George	14/06/1904	High Wycombe	1986	1922	1923		Wycombe Wan.	QPR	2	0	0	0	0	0	0	0	0	0
Harris NL	Neil	30/10/1894	Tollcross	1941	1925	1926	s	Newcastle United	Shelbourne	49	3	0	0	0	23	2	0	0	0
Harrison AW	Albert					1905			Ruddington		3	0	0	0	0	0	0	0	0	0
Harrisson AE	Alfred		1872	Holbeach	1947	1894				Nottm. Forest	1	0	0	0	0	0	0	0	0	0
Hart PA	Paul	04/05/1953	Golborne		1987			Birmingham City	Chesterfield	23	2	0	3	1	0	0	0	0	0
Hateley A	Tony	13/06/1941	Derby		1958	1962		Derby County	Aston Villa	188	13	6	0	0	109	4	1	0	0
					1970	1971		Birmingham C	Oldham Ath.										
Hatton C	Cyril	14/09/1918	Grantham	1987	1936	1938		Grantham Coop	QPR	62	3	0	2	0	8	0	0	0	0
Heathcote J	Jimmy	17/01/1894	Bolton		1922			Blackpool	Pontypridd	12	0	0	0	0	1	0	0	0	0

Name		D.o.B.	Place of Birth	Died	First Season	Last Season	Ints	Previous Club	Next Club	Appearances					Goals				
										Leg	FAC	FLC	Oth	PO	Leg	FAC	FLC	Oth	PO
Heffernan P	Paul	29/12/1981	Dublin		1999	2003		Newtown (Ireland)	Bristol City	100	4	5	5	0	36	1	1	0	0
Henderson WCP	Wayne	16/09/1983	Dublin		2004		r	Aston Villa (loan)		11	0	0	1	0	0	0	0	0	0
Hendon IM	Ian	05/12/1971	Ilford		1996	1998		Leyton Orient	Northampton Town	82	9	5	0	0	6	0	1	0	0
Hendry J	Jack		Scotland		1890	1895		Rangers	Heanor T	163	18	0	9	2	1	0	0	0	0
Hendry R	Robert	1876	Dumbarton		1897			Everton	Greenock Morton	7	0	0	0	0	0	0	0	0	0
Henrys A	Arthur	1867	Nottingham	1922	1896			Leicester Fosse		7	0	0	0	0	0	0	0	0	0
Henshall HV	Horace	14/06/1889	Hednesford	1951	1912	1921		Aston Villa	Sheffield Wed.	164	16	0	0	0	27	2	0	0	0
Hesford I	Iain	04/03/1960	Ndola, Zambia		1985			Sheffield Wed. (loan)		10	0	0	1	0	0	0	0	0	0
Higgins AK	Andy	26/04/1909	Gartsherrie	1966	1934			Newport County	Olympique Lillios (Fr)	10	0	0	0	0	2	0	0	0	0
Hill H	Harold	24/09/1899	Blackwell, Derbyshire	1969	1919	1924		New Hucknall Coll.	Sheffield Wed.	151	19	0	0	0	50	6	0	0	0
Hillhouse JT	John	14/01/1898	Hurlford		1926			Rochdale	Bury	4	0	0	0	0	0	0	0	0	0
Hills WJ	Walter	18/07/1898	Ferozepore, India	1985	1924	1926		Meadow Thursday	Grantham	3	1	0	0	0	0	0	0	0	0
Hilton F	Fred	08/07/1903	Sheffield		1924	1928		Grimsby Town	Scunthorpe U	109	5	0	0	0	3	0	0	0	0
Hindmarsh JS	John	29/01/1913	Ashington	1990	1937	1938		Burnley	Ashington	57	5	0	3	0	0	0	0	0	0
Hobson J	John	01/06/1946	Barnsley		1969	1970		Barnsley		49	1	2	0	0	6	0	0	0	0
Hodder W	Bill	1865	Stroud	1897	1888			Notts Rangers	Nottm Forest	20	2	0	0	0	3	0	0	0	0
Hodson SP	Simeon	05/03/1966	Lincoln		1983	1984		Swinderby FC	Charlton Ath.	27	0	3	0	0	0	0	0	0	0
Hogg GJ	Graeme	17/06/1964	Aberdeen		1994	1997		Hearts	Brentford	66	4	5	4	0	0	1	0	0	0
Hold O	Oscar	19/10/1918	Carlton, West Yorks	2005	1948			Norwich City	Chelmsford C	19	4	0	0	0	9	0	0	0	0
Holder DJ	Dave	15/12/1943	Cheltenham	2002	1963			Cardiff City	Barrow	8	1	2	0	0	0	0	0	0	0
Holder SW	Steve	21/04/1952	Nottingham		1969			Nottm schools	Corby T	1	0	0	0	0	0	0	0	0	0
Holland JH	Jack	1861	Bulwell		1886	1888			Nottm Forest	9	9	0	0	0	0	0	0	0	0
Holmes R	Richard	07/11/1980	Grantham		1998	2002		Bottesford	Harrowby U	59	4	4	3	0	0	0	0	0	0
Holmes WH	Harry	18/08/1908	Ambergate	1976	1933			Coventry City	Birmingham	2	0	0	0	0	0	0	0	0	0
Hooks P	Paul	30/05/1959	Wallsend		1976	1982		Aston Villa	Derby County	173	9	16	19	0	30	1	6	4	0
Hooley A					1891			Stapleford FC	Stapleford FC	3	0	0	0	0	1	0	0	0	0
Hooper WG	Bill	20/02/1884	Lewisham	1952	1912			Nottm. Forest	Barrow	16	1	0	0	0	1	0	0	0	0
Hopkins GH	George	11/05/1901	Sheffield	1974	1926	1927		Newark T	Scarborough	28	0	0	0	0	0	0	0	0	0
Horobin R	Roy	10/03/1935	Brownhills		1958	1961		West Bromwich A.	Peterborough Utd.	123	7	2	0	0	37	0	2	0	0
Hoten RV	Ralph	27/12/1896	Pinxton	1978	1919	1920		Pinxton Colliery	Portsmouth	4	0	0	0	0	1	0	0	0	0
Houghton R	Roy	31/03/1921	Billingborough		1937	1938			Boston United	8	0	0	3	0	0	0	0	0	0
Houghton WE	Eric	29/06/1910	Billingborough	1996	1946	1948	e	Aston Villa	Notts manager	55	5	0	0	0	10	0	0	0	0
Hoult AA	Aubrey	17/07/1915	Whitwick	1998	1934	1935		Oaks Parish Church	Northampton Town	8	0	0	1	0	0	0	0	0	0
Howe HA	Bert	01/04/1916	Rugby	1972	1947	1948		Leicester City	Rugby T	52	7	0	0	0	0	0	0	0	0
Howell DG	Dean	29/11/1980	Burton-on-Trent		1999			Stoke City	Crewe Alexandra	1	0	0	0	0	0	0	0	0	0
Hoyle CR	Colin	15/01/1972	Wirksworth		1994	1995		Bradford City	King's Lynn	5	0	0	1	0	0	0	0	0	0
Hubbard J	Jack	24/03/1925	Wath-on-Dearne	2002	1945	1947			Scarborough	13	6	0	0	0	2	1	0	0	0
Hughes AJ	Andy	02/01/1978	Manchester		1997	2000		Oldham Athletic	Reading	110	10	7	2	0	17	2	1	0	0
Hulme J	John	06/02/1945	Mobberley		1971			Bolton Wan. (loan)		8	0	0	0	0	0	0	0	0	0
Humphreys P	Percy	03/12/1880	Cambridge	1959	1901	1906	e	QPR	Leicester Fosse	189	13	0	0	0	66	7	0	0	0
Hunt D	David	17/04/1959	Leicester		1977	1986		Derby County	Aston Villa	336	22	29	21	0	28	2	5	2	0
Hunt JM	James	17/12/1976	Derby		1995	1996		Assoc. schoolboy	Northampton Town	19	1	0	4	0	1	0	0	1	0
Hunt SJ	Stephen	11/11/1984	Southampton		2006			Colchester Utd.		32	0	3	1	0	1	0	0	0	0
Hurst G	Glynn	17/01/1976	Barnsley		2004	2005		Chesterfield	Stockport Co.	59	5	2	1	0	23	0	0	1	0
Innes RA	Bob	23/07/1878	Lanark	1959	1901	1902		New Brompton	Nottm. Forest	48	3	0	0	0	0	0	0	0	0
Ireland CR	Craig	29/11/1975	Dundee		2000	2002		Airdrie	Barnsley	80	1	2	0	0	2	0	0	0	0
Iremonger A	Albert	15/06/1884	Wilford, Notts	1958	1904	1925		Nottm. Forest	Lincoln City	564	37	0	0	0	0	0	0	0	0
Jackson C	Craig	17/01/1969	Renishaw		1985	1987		Trainee		5	0	1	0	0	0	0	0	0	0
Jackson H	Harry	23/04/1864	Nottingham		1884	1888		Sneinton Wan.	Nottm Forest	5	21	0	0	0	3	19	0	0	0
Jackson J	Jimmy	26/03/1931	Glasgow		1948	1953		Mapperley Celtic	Toronto	113	10	0	0	0	47	3	0	0	0
					1954	1957		Toronto	Headington Utd										
Jackson JJ	Justin	10/12/1974	Nottingham		1997	1998		Woking	Halifax Town	25	5	0	2	0	1	0	0	0	0
Jacobsen A	Anders	18/04/1968	Oslo, Norway		2000		no	Stoke City	Skeid Oslo	29	5	0	0	0	2	0	0	0	0
Jakeman GJW	George	19/05/1903	Small Heath	1973	1929	1932		Aston Villa	Kidderminster H	70	1	0	0	0	0	0	0	0	0
James L	Lance	11/01/1890	Nottingham	1983	1910	1913				6	0	0	0	0	0	0	0	0	0
James WB	Wilf	19/02/1907	Cross Keys	1996	1928	1929	w	Owston Park Rgs	West Ham Utd.	16	0	0	0	0	5	0	0	0	0
Jardine RJ	Bob	1864	Partick	1941	1888	1894		Halliwell	Derby County	18	0	0	1	0	9	0	0	0	0
Jarvis H	Harry	08/10/1928	Maltby		1952	1954		Worksop T	Nottm. Forest	29	1	0	0	0	0	0	0	0	0
Jayes AG	Gordon	26/11/1923	Leicester	1997	1946	1947		Nuneaton Boro	Nuneaton Boro	27	3	0	0	0	7	1	0	0	0
Jemson NB	Nigel	10/08/1969	Preston		1994	1995		Sheffield Wed.	Oxford United	14	0	4	1	0	1	0	1	0	0
Jenkins SR	Steve	16/07/1972	Merthyr Tydfil		2003		w	Cardiff City	Peterborough Utd.	17	2	3	1	0	0	0	0	0	0
Jennings W	Bill	25/02/1891	Cinderhill	1953	1913	1914		Arnold St Mary's	Norwich City	42	1	0	0	0	0	0	0	0	0
Johnson J	Joe		Stamford		1919			Mansfield Mechanics	Watford	10	0	0	0	0	0	0	0	0	0
Johnson MO	Michael	04/07/1973	Nottingham		1991	1995	ja	Clifton All Whites	Birmingham City	107	4	9	16	0	0	0	0	0	0
Johnson T	Tommy	15/01/1971	Newcastle		1988	1991		Assoc. schoolboy	Derby County	118	5	9	11	6	47	1	5	0	4
Johnston TD	Tom	30/12/1918	Coldstream	1994	1948	1956		Nottm. Forest	Birmingham C (coach)	267	19	0	0	0	88	4	0	0	0
Jones A	Aaron	1882	Walsall	1950	1906	1907		Small Heath	Retired	22	4	0	0	0	6	2	0	0	0
Jones AF	Freddie	25/12/1888	Newstead		1907	1910		Sutton Town	Coventry City	86	5	0	0	0	27	4	0	0	0
					1912			Coventry City	Coventry City										
Jones AT	Albert	06/02/1883	Talgarth	1963	1905	1906	w	Nottm. Forest	Norwich City	30	1	0	0	0	0	0	0	0	0
Jones B	Barrie	31/10/1938	Barnsley		1961	1963		Army	King's Lynn	42	2	6	0	0	15	0	2	0	0
Jones F	Fred	26/08/1909	Pontypool	1994	1934			Swansea T	Millwall	1	0	0	0	0	0	0	0	0	0
Jones G	Gary	06/04/1969	Huddersfield		1995	1998		Southend Utd.	Hartlepool Utd.	117	10	6	1	2	38	7	1	0	0
Jones JW	Jimmy	1896	Warsop		1919	1920		Welbeck Coll.	Alfreton T	11	0	0	0	0	0	0	0	0	0
Jones MD	Mick	24/03/1947	Sunderland		1969	1972		Derby County	Peterborough Utd.	100	7	6	1	0	1	0	0	0	0
Jones MR	Mark	21/12/1965	Mansfield		1983	1984		App.		6	0	0	0	0	0	0	0	0	0
Jorgensen H	Henrik	12/01/1979	Bogense, Denmark		2000	2001		B1909 (Denmark)	B1909 (Denmark)	7	2	1	2	0	0	0	0	0	0
Joseph D	David	22/11/1976	Guadeloupe		2000			Montpellier (loan)		27	1	4	1	0	4	0	0	0	0
Joyce C	Chris	19/04/1933	Dumbarton	2002	1959	1961		Nottm. Forest	Nuneaton Boro	62	1	1	0	0	18	0	0	0	0
Joynes RA	Dickie	1877	Grantham	1949	1901	1902		Newark	Newark	46	1	0	0	0	3	0	0	0	0
Julian W	Walter	24/12/1914	Hucknall	1972	1934	1937		West Bridgford	Crewe Alexandra	14	0	0	3	0	0	0	0	0	0
Jupp DA	Duncan	25/01/1975	Guildford		2002		r	Wimbledon	Luton Town	8	1	0	0	0	0	0	0	0	0

Name		D.o.B.	Place of Birth	Died	First Season	Last Season	Ints	Previous Club	Next Club	Appearances					Goals				
										Leg	FAC	FLC	Oth	PO	Leg	FAC	FLC	Oth	PO
Kavanagh EM	Eddie	20/07/1941	Glasgow		1964			Cambuslang Rgs	Boston United	25	2	3	0	0	4	1	0	0	0
Kavanagh T	Terrence	1912	Dublin		1936			Everton	Exeter City	2	0	0	1	0	0	0	0	0	0
Kearton JB	Jason	09/07/1969	Ipswich, Australia		1994			Everton (loan)		10	0	0	2	0	0	0	0	0	0
Keeble WFW	Fred	30/08/1919	Coventry	1987	1947			Grimsby Town		4	0	0	0	0	1	0	0	0	0
Keeling P	Percy	1903	Basford	1939	1924			Alfreton T	Ilkeston T	6	0	0	0	0	0	0	0	0	0
Keetley TE	Tom	16/11/1898	Derby	1958	1929	1932		Doncaster Rovers	Lincoln City	103	7	0	0	0	94	4	0	0	0
Kelly EP	Eddie	07/02/1951	Glasgow		1980			Leicester City	Bournemouth	27	1	5	7	0	1	0	2	0	0
Kelly P	Peter	20/03/1901	Tyldesley	1950	1925	1927		New Brighton	New Brighton	69	1	0	0	0	19	0	0	0	0
Kelly W	Willie	27/03/1880	Kirkintilloch		1903			West Ham U	Brighton & Hove A.	2	0	0	0	0	0	0	0	0	0
Kemp H	Haydn	17/01/1897	Mosborough	1982	1920	1930		Chesterfield Mun.	Thames	286	26	0	0	0	6	0	0	0	0
Kennedy PHJ	Peter	10/09/1973	Lurgan		1996		n	Portadown	Watford	22	2	1	1	0	0	1	0	0	0
Kerr G	George				1893			Kilmarnock		23	1	0	5	0	6	0	0	1	0
Kevan DJ	David	31/08/1968	Wigtown		1985	1989		App.	Stoke City	89	6	4	9	0	3	1	0	0	0
Kiddier JF	James	1874	Nottingham	1935	1895				Bulwell United	15	0	0	0	0	4	0	0	0	0
Kilcline B	Brian	07/05/1962	Nottingham		1979	1983		Assoc. schoolboy	Coventry City	158	10	16	9	0	9	2	1	1	0
Kilford JD	John	08/11/1938	Derby		1958			Derby Corinthians	Leeds United	26	1	0	0	0	0	0	0	0	0
King JD	Jeff	09/11/1953	Fauldhouse		1975			Derby County (loan)		3	0	0	0	0	0	0	0	0	0
King LH	Louis	1873	Nottingham	1952	1892	1893		Greenhalgh's		3	0	0	1	0	0	0	0	0	0
King PG	Phil	28/12/1967	Bristol		1993			Sheffield Wed. (loan)		6	0	0	2	0	0	0	0	0	0
King TP	Tom	29/06/1909	Woolsthorpe-by-Belvoir	1993	1934			Sneinton	Bournemouth	2	0	0	0	0	0	0	0	0	0
Kinsey G	George	27/11/1866	Burton-on-Trent	1936	1896		e	Derby County	Eastville Rovers	4	0	0	0	0	0	0	0	0	0
Kirk JJ	James	1879	Southwell	1953	1902			Southwell St Mary's	Newark	1	0	0	0	0	0	0	0	0	0
Kirkham R	Royce	17/10/1937	Ollerton		1956			Ollerton Coll.	Workington	1	0	0	0	0	0	0	0	0	0
Kirkup FW	Frank	12/01/1939	Spennymoor		1965			Carlisle Utd.	Workington	29	1	2	0	0	3	0	0	0	0
Kiwomya AD	Andy	01/10/1967	Huddersfield		1997			Bradford City	Halifax Town	2	0	0	1	0	0	0	0	0	0
Knox T	Tommy	11/11/1905	Ushaw Moor		1933	1935		Hartlepools Utd.	Crystal Palace	72	5	0	1	0	0	0	0	0	0
Kuduzovic F	Faz	10/10/1984	Bosnia		2004			Derby County	Sligo Rovers	3	0	0	0	0	0	0	0	0	0
Kuhl M	Martin	10/01/1965	Frimley		1994			Derby County (loan)		2	0	0	0	0	0	0	0	0	0
Ladd IM	Ian	22/11/1958	Peterborough		1977				Cambridge Utd.	1	0	0	0	0	0	0	0	0	0
Lahtinen AA	Aki	31/10/1958	Oulu, Finland		1981	1984	fi	OPS Oulo (Finland)		45	3	5	0	0	2	0	0	0	0
Laird A	Alex	02/06/1926	Newmains	2004	1953			Corby Town	Cheltenham T	1	0	0	0	0	0	0	0	0	0
Lamb JA	Jack	1893	Birmingham		1913	1914		Worcester C	Worcester C	8	0	0	0	0	3	0	0	0	0
Lane F	Frankie	20/07/1948	Wallasey		1975			Liverpool	Kettering T	2	0	0	0	0	0	0	0	0	0
Lane JG	Jackie	10/11/1931	Selly Oak		1956	1958		Birmingham City	Hinckley Ath.	57	3	0	0	0	19	0	0	0	0
Langford JW	John	04/08/1937	Kirkby-in-Ashfield		1958			Nottm. Forest	Bourne T	16	0	0	0	0	0	0	0	0	0
Langham W	Billy	1876	Lenton		1896	1897		South Shore	Bristol City	47	3	0	0	4	15	0	0	0	1
Law N	Nicky	08/09/1961	Greenwich		1988	1989		Plymouth Argyle	Rotherham Utd.	47	1	4	4	0	4	0	0	0	0
Lawless PJH	Henry				1929			Calthorpe	Loghboro Corinthians	2	0	0	0	0	0	0	0	0	0
Lawrence E	Eddie	24/08/1907	Cefn Mawr	1989	1931	1935	w	Clapton Orient	Bournemouth	138	4	0	1	0	2	0	0	0	0
Lawton T	Tommy	06/10/1919	Bolton	1996	1947	1951	e	Chelsea	Brentford	151	15	0	0	0	90	13	0	0	0
Lee GM	Garnet	07/06/1887	Calverton	1976	1910					4	0	0	0	0	0	0	0	0	0
Lee JB	Jason	09/05/1971	Forest Gate		2006			Northampton Town		38	1	2	0	0	15	0	1	0	0
Legg A	Andy	28/07/1966	Neath		1993	1995	w	Swansea City	Birmingham City	89	8	11	15	0	9	2	0	3	0
Leonard J	John				1897			Derby County		1	0	0	0	0	1	0	0	0	0
Leonard MC	Mick	09/05/1959	Carshalton		1979	1988		Halifax Town	Chesterfield	204	20	15	13	2	0	0	0	0	0
Leuty LH	Leon	23/10/1920	Meole Brace	1955	1950	1955		Bradford		188	13	0	0	0	3	1	0	0	0
Leverton R	Ron 'Tot'	08/05/1926	Whitwell	2003	1953	1955		Nottm. Forest	Walsall	45	6	0	0	0	5	0	0	0	0
Lewis G	George	01/01/1875	Chasetown		1897	1901		Wellingborough T	Bristol City	129	8	0	0	0	1	1	0	0	0
Lewis HH	Harry	25/10/1910	Merthyr Tydfil	2006	1933	1934		Southend Utd.	West Ham Utd.	32	1	0	0	0	7	0	0	0	0
Liburd RJ	Richard	26/09/1973	Nottingham		1998	2002		Carlisle Utd.	Lincoln City	154	12	7	2	0	9	2	0	0	0
Lindley JE	Jimmy	23/07/1981	Sutton-in-Ashfield		1999	2000		Trainee	Gresley Rovers	3	0	1	0	0	0	0	0	0	0
Lindley T	Tinsley	27/10/1865	Nottingham	1940	1889		e	Nottm Forest	Nottm Forest	2	1	0	0	0	0	0	0	0	0
Linton JA	Jimmy	02/12/1930	Tollcross		1952	1958		Kirkintilloch RobRoy	Watford	114	6	0	0	0	0	0	0	0	0
Lister E	Eric	13/08/1933	Willenhall	2004	1954	1956		Wolves	Boston United	8	0	0	0	0	0	0	0	0	0
Livesey DR	Danny	31/12/1984	Salford		2003			Bolton Wan. (loan)		11	0	0	1	0	0	0	0	0	0
Locker W	Billy	16/02/1866	Long Eaton	1952	1890			Long Eaton Rgs	Loughborough T	21	6	0	0	0	12	2	0	0	0
Lockie AJ	Alex	11/04/1915	South Shields		1946			Sunderland		23	3	0	0	0	0	0	0	0	0
Logan J	Jimmy	24/06/1870	Troon	1896	1893	1894	s	Aston Villa	Dundee	41	7	0	7	2	31	6	0	0	0
Logan P	Peter 'Paddy'	1877	Glasgow		1898			Motherwell	Woolwich Arsenal	16	1	0	0	0	6	0	0	0	0
Long SW	Stacy	11/01/1985	Bromley		2005			Charlton Ath.		19	2	1	0	0	1	0	0	0	0
Lormor A	Tony	29/10/1970	Ashington		1997			Preston NE (loan)		7	0	0	0	0	0	0	0	0	0
Lovatt HA	Harry	18/08/1905	Audley	1984	1930	1931		Leicester City	Northampton Town	9	2	0	0	0	3	0	0	0	0
Lovell FW	Fred	18/06/1929	Crewe		1952	1953		RAF		7	0	0	0	0	2	0	0	0	0
Lowe E	Eddie	11/07/1925	Halesowen		1963	1964	e	Fulham	Plymouth (scout)	9	0	0	0	0	0	0	0	0	0
Loxley H	Bert	03/02/1934	Matlock		1954	1963		Bonsall (Derbys)	Mansfield Town	245	13	8	0	0	9	1	1	0	0
Ludlam C	Craig	08/11/1976	Sheffield		1996			Sheffield Wed. (loan)		1	0	0	0	0	0	0	0	0	0
Lund GJ	Gary	13/09/1964	Grimsby		1987	1994		Lincoln City	Chesterfield	248	16	18	29	5	62	4	5	7	1
Lunn H	Harry	20/03/1925	Lurgan	1980	1946			Glenavon	Portsmouth	24	3	0	0	0	5	0	0	0	0
Lyle D	David				1890			Wishaw Thistle		2	0	0	0	0	0	0	0	0	0
Lyman CC	Colin	09/03/1914	Northampton	1986	1947			Nottm. Forest	Nuneaton Boro	21	0	0	0	0	5	0	0	0	0
McCairns T	Tommy	22/12/1873	Dinsdale	1932	1899			Bristol Rovers	Lincoln City	4	0	0	0	0	0	0	0	0	0
McCall J	John	1877	Muirkirk		1903			Bristol Rovers		3	0	0	0	0	0	0	0	0	0
McCallum CJ	Neil	03/07/1868	Bonhill	1920	1895		s	Newark	Heanor T	13	2	0	0	0	3	0	0	0	0
McCann GS	Grant	14/04/1980	Belfast		2000		n	West Ham Utd.(loan)		2	0	1	0	0	0	0	0	0	0
McCann HA	Austin	21/01/1980	Alexandria		2006			Boston United		43	1	2	0	0	0	0	0	0	0
McCappin SA	Sam	1875	Kilburn	1945	1899			Ilford		7	0	0	0	0	0	0	0	0	0
McCarthy PR	Paddy	31/05/1983	Dublin		2002			Manchester C (loan)		6	0	0	0	0	0	0	0	0	0
MacCartney CW	Charlie	04/02/1910	Stamford	1982	1932	1934		Stamford T	Wrexham	50	1	0	0	0	19	0	0	0	0
McCavana WT	Terry	24/01/1921	Belfast		1948		n	Coleraine	Coleraine	3	0	0	0	0	0	0	0	0	0
McClelland J	John	07/12/1955	Belfast		1991		n	Leeds United (loan)		6	0	0	0	0	0	0	0	0	0
McCormack JC	Cec	15/02/1922	Chester-le-Street	1995	1951	1955		Barnsley		82	3	0	0	0	35	1	0	0	0
McCulloch JG	Gordon	03/03/1888	Hinckley	1918	1911			Sutton Town	Sutton Town	1	0	0	0	0	0	0	0	0	0
McCulloch JB	Iain	28/12/1954	Kilmarnock		1978	1983		Kilmarnock	Retired	215	11	17	17	0	51	2	1	0	0

Name		D.o.B.	Place of Birth	Died	First Season	Last Season	Ints	Previous Club	Next Club	Appearances Lge	FAC	FLC	Oth	PO	Goals Lge	FAC	FLC	Oth	PO
McDerment WS	Billy	05/01/1943	Paisley		1969			Luton Town	Morton	3	0	1	0	0	0	0	0	0	0
McDermott A	Andy	24/03/1977	Sydney, Australia		2000			West Bromwich A.	Northern Spirit (Aus)	25	1	4	0	0	0	0	1	0	0
McDonagh JM	Jim 'Seamus'	06/10/1952	Rotherham		1983	1984	r	Bolton Wanderers	Wichita Wings	35	4	7	0	0	0	0	0	0	0
McDonald E	Ted		1875	Newcastle-under-Lyme	1938	1899	1903		Burslem Port Vale	Portsmouth	139	13	0	0	0	3	0	0	0	0
MacDonald JS	John	23/09/1922	Edinburgh		1948			Carshalton Ath.	QPR	1	0	0	0	0	0	0	0	0	0
McFaul S	Shane	23/05/1986	Dublin		2003	2004		Cherry Orchard (Ire)		30	3	0	1	0	0	0	0	0	0
McGoldrick DJ	David	29/11/1987	Nottingham		2003 2005			Assoc. schoolboy Southampton (loan)	Southampton	10	0	0	1	0	0	0	0	0	0
McGorian IM	Ike	19/10/1901	Silksworth		1928			Sunderland	Carlisle Utd.	1	0	0	0	0	0	0	0	0	0
McGovern PM	Paddy	14/05/1948	Edinburgh		1967			Royston Boys' Club		3	1	0	0	0	0	0	0	0	0
McGrath J	Jimmy	04/03/1907	Washington	1950	1934			Port Vale	Bradford	11	0	0	0	0	3	0	0	0	0
McGrath J	John	21/03/1932	Tidworth		1955	1957		Aldershot	Darlington	54	3	0	0	0	5	0	0	0	0
McGregor AC	Andrew		1867	Wishaw		1890	1892		Wishaw Thistle		44	7	0	0	0	11	5	0	0	0
McHugh FJ	Frazer	14/07/1981	Nottingham		2003			Bradford City	Hucknall T	13	0	0	0	0	0	0	0	0	0
McInnes T	Tom	22/03/1870	Glasgow		1889	1892		Cowlairs	Rangers	73	13	0	0	1	20	7	0	0	0
McIntyre JA	Jimmy		1881	Darlaston	1954	1902			Walsall	Northampton Town	9	0	0	0	0	3	0	0	0	0
Mackey JA	Jim	25/11/1897	Ryton-on-Tyne	1990	1923			Carlisle Utd.	Lincoln City	3	0	0	0	0	1	0	0	0	0
McLachlan J	Jimmy					1893			Derby County	Derby County	2	0	0	0	0	0	0	0	0	0
McLean T	Tom		1866	Alexandria	1936	1888 1894	1891		Vale of Leven	Derby County	66	10	0	2	0	0	0	0	0	0
McLenahan H	Hugh	23/03/1909	West Gorton	1988	1936	1938		Manchester Utd.		54	2	0	2	0	1	0	0	0	0
McLeod W	Billy		1887	Hebburn		1919	1920		Leeds City	Doncaster Rovers	40	3	0	0	0	10	2	0	0	0
McMahon D	Daryl	10/10/1983	Dublin		2006			West Ham Utd.(loan)		7	0	0	0	0	0	0	0	0	0
McMahon LJ	Lewis	02/05/1985	Doncaster		2005			Sheffield Wed.		29	2	0	1	0	0	1	0	1	0
McMain J	Joe		1873	Preston		1899			Wolves	Kettering T	26	3	0	0	0	13	2	0	0	0
McManus CE	Eric	14/11/1950	Limavady		1972	1978		Coventry City	Stoke City	229	9	13	14	0	0	0	0	0	0
McMillan J	James					1889			Q of South Wan.		22	3	0	0	0	0	0	0	0	0
McMorran JW	Jimmy	29/10/1942	Muirkirk		1969			Walsall	Halifax Town	6	0	0	0	0	0	0	0	0	0
McNamara NA	Niall	26/01/1982	Limerick		2001			Nottm. Forest	Belper Town	4	0	0	0	0	0	0	0	0	0
McNamee P	Peter	20/03/1935	Glasgow		1965			Peterborough Utd.	March Town	3	0	0	0	0	0	0	0	0	0
Maconnachie A	Alex					1898	1900		Derby County	Third Lanark	76	5	0	0	0	26	2	0	0	0
McParland IJ	Ian 'Charlie'	04/10/1961	Edinburgh		1980	1988		Ormiston Primrose	Hull City	221	17	16	11	2	69	9	5	7	0
McPherson IB	Ian	26/07/1920	Glasgow	1983	1945 1951	1952		Rangers Arsenal	Arsenal Brentford	50	4	0	0	0	7	3	0	0	0
McPherson K	Ken	25/03/1927	Hartlepool		1950	1952		Hordern Coll.	Middlesbrough	26	4	0	0	0	10	4	0	0	0
McPherson L	Lacky	11/07/1900	Denistoun		1921	1923		Cambuslang Rgs	Swansea Town	32	0	0	0	0	5	0	0	0	0
McStay WJ	Willie	26/11/1961	Hamilton		1987	1989		Huddersfield T	Kilmarnock	45	0	4	5	2	1	0	0	0	0
McSwegan GJ	Gary	24/09/1970	Glasgow		1993	1995	s	Rangers	Dundee U	62	5	7	6	0	21	1	3	1	0
McVay DR	David	05/03/1955	Workington		1973	1978		Clifton All Whites	Peterborough Utd.	113	4	8	5	0	2	0	1	0	0
Mabbott J	John					1892	1893		Nottm St John's	Mansfield Town	2	0	0	0	0	0	0	0	0	0
Machin PU	Prestwood	01/07/1892	Nottingham		1913			Nottm. Forest		1	0	0	0	0	0	0	0	0	0
Maddison F	Frank	06/05/1934	Worksop	1993	1956	1957				15	0	0	0	0	0	0	0	0	0
Maidment JHC	Jimmy	28/09/1901	Monkwearmouth	1977	1931	1932		Lincoln City	Accrington Stanley	44	1	0	0	0	0	0	0	0	0
Mainman HL	Harry	07/04/1877	Liverpool	1953	1901	1906		Reading		130	7	0	0	0	0	0	0	0	0
Mair G	Gordon	18/12/1958	Bothwell		1976	1983		Fir Park BC	Lincoln City	131	4	14	6	0	18	0	2	1	0
Mann AF	Arthur	23/01/1948	Burntisland	1999	1972	1978		Manchester City	Shrewsbury Town	253	14	16	9	0	21	1	2	1	0
Mann RH	Ron	08/10/1932	Nottingham		1950			Coventry City	Aldershot	1	0	0	0	0	0	0	0	0	0
Manns PH	Paul	15/04/1961	Great Haywood		1979	1981		Cardiff City	Chester City	7	1	1	7	0	1	1	0	1	0
Mansley A	Allan	31/08/1946	Liverpool	2001	1971			Brentford (loan)		11	0	3	0	0	2	0	0	0	0
Mardon HJ	Harry	08/06/1914	Cardiff	1981	1936	1937		Hereford Utd.	Bournemouth	22	1	0	4	0	8	0	0	5	0
Marriott F	Frank	26/10/1894	Sutton-in-Ashfield	1947	1919	1922		Sutton Junction	Swansea Town	96	16	0	0	0	1	0	0	0	0
Marsden C	Chris	03/01/1969	Sheffield		1994	1995		Wolves	Stockport Co.	10	0	1	1	0	0	0	0	1	0
Marsh IW	Ike		1877	Burton-on-Trent		1899			Hucknall Portland	Newark	3	0	0	0	0	0	0	0	0	0
Marsh JK	Jack	08/10/1922	Mansfield	1997	1946	1948		Mansfield BC	Coventry City	42	5	0	0	0	18	3	0	0	0
Marshall SA	Shaun	03/10/1978	Fakenham		2005			Cambridge Utd.		1	0	0	1	0	0	0	0	0	0
Marshall SK	Stan	20/04/1946	Goole		1966	1967		Middlesbrough		49	1	2	0	0	17	1	0	0	0
Martin DA	Dan	24/09/1986	Derby		2005	2006		Derby County		51	0	4	1	0	8	0	1	0	0
Martin DK	Davy 'Boy'	01/02/1914	Belfast	1991	1938	1945	i	Nottm. Forest	Glentoran	26	4	0	0	0	16	1	0	0	0
Martindale G	Gary	24/06/1971	Liverpool		1995	1997		Peterborough Utd.	Rotherham Utd.	66	4	4	3	3	13	0	0	1	2
Masson DS	Don	26/08/1946	Banchory		1968 1978	1974 1981	s	Middlesbrough Derby County	QPR Biulova (HK)	402	17	23	13	0	92	3	1	1	0
Matthews CHW	Cyril	01/12/1901	Cowes	1973	1927	1929		Bury	Stockport Co.	15	0	0	0	0	0	0	0	0	0
Matthews LJ	Lee	16/01/1979	Middlesbrough		1998			Leeds United (loan)		5	0	0	0	0	0	0	0	0	0
Matthews RD	Rob	14/10/1970	Slough		1991	1994		Shepshed Chart'hse	Luton Town	43	5	2	7	0	10	2	0	0	0
Matthews W	Billy		1882	Derby	1916	1906	1911		Aston Villa	Derby County	177	11	0	0	0	37	6	0	0	0
Maw A	Arthur 'Digger'	29/12/1909	Frodingham	1964	1928	1931		Scunthorpe Utd.	Leicester City	35	1	0	0	0	11	0	0	0	0
May EH	Teddy		1865	Hull	1941	1888	1889		Burslem Port Vale	Nottm Forest	29	7	0	0	0	4	5	0	0	0
May WO	Billy		1865	Hull	1936	1888			Long Eaton Rgs	Notts Rangers	4	0	0	0	0	0	0	0	0	0
Mays AW	Billy	18/07/1902	Ynyshir	1959	1929		w	Wrexham	Burnley	8	0	0	0	0	4	0	0	0	0
Meads T	Tommy	02/11/1900	Grassmoor	1983	1935			Tottenham H	Frickley Coll.	18	2	0	1	0	2	0	0	0	0
Mellors M	Mark	30/04/1880	Basford	1961	1902	1903		Bulwell U	Brighton & Hove A.	9	0	0	0	0	0	0	0	0	0
Mendes AJHA	Junior	15/09/1976	Balham		2006		mn	Huddersfield T		37	1	4	1	0	5	0	0	0	0
Mendez G	Gabriel	12/03/1973	Buenos Aires, Argentina		1996		au	Parramatta (Aus)(loan)		3	0	0	0	0	0	0	0	0	0
Merritt R	Dicky	22/07/1897	Shiney Row	1978	1929			York City	Easington Coll.Welf.	1	0	0	0	0	0	0	0	0	0
Mildenhall SJ	Steve	13/05/1978	Swindon		2001	2004		Swindon Town	Oldham Athletic	76	6	5	3	0	0	0	1	0	0
Millington J	John		1912	Leigh		1935	1936		Clapton Orient	Birmingham	15	0	0	1	0	2	0	0	0	0
Mills BR	Paddy	23/02/1900	Multan, India	1994	1925	1928		Hull City	Birmingham	76	3	0	0	0	35	1	0	0	0
Mills GR	Gary	11/11/1961	Northampton		1987 1994	1988 1995		Nottm. Forest Leicester City	Leicester City Grantham T	122	9	11	15	2	8	0	1	0	0
Mills PC	Percy	10/01/1909	Barton-on-Humber	1967	1927	1938		Hull City		407	20	0	7	0	21	0	0	0	0
Mimms RA	Bobby	12/10/1963	York		1985			Everton (loan)		2	0	0	1	0	0	0	0	0	0
Mitchell A	Arnold	01/12/1929	Rawmarsh		1951			Nottm. Forest	Exeter City	1	0	0	0	0	0	0	0	0	0

Name		D.o.B.	Place of Birth	Died	First Season	Last Season	Ints	Previous Club	Next Club	Appearances					Goals				
										Leg	FAC	FLC	Oth	PO	Leg	FAC	FLC	Oth	PO
Mitchell MJ	Michael	04/10/1903	Glasgow		1924			Burnbank Ath.	New Bedford Whalers	5	0	0	0	0	0	0	0	0	0
Mitchell PR	Paul	08/11/1978	Nottingham		1996	1997		Trainee	Rolls Royce (Hucknall)	2	0	0	1	0	0	0	0	0	0
Molloy P	Paddy	1921	Athlone	1973	1947					1	0	0	0	0	0	0	0	0	0
Molloy W	William				1931			Dick, Kerr's	Dick, Kerr's	2	0	0	0	0	1	0	0	0	0
Montgomery J	Jack	18/06/1876	Chryston	1940	1898	1910		Tottenham H		316	23	0	0	0	2	0	0	0	0
Moore AE	Albert	1863	Nottingham		1884	1888				10	17	0	0	0	3	6	0	0	0
Moore B	Brian	24/12/1938	Hemsworth		1961	1962		Mansfield Town	Doncaster Rovers	27	1	1	0	0	3	0	1	0	0
Moore GW	George	1887	Newport, Shropshire		1907			Stafford Rgs		1	0	0	0	0	0	0	0	0	0
Moore H	Harry	05/08/1896	Worksop	1984	1921			Worksop T	Boston T	16	0	0	0	0	0	0	0	0	0
Moreau F	Fabrice	07/10/1967	Paris, France		2000			Airdrie		5	0	0	0	0	0	0	0	0	0
Morley H	Bert	1882	Kiveton Park	1957	1906	1914	e	Grimsby Town		258	11	0	0	0	0	0	0	0	0
Morley HA	Haydn	26/11/1860	Derby	1953	1886	1888		Derby County	Derby County	2	7	0	0	0	0	0	0	0	0
Morrad FG	Frank	28/02/1920	Brentford		1946			Southall	Leyton Orient	1	0	0	0	0	0	0	0	0	0
Morris JJ	Jack	11/02/1878	Liscard	1947	1900	1902		Blackpool	Bristol City	77	5	0	0	0	30	3	0	0	0
Mosley AE	Andrew	25/12/1885	Sneinton	1971	1906	1909		Sneinton FC		11	0	0	0	0	0	0	0	0	0
Moulden A	Tony	28/08/1942	Farnworth		1965			Peterborough Utd.	Rochdale	23	0	1	0	0	1	0	0	0	0
Moulson C	Con	03/09/1906	Clogheen	1989	1936	1938	r	Lincoln City		97	6	0	3	0	0	0	0	0	0
Mowl WJ	John	23/06/1922	Bulwell		1948			RAF	Mansfield Town	3	1	0	0	0	0	0	0	0	0
Muir RB	Bobby	14/04/1878	Kilmarnock	1953	1904			Celtic	Norwich City	19	1	0	0	0	0	0	0	0	0
Munro D	David	1885			1907			Third Lanark		12	2	0	0	0	1	0	0	0	0
Murphy FJ	John	16/08/1949	Edinburgh		1967	1968		Edina Juniors	St Johnstone	19	0	0	0	0	2	0	0	0	0
Murphy J	John	1872	Nottingham	1924	1896	1897		Hucknall St Johns	Bristol City	37	2	0	0	4	24	0	0	0	0
Murphy JB	Jim	29/11/1942	Glasgow		1967	1968		Raith Rovers	Motherwell	33	0	2	0	0	7	0	0	0	0
Murphy SP	Shaun	05/11/1970	Sydney, Australia		1992	1996	au	Perth Italia (Aus)	West Bromwich A.	109	6	7	10	3	5	0	0	2	0
Murray AD	Adam	30/09/1981	Birmingham		2003			Derby County	Kidderminster H	3	1	0	0	0	0	0	0	0	0
Murray S	Shaun	07/02/1970	Newcastle		1998	2000		Bradford City	Kettering T	55	10	3	1	0	3	1	0	0	0
Needham DW	Dave	21/05/1949	Leicester		1965	1976			QPR	429	17	21	4	0	32	2	1	0	0
Needham LP	Liam	19/10/1985	Sheffield		2005	2006		Gainsborough Trin.		23	0	2	1	0	0	0	0	0	0
Nelson GP	Garry	16/01/1961	Braintree		1990			Brighton & HA (loan)		2	0	0	0	0	0	0	0	0	0
Newsham S	Stan	24/03/1931	Farnworth	2001	1957	1961		Bournemouth	Wellington T	99	4	0	0	0	44	0	0	0	0
Newton AL	Adam	04/12/1980	Grays		2000		sk	West Ham Utd.(loan)		20	2	0	0	0	1	0	0	0	0
Newton J	John	19/01/1940	Edinburgh		1958	1960		Craiglea Thistle	York City	5	0	0	0	0	0	0	0	0	0
Nicholson KJ	Kevin	02/10/1980	Derby		2000	2003		Northampton Town	Scarborough	95	4	5	4	0	3	1	0	0	0
Nicol S	Steve	11/12/1961	Irvine		1994	1995	s	Liverpool	Sheffield Wed.	32	1	1	3	0	2	0	0	0	0
Nixon JC	Jon	20/01/1948	Ilkeston		1969	1974		Long Eaton U	Peterborough Utd.	179	13	8	1	0	32	3	3	0	0
Nogan LM	Lee	21/05/1969	Cardiff		1996		w	Reading (loan)		6	0	0	0	0	0	0	0	0	0
Noon H	Harry	06/10/1927	Sutton-in-Ashfield	1996	1957	1961		Bentinck Meths	Bradford City	122	6	3	0	0	0	0	1	0	0
Norris SM	Steve	22/09/1961	Coventry		1989			Scarborough (loan)		1	1	0	0	0	0	0	0	0	0
Norton DW	David	03/03/1965	Cannock		1988	1990		Aston Villa	Hull City	27	0	4	3	2	1	0	0	0	0
Notley WS	Wilf	25/05/1913	Bourne	1972	1935			Tottenham H	Boston United	20	3	0	0	0	9	0	0	0	0
N'Toya-Zoa T	Tcham	03/11/1983	Kinshasa, DR Congo		2006			Chesterfield		21	1	4	1	0	1	0	1	0	0
Nugent J	John				1904					3	0	0	0	0	0	0	0	0	0
Oakes DR	Dennis	10/04/1946	Bedworth		1967	1970		Coventry City	Peterborough Utd.	120	3	3	0	0	0	0	0	0	0
Oakes ST	Stefan	06/09/1978	Leicester		2003	2004		Walsall	Wycombe Wan.	45	3	1	0	0	5	1	0	0	0
O'Brien RC	Ray	21/05/1951	Dublin		1973	1982	r	Manchester Utd.	Boston United	323	11	25	27	0	31	0	4	4	0
O'Callaghan BP	Brian	24/02/1981	Limerick		2005			Worksop T		33	2	1	0	0	1	0	0	0	0
O'Donnell D	Dennis	1882	Willington Quay		1907			QPR	Bradford	18	1	0	0	0	4	0	0	0	0
O'Grady CJ	Chris	25/01/1986	Nottingham		2004			Leicester City (loan)		9	1	0	1	0	0	0	0	0	0
Oldershaw HJ	Harry	01/10/1898	Basford		1921			Magdala Ams	Boston T	1	0	0	0	0	0	0	0	0	0
O'Neill MHM	Martin	01/03/1952	Kilrea		1983	1984	n	Norwich City	Retired	64	7	10	0	0	5	0	2	0	0
Orgill H	Harry	01/10/1920	Hucknall	1979	1947			Nottm. Forest		2	0	0	0	0	0	0	0	0	0
O'Riordan DJ	Don	14/05/1957	Dublin		1988	1992		Grimsby Town	Torquay United	109	6	6	15	3	5	2	1	1	0
Osborne AW	Archie	1869	Lanarkshire	1913	1890	1893		Vale of Leven	Clyde	46	6	0	5	0	1	0	0	0	0
Oswald J	Jimmy	03/01/1868	Greenock	1948	1889	1892	s	Third Lanark	St Bernard's	95	11	0	0	1	55	10	0	0	0
Oswald J	John		Greenock		1889			Third Lanark	Burnley	22	3	0	0	0	6	3	0	0	0
Otto RJ	Ricky	09/11/1967	Hackney		1997			Birmingham C (loan)		4	0	2	0	0	0	0	0	0	0
Owen HGP	Hugh	19/05/1859	Bath	1912	1888			Corpus Christi (Camb)	Nottm Forest	1	0	0	0	0	0	0	0	0	0
Owers G	Gary	03/10/1968	Newcastle		1998	2001		Bristol City	Forest Green Rov.	154	13	11	2	0	12	2	0	0	0
Pace DJ	Derek 'Doc'	11/03/1932	Bloxwich	1989	1964	1965		Sheffield Utd.	Walsall	29	0	1	0	0	15	0	0	0	0
Pacey HC	Herbert	1890	Nottingham		1910	1911			Ericssons	3	0	0	0	0	0	0	0	0	0
Palmer CA	Charlie	10/07/1963	Aylesbury		1988	1993		Hull City	Walsall	182	10	9	14	6	7	0	0	2	0
Palmer CL	Chris	16/10/1983	Derby		2004	2005		Derby County	Wycombe Wan.	54	5	1	1	0	5	0	1	0	0
Pape AA	Albert	13/07/1897	Wath-on-Dearne	1955	1923			Rotherham County	Clapton Orient	6	2	0	0	0	2	1	0	0	0
Paris AD	Alan	15/08/1964	Slough		1990	1991		Leicester City	Slough T	42	4	2	2	3	1	0	0	0	0
Parke J		1871	Scotland		1892			Jordanhill		1	0	0	0	0	0	0	0	0	0
Parkin B	Brian	12/10/1965	Birkenhead		1998			Wycombe Wan.	Wimbledon	1	0	0	0	0	0	0	0	0	0
Parkinson AJ	Andy	27/05/1979	Liverpool		2003			Sheffield Utd. (loan)		59	1	2	0	0	8	0	0	0	0
					2006			Grimsby Town											
Parks A	Albert	09/02/1926	Lurgan		1946	1947		Glenavon	Glenavon	30	0	0	0	0	4	0	0	0	0
Parry C	Cyril	13/12/1937	Derby		1957	1958		Derby County	Bourne T	12	0	0	0	0	2	0	0	0	0
Paxton JW	John	24/03/1928	Wolverhampton		1950			Wolves	Kidderminster H	2	0	0	0	0	0	0	0	0	0
Pead CG	Craig	15/09/1981	Bromsgrove		2004			Coventry C (loan)		5	0	0	1	0	0	0	0	0	0
Pearce DA	Dennis	10/09/1974	Wolverhampton		1997	2000		Wolves	Peterborough Utd.	118	13	8	3	0	3	0	0	0	0
Peart JG	Jack	03/10/1888	South Shields	1948	1912	1919		Newcastle United	Birmingham	82	2	0	0	0	51	1	0	0	0
Pembleton A	Arthur	25/01/1895	Palterton	1976	1919	1921		Woodhouse Ex.	Millwall	71	9	0	0	0	0	0	0	0	0
Pennington H	Harry	21/04/1880	Salford	1961	1900	1904		Brentford	Atherton CH	126	10	0	0	0	0	0	0	0	0
Pepper FW	Frederick				1909	1911		Netherfield Rgs	Hamilton Lancs (Can)	5	0	0	0	0	0	0	0	0	0
Perry J	Joe	1893	Kingswinford		1914			Stourbridge	Ebbw Vale	18	0	0	0	0	0	0	0	0	0
Pike GA	Geoff	28/09/1956	Clapton		1987	1988		West Ham Utd.	Leyton Orient	82	5	6	6	2	17	2	1	0	0
Pilkington KW	Kevin	08/03/1974	Hitchin		2005	2006		Mansfield Town		84	3	1	0	0	0	0	0	0	0
Pimbley DW	Doug	19/06/1917	King's Norton	1988	1947	1949		Birmingham City		23	0	0	0	0	1	0	0	0	0
Pipe DR	David	05/11/1983	Caerphilly		2003	2006	w	Coventry City		141	7	5	1	0	4	0	0	0	0
Plackett S	Syd	21/09/1898	Sawley	1950	1926	1929		Derby County		84	1	0	0	0	0	0	0	0	0

Name		D.o.B.	Place of Birth	Died	First Season	Last Season	Ints	Previous Club	Next Club	Appearances					Goals				
										Leg	FAC	FLC	Oth	PO	Leg	FAC	FLC	Oth	PO
Platnauer NR	Nicky	10/06/1961	Leicester		1989	1990		Cardiff City	Leicester City	57	1	6	7	3	1	0	0	0	0
Platt CL	Clive	27/10/1977	Wolverhampton		2003			Rochdale	Peterborough Utd.	19	3	3	0	0	3	3	0	0	0
Platts R	Bob	1901	Anston		1920	1924		Anston U	Southend Utd.	50	3	0	0	0	3	0	0	0	0
Pollitt MF	Mike	29/02/1972	Farnworth		1996	1997		Darlington	Sunderland	10	0	0	2	0	0	0	0	0	0
Poole W	William	16/09/1900	Keyworth		1919			Basford United	Coventry City	1	0	0	0	0	0	0	0	0	0
Pope FJL	Frankie	1884	Brierley Hill	1953	1906			Wolves	Walsall	2	0	0	0	0	0	0	0	0	0
Poppitt J	James	1875	Oakengates	1930	1905	1906		Swindon Town	Lincoln City	15	0	0	0	0	2	0	0	0	0
Poric A	Adem	22/04/1973	Kensington		1997		au	Rotherham Utd.		4	0	0	0	0	0	0	0	0	0
Poskett TW	Tom	26/12/1909	Esh Winning	1972	1934			Lincoln City	Tranmere Rovers	10	0	0	0	0	0	0	0	0	0
Potter A	Arthur	1874	Nottingham		1897			Army	Bristol City	2	0	0	0	0	0	0	0	0	0
Povey VR	Vic	16/03/1944	Wolverhampton		1963	1964		Wolves	Pan Hellenic (Aus)	35	0	0	0	0	3	0	0	0	0
Praski J	Josef	22/01/1926	France	1998	1948			Jeanfield Swifts	Sutton Town	3	0	0	0	0	0	0	0	0	0
Prescott TG	Tom	08/01/1875	Attercliffe	1957	1896	1904		Liverpool South End	Notts trainer	212	14	0	0	4	1	0	0	0	0
Price LP	Lew	12/08/1896	Caersws	1969	1922	1927		Aston Villa	QPR	66	4	0	0	0	6	1	0	0	0
Pring KD	Keith	11/03/1943	Newport		1967	1968	w	Rotherham Utd.	Southport	44	1	2	0	0	2	0	0	0	0
Pritchard RT	Roy	09/05/1925	Dawley	1993	1957			Aston Villa	Port Vale	18	1	0	0	0	0	1	0	0	0
Probert EW	Eric	17/05/1952	South Kirkby	2004	1973	1977		Burnley	Darlington	122	3	9	5	0	13	0	0	0	0
Protheroe S	Syd	16/12/1910	Dowlais	1982	1938			Rochdale		2	0	0	0	0	0	0	0	0	0
Proudfoot J	Jimmy	31/01/1906	Usworth Colliery	1963	1932			Barnsley	Southend Utd.	10	0	0	0	0	0	0	0	0	0
Purvis B	Bart	15/10/1921	Gateshead	2001	1948	1950		Plymouth Argyle	Carlisle Utd.	25	2	0	0	0	0	0	0	0	0
Quayle ML	Mark	02/10/1978	Liverpool		1998			Everton	Grimsby Town	5	2	0	1	0	1	0	0	0	0
Quinn SJ	Jimmy	15/12/1974	Coventry		2001		n	West Brom (loan)		6	0	0	1	0	3	0	0	0	0
Ramage CD	Craig	30/03/1970	Derby		1999	2000		Bradford City		55	2	7	0	0	7	0	2	0	0
Ramsden SP	Simon	17/12/1981	Bishop Auckland		2002			Sunderland (loan)		32	1	1	0	0	0	0	0	0	0
Randall K	Kevin	20/08/1945	Ashton-under-Lyne		1972	1975		Chesterfield	Mansfield Town	121	7	7	0	0	39	4	4	0	0
Rankin JP	Johnnie	10/05/1901	Coatbridge		1934	1935		Chelsea	Buxton Town	25	1	0	0	0	2	0	0	0	0
Rapley KJ	Kevin	21/09/1977	Reading		1998	2000		Brentford	Colchester Utd.	52	2	3	1	0	5	1	0	0	0
Rawson K	Ken	18/09/1931	Ripley	1986	1954	1960		Ripley	Ilkeston T	34	0	0	0	0	0	0	0	0	0
Rayner JP	Jim	31/03/1935	Cornsay		1964			Grantham	Ilkeston T	32	2	2	0	0	13	1	0	0	0
Redmile MI	Matt	12/11/1976	Nottingham		1995	2000		Trainee	Shrewsbury Town	147	13	11	4	0	7	1	0	0	0
Reece PJ	Paul	16/07/1968	Nottingham		1994			Oxford United	West Bromwich A.	11	0	1	3	0	0	0	0	0	0
Read CW	Charlie 'Chick'	21/03/1912	Holbeach	1964	1938			Mansfield Town	Spalding United	36	3	0	0	0	2	0	0	0	0
Reeves DE	David	19/11/1967	Birkenhead		1992	1993		Bolton Wanderers	Carlisle Utd.	13	0	2	0	0	2	0	0	0	0
Regis DR	Dave	03/03/1964	Paddington		1990	1996		Barnet	Plymouth Argyle	56	0	2	3	3	17	0	0	1	1
Reid J	Jimmy	18/11/1879	Bellshill		1903	1904		Worksop T	Watford	16	1	0	0	0	2	0	0	0	0
Reid P	Peter	20/06/1956	Huyton		1993		e	Southampton	Bury	5	0	0	0	0	0	0	0	0	0
Reilly MM	Matt 'Gunner'	22/03/1874	Donnybrook	1954	1905		i	Dundee	Tottenham H	16	0	0	0	0	0	0	0	0	0
Rhodes CK	Chris	09/01/1987	Mansfield		2003			Scholar		1	0	0	0	0	0	0	0	0	0
Richards LG	Lloyd	11/02/1958	Jamaica		1975	1977		Derby Schools	York City	9	0	2	2	0	0	0	0	0	0
Richards P	Pedro	11/11/1956	Edmonton	2001	1974	1985		Notts Schools	Boston United	399	19	39	28	0	5	0	1	0	0
Richards S	Sam	1889	Bulwell	1962	1910	1921		Bulwell Forest Villa		179	6	0	0	0	69	2	0	0	0
Richardson IG	Ian	22/10/1970	Barking		1995	2004		Birmingham C		253	20	18	5	3	21	2	2	1	0
Richardson J	John	20/04/1945	Worksop		1971			Derby County	King's Lynn	2	0	1	0	0	0	0	0	0	0
Richardson LN	Leam	19/11/1979	Leeds		2001			Bolton Wan. (loan)		21	1	0	0	0	0	0	0	0	0
Rickards CT	Tom 'Tex'	19/02/1915	Giltbrook	1980	1932	1937		Johnson & Barnes	Cardiff City	112	7	0	5	0	22	3	0	2	0
Rideout PD	Paul	14/08/1964	Bournemouth		1991			Southampton	Rangers	11	1	2	2	0	3	0	0	0	0
Ridgway ID	Ian	28/12/1975	Reading		1994	1996		Balderton Jnrs	Kettering T	7	0	0	2	0	0	0	0	0	0
Rigby NE	Norman	23/05/1923	Warsop	2001	1947	1950		Newark Town	Peterborough Utd.	46	3	0	0	0	0	0	0	0	0
Riley H	Harry	22/11/1909	Hollinwood	1982	1933			Lincoln City	Cardiff City	16	0	0	0	0	3	0	0	0	0
Riley J	Joe	1910	Sheffield		1937			Bournemouth	Gloucester City	7	0	0	0	0	1	0	0	0	0
Riley PA	Paul	29/09/1982	Eastwood		2001	2003		Assoc. schoolboy	Grimsby Town	28	2	2	1	0	3	0	0	0	0
Rimmer SA	Stuart	12/10/1964	Southport		1988			Watford	Walsall	4	2	0	3	0	2	0	0	0	0
Robertson S	Sam	1882	Cowdenbeath		1905			Dundee		2	0	0	0	0	0	0	0	0	0
Robinson DA	David	14/01/1965	Haverton Hill		1992	1993		Peterborough Utd.	Retired, injury	3	0	1	0	0	1	0	1	0	0
Robinson GF	George	17/06/1925	Melton Mowbray	2000	1945	1946		Holwell Works	Grantham	29	5	0	0	0	0	0	0	0	0
Robinson LJ	Len	01/10/1946	Nottingham		1963	1964		Nottm. Forest		4	0	0	0	0	0	0	0	0	0
Robinson MJ	Mark	26/11/1960	Nottingham		1984	1985		Ilkeston T	Shepshed Charter.	26	1	1	1	0	1	0	0	0	0
Robinson MLStC	Marvin	11/04/1980	Crewe		2004			Chesterfield	Rushden & Diamonds	2	0	0	0	0	0	0	0	0	0
Robinson P	Peter	29/01/1922	Manchester	2000	1949	1952		Buxton	King's Lynn	82	2	0	0	0	0	0	0	0	0
Robinson PJ	Phil	06/01/1967	Stafford		1989	1997		Wolves	Huddersfield T	143	9	10	8	3	10	1	2	0	0
Robledo EO	Ted	26/07/1928	Iquique, Chile	1970	1957			Colo Colo (Chile)		2	0	0	0	0	0	0	0	0	0
Robson MA	Mark	22/05/1969	Newham		1997	1999		Charlton Ath.	Boreham Wood	32	3	2	1	0	4	0	0	0	0
Roby D	Don	15/11/1933	Wigan		1950	1960		Orrell Bisphan Meths	Derby County	226	6	1	0	0	37	0	0	0	0
Roeder GV	Glenn	13/12/1955	Woodford		1983			QPR (loan)		4	0	3	0	0	0	0	0	0	0
Rogers PA	Paul	21/03/1965	Portsmouth		1995	1996		Sheffield Utd.	Wigan Ath.	22	1	0	3	3	2	1	0	0	0
Rose MJ	Mick	22/07/1943	New Barnet		1966	1969		Charlton Ath.	E London (S Africa)	109	3	4	0	0	0	0	0	0	0
Ross I	Ian	26/11/1947	Glasgow		1976			Aston Villa (loan)		4	0	0	0	0	1	0	0	0	0
Ross I	Ian	13/01/1986	Sheffield		2006			Sheffield Utd. (loan)		36	1	4	1	0	1	0	0	0	0
Ross W	William	1874	Kiveton Park		1900	1903		Reading	Grimsby Town	110	8	0	0	0	28	1	0	0	0
Roy JR	Jack	23/03/1914	Woolston	1980	1937	1938		Sheffield Wed.	Tranmere Rovers	15	0	0	1	0	0	0	0	0	0
Rushton BWE	Brian	21/10/1943	Sedgley		1967			Birmingham City	Stourbridge	3	0	0	0	0	0	0	0	0	0
Russell D	Dave	08/04/1868	Airdrie	1918	1895					9	0	0	0	0	0	0	0	0	0
Russell ET	Eddie	15/07/1928	Cranwell		1958			Leicester City		9	0	0	0	0	0	0	0	0	0
Russell KJ	Kevin	06/12/1966	Portsmouth		1994			Bournemouth	Wrexham	11	0	0	0	0	0	0	0	0	0
Russell RI	Bobby	27/12/1919	Aberdour	2004	1948			Chelsea	Leyton Orient	2	0	0	0	0	0	0	0	0	0
Russell WP	Peter	16/01/1935	Gornal		1955	1958		Wolves	Hereford U	106	4	0	0	0	6	0	0	0	0
Ryan JO	John	28/10/1944	Liverpool		1969			Luton Town	Altrincham	24	1	0	0	0	0	0	0	0	0
Sanderson EJ	Edgar	16/03/1874	Elkington		1897	1898		Jarrow	Retired, injury	34	2	0	0	0	0	0	0	0	0
Sands JIB	Joseph	1882	Nottingham	1960	1903			Lawrence's Ath.	Nottm. Forest	2	0	0	0	0	0	0	0	0	0
Scanlon J	Ian	13/07/1952	Birkenshaw, Lanarks		1972	1977		East Stirling	Aberdeen	111	1	10	9	0	31	0	3	1	0
Scoffham S	Steve	12/07/1983	Munster, Germany		2003	2005		Gedling T	Burton Albion	52	1	1	0	0	7	0	0	0	0
Scully ADT	Tony	12/06/1976	Dublin		2003	2004		Tamworth		41	4	2	1	0	5	1	0	0	0
Sewell J	Jackie	24/01/1927	Kells, Cumberland		1946	1950	e	Whitehaven T	Sheffield Wed.	178	15	0	0	0	97	7	0	0	0

Name		D.o.B.	Place of Birth	Died	First Season	Last Season	Ints	Previous Club	Next Club	Appearances Lge	FAC	FLC	Oth	PO	Goals Lge	FAC	FLC	Oth	PO
Sharman J					1897	1899		Beeston Humber	Grimsby Town	2	0	0	0	0	0	0	0	0	0
Sharpe JW	Jack	09/12/1866	Ruddington	1936	1889				West Herts	3	0	0	0	0	0	0	0	0	0
Shaw AF	Arthur	01/08/1869	Basford	1946	1888	1889			Nottm. Forest	4	0	0	0	0	0	0	0	0	0
Shaw TF	Fred	27/03/1909	Hucknall	1994	1934	1936		Birmingham	Mansfield Town	56	1	0	2	0	20	0	0	1	0
Shelton A	Alf	11/09/1865	Nottingham	1923	1888	1895	e	Notts Rangers	Loughborough T	195	26	0	7	3	3	1	0	0	0
Shelton C	Charles	22/01/1864	Nottingham	1951	1888	1891	e	Notts Rangers		20	3	0	0	0	1	1	0	0	0
Shelton G	Gary	21/03/1958	Nottingham		1979			Aston Villa (loan)		8	0	0	0	0	0	0	0	0	0
Shepperson G	George				1893	1895		Northwich Victoria		5	0	0	4	0	0	0	0	1	0
Sheridan J	John	25/05/1938	Ramsgate		1957	1965		Linby Colliery	Hartlepools Utd.	287	11	10	0	0	9	1	2	0	0
Sheridan J	Jake	08/07/1986	Nottingham		2005	2006		Dunkirk		30	1	2	1	0	1	0	0	0	0
Sherlock PG	Paul	17/11/1973	Wigan		1993	1994		Notts Schools	Mansfield Town	12	2	1	3	0	1	0	0	0	0
Sherwin M	Mordecai	26/02/1851	Kimberley	1910	1883	1888				1	19	0	0	0	0	0	0	0	0
Shiels DP	Dennis	24/08/1938	Belfast		1965			Peterborough Utd.	Retford T	29	1	1	0	0	6	0	0	0	0
Shooter FA	Francis	21/01/1906	Ilkeston	1980	1930			Newark Town	Mansfield Town	2	0	0	0	0	0	0	0	0	0
Short CJ	Craig	25/06/1968	Bridlington		1989	1992		Scarborough	Derby County	128	8	6	11	5	6	1	1	1	1
Short CM	Chris	09/05/1970	Munster, Germany		1990	1995		Scarborough	Sheffield Utd.	94	5	7	7	2	2	0	1	0	0
Shrewsbury P	Phil	25/03/1947	Langley Mill		1966			Nottm. Forest	Long Eaton U	2	0	0	0	0	0	0	0	0	0
Shufflebotham J	Jack	11/04/1885	Macclesfield	1954	1904			Aston Villa	Small Heath	1	0	0	0	0	0	0	0	0	0
Silk GL	Gary	13/09/1984	Newport, Isle of Wight		2006			Portsmouth		30	1	4	1	0	0	0	0	0	0
Simcoe KE	Ken	14/02/1937	Nottingham		1960			Coventry City	Heanor T	2	0	0	0	0	0	0	0	0	0
Simpson A	Alec	24/11/1924	Glasgow		1949	1952		Wolves	Southampton	74	2	0	0	0	6	1	0	0	0
Simpson M	Michael	28/02/1974	Nottingham		1993	1996		Nottm. Forest	Wycombe Wan.	49	3	5	10	0	3	0	0	0	0
Simpson T	Tom	13/08/1879	Keyworth	1961	1899	1901		Keyworth	Leicester Fosse	7	0	0	0	0	0	0	0	0	0
Sims J	John	14/08/1952	Belper		1975	1977		Derby County	Exeter City	61	1	4	8	0	13	0	1	3	0
Sims SF	Steve	02/07/1957	Lincoln		1984	1986		Watford	Watford	85	7	9	3	0	5	0	1	0	0
Sissoko N	Noe	02/06/1983	Bamoko, Mali		2005			Creteil		3	0	0	0	0	0	0	0	0	0
Sisson T	Tom	19/10/1894	Basford	1976	1914			Player's Ath.	Hucknall Byron	3	0	0	0	0	0	0	0	0	0
Slawson SM	Steve	13/11/1972	Nottingham		1991	1994		Trainee	Mansfield Town	38	3	2	7	0	4	0	0	1	0
Smalley PT	Paul	17/11/1966	Nottingham		1985	1987		Notts Schools	Scunthorpe Utd.	118	10	4	12	0	0	0	0	0	0
Smith AW	Albert	23/07/1869	Nottingham	1921	1889		e	Nottm. Forest	Nottm. Forest	4	0	0	0	0	0	0	0	0	0
Smith DA	David	25/06/1961	Sidcup		1992			Plymouth Argyle	Retired, injury	37	1	2	2	0	8	0	0	0	0
Smith DF	Dave	11/03/1956	Nottingham		1975	1977		App.	Torquay United	50	2	5	6	0	0	0	0	1	0
Smith DW	David	07/07/1875	Lochgelly	1947	1900			Millwall Ath.	Middlesbrough	5	0	0	0	0	0	0	0	0	0
Smith G	George	20/05/1901	Glasgow		1924	1927		Strathclyde	West Ham Utd.	83	3	0	0	0	0	0	0	0	0
Smith GH	George	13/04/1936	Nottingham		1955	1966		Dale Rovers	Hartlepool Utd.	323	15	14	0	0	0	0	0	0	0
Smith GWC	Graham	02/11/1947	Liverpool		1968			Loughborough U	Colchester Utd.	10	0	0	0	0	0	0	0	0	0
Smith HR	Harold	12/03/1907	Watford	1979	1930	1934		Wealdstone	Cardiff City	117	5	0	0	0	0	0	0	0	0
Smith J	Jackie	24/04/1936	Hartlepool		1966	1968		Brighton & Hove A.	Margate	78	2	3	0	0	12	0	0	0	0
Smith JA	Jay	24/09/1981	Lambeth		2006			Southend Utd.		27	0	0	0	0	4	0	0	0	0
Smith JT	Jimmy	12/03/1902	Old Kilpatrick	1975	1936			Newport County	Dumbarton	4	0	0	0	0	1	0	0	0	0
Smith JW	Joe		Blackheath, Worcs		1932			Barnsley	Scunthorpe Utd.	23	1	0	0	0	1	0	0	0	0
Smith KW	Keith	15/09/1940	Woodville		1967	1969		Leyton Orient	Kidderminster H	89	3	4	0	0	7	0	0	0	0
Smith MC	Mark	21/03/1960	Sheffield		1992			Barnsley	Lincoln City	5	0	0	0	0	0	0	0	0	0
Smith RL	Roy	22/09/1916	Shirebrook		1948	1952		Sheffield Wed.		110	5	0	0	0	0	0	0	0	0
Smith W	William 'Tich'	10/11/1868	Sawley	1907	1889			Notts Rangers	Long Eaton Rgs	23	1	0	0	0	11	0	0	0	0
					1896			Long Eaton Rgs	Loughborough T										
Smith W	Walter				1899			South Liverpool		2	0	0	0	0	0	0	0	0	0
Smith WA	William	29/09/1900	Corsham	1990	1923	1926		Bath City	West Ham Utd.	41	4	0	0	0	4	0	0	0	0
Snook HD	Herbert	23/12/1867	Nottingham	1947	1888			Trent College		1	3	0	0	0	0	0	0	0	0
Sofiane Y	Youssef	08/07/1984	Lyon, France		2004			West Ham U (loan)		4	0	0	1	0	0	0	0	1	0
Somner MJ	Matt	08/12/1982	Isleworth		2006			Bristol Rovers		38	1	3	1	0	1	0	0	0	0
Soutar HW	Harry	18/09/1902	Invergowrie		1930			Accrington Stanley	Rotherham Utd.	7	2	0	0	0	0	0	0	0	0
Southwell AA	Aubrey	21/08/1921	Grantham	2005	1945	1956		Nottm. Forest	Boston United	328	29	0	0	0	2	0	0	0	0
Spencer F	Fred	1873	Nottingham		1900	1901		Nottm. Forest	St Andrews (Nottm)	15	1	0	0	0	2	0	0	0	0
Stabb GH	George	26/09/1912	Paignton	1994	1934			Torquay United	Port Vale	24	1	0	0	0	6	0	0	0	0
Stallard M	Mark	24/10/1974	Derby		1998	2003		Wycombe Wan.	Barnsley	201	10	14	2	0	69	3	7	0	0
					2004			Barnsley (loan)											
Staniforth AC	Chris	26/09/1895	Carrington	1954	1924	1925		Mansfield Town	Mansfield Town	66	1	0	0	0	22	0	0	0	0
					1927			Mansfield Town	Mansfield Town										
Stant PR	Phil	13/10/1962	Bolton		1989			Hereford Utd.	Fulham	22	1	2	5	0	6	0	1	0	0
Steele E	Ernie	28/10/1911	Leigh	1997	1934	1935		Torquay United	Bath City	54	4	0	1	0	9	1	0	0	0
Steele MA	Murray	1891	Mansfield	1922	1912			Mansfield Mechanics	Mansfield Mechanics	3	0	0	0	0	0	0	0	0	0
Stevens S	Sammy	18/11/1890	Netherton	1948	1920			Hull City	Coventry City	22	3	0	0	0	9	2	0	0	0
Stevenson AE	Alfred	01/04/1902	Broughton, Northants	1960	1926			Worksop T	Chatham T	3	0	0	0	0	0	0	0	0	0
Stewart A	Alec	1868	Greenock		1896	1897		Nottm. Forest	Bedminster	35	1	0	0	4	3	0	0	0	0
Still RG	Ron	10/06/1943	Aberdeen		1965	1966		Arsenal	Brentford	46	0	3	0	0	15	0	0	0	0
Stimpson GH	George	25/01/1910	Giltbrook	1983	1930	1933		Kimberley Ams	Rhyl	90	3	0	0	0	0	0	0	0	0
Stoakes JH	Jimmy	17/12/1895	Newark	1979	1919			Newark Ath.	Norwich City	2	0	0	0	0	0	0	0	0	0
Stokes A	Fred	1904	West Bromwich	1960	1926	1928		Allans Everett	Coventry City	13	0	0	0	0	0	0	0	0	0
Stone DJC	Danny	14/09/1982	Liverpool		2001	2002		Blackburn Rovers	Southport	21	3	0	3	0	0	0	0	0	0
Stone G	Geoff	10/04/1924	Mansfield	1993	1948	1949		Beeston Boy's Club	Darlington	4	0	0	0	0	0	0	0	0	0
Stone M	Mick	23/05/1938	Hucknall		1958			Linby Colliery	Sutton Town	7	0	0	0	0	0	0	0	0	0
Stothert J	James	1870	Blackburn		1894	1895		Lincoln City	Bacup	23	0	0	5	0	0	0	0	0	0
Streets GH	George	05/04/1893	Nottingham	1958	1919	1927		Sheffield Wed.		133	9	0	0	0	0	0	0	0	0
Strodder GJ	Gary	01/04/1965	Cleckheaton		1995	1998		West Bromwich A.	Hartlepool Utd.	121	11	9	4	3	10	0	0	0	0
Stubbs BH	Brian	08/02/1950	Keyworth		1968	1980		Loughborough U	Grantham	426	21	23	16	0	21	1	4	1	0
Sullivan JH	Jim	14/11/1904	Burnley		1925	1927		Crewe Alexandra	Grantham	22	2	0	0	0	10	0	0	0	0
Suter ER	Bob	10/07/1878	Epperstone	1945	1898	1901		Southwell St Mary's	Newark	42	5	0	0	0	0	0	0	0	0
					1906			Newark	Goole Town										
Swift GH	George	03/02/1870	Oakengates	1956	1902			Leicester Fosse	Leeds City	16	0	0	0	0	0	0	0	0	0
Tait BS	Barry	17/06/1938	York		1964			Crewe Alexandra	Scarborough	3	0	0	0	0	0	0	0	0	0
Tait RJ	Bobby	04/10/1938	Edinburgh		1962	1963		Aberdeen	Barrow	60	4	5	0	0	11	2	2	0	0
Tann AJ	Adam	12/05/1982	Fakenham		2005			Cambridge Utd.	Leyton Orient	5	1	0	0	0	0	1	0	0	0

Name		D.o.B.	Place of Birth	Died	First Season	Last Season	Ints	Previous Club	Next Club	Appearances					Goals				
										Leg	FAC	FLC	Oth	PO	Leg	FAC	FLC	Oth	PO
Tarplin W	Walter	30/03/1879	Small Heath	1937	1903	1907		Coventry City	Reading	97	6	0	0	0	25	2	0	0	0
Tasker E	Ernest	1898	Basford		1919			Hucknall Byron	Shirebrook	1	0	0	0	0	0	0	0	0	0
Taylor GA	George	1916	Grimsby		1938			Boston United		6	0	0	0	0	0	0	0	0	0
Taylor GT	George	23/04/1907	Walsall		1925	1933		Stourbridge	Bolton Wanderers	265	12	0	0	0	46	3	0	0	0
Taylor JE	Jack	11/09/1924	Chilton	1970	1953	1956		Wolves	Bradford	53	1	0	0	0	19	0	0	0	0
Taylor T	Tommy	1916	Walsall		1938			Steetly Works	Walsall	25	3	0	0	0	1	0	0	0	0
Tewkesbury KC	Ken	10/04/1909	Hove	1970	1932			Aston Villa	Aston Villa	7	0	0	0	0	0	0	0	0	0
Thomas DR	Dean	19/12/1961	Bedworth		1989	1993		Northampton Town	Bedworth U (mgr)	134	6	11	8	6	8	0	0	0	0
Thomas GR	Geoff	05/08/1964	Manchester		2000		e	Barnsley	Crewe Alexandra	8	0	0	0	0	1	0	0	0	0
Thompson DS	Dave	27/05/1962	Manchester		1986	1987		Rochdale	Wigan Ath.	55	3	4	2	0	8	0	0	0	0
Thompson TW	Terry	25/12/1946	Barlestone		1965	1967		Wolves		66	2	3	0	0	3	0	0	0	0
Thorne T	Terry	02/02/1947	Kirton-in-Lindsey		1966			Ipswich Town	Sydney FC (Aus)	2	0	0	0	0	0	0	0	0	0
Thorpe A	Adrian	25/11/1963	Chesterfield		1987	1988		Bradford City	Walsall	59	4	3	6	2	9	1	1	2	0
Thorpe AE	Ted	14/07/1910	Pilsley	1971	1931			Mansfield Town	Norwich City	1	0	0	0	0	0	0	0	0	0
Thraves J	Jimmy	01/01/1868	Darley Dale	1936	1890	1891		Notts St Johns	Leicester Fosse	4	5	0	0	0	0	0	0	0	0
Thurman AJ	Arthur	08/05/1874	Nottingham	1900	1898			Gedling Grove	Killed in action	2	0	0	0	0	0	0	0	0	0
Tierney F	Francis	10/09/1975	Liverpool		1998	1999		Crewe Alexandra	Witton Albion	33	5	1	2	0	4	1	0	0	0
Tomlinson ET	Tommy	1890	Sheffield		1912			Mexborough T	Newport County	7	0	0	0	0	0	0	0	0	0
Toone G	George	10/06/1868	Nottingham	1943	1889 1901	1898	e	Notts Rangers Bristol City	Bedminster Retired	265	22	0	11	5	0	0	0	0	0
Toone G	George	06/09/1893	Nottingham	1950	1913			Sneinton Inst.	Watford	1	0	0	0	0	0	0	0	0	0
Torpey SDJ	Steve	08/12/1970	Islington		1998			Bristol City (loan)		6	0	2	0	0	1	0	1	0	0
Toser EW	Ernie	30/11/1912	Old Ford, Bow, London	2002	1946			Millwall	Bognor Regis T	2	0	0	0	0	0	0	0	0	0
Towler BE	Bernard	13/03/1912	Ipswich	1992	1938			Lincoln City	Ruston Bucyrus	22	0	0	0	0	9	0	0	0	0
Tucker K	Ken	02/10/1925	Poplar		1956	1957		West Ham Utd.	Margate	28	2	0	0	0	2	1	0	0	0
Turner GW	George	05/05/1910	Mansfield	1996	1930			Sneinton	Luton Town	3	0	0	0	0	1	0	0	0	0
Turner P	Phil	12/02/1962	Sheffield		1988	1995		Leicester City	Grantham T (ass. mgr)	237	15	20	28	6	16	3	0	2	1
Turner RP	Robbie	18/09/1966	Littlethorpe		1992			Plymouth Argyle	Exeter City	8	1	0	0	0	1	0	0	0	0
Twigg RL	Dick	10/09/1939	Barry		1958			Barry T	Sutton U	2	0	0	0	0	0	0	0	0	0
Ullathorne R	Rob	11/10/1971	Wakefield		2004	2005		Northampton Town		69	3	3	1	0	0	0	1	0	0
Upton F	Frank	18/10/1934	Ainsley Hill		1966			Derby County	Worcester C	34	1	0	0	0	3	0	0	0	0
Vallance R	Bob	19/09/1901	Stanley Common	1980	1929			Grantham T	Grantham T	8	0	0	0	0	0	0	0	0	0
Vasey RH	Bob	16/12/1907	Annfield Plain	1979	1936	1937		Nottm. Forest	Brighton & Hove A.	27	1	0	3	0	1	0	0	0	0
Vincent R	Bobby	29/05/1949	Leicester		1965					1	0	0	0	0	0	0	0	0	0
Vinter M	Mick	23/05/1954	Boston		1972	1978		Boston United	Wrexham	166	8	10	10	0	54	5	1	3	0
Wade A	Allen	19/07/1926	Scunthorpe		1952	1955		Scunthorpe Utd.	Grantham	9	0	0	0	0	0	0	0	0	0
Wainwright T	Thomas	1879	Nantwich		1904	1905		Wellington Town	Wellington Town	8	0	0	0	0	0	0	0	0	0
Waitt MH	Mick	25/06/1960	Hexham		1984	1986		Keyworth U	Lincoln City	82	10	5	5	0	27	4	1	0	0
Walker A	Albert	1888	Ripley		1908	1911		QPR	Croydon Common	53	3	0	0	0	9	0	0	0	0
Walker G	George	24/05/1909	Musselburgh		1933	1935	s	St Mirren	Crystal Palace	100	4	0	1	0	1	0	0	0	0
Walker J	James	25/11/1987	Hackney		2006			Charlton Ath. (loan)		8	0	0	0	0	0	0	0	0	0
Walker JA	John	30/11/1871	Plumtree	1951	1891	1892		Derby County	Oxford Univ.	4	0	0	0	0	0	0	0	0	0
Walker JH	Harry	1890	Wirksworth	1934	1920			Derby County	Fulham	5	0	0	0	0	1	0	0	0	0
Walker RN	Richard	09/11/1971	Derby		1992	1996		Trainee		67	3	10	9	0	4	0	0	0	0
Walkerdine GC	Garnet	1882	Nottingham	1965	1903				Gainsborough Trin.	1	0	0	0	0	0	0	0	0	0
Walkerdine H	Harry	1870	Nottingham	1949	1889 1891	1892		Gainsborough Trin.	Gainsborough Trin.	38	2	0	0	1	16	0	0	0	0
Wall TH	Tom	29/05/1909	Nottingham	1989	1932			Clifton Colliery	Tottenham H	3	0	0	0	0	0	0	0	0	0
Warburton BF	Ben	1864	Worksop	1943	1888					2	2	0	0	0	0	0	0	0	0
Ward A	Alfred	1883	Eastwood	1926	1903			Clowne White Star	Brighton & Hove A.	7	1	0	0	0	0	0	0	0	0
Ward D	Darren	11/05/1974	Worksop		1995	2000	w	Mansfield Town	Nottm. Forest	251	23	18	7	3	0	0	0	0	0
Ward J	John	18/01/1948	Mansfield		1965			App.		5	0	0	0	0	0	0	0	0	0
Wardle ES	Edwin	11/01/1870	Nottingham		1888					2	4	0	0	0	0	1	0	0	0
Warner AC	Alf	1879	Hyson Green		1899	1907		Weal FC	Tottenham H	56	3	0	0	0	15	1	0	0	0
Warren MW	Mark	12/11/1974	Clapton		1998	2001		Leyton Orient	Colchester Utd.	84	1	9	4	0	1	0	0	0	0
Waterall A	Albert	01/03/1887	Radford	1963	1910	1912		Sneinton	Stockport Co.	26	1	0	0	0	1	0	0	0	0
Waterall I	Ike	03/10/1888	Radford	1970	1906 1909	1919		Heanor U Rotherham Town	Doncaster Rovers Millwall	184	7	0	0	0	12	1	0	0	0
Waterall TW	Tommy	24/10/1884	Radford	1951	1905	1907		Heanor U	Bradford	28	4	0	0	0	5	0	0	0	0
Wathey F	Frank	1888	Barnsley		1912				Mexborough	7	0	0	0	0	0	0	0	0	0
Watling BJ	Barry	16/07/1946	Walthamstow		1969	1971		Bristol City	Hartlepool Utd.	66	4	1	0	0	0	0	0	0	0
Watson AEC	Arthur	1870	Hucknall Torkard	1937	1893	1894		Mansfield Town	Mansfield Town	22	5	0	1	1	13	1	0	0	0
Watson CR	Charlie	10/03/1949	Newark		1967			Southwell City	Rainworth MW	1	0	0	0	0	0	0	0	0	0
Watson DV	Dave	05/10/1946	Stapleford		1966 1984	1967	e	Stapleford OB Fort Lauderdale	Rotherham Utd. Kettering T	50	1	2	0	0	2	0	0	0	0
Watson J	Joe				1932	1933		Derby Wednesday		10	0	0	0	0	0	0	0	0	0
Watson N	Norman	21/12/1899	Chester-le-Street		1932			Leicester City	Workington	5	0	0	0	0	0	0	0	0	0
Watson WJB	Jimmy	14/08/1910	Govan	1979	1938			Gillingham	Bristol Rovers	17	0	0	0	0	4	0	0	0	0
Watts AE	Ernie	1872	Woolhampton		1898			Reading	Reading	17	1	0	0	0	0	0	0	0	0
Watts TH					1906			Magdala Ams		3	0	0	0	0	0	0	0	0	0
Weaver E	Eric	01/07/1943	Rhymney		1967			Swindon Town	Northampton Town	17	1	0	0	0	4	0	0	0	0
Webster A	Adam	03/07/1980	Leicester		1999			Barwell FC	Bedworth U	1	0	0	0	0	0	0	0	0	0
Weightman FH	Fred	1863	Newark	1897	1888			Notts Wanderers	Nottm. Forest	1	0	0	0	0	1	0	0	0	0
Wells MA	Mark	15/10/1971	Leicester		1991	1992		Trainee	Huddersfield T	2	0	0	1	0	0	0	0	0	0
West A	Alf	15/12/1881	Nottingham	1944	1911	1914		Liverpool	Mansfield Town	130	4	0	0	0	4	0	0	0	0
West AK	Abe	1887	Cockermouth	1952	1912					1	0	0	0	0	0	0	0	0	0
Weston M	Myles	12/03/1988	Lewisham		2006			Charlton Ath (loan)		4	0	0	0	0	0	0	0	0	0
Whitcombe GC	George	21/01/1902	Cardiff	1986	1930			Port Vale	Ashton National	7	1	0	0	0	0	0	0	0	0
White A	Alan	22/03/1976	Darlington		2006			Boston United		35	1	3	1		5	0	0	0	0
White AD	Andy	06/11/1981	Swanwick		2005			Crewe Alexandra		26	1	1	1	0	2	0	0	0	0
White DW	Devon	02/03/1964	Nottingham		1994 1996	1995 1997		QPR Watford	Watford Shrewsbury Town	55	4	7	6	0	17	1	7	2	0
Whitelaw A	Andrew	19/05/1865	Jamestown	1938	1891	1892	s	Heanor Town	Heanor Town	41	3	0	0	1	0	0	0	0	0

Name		D.o.B.	Place of Birth	Died	First Season	Last Season	Ints	Previous Club	Next Club	Appearances					Goals				
										Leg	FAC	FLC	Oth	PO	Leg	FAC	FLC	Oth	PO
Whitley J	Jeff	28/01/1979	Ndola, Zambia		2001	2002	n	Manchester C (loan)		18	1	0	1	0	0	0	0	0	0
Whitlow MW	Mike	13/01/1968	Northwich		2004			Sheffield Utd.	Coaching staff	24	4	1	1	0	0	0	0	0	0
Whittaker FJ	Fred	12/10/1923	Vancouver, Canada		1946			Vancouver		10	0	0	0	0	2	0	0	0	0
Whyte P	Peter		Scotland		1902				Renton	3	4	0	0	0	0	0	0	0	0
Widdowson A	Albert	31/03/1864	Bingham	1938	1891			Nottm. Forest		3	0	0	0	0	0	0	0	0	0
Widdowson A	Alf	16/09/1900	Keyworth	1970	1919	1927		Boots Ath.	Coventry City	141	16	0	0	0	39	7	0	0	0
Widdowson TH	Tom		1862 Hucknall	1944	1888			Nottm. Forest	Nottm. Forest	12	2	0	0	0	0	0	0	0	0
Wilder CJ	Chris	23/09/1967	Wortley		1995	1996		Rotherham Utd.	Bradford City	46	4	2	1	0	0	0	0	0	0
Wileman RA	Richard	04/10/1947	Breedon		1966				Loughborough U	2	0	0	0	0	0	0	0	0	0
Wilkes TC	Tim	07/11/1977	Nottingham		1996			Trainee	Kettering T	3	0	0	2	0	0	0	0	0	0
Wilkie L	Lee	20/04/1980	Dundee		2001		s	Dundee (loan)		2	0	0	0	0	0	0	0	0	0
Wilkinson F	Frank	08/01/1867	Radcliffe-on-Trent		1889	1893		Wilkinson's (Beeston)		9	1	0	4	0	0	1	0	0	0
Wilkinson JW	John		1882 Hucknall Torkard		1904	1905		Hucknall White Star	Tottenham H	7	0	0	0	0	0	0	0	0	0
Williams A	Andy	29/07/1962	Birmingham		1991	1993		Leeds United	Rotherham Utd.	39	1	3	0	0	2	0	0	0	0
Williams DH	Dai		Liverpool		1912	1913		Glossop	Belfast Celtic	31	1	0	0	0	5	0	0	0	0
Williams JN	John	11/05/1968	Birmingham		1994			Coventry C (loan)		5	0	0	0	0	2	0	0	0	0
Williams M	Matt	05/11/1982	St Asaph		2003	2005		Manchester Utd.		26	3	2	1	0	1	0	0	0	0
Williamson A	Albert		1866 Sawley		1891			Derby County	Nottm. Forest	2	0	0	0	0	0	0	0	0	0
Wills GF	Gordon	24/04/1934	West Bromwich		1953	1957		Wolves	Leicester City	154	8	0	0	0	45	1	0	0	0
Wilson AP	Andy	13/10/1967	Maltby		1968			Rotherham U(loan)		1	0	0	0	0	0	0	0	0	0
Wilson KJ	Kelvin	03/09/1985	Nottingham		2003	2005		Notts Schools	Preston NE	78	5	3	2	0	3	0	1	0	0
Wilson KJ	Kevin	18/04/1961	Banbury		1991	1993	n	Chelsea	Walsall	69	2	4	6	0	3	0	0	0	0
Withe C	Chris	25/09/1962	Speke		1987	1988		Bradford City	Bury	80	5	4	10	2	3	0	0	1	0
Withers A	Alan	20/10/1930	Bulwell		1958	1962		Lincoln City	Wisbech Town	121	6	4	0	0	22	2	0	0	0
Wood GT	Gary	02/12/1955	Corby		1977	1980		Kettering T	Kettering T	11	1	3	4	0	0	0	0	0	0
Woodfield T	Terry	21/01/1946	Nottingham		1963					5	0	0	0	0	0	0	0	0	0
Woodford RM	Bobby	06/12/1943	Keyworth		1961			Keyworth U		3	0	0	0	0	0	0	0	0	0
Woodland A	Arthur	03/08/1891	Mount Pleasant	1941	1919	1921		Norwich City	Southend Utd.	48	1	0	0	0	1	0	0	0	0
Woolley JH	Jim		1889 Kegworth	1980	1912	1914		Kegworth		3	0	0	0	0	0	0	0	0	0
Woolley RA	Bob	29/12/1947	Nottingham	1971	1963	1965		Notts Schools		9	0	0	0	0	2	0	0	0	0
Worthington N	Nigel	04/11/1961	Ballymena		1981	1983	n	Ballrmena U	Sheffield Wed.	67	4	11	3	0	4	0	0	0	0
Worthington PR	Bob	22/04/1947	Halifax		1968	1973		Middlesbrough	Southend Utd.	232	15	10	0	0	1	0	0	0	0
Wren JE	Jack	30/01/1894	Bristol	1948	1922	1925		Bristol City	Southport	63	4	0	0	0	0	0	0	0	0
Wright BAW	Bernard	19/09/1923	Walthamstow		1946					2	0	0	0	0	0	0	0	0	0
Wright F	Fred		1908 Ruddington		1928			Ruddington	Grantham T	1	0	0	0	0	0	0	0	0	0
Wright JE	Jack		North Wingfield		1931			Matlock T	Ilkeston U	1	0	0	0	0	1	0	0	0	0
Wylie RM	Ron	06/08/1933	Glasgow		1951	1958		Clydesdale Jnrs	Aston Villa	227	11	0	0	0	36	3	0	0	0
Wyllie J	John		1914 Maybole		1938			Lincoln City		1	0	0	1	0	0	0	0	0	0
Wyness GD	George	12/08/1907	Monkwearmouth	1993	1936			Rochdale	Gateshead	10	0	0	0	0	0	0	0	0	0
Yates DR	Dean	26/10/1967	Leicester		1984	1994		Syston Jnrs	Derby County	314	20	24	30	6	33	0	0	2	2
Yeomans K	Kelvin	25/08/1947	Nottingham		1967			Beeston		1	0	0	0	0	0	0	0	0	0
Young A	Archie	01/01/1915	Paisley		1938			Portsmouth		11	0	0	0	0	0	0	0	0	0
Young AF	Alex 'Alan'	26/10/1955	Kirkcaldy		1984	1985		Brighton & Hove A.	Rochdale	43	5	6	0	0	13	1	2	0	0
Young RA	Richard	18/10/1968	Nottingham		1986			Trainee	Southend Utd.	35	3	2	2	0	5	1	0	0	0
Zadkovich RA	Ruben	23/05/1986	Fairfield, Australia		2004	2005		QPR		9	0	0	0	0	1	0	0	0	0

Three great goalscorers, pictured in 1976. Les Bradd (left) is presented with a silver salver to celebrate his record goals total. On his left are Jackie Sewell and Tony Hateley.

OTHER NOTTS PLAYERS

Played in F.A. Cup but made no League appearances

		First season	Last season	Date of birth	Place of Birth	Died	Previous Club	Next Club
Bausor TJ	Thomas	1881		1862	Southwell	1933		
Brown GN	Noel	1888		10/05/1867	Nottingham	1949		
Brown HH	Harold	1888		02/07/1864	Nottingham			
Burton FE	Frank	1886		18/03/1865	Nottingham	1948	Nottm High School	Nottm Forest
Chapman H		1880	1885					
Cotterill WH	William	1886	1888	1864	Ripley			
Coulby GA	George	1884		21/08/1866	Sherwood, Nottm	1933	Cambs Univ.	London Ams.
Cursham AW	Arthur	1878	1883	14/03/1853	Wilford	1884	Law Club	Emigrated
Cursham CL	Charles	1877	1881	29/10/1858	Wilford	1923		
Dixon JA	John	1883	1884	27/05/1861	Grantham	1931	Chignell G.S.	
Dobson ATC	Alfred	1881	1884	28/3/1859	Sherwood, Nottm	1932	Downside Col.	
Fletcher HS	Herbert	1881		31/05/1860	Nottingham			Bank FC
Gillet LF	Leonard	1882		21/1/1861	Derby	1915	O. Carthusians	Derby County
Greenhalgh EH	Ernest	1877	1882	06/03/1849	Mansfield	1922		
Greenhalgh H	Harold	1877	1880	1852	Mansfield			
Greenhalgh RJ	Richard	1877	1878	1856	Mansfield	1936		
Harris TK	Kevin	1945		20/02/1918	Dublin	1984	Carlisle Utd	Brentford
Henfrey AG	Arthur	1893		1868	Wellingborough	1929	Corinthians	
Hibbert C		1889					Heanor Town	
Jessop ECH	Ernest	1879		1860	Cheltenham			St Barts
Jessop HJ	Henry	1877	1882	1858	Exeter	1914		
Johnson F	Frank	1884						
Keely EM	Erasmus	1877			Woodthorpe, Nottm			
Keely SW	St John	1877		1848	Woodthorpe, Nottm	1908		
Kirby A	Alan	1945		19/12/1926	Barrow			Barrow
Macrae S	Stuart	1879	1886	1857	Port Bannatyne, Bute	1927		
Maltby CL	Charles	1880		1858	Farndon	1936		
Marshall AT	Arthur	1884					Nottm. Mellors	
Marshall JT		1888						
Meredith RG	Robert	1945		03/09/1917	Swansea	1994	Carlisle Utd	Carlisle Utd
Moore HT	Harry	1881	1887	27/6/1861	Nottingham	1939		
Morgan JR	John	1879		1854	Pengwern	1937		
Morse H	Harold	1878		04/12/1859	Birmingham			
Oliver TA	Thomas	1877	1879	13/09/1857	Nottingham			
Owen Rev. JRB	John	1878		1848	Reading	1921	Sheffield	Maldon (Essex)
Palmer S	Sam	1880						
Parker A	Albert	1945						
Peacock E	Ernie	1945		11/12/1924	Bristol	1973	Syston Town	Bristol C
Pearson AH	Alfred	1877		1851	Shardlow	1930		
Pennant JL	Jermaine	1998		15/01/1983	Nottingham		Assoc. schoolboy	Arsenal
Pye J	Jesse	1945		22/12/1921	Treeton	1984	Sheff. Utd.	Wolves
Ratcliffe P	Patrick	1945		31/12/1919	Dublin		Bohemians	Wolves
Seals G	George	1877	1882	1850	Radford, Nottm			
Smith SG	Stuart	1882	1883	1858	Lenton, Nottm		Manchester	
Smythe EM		1879						
Snook FW	Frederick	1883	1886	10/07/1864	Nottingham	1904		
Snook JB	James	1883	1883	15/11/1859	Nottingham	1943		
Snook WP	Percy	1888		23/10/1869	Nottingham	1955	Trent College	
Stancer LB	Leslie	1945		1925	Grantham			Grantham
Stevens THV	Harold	1888		21/12/1866	Nottingham	1958		
Widdowson SW	Sam Weller	1877		16/04/1851	Hucknall Torkard	1927	Nottm Forest	Nottm Forest
Woolley E		1883						

Played in Football League Cup

		First season	Last season	Date of birth	Place of Birth	Died	Previous Club	Next Club
King CW	Colin	1979		21/06/1955	Edinburgh		Clydebank	Mansfield T
Henshaw TR	Terry	1997	1998	29/02/1980	Nottingham		Trainee	
Stevens SD	Shaun	1997		28/09/1978	London		Millwall (jnrs)	

Played in Miscellaneous Games Only (including test matches and play-offs)

		First season	Last season	Date of birth	Place of Birth	Died	Previous Club	Next Club
Akers S	Steven	2006		20/09/1988	Derby		Littleover Dazzlers	
Chilaka C	Chibuzor	2005		21/10//1986	Nigeria		Youth team	
Dallman W	William	1938		08/08/1918	Mansfield	1988	Rufford Col.	Mansfield Town
Dunn MA	Mark	2000		18/09/1982	Newport, Gwent		Youth team	
Gellert B	Brian	2000		10/05/1977	Kolding, Denmark		Xanthi, Greece	
Rabat D	Didier	1998		02/08/1966	Noumea, New Caledonia		Trialist	
Randall D	Dean	1997		15/05/1979	Nottingham		Youth team	
Roberts D	Dennis	1937		05/02/1918	Monk Bretton	2001		Bristol City
Roddie AR	Andrew	1996		04/11/1971	Glasgow		Trialist	
Samuels JL	Jerome	1998		08/03/1976	Jamaica		Trialist	
Sissons HP	Henry	1893	1894	1874	Worksop	1961	Worksop Town	Mansfield T

Another 13 players only appeared in the United Counties League:
Askew, Broughton, Dean, Dugard, I Gadsby, W Garrett, F Haslam, Howkins, J McGinn, J Mounteney, WL Murray, W Oldershaw and J Goode

Made debut in 1939/40 League Matches

		First season	Last season	Date of birth	Place of Birth	Died	Previous Club	Next Club
Chester TH	Thomas	1939		07/11/1907	Glasgow		Burnley	
Knox JP	James	1939		08/08/1910	Glasgow		St. Mirren	
Mackenzie J	James	1939		1914	Sudbrook		Cardiff C	
Rayner FW	Frank	1939		1913	Goldthorpe		Burnley	
Ringrose A	Alfred	1939		18/11/1916	Edmonton	1968	Tottenham H	
Weightman E	Eric	1939		04/05/1910	York		Chesterfield	

WARTIME PLAYERS

World War One

Guest players whose club is unknown are marked with an asterisk

	Apps	Gls	Guest From:
Allsebrook R	27	1	
Atkin J	1		Derby County
Bache JW	19	6	Aston Villa
Bacon T	1		
Bagshaw JJ	86	3	Derby County
Barraclough	1		
Bartrop W	1		
Bell	1		
Bell JJ	1		Nottm. Forest
Bird W	31	4	
Blackburn G	1		
Bowser S	14		West Bromwich A.
Boyne R	1		
Branston JT	25		
Brooks	1		
Brownlow W	1		
Bryan JJ	31		
Cantrell J	127	78	Tottenham H
Charles F	1		
Charlesworth G	51	3	
Clamp A	11		
Clarke	1		
Clay T	21	3	Tottenham H
Cook J	7	3	
Cooke JR	5	1	
Crossley CH	1		
Cumming J	19	2	
Dale GH	3	2	
Davis	1		
Davis F	1		
Dexter F	2		
Dexter G	2		
Driver T	1		
Dunn R	23	3	
Edleston	1		
Fearnley	1	1	
Feebery J	3		Bolton Wan.
Flint WA	100	13	
Foster JH	19	1	
Foster WH	3		
Goodman T	1		
Graham DC	2		
Hasell AA	2		
Hawley F	12	1	
Hayes J	2		
Henshall HV	63	15	
Hill H	1		
Housley H	12	6	Mansfield Town
Iremonger A	93		
James W	6	1	
Jennings W	46	2	
Johnson H (Jr)	1		
Johnson J	19		
Jones B	1		
Kay H	1		
Keeling S	2		
Kemp H	3	1	
Laxton LE	4		
Leafe D	1		
Leatherland J	1		
Leonard H	1	2	Derby County
Lilley B	1		
Loversuch A	1		
Mann J	1	1	
Marriott F	45		
McNeal R	10		West Bromwich A.
Mee GW	11	1	
Morley H	43		
Morris W	1		
Neal G	7		
Newman GW	3	2	
Orme JH	1		
Parrish J	4	2	
Peart JG	1		
Pennington J	25		West Bromwich A.
Perry J	30		
Plant	1		
Poole WS	1		

	Apps	Gls	Guest From:
Price W	1		
Pykett B	4		
Reider J	1		
Richards S	100	50	
Robson M	2		
Sambrooke C	6		
Sankey T	1		
Scrimshaw A	16	1	
Scrimshaw H	5		
Sheldon L	34	1	
Short J	42	20	Lincoln City
Sissons W	1		
Smith G	5		
Smith J	4		West Bromwich A.
Starkey G	1		
Steele MA	6		
Storer H	1	1	
Storey	1		
Tattershall W	2		
Thompson	1		
Thurman M	1		
Timmins W	24		
Tinsley W	1	1	
Toone G (Jr)	3		
Tremelling S	2	1	
Turner H	1		
Walker JH	39	8	Derby County
Walkerdine	1		
Waterall A	10		Stockport County
Waterall I	72	6	
Waterall T	16		Watford
West, Alf	5		
White	1		
White J	1		
White T	15		
Wield T	2		
Willis AS	1		
Wilson J	1		
Woodland A	15		
Woods J	2	1	
Woolley J	2		
Wright H	5		
Yates A	1		

World War Two

	Apps	Gls	Guest from:
Airlie S	2	1	*
Akers W	1	0	Mansfield T
Alderton JH	1	0	Wolves
Alexander T	3	0	
Allen RHA	21	0	
Allen W	2	1	
Anderson J	1	1	Queen o' South
Andrews G	1	0	
Antonio GR	24	7	Stoke C
Ashton P	3	0	Nottm. Forest
Ashworth	1	0	Blackpool
Bacuzzi J	4	0	Fulham
Bagnall R	3	1	
Bailey L	2	0	*
Baker D	12	1	Sheff. Utd.
Ball E	1	0	
Ball WJE	1	0	
Barke JL	15	0	Mansfield T
Barker JW	8	0	Derby Co.
Barnard CH	2	0	*
Barsby CF	1	0	
Barton P	8	0	
Bartram S	2	0	Charlton Ath.
Baxter WA	1	0	Nottm. Forest
Beattie A	20	1	Preston NE
Beattie R	1	0	Preston NE
Becci A	1	0	Arbroath
Bell T	1	0	*
Bellis A	1	0	Port Vale

	Apps	Gls	Guest From:
Benner R	23	0	
Beresford R	28	10	
Berry	1	0	
Bicknell R	5	0	Wolves
Bingham	1	0	
Blagg EA	1	0	Nottm. Forest
Bland P	1	0	*
Blood JF	3	0	Exeter City
Bloomfield W	1	0	
Boileau HA	4	0	Coventry C
Booth LJ	7	2	
Bowers J	16	8	Leicester C
Brader FW	5	2	
Bradley G	2	0	Leicester C
Bradshaw	2	0	
Bramley E	4	0	Mansfield T
Bridges	1	0	Sheffield Utd.
Briggs R	1	0	
Brook R	2	0	Bristol City
Brookbanks E	2	0	
Brooks	5	0	Burnley
Broome FH	20	15	Aston Villa
Brown AW	4	1	Burnley
Brown E	4	0	
Brown GR	10	0	QPR
Brown M	1	0	
Brunt GR	2	0	
Buckley FL	14	3	
Burgess R	16	0	Tottenham H
Butler S	2	0	West Bromwich A.
Bye JH	1	0	Birmingham C
Cairns WH	3	0	Newcastle U
Carrick R	1	0	*
Carter	1	0	
Carter HS	1	0	Sunderland
Carter J	2	0	
Challinor C	1	0	
Challinor J	6	0	Stoke City
Chapman RJF	1	0	QPR
Chester TH	4	0	
Clack FE	5	0	Brentford
Clarke GA	14	1	
Clayton S	7	2	
Clements	1	0	
Clift BC	3	1	West Brom.
Clover G	1	0	
Coen L	15	2	Coventry C
Coleman E	1	0	Norwich City
Collindridge C	35	20	Sheff. Utd.
Collins AD	3	0	Chesterfield
Connor	1	0	
Cooper EJ	6	0	
Cooper S	6	0	
Corkhill WG	83	1	Cardiff C
Coulston W	8	0	
Crisp GH	1	0	Nottm. Forest
Crooks SD	38	16	Derby Co.
Davidson DBL	15	0	Bradford PA
Davidson RT	2	0	Coventry C
Davie J	13	6	Brighton & HA
Davies RG	1	0	Nottm. Forest
Davies W	4	0	*
Davis RD	2	2	Sunderland
Dean	1	0	
DeLisle	1	0	
Dickson W	1	0	
Dimond S	5	3	Man. Utd.
Dixon W	1	0	
Donaldson HA	6	0	
Drinkwater	1	0	
Drury GB	2	2	Arsenal
Drysdale J	1	0	*
Duggan	1	0	Bradford PA
Duncan D	39	10	Derby Co.
Duns L	5	1	Sunderland
Edwards GR	16	6	Aston Villa
Edwards WJ	3	0	

WARTIME PLAYERS - CONTINUED

Player	Apps	Gls	Guest from:
Elliott CS	4	0	Coventry C
Ellmer FB	7	0	
Everett HP	13	0	
Fell J	1	0	*
Fenton M	2	1	*
Findlay PA	1	0	
Flaherty E	2	1	
Fletcher	1	0	Blackpool
Flint K	14	1	
Flintson	1	0	
Flower T	9	0	
Foster J	1	0	
Gallacher P	2	0	Stoke City
Gallago	1	0	
Gardner	1	0	
Gascoigne D	1	0	
Gascoigne D	2	2	
Gilson H	1	0	
Girdham A	3	0	
Glover P	3	0	*
Godfrey L	10	0	Aston Villa
Goodman	1	0	
Goodwin FN	2	0	
Graham R	1	0	Leicester C
Grant AF	1	0	Leicester C
Grant EA	1	0	
Gray R	25	2	Oldham Ath.
Greaves	1	0	
Green T	3	0	Coventry C
Gregory H	1	0	
Griffiths J	9	0	Man. Utd.
Griffiths K	1	0	
Groves A	5	2	Portsmouth
Guttridge R	5	0	Aston Villa
Hague JK	3	0	Southend U
Haines J	5	0	*
Haines JTW	4	1	Swansea T
Hall B	11	0	
Hann R	19	0	Derby Co.
Harris K	18	1	
Harrison R	5	2	*
Hatfield B	3	1	Bradford PA
Hatton C	16	8	
Haycock F	1	0	Aston Villa
Hazel	1	0	
Hepworth R	36	2	Bradford PA
Hewitt H	1	0	Northampton
Higson S	1	0	
Hilliard G	1	0	*
Hinchcliffe T	1	0	Derby Co.
Hinsley G	5	2	Bradford City
Hinton E	1	0	Lincoln City
Hodgkins JS	1	0	
Hogg F	20	0	Luton T
Hollis KB	1	0	Nottm. Forest
Holmes E	2	1	
Houghton WE	3	0	
Howard	1	0	
Howarth G	2	0	
Hoyle D	3	0	
Hubbard J	27	4	
Hughes A	1	0	*
Hughes S	11	0	Brighton &HA
Hunter J	3	2	Preston NE
Huntley	1	0	
Hutchinson J	4	0	
Iceton OL	1	0	Preston NE
Iddon H	1	0	Preston NE
Iverson RT	4	0	Aston Villa
Jackson H	4	0	
James J (1)	1	0	
James J (2)	1	0	
Jepson A	4	0	Port Vale
Jessop W	3	0	Preston NE
Johnson J	1	0	*
Johnson JT	9	0	*
Johnson JW	4	1	Huddersfield T
Johnston TD	1	0	Nottm. Forest
Jones A	1	0	
Jones B	1	0	
Jones DO	13	0	Leicester C
Jones H	2	0	Burton T
Jones JT	2	0	
Jones LJ	50	11	Arsenal
Keen E	4	0	Derby Co.
Kingwell LE	1	0	Torquay Utd.
Kirby N	9	0	
Kirkham R	1	0	
Kirkpatrick S	2	0	
Kirton J	25	0	Stoke City
Knott H	1	1	Hull City
Knowles C	1	1	
Knox JP	2	1	
Lager EW	2	2	Coventry C
Lamb W	1	0	
Lamb HE	1	0	
Lambert R	1	0	
Lane H	4	1	*
Lawton T	1	0	Everton
Ledger JK	16	2	
Leuty LH	12	0	
Lewis G	6	2	Crystal P.
Liddle D	12	4	Leicester C
Lilley K	1	0	
Long D	3	0	
Lovering W	2	0	*
Lunn	1	0	
Lyman CC	2	1	Tottenham H
Mackenzie J	14	6	
Major L	1	0	Leicester C
Marsh JK	5	5	
Marshall JG	20	0	Burnley
Martin DK	4	3	
Martin EJ	1	0	
Martin FA	1	1	
Mason J	5	0	
Massie A	9	0	Aston Villa
Maund JH	2	1	Nottm. Forest
McEwan F	1	0	QPR
McMullen J	2	0	*
McNaughton GN	2	0	
McPherson IB	41	12	Glasgow Rangers
Melling F	1	0	
Meredith RD	10	2	
Middleton L	2	0	
Mills A	1	0	*
Mills PC	27	2	
Moran A	2	0	
Morby JH	8	0	Aston Villa
Mordue J	1	0	
Morgan	1	0	
Morley J	3	0	
Morrad FG	20	6	
Moss G	10	3	
Moulson C	14	0	
Mowl WJ	10	0	
Munks JA	5	0	
Murphy G	2	0	Bradford C
Musson WU	5	0	Derby County
Mynard LD	1	0	Wolves
Newman	1	2	
Nicholas J	1	0	
Nicholas JT	43	2	Derby Co.
Nicholls H	13	0	Northampton
Nugent S	1	0	
O'Donnell F	3	1	
O'Neill T	6	0	
Oakley JC	4	0	Chesterfield
Openshaw	1	0	
Padman	1	0	
Page D	1	0	
Parker A	8	1	
Parkin FW	4	0	
Parks A	15	2	
Parr J	3	0	Derby Co.
Pavlov M	1	0	Lincoln City
Peacock E	15	0	
Pettitt	1	0	
Piercy C	5	0	Chester
Pithie DS	1	0	*
Pomphrey EA	10	0	
Potts	1	0	
Pritchard R	1	0	*
Probert	1	0	
Pye J	30	16	
Ramage PMF	5	0	Derby Co.
Ratcliffe PC	19	0	
Rawcliffe F	16	5	Wolves
Rayner F	6	1	
Read CW	7	2	
Renshaw	1	0	
Rhodes K	1	0	
Rickards CT	20	9	Cardiff City
Rigby NE	11	0	
Ringrose A	1	0	
Rist FH	1	0	Charlton Ath.
Roberts D	3	0	Wolves
Robinson GF	5	0	
Robinson GH	1	1	Charlton Ath.
Robinson P	1	0	
Rollett E	3	0	
Rollinson	1	0	
Ross J	1	0	*
Rossington K	1	0	*
Rothwell E	2	0	Bolton Wan.
Rowley W	1	0	
Ruecroft EJ	1	0	Halifax T
Russell D	1	0	*
Sail GH	1	0	
Sewell J	28	8	
Sharman F	22	0	Leicester C
Sheen J	4	0	Sheff. Utd.
Shell FH	2	0	Aston Villa
Siddons F	2	1	
Sidlow C	7	0	Wolves
Simpson C	2	1	
Skidmore W	2	0	Wolves
Slack L	1	0	Derby Co.
Smallwood E	1	0	
Smeeton J	1	0	
Smith J	4	0	
Smith JT	4	0	*
Smith L	7	0	*
Smith R	1	0	
Sneddon T	1	0	Rochdale
Southwell AA	66	1	
Sparrow	2	0	
Stancer LB	19	0	
Stanowski	1	0	
Steele FC	7	3	Stoke City
Steen AW	3	0	Wolves
Stephenson R	7	0	
Stewart R	1	0	*
Stillyards G	1	0	Lincoln C
Strain N	14	4	
Streten BR	19	0	
Somerfield AG+A	1	0	Wolves
Summers	1	0	
Sweet	2	0	
Swinburne TA	1	0	Newcastle U
Tapping FH	4	0	Blackpool
Taylor J	1	0	
Taylor GT	5	0	Coventry C
Taylor JL	3	0	
Taylor WB	1	0	Grimsby T
Thorne	1	0	
Thorpe A	4	0	
Toothill R	4	0	
Towler BE	43	15	
Townrow RF	1	0	*
Trim RF	1	0	Nottm. Forest
Tweed GE	1	0	*
Tyroll	1	0	
Unwin S	6	0	
Vallance	4	1	
Van Gelden J	2	0	
Vause PG	1	0	Rochdale
Vincent NE	3	0	Grimsby T
Waite JH	1	0	
Wakeman A	2	0	
Walker E	3	1	Bradford
Walsh W	14	2	Derby Co.
Walters H	8	0	Wolves
Warburton G	3	1	
Ward TV	11	0	Derby Co.
Waterall K	2	0	
Weaver S	1	1	Chelsea
Weightman E	5	0	
Wheldon E	2	0	
White A	3	0	
Whitehead J	2	0	
Wilcox GE	10	0	Derby Co.
Wildgoose C	1	0	
Wilkinson N	40	0	Stoke City
Wilson	1	1	
Windle R	5	0	
Wiseman G	20	0	
Wood CC	1	0	
Woodcock E	2	0	
Woolacott H	1	0	*
Wright	2	0	
Wright H	1	0	*
Wright J	2	3	
Wright WA	5	1	Wolves

FRIENDLY GAMES SINCE 1888

Games listed as "CC" were for the Notts FA County Cup (1936/37 onwards)

1888/89
Sep	8	Grantham Rovers	a	3-0
	13	Wirksworth	a	2-0
	27	Boston	a	3-0
Oct	4	Canadians	h	2-0
Dec	1	Nottingham Forest	a	0-3
	26	Nottingham Forest	h	4-1
Jan	3	Casuals	h	1-0
Feb	9	Queen's Park	h	0-6
Mar	2	Notts Rangers	h	3-1
	23	Long Eaton Rangers	h*	1-1
	30	Nottingham Forest	a	5-2

Benefit for H Emmitt & S. Norman (Forest)
* Castle Ground

1889/90
Sep	2	Nottm Jardines	h*	3-1
Oct	3	Sheffield Wednesday	h	6-1
	21	Sheffield United	a	3-2
	31	South of England	h	6-3
Nov	30	Nottingham Forest	a	4-2
Dec	26	Nottingham Forest	h	1-1
	28	Dumfries	h	13-3
Feb	8	Halliwell	h	3-2
Mar	22	Sunderland Albion	h*	2-0
	29	Derby County	a	2-3
Apr	4	Lincoln City	a	2-2
	6	Bootle	h*	2-0
	7	Aston Villa	a	1-3
	8	Rotherham Town	a	0-4
	12	Celtic	a	1-1
	14	Third Lanark	a	0-4
	15	St. Bernards	a	0-7
	19	Sunderland	a	1-2
	21	Sunderland Albion	a	3-6
	22	Newcastle East End	a	1-1
	23	Middlesbro' Ironopolis	a	0-0
	24	Grimsby Town	a	1-1
	26	Bootle	a	2-4
	28	Burslem Port Vale	a	0-2
May	1	Everton	a	1-0

* Castle Ground

1890/91
Sep	1	Nottm. Jardines	h*	7-0
	3	Burton Wanderers	a	4-0
	11	Newark	a	6-0
Oct	4	Sheffield Wednesday	h	3-1
Dec	26	Nottingham Forest	h	0-0
Feb	7	Stoke	h	3-1
	21	Corinthians	h	1-2
Mar	23	Derby County	a	0-2
	27	Lincoln City	a	1-0
	28	Stoke	a	1-1
	30	Sheffield Wednesday	a	2-3
	31	Preston North End	h	0-4
Apr	4	Everton	a	0-1
	8	Burton Swifts	a	3-4

Bass Charity Vase

	11	Sunderland	a	0-6
	13	Aston Villa	a	0-2
	18	Nottingham Forest	a	4-2
	23	Everton	h*	0-1
	25	Wolves	a	1-2
	27	Leicester Fosse	a	2-2
	30	Newark	a	4-0

* Castle Ground

1891/92
Sep	2	Lincoln City	a	4-0
	7	Sheffield United	a	1-4
	10	Newark Town	h*	6-1
	14	Leicester Fosse	a	4-3
	23	Mansfield Town	a	2-1
Oct	3	Nottingham Forest	h	1-3
	22	Newark Town	a	5-0
Nov	5	Royal Arsenal	h	4-3
	11	Cambridge University	a	3-0
	19	Oxford University	h	8-0
Dec	26	Nottingham Forest	h	0-1

1891/92 - continued
Jan	25	Preston North End	a	2-6

Ordered by Football League

	30	Derby County	h	5-1
Feb	8	Oxford University	a	4-2
	13	Sheffield United	a	0-0
Mar	5	Cambridge University	h	5-2
	12	Burton Swifts	a	5-0

Bass Charity Vase

	14	Sheffield Wednesday	a	5-2
	17	Sheffield United	h	2-0
	31	Royal Arsenal	a	4-2
Apr	2	Sheffield Wednesday	h	2-5
	6	Wolves	a	2-1

Bass Charity Vase, at Burton

	18	Ardwick	a	1-2
	19	Distillery	a	5-2
	24	Wolves	h*	2-0
	27	Derby County	a	0-5

Bass Charity Vase, at Burton

	30	Newton Heath	a	0-0

* Castle Ground

1892/93
Sep	1	Gainsborough Trinity	h*	3-1
	12	Middlesbro' Ironopolis	a	0-4
Oct	13	Newark	a	4-0
	24	Kimberley	a	7-0
	27	Cambridge University	h	10-1
Nov	2	Greenhalgh's	a	4-2
	7	Bulwell United	a	1-2
	24	Grantham Rovers	a	2-0
Dec	3	Ardwick	a	3-3
	26	Nottingham Forest	h	0-1
	27	Preston North End	h	1-1
Jan	2	Aberdeen	a	4-0
	3	Celtic	a	1-1
	4	Wishaw Thistle	a	2-5
Feb	18	Newcastle United	a	2-3
	20	Aston Villa	a	2-6
Mar	4	Bootle	a	3-4
	23	Stoke	a	0-2

Bass Charity Vase

Apr	1	Middlesbro' Ironopolis	h*	3-0
	10	Kettering Town	a	4-0
	12	Mansfield Town	a	4-1
	15	Bury	a	2-5
	25	Hucknall	a	3-1
	26	Sutton	a	3-2
	29	Grimsby Town	a	1-3

* Castle Ground

1893/94
Sep	4	Bulwell United	h*	9-0
	18	Greenhalgh's	h	3-2
	23	Chester	h	5-1
	25	Leicester Fosse	a	2-1
	28	Burton Wanderers	h	1-2
Oct	2	West Bromwich Alb.	a	0-2
	7	Chatham	a	7-0
	9	Sheffield Wednesday	a	2-1
Nov	10	Loughborough	a	1-4
	11	Nottingham Forest	a	2-1
	13	Wolves	a	1-4
Dec	7	Aston Villa	h	0-2
	21	Everton	h	0-0
	23	Corinthians	h	4-1
	26	Nottingham Forest	h	1-1
Jan	1	Kettering T	a	5-0
	4	WBA	h	3-1
Apr	5	Wolves	h*	2-0

Bass Charity Vase

	12	Stoke	a	0-2

Bass Charity Vase, at Burton

	14	Crouch End	a	6-1
	16	Burton Wanderers	a	1-2
	21	Newark Town	a	2-1
	23	Everton	a	0-3
	30	Rangers	a	1-3

* Castle Ground

1894/95
Oct	20	Nottingham Forest	a	0-2
Nov	1	Vampires	h	5-2
	8	Derby County	h	0-6

HB Daft's benefit

	12	Bulwell United	a	3-0
	17	Corinthians	a	4-3
Dec	26	Nottingham Forest	h	1-1
Feb	16	Small Heath	h	3-3
	27	Midlands XI	h	4-4

E May's benefit

Mar	2	Grimsby Town	a	0-4
	28	Norfolk County	a	3-0
Apr	3	Mansfield Town	a	0-2
	15	Rangers	h	1-0

At Town Ground

1895/96
Sep	2	Loughborough	h	3-1

At Castle Ground

	9	Hucknall St. John's	a	2-1
Oct	21	Kimberley	a	8-0
Nov	11	Bulwell United	a	5-2
Dec	5	Sheffield Wednesday	h	1-3

Calderhead's benefit

	19	Notts Olympic	h	7-1
	26	Nottingham Forest	h	1-1
Jan	4	Millwall Athletic	a	1-5
	23	Barking Woodville	a	5-0
	25	Tottenham Hotspur	a	5-1
Feb	15	Nottingham Forest	a	1-3
Mar	28	Small Heath	a	4-3
Apr	16	Derby County	h	6-1
	18	Gravesend United	a	1-1
	22	Mansfield Town	a	3-2
	23	Hucknall Torkard	a	2-3
	25	Liverpool South End	a	0-4
	27	Worksop	a	2-1

1896/97
Sep	1	Millwall Athletic	a	1-2
	2	Luton Town	a	1-2
	7	Hucknall St. John's	a	1-1
	14	Mansfield Town	a	2-0
	22	Sheffield United	a	1-0

At Huddersfield

Oct	19	Kimberley	a	7-1
Nov	5	Vampires	h	7-3
	9	Bulwell United	a	3-1
	12	Wolves	h	3-1

G. Toone's benefit

Dec	26	Nottingham Forest	h	1-2
	29	Corinthians	h	4-1
Feb	17	Burton Swifts	a	1-0

Burford Cup

	20	Stockport County	a	4-1
Mar	11	Lincoln City	h	3-1

Burford Cup

	18	Casuals	a	2-1
Apr	5	Fairfield	a	1-1
	28	Leicester Fosse	h*	0-2

Burford Cup

	29	Aston Villa	h*	1-2

C Bramley's benefit
* At Town Ground

1897/98
Sep	13	Lincoln City	a	2-0
	27	Wolves	a	1-1
Oct	18	Kimberley	a	4-2
Nov	8	Bulwell United	a	1-2
	10	Mansfield Town	a	6-2
	13	Manchester City	a	2-3
	20	Small Heath	a	3-2
Dec	27	Nottingham Forest	h	0-1
	28	Sheffield Wednesday	a	1-1
Jan	8	Grimsby Town	a	1-2
	19	Loughborough	a	1-1
Feb	12	Bristol City	a	2-2

1897/98 - continued
Mar	23	Ilkeston	a	3-1
	26	Corinthians	a	0-1
Apr	16	Walsall	a	2-3
	25	Leicester Fosse	a	1-2
		Burford Cup tie		

1898/99
Sep	1	Grimsby Town	a	2-1
Oct	20	Grimsby Town	h	3-1
Dec	26	Bristol City	h	2-4
Jan	30	Sheffield Wednesday	a	3-1
Feb	25	Brighton United	a	2-1
Mar	2	Derby County	h	2-0
		TG Prescott's benefit		
	4	Corinthians	a	2-1
	31	Nottingham Forest	a	5-1
Apr	24	Woolwich Arsenal	a	1-2

1899-1900
Sep	4	Tottenham Hotspur	a	1-4
	27	Brighton United	a	1-3
Nov	27	Burslem Port Vale	a	2-3
Dec	26	Nottingham Forest	h	2-4
Feb	24	Corinthians	a	1-1
Mar	27	Lincoln City	a	1-3

1900/01
Sep	27	Tottenham Hotspur	h	4-1
		Calderhead's second benefit		
Oct	8	Tottenham Hotspur	a	1-1
Nov	12	Bulwell United	a	4-1
Dec	8	Corinthians	a	1-4
	24	Leicester Fosse	a	4-3
Mar	14	Sheffield Wednesday	h	1-2
	30	Aberdare	a	7-1
Apr	1	South Wales League	a	2-0
		At Cardiff		
	20	Woolwich Arsenal	a	0-3
	27	Celtic	a	2-1

1901/02
Sep	2	Chesterfield	a	4-1
Dec	25	Rangers	h	2-3
	30	Wolves	a	2-5
Jan	2	Rangers	a	3-2
	16	Wolves	h	2-3
		J. Goode's benefit		
Feb	22	Clapton	a	2-2
Mar	1	Walsall	a	1-1
	15	Corinthians	a	4-2

1902/03
Sep	1	Northampton Town	a	4-1
Nov	10	Bulwell United	a	2-0
	25	Oxford University	a	2-2
Dec	11	Oxford University	h	4-4
	13	Clapton	a	3-3
Mar	14	Corinthians	a	2-1
	21	Coventry City	a	2-0
Apr	25	Sheffield Wednesday	a	0-2
		At Plymouth		
	27	Aberaman	a	1-2

1903/04
Sep	8	Grimsby Town	a	3-4
	14	Leicester Fosse	a	2-0
Nov	18	Oxford University	a	2-0
Dec	10	Oxford University	h	5-1
		J Montgomery's benefit		
	28	Corinthians	h	3-5
Mar	5	Northampton Town	a	2-2
	12	Corinthians	a	1-2
Apr	9	Clapton	a	2-0
	16	Plymouth Argyle	a	1-0
	30	Grimsby Town	a	2-2

1904/05
Sep	1	Hull City	a	2-2
Dec	10	Clapton	a	3-1
Mar	4	Corinthians	a	5-2
Apr	12	Stafford Rangers	a	1-0

1905/06
Mar	10	Corinthians	a	3-3
Apr	17	Leicester Fosse	a	1-1

1906/07
Sep	26	Lincoln City	a	3-3
Feb	16	Corinthians	a	1-4
Apr	30	Grimsby Town	a	2-0

1907/08
Sep	16	Norwich City	a	2-2
	23	Leicester Fosse	a	3-6
Feb	22	Brighton & Hove Alb.	a	1-3

1908/09
Nov	11	Lincoln City	a	1-1
Feb	6	Hull City	a	1-1

1909/10
Apr	27	Chesterfield	a	3-0
Jun	1	Danish XI	a	2-2
	3	Danish XI	a	4-2
	5	Danish XI	a	2-1

1910/11
Sep	13	Grimsby T	a	1-2

1911/12, 1912/13 no games

1913/14
Jan	31	Nottingham Forest	h	0-5
		Notts FA Senior Cup		
Apr	25	Swansea Town	a	2-2
	27	Merthyr Town	a	0-1
May	31	Barcelona	a	3-1
Jun	4	Barcelona	a	4-2
	7	Barcelona	a	10-3

1914/15
Apr	17	Rangers	a	1-1

1915/16
May	6	Nottingham Forest	a	2-1
		War Charities Fund		

1916/17
Apr	28	Dr. Coutts-Wood's XI	a	4-1
		At Bulwell		

1917/18
Oct	6	Local, Works XI	a	1-0
		At Beeston Rugby Ground		
Apr	20	Nottingham Forest	a	0-1
		Notts FA Senior Cup		

1918/19
Apr	26	West Ham United	a	1-1
May	17	Coventry City	a	2-3
		Bass Charity Vase		

1919/20
Jul	19	Derby County	a	4-5
		Armistice Celebrations		
May	8	Nottingham Forest	h	0-2
		Nottm Hospital Fund		

1921/22
Apr	24	Norwich City	a	2-0
		Norwich Hospital Cup		
May	25	St. Mirren	a	1-2e
		In Barcelona		
	27	Barcelona	a	4-2
	28	Barcelona	a	1-1

1922/23
Dec	13	Nottingham Forest	a	0-2
		Notts Senior Cup (for Children's Xmas Fund)		
May	7	Boston	a	2-0
		Boston Hospital Cup		
	?	Copenhagen XI	a	3-0
	27	Copenhagen XI	a	1-0
	?	Danish XI	a	3-2

1923/24
Apr	3	RAF	a	0-0
		At Cranwell		
	30	Lincoln City	a	0-3
		Wilson Hospital Cup		

1924/25
Mar	23	Mansfield & Dist.	a	2-0
		Mansfield Hospital Charity Cup		
Apr	20	Lincoln City	a	0-0
		Wilson Hospital Cup		
	22	Burton Town	a	0-1
		Bass Charity Vase		
May	7	Vienna Sports Club	a	1-0
	11	Prague	a	0-1
	?	Prague	a	1-1
	?	Ostrau	a	1-3

1925/26
Oct	25	Nottingham Forest	h	2-2
		For Notts CCC funds		
Apr	26	RAF	a	1-2
		For RAF Memorial Fund, at Cranwell		

1928/29
May	4	Carlisle United	a	2-5

1930/31
Apr	20	Grimsby Town	a	4-2
		Grimsby Hospital Cup		
	29	Wealdstone	a	8-3
May	4	Chesterfield	a	2-2
		Chesterfield Hospital Cup		

1932/33
Jan	28	Airdrie	h	4-1
May	1	Coventry City	a	0-2
		Coventry Hospital Cup		

1933/34
Apr	23	Dolphin	a	5-2
	30	Exeter City	a	5-5

1934/35
May	6	Nottingham Forest	h	3-2e
		Notts FA Senior Cup Final		

1935/36
Sep	30	Hearts	h	2-4
		Testimonial for Alf Feebery		
Apr	20	Heanor Town	a	3-1

1936/37
Oct	14	Mansfield Town	a	5-1	CC
	28	Nottingham Forest	h	1-0e	CC

1937/38
Oct	13	Nottingham Forest	a	0-1	CC
May	9	Chesterfield	a	1-2	
		Chesterfield Hospital Cup			

1938/39
Aug	20	Nottingham Forest	a	1-4	
		Football League Jubilee Fund:			
		Flower; Mills, Blood; Young,			
		Gallagher, Burditt; Houghton,			
		Watson, Gaughran, Read,			
		Protheroe. Scorer: Protheroe.			
		Att. 9,505			
Sep	19	Boston	a	2-1	
Oct	19	Mansfield Town	h	2-3	CC

1939/40 - see main section

1940/41
Sep	14	Sheffield Wednesday	a	1-3
	21	Army XI	h	1-1
Dec	14	FA XI	h	2-1
Mar	8	Services XI	h	3-1

1941/42
Dec	13	Polish XI	h	1-3

1942/43 to 1943/44 - no matches

1944/45
Mar 17 Aston Villa Res. h 4-1

1945/46
Aug 15 Nottingham Forest a 2-3
Celebration of VJ Day
Oct 10 British Army XI a 5-2
In Cologne
Apr 27 Cardiff City a 1-5
May 11 Leicester City h 5-0
Bolton Disaster Relief Fund

1946/47
Sep 30 Coventry City a 1-4
Testimonial for George T. Taylor

1947/48
Dec 6 Port Vale h 2-2
Apr 26 Brighton & Hove Alb. a 7-1
May 8 Chesterfield a 1-2
Chesterfield Hospital Cup
22 Shelbourne a 4-1

1948/49
Apr 11 Airdrie h 1-1
27 Celtic h 2-1

1949/50
May 2 Clyde h 2-0
3 Leicester City a 0-3

1950/51
Oct 11 Chesterfield h 4-1
Creswell Col. Disaster Fund
Jan 27 Everton a 2-3
Feb 10 Everton h 0-3
Apr 16 Third Lanark h 2-4
18 Buxton a 2-1
May 10 FC Austria h 1-1
Festival of Britain match

1951/52
Feb 23 Middlesbrough a 1-2
Apr 28 Dudley Town a 6-1

1952/53
Feb 28 Middlesbrough h 4-1
Mar 16 Derby County a 0-3
23 Derby County h 1-1
Apr 9 East Fife h 2-5
16 Hartlepools United a 1-2
27 Dudley Town a 0-1
Andy Langford benefit

1953/54
Dec 1 Admira Wien h 3-5
Apr 28 Mansfield Town XI a 6-3
E Barks/S Watson benefit
29 All Stars XI h 6-1
May 5 Apeldoorn a 2-3
8 Wageningen a 2-2
12 North Holland Select a 1-1

1954/55
Oct 11 Clyde h 0-2
T. Dean's benefit (floodlit)
Nov 3 Maccabi, Tel Aviv h 4-2
May 4 All Stars XI a 3-3
Oscar Hold's benefit, at March Town

1955/56
Jan 28 Brentford a 4-0
May 3 Wolves h 4-2
L. Leuty fund

1956/57
Feb 16 Manchester City h 1-2
Mar 2 Queen of the South h 3-0
Apr 29 King's Lynn a 0-1
Peter Robinson benefit

1957/58
Oct 30 Budowlani (Poland) h 3-0
Apr 29 Select XI (at March) a 6-1
S Garratt/M Reagan benefit
May 1 Kettering Town h 4-0

1958/59
Dec 6 Exeter City a 0-2
Jan 24 Man. Utd. Reserves a 0-4
13,770 spectators

1959/60
Oct 26 Nottingham Forest h 3-1
Nov 4 Headington United a 2-2

1960/61
May 8 Nottingham Forest a 3-4e *CC*

1961/62
May 2 England XI h 1-3
Centenary match
8 Nottingham Forest h 1-2 *CC*

1962/63
Aug 11 Ilkeston Town a 5-3
Nov 24 Oldham Athletic a 0-2
May 23 Mansfield Town h 4-3 *CC*
27 Nottingham Forest a 2-1e *CC*

1963/64
Apr 14 Nottingham Forest h 1-5 *CC*

1964/65
Aug 10 Grantham a 0-6
17 Burton Albion a 4-3
18 Sutton Town a 0-0
Jan 30 Bury h 1-2
May 3 Mansfield Town a 0-1 *CC*

1966/67
Aug 10 Birmingham City h 2-2
13 Cambridge United a 1-2
Oct 3 All Stars h 6-3
Testimonial for Mike Barber
25 Mansfield Town h 4-0 *CC*
Apr 18 Partick Thistle h 1-4
May 9 Nottingham Forest a 0-2 *CC*

1967/68
Mar 25 Mansfield Town a 1-0 *CC*
May 14 Nottingham Forest a 0-3 *CC*

1968/69
Aug 5 Nuneaton Borough a 0-1
May 3 Mansfield Town a 3-1 *CC*
7 Nottingham Forest a 1-2 *CC*

1969/70
Oct 22 Mansfield Town h 2-0 *CC*
Dec 6 Chesterfield a 1-2
Apr 28 Nottingham Forest a 0-2e *CC*

1970/71
Aug 1 Sheffield Wednesday h 1-2
4 Leicester City h 1-2
7 South Shields a 0-0
10 Sutton Town a 3-0
Mar 30 Mansfield Town h 0-1 *CC*
May 10 Nottingham Forest a 1-4
Alan Hill testimonial
Jun 1 Rimini a 4-2
10 Cesena a 2-1

1971/72
July 31 Bohemian CKD Prague h 3-1
Aug 7 Watford a 3-3
Nov 8 Nottingham Forest h 0-2
Jack Wheeler's testimonial
May 10 Nottingham Forest h 3-0 *CC*
15 Mansfield Town a 1-3 *CC*
17 Boston United a 0-2
Lakin and Howell's testimonial

1972/73
Aug 2 Lincoln City a 0-1
5 Wolves h 0-3
7 Nuneaton Borough a 1-2
Mar 27 Gibraltar a 7-0
May 2 Nottingham Forest h 0-1 *CC*

1973/74
Jul 30 Arbroath a 0-3
Aug 1 Elgin City a 2-0
3 Inverness Thistle a 4-2
11 Leicester City h 1-2
15 Hereford United a 1-2
18 Coventry City h 0-2
May 1 Mansfield Town h 4-2 *CC*
7 Nottingham Forest a 2-3 *CC*

1974/75
Aug 3 Torquay United a 1-1
6 Exeter City a 2-0
9 Swindon Town a 1-1
May 1 Mansfield Town a 0-0 *CC*
Won 5-4 on penalties
8 Nottingham Forest a 1-0 *CC*
9 Minsk Dynamo h 4-4
30th anniversary of VE day; lost on pens 4-3
13 Fulham a 2-2
In Gibraltar
15 Fulham a 3-2
In Gibraltar

1975/76
Aug 2 Peterborough United h 3-2
5 Cambridge United a 0-1
9 Kettering Town a 4-3
Above three games for Shipp Cup
11 Colchester United a 2-0
Jan 24 Sheffield United h 3-0
May 29 Abaluhya (Nairobi) a 2-0
30 Gor Mahia (Nairobi) a 3-1
Jun 5 Kenya Breweries(M'basa) a 0-2
6 Mwenge (Mombasa) a 1-2

1976/77
Oct 26 Nottingham Forest h 1-0 *CC*
Held over from 1975/76
Apr 18 Midlands International XI h 2-1
*Testimonial for Dave Needham.
Played by "Nottingham XI"*
May 25 St. Mirren a 2-2
In Gibraltar
26 St. Mirren a 2-1
Jubilee Cup won 4-3 on aggregate

1977/78
Aug 15 Nottingham Forest a 1-1 *CC*
Held over from 1976/77. Lost 2-3 on pens.
Apr 12 Nottingham Forest h 0-1
Testimonial for Les Bradd
May 8 Mansfield Town a 0-2 *CC*

1978/79
Mar 5 Mansfield Town a 0-3 *CC*

1979/80
Aug 1 Oxford United a 3-1
Nov 12 Mansfield Town a 2-2 *CC*
Won on penalties 9-8
Feb 16 Crystal Palace a 2-2
Mar 7 Manchester City h 0-2
May 6 Nottingham Forest a 1-2 *CC*

1980/81
Sep 8 Nottingham Forest h 2-3
Testimonial for Brian Stubbs
Apr 13 Mansfield Town h 1-2 *CC*
May 7 Nottingham Forest a 0-3
Testimonial for Jimmy Gordon

1981/82
Nov 3 Forest "All Star XI" h 3-5
Testimonial for Jimmy Sirrel
Dec 19 Queens Park Rangers a 0-3
Mar 8 Gibraltar a 1-0
Apr 6 International XI h 5-5
Don Masson's testimonial
19 Mansfield Town a 1-1 *CC*
Won on penalties 5-4
May 18 Nottingham Forest a 1-7 *CC*

1982/83
Aug	14	Sheffield Wednesday	a	0-5	
	17	Barnsley	a	1-0	
	23	Leicester City	a	1-2	
Mar	23	Boston U	a	5-5	
		John Moyes testimonial			
Apr	26	Mansfield Town	h	2-1	CC
May	9	Nottingham Forest	a	3-4	CC

1983/84
Aug	5	Jerez	a	1-1	
		Won on penalties			
	6	Americo di Mexico	a	1-3	
		4 team tournament in Jerez			
	13	Grimsby Town	a	1-1	
	17	Doncaster Rovers	a	3-1	
	20	Derby County	h	2-1	
Feb	9	Real Mallorca (Spain)	a	0-1	
	28	Mansfield Town	a	0-4	CC
May	28	Cargo (Kenya)	a	5-4	
Jun	1	Leopards	a	2-4	
	3	Gor Mahia	a	2-1	
		Kenya tour			

1984/85
Aug	4	Burton Albion	a	1-3	
	11	Lincoln City	a	0-4	
	13	Exeter City	a	1-0	
	15	Bristol City	a	2-2	
	18	Sheffield Wednesday	h	1-1	
		Ray O'Brien testimonial			
Dec	11	Lincoln C	a	3-1	
Feb	19	Lincoln City	a	2-0	
	26	Nottingham Forest	h	1-2	
		Pedro Richards testimonial			

1985/86
Aug	3	Ipswich Town	h	1-1	
	10	Mansfield Town	h	2-2	CC*
		Won on penalties 3-2			
	12	Leicester City	h	2-1	
Sep	11	Nottingham Forest	a	2-1	CC*
		CC games held over from 1984/85			
Oct	24	Manchester United	h	1-2	
		Iain McCulloch testimonial			
Feb	15	Queens Park Rangers	a	2-2	
	18	Luton Town	a	2-4	
	24	Nottingham Forest	a	1-4	
		Loughborough Univ. artificial surface			
May	8	Nottingham Forest	a	0-2	CC

1986/87
Jul	26	Grantham	a	0-3	
	30	Boston United	a	1-1	
Aug	9	Sheffield Wednesday	h	0-3	
	12	Mansfield Town	a	0-3	CC
	16	Coventry City	h	0-2	
Oct	14	Nottingham Forest	h	2-5	
		For Lifeline trophy			

1987/88
Jul	25	Buxton	a	0-2	
	28	Kettering Town	a	4-3	
Aug	1	Hednesford Town	a	0-1	
	4	Derby County	a	3-3	
	9	Nottingham Forest	h	4-4	CC
		Won on penalties 4-3			
	11	Mansfield Town	a	2-2	CC
		Lost on penalties 4-5			
Oct	14	Hinckley Town	a	4-1	
Mar	6	Shepshed Charterhouse	a	2-1	
		Mark Robinson testimonial			

1988/89
Aug	6	Sheffield Wed.	a	0-0	
	8	Shepshed	a	1-1	
	9	Derby County	a	1-2	
	13	Aston Villa	h	3-2	
	16	Gainsborough Trin.	a	7-1	
	21	Nottingham Forest	h	1-1	CC
		Won on penalties 4-2			
	23	Mansfield T	a	2-3	CC

1989/90
Jul	22	Warminster	a	5-0	
	25	Stapenhill	a	3-1	
	29	Boston U	a	2-1	
Aug	1	Sheffield Utd.	h	0-1	
	5	Luton T	h	2-0	
	8	Whitby T	a	2-0	
	13	Nottingham Forest	a	1-3	CC

1990/91
Jul	31	Stapenhill	a	3-0	
Aug	4	Boston U	a	4-0	
	7	Barnet	a	1-1	
	9	Sheffield Utd.	h	2-0	
	13	Darlington	a	3-0	
	15	Pickering T	a	6-0	
Aug	22	Mansfield T	a	3-3	CC
		Lost 1-4 on penalties			
Dec	4	Karpaty (Ukraine)	h	2-0	
May	13	Nottingham Forest	h	2-1	
		Mick Walker testimonial			

1991/92
Jul	27	Burton Albion	a	4-1	
	29	Boston U	a	4-0	
	31	Tranmere Rovers	h	1-0	
Aug	2	Armitage	a	4-1	
	3	Pickering T	a	2-1	
	7	Mansfield T	h	4-0	CC
	11	Nottingham Forest	a	1-2	CC
Jan	2	Hucknall T	a	5-0	

1992/93
Jul	23	Romsey	a	9-0	
	25	Waterlooville	a	4-1	
	28	Lincoln C	a	1-0	
Aug	1	Boston U	a	2-0	
	4	Hartlepool U	a	1-2	
	6	Pickering T	a	4-0	
	8	Scarborough	a	0-0	
Mar	26	Gibraltar	a	4-0	
Apr	20	Mansfield T	h	3-0	CC
May	11	Nottingham Forest	a	0-3	CC
		Att. 12,493; Brian Clough's farewell			

1993/94
Jul	16	Armitage	a	6-1	
	20	Shepshed Albion	a	6-0	
	29	Stafford Rangers	a	1-3	
Aug	4	Chester City	a	0-1	
	8	Mansfield T	h	2-1	CC

1994/95
Jul	16	Armitage	a	6-0	
	19	Slovan Bratislava	a	0-1	
	19	Kosice	a	1-0	
		Mini-tournament; 50 min. games			
	23	Northampton T	a	1-1	
		At Wellingborough			
Aug	3	Rotherham U	a	1-0	
	6	Birmingham C	a	2-0	
		At Bescot Stadium, Walsall			
	9	Ipswich T	a	0-1	
		At Grantham			
Nov	11	Nottingham Forest	a	1-3	CC
		Final held over from 1993/94			

1995/96
Jul	21	Gedling Town	a	5-0	
	28	Ipswich Town	a	2-0	
		At Grantham			
Aug	2	Leicester United	a	5-0	
	5	Leicester City	h	2-1	
	7	Mansfield Town	a	2-0	CC
		Semi-final held over from 1994/95			

1996/97
Jul	23	Ilkeston Town	a	2-2	
	27	Boston United	a	1-0	
Aug	1	Glenavon	a	3-0	
	3	Glentoran	a	1-0	
		John Devine testimonial			
	7	Nottingham Forest	a	1-1	CC
		Won 3-1 on penalties			
		Final held over from 1994/95			
	10	Crystal Palace	h	2-1	

1997/98
Jul	16	Birmingham City	h	0-1	
	19	Bolton Wanderers	h	3-4	
	23	Leicester City	h	1-2	
	31	Ilkeston Town	a	5-2	
Aug	4	Nottingham Forest	h	1-6	CC
		Final held over from 1996/97			

1998/99
Jul	21	Ilkeston Town	a	2-2	
	25	Mansfield Town	a	1-1	CC*
		Won 8-7 on penalties			
	29	West Bromwich Albion	h	2-3	
	31	Sheffield United	h	0-0	
Aug	4	Nottingham Forest	a	0-5	CC*
		**CC games held over from 1997/98*			
May	11	Mansfield Town	h	2-1	CC

1999/2000
Jul	14	Ilkeston Town	a	4-0	
	17	Arsenal	h	1-2	
	23	Thailand	a	1-4	
	25	Brunei XI	a	2-0	
	27	Port Authority	a	0-0	
	28	Bangkok Metro Admin	a	3-1	
May	1	Nottingham Forest	a	0-1	CC
		Final held over from 1998/99			

2000/01
Jul	19	Boston United	a	1-2	
	22	Ilkeston Town	a	1-1	
	25	Kettering Town	a	2-0	
	28	West Bromwich Albion	h	0-3	
Aug	1	Sheffield United	h	3-3	
	5	Mansfield Town	h	2-0	CC
Nov	14	Nottingham Forest	a	0-1	CC
		CC games held over from 1999/2000			

2001/02
Jul	26	Stirling Albion	a	4-1	
	28	Partick Thistle	a	1-0	
	30	East Fife	a	6-1	
Aug	3	West Ham United	a	2-1	
Sep	2	Mansfield Town	h	2-1	CC
	2	Nottingham Forest	h	0-1	CC

2002/03
Jul	17	Hucknall Town	a	2-1	
	24	Porthleven AFC	a	3-0	
	26	Newquay AFC	a	15-1	
	30	Leicester City	h	0-2	
Aug	2	Derby County	h	1-3	

2003/04
Jul	19	Ilkeston Town	a	3-1	
	27	Skoda Xanthi (Greece)	a	0-0	
		Lost on penalties			
	27	Italian triallists	a	0-1	
		Trentino Trophy mini-tournament at Pinzolo, Italy, two 45-minute games			
	29	Stoke City	h	1-1	
Aug	1	Royal Antwerp	h	2-0	

2004/05
Jul	13	Northwich Victoria	a	4-0	
	17	Bideford AFC	a	4-2	
	21	Swindon Town	a	1-3	
		At Bideford			
	24	Shildon	a	2-0	
	28	Coventry City	h	2-2	

2005/06
Jul	7	Hucknall Town	a	2-0	
	16	Gillingham	h	2-1	
	22	Doncaster Rovers	a	2-1	
	26	Derby County	h	1-0	
	30	Hereford United	a	1-2	
Mar	7	Radford FC	a	4-0	
		New floodlights opening			

2006/07
Jul	15	Hucknall Town	a	1-1	
	23	Coventry City	h	0-2	
	25	Doncaster Rovers	h	2-1	
Aug	1	Sheffield United	h	0-0	
May	2	Mansfield Town	h	0-1	CC

THE AUTHORS

Keith Warsop's career in the newspaper industry doesn't quite date back to the days when carrier pigeons brought the latest score from the ground to the presses; it just feels that way! Perhaps that is because he saw Tommy Lawton's first goal at Meadow Lane, though he claims he was a short-trousered schoolboy at the time. Keith was on duty for the Nottingham Post Saturday football editions in the days of Bradd and Masson, before leaving the East Midlands to work for other newspapers. Now retired and back in Nottingham, he has time for the garden as well as maintaining his records of County and Notts cricket. His previous published titles include The Magpies (Sporting & Leisure Press 1984) and The Early FA Cup Finals and the Southern Amateurs (Soccerdata, 2004).

Tony Brown saw his first match at Meadow Lane in 1956 and was on the terraces for the Centenary Match in 1962: he looks forward to celebrating the club's 150th anniversary in 2012. A career in computing and telecoms left him forcibly retired in 1994, since when his new life as a writer and publisher of football titles has kept him busy. His previous titles include The Official History of Notts County (Yore, 1996) and many Soccerdata publications, including Complete Records of the FA Cup, Football League Cup, FA Trophy and FA Vase, and The Forgotten Cup of 1945/46 (with Jack Rollin).

ACKNOWLEDGEMENTS

Both authors are indebted to many people who helped with their earlier publications, particularly the staff at the Nottingham Local Studies Library in Angel Row. For this volume, we would like particularly to mention Garth Dykes (the author of Meadow Lane Men), Michael Joyce (for the use of his players' database), Brian Tabner (for his attendance records), Ian Mills and Michael Harrison (for details from their collections of County statistics and programmes) and Peter Wynne-Thomas (for his input on the cricket side of things).

PHOTOGRAPHIC CREDITS

Copyright photographs used in the book are published by arrangement with John Sumpter (of JMS Photography, the official photographer of Notts County), Colorsport, the Nottingham Evening Post, and Picture the Past. The authors are also indebted to the executors of the late Paul Wain for the use of archive material from Paul's collection.

The back cover of this book features a scroll presented to the club by the Football League in 1909, to celebrate the first 21 years of the League. A full-size facsimile of the scroll can be purchased from the club shop.

Every effort has been made to identify the copyright holders of the photographs used in the book. In some instances, the copyright holder is unknown. If we have accidentally infringed copyright please notify the publisher so that it can be rectified in any future editions of the book.

Three Magpies, May 2006.